UNIVERSITY CASEBOOK SERIES®

HISTORIC PRESERVATION LAW

SECOND EDITION

SARA C. BRONIN
Professor
Cornell University College of Architecture, Art and Planning and
Associate Member of the Faculty, Cornell Law School

J. PETER BYRNE
John Hampton Baumgartner, Jr. Professor of Real Property Law
Georgetown University Law Center

FOUNDATION
PRESS

University Casebook Series is a trademark registered in the U.S. Patent and Trademark Office.

© 2012 by THOMSON REUTERS/FOUNDATION PRESS
© 2021 LEG, Inc. d/b/a West Academic
    444 Cedar Street, Suite 700
    St. Paul, MN 55101
    1-877-888-1330

Printed in the United States of America

ISBN: 978-1-68467-634-7

For students and stewards of the past.
S.C.B.

For Tersh Boasberg,
champion of historic preservation, colleague, and friend.
J.P.B.

PREFACE

This book was written for anyone interested in the increasingly important area of historic preservation law. With this book, we hope to advance and encourage the teaching of preservation law, shape the way the field is conceived, and create a practical resource that will be consulted by attorneys and other preservation professionals. With this second edition, we also hope to have tackled modern challenges to historic preservation—including climate change, cultural exclusion, and economic inequality—in a way we did not do in the first.

Our approach to the subject is reasonably straightforward. We present the most significant legal issues in preservation and place them in a contemporary context, identifying contested questions and areas of reform. The format of the book is traditional: edited leading cases with notes that provide explanation, extension, and issues for discussion. Given the interdisciplinary nature of the field, we believe that the legal issues can only be understood in light of historical, aesthetic, political, and administrative issues that make up the larger realm of preservation. Accordingly, we provide secondary materials, both legal and non-legal.

Because we focus on preservation of buildings and sites, we present preservation as part of land use or urban development law. Thus, we provide extensive treatment of local preservation law, which regulates private property, as well as relevant issues in real estate finance and project development. We also provide comprehensive treatment of federal law, including the National Historic Preservation Act and related statutes. In addition, we explore federal laws that address preservation vis-a-vis cultural property issues, particularly regarding Native American and archaeological sites. Preservation has also generated important and interesting constitutional questions related to takings, religious freedoms, and free speech rights, which we address. We have added a chapter in this edition focused exclusively on international cultural heritage law, which domestic practitioners must be well-versed in, in an increasingly global age.

A word about the editing of the cases and other secondary materials is in order. The disposition of cases in the historic preservation context often hinges on details—such as the history or architecture of a structure—which we include to the extent needed to ensure meaningful comprehension of the underlying legal results. With respect to secondary materials, we have often focused on a few key points, rather than full arguments. We nonetheless hope that these materials will be used to expand readers' perspective on the field.

As far as formatting, we follow standard casebook editorial shorthand, including the convention of using three stars (* * *) for any deletions of more than one or two words in source materials. We often delete citations and quotation marks, or edit internal citations to conform with modern usage, without indication. Many sources, including institutional reports and scholarly articles, may be found online, but given the speed with which website addresses change, we have declined to include URLs in our text. We have included only original footnotes, and have not offered any of our own. For our notes within the text, we use "EDS." offset by brackets.

We would like to thank the Georgetown University Law Center and the University of Connecticut School of Law for providing research support. We also thank the consistently helpful staff of those institutions, including Betsy Kuhn, Jennifer Lane, Anna Selden, and Teresa Thomas. The book has benefitted from the efforts of many research assistants over the years, including Emma Avery, Jennifer Conroy, David Ewen, Carlene Felix, Alison Gillis, Edward Imperatore, Bart Kempf, Jemma McPherson, Kirk MacKinnon Morrow, Deborah Newburg, Brendan Pilver, Mia Fioritto Rubin, Sana Sheikh, Kaitlyn Stewart, Anne Thibadeau, and Bethany Tindall. In addition, we would like to thank Albert G. Lauber for his assistance in reviewing the section on tax credits although any mistakes are ours.

ACKNOWLEDGMENTS

The authors gratefully acknowledge the following authors, photographers, publishers, and copyright holders for their permission to reprint their work in our book.

Books & Articles

Avrami, Erica. *Building a Foundation for Action: Anti-Racist Historic Preservation Resources.* © 2021 by Erica Avrami. Reprinted with permission.

Fitch, James Marston. *Historic Preservation: Curatorial Management of the Built World.* pp. 1, 7–8, 10–12. © 1990 by the Rector and Visitors of the University of Virginia. Reprinted with permission.

Holleran, Michael. *Boston's "Changeful Times": Origins of Preservation and Planning in America.* p. 84. © 1998 The Johns Hopkins University Press. Reprinted with permission of The Johns Hopkins University Press.

Miller, Julia H. *A Layman's Guide to Historic Preservation Law.* © 2008 by the National Trust for Historic Preservation. Reprinted with permission.

National Trust for Historic Preservation. *Assessing Economic Hardship Claims Under Historic Preservation Ordinances.* pp. 4–5. © 2009 by the National Trust for Historic Preservation. Reprinted with permission.

National Trust for Historic Preservation. *The Greenest Building: Quantifying the Environmental Value of Building Reuse.* pp. vi & viii. © 2011 by the National Trust for Historic Preservation. Reprinted with permission.

PlaceEconomics, *Twenty-Four Reasons Historic Preservation is Good for Your Community*, pp. 1–7. © 2020 by the National Trust for Historic Preservation. Reprinted with permission.

Rose, Carol M. *Preservation and Community: New Directions in the Law of Historic Preservation.* 33 Stanford Law Review 473. pp. 476–479, 488–491. © 1981 Carol M. Rose, Stanford Law Review. Reprinted with permission.

Tyler, Norman, Ilene R. Tyler, & Ted Ligibel. *Historic Preservation: An Introduction to its History, Principles, and Practice.* pp. 37–47. © 2018 by Norman Tyler, Ilene R. Tyler, & Ted Ligibel. © 2018, 2000, 1994 by Norman Tyler. Used by permission of W.W. Norton & Company, Inc.

Uniform Conservation Easement Act. © 2007 National Conference of Commissioners on Uniform State Laws. Reprinted pursuant to a blanket copyright agreement between the Uniform Law Commission and Thomson Reuters.

Images

1-1: Mount Vernon Mansion, Mount Vernon, VA. © Sara C. Bronin 2007.

1-2: Mount Vernon Reconstructed Cabin of an Enslaved Person, Mount Vernon, VA. © Sara C. Bronin 2007.

1-3: Independence Hall, Philadelphia, PA. © Sara C. Bronin 2010.

1-4: Mies van der Rohe's Farnsworth House, Plano, IL. © Sara C. Bronin 2005.

1-5: A Current View of the Gettysburg Battlefield, Gettysburg, PA. © Sara C. Bronin 2009.

1-6: The Historic Willard Hotel, Washington, DC. © Sara C. Bronin 2011.

1-7: Fells Point National Historic District Building Marker, Baltimore, MD. © Sara C. Bronin 2011.

1-8: Modern Glass Courtyard of the Patent Office Building, Washington, DC. © Sara C. Bronin 2009.

1-9: French Quarter View 1, New Orleans, LA. © Sara C. Bronin 2008.

1-10: French Quarter View 2, New Orleans, LA. © Sara C. Bronin 2008.

1-11: James Madison's Montpelier: A National Trust Historic Site, Orange, VA. © Sara C. Bronin 2009.

2-1: Elements of the Hiram M. Chittenden Locks and Lake Washington Ship Channel Historic District, Seattle, WA. © Sara C. Bronin 2006.

2-2: Designation Marker of the Hiram M. Chittenden Locks and Lake Washington Ship Channel Historic District, Seattle, WA. © Sara C. Bronin 2006.

2-3: Grant Park Stadium (Soldier Field) in 1932, Chicago, IL. Photograph from the Collection of the National Historic Landmark Program.

2-4: Grant Park Stadium (Soldier Field) in 2005, Chicago, IL. © Sara C. Bronin 2005.

2-5: The 16th Street Building, Originally the Italian Ambassador Residence, Washington, DC. © Sara C. Bronin 2011.

2-6: The Fuller Street Building, Originally the Chancery, Washington, DC. © Sara C. Bronin 2011.

3-1: Porch of the Maidens at the Aloha House at the National Park Seminary Site, Silver Spring, MD. © Sara C. Bronin 2011.

3-2: The Main Building at the National Park Seminary Site, Silver Spring, MD. © Sara C. Bronin 2011.

3-3: Continued Neglect at an Auxiliary Building of the National Seminary Site, Silver Spring, MD. © Sara C. Bronin 2011.

3-4: Continued Neglect at the Gymnasium of the National Seminary Site, Silver Spring, MD.   © Sara C. Bronin 2011.

4-1: Exterior View of the Gettysburg Cyclorama Building Designed by Richard Neutra, Gettysburg, PA. Historic American Buildings Survey, Library of Congress, Prints and Photographs Division. Photograph catalogued at HABS PA-6709-7.

4-2: Interior View of the Gettysburg Cyclorama Building Designed by Richard Neutra, Gettysburg, PA. Historic American Buildings Survey, Library of Congress, Prints and Photographs Division. Photograph catalogued at HABS PA-6709-42.

5-1: The Lake Keechulus Snowshed Bridge, Hyak, WA. Lake Keechelus Bridge. Historic American Engineering Record, Library of Congress, Prints and Photographs Division. Photograph catalogued at HAER WASH,19-HYAK.V,1.

5-2: The Main Avenue Bridge on the Merritt Parkway, Norwalk, CT. *View Along Main Avenue to Bridge Carrying Merritt Parkway, ca. 1940.* Collection Connecticut Department of Transportation. Historic American Engineering Record, Library of Congress, Prints and Photographs Division. Photograph catalogued at HAER CONN,1-NOWA,7.

5-3: The Norwalk River Bridge on the Merritt Parkway, Norwalk, CT. *Merritt Parkway, Norwalk River Bridge, Spanning Norwalk River, Norwalk, Fairfield, CT.* Historic American Engineering Record, Library of Congress, Prints and Photographs Division. 1993. Photograph catalogued at HAER CONN,1-NOWA,10.

6-1: Gondleman's Berm and Berms Beyond, Belmont Street, Washington, DC. © Sara C. Bronin 2011.

6-2: Across the Street from Gondleman's Home, Belmont Street, Washington, DC. © Sara C. Bronin 2011.

6-3: Meridian Hill Park, Washington, DC. © Sara C. Bronin 2011.

6-4: Landscape Preservation at Gettysburg Battlefield, Gettysburg, PA. © Sara C. Bronin 2009.

6-5: 901 F Street's F Street Façade, Washington, DC. © Sara C. Bronin 2011.

6-6: 901 F Street's 9th Street Façade, Washington, DC. © Sara C. Bronin 2011.

6-7: 614 and 616 North Kenilworth Avenue, Oak Park, IL. © Sara C. Bronin 2011.

6-8: Frank Lloyd Wright's Home & Studio Masonry Detail, Oak Park, IL. © Sara C. Bronin 2005.

6-9: The Prairie Style Hills-DeCaro House Being Rehabilitated, Oak Park, IL. © Sara C. Bronin 2005.

6-10: The Woodward Building, Washington, DC. © Sara C. Bronin 2011.

6-11: A Hulking Black Glass Building in Foggy Bottom, Washington, DC. © Sara C. Bronin 2010.

6-12: The International Spy Museum Addition, Washington, DC. Tersh Boasberg, Photographer. Reprinted with permission.

6-13: The Vibrant Wooster Street in the SoHo Neighborhood, Manhattan, NY. © Sara C. Bronin 2007.

7-1: Marcel Breuer's Proposal for the "Air Rights Building" at Grand Central Terminal. "Grand Central Air Rights Building, proposal drawing, ca. 1969" by an unidentified photographer. Marcel Breuer papers, Archives of American Art, Smithsonian Institution.

7-2: 42nd Street Façade of Grand Central Terminal, Manhattan, NY. © Sara C. Bronin 2008.

7-3: Towering Skyscrapers North of Grand Central Terminal, Manhattan, NY. © Grace E. Yu 2011. Reprinted with permission of g.Yu fotografie.

7-4: The Lawns of Cathedral Mansions South, Washington, DC. © Sara C. Bronin 2011.

7-5: Forrest Myers' Sculpture at 599 Broadway, Manhattan, NY. © Grace E. Yu 2011. Reprinted with permission of g.Yu fotografie.

7-6: The St. Bartholomew's Church Complex, Manhattan, NY. © Grace E. Yu 2011. Reprinted with permission of g.Yu fotografie.

7-7: The Façade of the Canterbury House, Ann Arbor, MI. Matt DeLand, Photographer. Reprinted with permission.

7-8: Newbury Street, Boston, MA. © Sara C. Bronin 2004.

7-9: Back Bay Residential Street, Boston, MA. © Sara C. Bronin 2004.

8-1: The African Burial Ground, Manhattan, NY. © Grace E. Yu 2011. Reprinted with permission of g.Yu fotografie.

10-1: The "Chipped Tooth" at 952 Fifth Avenue, Manhattan, NY. © Grace E. Yu 2011. Reprinted with permission of g.Yu fotografie.

11-1: The Exterior of the Pre-Renovation Octagon Tower, Roosevelt Island, NY. Reprinted with permission from Becker & Becker Associates, Inc.

11-2: The Interior of the Pre-Renovation Octagon Tower, Roosevelt Island, NY. Reprinted with permission from Becker & Becker Associates, Inc.

11-3: The Finished Octagon at Roosevelt Island Development Project, Roosevelt Island, NY. © Paul Warchol. Reprinted with permission from Becker & Becker Associates, Inc.

11-4: The Philcade Building in 1962, Tulsa, OK. Reprinted with permission from Beryl Ford Collection/Rotary Club of Tulsa, Tulsa City-County Library, and Tulsa Historical Society.

11-5: The Philcade Building in 2011, Tulsa, OK. Hannah Wiseman, Photographer. Reprinted with permission.

11-6: A Modern, ADA-Compliant Addition to the D.C. Court of Appeals, Washington, DC. Tersh Boasberg, Photographer. Reprinted with permission.

11-7: The Copley Square Façade of the Boston Public Library, Boston, MA. © Sara C. Bronin 2008.

11-8: The Copley Station Elevator in Front of the Boylston Street Façade of the Boston Public Library, Boston, MA. Abigail Byrne, Photographer. Reprinted with permission.

11-9: The Copley Station Elevator in Front of the Old South Church, Boston, MA. Abigail Byrne, Photographer. Reprinted with permission.

11-10: Elvis Presley's Graceland, Memphis, TN. © Sara C. Bronin 2008.

11-11: Frank Lloyd Wright's Taliesin West, Scottsdale, AZ. © Sara C. Bronin 2009.

12-1: The Historic Mostar Bridge Under Reconstruction in 2000, Mostar, Bosnia. © Sara C. Bronin 2000.

12-2: Machu Picchu, Urubamba Province, Peru. © Sara C. Bronin 2003.

12-3: The Taj Mahal, Agra, India. David Castor, Creative Commons CC0 License 2.0 2008.

12-4: A Dugong. Ruth Hartnup, Creative Commons CC0 License 2.0 2004.

SUMMARY OF CONTENTS

TABLE OF CONTENTS

TABLE OF CASES

The principal cases are in bold type.

UNIVERSITY CASEBOOK SERIES®

HISTORIC PRESERVATION LAW

SECOND EDITION

CHAPTER ONE

HISTORIC PRESERVATION LAW IN CONTEXT

Historic preservation law encompasses the rules, processes, and institutions that afford special protections to properties considered important for their ability to convey historic or cultural meaning to people today. Every year, more and more properties undergo the formal process of being "designated" historic—that is, they are deemed to be worthy of recognition or protection under the law. Historic preservation law thus has become increasingly important.

This Chapter provides a broad overview of historic preservation law, providing both necessary background and analysis of current issues. It first covers the history of the preservation movement, explaining its transition from an elite, private movement to the more egalitarian, publicly-supported movement of today. It then asks fundamental questions that underlie all preservation law and policy: what do we preserve, why and how do we preserve it, and who does the preserving? The Chapter concludes by identifying three modern global challenges— climate change, cultural exclusion, and economic inequality—and argues that historic preservation law presents a unique opportunity to meaningfully address these challenges.

This Chapter sets the stage for later Chapters, which will cover the aspects of property, land use, real estate, environmental, local government, cultural resources, administrative, and constitutional law that comprise historic preservation law.

A. A BRIEF HISTORY OF THE PRESERVATION MOVEMENT

The preservation movement in the United States began slowly, at first focusing on a few nationally significant sites related to the Founding Fathers or military battles. Over time, preservation efforts expanded to include sites with architectural or cultural significance. By the second half of the twentieth century, preservation activity began to encompass sites reflecting the histories of "everyday" people. In the twenty-first century, the movement has a "bigger tent" approach, with more preservationists recognizing the need to protect the histories of diverse and underrepresented populations. Despite recent progress, the movement has been dominated from its inception by the values and stories of people of privilege. Later in this Chapter, we explore how preservation has begun to reckon with these origins, but for now consider the following general description of early developments in the field.

Norman Tyler, Ilene R. Tyler, & Ted J. Ligibel, Historic Preservation: An Introduction to Its History, Principles, and Practice
(2018)

Many early preservation activities took place throughout the nation in the eighteenth and more prominently in the nineteenth century, but often under the banner of *antiquarianism*. Genealogists, historians, conservationists, collectors, associations and societies, and individuals often carried out preservation work before it was known as such. Over time, these activities became more recognized as historic preservation.

* * *

One of the first acts of preservation was the successful effort in 1816 to save Independence Hall (then known as the Old State House) from demolition. This Philadelphia building has tremendous historical significance, as every student of American history recognizes. At the time, however, the building was not revered for its association with the founding of the United States. That changed in 1824, when the French Marquis de Lafayette visited Philadelphia as part of an extensive tour of the United States. Preparations for his visit drew attention to the state of disrepair inside the building and sparked interest that resulted in restoring the Assembly Room as the Hall of Independence and the State House Yard as Independence Square. In 1852, the City of Philadelphia decided to celebrate July 4 each year in the State House, and it established the name Independence Hall to denote the entire building.

The Mount Vernon Ladies' Association of the Union is generally considered the first nationwide preservation group organized in the United States. It was founded in 1853 to save deteriorating Mount Vernon, George and Martha Washington's homestead. The association presented a petition to Congress for "The Proposed Purchase of Mount Vernon by the Citizens of the United States, in Order that They May at All Times Have a Legal and Indisputable Right to Visit the Grounds, Mansion, and Tomb of Washington." The petition failed, and the federal government showed no interest in taking care of the property. As a result, Ann Pamela Cunningham chartered the Mount Vernon Ladies' Association. Motivated primarily by patriotism, she offered the challenge, "Those who go to the Home in which he lived and died, wish to see in what he lived and died! Let one spot in this grand country of ours be saved from change!"

Cunningham found other women of means who had both the time and inclination to help, and through this private organization, they raised the money to acquire Mount Vernon. The association's members, who were located in each of the states of the Union at that time, spearheaded a bold and successful campaign that saved and allowed for restoration of the structure. The association served as an early model for organizations involved in saving landmark structures threatened by the encroachment of development or by time. Their significant effort also helped form some of the early trends of the preservation movement of the United States—for example, the early tradition that preservation activities were largely supported by private individuals, and that women had a prominent role in these activities. Out of the founding traditions also came the commonly adopted goal of saving individual landmark buildings.

With the emphasis by early preservationists on saving landmarks, there was little interest in preservation for the sake of architectural history. Nineteenth-and early-twentieth-century organizations, including historical or patriotic societies, family organizations, and government agencies, saved landmark buildings more for patriotic reasons than for their architectural ones. During that period, the historical connections of structures to great men and important events, the earlier the better, were the only criteria worth considering for preservation of a structure.

Throughout the nineteenth century, the federal government took virtually no active role in preservation and showed no inclination to recognize or protect buildings of potential historical significance. Instead, the government's interest was oriented toward the protection of the expanding nation's natural features, especially in the West. In 1872, the federal government established Yellowstone National Park as a protected area and the world's first national park comprising land in three states.

In the Southwest, the federal government showed interest in preserving adobe dwellings, some of which dated to the fourteenth century. Settlers exploring this new territory often looted and destroyed these dwellings to get artifacts to sell back east. In 1889, Congress designated the Casa Grande ruin in Arizona, abandoned in the mid-1400s, as the nation's first National Monument and appropriated $2,000 to protect it—the first federal funding ever allocated for preservation.

At the same time, two cowboys looking for cattle in Arizona came across a spectacular site, the Cliff Palace dwellings of Mesa Verde. For the next eighteen years, word of the site spread back to the East Coast. Scavengers came to take well-preserved artifacts, selling them on the international market for good profits. Recognizing the loss at this significant site, Congress established Mesa Verde National Park with the intention of preserving the dwellings and remaining artifacts. * * *

The Antiquities Act of 1906, signed into law by President Theodore Roosevelt, established stiff penalties for destroying federally owned sites. The act was the nation's first historic preservation legislation, giving the president authority to designate "historic landmarks, historic and prehistoric structures, and other objects of historic or scientific interest" situated on federal lands. It prompted the surveying and identification of historic sites throughout the country and transferred authority for administering preservation activities from the federal level from

Congress to the executive branch of government, allowing for more efficient management. These designations are known as national monuments, and they normally represent sites of overriding cultural and natural significance. They can be created by presidential proclamation or designated by congressional legislation. The addition or elimination of a designation can be politically charged, especially when made toward the beginning or end of a president's term. The Antiquities Act further established the administration of preservation efforts through the Office of the Secretary of the Interior, where it remains today. * * *

The National Park Service (NPS) was established in 1916 within the U.S. Department of the Interior as the administrative agency responsible for national parks. The goal was to establish an apparatus to handle sites too large for private protection or preservation, such as the Jamestown and Yorktown sites in Virginia, which were combined to form the Colonial National Historical Park. It also began a program of acquiring Civil War battlefield sites to protect them from development.

Because of its early involvement with the protection of natural sites, the National Park Service has always played an integral role in preservation at the federal level. Today its role has expanded well beyond the protection of the natural environment to include the administration of most federal historic preservation programs. It works with state and local governments, nonprofit organizations, historic property owners, Native American tribes, and others. These preservation activities include managing the ninety thousand sites listed in the National Register of Historic Places, the 2,500 sites listed as National Historic Landmarks, and the thirty-seven sites listed as National Heritage Areas; administering preservation grants; and reviewing historic rehabilitation tax credit applications. The NPS developed standards and guidelines used for historic rehabilitation projects that have become the standard used nationally. * * *

The first city to establish a historic district with regulatory control was Charleston, South Carolina. To protect against a proposed new gas station in its historic center and to counter a threat from outsiders who were dismantling many beautiful Charleston houses, local citizens and planners in 1931 established an unprecedented zoning ordinance that made it illegal to erect or institute any service or filling stations, automobile repair shops, factories or other buildings or businesses which would detract from the architectural and historical setting. This ordinance is significant because it had no legal precedent and was established without enabling legislation from the state, typically required for new regulatory procedures. The ordinance also included a provision that "applications for building permits and for Certificates of Occupancy . . . must be approved as to exterior architectural features which are subject to public view from a public street or highway." A board of architectural review was established that had authority to review exterior changes to buildings within the district and to issue "Certificates of Appropriateness" if such changes were deemed acceptable. Without a firm legal basis for this review authority, the regulatory district was vulnerable to litigation, but it remained viable largely because it had general community support. It is interesting to note that this is the same era in which zoning efforts were first instituted and upheld across the nation as a legal and necessary "police power" to control land use.

Charleston became a prototype for other early historic districts, including the Vieux Carré section of New Orleans, authorized through a Louisiana state constitutional amendment in 1936. San Antonio, Texas, followed suit in 1939; Alexandria, Virginia, in 1946; Williamsburg in 1947; Winston-Salem, North Carolina, in 1948, and the Georgetown section of Washington, D.C., in 1950.

The initiatives mentioned in the excerpt were only the beginning of the story. In the 1940s and 1950s, demographic movement from urban to suburban areas, the rise of the automobile and the interstate transportation system, failures in centralized planning, and assorted environmental disasters inspired many to take up the preservation mantle, particularly in urban areas.

The book *The Death and Life of American Cities*, published in 1961 by a New York City activist named Jane Jacobs, became one of the movement's central texts. The book decried the large-scale "urban renewal" projects that characterized urban planning at the time, and encouraged readers to protect a human-scale built environment that fostered vibrant community life and changed only organically. Jacobs's book heralded the rise of the historic district across the country as a means of preserving groups of buildings whose components, perhaps, lacked architectural merit but nonetheless formed a coherent landscape. The fight against urban renewal had racial and socioeconomic consequences, as people most affected by urban renewal were from marginalized groups more vulnerable, and more worthy of protection, than the buildings themselves. At the time, however, people fighting urban renewal for historic preservation purposes did not always see their effort in these terms, though in some places, including Washington, D.C., people who opposed "white men's roads through black men's communities" joined the movement and attempted to use preservation law to shield their neighborhoods from destruction.

The destruction of the magnificent Roman-inspired Pennsylvania Station in Manhattan in 1963 further catalyzed the preservation movement nationwide. By the end of the 1960s, the key components of the federal system were in place, including the National Historic Preservation Act, the National Environmental Policy Act, and the Transportation Act, which are fully covered in later Chapters. States adopted versions of these federal laws, while local preservation commissions and tribal governments set up their own registers and protections for historic properties. More recently, new legal protections, like conservation and preservation easements, intended to cover structures, scenic areas, and public economic incentives, such as tax credits and grants, have been incorporated into the law. These too, will be discussed further in later Chapters.

NOTES & QUESTIONS

1. Why were early preservationists drawn to preservation? Do any of their rationales seem less important or less relevant today? More important or more relevant? Consider these excerpts from histories of early preservation in Boston and New York City:

> Even in the mid-nineteenth century, people found the disappearance of prominent old buildings disturbing because they believed, despite the culture of change, that at least some of them were supposed to be permanent. Ideas about environmental permanence were tied up in attitudes about social and institutional stability, and instability was uncomfortable. Growing antiquarian sensibility allowed people to appreciate buildings and scenes of great age even while applauding the progress that was relegating them to memory. These conflicting ideas did not get sorted out, because they were seldom translated into action. Starting around the time of the Civil War, however, the combination of increasingly pervasive urban change together with an increasing awareness of history forced Americans to recognize these contradictions and to consider, at first tentatively and unsuccessfully, what to do with old but valued pieces of the urban environment.

MICHAEL HOLLERAN, BOSTON'S "CHANGEFUL TIMES": ORIGINS OF PRESERVATION AND PLANNING IN AMERICA 84 (1998).

> Preservation was seen by its proponents as an integral part of building the modern city. * * * Preservationists were the imagineers of a memory infrastructure serving the great project of urban "improvement." * * * Memory sites such as parks, preserved buildings, monuments, and so on, represented the cultural aspect of "improvement" ideal—opposed to the bugaboos of disorder and congestion—and provided New York with historical memory "commensurate with the dignity of the metropolis of the New World." * * * Preservation, at its roots, was about an *engagement* with modernity, not a rejection of it.

Randall Mason, *Historic Preservation, Public Memory, and the Making of Modern New York City, in* GIVING PRESERVATION A HISTORY: HISTORIES OF HISTORIC PRESERVATION IN THE UNITED STATES 131, 157 (Max Page & Randall Mason, eds., 2004).

Figures 1-1 & 1-2:
Mount Vernon Mansion and Reconstructed
Cabin of an Enslaved Person,
Mount Vernon, VA

2.   Critics of preservation often dismiss the movement as elitist. This criticism accurately characterized early preservation efforts. After all, the Founding Fathers, on whom early preservationists were particularly focused, were members of an elite group, from both racial and socioeconomic perspectives. At Mount Vernon, for example, the Ladies' Association at first aimed exclusively at preserving George Washington's primary residence, shown in Figure 1-1, and his personal history. Numerous auxiliary structures in various states of repair also existed on the sprawling estate, but these structures were largely neglected. Visitors during the late nineteenth century had an accordingly limited perspective of the estate's full history.

More recently, however, the Ladies' Association (which continues to operate Mount Vernon) has made efforts to expand the history presented to the approximately one million visitors it receives each year. Most interestingly, the public tour now includes a reconstruction of a typical cabin of an enslaved person, shown in Figure 1-2, and extensive interpretative exhibits describing enslaved people's significant role in the day-to-day operations of such a large estate. When Washington died, 316 people he enslaved lived at Mount Vernon. Unique among the Founding Fathers, his will stipulated that all of the people he enslaved were to be freed once his wife Martha died. How does the expansion of Mount Vernon's interpretive displays reflect changes in the preservation movement more generally?

Especially in modern real estate development projects, preservation continues to bring racial and socioeconomic tensions to the fore, as the discussion on gentrification in Chapter 11 will describe in greater detail.

3.   The excerpt mentions the Antiquities Act of 1906, the first federal preservation statute that did not focus on a specific site. What kinds of resources are protected by the Antiquities Act? By excluding resources not on federal land, the Antiquities Act has a fairly limited scope. Over time, all levels of government—federal, tribal, state, and local—began to offer a more diverse array of protections to many different kinds of properties. Chapter 8 chronicles how the federal government has provided greater protection for archaeological sites and objects since the passage of the Antiquities Act.

4.   This excerpt provides a preview of the next section, which describes what kinds of things Americans have collectively chosen to preserve. So far, what have you learned about what things belong on this list?

B. FUNDAMENTAL QUESTIONS: WHAT, WHY, HOW, AND WHO?

With the history of the preservation movement in mind, we turn now to four fundamental questions in historic preservation law: what, why, and how do we preserve, and who are the key players?

1. WHAT DO WE PRESERVE?

Historic preservation laws have been written to protect many different kinds of real and personal property, as long as such properties are deemed to be "significant" and have "integrity." The most widely used definitions of significance and integrity may be found in the criteria for determining whether a property is historic enough to be listed on the National Register. "Significant" means having an attribute that is associated with important historical events; associated with the lives of significant persons; emblematic of the architectural characteristics of a type, period, or method of construction; and instructive (or likely to be instructive) in the fields of either prehistory or history. 36 C.F.R. § 60.4. "Integrity" encompasses "integrity of location, design, setting, materials, workmanship, feeling, and association." *Id.* These definitions have been incorporated countless times into similar tribal, state, and local laws across the country.

Figure 1-3:
Independence Hall,
Philadelphia, PA

Figure 1-4:
Mies van der Rohe's Farnsworth House,
Plano, IL

Chapter 2 more fully covers the process of designation to the National Register and to state and local registers, as well as the legal criteria for finding that a property has both significance and integrity. In this section, we aim merely to expose readers to broader questions relating to what our society has found most worthy of protection.

Among protected properties, buildings and other inhabitable structures—either listed individually or as part of historic districts—comprise the largest portion. Grand civic structures, such as Independence Hall in Philadelphia and the Jefferson Memorial in Washington, D.C., have been designated historic. Famous houses, including Frank Lloyd Wright's Fallingwater in Bear Run, Pennsylvania, and Mies van der Rohe's Farnsworth House near Plano, Illinois, have merited protection. Rural barns, neighborhood schoolhouses, urban skyscrapers, and early industrial buildings have been protected across the country. Small and modest structures have also been included. For example, listed on the National Register is a rock outhouse—with cast iron toilets from the 1920s that constantly flush when someone is seated on them—at an early rural service station along Route 66 in Warwick, Oklahoma.

Beyond buildings, engineering marvels and public works infrastructure, including roads and bridges, have been protected by preservation law. Freestanding, sculptural structures, such as the Statue of Liberty and the Jefferson National Expansion Memorial (the Gateway Arch) in St. Louis, have merited designation. Archaeological and tribal resources, including both sites and objects, have found protection in historic preservation and cultural resources laws discussed further in Chapters 8 and 9.

Significant landscapes and open spaces, including military battlefields, have also been preserved. The preservation of the battlefield at Gettysburg was a particularly important focus of early presentation efforts. The battle of Gettysburg, during which the Union Army beat back advances by General Robert E. Lee's Confederate troops, was the turning point of the Civil War. It was also the bloodiest battle of that conflict, with both sides together suffering over 51,000 casualties (soldiers killed, wounded, missing, or captured). An adjacent cemetery for Union soldiers was the site of President Abraham Lincoln's famous recitation of what is now known as the Gettysburg Address. In the late nineteenth century, local entrepreneurs erected a railway on private land ringing the battlefield, to shuttle tourists around the site. The federal government and local preservationists objected to the railway on the grounds that it disrupted visitors' perceptions of the battlefield. The following Supreme Court opinion resolved that conflict and contains an important defense of the role of government in preservation.

United States v. Gettysburg Electric Railway Company
160 U.S. 668 (1896)

■ MR. JUSTICE PECKHAM, after stating the facts in the foregoing language, delivered the opinion of the court.

[EDS.: After Congress authorized a commission to "preserv[e] the lines of battle," the commission condemned the land over which railway lines of the Gettysburg Electric Railway Company ran. The railway company challenged the constitutionality of the federal government's use of eminent domain to acquire ownership of land for purposes of historic preservation.]

The really important question to be determined in these proceedings is whether the use to which the petitioner desires to put the land described in the petitions is of that kind of public use for which the government of the United States is authorized to condemn land.

It has authority to do so whenever it is necessary or appropriate to use the land in the execution of any of the powers granted to it by the constitution.

Is the proposed use to which this land is to be put a public use, within this limitation? The purpose of the use is stated in the first act of congress, passed on the 3d day of March, 1893 (the appropriation act of 1893), and is quoted in the above statement of facts. The appropriation act of August 18, 1894, also contained the following: "For continuing the work of surveying, locating and preserving the lines of battle at Gettysburg, Pa., and for purchasing, opening, constructing and improving avenues along the portions occupied by the various commands of the armies of the Potomac and Northern Virginia on that field, and for fencing the same; and for the purchase, at private sale or by condemnation, of such parcels of land as the secretary of war may deem necessary for the sites of tablets, and for the construction of the said avenues; for determining the leading tactical positions and properly marking the same with tablets of batteries, regiments, brigades, divisions, corps and other organizations with reference to the study and correct understanding of the battle, each tablet bearing a brief historical legend, compiled without praise and without censure; fifty thousand dollars, to be expended under the direction of the secretary of war."

In these acts of congress, and in the joint resolution, the intended use of this land is plainly set forth. It is stated in the second volume of Judge Dillon's work on Municipal Corporations (4th Ed. § 600) that, when the legislature has declared the use or purpose to be a public one, its judgment will be respected by the courts, unless the use be palpably without reasonable foundation. Many authorities are cited in the note, and, indeed, the rule commends itself as a rational and proper one.

As just compensation, which is the full value of the property taken, is to be paid, and the amount must be raised by taxation, where the land is taken by the government itself, there is not much ground to fear any abuse of the power. The responsibility of congress to the people will generally, if not always, result in a most conservative exercise of the right. It is quite a different view of the question which courts will take when this power is delegated to a private corporation. In that case the presumption that the intended use for which the corporation proposes to take the land is public is not so strong as where the government intends to use the land itself.

In examining an act of congress, it has been frequently said that every intendment is in favor of its constitutionality. Such act is presumed to be valid unless its invalidity is plain and apparent. No presumption of invalidity can be indulged in. It must be shown clearly and unmistakably. This rule has been stated and followed by this court from the foundation of the government.

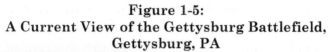

Figure 1-5:
A Current View of the Gettysburg Battlefield,
Gettysburg, PA

Upon the question whether the proposed use of this land is public one, we think there can be no well-founded doubt. And also, in our judgment, the government has the constitutional power to condemn the land for the proposed use. It is, of course, not necessary that the power of condemnation for such purpose be expressly given by the constitution. The right to condemn at all is not so given. It results from the powers that are given, and it is implied because of its necessity, or because it is appropriate in exercising those powers. Congress has power to declare war, and to create and equip armies and navies. It has the great power of taxation, to be exercised for the common defense and general welfare. Having such powers, it has such other and implied ones as are necessary and appropriate for the purpose of carrying the powers expressly given into effect. Any act of congress which plainly and directly tends to enhance the respect and love of the citizen for the institutions of his country, and to quicken and strengthen his motives to defend them, and which is germane to, and intimately connected with, and appropriate to, the exercise of some one or all of the powers granted by congress, must be valid. This proposed use comes within such description. The provision comes within the rule laid down by Chief Justice Marshall in *McCulloch v. Maryland*, 4 Wheat. 421 (1819), in these words: "Let the end be legitimate, let it be within the scope of the constitution, and all means which are appropriate, which are plainly adequate to that end, which are not prohibited but consistent with the letter and spirit of the constitution, are constitutional."

The end to be attained, by this proposed use, as provided for by the act of congress, is legitimate, and lies within the scope of the constitution. The battle of Gettysburg was one of the great battles of the world. The numbers contained in the opposing armies were great; the sacrifice of life was oreadful [sic]; while the bravery, and, indeed, heroism, displayed by both the contending forces, rank with the highest exhibition of those qualities ever made by man. The importance of the issue involved in the contest of which this great battle was a part cannot be overestimated. The existence of the government itself, and the perpetuity of our institutions, depended upon the result. Valuable lessons in the art of war can now be learned from an examination of this great battlefield, in connection with the history of the events which there took place. Can it be that the government is without power to preserve the land, and properly mark out the various sites upon which this struggle took place? Can it not erect the monuments provided for by these acts of congress, or even take possession of the field of battle, in the name and for the benefit of all the citizens of the country, for the present and for the future? Such a use seems necessarily not only a public use, but one so closely connected with the welfare of the republic itself as to be within the powers granted congress by the constitution for the purpose of protecting and preserving the whole country. It would be a great object lesson to all who looked upon the land thus cared for, and it would show a proper recognition of the great things that were done there on those momentous days. By this use the government manifests for the benefit of all its citizens the value put upon the services and exertions of the citizen soldiers of that period. Their successful effort to preserve the integrity and solidarity of the great republic of modern times is forcibly impressed upon every one who looks over the field. The value of the sacrifices then freely made is rendered plainer and more durable by the fact that the government of the United States, through its representatives in congress assembled, appreciates and endeavors to perpetuate it by this most suitable recognition. Such action on the part of congress touches the heart, and comes home to the imagination of every citizen, and greatly tends to enhance his love and respect for those institutions for which these heroic sacrifices were made. The greater the love of the citizen for the institutions of his country, the greater is the dependence properly to be placed upon him for their defense in time of necessity, and it is to such men that the country must look for its safety. The institutions of our country, which were saved at this enormous expenditure of life and property, ought to and will be regarded with proportionate affection. Here upon this battlefield is one of the proofs of that expenditure, and the sacrifices are rendered more obvious and more easily appreciated when such a battlefield is preserved by the government at the public expense. The right to take land for cemeteries for the burial of the deceased soldiers of the country rests on the same footing, and is connected with, and springs from, the same powers of the constitution. It seems very clear that the government has the right to bury its own soldiers, and to see to it that their graves shall not remain unknown or unhonored.

No narrow view of the character of this proposed use should be taken. Its national character and importance, we think, are plain. The power to condemn for this purpose need not be plainly and unmistakably deduced from any one of the particularly specified powers. Any number of those powers may be grouped together, and an inference from them all may be drawn that the power claimed has been conferred.

It is needless to enlarge upon the subject, and the determination is arrived at without hesitation that the use intended, as set forth in the petition in this proceeding, is of that public nature which comes within the constitutional power of congress to provide for by the condemnation of land.

NOTES & QUESTIONS

1.   This opinion deals with eminent domain, the public power to condemn property and put it toward a public use. The U.S. Constitution does not expressly give Congress the power of eminent domain, but it is considered incidental to, or "necessary and proper" for, the exercise of powers Article I does confer. In this decision, the Supreme Court considers whether the use of eminent domain to create a national battlefield park is within the powers given to Congress. Would you say that the Court takes a broad or narrow view of Congress's power to engage in historic preservation? What moves the Court to adopt that view? Congress's power of eminent domain is constrained by the Fifth Amendment takings clause, which states: "nor shall private property be taken for public use, without just compensation." The takings clause is now considered to apply to the states via the Fourteenth Amendment and is further discussed in Chapter 7.

2.   Efforts to preserve the battlefield at Gettysburg began even before the Civil War ended. The first steward of Gettysburg was the Pennsylvania legislature, which incorporated the cemetery, and an association of Pennsylvania Civil War veterans, which began accumulating the land on which the historic battle took place. By 1870, the federal government had taken ownership of the cemetery and by 1895 (as affirmed by the preceding opinion), it controlled the battlefield as well. Since 1933, the site—now known as Gettysburg National Military Park and including both cemetery and battlefield—has been overseen by the National Park Service. Various monuments, structures, markers, observation towers, and objects have been erected and taken down over the years as our understanding of the site and approach to its preservation has evolved.

3.   Disputes about activities on land adjacent to the Gettysburg battlefield endured long after *Gettysburg Electric Railway* was decided. The erection of a 307-foot commercial observation tower built on nearby private land in 1974, for example, also inspired litigation. *See Commonwealth v. Nat'l Gettysburg Battlefield Tower, Inc.*, 311 A.2d 588 (Pa. 1973). In that case, the parties agreed to a land swap in which the tower would be moved

further from the battlefield. (Ultimately, however, the National Park Service condemned the tower and demolished it in 2000.) That messy dispute turned public opinion in favor of systematic battlefield preservation. By 1975, the citizens of Gettysburg established the Gettysburg Battlefield Historic District covering the battlefield and adjacent areas. Listed on the National Register, the Historic District helps to protect, through regulation, what preservationists had previously tried to protect through piecemeal litigation and public pressure.

4.   Another major question has been how to preserve the interpretive facilities that have been erected to help visitors understand Gettysburg. Consider the case of the Park Service's first permanent visitors' center, built in 1962 and designed by renowned modernist architect Richard Neutra. The critically-acclaimed Neutra center was designed to house a massive cyclorama painting by Paul Philippoteaux, depicting key battlefield events. The Park Service later proposed to demolish the building, located within the battlefield area, so that it could reconstruct the landscape to approximate its appearance at the time of the battle. Preservationists were divided, though through the Section 106 process of the National Historic Preservation Act, the Park Service and the nonprofit National Trust for Historic Preservation signed a memorandum of agreement acknowledging the Park Service's ability to demolish the Neutra center. Other groups, unhappy with this result, filed suit to enjoin demolition. *Network v. Latschar*, 701 F. Supp. 2d 49 (D.D.C. 2010), and the eventual demolition of the building is considered in greater detail in Chapter 4. Visitors to Gettysburg may now visit a new, 22,000 square foot museum that includes a special room for the cyclorama painting.

5.   These and other fascinating legal issues regarding what to preserve at Gettysburg have been chronicled by Professor J. Peter Byrne. *See Hallowed Ground: The Gettysburg Battlefield in Historic Preservation Law*, 22 TUL. ENVTL. L.J. 203 (2009). He concludes:

> Decisions about preservation and presentation of a historic site of central cultural and political significance will always reflect the perspectives of contemporary society, especially those with power. When we look behind the patriotic purposes supporting public preservation of the Gettysburg battlefield, we find evolving over time a memorial to the sacrifice of the soldiers, veterans asserting their ongoing political power, the promise of emancipation and equal citizenship, assertions of national unity, white supremacy, conservative stability, renewal of an American mission to promote global freedom, nostalgia for pastoralism in the face of monotonous sprawl development, martial valor in a world of nuclear destruction, the fun of family outings, and the business of heritage tourism. In all this, the dramatic stories of the Battle and its significance for our history comes alive in different manners for different visitors.

Id. at 268. Consider this view, and the reasoning of the Supreme Court in *Gettysburg Electric Railway*, when reading the next section, on why we preserve.

Case Studies: Trees and Dugongs

Perhaps the more thought-provoking recent questions about what may be worth preserving have revolved around objects found in nature. In *Hatmaker v. Georgia Department of Transportation,* 973 F. Supp. 1058 (M.D. Ga. 1997), the court considered whether a single tree—named the Friendship Oak—could be considered historic under federal eligibility guidelines. The Secretary of the U.S. Department of Transportation had determined that the tree was not eligible to be listed on the National Register, and therefore that the Secretary could proceed with a federal road-widening project requiring the tree's removal. Two licensed arborists sued the Secretary for failing to follow proper procedures to determine whether the tree was eligible for the National Register, including failing to adequately weigh the evidence of the tree's historicity. At the time, only 4 trees were individually listed on the National Register (then containing 65,000 listings).

Both sides presented evidence about the tree's historical significance. The evidence showed no connections between that specific tree and Native American groups, historic trails or transportation routes, military events, or lynchings (a brutal but all too common type of "event" in Georgia's history). However, the tree was listed on a statewide "Historic Tree Register," was an attraction in an official state travel publication, and may possibly have been the last surviving feature of an encampment for American soldiers during the Spanish-American War. Moreover, outside the courtroom, the publicity campaign for the tree's survival, and the litigation itself, gave the tree special contemporary meaning.

Ultimately, the court found that there was not enough evidence to support a finding that the Secretary's determination was "clearly erroneous," which would have been required for the court to demand that the Secretary re-evaluate the tree. The *Hatmaker* case presents two central puzzles for preservationists. First, to what extent should litigation or publicity concerning a resource contribute to a finding of significance? Second, if a resource is "the last remaining vestige of times" past, should it be protected simply for its historic value, or should it not be protected because it lacks the historical context in which it could be best understood?

International sites, too, have raised provocative questions about what should be protected under U.S. preservation laws. You will read more about international preservation issues in Chapter 12. But for now, consider *Okinawa Dugong v. Gates*, 543 F.Supp.2d 1082 (N.D. Cal. 2008), which dealt with whether the Department of Defense was required to take into account the effects of a construction of military air station in Okinawa on the dugong, "a marine mammal of cultural and historical significance to the Japanese people." Among other indicators of its significance, the dugong is listed as a "natural monument" on the

Japanese Register of Cultural Properties. As you will learn in Chapter 3, the National Historic Preservation Act requires that federal agencies such as the Department of Defense take into account the effect of certain federal "undertaking[s]" on historic properties. *See* 54 U.S.C. § 306108. Section 402 of the National Historic Preservation Act clarifies that Congress intended to protect not just domestic undertakings, but "undertaking[s] outside the United States that may directly and adversely affect a property that is on the World Heritage List or on the applicable country's equivalent of the National Register." 54 U.S.C. § 307101(e). The court concluded that the Okinawa dugong was protected by the National Historic Preservation Act because the Japanese Register of Cultural Properties was the equivalent of the National Register.

Consider the protection of the dugong in light of types of property which have been more commonly protected by American historic preservation laws. How do domestic concepts of "significance" and "integrity" come into play in this case? Should the impact on the dugong have been considered under federal or international laws relating to endangered species instead? Or is the dugong more like a scenic landscape—a critical part of a coherent ecosystem, albeit underwater? Or like cultural patrimony, given its significance to Japanese culture? What does Japan's protection of the dugong say about our respective cultures or legal systems?

2.   WHY DO WE PRESERVE?

Justifications for preservation have evolved over time. Congress has expressed the national interest in preservation several times, most notably in its findings and declarations introducing the National Historic Preservation Act of 1966. The National Historic Preservation Act is a sweeping federal law that forms the heart of our federal preservation regime; it will be the subject of Chapter 3. Before it was eliminated in a recodification, the following excerpt summarized why Congress identified preservation as a national goal.

Findings and Declarations of the National Historic Preservation Act
The former 16 U.S.C. § 470(b)

The Congress finds and declares that—

(1) the spirit and direction of the Nation are founded upon and reflected in its historic heritage;

(2) the historical and cultural foundations of the Nation should be preserved as a living part of our community life and development in order to give a sense of orientation to the American people;

(3) historic properties significant to the Nation's heritage are being lost or substantially altered, often inadvertently, with increasing frequency;

(4) the preservation of this irreplaceable heritage is in the public interest so that its vital legacy of cultural, educational, aesthetic, inspirational, economic, and energy benefits will be maintained and enriched for future generations of Americans;

(5) in the face of ever-increasing extensions of urban centers, highways, and residential, commercial, and industrial developments, the present governmental and nongovernmental historic preservation programs and activities are inadequate to insure future generations a genuine opportunity to appreciate and enjoy the rich heritage of our Nation;

(6) the increased knowledge of our historic resources, the establishment of better means of identifying and administering them, and the encouragement of their preservation will improve the planning and execution of Federal and federally assisted projects and will assist economic growth and development; and

(7) although the major burdens of historic preservation have been borne and major efforts initiated by private agencies and individuals, and both should continue to play a vital role, it is nevertheless necessary and appropriate for the Federal Government to accelerate its historic preservation programs and activities, to give maximum encouragement to agencies and individuals undertaking preservation by private means, and to assist State and local governments and the National Trust for Historic Preservation in the United States to expand and accelerate their historic preservation programs and activities.

A variety of economic and social movements led Congress to enact the National Historic Preservation Act in 1966. For example, suburbs were rising in popularity, and the resulting flight from cities led to neglect of historic resources. Urban renewal, which often involved clearing entire historic neighborhoods for large-scale public housing and infrastructure, occurred around this time as well. A single event that focused the nation's attention on preservation was the demolition, which began in 1963, of the Beaux-Arts Pennsylvania Station in Manhattan to make way for Madison Square Garden and a new, soulless, underground Penn Station. In 2021, Moynihan Station opened in another Beaux Arts marvel, the Post Office across the street from the demolished Pennsylvania Station. This new station restored dignity to the experience of train travelers arriving in New York City. It was named after Senator Daniel Patrick Moynihan, a politician who championed historic preservation.

In light of the purposes identified by Congress, consider the following four readings, each presenting a different view about why we might choose to preserve.

a.   THE COMMUNITY-BUILDING RATIONALE

Carol M. Rose, Preservation and Community: New Directions in the Law of Historic Preservation
33 STAN. L. REV. 473 (1981)

The phrase "historic preservation" is so elastic that any sort of project can be justified—or any change vilified—in its name. In a sense, every event is "history," and it is a cliché among professional historians that views of "historic significance" alter considerably with shifting social interests—a point amply attested by the sudden discovery of black history, the boom in the history of women's movements, and the reinterpretation of the Cold War. Art and architectural historians, especially important to preservation, are equally flexible in their views of "historic significance," as shown by their recent interest in the art deco Coca-Cola signs, quonset hut offices, and White Tower diners that once horrified historic preservationists.

Like "historic significance," "preservation" is a varying concept. Does "preservation" mean maintenance, or restoration, or indeed reconstruction and adaptive alteration? Is it merely photographing old things or describing them in words? Does it include something new that further develops an older tradition? Because historic significance is so open-ended and preservation so ambiguous, publicly supported historic preservation is singularly vulnerable to the charge of arbitrariness.

This is no matter of merely academic significance. Despite a certain little-old-lady aura about preservation in the abstract, disputes over preservation can carry an extraordinary emotional force: Witness the Hawaiians who risked criminal trespass charges to prevent the armed services' practice bombing on ancient [indigenous] shrines. Money stakes also run high. In 1978, lease arrangements worth millions of dollars were lost when the United States Supreme Court decided in *Penn Central Transportation Company v. New York* that New York's preservation controls on Grand Central Station did not amount to a "taking" and that the owners could thus be prevented from adding a multi-story tower to the old building. As the courts begin to interpret the wave of preservation statutes, some property owners are resisting landmark designation under the statutes. Once viewed as a merely honorary embellishment, designation is now fraught with tax consequences and use restrictions.

Aside from direct financial considerations, historic preservation activities may have consequences that give pause to the most socially conscious citizen: A preservation board's permit denial may block nursing home facilities, a low-income housing project, or a rapid transit facility;

and, perhaps most significant, in the wake of increased attention to historic structures, the low-income residents of old neighborhoods may be forced out by steeply rising rents.

The displacement of low-income residents, to which I shall return later, may be the albatross of the modern historic preservation movement, evoking as it does the overtones of snobbery and special interest that have long dogged preservationists. Almost a decade ago, Michael Newsome warned that poor black families might be displaced as middle class whites moved into spruced-up "historic" neighborhoods—and observed that it wasn't *black* history that the preservationists had in mind.

The displacement issue raises the central problems in historic preservation law: What elements of the past are to be preserved, and why should their preservation take the form of maintaining buildings or groups of buildings? The answers clearly entail choices among political constituencies and preferences. But without a coherent rationale to explain and direct public involvement in preservation activities, the legal techniques for preservation become little more than new weapons for the politically adroit. Precisely because preservation calls for political choices, it is imperative to identify the public purposes of preservation so that preservation law can be made intelligible by reference to those purposes.

Can any coherent rationale give shape to the amorphous activities that might conceivably gather under the aegis of historic preservation? Just such a rationale has been emerging in the recent profusion of preservation programs—a rationale slightly unexpected and seldom fully articulated, yet repeatedly glimpsed in the major preservationist legislation and litigation over the last 15 years. According to this implicit rationale, the chief function of preservation is to strengthen local community ties and community organization.

The very inchoacy of the community-building purpose in preservation—not to speak of the many preservation activities that seem to diverge from such a purpose—suggests that this emerging rationale requires exploration and elaboration. This article undertakes that task, first crystallizing the main features of a community-building rationale for preservation, and then using the rationale as a standard for evaluating current preservation programs. * * *

The third phase of historic preservation [EDS.: after a first phase of preservation as "inspiration" and a second phase of preservation for architectural or artistic merit] builds on elements of the past by expanding the substantive considerations implicit in *Gettysburg* and by increasing the attention paid to procedure. Although the effects of urban renewal and the urban freeway projects scarcely rival the effects of the Civil War battles that gave emotional resonance to *Gettysburg*, the saga of shattered neighborhoods did move architects and urbanologists to reconsider the political ramifications of the physical environment. The focus of this reconsideration, as in *Gettysburg*, was the contribution of the physical environment to the maintenance of community—not the national community as in *Gettysburg*, but the smaller community of the city and neighborhood. Jane Jacobs's 1961 book, *The Death and Life of Great American Cities*, stressed the city dweller's need for buildings of varying ages and uses, discussed the psychological and social consequences of structural layout, and prescribed architecture that contributes to neighborly interest in the community. More recently, Oscar Newman's *Defensible Space* used many of Jacobs's ideas in exploring the use of architecture to encourage neighborhood crime prevention. And in his *Image of the City*, Kevin Lynch took the simple phenomenon of *not feeling lost* as a starting point for examining the architectural qualities—scale, border, direction, the punctuation of an occasional singular "landmark"—that make a neighborhood or a city "legible" or "imageable" in the viewer's mind. In the legible city, not only can urban dwellers find their way, but the architectural qualities themselves lend drama, interest, an occasion for anecdotes about the past, and thus a framework for identification with the shared experience of the community.

Although the contribution of architecture to community requires further definition, this discussion does suggest a consistent and substantive foundation for public involvement in preservation efforts.

In the past 15 years, the community-oriented architectural discussion has influenced the direction of public preservation activities, and its vocabulary has entered the legal terminology of historic preservation. In the U.S. Conference of Mayors report, *With Heritage So Rich*, a volume widely regarded as the seminal work behind the 1966 National Historic Preservation Act (NHPA), one finds the claim that an historic district is a legislative attempt to preserve the "village within the city." Herbert Gans first used the phrase to describe Boston's West End, an ethnic neighborhood ultimately cleared by urban renewal and something of a *cause célèbre* in the anti-urban renewal literature. The NHPA's stated purpose of providing a "sense of orientation to the American people" reflects Lynch's language. Local ordinances for historic districts routinely regulate the scale of buildings in the districts, and guidelines for preservation rehabilitation often discuss the relationship of structures to the visual definition of the entire street.

As for the importance of orientation, when a Congressman asked why Washington's embattled Willard Hotel was "historic" though only 70 years old, a Park Service representative responded:

> [A] lot of things make things historic. It is anything that gives a place a sense of place ... And if we keep tearing down everything which gives the city a sense of identity, and putting up duplicates of commercial glass boxes ... how do you know where you are?

Figure 1-6:
The Historic Willard Hotel,
Washington, DC

The Willard controversy gave courts an opportunity to comment on a community-building rationale for preservation. The decision in *Commissioner of the District of Columbia v. Benenson*, one step in the protracted litigation over the Willard, favored the hotel's owners over the preservationists but acknowledged the ways in which historic structures strengthen the links of a community:

> There may well be those who think it lamentable that this handsome old hotel may soon be demolished. Retention of fine architecture, especially in the capital of a relatively young country such as ours, lends a certain stability and cultural continuity, which can only contribute over the years to national substance. If one looks at the architecture of a city and sees only the present, the feeling of character is missing.

If community-building is the central direction of recent preservation activity, several consequences follow. First, the age and fame of a structure are only two among several elements, including scale, distinctiveness of design, and location, that should be considered in assessing a building's importance to the community. Second, because a community exists over time, the present members are to be considered valuable. However important it may be to conserve the indicia of the past, some latitude must remain for the contributions of the present. Third, a community-building rationale should place preservation—and the physical surroundings generally—in a larger perspective of community needs. Finally, if it is recognized that physical surroundings play a political role in the community, the treatment of those surroundings cannot be viewed as the preserve of aesthetes and bluebloods, but must become an issue for a broader constituency.

b.   PRESERVING THE PROTOTYPE

James Marston Fitch, Historic Preservation: Curatorial Management of the Built World
(1990)

The outstanding accomplishment of modern industrial technology has been what we may call the democratization of material culture. It goes without saying that the consumption or enjoyment of a given cultural artifact—a book, a picture, a chair, a sherbet—by the masses of the people awaited the technical means for multiplying that artifact; only then could there be wider access to the forms of material culture. Depending upon the artifact in question, this multiplication has been achieved by replica, duplicate, or facsimile. Generally speaking, the replica, an expression of handicraft production, has disappeared. The duplicate and the facsimile have, therefore, become the standard expressions of modern industrial production. * * *

In no other sector of material culture * * * has the means of replicating a prototype—and replicating it anywhere in the world—been as pervasive as in architecture. Earlier European conquerors of Asia, Africa, and the Americas had, of course, brought with them their own vocabulary of architectural forms. But the extent to which they were able to apply them in the new environment was sharply limited by their own relatively primitive preindustrial technologies. All of this is quite changed today. The great prototypical forms of contemporary architecture—the mass-housing projects of Gropius, the skyscrapers of Le Corbusier, the glass pavilions of Mies van der Rohe—have been endlessly replicated around the world. In this proliferation of a few basic prototypes, we face in microcosm all of the paradoxes of modern industrialized mass production. The ability to produce a 40-story high-rise office building as easily in Lagos as in Los Angeles is, in abstract terms, a remarkable accomplishment. Such an exportation of exotic architectural forms would have been inconceivable a century ago. Moreover, it can be argued that the need for multistory construction in a rapidly growing city like Lagos may be quite as justifiable there as in American cities where the type was invented.

Nevertheless, the efflorescence of these internationalized prototypes has serious consequences * * * Here in America [we see] * * * the endless replication of a handful of discredited clichés: the ranch-type house, the "colonial" shopping center. It may be argued that the industrialized multiplication of this limited range of artifacts has brought a higher level of privatized comfort to middle-class American families than ever before. But it can scarcely be denied that it has been accompanied by the degradation of the style itself. It is probably an instinctive response to this vulgarization that the same middle-class families visit in increasing numbers such historic sites as Deerfield, Williamsburg, and Savannah, for there they can experience the original, the prototype, in all its sensuous and associational appeal. * * *

The dilemma is clear enough; yet we scarcely admit it to thought. Modern industrial technology constitutes the indispensable agent of material abundance and hence of political democracy. But in the very process of mass-producing the artifacts of material culture, it subjects the prototypes of these artifacts to remorseless attrition. The industrial duplicate or facsimile cannot, under any circumstances, be the qualitative equal of its prototype, no matter how socially useful it may be. * * * Both the uniqueness and the integrity of the artifact are in jeopardy because, left to itself, the facsimile tends to supplant and then to destroy the original. Already, in the highly developed countries of the West, this process has advanced far enough that a new generation is among us whose aesthetic experience and hence aesthetic judgment are based upon private contact with duplicate and facsimile, rather than upon public participation in the exposure to great originals. Such a development, indefinitely extended, can only lead to the impoverishment of the sensual and aesthetic life of each individual and a drastic alteration in the tone of the entire culture. * * *

The field of historic preservation, for all its pragmatic, ad hoc development up to date, already displays a high order of social innovation and invention. These activities already display many of the elements of a comprehensive national program by which we shall be able to preserve the prototypical forms—settlements, districts, individual buildings, and gardens—against which all material culture must be judged.

c.   THE ECONOMIC DEVELOPMENT RATIONALE

PlaceEconomics, Twenty-Four Reasons Historic Preservation Is Good For Your Community
(2020)

We measure the contributions of historic preservation that can be measured. Over the last five years PlaceEconomics has done analyses of the impacts of historic preservation in nearly a dozen cities of all sizes throughout the United States. From that research we've assembled the twenty-four reasons why historic preservation is good for your city.

1.   Jobs

Historic rehabilitation means jobs—generally well-paid jobs, particularly for those without advanced formal education. Rehabilitation tends to be more labor intensive than new construction, so work restoring historic buildings has a greater job creating impact per dollar spent than new construction. In Savannah, for example, one million dollars spent on the rehabilitation of a Savannah historic building will generate about 1.2 more jobs and $62,000 more in income for Georgia citizens than the same amount spent on new construction.

In New York City, more than $800 million is invested annually in New York's historic buildings, creating jobs for 9,000 New Yorkers and providing paychecks of over $500 million each year.

In Pittsburgh, just the projects using the federal historic tax credit have added an average of 500 jobs and $18 million in salaries and wages every year for the past 35 years.

But jobs don't just come from historic rehabilitation activities. Designated local historic districts are job magnets. In Nashville, while only 3% of jobs are located in historic districts, 11% of all job growth in the city has gone to historic districts. * * * In Nashville designated historic districts also saw 24% of all job growth in accommodation and food service jobs, playing a key role in the tourism industry. In New York City, while 8% of all jobs are in designated historic districts, 12.7 % of all food service and accommodations jobs are there. As anyone in the food service industry knows, success depends not just on the quality of the food, but the atmosphere and character of the restaurant. That's why in Rhode Island, 14 of the 25 highest rated restaurants on Yelp are in historic districts. In Raleigh 9 of the top 20 Yelp rated restaurants are in historic districts. It's not just that cities providing dining are thriving, those restaurants are particularly thriving in designated historic districts.

2.   Downtown Revitalization

Thirty years ago, the conventional wisdom was that downtowns had been replaced by shopping centers, and if downtowns survived at all it would be exclusively because local government and financial institutions were located there. Of course, that was a prescription for a nine to five, five day a week economic, social, and cultural desert. Thankfully not everyone accepted that premise. In large cities and small towns, the most common and ultimately successful strategy was to identify, protect, reuse, and enhance the historic buildings that differentiated downtown from the mall. For those places wise and farsighted enough to reinvest and redevelop their historic structures rather than raze them, the payoff is clear.

In Indianapolis, while about 11% of downtown is made up of historic districts, they contribute a disproportionate amount of income generation, containing nearly 39,000 jobs, 26% of all of the jobs downtown. In Nashville commercial property values in downtown historic districts increased in value by 425% between 2007 and 2017, compared to the rest of downtown at 236%. Two-thirds of new businesses in downtown Raleigh chose historic and other older buildings for their location. In Saratoga Springs, New York, the downtown Broadway Historic District is the cultural and economic hub of Saratoga Springs where 22% of all jobs in the city are located. In Tybee Island, Georgia (population 3,127) the concentrated efforts towards the Main Street Corridor commercial area creates a fertile environment for small businesses. Nearly 250 net new jobs have been created in the Tybee Island Main Street Corridor alone.

Main Street is an economic revitalization program based on utilizing each downtown's historic buildings. There is no more cost-effective program of economic development of any kind in the United States today. Since 1980, Main Street districts in more than 2000 communities have seen cumulative investment of $79 billion, 285,000 buildings rehabilitated, more than 640,000 net new jobs, and nearly 144,000 net new business. Many of these are small towns in rural America. This historic preservation-based program didn't ruin those towns; in many cases it literally saved them.

3.   Heritage Tourism

Often when "economics" and "historic preservation" appear in the same sentence, the reaction is, "Oh, you must mean heritage tourism." In fact, tourism is just one economic contributor of historic preservation, but it is an important one. Consistent findings in both the US and internationally indicate that heritage visitors stay longer, visit more places, and spend more per day than do tourists with no interest in historic resources.

New York City's historic sites, places, and landmarks are a major draw for visitors. For domestic tourists who only come to the City for a day, nearly one-third (31.2%) fall into the "heritage visitor" category. The share is even larger for overnight visitors, with 4 in 10 putting a high priority on visiting historic places. While New York's tourism industry has a huge impact on the City's overall economy, just the domestic heritage tourism component represents direct spending of more than $8 billion each year. Those expenditures mean jobs—nearly 135,000 jobs a year. Over 98,000 are jobs directly related to the heritage tourism industry and an additional 36,000 indirect and induced jobs are generated by heritage tourism. These heritage tourism jobs result in nearly $6 billion in direct wages to New York City residents and $738 million in local tax revenue. Each heritage visitor in New York City spends on average $83 more during the trip than the non-heritage tourist.

In Pittsburgh 45.6% of overnight visitors and 44.8% of day visitors fall within the definition of heritage tourist. Tourism is a large and growing industry there, but just the heritage portion of that industry is responsible for nearly $812 million annually in expenditures in the Pittsburgh area. What is particularly important about these visitors is that they spend more each day in Pittsburgh as compared to visitors with no interest in historic resources. This difference is the heritage premium. Pittsburgh sees nearly $64 million per year in additional economic activity based on the additional amount heritage visitors spend each day compared to other tourists.

Just the heritage portion of Pittsburgh's tourism industry is responsible for 12,300 direct jobs and an additional 4,500 indirect jobs. The salary and wages paid to workers meeting the needs of Pittsburgh's heritage visitors is $310 million per year with another $223 million to indirect and induced jobs.

Nearly all expenditures of tourists fall into five categories: lodging; food and beverage; local transportation; retail purchases; and entertainment/admissions/amusements. In San Antonio, not only do heritage visitors spend more in total, they spend more in each of the five areas than do tourists with no interest in historic preservation. Those tourism expenditures create both jobs and paychecks. Over 14,000 food and beverage workers, nearly 12,000 retail employees, and 9,000 workers in hotels, motels, and B&Bs owe their jobs to San Antonio's heritage visitors. Those food and beverage workers take home over $400 million in salary and wages, $350 million for those in retail, and an additional $317 million in paychecks for hotel and motel workers.

Travel experts understand the appeal of historic preservation—and far beyond just the occasional monument or mansion. *The New York Times* regularly runs a feature named, "36 hours in. . ." When Raleigh, North Carolina was covered 15 of the 22 recommended businesses to visit were located in designated historic districts. A similar article appeared in the *Washington Post* entitled, "What to do in Indianapolis," recommend[ing] sixteen places to go, eat, shop, stay, and explore. Eleven of them were in designated historic districts.

4.   Property Values

There is no area of preservation economic analysis that has been done more often than measuring the impact of local historic districts on property values. Regardless of the researcher, the methodology, or the location of the study, the results of these analyses have been remarkable consistent: In nearly every instance properties in local historic districts have greater rates of appreciation than properties elsewhere in the same city. Thirty years ago, opponents to the creation of a local historic district usually claimed, "Historic districts mean one more layer of regulation. More regulation means, prima facie, lower property values." Of course, study after study has demonstrated the opposite has been true; the values of properties have significantly benefited from local district designation. Today the argument—often from the same people who opposed districts early—is more likely to be, "Those damn historic districts will mean my property value is going up, so I'll have to pay more property taxes."

In Indianapolis, between 2002 and 2016, a single-family house in a local historic district has on average increased in value 7.3% each year, compared with just under 3.5% for houses not in historic districts. This market preference also extends to the amount of activity. Historic districts, which only make up 5.5% of properties in the city, represented nearly 20% of all sales and almost 35% of the aggregate sale amount.

Between 2000 and 2008, single-family residential properties in Raleigh increased in value 49% on a per square foot basis. Over that same time period value increases in three local historic districts increased in value between 84% and 111%.

The square foot value for single family homes in Pittsburgh not in historic district increased 45% between 2001 and 2014. Every local historic district saw a value increase greater than the average of the rest of the city.

Saratoga Springs is fortunate to have a large inventory of older and historic houses, many of which are not located in one of the local historic districts. Some buyers are specifically attracted to these older properties. Comparisons were made for both median and mean by age, by style, by "typical house," by total value, by value per square foot, and by rate of change in value over time. In every instance, properties in designated local historic districts outperformed comparable properties not within local districts.

It is true that higher values usually mean higher property taxes. And for those with modest resources or living on fixed incomes, that can create difficulties. Often led by preservation advocates, many cities have adopted taxation policies that mitigate those problems. But the reality is this—rising property values resulting in rising taxes may be a cash flow problem, but a wealth enhancement.

Around the United States, the effective property tax rate is typically between 1.5% and 2.5% of the value of the property each year. Thus, a property worth $100,000 would have annual taxes of between $1,500 and $2,500. For example purposes only, assume the market as a whole goes up 3% per year while properties in the historic district go up 4% per year. Next year the non-historic house would have a value increase of $3,000 and increased taxes of between $45 ($3,000 x 1.5%) and $75 ($3,000 x 2.5%) while the historic house would have a value increase of $4,000 and increased taxes of between $60 ($4,000 x 1.5%) and $100 ($4,000 x 2.5%). So here is the effect on the owner of the historic house—she had to pay additional taxes of between $15 and $25 more than her neighbor, the owner of the non-historic house. But the value of her home increased $1,000 more than did her neighbor. She would be hard pressed to find any investment on Wall Street where an additional $15 to $25 in outlay was rewarded with another $1,000 in wealth.

That does not mean that rising property taxes which cause financial difficulties for some owners should not be addressed. But the short-term cash flow problem is offset 40 to 67 times by the increased wealth.

d.   THE SUSTAINABILITY RATIONALE

National Trust for Historic Preservation, The Greenest Building: Quantifying the Environmental Value of Building Reuse
(2011)

Until now, little has been known about the climate change reductions that might be offered by reusing and retrofitting existing buildings rather than demolishing and replacing them with new construction. This groundbreaking study concludes that building reuse almost always offers environmental savings over demolition and new construction. Moreover, it can take between 10 and 80 years for a new, energy-efficient building to overcome, through more efficient operations, the negative climate change impacts that were created during the construction process. However, care must be taken in the selection of construction materials in order to minimize environmental impacts; the benefits of reuse can be reduced or negated based on the type and quantity of materials selected for a reuse project.

This research provides the most comprehensive analysis to date of the potential environmental impact reductions associated with building reuse. Utilizing a Life Cycle Analysis (LCA) methodology, the study compares the relative environmental impacts of building reuse and renovation versus new construction over the course of a 75-year life span. LCA is an internationally recognized approach to evaluating the potential environmental and human health impacts associated with products and services throughout their respective life cycles.

This study examines indicators within four environmental impact categories, including climate change, human health, ecosystem quality, and resource depletion. It tests six different building typologies, including a single-family home, multifamily building, commercial office, urban village mixed-use building, elementary school, and warehouse conversion. The study evaluates these building types across four U.S. cities, each representing a different climate zone, i.e., Portland, Phoenix, Chicago, and Atlanta. * * *

Building reuse almost always yields fewer environmental impacts than new construction when comparing buildings of similar size and functionality. The range of environmental savings from building reuse varies widely, based on building type, location, and assumed level of energy efficiency. Savings from reuse are between 4 and 46 percent over new construction when comparing buildings with the same energy performance level. The warehouse-to-multifamily conversion—one of the six typologies selected for study—is an exception: it generates a 1 to 6 percent greater environmental impact relative to new construction in the ecosystem quality and human health impact categories, respectively. This is due to a combination of factors, including the amount and types of materials used in this project. * * *

Reuse-based impact reductions may seem small when considering a single building. However, the absolute carbon-related impact reductions can be substantial when these results are scaled across the building stock of a city. For example, if the city of Portland were to retrofit and reuse the single-family homes and commercial office buildings that it is otherwise likely to demolish over the next 10 years, the potential impact reduction would total approximately 231,000 metric tons of CO_2— approximately 15% of their county's total CO_2 reduction targets over the next decade. When scaled up even further to capture the potential for carbon reductions in other parts of the country, particularly those with a higher rate of demolition, the potential for savings could be substantial. Given these potential savings, additional research and analysis are needed to help communities design and employ public-policy tools that will remove obstacles to building reuse.

Reuse of buildings with an average level of energy performance consistently offers immediate climate-change impact reductions compared to more energy-efficient new construction. It is often assumed that the CO_2-reduction benefits gained by a new, energy efficient building outweigh any negative climate change impacts associated with the construction of that building. This study finds that it takes 10 to 80 years for a new building that is 30 percent more efficient than an average-performing existing building to overcome, through efficient operations, the negative climate change impacts related to the construction process. As indicated in the following table, an exception also exists here for the warehouse-to-multifamily building conversion. Upon analysis, this adaptive use scenario does not offer the carbon savings provided by other reuse scenarios.

Building reuse alone cannot fulfill the urgent task of reducing climate change emissions. . . . [R]euse and retrofitting for energy efficiency, together, offer the most significant emissions reductions in the categories of climate change, human health, and resource impact. Certainly, the barriers to retrofits are numerous. However, a variety of organizations are presently working to address the obstacles to greening existing buildings. This study finds that reuse and retrofit are particularly impactful in areas in which coal is the dominant energy source and more extreme climate variations drive higher energy use.

Materials matter: the quantity and type of materials used in a building renovation can reduce, or even negate, the benefits of reuse. In general, renovation projects that require many new materials—for example, an addition to an elementary school or the conversion of a warehouse to a residential or office use—offer less significant environmental benefits than scenarios in which the footprints or uses of the buildings remain unchanged. In the case of the warehouse-to-multifamily conversion scenario, the newly constructed building actually demonstrated fewer environmental impacts in the categories of ecosystem quality and human health.

NOTES & QUESTIONS

1.   Which of these four justifications for historic preservation are most likely to appeal to the broadest audience? Which is the least appealing? Is the answer different now than it was fifty years ago?

2.   Measuring impact or outcomes often presents methodological challenges in fields such as historic preservation. In a 2008 report, the National Trust for Historic Preservation acknowledged that embodied energy calculations often rely on outdated values for materials, and that analyses for whole buildings may either be under-or over-inclusive in terms of the amounts or types of materials. Patrice Frey, Nat'l Trust for Historic Pres., *Building Reuse: Finding a Place on American Climate Policy Agendas* 10–11 (2008). Because embodied energy analyses are often incorporated into life cycle analyses, life cycle analyses too may be compromised. *Id.* at 15–16.

Similarly, assessing the economic impact of preservation can be challenging. In 2005, the Brookings Institution published a paper on the relevant literature, which stated:

> The economic costs and benefits of historic preservation are the subject of persistent and urgent questioning in public debates. Whenever historic preservation comes up in public discourse, it seems, economic arguments figure prominently. Sometimes the discussion is about whether historic preservation has some economic value, and the answer generally is "yes." And sometimes the tougher questions are ventured: does historic preservation of a certain site have more economic value than an alternative investment might have? What are the costs and benefits of regulation? Is preservation an effective way to stimulate economic development? * * *

> A growing number of studies and research projects take on issues in this realm of understanding the economic values of historic preservation. The specific kinds of questions and themes addressed include: Justification of public policies and other investments (especially rehabilitation tax credits); rationales for advocating preservation over new construction; rationales for promoting generally conservative approaches to managing the built environment (falling under the rubrics of "sustainability" or "smart growth"); justifying material support for preservation as an expression of culture (in which a lot of the questioning is identical to that plaguing the arts and culture sectors in general, whether the topic is funding for museums, art, music, or other

forms); and how to use economic analysis to inform management decisions for historic preservation sites and programs.

Despite the growing number, range, and sophistication of studies, however, this review concludes that the field is not thoroughly studied, nor is there much agreement on answers to basic pragmatic and policy questions.

Randall Mason, Brookings Institution, *Economics and Historic Preservation: A Guide and Review of the Literature* 1 (2005).

For a compilation of economic studies of historic preservation, *see* DONOVAN D. RYPKEMA, THE ECONOMICS OF HISTORIC PRESERVATION: A COMMUNITY LEADER'S GUIDE (3d ed. 2014). For a more skeptical account, see EDWARD L. GLAESER, TRIUMPH OF THE CITY: HOW OUR GREATEST INVENTION MAKES US RICHER, SMARTER, GREENER, HEALTHIER, AND HAPPIER 148–52 (2011).

If the numbers do not or cannot tell the full story, how should society value the immeasurable benefits of preservation mentioned by Mason? As he asks in the same report, is it useful, or even possible, to "price the priceless"?

3.   Professor William Fischel has posited that concern for home values is a central motivator of citizen involvement and of local government behavior because homeowners are politically influential, guided by concern for the value of their homes, and cognizant of how local government choices affect home values. WILLIAM A. FISCHEL, THE HOMEVOTER HYPOTHESIS: HOW HOME VALUES INFLUENCE LOCAL GOVERNMENT TAXATION, SCHOOL FINANCE, AND LAND-USE POLICIES (2005). How might so-called homevoters view historic preservation? Do their interests explain why so many local governments have adopted preservation laws in recent decades?

Many studies have confirmed that property values rise after historic preservation designation. One study reviewed the impact of historic district designation on the New York City housing market. When development is limited in neighborhoods designated as historic, housing supply becomes limited, the cost of housing rises in those districts, and issues of affordability arise. *See* Vicki Been et al., *Preserving History or Hindering Growth? The Heterogeneous Effects of Historic Districts on Local Housing Markets in New York City*, NATIONAL BUREAU OF ECONOMIC RESEARCH WORKING PAPER SERIES, Working Paper 20446, at 2 (2014). Another researcher, studying Denver, found that historic district designation correlates with a rise in property values by 12 to 23 percent. Yang Zhou, *The Political Economy of Historic Districts: the Private, the Public, and the Collective*, 86 REGIONAL SCI. & URBAN ECON. (2021). Is all preservation necessarily inequitable?

We think not. Consider the twenty other "reasons historic preservation is good for your community," which we did not excerpt above. They include lower foreclosure rates, relative resiliency in up and down real estate markets, and use of historic places by small businesses. Moreover, and perhaps a counterpoint to the New York City study, historic places have a higher incidence of affordable housing, and more diverse income levels of resident.

4.   What role does self-interest play among those who support preservation? Do property owners pat themselves on the back when they mount a "Historic Property" plaque, indicating that their property is worthy of special attention? See, as an example, this historic marker on a building in Baltimore, which reads: "This property is listed on the National Register as a part of Fell's [sic] Point National Historic District and is registered with the Preservation Society." What is your reaction when you see one of these markers?

Figure 1-7:
Fells Point National Historic District Building Marker,
Baltimore, MD

5.   Can historic preservation be justified on the grounds that it is a public duty? Professor Joseph L. Sax explored the history of the Abbé Grégoire (a religious figure) and the origins of heritage preservation ideology in France. Sax concludes that historic preservation was seen "as a state responsibility; cultural property as 'belonging' to the nation regardless of formal ownership; and creative achievement as a national asset." Joseph L. Sax, *Heritage Preservation as a Public Duty: The Abbé Grégoire and the Origins of an Idea*, 88 MICH. L. REV. 1142, 1168–69 (1990). Given what you know about historic preservation law so far, does our preservation program reflect the fulfillment of this public duty, or a desire to fulfill it?

6.   There is also a purely aesthetic justification for historic preservation. Robert E. Stipe advocates for preserving the appearance of historic buildings and monuments, primarily for their "intrinsic value as art." Robert E. Stipe, *Why Preserve?*, A RICHER HERITAGE: HISTORIC PRESERVATION IN THE TWENTY-FIRST CENTURY xiv (Robert E. Stipe, ed.,

2003). If you were a decision-maker, would you be more likely to preserve certain styles of historic buildings?

7.   Not everyone views historic buildings as visually appealing. Some have argued that the growing formalization and standardization of historic preservation techniques detracts from architectural variety and experiential vitality. Herbert Muschamp, the longtime *New York Times* architectural critic, wrote in 1993 that:

> What has taken the place of architecture is architectural history: landmarks preservation, connoisseurship of period styles and design guidelines that require new buildings to emulate the appearance of old ones. * * * Architecture is an urban intruder: a destroyer of memories, a painful reminder that people have little control over their surroundings. Three decades ago, the preservation movement dramatically increased that control. A movement that had been regarded as an elitist pastime became one of the most powerful tools with which citizens could exercise power over the urban landscape. It was a tool directed against real estate development, but inevitably it was turned against architecture. Its particular target was modern architecture, a style whose path had been paved with gestures of contempt for the Beaux-Arts and other facets of the city's rich stylistic mix.

Fear, Hope, and the Changing of the Guard, N.Y. TIMES, Nov. 14, 1993. What did Muschamp mean by "architecture"? What do you think of his critique of the preservation movement as anti-creative? Does his allegation that preservationists are anti-modernists ring false given preservationists' embrace of modernist icons like the Farnsworth House?

Now read an excerpt from a book by *Wall Street Journal* architectural critic, Ada Huxtable:

> [W]e like our memories better all cleaned up. The gritty and sometimes unlovely accumulations that characterize cities are the best and worst of what we have produced; they exert a fascination that no neatly edited version can inspire. * * *

> The act of preservation turns what has been "saved" into something else, at the same time that the improvements provide the economic base that "saves" it. This is classic Catch-22. Sooner or later, image and function are defined and fixed in an artificial formula that combines sentiment, fashion, and tourist appeal. * * *

> What the perfect fake or impeccable restoration lacks are the hallmarks of time and place. They deny imperfections, alterations, and accommodations; they wipe out all the incidents of life and change. The worn stone, the chafed corner, the threshold low and uneven from many feet, the marks on walls and windows that carry the presence and message of remembered hands and eyes—all of those accumulated, accidental, suggestive, and genuine imprints that imbue the artifact with its history and continuity, that have stayed with it in its conditioning passage through time—are absent

or erased. * * * These objects and places simply do not resonate. They are mute. They are hollow history.

ADA LOUISE HUXTABLE, THE UNREAL AMERICA: ARCHITECTURE AND ILLUSION (1999). What kinds of "gritty" or imperfect aspects of a place might some preservation developers seek to remove? Is there anything the law can do about preserving the grittiness? Should it try to? Think about these critiques when you read about the Secretary's Standards, next.

3.   HOW DO WE PRESERVE?

The question "How do we preserve?" really requires two answers. The first answer relates to physical techniques and methods used to preserve older buildings, and the second relates to the law. This section will focus on the first answer only briefly; the remainder of this section, and, of course, the remainder of this book deals more deeply with the second.

a.   THE PHYSICAL "HOW"

The question of "how," physically, we should preserve properties is perhaps best addressed in the Secretary of the Interior's Standards for the Treatment of Historic Properties (the "Standards"). The Standards, codified at 36 C.F.R. Part 68, were developed as best practices to be consulted by anyone undertaking a preservation project. They are intended to apply broadly to many types of protected properties, including buildings, sites, structures, objects, and districts, but are not intended to cover exceptional properties or circumstances. The Standards have been either adopted or adapted by local, state, and tribal governments; in certain jurisdictions, for certain projects, compliance with the Standards is mandatory.

Substantively, the Standards include suggestions for four different treatments of historic properties, which from greatest to least amount of fidelity to existing conditions are: preservation, rehabilitation, restoration, and reconstruction. The Federal Regulations provide the following general rules for each treatment type.

Secretary of the Interior's Standards for the Treatment of Historic Properties
36 C.F.R. § 68.3

(a) Preservation.

(1) A property will be used as it was historically, or be given a new use that maximizes the retention of distinctive materials, features, spaces and spatial relationships. Where a treatment and use have not been identified, a property will be protected and, if necessary, stabilized until additional work may be undertaken.

(2) The historic character of a property will be retained and preserved. The replacement of intact or repairable historic materials or alteration of features, spaces and spatial relationships that characterize a property will be avoided.

(3) Each property will be recognized as a physical record of its time, place and use. Work needed to stabilize, consolidate and conserve existing historic materials and features will be physically and visually compatible, identifiable upon close inspection and properly documented for future research.

(4) Changes to a property that have acquired historic significance in their own right will be retained and preserved.

(5) Distinctive materials, features, finishes and construction techniques or examples of craftsmanship that characterize a property will be preserved.

(6) The existing condition of historic features will be evaluated to determine the appropriate level of intervention needed. Where the severity of deterioration requires repair or limited replacement of a distinctive feature, the new material will match the old in composition, design, color and texture.

(7) Chemical or physical treatments, if appropriate, will be undertaken using the gentlest means possible. Treatments that cause damage to historic materials will not be used.

(8) Archeological resources will be protected and preserved in place. If such resources must be disturbed, mitigation measures will be undertaken.

(b) Rehabilitation.

(1) A property will be used as it was historically or be given a new use that requires minimal change to its distinctive materials, features, spaces and spatial relationships.

(2) The historic character of a property will be retained and preserved. The removal of distinctive materials or alteration of features, spaces and spatial relationships that characterize a property will be avoided.

(3) Each property will be recognized as a physical record of its time, place and use. Changes that create a false sense of historical development, such as adding conjectural features or elements from other historic properties, will not be undertaken.

(4) Changes to a property that have acquired historic significance in their own right will be retained and preserved.

(5) Distinctive materials, features, finishes and construction techniques or examples of craftsmanship that characterize a property will be preserved.

(6) Deteriorated historic features will be repaired rather than replaced. Where the severity of deterioration requires replacement of a distinctive

feature, the new feature will match the old in design, color, texture and, where possible, materials. Replacement of missing features will be substantiated by documentary and physical evidence.

(7) Chemical or physical treatments, if appropriate, will be undertaken using the gentlest means possible. Treatments that cause damage to historic materials will not be used.

(8) Archeological resources will be protected and preserved in place. If such resources must be disturbed, mitigation measures will be undertaken.

(9) New additions, exterior alterations or related new construction will not destroy historic materials, features and spatial relationships that characterize the property. The new work will be differentiated from the old and will be compatible with the historic materials, features, size, scale and proportion, and massing to protect the integrity of the property and its environment.

(10) New additions and adjacent or related new construction will be undertaken in such a manner that, if removed in the future, the essential form and integrity of the historic property and its environment would be unimpaired.

(c) Restoration.

(1) A property will be used as it was historically or be given a new use that interprets the property and its restoration period.

(2) Materials and features from the restoration period will be retained and preserved. The removal of materials or alteration of features, spaces and spatial relationships that characterize the period will not be undertaken.

(3) Each property will be recognized as a physical record of its time, place and use. Work needed to stabilize, consolidate and conserve materials and features from the restoration period will be physically and visually compatible, identifiable upon close inspection and properly documented for future research.

(4) Materials, features, spaces and finishes that characterize other historical periods will be documented prior to their alteration or removal.

(5) Distinctive materials, features, finishes and construction techniques or examples of craftsmanship that characterize the restoration period will be preserved.

(6) Deteriorated features from the restoration period will be repaired rather than replaced. Where the severity of deterioration requires replacement of a distinctive feature, the new feature will match the old in design, color, texture and, where possible, materials.

(7) Replacement of missing features from the restoration period will be substantiated by documentary and physical evidence. A false sense of history will not be created by adding conjectural features, features from

other properties, or by combining features that never existed together historically.

(8) Chemical or physical treatments, if appropriate, will be undertaken using the gentlest means possible. Treatments that cause damage to historic materials will not be used.

(9) Archeological resources affected by a project will be protected and preserved in place. If such resources must be disturbed, mitigation measures will be undertaken.

(10) Designs that were never executed historically will not be constructed.

(d) Reconstruction.

(1) Reconstruction will be used to depict vanished or non-surviving portions of a property when documentary and physical evidence is available to permit accurate reconstruction with minimal conjecture and such reconstruction is essential to the public understanding of the property.

(2) Reconstruction of a landscape, building, structure or object in its historic location will be preceded by a thorough archeological investigation to identify and evaluate those features and artifacts that are essential to an accurate reconstruction. If such resources must be disturbed, mitigation measures will be undertaken.

(3) Reconstruction will include measures to preserve any remaining historic materials, features, and spatial relationships.

(4) Reconstruction will be based on the accurate duplication of historic features and elements substantiated by documentary or physical evidence rather than on conjectural designs or the availability of different features from other historic properties. A reconstructed property will re-create the appearance of the non-surviving historic property in materials, design, color and texture.

(5) A reconstruction will be clearly identified as a contemporary re-creation.

(6) Designs that were never executed historically will not be constructed.

––––––––––

Additional guidelines are provided in 36 C.F.R. §§ 68.1 and 68.2. Each of these four treatments requires different methods and produces different outcomes. How might one choose which treatment to use? One should consider the building's significance and relevant importance, physical condition, proposed use, relevant code requirements, availability of documentation, and economic and technical feasibility. For instance, a property which is the last surviving example of a particular style of architecture in a city might be a candidate for preservation, which involves careful fidelity to the property's existing physical features. A project involving a change of use—say, the conversion of a historic neighborhood school into luxury condominiums—might benefit from the more flexible standards of rehabilitation. An example of a reconstruction is the cabin of enslaved people at Mount Vernon, mentioned above. Because of the temporal materials and poor quality of such homes, none survived to the present day, yet a facsimile, clearly labeled as such, could help visitors better understand the history of the estate.

NOTES & QUESTIONS

1.   How would you characterize each of the four treatments? What subtle differences between them have the most impact on the physical results of an alteration?

2.   Various levels of government incorporate the Standards. Yet for the most part, property alterations are held to the rehabilitation standard. Should these requirements vary? What are the advantages and disadvantages of having more rigorously-tiered preservation laws?

Figure 1-8:
Modern Glass Courtyard of the Patent Office Building,
Washington, DC

3.   What is the physical impact of 36 C.F.R. § 68.3(b)(9) & (10), regarding new additions to historic properties? Figure 1-8 depicts an elegant example of a project that fully complies with those sections of the Standards. It shows the interior courtyard of the Greek Revival Patent Office Building (now housing the Smithsonian American Art Museum and National Portrait

Gallery) in Washington, D.C., which is one of only about 2,500 National Historic Landmarks in the country. While the walls of the courtyard date back to the nineteenth century, the roof was completed in 2007. The undulating glass, aluminum, and steel roof were erected as part of a renovation to allow the courtyard to be used year-round for a variety of events. The architect, Foster + Partners, designed the roof so that it would complement the existing structure, but it is clearly modern and differs from the Patent Office Building in material, texture, and scale. Because it is independently supported by eight steel columns resting just within the courtyard walls, the roof can be removed without harming any historic fabric.

4.   Discuss (perhaps with others) examples of preservation projects in your community that have been undertaken using each of the four treatments described above. Based on your observations, how closely have such projects adhered to the Secretary's Standards?

5.   Review the Standards again while thinking about the challenges of climate change. The Standards take a very formal approach to restoring specific materials and retaining integrity of location. Yet this formality may preclude the kind of flexible response that will be needed as wildfires, mudslides, floods, extreme heat, and sea level rise batter the planet. Should there be a climate change exception, which allows property owners to apply fireproofing materials, or raise buildings above flood levels, even though the Standards today would not allow either? Could you make a case for a "relocation" treatment, which would allow historic resources to be moved out of harm's way? And what about a "deconstruction" treatment, which would allow historic resources that must be taken down to save people to be salvaged for reuse? For a proposal that the Standards be augmented to include both treatments, see Sara C. Bronin, *Adapting National Preservation Standards to Climate Change*, for TOWARDS SUSTAINABILITY AND EQUITY: ENVISIONING PRESERVATION POLICY REFORM (Erica Avrami, ed. 2021).

b.   THE LEGAL "HOW"

We turn now to how our legal system promotes historic preservation—a necessarily brief introduction to the issues considered in most of the remainder of this book. The law utilizes four primary methods: regulation, procedural requirements, incentives, and information.

Regulation, the method having the largest impact and used as the basis for the largest number of laws, simply means imposing rules on activities relating to historic preservation. Regulations range in scope and scale—from a local ordinance mandating that certain paint colors be used within a historic district to a federal law describing how archaeological artifacts found on public land should be handled. Although regulatory historic preservation laws primarily target the actions of private actors, public bodies may also have to comply with certain regulations.

Procedural requirements mandate that, within the course of decision-making about a particular action, public or private actors consider impact on historic sites or consult with interested third parties, but such requirements do not dictate particular substantive results. Federal and state environmental protection laws, as well as the National Historic Preservation Act (the subject of Chapter 3), have procedural requirements that have saved important historic sites from harm. Local laws such as demolition delay ordinances, which mandate a period of time during which no demolition of a historic property may occur, allow the property owner to consider alternatives and also fall under this category. Note that in contrast to procedural requirements, a handful of laws impose substantive results, such as requiring that actors minimize all harm to protected properties.

Public incentives—ranging from low-interest loans, to lump sum grants, to tax credits, to exemptions from building codes or zoning requirements—have encouraged private parties to invest in historic preservation projects. Some of these incentives will be discussed further in Chapters 10 and 11.

Finally, various levels of government have set up institutions that both gather and disseminate information intended to promote or support preservation. Such information may include property surveys, thematic histories, and archaeological techniques. For example, in 1933, Congress created the Historic American Buildings Survey, an office within the Department of the Interior, that collects and makes publicly-available drawings, photographs, written reports, and other media depicting various aspects of American architectural heritage. As another example, planning offices may fulfill an educational mission by running workshops or creating pamphlets for property owners seeking to do small-scale projects, such as energy efficiency improvements, on their historic homes.

All levels of government have enacted laws evidencing the four primary methods of promoting preservation, along with numerous secondary methods. Within our federal system, governments may either work together on overlapping areas of concern or divide duties based on respective legal authority.

Underlying all historic preservation laws at the state and local levels is the authority to act pursuant to the "police power." The police power, reserved to the states by the Tenth Amendment to the U.S. Constitution, authorizes states to make laws that promote public health, safety, morals, or general welfare. States may delegate all or part of this authority to localities but must specify the scope of such delegation. The police power has been used by both states and localities to justify their authority to enact zoning laws, building codes, nuisance prohibitions, and historic preservation ordinances. To violate the police power, a preservation ordinance would have to be clearly arbitrary or unreasonable, or would have to bear no substantial relation to the public health, safety, morals, or general welfare. *See Vill. of Euclid v. Ambler Realty Co.*, 272 U.S. 365, 395 (1926) (establishing the reasonableness standard for judicial reviews of exercises of local zoning authority).

A preservation law otherwise justified by the police power may be invalidated if it is found to violate certain rights granted by the U.S. Constitution (or by state constitutions). Many of these rights are discussed in Chapter 7. As we set the stage for later discussions, it is worth mentioning one constitutional right—the right to due process—which is guaranteed by the Fifth Amendment and made applicable to the states by the Fourteenth Amendment. According to the Constitution and to Supreme Court interpretations thereof, neither the state nor the federal government may deprive any individual "of life, liberty, or property, without due process of law." U.S. CONST. amend. V. Due process challenges have frequently been filed against preservation ordinances. The following case highlights key issues.

Maher v. City of New Orleans
516 F.2d 1051 (5th Cir. 1975), *cert. denied*, 426 U.S. 905 (1976)

■ ADAMS, CIRCUIT JUDGE:

The issues posed in the case at hand, although they concern a municipal ordinance, nevertheless carry implications of nationwide import.

Plaintiff Maher, on the basis of the Fifth Amendment, assails an ordinance of the City of New Orleans that regulates the preservation and maintenance of buildings in the historic Vieux Carre section of that city, popularly known as the French Quarter. Maher asserts that, on its face, the Vieux Carre Ordinance affronts the due process clause, because it provides no objective criteria to guide the Commission charged with its administration. * * *

I.   Factual Background.

By amendment to the Louisiana Constitution in 1936, authority was vested in the City of New Orleans to create a Commission whose purpose was stated to be:

> The preservation of such buildings in the Vieux Carre section of the City of New Orleans as, in the opinion of said Commission, shall be deemed to have architectural and historical value, and which buildings should be preserved for the benefit of the people of the City of New Orleans and the State of Louisiana, and to that end the Commission shall be given such powers and duties as the . . . City of New Orleans shall deem fit and necessary.

To implement the historical preservation plan, the City enacted the Vieux Carre Ordinance. That Ordinance establishes the Vieux Carre Commission and creates a framework of rules governing its powers, duties and operations. Among its other provisions, the Ordinance stipulates that, to perform construction, alteration or demolition work within the geographic boundaries controlled by the legislation, one must procure a permit approved by the Commission.[5]

The present controversy centers on the fate of the Victorian Cottage situated at 818–22 Dumaine Street, adjacent to the Maher residence in the Vieux Carre. Mr. Maher, who owned the property until his recent death, had sought since 1963 to demolish the cottage and to erect a seven-apartment complex on the site.

Following a preliminary approval of Maher's proposal by its Architectural Committee, the Commission on April 16, 1963, disapproved Maher's application to raze the cottage. Almost from the time of the original application, interested individual neighborhood owners, as well as organized groups including the Vieux Carre Property Owners and Associates, Inc., the French Quarter Residents Association and the Louisiana Council for the Vieux Carre vigorously opposed the Maher plan to tear down the cottage and to develop the property.

Maher undertook a succession of attempts to secure approval of his plans from the Commission. After several refusals, the Commission was finally prevailed upon to issue the permit. Ultimately, however, construction was prohibited when on August 16, 1966, the City Council for New Orleans, on the basis of an appeal, forbade the grant of a demolition permit. * * *

[I]n 1971, Maher filed the present federal suit under the civil rights act against the City and its agencies, seeking a declaratory judgment that the Ordinance is unconstitutional and an injunction against its enforcement. * * *

III. The Vieux Carre Ordinance is a Proper Exercise of the Police Power.

The Supreme Court has erected wayposts to guide our consideration whether an enactment such as the Vieux Carre Ordinance violates due process. A legislative determination is generally accorded a presumption of constitutionality,[34] but it is nevertheless subjected to several tests before its validity is established. To be sound, the enactment must be within the perimeter of the police power, an authority residing in the law-making body to secure, preserve and promote the general health, welfare and safety. A regulatory ordinance, to be sustained as a suitable exercise of the police power, must bear a real and substantial relation to a legitimate state purpose. The means selected must be reasonable and of

---

[5] Before the commencement of any work in the erection of any new building or in the alteration or addition to, or painting or repainting or demolishing of any existing building, any portion of which is to front on any public street or alley in the Vieux Carre Section, application by the owner for a permit therefor shall be made to the Vieux Carre Commission, accompanied by the full plans and specifications thereof so far as they relate to the proposed appearance, color, texture of materials and architectural design of the exterior, including the front, sides, rear and roof of such building, alteration or addition or of any out building, party wall, courtyard, fence or other dependency thereof.

[34] Goldblatt v. Hempstead, 369 U.S. 590 (1962); Village of Euclid v. Ambler Realty Co., 272 U.S. 365 (1926).

general application, and the law must not trench impermissibly on other constitutionally protected interests.[38] * * *

Throughout the country, there appears to be a burgeoning awareness that our heritage and culture are treasured national assets. Many locales endowed with historic sites have enacted protective measures for them. The Vieux Carre Ordinance is among the earliest efforts in this regard, and has served as a prototype for similar enactments elsewhere. * * *

The Court is not free to reverse the considered judgment of the legislature that it is in the public interest to preserve the status quo in the Vieux Carre and to scrutinize closely any proposed change in the ambiance by private owners. Where a legislative determination is "fairly debatable, the legislative judgment must be allowed to control." We thus conclude that, considering the nationwide sentiment for preserving the country's heritage and with particular regard to the context of the unique and characteristic French Quarter, the objective of the Vieux Carre Ordinance falls within the permissible scope of the police power. * * *

The Ordinance is of general application to a well-defined geographic area. In addition, it establishes a Commission whose professional qualifications and means of selection are delineated. Within the boundaries of the French Quarter, the Commission is directed to review plans for all proposed demolition or construction and its duties and procedures are specific. After due consideration the Commission reports its recommendations to the Director of the Department of Safety and Permits, whereupon a permit for the proposed work may issue. Provision is made for review by the City Council.

Though generally the procedures ordained are not faulted,[57] Maher attacks the schema as violative of due process because, in his view, it provides inadequate guidance to the Commission for the exercise of its administrative judgment. The City concedes that no official objective standards have been promulgated in this regard. Maher suggests that formal standards are mandatory to guide the Commission in its resolution of the buildings deserving of preservation. * * *

While concerns of aesthetic or historical preservation do not admit to precise quantification, certain firm steps have been undertaken here to assure that the Commission would not be adrift to act without standards in an impermissible fashion. First, the Louisiana constitution,

---

[38] Pennsylvania Coal Co. v. Mahon, 260 U.S. 393 (1922).

[57] The suggestion was advanced that the Ordinance has been, and continues to be, enforced in an arbitrary fashion and not altogether free from influence. Evidence, including a federally funded report on the Commission's operations, was inserted in the record to support such claims. Charges that improper considerations play a role in decision making respecting the French Quarter merit serious attention by the Court. The district court decided that on balance, the allegations in this respect were not substantiated by the record. On review, we affirm the district court on the basis that its result finds support in the record and is not clearly erroneous. In so affirming, however, we pause to note that past enforcement of the Ordinance does not seem to have been uniformly predictable.

the Vieux Carre Ordinance and, by interpretation, the Supreme Court of Louisiana, have specified their expectations for the Vieux Carre, and the values to be implemented by the legislation.

Further, the legislature exercises substantial control over the Commission's decision-making in several ways. Where possible, the ordinance is precise, as for example in delineating the district, defining what alterations in which locations require approval, and particularly regulating items of special interest, such as floodlights, overhanging balconies or signs.

Another method by which the lawmaking body curbed the possibility for abuse by the Commission was by specifying the composition of that body and its manner of selection. Thus, the City is assured that the Commission includes architects, historians and business persons offering complementary skills, experience and interests.

The elaborate decision-making and appeal process set forth in the ordinance creates another structural check on any potential for arbitrariness that might exist. Decisions of the Commission may be reviewed ultimately by the City Council itself. Indeed, that is the procedure that was followed in the present case.

It is true, as Maher observed, that no officially promulgated regulations pinpoint each decision by the Commission. Nonetheless, apart from the evident purpose of the legislation and the taut lines of review maintained by the legislature over the operation of the Commission, other fertile sources are readily available to promote a reasoned exercise of the professional and scholarly judgment of the Commission. It may be difficult to capture the atmosphere of a region through a set of regulations. However, it would seem that old city plans and historic documents, as well as photographs and contemporary writings may provide an abundant and accurate compilation of data to guide the Commission. And the district court observed,

> In this case, the meaning of a mandate to preserve the character of the Vieux Carre "takes clear meaning from the observable character of the district to which it applies."

Aside from such contemporary indicia of the nature and appearance of the French Quarter at earlier times, the Commission has the advantage at present of a recent impartial architectural and historical study of the structures in the area. The Vieux Carre Survey Advisory Committee conducted its analysis under a grant to Tulane University from the Edward G. Schleider Foundation. Building by building, the Committee assessed the merit of each structure with respect to several factors. For example, regarding the Maher cottage at issue here, the Louisiana Supreme Court noted that the Survey Committee "was of the opinion that this cottage was worthy of preservation as part of the over-all scene." While the Schleider survey in no way binds the Commission, it does furnish an independent and objective judgment respecting the edifices in the area. The existence of the survey and other historical source material assist in mooring the Commission's discretion firmly to the legislative purpose.

We thus conclude that the present zoning ordinance, enacted to promote the social and economic goals of preserving a historical district judged of public value, does not delegate unfettered authority to the Vieux Carre Commission. Rather, the legislature has provided adequate structure and guidelines to that administrative body. * * *

V.   Conclusion.

The Vieux Carre Ordinance was enacted to pursue the legitimate state goal of preserving the "tout ensemble" of the historic French Quarter. The provisions of the Ordinance appear to constitute permissible means adapted to secure that end. Furthermore, the operations of the Vieux Carre Commission satisfy due process standards in that they provide reasonable legislative and practical guidance to, and control over, administrative decision-making.

Once the district court concluded it was at liberty, under principles of finality, to reach the merits of Maher's case, that court was not persuaded that the denial of a demolition permit was arbitrary. It did not find that the ordinance as applied to Maher constituted a taking of Maher's property for which compensation was indicated. These determinations, based on the proof proffered there, are not clearly erroneous.

An order will, therefore, be entered affirming the judgment of the district court.

Affirmed.

NOTES & QUESTIONS

1.   What two levels of government were involved in the creation of the Vieux Carré Ordinance? Why was it enacted? The panel deferred to the legislature by referencing the legislature's "considered judgment" exercised during the drafting process of the Ordinance. To which aspect of the Ordinance's drafting process did the court defer?

2.   Figures 1-9 and 1-10 present views of structures within the Vieux Carré Historic District, better known as the French Quarter, of New Orleans. Based on these photographs and any other knowledge you may have of the neighborhood, do you agree with the district court and the Fifth Circuit that the meaning of the preservation mandate within the ordinance is clarified by the district's observable character? Would this approach work in historic districts with more eclectic architecture? If not, what might circumvent due process challenges aimed at regulations in those historic districts?

3.   What do you make of Footnote 57? Should the lack of predictability have been fatal to the ordinance? Or is there a certain amount of flexibility appropriate—or even desirable—in preservation laws?

Figures 1-9 & 1-10:
Two Views of the French Quarter,
New Orleans, LA

4.   The Fifth Circuit panel cited the *Euclid* case, the 1926 Supreme Court decision that upheld the zoning ordinance of Euclid, Ohio, against due process and equal protection challenges. *Vill. of Euclid v. Ambler Realty Co.*, 272 U.S. 365 (1926). The Supreme Court rejected those challenges, holding that Euclid's zoning ordinance was a valid exercise of the police power. At the time, Euclid's ordinance was typical of zoning laws across the country, which regulated the way property owners used land to ensure that undesirable land uses or nuisances were segregated from more desirable uses. Enacted primarily at the local level, zoning laws today still regulate use, but have added regulations involving building size, shape, and placement.

For many years, state and local governments assumed that the same authority—the police power—upheld in the *Euclid* case for zoning ordinances could be used to justify historic preservation ordinances. As the *Maher* case reveals, however, property owners sometimes had a different view. The Supreme Court addressed the historic preservation question in 1978, a few years after *Maher* was decided. *See Penn Cent. Transp. Co. v. City of N.Y.*, 438 U.S. 104 (1978). *Penn Central* upheld New York City's Landmarks Law as a valid exercise of the city's police power against a challenge focusing on the takings clause of the U.S. Constitution. A full treatment of *Penn Central* is included in Chapter 7.

5.   Around the same time *Euclid* was decided, the Supreme Court held a zoning ordinance invalid for violating the due process clause. In *Washington ex rel. Seattle Title Trust Co. v. Roberge*, 278 U.S. 116 (1928), the Court considered the following provision of the Seattle zoning ordinance: "A philanthropic home for children or for old people shall be permitted in [a particular zone] * * * when the written consent shall have been obtained of the owners of two-thirds of the property within four hundred (400) feet of the proposed building." *Id.* at 118. The trustee of a philanthropic home unable to locate a new home in the affected zone sued, and the Court found that the consent requirement was "repugnant to the due process and equal protection clause," stating:

> [T]here is no legislative determination that the proposed building and use would be inconsistent with public health, safety, morals, or general welfare. The enactment itself plainly implies the contrary. * * * The section purports to give the owners of less than one-half the land within 400 feet of the proposed building authority—uncontrolled by any standard or rule prescribed by legislative action—to prevent the trustee from using its land for the proposed home. The superintendent is bound by the decision or inaction of such owners. There is no provision for review under the ordinance; their failure to give consent is final. They are not bound by any official duty, but are free to withhold consent for selfish reasons or arbitrarily and may subject the trustee to their will or caprice.

Id. at 121–22. Ordinances that require neighbors' consent to either allow or prohibit certain preservation activities should be considered in light of *Roberge* and related cases to ensure that they do not run afoul of the due process clause.

6.   Although the *Maher* opinion has proven to be influential, it has not been the last word on due process challenges to preservation ordinances. A handful of state appellate-level courts have found violations of procedural due process in certain local historic review processes. *See, e.g., Unruh v. City of Asheville*, 388 S.E.2d 235 (N.C. Ct. App. 1990); *S. Nat'l Bank of Hous. v. City of Austin*, 582 S.W.2d 229 (Tex. Civ. App. 1979).

In 2009, preservationists across the country were alarmed when an Illinois court upheld the ability of property owners in a Chicago historic district to challenge the Chicago Landmark Ordinance on the basis that the Ordinance was unconstitutionally vague. *See Hanna v. City of Chi.*, 907 N.E.2d 390 (Ill. App. 2009). (The challenged portion of the Ordinance may be found in the State and Local Designation Part of Chapter 2.) The opinion's most controversial language included the following statements: "We believe that the terms 'value,' 'important,' 'significant,' and 'unique' are vague, ambiguous, and overly broad. We are unpersuaded by the City's argument that the Commission members can be well guided by these terms." *Id.* at 396. Can you see why numerous Illinois cities and preservation groups filed amicus briefs on behalf of the city? This decision was eventually reversed.

4.   WHO ARE THE KEY PLAYERS?

This Chapter has identified a few of the key players in historic preservation, but further clarification of their role may be in order. Most key players fall into one of three categories: property owners, public entities and officials, and nonprofit organizations.

a.   PROPERTY OWNERS

Property owners, including their agents and affiliates, play perhaps the largest role in the preservation story because of their inherent power over historic resources they own. Where preservation laws govern modifications or demolition, property owners may choose to adhere strictly to the laws, challenge them, or ignore them (either by neglecting or by actively damaging historic resources). At the same time, an owner of a property that is designated neither historic nor otherwise protected may nonetheless follow best practices, such as the Secretary of the Interior's Standards for the Treatment of Historic Properties, in taking any action. Where no protections exist, property owners may lead a movement within their communities to put a preservation regime in place.

Property owners may be either private or public entities. The applicability of some laws depends on the identity of the property owner. Many laws that incorporate procedural requirements, for example, target public agencies acting as owners. Laws that have a regulatory focus tend to exempt public property owners and apply only to private entities. Similarly, incentive programs are geared toward private property owners.

We should not understate the impact of governments acting as property owners, particularly with respect to archaeological and Native American resources. The federal government alone owns about 644 million acres of land, or about 30 percent of the land in the United States. In addition, it serves as a trustee for 56 million acres of tribal lands, on behalf of over 300 tribes. State and local governments own about 195 million acres, comprising about 9 percent of land in this country. Thus only about 60 percent of land (about 1.37 billion acres) in the United States is privately owned. *See* U.S. DEP'T OF AG. ECON. RES. SERV., MAJOR USES OF LAND IN THE UNITED STATES, 2011 (2012). These figures suggest that preservation legal regimes must consider public as well as private actors, although given the nature of their respective properties the treatments may well differ.

Developers who are property owners or are working on behalf of property owners have also had impacts on the field. They have helped to advance the preservation movement through legislative advocacy, particularly for rehabilitation tax credits discussed in Chapter 11. Their challenges to historic preservation laws, however, have sometimes resulted in the demolition of valuable historic places.

b.   PUBLIC ENTITIES AND OFFICIALS

There are four primary levels of government in this country: federal, state, local, and tribal. All have a role in historic preservation. Government regulates preservation-related activities, finances historic development projects, administers registers of historic places, educates private property owners, serves as a clearinghouse of information, and coordinates various stakeholders.

At the federal level, Congress, as the elected legislative body, may choose to pass, modify, or reject statutes related to preservation nationwide. An important federal law related to preservation, the National Historic Preservation Act, will be covered in Chapters 2 and 3. Another procedural law, the National Environmental Policy Act, will be discussed in Chapter 4. Section 4(f) of the Department of Transportation Act provides substantive (as opposed to merely procedural) protections for historic properties threatened by certain federal road projects and is the subject of Chapter 5. Chapters 8 and 9 will focus on four federal laws related to the preservation of archaeological resources and Native American sites: the Antiquities Act, the Historic Sites Act, the Archaeological Resources Protection Act, and the Native American Graves Protection and Repatriation Act. And finally, Congress has passed laws related to conservation and preservation easements, which will be described in Chapter 10, as well as financial incentives, covered in Chapter 11. While many other federal statutes have a significant impact on preservation, an understanding of these pieces of legislation provides an excellent overview of the role of the federal legislative branch in the realm of preservation.

Congress does not bear exclusive authority to make rules affecting preservation nationwide. Within certain limited authority, the President may issue executive orders directing federal agencies to address preservation. For example, in 1996, President Bill Clinton issued Executive Order No. 13006, *Locating Federal Facilities on Historic Properties in Our Nation's Central Cities*, which required federal agencies locating federal facilities to "give first consideration to historic properties within historic districts," then consider other sites within historic districts, and only after considering both types of sites, consider historic properties outside of historic districts. In 2003, President George W. Bush issued Executive Order No. 13287, *Preserve America*, which required agencies to create an inventory of their historic properties in accordance with the National Historic Preservation Act, assess their general condition and management needs, and make plans to meet those needs. The President directed agencies to include the economic development potential (e.g., heritage tourism) of their historic properties in their evaluation.

As the executive orders mentioned above imply, federal agencies are an important public actor in the preservation context. Every agency, no matter what their function, owns or manages historic resources and must treat those resources as Congress or the President dictates. A few agencies have more specific roles. The Department of Transportation, for example, evaluates projects subject to Section 4(f) of the Transportation Act, while the Environmental Protection Agency helps implement and support the National Environmental Policy Act. The Advisory Council on Historic Preservation, a Cabinet-level body appointed by the President, advises the President and Congress on preservation policy; promotes coordination among federal agencies, states, localities, tribes, and private stakeholders; reviews federal programs and policies to promote effectiveness and coordination; and administers the National Historic Preservation Act.

The agency with perhaps the largest role in preservation policy and programming is the Department of the Interior. The National Park Service (NPS), one of the Department's nine bureaus, administers numerous programs that affect preservation and heritage, including programs for American Indians and museums. The Bureau of Indian Affairs, another division of the Department of the Interior, administers land held in trust for tribes by the federal government and helps to manage certain cultural resource programs. Finally, as its name implies, the Bureau of Land Management manages the vast majority of federal public land, including 245 million acres of surface land (including 35 million acres of national conservation lands) and 700 million acres of subsurface mineral estates (under both public and private land).

State governments are a second public player in preservation. State legislatures have sometimes passed preservation laws similar to those passed by Congress. State registers of historic places, for example, are based by and large on the National Register of Historic Places. As another example, state versions of the National Environmental Policy Act may provide similar, but not exactly the same, protections. Connecticut's Environmental Protection Act, for example, allows any individual to sue to prevent "the unreasonable destruction of historic structures and landmarks of the state," which protects resources either listed or under consideration for listing on the National Register of Historic Places. CONN. GEN. STAT. §§ 22a–15 to 22a–19b. State legislatures also have the power to establish localities' abilities to engage in preservation-related activities, passing various versions of enabling statutes that allow local governments to consider historic resources in planning and zoning decisions, create historic districts, and/or establish local registers of historic places.

In the state executive branch, a governor may have powers similar to the President's executive order authority. In addition, to comply with the National Historic Preservation Act, governors of all fifty states must appoint State Historic Preservation Officers (SHPOs) who support federal, state, and local preservation activities. These SHPOs administer the National Historic Preservation Act at the state level, consult with federal agencies undertaking projects on historic properties within the state, review nominations to the National Register of Historic Places, and administer the state register of historic places. They may also operate historic sites, research history, conduct surveys, or finance private or public preservation projects.

Local governments must work within statutory grants of authority from the state when dealing with preservation issues. As we will see particularly in Chapters 2 and 6, localities have an important regulatory function. Of the various levels of government, localities are most likely to interact with private property owners through education programs, through the enforcement of preservation regulations, or through the administration of other municipal functions, such as the planning and zoning authority. Local officials enforcing historic preservation ordinances are subject to the fundamental fairness doctrine, conflict of interest rules, and the appearance of impropriety. *See Barry v. Historic Dist. Comm. of Borough of Litchfield*, 108 Conn. App. 682 (2008). As Chapter 7 reveals, the expansive role of localities in garden-variety preservation decisions often leads to conflict. In fact, all of the major cases excerpted in that Chapter involve a claim that a local government violated a property owner's constitutional rights. Note that regional governments, where authorized, may have functions similar to local governments but have not historically played a key role in preservation.

Some localities are eligible to participate in the federal program for "certified local governments" (CLG). CLGs are eligible for grants (administered through the State Historic Preservation Office) and technical assistance from the National Park Service and SHPO. CLGs must have a historic preservation commission, designate and regulate historic properties, and maintain a local register of historic places, among other things. As of March 2021, there were 2,037 CLGs nationally, each participants in the federal regulatory regime.

Native American tribes, as sovereign nations, as well as Native Hawaiian groups, have special statutory roles derived from federal law. Like states that appoint SHPOs, tribes appoint THPOs: Tribal Historic Preservation Officers, who share many of the same responsibilities as the SHPOs. Tribes and Native Hawaiians often serve as stewards not just of the built environment, but also of cultural artifacts. Their role in preservation is further discussed in Chapter 3, with respect to the National Historic Preservation Act, and in Chapters 8 and 9, which deal with archaeological and Native American protections.

c.   NONPROFIT ORGANIZATIONS

As the first section of this Chapter revealed, nonprofit organizations, such as the Mount Vernon Ladies' Association, of the Union were critical to the development of the historic preservation movement in this country. They continue to be critical in the advancement of preservation policy and in bolstering private preservation activity. As Chapters 2 and 3, in particular, will highlight, nonprofit organizations have also been integral to important litigation that has clarified aspects of preservation law.

Figure 1-11:
James Madison's Montpelier: A National
Trust Historic Site,
Orange, VA

The most important national nonprofit organization, the National Trust for Historic Preservation, was chartered in 1949 by Congress. *See* 54 U.S.C. § 312101. Dedicated to saving historic resources and revitalizing communities, the Trust has an expansive mission. Its main office in Washington, D.C., and several regional offices, engage in advocacy and education projects. Its legal department leads the way on preservation litigation in federal court and deploys attorneys to lend a hand in local preservation battles. The Trust's economic development projects extend from the National Main Street Center, which provides technical and financial assistance to small towns eager to enhance their historic commercial cores, to the Heritage Tourism program, which includes a network of historic hotels. To raise awareness about specific sites, it annually publishes a "List of 11 Most Endangered Places." The Trust also owns and operates twenty-seven historic sites across the country, including President James Madison's home Montpelier, shown in Figure 1-11, and the Philip Johnson Glass House in Connecticut. Special programs have highlighted African-American historic resources, urban schoolhouses, and rural heritage development, among other resources. A related community investment corporation provides financial investments to those engaged in real estate development projects involving historic sites. As a result of its fundraising partnerships and membership expansion, the Trust no longer receives any of its funding from the federal government.

While the Trust's activities and mission are broad, many national nonprofits focus on more specific aspects of preservation. For example, DOCOMOMO, an acronym for the DOcumentation and COnservation of buildings, sites and neighborhoods of the MOdern MOvement, promotes the study, interpretation, and protection of modern structures and landscapes. In addition, there are two organizations, the National Conference of State Historic Preservation Officers and the National Association of Tribal Historic Preservation Officers, that help coordinate and convey the needs and concerns of SHPOs and THPOs, respectively. They testify before Congress, guide policy, and support members in their respective statutory missions. The National Alliance of Preservation Commissions plays a similar role for the members of local historic preservation commissions. Meanwhile, the National Preservation Institute offers professional training for individuals in the public and private sectors in historic preservation and cultural resource management.

Statewide nonprofit organizations mirror national organizations, but they do so on a smaller scale. As one example, Preservation Connecticut, like the National Trust for Historic Preservation, serves advocacy and education functions and is funded primarily through private donations. In addition, it receives several hundred thousand dollars' worth of grant money from the state legislature each year to administer and distribute to various public entities, private organizations, and individuals. Among its staff are three "circuit riders," who consult with local communities about, among other things, technical feasibility, financial strategies, and the practices of local historic district commissions. Preservation Connecticut also sponsors a historic properties exchange and a "find a professional" program that connects preservation professionals with property owners doing work on historic resources. Many other statewide nonprofit organizations around the country operate programs similar to those of Preservation Connecticut.

At the local level, preservation groups abound. They range in scale, purpose, and duration. For example, the Providence Preservation Society was founded in 1956, when demolition of the city's "College Hill" neighborhood was proposed. It monitors local commission meetings, meets with neighborhood associations, maintains a "most endangered properties" list, and recognizes preservation successes through an awards program. On the other side of the country, the Preservation Resource Center of New Orleans, established in 1974, advocates for historic buildings, publishes a popular magazine, and highlights vernacular architecture (including shotgun houses) of the city. It played a prominent role in the preservation of the city after Hurricane Katrina, restoring and reselling vacant and blighted properties and helping homeowners repair historic homes.

C. MODERN CHALLENGES TO PRESERVATION

In the twenty-first century, all fields of law must address three pressing global challenges: climate change, cultural exclusion, and economic inequality. To some extent, historic preservation law is well-suited to address these challenges, because it provides a flexible framework for decision-making rooted in interpretation and nuance. Indeed, preservationists are already grappling with how to update existing laws. Accelerating these efforts can ensure preservationists take advantage of the unique characteristics of their field to make preservation is a key part of the solution.

1. CLIMATE CHANGE

The climate crisis and ensuing natural hazards threaten not only our historic places but also our very existence. Extreme weather events—such as hurricanes, tropical storms, tornadoes, blizzards, earthquakes, heat waves, and droughts—are becoming more frequent. Such events directly threaten historic resources. *See* DEBRA HOLTZ ET AL., UNION OF CONCERNED SCIENTISTS, NATIONAL LANDMARKS AT RISK: HOW RISING SEAS, FLOODS, AND WILDFIRES ARE THREATENING THE UNITED STATES' MOST CHERISHED HISTORIC SITES (2014).

Fortunately, historic preservation law is well-positioned to help us both mitigate the negative impacts of human activities that cause climate change, and adapt to the changing climate.

a.   MITIGATION

Mitigating climate impacts means reducing the emission of greenhouse gases that make our planet warm faster. Preservation, at its core, is an exercise in sustainability. As Part B.2.D. of this Chapter notes, reusing existing buildings results in far less environmental degradation than demolishing and replacing them with new construction. The preservation of historic places for reuse—a central aim of historic preservation law—is already consistent with mitigation goals.

Mitigation measures beyond simply maintaining and reusing older buildings are also important. Currently, the Secretary of the Interior's Standards for the Treatment of Historic Properties, excerpted in Part B.3.A. of this Chapter, do not clearly allow for enhanced climate mitigation measures, such as on-site renewable energy generation, energy-efficient windows, high-tech insulation, and even small features, like thermal breaks. National Park Service guidelines clarify agency interpretation of the Standards, but they have been somewhat disappointing. NAT'L PARK SERV., ILLUSTRATED GUIDELINES ON SUSTAINABILITY FOR REHABILITATING HISTORIC BUILDINGS (2013). Among other recommendations, the guidelines advocate retaining existing heating, ventilating and air conditioning systems and recommends renewable energy technology only as a last resort after all other measures are taken to make a building's historic or existing systems more efficient. *Id.* at 10–14.

Renewable energy has been a particular source of litigation in recent years. The best-known litigation over a large-scale installation involved Cape Wind: one hundred and thirty offshore wind turbines, each more than four hundred feet (about forty stories) tall, covering twenty-six square miles of Nantucket Sound. The Keeper of the National Register placed the Sound on the Register in 2010, stating that it met all four criteria of national significance contained in 36 C.F.R. § 60.4, further discussed in Chapter 2. The Section 106 process, triggered by this designation, resulted in the agency in charge of the permit (the Mineral Management Service) admitting that an adverse effect would occur to thirty-four protected sites. The State Historic Preservation Office, tribal consulting parties, and the Advisory Council for Historic Preservation all reviewed and rejected the mitigation measures proposed. Ultimately, the Secretary of the Interior—who had statutory authority to make a final decision—sided with the proponents of the project, who touted its potential for economic development and its ability to help Americans increase their "energy independence." Despite the Secretary's approval, after sixteen years, the developers abandoned the project, bearing a $100 million loss. *See* J.B Ruhl & James Salzman, *What Happens When the Green New Deal Meets the Old Green Laws?*, 44 VT. L. REV. 693, 693–720 (2020), for an analysis of the immense challenges that modern environmental projects face under the existing federal, state, and local siting and environmental protection regimes.

At the local level, too, renewable energy installations have been challenged. Historic preservation review boards sometimes reject solar panels, sometimes on mistaken local interpretations of the Secretary's Standards. Some states, such as California and Connecticut, have intervened to restrict local boards' ability to deny solar panels. *See* CAL. GOV'T CODE § 65850.5 (denials allowed only if system has a "specific, adverse impact upon the public health and safety, and there is no feasible method to satisfactorily mitigate or avoid the specific, adverse impact"); CONN. GEN. STAT. § 7–147f(a) (denials only allowed if system "cannot be installed without substantially impairing the historic character and appearance of the district"). These state reforms are a step in the right direction and show how the law can adjust to harmonize both sustainability and preservation values.

b.   ADAPTATION

Historic preservation is inherently adaptive: evolving over time to meet present day conditions. It is a misconception that historic preservation law aims to lock places in amber. Of the four treatments of historic properties outlined by the Secretary's Standards, only properties receiving the restoration treatment require adherence to a particular period of significance. The vast majority of preservation activity takes the rehabilitation-treatment approach, one that recognizes that changes in uses and materials are inevitable.

Accordingly, preservationists have started to grapple with the need to adjust as our weather becomes more extreme. Disaster law, which deals with climate threats most directly, offers a window into current efforts. Federal laws dealing with disaster planning and response modestly address historic places. Thirty-two of fifty states incorporate historic preservation in disaster management planning. Douglas Appler & Andrew Rumbach, *Building Community Resilience Through Historic Preservation*, 82 J. AMER. PLANNING ASS'N 95 (2016). Very few local governments have begun to integrate planning, hazard mitigation, and heritage protection, a fact confirmed by a study of 863 Colorado municipalities. Andrew Rumbach et al., *Are We Protecting Our History? A Municipal-Scale Analysis of Historic Preservation, Flood Hazards, and Planning*, J. PLANNING ED. & RESEARCH (2020) (finding that 74 percent of Colorado's National Register-listed historic districts overlapped with floodplains yet lacked basic protections). Interestingly, cities doing more to address natural hazards to historic places, including Philadelphia, Charleston, and New Orleans, have the oldest local regulatory regimes in the country.

But more must be done. At a very basic level, preservationists must do more on the data-collection side of things, because we do not know where historic resources are located, or the natural hazard risks associated with them. Without knowing that, preservationists will not be able to understand how historic places can be part of our national adaptation strategy. In addition, Congress should change the National Flood Insurance Program to encourage the modification or moving of historic structures. *See* Sara C. Bronin, *Law's Disaster: Heritage at Risk*, 46 COLUMBIA J. ENVTL. L. 487 (2021).

And finally, the Secretary's Standards may need to be augmented with new treatments that recognize the severity of the threats. One new Standard, relocation, could articulate the means by which a historic property could be relocated to safer ground. Another new Standard, deconstruction, could be used in situations where managed retreat is the only responsible choice. *See* Sara C. Bronin, *Adapting National Preservation Standards to Climate Change*, for TOWARD SUSTAINABILITY AND EQUITY: ENVISIONING PRESERVATION POLICY REFORM (Erica Avrami, ed. 2021).

Given the urgency of our climate response, preservationists will have to clarify rules that state how energy-saving mitigation measures and adaptation strategies can be incorporated into historic sites. We think this is possible, and even inevitable, given the characteristics of the field and the legal framework in which it operates.

2. CULTURAL EXCLUSION

Since its inception, the American experiment has been marked by constant tension between ethnic and racial groups, the oppression and expulsion of Native people, and the dominance of White perspectives and values. Historic preservation, and historic preservation law, has unfortunately, in many ways, exemplified and reinforced this hierarchy.

The focus of early preservation efforts on sites associated with White people has endured. Today's registers of historic places testify to that unfortunate fact. Of 95,214 properties on the National Register in 2020, 2% are related to African-American history, 0.42% are related to women's history, 0.14% are related to Latino history, 0.10% are related to Asian history, and 0.03% are related to LGBTQ history. Jeremy C. Wells & Priya Chhaya, A Guide to Becoming an Historic Preservation Professional 2 (2020). Exceptions to this pattern of exclusion have been world-famous sites, such as the Dexter Avenue Baptist Church (1974) from which Martin Luther King, Jr. organized the Montgomery bus boycott, and the Stonewall Inn (1999), in New York City, where the first large public resistance to discrimination against LGBTQ people occurred.

Why are the numbers so low? Of course, they reflect broad patterns of subordination. But the law, too, embodies discriminatory structures. The designation process more fully detailed in Chapter 2 is a formal process that adheres to strict interpretations of what has sufficient material "integrity," a concept enshrined in designation standards at the local, state, and federal levels. Often, the integrity standard leaves out resources associated with low-income people or people of color, who may have a harder time maintaining their historic resources to satisfy the standard. *See* Raymond W. Rast, *A Matter of Alignment: Methods to Match the Goals of the Preservation Movement*, 28 FORUM J. 14 (2014); Vince Michael, *Diversity in Preservation: Rethinking Standards and Practices*, 28 FORUM J. 5 (2014). The integrity bar also diminishes the formal protection available for resources associated with American Indian, Alaska Native, and Native Hawaiian people, a topic covered more fully in Chapters 8 and 9.

Beyond the designation process, political leaders have made value judgments about whose history to celebrate by erecting public monuments focused on particular histories. Monuments to the Confederacy have been a hot topic in recent years, and at times public commentators have blamed historic preservation law for their endurance. As Chapter 2 reveals, however, historic preservation law does not typically see monuments as worthy of preservation. The National Park Service explains that commemorative properties "are not directly associated with the event or with the person's productive life, but serve as evidence of a later generation's assessment of the past." Patrick W. Andrus, *How to Apply the National Register Criteria for Evaluation* 15 (Nat'l Park Serv., Nat'l Register Bull. No. 15, 2002). There have been some exceptions to this rule, including Confederate monuments included in a National Historic Landmark designation as integral to the design of Monument Avenue in Richmond, Virginia. In addition, various state legislatures have adopted statutes that prohibit the removal of Confederate monuments. Professor Byrne has argued that this recent phenomenon is inconsistent with the methods and values of historic preservation law. J. Peter Byrne, *Stone Monuments and Flexible Laws: Removing Confederate Monuments Through Historic Preservation Laws*, 71 FLA. L. REV. 169 (2020). In 2020, the National Trust for Historic Preservation issued a statement sanctioning the removal of these monuments from public spaces, recognizing that even though some Confederate monuments have been designated historic, "removal may be necessary to achieve the greater good of ensuring racial justice and equality." Many Confederate monuments have been removed, with others on their way out.

The statement from the National Trust reflects an ongoing recognition that the field must adapt to reverse past practices, and also that it has a role to play in guiding the transition toward a more inclusive society. If, as we believe, preservation fundamentally encompasses an adaptation ethic, then the field is inherently well-positioned to help with these shifts. Consider the following excerpt, which frames the key issues.

Erica Avrami, Building a Foundation for Action: Anti-Racist Historic Preservation Resources
(2021)

Black Lives Matter and other social justice movements mobilized much needed focus on structural legacies of anti-Black racial injustice and, in 2020, engendered widespread statements of support within the preservation community. Efforts to bring greater recognition to BIPOC (Black, Indigenous, People of Color) histories, publics, and practitioners within the preservation enterprise have been growing through groundbreaking initiatives such as the National Trust's African American Cultural Heritage Action Fund, Asian and Pacific Islander Americans in Historic Preservation, the Texas Freedom Colonies Project, Latinos in Heritage Conservation, BlackSpace, and other advocacy and funding entities. Debates surrounding the removal of Confederate and other controversial monuments have also fostered dialogue around racial injustice in public spaces, and compelled the preservation field to reconsider longstanding normative standards, which privilege particular values often rooted in Whiteness[1], and to plumb questions of intent with greater scrutiny.

However, there are growing calls to more critically analyze the role of preservation in contributing to and promulgating systemic racism, through the broader realm of the built environment as well as through its own policy infrastructure, such as the Response to the National Council for Preservation Education's Open Letter. This resource list seeks to further these calls by creating a platform to share knowledge in support of action.

There are long histories of marginalizing BIPOC peoples, thereby limiting the power of BIPOC individuals and publics to claim space and property. Such legacies of racism, subjugation, and exclusion are embedded in personal and social identities and positionalities, in our physical world, and in how publics and professionals define and value heritage. They are often designed, protected, and propped up by disciplinary norms and codes. As the primary objects of historic preservation policy and practice, the built environment and landscapes fundamentally reflect:

- who had/has the right to freedom and self-determination
- who could/can make or break laws, rules, and standards
- who had/has the right to occupy land
- who could/can own property

---

[1] There is ongoing debate around the capitalization of "White." The choice to capitalize it in this document is in support of scholars, activists, media professionals, and others who have argued that not capitalizing it "frames Whiteness as both neutral and the standard" (Nguyên & Pendleton, 2020). As sociologist Eve Ewing argues, "When we ignore the specificity and significance of Whiteness—the things that it is, the things that it does—we contribute to its seeming neutrality and thereby grant it power to maintain its invisibility" (Ewing, 2020).

- who could/can live in certain neighborhoods
- who had/has access to capital and financing
- who had/has political and narrative power.

Whiteness is a defining agent of socio-spatial conditions, historically and today. As such, it inextricably underpins the preservation systems and institutions through which heritage and its evidence are legitimized and valorized. There are also equally long legacies of BIPOC groups and collaborators preserving and conserving BIPOC heritage despite efforts—including by public institutions—to omit, erase, and underinvest in such assets.

Confronting these antecedents and their implications in contemporary preservation policy, practice, and education requires intentionality, collaboration, and the ceding of power. While the preservation field is becoming more diverse, fewer than one percent of professional preservationists are African-American (Cep, 2020), and 80 percent of National Park Service staff are White (Chari, 2020). White preservationists and predominantly White preservation institutions must be more than just allies to BIPOC colleagues; allyship alone places too heavy a burden on the excluded few to effect systemic change in a field so dominated by Whiteness. To reform standards, processes, and policy infrastructure, White preservationists must be, in the words of Dr. Alexandra Jones, "active accomplices."

This excerpt forms the introduction to a bibliography, available by contacting Professor Avrami, that includes a regularly-updated list of resources from scholars that have delved deeply not only into the issues we cover here, but also into stakeholder engagement, preservation education, and the demographics of the field.

Recent years have seen substantial movement toward prioritizing a more inclusive preservation system. For example, the National Trust has instituted the African American Heritage Action Fund, led by African American preservationist Brent Leggs, which made grants exceeding $4 million to more than 60 projects since 2017 and the date of publication. Grantees include the former home in Durham, North Carolina, of Pauli Murray, a remarkable African American human rights activist, lawyer, feminist, poet, Episcopal priest, and member of the LGBTQ community; and, While We Are Still Here, an organization of Harlem residents seeking to preserve and narrate the full history of their community.

Local designations in several cities have demonstrated a promising turn to sites of minority history. Washington, D.C., has landmarked several sites important to LGBTQ history, including the home of Frank Kameny, a leading organizer against discrimination in federal employment, and the house of The Furies, a groundbreaking lesbian collective in the 1960s and 70s. The city also designated the Kingman

Park Historic District, which preserves a row house neighborhood developed for African Americans during the period of de jure segregation. In 2021, New York City landmarked a house in Brooklyn connected with antebellum anti-slavery activity, after twenty years of advocacy. Many other cities have undertaken serious reorientations of their designation goals.

3.   ECONOMIC INEQUALITY

Economic inequality globally has worsened in recent years, with the gap between the rich and poor widening as a result of a variety of factors, including trade policies, structural racism, tax advantages for the wealthy, and a housing shortage. Admittedly, historic preservation as a field plays only a minor role in efforts to provide economic opportunity to those who need it most. But we want to recognize in a few words the role historic preservation does and can play, focusing specifically on the extent to which preservation offers affordable housing opportunities, which is one key to reducing economic inequality.

Older houses, "filtering down" in value as they deteriorate or fall out of fashion, have long provided affordable living options for low income individuals. A remaining question is whether historic preservation law—and, most relevantly, local historic district ordinances—prevent or promote the provision of affordable housing. Such ordinances prevent construction of high-rise public housing when out of scale with the district, but such projects are now disfavored for reasons independent of historic preservation. They also raise costs for repairs to or rehabilitation of contributing buildings, both through an additional layer of permitting and by requiring additions or replacements that are compatible with the original fabric; requiring wood rather than less expensive vinyl replacement windows is a classic example. Some jurisdictions have grant programs to assist low income homeowners in complying with preservation ordinances. The Providence, Rhode Island, Revolving Fund, for example, lends money in low and moderate income historic neighborhoods for redeveloping buildings as owner-occupied affordable housing.

Preservationists plausibly argue that preservation laws encourage affordable housing. Existing older housing provides most of the affordable housing in many cities. Local ordinances may slow gentrification by prohibiting developers in hot historic neighborhoods from demolishing existing housing to replace them with higher density luxury buildings. Moreover, as discussed in Chapter 11, developers frequently combine historic rehabilitation tax credits with low-income housing tax credits to amass the subsidy needed to create new affordable housing.

At times, it may be more expensive to adapt a historic building for affordable housing than construct new housing on a vacant lot, especially if the developer needs to comply with the Secretary's Standards to obtain tax credits. But there should be significant advantages to the residents of such a building that may balance higher costs. Neighbors may accept low-income housing more readily if the project rehabilitates an older building, improving the appearance of the area. Integration with neighbors of mixed income seems beneficial for low-income persons. From the exterior, it may be impossible to determine which rehabilitated buildings are subsidized and which are market rate. Moreover, if the affordable housing is in a gentrifying neighborhood, residents will be able to remain at affordable prices, providing them with the desirable amenities of such a neighborhood, while preserving the social benefits of a mixed income neighborhood. *See* J. Peter Byrne & Michael Diamond, *Affordable Housing, Land Tenure, and Urban Policy: The Matrix Revealed,* 34 FORDHAM URB. L. J. 527, 551–74 (2007).

A striking example is provided by the story of a property familiar to most law students from their first-year Property class, the Clifton Terrace apartment complex in Washington, D.C., made notorious in *Javins v. First National Realty Corp.,* 428 F.2d 1071 (D.C. Cir. 1970). That decision adopted the implied warranty of habitability in landlord tenant law. The innumerable housing code violations alleged in the case, creating conditions that the D.C. Corporation Counsel later described as "subhuman," became a national emblem of the slum rental housing to which many inner city minorities were consigned at that time. *See* Richard H. Chused, *Saunders (a.k.a. Javins) v. First Nat'l Realty Corp.,* 11 GEO. J. POVERTY L. & POL. 191, 218 (2004) (describing contemporary accounts of building conditions). After numerous failed efforts to improve conditions in the buildings, despite their notoriety, they have in recent years been successfully renovated using historic preservation and low-income housing tax credits, as subsidized mixed income rentals and condominiums subject to resident income restrictions. Restored to its original name of Wardman Court, the complex, constructed in 1914–15, was added to the National Register in 2001. Today, it provides attractive, affordable housing in a gentrifying neighborhood. Projects of this quality require substantial public investments, as well as imaginative private developers.

We cover the more specific issue of gentrification—displacement caused by development activity—in Chapter 11. But we thought it was important to use the framing function of Chapter 1 to demonstrate early the link between preservation, affordability, and economic opportunity.

CHAPTER TWO

DESIGNATION

Which properties should be preserved? Not all old buildings or sites can or should be saved. In the absence of legislative prohibitions, property owners retain the authority to replace or destroy their structures. Who should decide which properties merit special protection? What criteria help make such decisions? What procedures are fair? Answering these questions reveals the scope of historic preservation law and the properties to which it applies. In this Chapter, we consider these questions, first at the federal level, and then at the state and local levels, where designation draws heavily from federal law.

A. FEDERAL DESIGNATION

Federal law has established very influential criteria for designation. This section discusses the administration of the National Register, which has provided the most influential criteria for identifying historic properties worthy of presentation.

1. STATUTORY FRAMEWORK FOR THE NATIONAL REGISTER

Congress created the modern National Register of Historic Places in 1966, when it passed the National Historic Preservation Act (NHPA). Its origins lie in the Historic Sites Act of 1935, which will be further discussed in Chapter 8. Briefly, the Historic Sites Act authorized the National Park Service to conduct a national survey, to identify buildings and sites of national significance, and to accept or acquire them as elements of the national park system. At first, the properties surveyed were viewed as candidates to become national parks, and the list was kept confidential so as not to inflate prices. In the late 1950s, the Park Service began to consider the value of a list of historically-significant buildings without regard to acquisition, and it publicly announced the first list of National Historic Landmarks in 1960. There has also been a Historic American Buildings Survey (HABS) since 1933. Originally a New Deal make-work program for architects, it is now a rich repository of drawings and photographs of historic buildings, administered by the National Park Service and housed at the Library of Congress. Over time, HABS has been joined by the Historic American Engineering Record, the Historic American Landscapes Survey, and the Cultural Resources Geographic Information Systems.

A prime motive for enactment of the NHPA was to enlarge the criteria, participation, and funding for a national survey of historic properties. H.R. REP. No. 89–1916, at 3309–11 (1966). Section 101(a)(1)(A) of the NHPA authorized the Secretary of the Interior (the

"Secretary") to "expand and maintain a National Register of Historic
Places composed of districts, sites, buildings, structures, and objects
significant in American history, architecture, archeology, engineering,
and culture." 54 U.S.C. § 302101. In addition, Congress conferred broad
authority on the Secretary to establish the criteria for inclusion. Finally,
the NHPA authorized the Secretary to establish procedures for
designation—that is, the process by which the decisions about inclusion
are made. The Secretary in turn assigned all of these responsibilities to
the National Park Service. That delegation recognizes the accumulation
of expertise about the identification and treatment of historic properties
in the Park Service.

The Park Service is not the only public entity that influences the
Register. The NHPA provided a central role for the State Historic
Preservation Officer (SHPO), who has the responsibility to "identify and
nominate eligible property to the National Register and otherwise
administer applications for listing historic property on the National
Register." 54 U.S.C. § 302303(b)(2). In addition, through amendments
made to the NHPA in 1992, Congress permitted each Indian tribe to
qualify a Tribal Historic Preservation Officer (THPO), who serves a
function similar to that of the SHPO with respect to nominating
properties on tribal lands. More on the functions and characters of the
SHPO and of the THPO will be explored below.

In addition to the text of the NHPA, agency regulations published in
the Federal Register and other Park Service publications describe how
the National Register should be administered. The regulations of the
Department of the Interior providing the criteria for eligibility and the
procedures for listing are found at 36 C.F.R. Part 60. These regulations
have the force of law and receive substantial judicial deference as a
reasonable exercise of the authority delegated to the Secretary by the
NHPA. In addition, the Park Service has issued a series of Bulletins that
clarify how certain aspects of the NHPA and its regulations should be
interpreted by the public. The Park Service's Bulletin No. 15, *How to
Apply the National Register Criteria for Evaluation*, is most relevant
here. It further defines terms and provides guidance for their application.
Other official bulletins cover distinct types of resources or other aspects
of the evaluation process. These should receive some limited judicial
deference as interpretive guides for construing ambiguous terms in the
statute or in the regulations, but not as much as the regulations
themselves. The Park Service official who administers the National
Register process and makes final decisions about listing or eligibility has
the title "Keeper of the National Register of Historic Places."

2.   THE NATIONAL REGISTER CRITERIA

In an important sense, the criteria for inclusion within the National
Register defines the scope of federal historic preservation law—the range
of resources upon which the law acts. The breadth of the Register is

striking, encompassing many kinds of places and constructions, as well as touchstones of national, state, and local significance.

a. FIVE TYPES OF PROPERTY

Many types of tangible property can be listed on the National Register. As noted above, the NHPA authorization encompasses five kinds of tangible resources: buildings, objects, structures, sites, and districts. 54 U.S.C. § 302101. The regulations provide definitions of the categories of historic properties. *See* 36 C.F.R. § 60.3. These categories are not mutually exclusive. The collective scope of these definitions reveals the breadth of the National Register. Intangible resources, such as skills or practices, cannot be listed, but the association with such intangibles may qualify some tangible places as historic properties. Thus, a musical style cannot be listed, but an auditorium could be listed due to its association with that style.

A *building* should be the most familiar form of historical property. The definition makes it clear that the term includes any "structure created to shelter any form of human activity, such as a house, barn, church, hotel or similar structure." *Id.* § 60.3(a). A building also encompasses any "historically related complex such as a courthouse and jail." By contrast, a *structure* includes any other human construction "made up of interdependent and interrelated parts in a definite pattern of organization." *Id.* § 60.3(p). This category includes bridges, railways, and highways. The line between a building and a structure may waver; a lighthouse might be a building if human-operated but a structure if automated. The distinction is important primarily for the federal rehabilitation tax credit, further discussed in Chapter 11, which can be obtained only for rehabilitation of a certified *building*.

An *object* is a "material thing" that may be "movable yet related to a specific setting or environment." *Id.* § 60.3 (j). In certain cases, it may be difficult to distinguish between structures and objects. For example, the regulations list a steamboat as an object, but the National Park Service has distributed a publication, Bulletin No. 15, *How to Apply the National Register Criteria for Evaluation*, which treats a steamboat as a structure. Bulletin No. 15 limits objects to "constructions that are primarily artistic in nature," Patrick W. Andrus, *How to Apply the National Register Criteria for Evaluation* 5 (Nat'l Park Serv., Nat'l Register Bull. No. 15, 2002), although the regulatory definition includes things of "functional, aesthetic, cultural, historical or scientific value." 36 C.F.R. § 60.3(j). Both the regulations and the Bulletin seem to agree that to qualify, an object, even if moveable, needs some meaningful relation to a specific place.

A *site* need not involve any human construction but is a "location of a significant event, a prehistoric or historic occupation or activity, or a building or structure, whether standing, ruined, or vanished, where the location itself maintains historical or archeological value regardless of the value of any existing structure." *Id.* § 60.3(*l*). Thus, a site would include a battlefield, ruins, or a place (such as a sandbar) where Native Americans have engaged in traditional cultural practices.

Figures 2-1 & 2-2:
Scenes from the Hiram M. Chittenden Locks and Lake Washington Ship Channel Historic District, Seattle, WA

"A *district* is a geographically definable area, urban or rural, possessing a significant concentration, linkage, or continuity of sites, buildings, structures, or objects united by past events or aesthetically by plan or physical development." *Id.* § 60.3(d) (emphasis added). Thus, a district is an array of other properties, which may be significant as a group even if the individual elements may not. One example of a designated district is the Hiram M. Chittenden Locks and Lake Washington Ship Channel Historic District in Seattle, Washington, listed on the National Register. Among other structures and objects, it includes a boathouse, an administration building and house, boat locks, and a salmon ladder. Scenes from this district are depicted in Figures 2-1 and 2-2.

b. SIGNIFICANCE

In addition to fitting into one of the five categories of protected resources, a resource must be "significant" to be listed on the National Register. Nominally, the statute limits the term "significance" to "American history, architecture, archeology, engineering, and culture," 54 U.S.C. § 302101, but this language is too broad to provide guidance. The real limitations on significance come from the regulations, which define significance as encompassing one of four broad categories of historical significance *plus* "integrity of location, design, setting, materials, workmanship, feeling, and association." 36 C.F.R. § 60.4. The two key requirements for listing on the National Register are thus *historical significance* and *integrity*.

The four categories of historical significance relate directly to the values embodied in historic preservation generally. As the Federal Register defines it, those properties have significance that possess integrity and:

(a) that are associated with events that have made a significant contribution to the broad patterns of our history; or

(b) that are associated with the lives of persons significant in our past; or

(c) that embody the distinctive characteristics of a type, period, or method of construction, or that possess high artistic values, or that represent a significant and distinguishable entity whose components may lack individual distinction; or

(d) that have yielded, or may be likely to yield, information important in prehistory or history.

Id. Significance thus embraces places made historically important by association with important events or persons, those with aesthetic or cultural value, and those (including archeological sites) that may provide useful information to the trained eye.

Despite the curious references to "our" history or past, the criteria do not intend to enshrine only properties of national significance, but also those of state and of local significance. The breadth of the listed criteria permits neighborhoods and cultural communities to argue for the "significance" of places as a result of events, people, or architecture that embody their particular identities. The "criteria are worded in a manner to provide for a wide diversity of resources." *Id.* Decisions about significance in history require both serious scholarship and sensitivity to diverse popular estimations of what is important in the past.

c.   INTEGRITY

In addition to satisfying one of the four categories for historical significance, a property must have "integrity." This requirement is important, as it must be met for any National Register listing and most often will be contested by those opposing any finding of eligibility. According to the Park Service Bulletin No. 15, "Integrity is the ability of a property to convey its significance." Andrus, *supra*, at 44. Properties that have been neglected or modified may lack those physical features that impress upon a viewer the associations or values for which the property might be preserved. The regulations specify seven aspects of integrity: location, design, setting, materials, workmanship, feeling, and association. Bulletin No. 15 defines and gives examples of their applications.

Although an eligible property should contain several of these aspects, those that are crucial will depend upon the ground of significance for which the property could be designated. For example, moving a house might destroy its integrity if its primary significance lays in its association with an event that occurred at the original location, but might not if its primary significance lays in its architectural details.

Additionally, a district proposed for the Register may be rejected if the neighborhood character has been fundamentally altered by redevelopment. For example, an effort to designate a district centered around Maxwell Street in Chicago—reflecting the experiences of successive groups of immigrants and the birth of African-American, electric blues music—failed when the SHPO and the Keeper felt that the buildings in that area lacked integrity due to ongoing demolitions which were primarily made by an expanding university. *See Maxwell St. Historic Pres. Coal. v. Bd. of Trs. of the Univ. of Ill.*, 2000 WL 1141439 (N.D. Ill. 2000) (finding it unlikely that the plaintiff nonprofit organization would prevail over the SHPO and the Keeper to reverse their decision that the district lacked integrity, thus denying its request for a temporary restraining order against construction by the defendant university).

The Maxwell Street example illustrates an unfortunate consequence of integrity evaluations, which is that sites associated with people of color are often excluded from listing on the grounds that they do not maintain sufficient historic fabric at acceptable levels. Because of the way income correlates with race and ethnicity, these groups are less likely to have the funding to maintain their properties or the expertise to avoid damaging alterations that jeopardize a finding of integrity. Historic resources that change too much over time will be deemed to lack integrity, under strict notions of authenticity that fail to take into account broader notions of cultural heritage preservation. Various scholars have advocated to rethinking how the law treats the integrity criterion for designation at the federal, state, and local levels. *See, e.g.,* Sara C. Bronin, *Integrity as a Legal Concept* (unpublished manuscript on file with the author); Raymond W. Rast, *A Matter of Alignment: Methods to Match the Goals of the Preservation Movement*, 28 FORUM J. 14 (2014); Vince Michael, *Diversity in Preservation: Rethinking Standards and Practices*, 28 FORUM J. 5 (2014).

d.   ADDITIONAL CRITERIA

Congress continues to expand the types of properties eligible for National Register designation. Section 101(d)(6)(A), added in 1992, clarifies, and potentially stretches, the Register's scope by providing that "[p]roperty of traditional religious and cultural importance to an Indian tribe or Native Hawaiian organization may be determined to be eligible for inclusion on the National Register." 54 U.S.C. § 302706(a). Neither the statute nor the regulations define the relevant terms nor expand the criteria for including traditional cultural properties. National Register Bulletin No. 38, *Guidelines for Evaluating and Documenting Traditional Cultural Properties*, defines traditional cultural properties as those associated "with cultural practices or beliefs of a living community that (a) are rooted in that community's history, and (b) are important in maintaining the continuing cultural identity of the community." Patricia L. Parker & Thomas King, *Guidelines for Evaluating and Documenting Traditional Cultural Properties* 1 (Nat'l Park Serv., Nat'l Register Bull. No. 38, 1992). But traditional cultural properties still must meet the criteria set out in the general regulations for listing at 36 C.F.R. Part 60, which makes no mention of them.

Moreover, as knowledge and understanding about our material heritage has grown, the Park Service has developed criteria to evaluate a growing number of property types. For example, the Park Service has published a Bulletin in which it describes criteria specific to suburban developments and provides instructions on preparing a nomination form for eligible resources. *See* David L. Ames & Linda Flint McClellan, *Historic Residential Suburbs: Guidelines for Evaluation and Documentation for the National Register of Historic Places* (Nat'l Park Serv., Nat'l Register Bull. Series, 2002). Similar bulletins have been developed for rural historic landscapes, historic aviation properties, and designed historic landscapes. Such efforts have brought mines, airports, traditional agricultural layouts, and vernacular urban streetscapes within the purview of federal preservation rules.

3.   EXCEPTIONS AND SPECIAL CASES

The National Register regulations "ordinarily" exclude from eligibility several categories of places that might meet the above criteria: "cemeteries, birthplaces, or graves of historical figures, properties owned by religious institutions or used for religious purposes, structures that have been moved from their original locations, reconstructed historic buildings, properties primarily commemorative in nature, and properties that have achieved significance within the past 50 years." 36 C.F.R. § 60.4. For each of these exclusions, there are exceptional circumstances under which they may be listed, including:

(a)   A religious property deriving primary significance from architectural or artistic distinction or historical importance; or

(b)   A building or structure removed from its original location but which is significant primarily for architectural value, or which is the surviving structure most importantly associated with a historic person or event; or

(c)   A birthplace or grave of a historical figure of outstanding importance if there is no appropriate site or building directly associated with his productive life.

(d)   A cemetery which derives its primary significance from graves of persons of transcendent importance, from age, from distinctive design features, or from association with historic events; or

(e)   A reconstructed building when accurately executed in a suitable environment and presented in a dignified manner as part of a restoration master plan, and when no other building or structure with the same association has survived; or

(f)   A property primarily commemorative in intent if design, age, tradition, or symbolic value has invested it with its own exceptional significance; or

(g)   A property achieving significance within the past 50 years if it is of exceptional importance.

36 C.F.R. § 60.4. While exceptions for each category raise interesting legal questions, two are of broad legal significance.

First, "[a] religious property deriving primary significance from architectural or artistic distinction or historical importance" may be eligible. This seems noteworthy in light of the ongoing constitutional dispute about the application of historic preservation to religious properties, discussed further in Chapter 7. Bulletin No. 15 explains:

A religious property requires justification on architectural, artistic, or historic grounds to avoid any appearance of judgment by government about the validity of any religion or belief. Historic significance for a religious property cannot be

> established on the merits of a religious doctrine * * * . A religious property's significance * * * must be judged in purely secular terms. A religious group may, in some cases, be considered a cultural group whose activities are significant in areas broader than religious history.

Andrus, *supra*, at 26. However conceptually persuasive such a distinction between the religious and secular significance of a religious property may be, it has practical importance. It allows officials to disclaim any views about religious value. It also allows preservationists to seek eligibility determinations on any religious properties based upon both broad and standard preservation values. Finally, it provides a national standard as to the appropriateness of preservation consideration for religious buildings, even if the National Register does not impose restraints on the treatment of the building by a religious owner.

Second, a property less than fifty years old may be designated if it has "exceptional importance." 36 C.F.R § 60.4(g). The fifty-year standard provides a rule of thumb for the period of time "needed to develop historical perspective and to evaluate significance." Andrus, *supra*, at 41. Conceptual and practical problems would abound if properties generally were considered for some *historic* preservation protections immediately upon construction or upon the occurrence of some event. But historical perspective does not advance at a uniform pace; some places can be understood to have historic or architectural significance much sooner. Some important designation ordinances operate without an age minimum. The criterion of "exceptional significance" permits exceptions to be made. Thus, the Chrysler Building and the launch pad at Cape Canaveral could be confidently designated before the passage of fifty years. *Id.* at 42. Bulletin No. 15 emphasizes the need for scholarly research to provide historical perspective about the context for and importance of recent buildings or structures; scholarly understanding accrues over time.

4. FEDERAL DESIGNATION PROCEDURES

The procedures for considering a historic resource for listing on the National Register are provided entirely by Department of the Interior's regulations, found at 36 C.F.R. Part 60. Nominations of historic resources for the National Register may come from three primary sources: federal agencies, state historic preservation officers (SHPO), and tribal historic preservation officers (THPO) where tribes have qualified their programs. (Chapter 9 covers the role of the THPO in designation and explains when the THPO can assume the obligations of an SHPO; that discussion is not duplicated here.) Final decisions are made by the Keeper of the National Register. An explanation of the nomination procedures by federal agencies and by SHPOs reveals the federalism and shared enterprise character of the NHPA structure as a whole.

a.   AGENCY NOMINATIONS

Each federal agency must nominate eligible properties under its ownership or control. Section 110 of the NHPA requires each federal agency to establish a preservation program headed by a Federal Preservation Officer, who is an official, designated by the agency leader, through whom the agency identifies, evaluates, and nominates suitable properties. 54 U.S.C. § 306102. The federal agency must submit such nominations to the SHPO or to the THPO and to local elected officials for review and comment. 36 C.F.R. § 60.9(c). After receiving comments from these parties, the Federal Preservation Officer may approve the nomination and submit it, with all comments appended, to the Keeper. After the federal agency provides public notice of the proposed nomination in the Federal Register, any interested person may "petition the Keeper during the nomination process either to accept or reject" the nomination. *Id.* § 60.9(i). The Keeper must consider all timely, written submissions received before making a final decision.

b.   SHPO NOMINATIONS

SHPOs (and THPOs, where applicable) have primary responsibility for nominating to the Register properties located within their jurisdictions, given that qualified local governments have a right of consultation. 54 U.S.C. §§ 302104(a)–(b), and 302504. The SHPO may choose which properties to nominate in light of the priorities established in the State's historic preservation plan and in light of applications or suggestions received from localities, private individuals, or organizations. Members of the public and local governments who want to initiate the process for listing a property on the National Register must submit a nomination form with documentation to the SHPO, who may determine whether the property meets the criteria and whether submitting the nomination meets the state's priorities. The regulations provide that private persons may submit nominations directly to the Keeper in states without an approved State Historic Preservation Program, but none exist today!

The SHPO must submit draft nomination forms and any comments received from consulting parties to a State Review Board, whose members include representatives from the main professional fields concerned with preservation: history, architecture, architectural history, and archeology. 36 C.F.R. § 60.3(*o*). If the SHPO and the State Review Board disagree about whether the property meets the criteria, the SHPO *may* submit the nomination to the Keeper with the differing opinions, and the SHPO must do so if requested by the Review Board or by the chief elected official of the local government where the property is located. *Id* § 60.6 (*l*). Nominations submitted by an SHPO for a property that she does not believe meets the criteria should explain her views and certify that procedural requirements have been met and that the nomination is adequately documented and technically sufficient.

The SHPO nomination process involves notice requirements more elaborate than those involved in the federal agency nomination process. Before any nomination may be submitted to the Keeper, the SHPO must give notice of intent to nominate to the chief elected official of the local jurisdiction. In addition, Section 101(c)(2)(A) provides a mechanism for comment by officials of a certified local government on proposed designations of properties within its boundaries before the SHPO makes a recommendation to the Keeper. 54 U.S.C. § 302504. (The SHPO and the Secretary of the Interior should certify local governments within each state when they meet the criteria contained in the NHPA, which requires setting up a satisfactory local preservation law and review commission.) Section 101(c)(2)(A) further provides that when both the local historic preservation review commission and the chief elected local officer, usually the Mayor, recommend that a property not be designated, the SHPO should not act, unless some advocate files an appeal. *Id.* The SHPO then must forward the nomination to the Keeper but may do so with a negative recommendation. The NHPA thus promotes an active preservation program at the local level, while facilitating input from local politicians, as well as from local review boards.

In addition, the SHPO nomination process requires the notification of private owners of a proposed nomination of their property. These requirements implement the right given private owners by the 1980 amendments to the NHPA not to have their property listed on the National Register but only determined to be eligible for inclusion. 54 U.S.C. § 302105. In general, owners must be notified in writing of the proposed nomination and their right to object, but notice by publication is permitted when there are more than fifty property owners, as in the case of many historic districts; in such cases written notice also must be given to the chief elected local official. Owners may object by submission of a notarized statement to the SHPO, which records their objection. In the case of historic districts (or for individual properties owned by multiple parties), a majority of owners must submit notarized statements for an objection to be counted by the SHPO. 36 C.F.R. § 60.6(g). Once owners have objected and the Keeper has determined that the property is eligible for listing, the regulations provide that notice should be given to the owners and a local official. *Id.* § 60.6(v). The Park Service maintains separate records of listed and eligible properties.

The regulations also require general public notice of a proposed nomination by publication in the Federal Register upon submission to the Keeper. "Any person or organization which supports or opposes the nomination" can submit written arguments to the Keeper, who should consider them before making a decision. *Id.* § 60.6(t).

What happens when an SHPO considers, but then fails to nominate, a property to the Register? Any person or local government may appeal, to the Keeper, "the failure or refusal" of a SHPO to nominate, provided she makes her case in writing. *Id.* § 60.12(a). If the Keeper agrees with the appeal, she requests the SHPO to complete and forward the nomination to the Keeper. When the SHPO determines that a site is not eligible for inclusion, any person or local government may appeal that decision to the Keeper. *Id.* § 60.12. Failure to appeal precludes a finding that the person has exhausted her administrative remedies, *id.* § 60.12(e), and precludes judicial review of the decision. *See Hoonah Indian Ass'n v. Morrison*, 170 F.3d 1223, 1231 (9th Cir. 1999).

c.   THE ROLE OF THE KEEPER

Whichever party—an agency, an SHPO, or a THPO—nominates a historic resource, the final decision on nomination is made by the Keeper. The Keeper maintains independent judgment about substantive eligibility. As the Second Circuit has put it, "Where a nomination comes through a state historic preservation program, the regulations reserve final authority for the Park Service to determine whether the property will be added to the National Register." *Moody Hill Farms Ltd. P'ship v. U.S. Dep't of the Interior, Nat'l Parks Serv.*, 205 F.3d 554, 558 (2d Cir. 1999). Similarly, the Keeper's "determination that [a site] is eligible for inclusion on the National Register as a site of local historic importance is not vitiated, and cannot be vitiated, by the State Review Board's finding that the [site] has only 'marginal' significance." *Stop H-3 Ass'n v. Coleman*, 533 F.2d 434, 441 (9th Cir. 1976).

The Keeper's decisions can be reviewed in court only on the reasonableness standard embodied within the Administrative Procedure Act. *See Moody Hill Farms*, 205 F.3d at 561. In no published decision (other than that of the district court reversed in *Moody Hill Farms*) has any court set aside a decision made by the Keeper. Similarly, no person seeking a listing can force a dispute into court before the Keeper has ruled; the regulations make it plain that such a person has neither exhausted administrative remedies nor obtained a final decision, 36 C.F.R. § 60.12(e), thus precluding judicial review.

d.   AGENCY DETERMINATIONS OF ELIGIBILITY

As noted above, Section 106 of the NHPA requires federal agencies to consider the effects of their undertakings on any properties that are "included on" or "eligible for inclusion" on the National Register. 54 U.S.C. § 302105. Federal agencies that are in the process of considering an undertaking cannot limit their Section 106 reviews to properties previously listed or determined to be eligible by the Keeper. The regulations of the Advisory Council on Historic Preservation (ACHP)— an independent federal agency that, among other things, evaluates how federal agencies can better promote historic preservation—address this issue. The ACHP regulations require federal agencies themselves to assess the eligibility of properties potentially affected by their undertakings in consultation with the SHPO or the THPO. An "agency official shall take the steps necessary to identify historic properties within the area of potential effects." 36 C.F.R. § 800.4(b). If the relevant agency official and the SHPO, applying the National Register criteria, agree either that the property is eligible or that it is not, that determination shall govern. If they disagree, or if the Council or Secretary request, the agency official must obtain a determination from the Keeper. *Id.* § 800.4(c)(2). This duty of federal agencies to search for and to identify eligible properties both expands dramatically the scope of the NHPA's application and generates extensive information about previously unlisted properties.

The ACHP's interpretation of "eligible for inclusion" was upheld in the important decision, *CTIA-The Wireless Ass'n v. Fed. Commc'ns Comm'n*, 466 F.3d 105 (D.C. Cir. 2006). Petitioner, an association of cell phone companies, argued that Section 106 applied only to resources previously determined by the Keeper to be eligible. The court held that the ACHP's broader interpretation was reasonable and therefore controlling. The court held that the term was ambiguous in the NHPA and that the Federal Communications Commission had properly deferred to the ACHP's reasonable regulations. This holding seems eminently sensible because protection for a historic resource should not depend on whether it had previously been proposed for inclusion. There are many valuable unlisted resources, and the foreseeable possibility of harm is often a necessary prod to consideration of their worth.

This interpretation also seems consistent with the legislative history of the adoption of the "eligible for" language, which was added by statutory amendment in 1976. The ACHP's regulations already had required agencies to identify and to consider properties eligible for listing, in order to meet the agency's duties under the NHPA, the National Environmental Policy Act of 1969, and Executive Order 11593 (which was signed in 1971 by President Richard Nixon and required federal agencies to undertake surveys of any and all of their historic properties). The ACHP asked Congress to amend Section 106 to protect "eligible" properties, which would "clarify and support the council's present project review activities." *See* The Status of the Advisory Council on Historic Preservation Under the National Historic Preservation Act of 1966: Report of the Advisory Council on Historic Preservation to the Senate Committee on Interior and Insular Affairs, June 1975, *in* S. REP. No. 94–367 (1976), *reprinted in* 1976 U.S.C.C.A.N. 2460–61.

e.   RIGHTS OF PRIVATE PROPERTY OWNERS

Federal law does not impose any direct restriction on how a private owner may use or alter her property on account of inclusion on the National Register. Listing (or other determination of eligibility), however, may indirectly restrict the choices of the owner in at least two ways.

First, listing may obstruct the owner in obtaining federal funding or a license for a project favored by the owner because it would place some preservation duty on the relevant federal agency. For example, a private developer using a federal grant to renovate affordable housing, a state transportation agency seeking a federal permit to fill navigable waters, or a local government planning future use of a decommissioned military base may find their projects complicated by the duty placed on their partner federal agencies to comply with Section 106. Indeed, such non-federal entities often prepare much of the documentation used by the agency to comply.

Second, some state and local governments place, on state or local registers, any properties within their jurisdiction listed on the National Register. The Dade County Historic Preservation Ordinance discussed below in *Metro. Dade Cty. v. P.J. Birds, Inc.*, 654 So. 2d 170 (Fla. Dist. Ct. App. 1995), is just one example of a local ordinance that automatically includes historic resources that are listed on the National Register. This cross-listing, also known as "regulation by reference," may impose powerful substantive constraints on demolition or alteration under state or local law.

As we have seen, owners of nominated properties can object and prevent the listing of their properties on the National Register. 54 U.S.C. § 302105. But, avoiding listing will not necessarily free owners from these indirect effects. Owner objection does not prevent designating the property as "eligible" for inclusion on the Register, which would have the same consequences for federal funding or licensing of projects affecting the property as listing would. Moreover, many state and local preservation laws do not permit owners to prevent the listing of their properties. On the other hand, listing a property on the National Register (or within a district on a state or local register) is necessary to qualify for federal rehabilitation tax credits and other federal benefit programs. The irony of the owner objection provisions, then, is that they cannot exempt the owner from any significant regulatory restriction, but they can bar her from federal preservation benefits.

Property owners cannot challenge a federal listing for violating due process. The Fifth Amendment only requires due process before someone is "deprived" of life, liberty, or property. U.S. CONST. amend. V. However, as the Second Circuit has ruled, "national listing on its own does not impose any burdens on plaintiffs' use of their property. National listing constrains only the ability of departments of the federal government to take action affecting a listed property." *Moody Hill Farms Ltd. P'ship*, 205 F.3d at 563. Even if some states automatically add federally listed properties to state registers and then subject them to state regulation, due process rights are not implicated against federal officials, who are not responsible for the additional regulatory burdens.

NOTES & QUESTIONS

1. The need for objective evidence meeting scholarly standards of reliability is an important general principle in meeting the designation

criteria. This point is illustrated in *Hoonah Indian Ass'n*, 170 F.3d, a key case in Chapter 9. There, an Indian tribe in Alaska contested the Forest Service's conclusion that the region of a historic march by tribal members to escape hostile Russian forces was not eligible for listing because the path taken could not be reliably located. The reviewing court found the agency's decision reasonable and in accord with legal requirements, stating: "That important things happened in a general area is not enough to make the area a "site." There has to be some good evidence of just where the site is and what its boundaries are, for it to qualify for federal designation as a historical site." *Id.* at 1232. The court ruled that the agency properly disregarded oral legend even when accepted by the tribe as normative.

The Park Service's National Register Bulletin No. 38, *Guidelines for Evaluating and Documenting Traditional Cultural Properties*, provides sophisticated guidance on reconciling scholarly evidence with contemporary claims and oral tradition about sites of traditional cultural and religious significance to Native Americans. *See* Patricia L. Parker & Thomas King, *Guidelines for Evaluating and Documenting Traditional Cultural Properties* 1 (Nat'l Park Serv., Nat'l Register Bull. No. 38, 1992).

2. A subset of properties listed in the National Register meet the heightened requirements for designation as National Historic Landmarks. 54 U.S.C. § 306107. The criteria for Landmarks can be found at 36 C.F.R. Part 65. In general, a Landmark must possess nationally significant qualities of exceptional value or quality with a high degree of integrity. But, it is unclear how much more protection federal law provides to Landmarks. The U.S. Conference of Mayors had recommended that Congress prohibit demolition or alteration of such Landmarks, regardless of ownership, without the prior approval of the ACHP. *See* BYRD WOOD, WITH HERITAGE SO RICH: U.S. CONFERENCE OF MAYORS SPECIAL COMMITTEE ON HISTORIC PRESERVATION 195 (Nat'l Trust for Historic Pres. ed., 1999) (1966). Congress took the lesser step of providing a somewhat more stringent Section 106 protection for designated National Landmarks. Section 110(f) provides that the agency "shall to the maximum extent possible undertake such planning and actions as may be necessary to minimize harm to the landmark." 54 U.S.C. § 306107.

National Historic Landmarks also are more likely to qualify for the federal preservation grants that may be available. The executive branch of the federal government also has the power to preserve and maintain historic sites, granted by the Historic Sites Act of 1935, which will be discussed in greater detail in Chapter 8.

3. Owners of private property have a statutory right to notice in the federal designation process. After the designation process is over and a historic resource has been designated, ownership of the resource may change hands. How would a property owner know that her real property has been listed on the National Register, if the designation occurred prior to her tenure? The answer is not always simple. If she suspects that the property is on the National Register and she is Internet-savvy, she can review an online database of designated properties maintained by the National Park Service. If her property is part of a historic district, however, its address will

not be individually listed in the database, and she will have to examine a map of the district to determine if her property falls within it. The process of determining whether a property is on a state or local register may be even more difficult, especially where property records are not centrally kept or made available online.

If she has no idea that the property may be designated, she may be surprised to learn about its designation, for the first time, when she files for a building permit. This circumstance may occur if the locality requires a certificate of appropriateness for alterations or new construction on properties designated on the National Register or on state and local counterparts. In the vast majority of localities, there are no historic commissions with powers of review, and thus there may be no "trigger" for notice of the designation.

There are at least three viable alternatives to ensuring that subsequent owners or potential purchasers know about historic designation. The first is requiring disclosure of historic designation upon the sale or transfer of real property. But assuming that prior owners must only meet a "good faith" requirement, disclosure may be incomplete if the prior owners do not know that the property has been designated. Another alternative is for statements of designation to be recorded in the chain of title. Yet another is requiring professional real estate brokers to do the research and to disclose findings regarding a property's historic status, although this requirement would not include properties that change hands without the assistance of a broker. Localities with historic district commissions have only begun to explore these and other strategies of providing adequate notice to later property owners.

The notice-providing function of recordation is well-known; Chapter 10 discusses the recordation of conservation and preservation restrictions, which impose restrictions on owners. National Register designation, of course, may not impose any restrictions at all. Do you think that notice to subsequent owners or potential purchasers is necessary? If so, can you think of any other ways to ensure that designation of a parcel is clearly communicated?

4.   National Register Bulletin No. 16A described in detail how to prepare nominations for listing properties in the National Register. National Park Service, *How to Complete the National Register Registration Form* (1997). It directs nominators to "[r]elate information about each resource, such as date, function, associations, information potential, and physical characteristics, to the significance of the overall property to determine whether or not the resource contributes." *Id.* at 16. The Bulletin gives detailed advice on determining significance and also defines a noncontributing building as one that:

> does not add to the historic architectural qualities, historic associations or archaeological values for which a property is significant because it was not present during the period of significance or does not relate to the documented significance of the property; due to alterations, disturbances, additions or other changes, it no longer possesses historic integrity reflecting its

character at that time or is incapable of yielding important information about the period; or it does not independently meet the National Register criteria.

Id.

5.   Another path to federal designation occurs when a building not listed on the National Register becomes the subject of a federal historic rehabilitation tax credit application. According to 26 U.S.C. § 47(c)(3), any structure receiving tax credits must be listed on the National Register individually or must be a contributing structure to a registered historic district. When a taxpayer applies for a tax credit for a non-designated property, the State Historic Preservation Office automatically reviews its historical significance. As Chapter 11 describes, this review is a necessary first step to any tax credit application; applicants may not proceed without the National Register designation. Thus even if the applicants never actually rehabilitate the property or receive tax credits, the building would remain listed on the National Register. Is there a case to be made for a "contingent" designation in such circumstances, whereby applicants who do not successfully obtain tax credits within a certain amount of time can quietly de-list their building?

6.   The procedural formalities described in this section should not obscure the potential for the process to be influenced, at times, by politics. While most parties involved in the process possess significant expertise about historical resources and preservation, each of these officials is either appointed by a politician or elected in her own right. Consider a student author's account of the role of the City of Chicago in persuading the Illinois SHPO not to recommend designation of a district, where designation would have complicated a politically favored expansion of a college campus. Mark D. Brookstein, *When History is History: Maxwell Street, "Integrity," and the Failure of Historic Preservation Law*, 76 CHI. KENT L. REV. 1847 (2001).

Whatever the merits of the author's criticism of that case, he understates the benefits of stability, coverage, and endurance for preservation law that are gained over time by involving local powers in designation decisions. Final judgments made by the Keeper and opportunities for appeal, more often than not, keep political considerations in check.

7.   What is the impact of historic designation on property values? A study from the NYU Furman Center analyzed the effect of historic district designation in New York City. Generally, the research shows that property values increase in the areas in the historic district or within 250 feet of it. Citywide, property values within historic districts also tend to appreciate more rapidly over time. However, the study found that in Manhattan, the designation of a historic district may reduce the value of properties within the district.

Impacts systematically vary across neighborhoods: they increase more when the value of the lost option to redevelop is lower, and they may even decline in areas where the option to redevelop carries a very high value. The study's models, however, do not capture the value of preservation to city residents and to others more broadly, nor do they capture the increase in housing prices, citywide, that might result from supply restriction. *See* Vicki Been, Ingrid Gould Ellen, Michael Gedal, Edward Glaeser & Brian J. McCabe, *Preserving History or Hindering Growth? The Heterogeneous Effects of Historic Districts on Local Housing Markets in New York City* (N.Y. Univ. Furman Ctr., White Paper, 2014).

Would you be willing to pay more or to pay less for a property designated as historic?

8.   An issue of current controversy is whether sites that memorialize injustice—most particularly, Confederate monuments—can be designated on or removed from registers of historic places. The National Register eschews listing sites that are "primarily commemorative in nature," such as war memorials, 36 C.F.R. § 60.4, though some sites have been listed, as Part C.2. of Chapter 1 describes. Local preservation commissions have also exercised their authority to designate Confederate monuments, although Confederate monuments that are on municipal land can be removed by local legislation, regardless of prior designation. Historic preservation law may serve as a vehicle to remove Confederate monuments in a process that promotes public understanding. *Compare* Jess R. Phelps & Jessica Owley, *Etched in Stone: Historic Preservation Law and Confederate Monuments*, 71 FLA. L. REV. 627 (2019) *with* J. Peter Byrne, *Stone Monuments and Flexible Laws: Removing Confederate Monuments Through Historic Preservation Laws*, 71 FLA. L. REV. F. 169 (2020).

9.   The moon, though not within the boundaries of the United States (or even the Earth), contains relics worth preserving, including Neil Armstrong's footprints, "the bottom half of the first lunar lander, the scientific experiments, [and] the urine bags." Kenneth Chang, *To Preserve History on the Moon, Visitors are Asked to Tread Lightly*, N.Y. TIMES, Jan. 9, 2012. Following international law, everything that was left on the moon from the first lunar landing still belongs to the United States. However, the Outer Space Treaty, signed by 100 nations, including the United States, restricts any participating country from claiming sovereignty on any portion of the moon. Since the Apollo 11 and Apollo 17 landing sites are not within U.S. territory, do you think that the United States can designate them as national historic landmarks? Why or why not?

5.   FEDERAL DE-LISTING PROCEDURES

A property once listed as historic may be stripped of that designation when it has been altered to such an extent that its historic features lack integrity. Perhaps the highest-profile de-listing is that of Soldier Field, the home of the football team, the Chicago Bears. It opened in 1924, with a unique, Greco-Roman design that included Doric columns lining the façade. In 2003, ostensibly to alleviate safety and maintenance concerns, the stadium underwent a renovation so dramatic that a federal advisory board voted to remove the property from the list of National Historic Landmarks—the most elite designation status in the country. In considering the photographs below, do you see the differences between the original and the renovation? Could you make an argument that the renovation itself was part of the history of the site?

Figures 2-3 & 2-4:
Grant Park Stadium (Soldier Field) in 1932 and 2005,
Chicago, IL

Soldier Field, in 1932, before construction of the Park Administration Building. (Felix Mendelsohn, Chicago, Yesterday and Today, 1932).

Essentially the same process and criteria can be used to remove a property from the National Register. 36 C.F.R. § 60.15. Determinations of eligibility where owners had objected to a listing also can be reconsidered. *Id.* § 60.15(c). Generally, petitions for reconsideration or removal must come through the SHPO or through a Federal Preservation Officer when a federal property is implicated, although the Keeper may remove a property on her own motion. 36 C.F.R. § 60.15(k). A property may lose integrity through destruction of significant elements. When a property is physically moved, it will be removed from the National Register unless the SHPO or a federal agency shows that it retains integrity. *Id.* § 60.14(b). A property may also be removed upon a showing of new information, an "[e]rror in professional judgment" about meeting the criteria, or by a "[p]rejudical procedural error." *Id.* § 60.15(a). Properties removed for procedural errors continue to be considered eligible. *Id.* § 60.15(a)(4).

The Keeper makes final decisions about removal. In *White v. Shull*, 520 F. Supp. 11 (S.D.N.Y. 1981), the court held that it lacked jurisdiction to entertain an action seeking to remove a historic district from the National Register, when the plaintiffs had not first exhausted their available administrative remedies to request the Keeper to do so. Also, a state's decision to void a listing on the state register on procedural grounds would not vitiate a concurrent federal listing, unless the Keeper found that a prejudicial error occurred in the federal nomination. *Moody Hill Farms Ltd. P'ship*, 205 F.3d at 560. *But see Historic Green Springs, Inc. v. Bergland*, 497 F. Supp. 839 (E.D. Va. 1980) (removing a property from the National Register), for an example of a court that was not so deferential. The D.C. Circuit has liberally interpreted standing to challenge the Keeper's removal of a resource. *Sierra Club v. Jewell*, 764 F.3d 1 (D.C. Cir. 2014) (holding that environmental and historic preservation organizations have standing to challenge the removal of a historic resource by the Keeper of the National Register's decision).

B. STATE AND LOCAL DESIGNATION

State and local historic preservation designation processes generally resemble those in the National Register in essentials. Each level will require detailed scholarly documentation about the historic resource or resources, and each will generally require some type of notice to or involvement from affected property owners.

The primary difference may be the impact of designation. The National Register, discussed in detail in the preceding section, does not itself restrict property owners' discretion. Other local, state, and federal laws, however, may be passed to protect properties on the National Register by imposing affirmative duties upon their owners, neighbors, or others. By contrast, local ordinances or state laws that designate historic properties by and large do couple designation with certain restrictions on the rights of owners or of others. So designation may be more hotly contested in the state and local context.

The following two cases deal with the criteria and process that two different localities have used to designate properties as historic.

1.   STATE AND LOCAL CRITERIA

a.   A GENERAL STANDARD

A-S-P Associates v. City of Raleigh
258 S.E.2d 444 (N.C. 1979)

Plaintiff brought this action seeking a declaratory judgment that two ordinances adopted on 3 June 1975 by the City of Raleigh are invalid both on constitutional and statutory grounds. The two ordinances (hereinafter referred to collectively as the Oakwood Ordinance) amended the City's zoning ordinance to create a 98 acre, overlay historic district in the City's Oakwood neighborhood (hereinafter referred to as the Historic District), established the Raleigh Historic District Commission (hereinafter referred to as the Historic District Commission), adopted architectural guidelines and design standards to be applied by the Historic District Commission in its administration of the Oakwood Ordinance, and provided civil and criminal penalties for failure to comply with the Oakwood Ordinance. *See* RALEIGH, N.C., CODE, §§ 24–57 through 57.8 (1959).

The Ordinance was adopted pursuant to N.C. GEN. STAT. §§ 160A–395 through 399, which authorize municipalities to designate historic districts and to require that after the designation of a historic district any property owner within it who desires to erect, alter, restore, or move the exterior portion of any building or other structure first obtain a certificate of appropriateness from a historic district commission. A historic district commission's action is limited by N.C. GEN. STAT. § 160A–397 to "preventing the construction, reconstruction, alteration, restoration, or moving of buildings, structures, appurtenant fixtures, or outdoor advertising signs in the historic district which would be incongruous with the historic aspects of the district."

In May of 1974, the Division of Archives and History of the North Carolina Department of Cultural Resources nominated Raleigh's Oakwood neighborhood for inclusion on the United States Department of Interior's National Register of Historic Places. In the required statement of significance, the Division's Survey and Planning Unit observed:

> Oakwood, a twenty-block area representing the only intact nineteenth century neighborhood remaining in Raleigh, is composed predominantly of Victorian houses built between the Civil War and 1914. Its depressed economic state during most of the twentieth century preserved the neighborhood until 1971,

when individuals began its revitalization. The great variety of Victorian architectural styles represented by the houses reflects the primarily middle-class tastes of the business and political leaders of Raleigh for whom they were built, as well as the skill of local architects and builders. Oakwood is a valuable physical document of Southern suburban life during the last quarter of the nineteenth century.

On 25 June 1974, the Oakwood neighborhood was placed on the National Register.

At the request of The Society for the Preservation of Historic Oakwood, the Planning Department of the City of Raleigh conducted a study of the Oakwood neighborhood in 1974. Those conducting the study found that a high rate of absentee ownership existed in the neighborhood, that banks were reticent to lend money in the Oakwood area as a result of its unstable property values, that significant private efforts to preserve the historic aspects of the neighborhood had been undertaken, and that the neighborhood was at a transition point with an uncertain future. The recommendation of the study was that the City take affirmative action in one of two ways: (1) Plan and zone the neighborhood for high density residential and commercial development, which would result in the loss of most aspects of the historic significance of the neighborhood, or (2) maintain the neighborhood as medium density residential with an emphasis on preserving its historic aspects.

In January of 1975, the Planning Department submitted to the City Council *A Proposal for the Designation of Oakwood as an Historic District*. A proposed ordinance was submitted to the State Division of Archives and History for review, and recommended changes were made. On 10 April 1975, a joint public hearing was held before the Raleigh City Council and Planning Commission at which both proponents and opponents of the ordinance presented their views. On 3 June 1975 the City Council adopted the Oakwood Ordinance.

The Historic District thus created is an overlay zoning district. All zoning regulations in the area in effect prior to passage of the Oakwood Ordinance remain in effect. Compliance with the Oakwood Ordinance is required in addition to compliance with the preexisting, underlying zoning regulations. Most of the area covered by the Historic District is zoned residential. A relatively small portion of the area covered by it is zoned as office and institutional. Associates own a vacant lot, located within the Historic District at 210 North Person Street. The lot is within the office and institutional zoning district.

On 22 July 1975 Associates brought this action challenging the validity of the Ordinance on constitutional and statutory grounds. * * *

N.C. GEN. STAT. § 160A–395 authorizes any municipal governing body to designate one or more historic districts as a part of its general zoning ordinance. Municipal governing bodies (which term includes governing boards of counties as well) are thereby delegated the legislative power to determine whether or not to designate a historic district or districts. * * *

The delegation of legislative power to municipal governing bodies is not in this instance an unlimited delegation. *Id.* § 160A–396 provides that before a city or county may designate one or more historic districts it must establish a historic district commission. *Id.* § 160A–396 further limits the delegation of power by specifying that, "(a) majority of the members of such a commission shall have demonstrated special interest, experience, or education in history or architecture." *Id.* § 160A–397 imposes another limitation by specifying the method by which a historic district ordinance adopted by a city or county is to be enforced:

> From and after the designation of a historic district, no exterior portion of any building or other structure (including stone walls, fences, light fixtures, steps and pavement, or other appurtenant features) nor above-ground utility structure nor any type of outdoor advertising sign shall be erected, altered, restored, or moved within such district until after an application for a certificate of appropriateness as to exterior architectural features has been submitted to and approved by the historic district commission. * * *

Although the neighborhood encompassed by the Historic District is to a considerable extent an architectural meelange [sic], that heterogeneity of architectural style is not such as to render the standard of "incongruity" meaningless. The predominant architectural style found in the area is Victorian, the characteristics of which are readily identifiable. City of Raleigh, Planning Department, *A Proposal to Designate Oakwood as a Historic District* 1 (1975); N.C. Department of Cultural Resources, *National Register Nomination Form, Oakwood Historic District* (1974). In his deposition, Raleigh's Planning Director, A. C. Hall, Jr., testified:

> (T)he remaining part of Oakwood, yes, has been developed since that time, with varying types of architectures, filling in the holes, so to speak, in the neighborhood, but still this is in my opinion and my recollection, this is the only and the best example, and has a majority of worthwhile Victorian or Victorian Era structures in it, in the neighborhood that we have.

The characteristics of other architectural styles of historical interest found in the Historic District are equally distinctive and objectively ascertainable. The architectural guidelines and design standards incorporated into the Oakwood Ordinance provide an analysis of the structural elements of the different styles and provide additional support for our conclusion that the contextual standard of "incongruity" is a sufficient limitation on the Historic District Commission's discretion.

It will be remembered that N.C. GEN. STAT. § 160A–396 requires that a majority of the members of a historic district commission shall have demonstrated special interest, experience, or education in history or architecture. There is no evidence that Raleigh's Historic District Commission is not so constituted. To achieve the ultimate purposes of historic district preservation, it is a practical necessity that a substantial degree of discretionary authority guided by policies and goals set by the legislature, be delegated to such an administrative body possessing the expertise to adapt the legislative policies and goals to varying, particular circumstances. It is a matter of practical impossibility for a legislative body to deal with the host of details inherent in the complex nature of historic district preservation. * * *

[EDS.: The Court of Appeals found the ordinance unlawful on several grounds. The Supreme Court first held that the historic preservation ordinance did not violate the Due Process Clause or constitute an unconstitutional delegation of authority to the local government.]

Associates' third contention is that the superior court erred in concluding that defendant City did not deny Associates' equal protection of the laws by including Associates' property in the Historic District while excluding property owned by the North Carolina Medical Association, which is located in the same block. * * *

[T]he facts are as follows. Associates' vacant lot is located at 210 North Person Street. Adjacent to it at 216 North Person Street is the former Mansion Square Inn, built in the nineteenth century. The State Medical Society's large, four story office building is located at 222 North Person Street. These three pieces of property and a fourth at 204 North Person have been included since 1961 in an office and institutional zoning district. At the request of the State Medical Society, the property on which its building is located and two other adjacent lots owned by the Society in the same block were excluded from the overlay, Historic District. Associates' request that their vacant lot be similarly excluded was denied and theirs and all other property in the same block was included in the Historic District. Associates' equal protection claim is based on its allegations that defendant City acted arbitrarily and capriciously in setting the boundaries of the Oakwood Historic District because the included and excluded pieces of property are similarly located.

Without considering the questions raised by this contention, the Court of Appeals held that Associates had made a prima facie showing of arbitrary and capricious spot zoning. The Court of Appeals further held * * * that a major part of defendant City's evidence offered to show a reasonable basis for exclusion of the Medical Society's property should not have been considered because "it is (impermissible) in this jurisdiction to prove the intent of a legislative body by statements of one of its members." *A-S-P Assocs. v. City of Raleigh*, 247 S.E.2d 800, 804 (N.C. Ct. App. 1978). Disregarding defendant City's evidence, the Court of Appeals reversed the judgment of the superior court and ordered the case remanded for further proceedings on the question of whether or not defendant City had engaged in impermissible spot zoning.

Spot zoning is "(a) zoning ordinance, or amendment, which singles out and reclassifies a relatively small tract owned by a single person and surrounded by a much larger area uniformly zoned, so as to impose upon the small tract greater restrictions than those imposed upon the larger area, or so as to relieve the small tract from restrictions to which the rest of the area is subjected . . . ." *Blades v. City of Raleigh*, 187 S.E.2d 35, 45 (N.C. 1972). So defined, it is apparent that defendant City has not, in this instance, engaged in spot zoning at all. The City by passing the Oakwood Ordinance created a 102 acre overlay, zoning district (as it is authorized to do by N.C. GEN. STAT. § 160A–395), the restrictions of which apply to numerous individual property owners. In drawing the boundaries of the Historic District the City merely decided not to include certain property owned by the Medical Society, while including that owned by Associates and others in the same block. Reclassification of a relatively small tract owned by a single person surrounded by a much larger area, uniformly zoned, is simply not the issue involved. Thus we need only consider the equal protection of the laws claim raised by Associates.

The applicable rule of law by which our consideration must be guided is well stated in *Guthrie v. Taylor*, 185 S.E.2d 193 (N.C. 1971), *cert. denied*, 406 U.S. 920 (1972).

> Neither the Equal Protection Clause of the Fourteenth Amendment to the United States Constitution nor the similar language in Art. I, § 19, of the Constitution of North Carolina takes from the State the power to classify persons or activities when there is reasonable basis for such classification and for the consequent difference in treatment under the law.
>
> The test is whether the difference in treatment made by the law has a reasonable basis in relation to the purpose and subject matter of the legislation.

Id. at 201.

The reasonableness of a particular classification is a question of law for determination by the court. In its consideration of a particular legislative classification, which term encompasses the setting of zoning district boundaries, a court is bound, however, by two fundamental, related limitations. First, there is a presumption that a particular exercise of the police power is valid and constitutional, and the burden is on the property owner to show otherwise. Second, it must be remembered that classification is exclusively a legislative function. Because it is such, a court may not substitute its judgment of what is reasonable for that of the legislative body, particularly when the reasonableness of a particular classification is fairly debatable. This second limitation is reflected in former Chief Justice Bobbitt's observation in *State v. Greenwood*, 187

S.E.2d 8, 13 (N.C. 1972) that: "The equal protection clauses do not require perfection in respect of classifications. In borderline cases, the legislative determination is entitled to great weight." * * *

The evidence presented at the hearing on the motion for summary judgment showed: The State Medical Society's building is a large (four story), modern structure; virtually all elements of its architectural style are, by contrast with the structures on property included in the Historic District, extremely incongruous with its historic aspects; The Medical Society made substantial investments in the foundations of the building in order that two additional stories can be added at some point in the future; the adjacent lots owned by the Society, which were also excluded from the District, were acquired to provide additional off-street parking necessary to future expansion of the building; Associates' property, when purchased in 1972 had on it a dilapidated structure, which was subsequently demolished, and the property has remained vacant since; other pieces of property in the same block are either vacant or have structures on them which are reasonably compatible in terms of scale, orientations, setback and architectural style with the historic aspects of the District.

Bearing in mind the touchstone of judicial review of a particular legislative classification, the object of the legislative exercise of the police power, we cannot say that the superior court erred in its conclusion of law that a reasonable basis existed for the exclusion of the Medical Society's property while other property in the same block was included in the Historic District. Associates' property, other property in the same block, and that owned by The Medical Society are indeed Similarly located. They are not, however, Similarly situated, insofar as the purpose of the Historic District Ordinance is concerned. Substantial and material differences exist, as clearly shown by the uncontroverted evidence presented, which support the superior court's conclusion of law.

Exclusion from the Historic District of only that property owned by the Medical Society on which its building is located might have been a wiser choice. But is well settled that legislative bodies may make rational distinctions with substantially less than mathematical exactitude. *New Orleans v. Dukes*, 427 U.S. 297 (1976).

The decision of the Court of Appeals on this aspect of the case is reversed and the judgment of the superior court is affirmed.

NOTES & QUESTIONS

1.   Notice that the Oakwood District was first listed in the National Register of Historic Places and then later designated under the City of Raleigh ordinance. Designation under Raleigh's ordinance required the property owner to obtain regulatory approval before demolishing or significantly altering any building or erecting a new building on a site within the district. The property owner here objected to the inclusion of its vacant lot within the district because it meant that the Historic District Commission

could prohibit it from erecting a building that it found "incongruous" with the architectural character of the district.

2.   Local governments vary with respect to the roles of expert historic preservation commissions and elected local legislative bodies in the designation process. In Raleigh, the designation process is handled by the local legislative body (the City Council), with no role played by the city's recently renamed Historic Development Commission. As the court notes, the Oakwood District was designated by the Raleigh City Council, acting upon a recommendation of the city's Planning Department, by creating an "overlay district" within the city's Zoning Ordinance. In Washington, D.C., the Historic Preservation Review Board designates properties applying statutory standards, with no involvement by the D.C. Council. D.C. CODE § 6–1103. In other cities, decisions by expert boards may be appealed to, or must be approved by, the city council. In New York City, for example, the City Council, by majority vote, may modify or disapprove any designation by the Landmarks Preservation Commission within 120 days of the filing of the Commission's resolution. N.Y.C. ADMIN. CODE § 25–303(g)(2). In Chicago, the City Council may designate any area, district, building, or work of art, acting upon the recommendation of the Commission on Chicago Landmarks, but if the Council fails to act within a year of the submission of the Commission's recommendation, the designation is automatically granted. CHI., ILL., MUN. CODE 2–120–700, –705.

3.   Why was the State Medical Society building excluded from the district? Why were its two adjacent vacant lots excluded? Why was Associates' vacant lot included? What are the arguments for leaving such line-drawing to the City Council or a historic commission, or for having a court scrutinize it?

b.   AN EXCEPTIONAL IMPORTANCE STANDARD

Metropolitan Dade County v. P.J. Birds, Inc.

654 So. 2d 170 (Fla. Dist. Ct. App. 1995)

■ COPE, JUDGE. * * *

I.

Late in 1990, the Dade County Historic Preservation Board ("the Board") decided to consider Parrot Jungle for designation as a historic site. The Board's staff prepared a detailed report recommending a twelve acre portion of the Parrot Jungle property for such designation. After a public hearing, the Board voted in favor of the designation.

The owner, P.J. Birds, Inc., appealed to the Board of County Commissioners, arguing that it had not been given a full and fair opportunity to present its case in opposition to the designation. At the owner's request, the County Commission returned the matter to the Historic Preservation Board for a new hearing.

At the new hearing, the staff report and recommendations were again submitted to the Board. There was extensive testimony from the Board's Executive Director and the public. A number of written submissions were also accepted into the record. Although the owner had requested the second hearing, the owner did not present any evidence and the principals of the owner corporation declined to answer any questions put by the Board. The owner's input was confined solely to having the owner's counsel cross-examine the witnesses who testified, and in making legal argument.

The Historic Preservation Board again voted, without dissent, in favor of the designation as a historic site. The owner again appealed to the County Commission, which conducted a hearing. The County Commission upheld the historic designation. * * *

II.

Under the Dade County Historic Preservation Ordinance, there are two distinct sets of historic designation criteria. There is a set of general criteria which applies to sites which attained significance fifty or more years ago (the "General Criteria"). The General Criteria are set forth in the Historic Preservation Ordinance as follows:

§ 16A–10.   Designation process and procedure.

(I)   [Criteria.] The Board shall have the authority to designate areas, places, buildings, structures, landscape features, archeological sites and other improvements or physical features, as individual sites, districts or archeological zones that are significant in Dade County's history, architecture, archeology or culture and possess an integrity of location, design, setting, materials, workmanship or association, or:

(a)   Are associated with distinctive elements of the cultural, social, political, economic, scientific, religious, prehistoric and architectural history that have contributed to the pattern of history in the community, Dade County, south Florida, the State or the nation; or

(b)   Are associated with the lives of persons significant in our past; or

(c)   Embody the distinctive characteristics of a type, period, style or method of construction or work of a master; or that possess high artistic value; or that represent a distinguishable entity whose components may lack individual distinction; or

(d)   Have yielded, or are likely to yield information in history or prehistory; or

(e)   Are listed in the National Register of Historic Places.

Ch. 16A, METROPOLITAN DADE COUNTY CODE.

There is an additional criterion for sites attaining significance within the past fifty years. Pertinent here is the following:

(II) [Properties not generally considered; exceptions.] ... *[P]roperties that have achieved significance within the last fifty (50) years, will not normally be considered for designation. However, such properties will qualify* if they are integral parts of districts that do meet the criteria, or *if they fall within the following categories: * * **

> (f)   A property or district achieving significance within the past fifty (50) years if *it is of exceptional importance.*

Id. § 16A–10 (II) (emphasis added). A less-than-fifty-year-old property must not only meet the General Criteria, but in addition the site must be of "exceptional importance."

Thus, the ordinance creates what may be described as an "Over-fifty Rule," and an "Under-fifty Rule." * * *

III.

The question considered by the Historic Preservation Board in this case was how to apply the designation standards where the tourist attraction came into existence over fifty years ago, but where additional structures have been added within the past fifty years.

The Historic Preservation Board's Staff Summary states in part:

Parrot Jungle and Gardens which lies a few miles south of Miami is one of Florida's most unique tourist attractions. When it opened on December 20, 1936 it was billed as the "Only One in the World." For fifty-four years visitors have enjoyed the subtropical and tropical landscaping, man-made paths, and limestone structures that make up the jungle where hundreds of exotic birds are allowed to fly free.

The Staff Summary explains that the Parrot Jungle tourist attraction became commercially successful immediately and has operated continuously since its opening. The summary outlines the areas of Parrot Jungle which constituted the original tourist attraction and the structures built prior to World War II. The Staff Summary then goes on to explain that a duck pond and flamingo lake were added in the 1940's, a new entrance in 1954, and an amphitheater in 1974. The original and newer features are all integral to the tourist attraction.

The Staff Report recommended that twelve acres be designated as a historic site, out of Parrot Jungle's total of 31 acres. At the public hearing, the Board's Executive Director, Margot Ammidown, testified that from a historic preservation point of view, the property had attained significance over fifty years ago, and the "Over-fifty" standard applied. The original buildings are over fifty years old. The Parrot Jungle and Gardens became commercially successful over fifty years ago and have been operating continuously for over half a century. Indeed, Parrot Jungle's own present-day promotional brochure prominently states "Parrot Jungle and Gardens . . . Over 50 Years of Beauty and Tradition."

Ms. Ammidown then pointed out that in addition to the over fifty-year-old buildings, the site also includes some buildings and landscape features which were added within the last fifty years. Ms. Ammidown addressed the interpretation of the Historic Preservation Ordinance in such a case:

> In terms of some specific issues I think might come up, I would like to address one in particular since this is a very complicated site. We are not talking about an individual building. We are talking about a site that contains numerous buildings on a number of acres. *I would like to point out that even though buildings were added mostly throughout the 1940's that does not disqualify them from the designation. . . . You can designate since the Board considers an area in terms of all the contributing factors to the overall historic character of the property.* We think certainly that the areas of the Parrot Jungle that were added in the 1940's represent areas that *contributed to the overall historic character of the park.* Also the alterations that were done—they also were done in a fashion that greatly contributed to the historic aspect of the park.

(Emphasis added).

Simply put, if a property has attained significance dating back over fifty years, it does not lose that significance simply because there has been additional construction or modification within the past fifty years, so long as the additional construction or modification has contributed to the overall historic character. Particularly for a working commercial property, this is a rule of practical necessity. * * *

The Board decided to make the designation under both alternatives. * * *

IV. * * *

Here, the Board interpreted the "Over-fifty" portion of the ordinance to be applicable where the site achieved significance over fifty years ago, so long as more recent structures are consistent with, and contribute to the overall historic character of, the historic site.

The circuit court was obliged to defer to the agency's interpretation of the ordinance on this point. The Board's interpretation of the "Over-fifty" standard in this case represented a reasonable construction of the Historic Preservation Ordinance. That is especially so where, as here, the County Commission—the legislative body which enacted the ordinance—has specifically reviewed and approved the Board's interpretation. The historic designation should have been sustained on the basis of the "Over-fifty" rule.

V.

The Historic Preservation Board and the County Commission also found that the Parrot Jungle site qualified for designation pursuant to the "Under-fifty" rule. * * *

The circuit court panel found fault with the fact that the Historic Preservation Board had not heretofore adopted a rule to define "exceptional importance," and that explicit criteria defining "exceptional importance" had been announced by the Historic Preservation Board in the course of its administrative hearing on the Parrot Jungle designation. We conclude that here, too, the circuit court panel applied the incorrect law.

A.

Where a statute or ordinance delegates powers to an administrative body, there must be sufficient standards to guide the agency in the administration of the law.

This rule must be flexibly applied. * * *

The circuit court noted that the ordinance itself does not define "exceptional importance" and the Historic Preservation Board had not adopted rules to define it. The court concluded, in part, that the term itself did not give the Board sufficient guidance.

In so ruling the circuit court overlooked the administrative law cases which allow reference to generally recognized professional standards in interpreting the meaning of a statutory term. *See Fla. State Bd. of Architecture v. Wasserman*, 377 So. 2d 653, 656 (Fla. 1979) (referring to standards recognized in professional field of architecture); *Jones v. Dep't of Revenue*, 523 So. 2d 1211, 1213 (Fla. 1st Dist. Ct. App. 1988) (referring to professional standards for assessment levels). * * *

As a matter of state policy, Florida follows the objectives of the National Historic Preservation Act. *See* FLA. STAT. ANN. §§ 267.021(5), 267.061(2)(c), (3)(c), (3)(h) (Supp. 1994). All fifty states have adopted historic preservation laws, and numerous local preservation ordinances exist as well.

The Dade County Historic Preservation Ordinance is patterned on the federal historic preservation regulations. The Dade County "exceptional importance" standard for "Under-fifty" properties is drawn directly from 36 C.F.R. section 60.4. The National Park Service has issued a publication delineating the professional standards that apply to the "exceptional importance" term as used within the Federal Historic Preservation Regulations—the source from which the Dade Ordinance drew that term. *See* Arcella Sherfy & W. Ray Luce, *Guidelines for Nominating and Evaluating Properties that have Achieved Significance Within the Last Fifty Years* (Nat'l Park Serv., Nat'l Register Bull. No. 22, 1979).

At the hearing before the Historic Preservation Board, Ms. Ammidown testified regarding the "exceptional importance" standard in the Dade Historic Preservation Ordinance:

Q   Now the reference to that Section of the Code that refers to "exceptional importance": Is exceptional importance defined in the Code?

A   It's not specifically defined.

Q   Would you, therefore, agree that its definition is somewhat subjective?

A   Because there is such a wide array of historical and archeological sites, yes.

Q   It would be a subjective definition? * * *

Ms. Ammidown: Well, I would apply a couple of questions to such a site. One is: *Is it one of a kind, is it a unique historic site.* We may have numerous Art Deco buildings. Is it something that is one of a kind. Another question is: *Is it a site that is significant in multiple areas?* The Board has the obligation of designating sites for either historical significance, architectural significance, landscape design significance, archeological significance. Is it a site that is significant in more than one area and also *is it particularly significant to the cultural history of an area?* For example, in this case, tourism has been a principal industry of Dade County and you know in that respect that the property take[s] on added significance because it reflects something unique about our area.

[County Attorney]: *Among historic preservation professionals, is that the generally accepted standard?*

Ms. Ammidown: *Those are the types of things that are considered exceptional*—its contribution to an area of growth and development.

In sum, there are professional standards which are generally accepted within the field of historic preservation and which are applied on a case-by-case basis.[7] Applying those standards, the Historic Preservation Board's resolution states, in part, that "Parrot Jungle and Gardens . . . is a property of exceptional importance because: it is one of a kind; directly related to major themes in this community's history; and significant in multiple areas, including architecture, history, and landscape design[.]" The County Commission adopted the Historic Preservation Board's position on this point.

---

[7]   The Historic Preservation Board's transmittal memorandum to the County Commission states, in part:

Professional standards used to determine exceptional merit include consideration of whether the site is: a) one of a kind; b) directly related to a major theme in the region's development; c) significant in multiple areas which can include history, architecture, landscape design, and archaeology.

B.

Alternatively, assuming arguendo that there was an unlawful delegation problem, that problem was cured when the County Commission—the legislative body which enacted the Ordinance—passed its resolution ratifying the Historic Preservation Board's interpretation of the term "exceptional importance." Such a ratification procedure is specifically authorized by *Askew v. Cross Key Waterways*, 372 So. 2d 913, 925 (Fla. 1978). In that case the Florida Supreme Court addressed the remedies available to the legislature where there has been an unlawful delegation of legislative authority. *Id.* The court stated:

> [T]he legislature need only exercise its constitutional prerogative and duty to identify and designate those resources and facilities [which are areas of critical state concern]. It *may be done in advance* as with [the statutory designation of] the Big Cypress area of critical state concern, Section 380.055, Florida Statutes (1975), *or through ratification of administratively developed recommendations . . .*

Id. at 925 (emphasis added).

Here, the Historic Preservation Board adopted a definition of "exceptional importance" and included it in the Board's resolution designating Parrot Jungle as a historic site. The County Commission approved that designation, and in its resolution reiterated the Board's definition. This constitutes ratification within the latitude allowed by *Askew v. Cross Key Waterways*.

C.

The circuit court held that the "ad hoc determination of rules and criteria by the Board during the designation hearing was an abuse of the rule-making process which violated Appellant's [owner's] due process rights guaranteed under the Florida and U.S. Constitutions." * * * The court faulted the Historic Preservation Board for not having previously adopted a rule to define the "exceptional importance" standard.

We respectfully disagree with the circuit court's position on this legal issue. Writing in the context of the Florida Administrative Procedure Act, the Florida Supreme Court has said, "There are quantitative limits to the detail of policy that can effectively be promulgated as rules, or assimilated; and even the agency that *knows* its policy may wisely sharpen its purposes through adjudication before casting rules." *Gulf Coast Elec. Coop., Inc. v. Fla. Pub. Serv. Comm'n*, 462 So.2d 1092, 1094 (Fla. 1985) (citation omitted; emphasis in original). * * *

The Florida Supreme Court has thus explicitly recognized that an administrative agency may proceed with case-by-case adjudication, and that incipient policy may be allowed to develop before the agency adopts rules.

The historic preservation literature makes clear that the "exceptional importance" standard is one best suited for development through case-by-case adjudication. Discussing the counterpart federal historic preservation criteria, the National Park Service has said:

> The National Register Criteria for Evaluation encourage nomination of recently significant properties if they are of exceptional importance to a community, a State, a region, or the Nation. The criteria do not describe exceptional, nor should they. Exceptional, by its own definition, cannot be fully catalogued or anticipated. It may reflect the extraordinary impact of a political or social event. It may apply to an entire category of resources so fragile that survivors of any age are unusual. It may be the function of the relative age of a community and its perceptions of old and new. It may be represented by a building or structure whose developmental or design value is quickly recognized as historically significant by the architectural or engineering profession. It may be reflected in a range of resources for which a community has an unusually strong associative attachment.

> Thus a complete list of exceptionally significant resources cannot be prepared or precise indicators of exceptional value prescribed.

Sherfy & Luce, *supra* at 3.

Therefore, under Florida Supreme Court authority, the Historic Preservation Board was not required to adopt a rule to define the standard of "exceptional importance." It had the latitude to proceed in case-by-case adjudication. The circuit court order on this point did not apply the correct law.

D.

The next question is whether, apart from the failure to adopt rules, it can be said that there was any violation of the owner's due process rights under the Florida or federal Constitutions. That question must be answered in the negative.

The Historic Preservation Board staff in this case prepared a detailed analysis of the Parrot Jungle site. The principal position of the Staff Report was that the Parrot Jungle site qualified for designation under the "Over-fifty" standard. In the Report and in the testimony, there was a thorough evaluation of the Parrot Jungle property under the General Criteria which are spelled out at length in the Dade Historic Preservation Ordinance. At no time has the owner suggested that there is any infirmity in the General Criteria.

The owner was given notice and an opportunity to be heard on the issue of historic designation. The owner was represented by very able counsel at all stages. The owner had not one, but two, plenary hearings before the Historic Preservation Board. * * *

In sum, the Staff Report in this case had thoroughly delineated the different factors which supported the designation of this property as a historic site. These were all set forth in writing well in advance of both hearings, and provided to the owner and the Board. All of these factors were pertinent to the General Criteria set forth in section 16A–10(I).

An agency is entitled to engage in administrative adjudication. The interpretation of the term "exceptional importance" was well within the competence of the Historic Preservation Board to decide. This matter was heard on proper notice twice by the Historic Preservation Board, and twice by the County Commission. There is simply no viable claim that the owner's due process rights were violated.

VI.

The Parrot Jungle site qualified for designation under both the "Over-fifty" and "Under-fifty" rules. Either rule alone would be sufficient to support the designation. The circuit court order is quashed and the matter remanded with directions to reinstate the historic designation.

NOTES & QUESTIONS

1. What was historically significant about Parrot Jungle that merited designation as a landmark? If it has such significance should it matter whether it was fifty years old or not? What function do you think a fifty-year minimum plays? Do you find the "exceptional importance" criterion for sites less than fifty years old to be confusing?

2. Why did the owner contest the designation of Parrot Jungle as a landmark? What arguments did the owner make to the Historic Preservation Board or to the County Commission against the designation? What sort of facts should be relevant to deciding whether the property is significant? Would the owner normally have any special knowledge or expertise on these issues?

3. As you can see, the owner can appeal decisions to designate by the Historic Preservation Board to the County Commission. While the Board consists of persons with expertise or interest in history, architecture, or archeology, appointed by the Commission, the County Commission is the elected legislature of Dade County. What kinds of arguments might appeal to the Commission and to the Board, respectively? Is it good policy to allow property owners to make both kinds of arguments, to both professional and to legislative bodies, in the designation process?

c. VAGUE STANDARDS ✱

As *P.J. Birds* reveals, drafting criteria for the designation of historic properties can be a tricky balancing act. On one hand, it is important for criteria to be broadly worded, so that they may be flexibly applied. For example, drafters should not specify the exact architectural styles available for designation, because doing so would preclude the designation of buildings representing other architectural styles, including those styles that did not exist when the ordinance was drafted. On the other hand, criteria that are too broadly worded may be challenged for being unconstitutionally vague.

A case out of Chicago highlights the difficulties in striking the right balance. According to the city's Landmarks Ordinance, the Commission on Chicago Landmarks may only designate a property if it finds that two of the following seven criteria are satisfied:

✱ 1.   Its value as an example of the architectural, cultural, economic, historic, social, or other aspect of the heritage of the City of Chicago, State of Illinois, or the United States.

2.   Its location as a site of a significant historic event which may or may not have taken place within or involved the use of any existing improvements.

3.   Its identification with a person or persons who significantly contributed to the architectural, cultural, economic, historic, social, or other aspect of the development of the City of Chicago, State of Illinois, or the United States.

4.   Its exemplification of an architectural type or style distinguished by innovation, rarity, uniqueness, or overall quality of design, detail, materials, or craftsmanship.

5.   Its identification as the work of an architect, designer, engineer, or builder whose individual work is significant in the history or development of the City of Chicago, the State of Illinois, or the United States.

6.   Its representation of an architectural, cultural, economic, historic, social, or other theme expressed through distinctive areas, districts, places, buildings, structures, works of art, or other objects that may or may not be contiguous;

7.   Its unique location or distinctive physical appearance or presence representing an established and familiar visual feature of a neighborhood, community, or the City of Chicago.

CHICAGO, ILL., MUN. CODE § 2–120–620. Although these criteria are organized differently from the National Register criteria, they differ in substance primarily in Criterion 7, which emphasizes the sense of continuity that a characteristic structure provides psychologically to residents and requires no judgment about historical significance as such.

In *Hanna v. City of Chicago,* 907 N.E.2d 390 (Ill. App. Ct. 2009), property owners challenged the above designation criteria on the ground that they were unconstitutionally vague. An early decision by the trial court held for the property owners. Although it merely found that the complaint stated a cause of action, the court left no doubt that it viewed terms like "significant" and "value" to be "vague, ambiguous, and overly broad." *Id.* at 396. The city's petition for leave to appeal was denied, which meant that the case was remanded to the trial court for a decision on the merits. *See Hanna v. City of Chi.*, 910 N.E.2d 1127 (Ill. 2009). On remand, the trial court found that the words used "provide a description of the observable historic character of the districts" and were not void for vagueness. *Hanna v. City of Chi.*, No. 06 CH 19422 (Cook County, Ill. Chancery Div. May 2, 2012). Six years and several appeals and remands later, the trial court again granted judgment in favor of the defendants. *Hanna v. City of Chi.*, 2018 WL 8949747 (Ill. Cir. Ct. 2018). It is worth considering what makes designation decisions sufficiently predictable or reasonable so that owners' rights of due process are respected.

In *Handicraft Block Ltd. P'ship v. City of Minneapolis*, 611 N.W.2d 16 (Minn. 2000), the Minnesota Supreme Court considered an analogous issue: whether designation decisions employ sufficiently distinct criteria to be subject to judicial review under ordinary administrative law principles. Although the relevant Minneapolis ordinance uses the key terms "historic or aesthetic merit" rather than significance, the underlying inquiry appears to be the same. *Id.* at 22. Ironically, in this case, the property owner argued that the criteria are sufficiently determinate to permit judicial review, nearly the opposite of the argument in *Hanna* that they are unconstitutionally vague.

The Historic Preservation Commission had recommended designation of a 1907 Georgian revival building, flanked by skyscrapers, in downtown Minneapolis. When the owner sought judicial review, the court held that the Commission's decision sufficiently involved "investigating and determining facts for the purpose of reaching a legal conclusion regarding [a] disputed claim," and also "applied a prescribed standard to the facts" to be considered quasi-judicial and subject to review. *Id.* at 20–21. The court explained the nature of the standard:

> [T]hough the four primary considerations that must be satisfied are distinct, they are not inconsistent or lacking in specificity. The standards require an investigation of specific types of facts relating to a specific property that is selected for heritage designation. In order for a building to be designated, it must either be associated with a significant historical trend or counter-trend, historic persons or events, distinctive architecture, or notable architects or craftsmen. The standards are not merely goals, they are specific criteria for the City to consider. They provide the framework for the facts the City investigates and findings the City makes regarding the property, its use, its history and its owners in order to justify designation. It is well within the province of a reviewing court to determine whether the evidence gathered to support one of these specific guidelines provides a "substantial basis" for the challenged decision.

Id. at 23. The gist of the court's analysis is that a criterion like having historical merit by "display[ing] the distinguishing characteristics of an architectural style inherently valuable for study or method of construction," *id.* at 22 n.3, has enough substance to permit a court to decide whether there are substantial facts supporting the conclusion that the criteria are satisfied. The Commission recommends buildings for designation to the City Council, but the court did not address what increase of discretion that political check builds into the designation decision.

2.   STATE AND LOCAL DESIGNATION PROCEDURES

In state and local preservation law, designation is usually necessary to compel property owners to take on certain affirmative duties or to prevent them from taking certain actions toward their properties. Thus, the process of designation at the state and local levels is often far more important and contested than in federal law, which imposes few such obligations on property owners. Should designation procedures contain broad discretion to consider economic and political consequences, or should they be based primarily on the historic significance of the properties?

There are a few examples of powerful local commissions, such as the New York City Landmarks Preservation Commission and the Boston Landmarks Commission, which actually designate. Questions have been raised about the processes these commissions use to process applications for designation of resources. In one instance, the New York City commission was sued because it allowed nominations to languish for years. While a lower court allowed the challenge to proceed, the appellate court found the challengers had no standing. *See Citizens Emergency Committee to Preserve Preservation v. Tierney*, 896 N.Y.S.2d 41 (App. Div. 2010) (confirming the commission chair's authority to set meeting agendas, even if delays in processing nominations occur, reversing the lower court decision, 2008 WL 5027203 (N.Y. Sup. Ct. 2008)).

Embassy Real Estate Holdings, LLC v. District of Columbia Mayor's Agent for Historic Preservation
944 A.2d 1036 (D.C. 2008)

■ RUIZ, ASSOCIATE JUDGE.

This case arises out of a plan to convert, by partially demolishing and adding new construction to, the former Italian Embassy ("the property"), which is owned by petitioner, Embassy Real Estate Holdings, LLC, into condominium residences. After petitioner's construction team had applied for pre-construction and construction permits, the Historic Preservation Office ("HPO") applied to designate the property an historic landmark under the Historic Landmark and Historic Protection Act of 1978 ("the Act"). *See* D.C. CODE § 6–1101 *et seq.* (2001). The Department of Consumer and Regulatory Affairs ("DCRA") issued some of the requested permits before the Historic Preservation Review Board ("HPRB") completed its review of the designation application, which ultimately resulted in designation of the property as an historic landmark. As a result, the HPRB determined, the construction permits had been issued in error by DCRA, because the development that petitioner proposed for the property was inconsistent with the purposes of the Act. Petitioner appealed to the Mayor's Agent for Historic Preservation ("Mayor's Agent"), who affirmed HPRB's determination that issuance of the permits was inconsistent with the property's designation as an historic landmark.

Before this court, petitioner challenges the decision of the Mayor's Agent on various grounds: [including] that the permit applications are not subject to review under the Act because they were filed before the landmark designation, and, therefore, HPRB and the Mayor's Agent acted without jurisdiction. * * *

I. Background

The property is a free-standing urban mansion, located at 2700 16th Street and 1651 Fuller Street, N.W., which consists of a main building containing the former Italian ambassador's residence, a chancery wing, and a courtyard. It is designed in Italian Renaissance Revival Style and "is a primary and integral component of the boulevard of distinguished buildings that line 16th Street on Meridian Hill." The buildings and grounds are described in the HPRB's landmark designation:

> The three-story hip-roofed main block contains the original ambassador's residence, with one-story flat-roofed wings enclosing three sides of an open-air courtyard at the rear. The fourth side of the court is formed by the side of the original chancery wing, originally a long two-story hip-roofed block with its short end facing onto Fuller Street. A circa 1930s addition extends the original chancery in a similar two-story configuration along Fuller Street, creating an L-Shaped footprint overall. The embassy is faced in limestone with a terra cotta tile roof and sculptural embellishment concentrated at window and door surrounds; the simpler chancery is stucco with limestone trim and tile roofs.

In 2001, Bruce Bradley purchased the property, planning to either sell it for continued use as an embassy or develop it as a residential property. He sought the advice of an architectural design team, Shalom Baranes and Patrick Burkhart. Mr. Baranes advised that, although the property was not in an historic district or designated as an historic landmark, it was "clearly eligible for designation," and that, "should anyone file a designation application, it was our opinion that application would succeed."

To address this possibility, Mr. Baranes presented Mr. Bradley with two options. Under one option, Mr. Bradley would apply for the designation landmark and "then subject the whole property to the normal HPRB review," a course that would definitively establish whether the property would be designated an historic landmark and its development subject to review and, possibly, restrictions under the Act. The other option—which Mr. Baranes told Mr. Bradley would involve "some risk"— consisted of negotiating a private agreement with members of the preservation community most likely to file an application to designate the property as historic. Under such an agreement, the property owner typically offers certain concessions in the development plan in exchange for a promise not to file for historic designation of the property. Mr. Baranes explained that this option would be successful in "a situation where there was no other interested party in proceeding with a designation."[1]

Mr. Bradley's design team members testified that they first met with State [i.e., D.C.] Historic Preservation Officer David Maloney to discuss the project in the fall of 2001. * * *

According to Mr. Baranes, Mr. Maloney told the design team that the HPO had "no intent at the time" to file an application to designate the property as an historic landmark, but the team did not ask for an "absolute assurance that [the HPO] would never file a designation application;" Mr. Burkhart testified that he left this meeting with the understanding that, although Mr. Maloney did not intend to file a landmark application on behalf of the HPO, some community groups might do so, and that they should contact these groups. While Mr. Maloney agreed that he likely told the design team to contact community organizations, he testified that he was "100 percent certain" that he had not suggested that they enter into private agreements with these groups in an effort to bypass formal HPRB review under the Act.

In the economic aftermath of September 11, 2001, plans to renovate the property were put on hold. In the spring of 2004, Mr. Bradley brought new investors into the project and created the petitioner, Embassy Real Estate Holdings, LLC. In August 2004, the design team met again with Mr. Maloney of the HPO, to discuss a different plan to renovate the property. This time, Mr. Maloney raised concerns about the negative impact that the new design, which included a ninety-foot tower, would have on existing views and the courtyard, as well as the significant demolition required for its construction. Mr. Burkhart testified that, notwithstanding these concerns, he left that meeting as well with the understanding that the "HPO had no plans to designate the building."

---

[1]   According to Mr. Baranes's testimony, applications for designation are usually filed by private entities who are actively involved in the preservation of historic properties in the city. The regulations provide, however, that "[a]pplication for designation of a property as a historic landmark or historic district [may] be made . . . by the [Historic Preservation Review] Board, a public agency, governmental unit or department, [and] Advisory Neighborhood Commission . . . ." 10A D.C. [MUN. REGULATIONS] § 203.1 (2007). The parties agree that it was not common for the HPRB to apply for landmark designation.

Figures 2-5 & 2-6:
The Former Italian Embassy,
Washington, DC

Petitioner had no further contact with the HPO regarding the project. On January 24, 2006, petitioner entered into an agreement with the D.C. Preservation League ("DCPL"), a private group dedicated to preserving and enhancing historic properties in the District of Columbia, in which certain changes were made to the design of the proposed renovation, and petitioner agreed to preserve some of the historic interior features of the property—the latter being matters beyond the protection of the Act. In exchange, DCPL agreed not to file for a landmark designation.[3] Petitioner's negotiations also resulted in an April 26, 2006 resolution by the Advisory Neighborhood Commission IC ("ANC IC") supporting the project.

On January 26, 2005, petitioner applied for a permit to subdivide the property for sale as seventy-nine condominium units. The permit was issued, with the approval of the HPRB, on July 26, 2005. On September 14, 2005, petitioner filed applications with the D.C. Department of Regulatory and Consumer Affairs ("DCRA") for permits to prepare the site for construction (including construction staging, excavation, sheeting, and shoring), to alter and renovate the existing buildings, and to build new structures. The permit for construction staging and sidewalk usage was issued on December 12, 2005. The HPO filed an application for historic landmark designation on January 6, 2006—after the permit for construction staging and sidewalk usage was issued, but while the permits for excavation, sheeting, shoring, alteration/renovation and new construction were still pending. After the application for landmark designation was filed, the DCRA was notified immediately and petitioner was notified a few days later. Despite having been given notice of the landmark application in early January, the DCRA issued permits for excavation, sheeting and shoring on February 1 and for new construction on February 8, 2006. At a hearing held by the HPRB on February 2, 2006, on the application for landmark designation, petitioner "[did] not question the historic merit of the building," but complained about the timing of the landmark application. On February 23, 2006, the HPRB voted to designate the property an historic landmark and further recommended its nomination to the National Register of Historic Places. On March 1, 2006, the DCRA was notified of the landmark designation and was asked by the HPO to void the two permits (for excavation, sheeting and shoring, and for construction) that had been issued after the application for landmark designation was filed. Petitioner received notification, dated March 6, 2006, that the HPRB had designated the property an historic landmark.

Specifically, the HPRB determined that petitioner's construction permits had been issued in error by the DCRA due to the HPRB's designation of the property as an historic landmark, and should be voided, noting that: "permit applications related to this property cannot be issued without historic preservation review pursuant to D.C. Official

---

[3] The DCPL has filed a brief *amicus curiae* in this case. It is "neither in support of nor opposition to the parties in this case," although it continues to support the agreement it reached with petitioner in favor of renovating the property. As DCPL recognizes, such an agreement is "not binding on third parties, cannot be enforced by the public at large, and, unless they include the HPRB and HPO, do not reflect the opinion of the agencies that implement the public policy of the District reflected in the Preservation Act." The thrust of DCPL's brief is to support the authority of the HPRB and Mayor's Agent to review permits for construction that are pending when an application for landmark designation is filed.

Code § 6–1104 through 6–1108. That is the basis for this request for revocation." The HPRB also recommended that the petitioner's proposed development for the property was inconsistent with the purposes of the Act, and, therefore, the permits should not be issued.

Petitioner requested a hearing before the Mayor's Agent to reject the HPRB's recommendation and uphold the validity of the permits that had been issued by DCRA. * * * After the hearing, the Mayor's Agent, agreeing with the HPRB's recommendation, voided the permits that had been issued by DCRA after the landmark designation application had been filed, finding that:

> The project as submitted requires the demolition of significant exterior historic features, including the chimneys and major portions of the building that are visible from the courtyard, all of which are otherwise protected by the Act. Such a demolition would hardly be contributory to efforts to retain or enhance the landmark, despite [petitioner's] assertion that its proposal would encourage the adaptation of the property for current use. HPRB, in adopting the staff [HPO] report, specifically found that, "[c]construction [sic] of the tower would require demolition of significant parts of the embassy and chancery." * * *

II. Discussion

  A. The Historic Landmark and Historic District Protection Act, D.C. CODE § 6–1101, *et seq.*

Under the Act, the HPRB is empowered to "[d]esignate and maintain a current inventory of historic landmarks." D.C. CODE § 6–1103(c)(3).[6] The HPRB has authority to "initiate a historic landmark or historic district designation by directing the staff to prepare an application. . . ." 10A D.C. MUN. REGULATIONS § 207.1. The HPRB is also tasked with "[a]dvis[ing] the Mayor on the compatibility with the purposes of [the Act] of the applications pursuant to § 6–1104 through 6–1108 [for demolition, alteration, division, new construction, and preliminary review]." D.C. CODE § 6–1103 (c)(*l*). The HPO is "the administrative staff of the. . . Historic Preservation Review Board." 10A D.C. MUN. REGULATIONS § 9901 (2007). The Mayor's Agent is the person appointed to exercise the Mayor's authority under the Act, to make "the final determination on the approval or denial of applications for demolition, alteration, new construction, and subdivision subject to the Historic Protection Act . . . ." 10A D.C. MUN. REGULATIONS § 400.1. "The Mayor's Agent shall make these findings after having received and duly considered the recommendations from . . . the [HPRB] . . . ." 10A D.C. MUN. REGULATIONS § 400.2.

---

[6] The HPRB is composed of members appointed by the Mayor and confirmed by the Council of the District of Columbia. *See* D.C. CODE §§ 6–1102 (7) & 1103(a). * * *

B. Jurisdiction

As a preliminary matter, petitioner argues that the plain language of the Act bars the HPRB and the Mayor's Agent from asserting jurisdiction to review applications for permits that were already pending before the application for landmark designation was filed. It further suggests that allowing "late-filed" designation applications to apply to pending applications for building permits could result in indefinite delays, and would eviscerate the protection of the two ninety-day periods the statute mandates for a hearing and decision on applications for landmark designation. Petitioner relies primarily on the statutory language which provides that "[b]efore the Mayor may issue a permit" to demolish, alter, subdivide, or build new construction on the site of an "historic landmark," the "Mayor shall review" the permit application in accordance with the Act. D.C. CODE §§ 6–1104(a) (demolitions), –1105(a) (alterations), –1106(a) (subdivisions), –1107(a) (new construction). This language implies, petitioner argues, that the site for which permits are sought has to be designated a historic landmark *before* the Mayor can base the issuance (or denial) of permits on a review pursuant to the Act. Therefore, according to petitioner, since the property in this case had not yet been designated an historic landmark when petitioner applied for the permits, the Act should not have played a role in the issuance of the permits.

We conclude that petitioner's argument is foreclosed by the Act's definition of "historic landmark," as implemented by regulations issued pursuant to the Act. The statute's definition of "historic landmark" includes a "building . . . and its site . . . for which an application for [historic landmark designation] is pending" with the HPRB. D.C. CODE § 6–1102(6)(B). The regulations further provide that upon the "official filing" of an application for landmark designation, "the application is considered a pending application, and if the property is a proposed historic landmark, it is protected by the Act." 10A D.C. MUN. REGULATIONS § 208.2. This includes properties for which permit applications have already been filed. *See* D.C. CODE § 6–1102(6)(B) (providing that the HPRB "will determine within 90 days of *receipt of an application pursuant to* §§ 6–1104 to 6–1108 [referring to permits for demolition, alteration, subdivision and new construction] whether to list such property as an historic landmark.") (emphasis added). As the application was filed by HPO on January 6, 2006, and officially filed as of the same date, it was deemed a "pending application" and since the application was for historic landmark designation, the property was "protected by the Act" as of that date.[10]

---

[10] Petitioner argues that the HPO's application was not "official" until February 2, 2006, when the HPRB accepted the nomination for consideration as a District of Columbia landmark. However, 10A D.C. MUN. REGULATIONS § 208.2 provides that an application is "considered a pending application, and if the property is a proposed historic landmark, it is protected by the Act" when the HPRB's "staff has completed the official filing" of the application for landmark designation. The HPRB's staff has ten days to determine whether an application is complete.

The regulations seek to mitigate any potential unfairness from such interim protection by the requirement that when construction permits are pending, the HPRB must both hold a hearing *and* come to a final decision within ninety days of the application for landmark designation. *See* 10A D.C. MUN. REGULATIONS § 209.5. ("If a historic landmark application is filed *when a permit application subject to review under the Act is pending at DCRA*, the ninety (90) day period for a determination on the designation shall be counted from the date the historic landmark application is filed.") (emphasis added). To meet this goal, the regulations provide that DCRA is to be notified "[i]mmediately" after an application is officially filed, and the owner of the property subject to an application for landmark designation is to be notified of same "[w]ithin ten days of an official filing." 10A D.C. MUN. REGULATIONS §§ 209.1 & 209.2. Upon being notified of the application for landmark designation, the property owner is to advise the HPO within five days if there are any permit applications pending before DCRA, *see* 10A D.C. MUN. REGULATIONS § 209.6, so as to trigger the HPRB's expedited consideration.

Petitioner applied for its permits on September 14, 2005, and the HPO applied for landmark designation on January 6, 2006. Since the historic landmark application was filed "when a permit application subject to review under the Act [was] pending at DCRA," 10A D.C. MUN. REGULATIONS § 209.5, the Act's provisions applied to consideration of the permits, so long as HPRB made a decision concerning landmark designation within ninety days after the application was made. The HPRB did so; it designated the property an historic landmark on February 23, 2006, and communicated its decision to petitioner on March 6, 2006, well within the ninety-day deadline in the regulation. * * *

We defer to an agency's interpretation of the statute it is charged with administering unless it is unreasonable, plainly wrong or inconsistent with the purpose of the legislation. *See D.C. Pres. League v. D.C. Dep't of Consumer & Regulatory Affairs*, 711 A.2d 1273, 1275 (D.C. 1998). In light of the amendment to the statute's definition of "historic landmark," and the purpose of the Act, we cannot say that the agency's specification of the procedures to be followed, and the timetable to be applied, in the limited class of cases where a landmark application is filed after permit applications is unreasonable. At most, a property owner with pending permit applications will have to wait ninety days for a final decision on landmark designation. The agency's regulations create a logical continuum that balances the interest of property owners and the public interest in historic preservation: where there are no permit

---

10A D.C. MUN. REGULATIONS § 208.1. "If the application is complete, and the applicant has paid the applicable filing fee, the staff shall assign a case number, date stamp, and *officially file* the application." *Id.* (emphasis added). Applications initiated by the HPRB are processed "according to the procedures required for any other application, except that the filing fee shall be waived." 10A D.C. MUN. REGULATIONS § 207.2. The letter from the HPRB, on which petitioner relies, states that the application was "officially on file" with the HPRB as of January 6, 2006, the day it was filed. The record supports that the application was complete, and thus, "official" and considered a "pending application" under the statute, as of January 6, 2006.

applications pending, the HPRB has ninety days to schedule a hearing on an application for landmark designation, but there is no prescribed deadline within which a decision must be made, see 10A D.C. MUN. REGULATIONS § 209.4; where a landmark designation is filed followed by permit applications, the HPRB must hold a hearing within ninety days of the landmark application and come to a decision within ninety days of the permit application, see D.C. CODE § 6–1102(6)(B); but where a landmark designation application is filed after permit applications, the HPRB must both hold a hearing and decide whether to make the designation within ninety days, counted from the date the designation application is official. *See* 10A D.C. MUN. REGULATIONS § 209.5.

As the application for landmark designation brought the property within the purview of the Act, and HPRB acted to designate the property an historic landmark within the ninety-day period prescribed in the regulation, we conclude that the Mayor's Agent and the HPRB had jurisdiction to review petitioner's construction permits for consistency with the purposes of the Act. * * *

For the foregoing reasons, we hold that the HPRB and the Mayor's Agent had jurisdiction to review the permits under the Historic Preservation Act, and that denial of these permits was neither arbitrary nor capricious, and was supported by substantial evidence of record. The petition to reverse the Mayor's Agent is, therefore, denied.

NOTES & QUESTIONS

1. Does the District of Columbia statute adequately protect the interests of the property owner by not cancelling permits already granted and by requiring the Historic Preservation Review Board to make its decision within ninety days? Should all requests for demolition permits be stayed to permit consideration of designation requests?

2. Did Embassy Real Estate have a strong argument that it reasonably relied on the non-landmark status of the Italian Embassy Building when it committed to its development plan? What additional factors not present in that case would make their claim stronger?

3. Figures 2-5 and 2-6 depict two of the facades described in the Historic Preservation Review Board's landmark designation. The grander 16th Street building includes the original ambassador's residence. The more modest Fuller Street building is the two-story chancery addition, which still has a "Cancelleria" sign cut into the ornamental stonework above the doorway.

4. Some jurisdictions protect undesignated properties that may be eligible for designation by delaying the issue of a demolition permit for any older property. Yonkers, New York, for example, mandates a review by the Landmarks Commission whenever a demolition permit is requested for a building more than seventy-five years old. If the board concludes that the property is eligible for designation, it can stay demolition for one hundred

and eighty days to consider a designation application. Is such an approach better than a race between designation and demolition?

5.   Mention is made in the case of interior historic features. Local governments generally designate only the exteriors of buildings or those parts visible from public space. Some can designate interiors but do so only rarely because the regulation that follows such designation of interior spaces can interfere with the owner's use or adaption of property as to threaten a violation of constitutional property rights. *See Teachers Ins. & Annuity Ass'n of America v. City of N.Y.*, 623 N.E.2d 526 (N.Y. 1993) (upholding designation of the interior of the Four Seasons Restaurant, designed by architect Phillip Johnson); *United Artists' Theater Circuit, Inc. v. City of Phila.*, 635 A.2d 612 (Pa. 1993) (holding that although designation of a building interior is not an unconstitutional taking of property, the Philadelphia Historical Commission lacked statutory authority to designate an interior).

Religious interiors present special issues. A Massachusetts court found that the designation of the interior of a church sanctuary violated the free exercise provision of the state constitution. *See Soc'y of Jesus of New England v. Boston Landmarks Comm'n*, 564 N.E.2d 571 (Mass. 1990). Should religious buildings and structures be entirely exempt from historic designation—or just interior worship facilities?

6.   Scholars have worried that the threat of preservation regulation might drive owners to demolish their buildings before designation can occur. *See, e.g.*, THOMAS W. MERRILL & HENRY E. SMITH, PROPERTY: PRINCIPLES AND POLICIES 1254 (2017). Anecdotal evidence supports the concern and sometimes raises the additional worry that government officials may connive in such destruction. *See, e.g.*, Robin Pogrebin, *Preservation and Development, Engaged in a Delicate Dance*, N.Y. TIMES, Dec. 1, 2008, at C1. The following case shows how procedures can evolve to address that risk.

7.   State law in Oregon allows for a "property owner" to seek a de-listing from a local register of historic places. Or. Rev. Stat. § 197.772(3). The Oregon Supreme Court interpreted this provision to mean that only the property owner at the time of the designation could successfully petition for removal from a register. *See Lake Oswego Pres. Soc'y v. City of Lake Oswego*, 360 Or. 115 (2016). The availability of the objection is therefore finite, and does not transfer with the land. What are the advantages and disadvantages to this decision?

CHAPTER THREE

THE NATIONAL HISTORIC PRESERVATION ACT

The National Historic Preservation Act of 1966 (NHPA) for the first time set forth a comprehensive federal historic preservation program. Chapter 2 discussed one product of the NHPA: the National Register of Historic Places. The National Register is a curated list of significant districts, sites, buildings, structures, and objects that meet certain criteria. Once a property is listed on (or deemed eligible for) the National Register, it is granted broad protection by the most significant provision of the NHPA: Section 106. Section 106 establishes a review process through which federal agencies may assess the impact of their undertakings on such properties.

This Chapter will focus primarily on the review process contained in Section 106, but other critically important provisions of the NHPA will be discussed and deserve mention at the outset. For example, the NHPA created the Advisory Council on Historic Preservation, a federal agency devoted to historic preservation policy, which advises the President and plays a key role in the Section 106 review process. Other federal agencies, which must comply with Section 106, have additional responsibilities for the management of historic properties they own or control. They are required to inventory and identify historic properties and to incorporate historic preservation planning in agency programs. Federal agencies must also designate a federal historic preservation officer who helps the agency carry out its mandates under the NHPA. For a special class of historic properties—National Historic Landmarks—the NHPA requires federal agencies to apply a heightened level of review and to take steps necessary to minimize harm.

Apart from its impact on the federal government, the NHPA created a network of state historic preservation officers (SHPOs), which provide leadership in each state and facilitate the nomination of properties to the National Register. Finally, the NHPA created a role for tribal governments, tribal historic preservation officers (which in some situations can take the place of SHPOs), and Native Hawaiian organizations, each of which may act as consulting parties during the decision-making process.

A. INTRODUCTION TO SECTION 106

Section 106 of the National Historic Preservation Act (NHPA) constitutes the heart of federal historic preservation law. Courts have repeatedly relied on Section 106's precise language to decide important questions about the scope and character of federal preservation law, so the key provision merits full quotation:

> The head of any Federal agency having direct or indirect jurisdiction over a proposed Federal or federally assisted undertaking in any State and the head of any Federal department or independent agency having authority to license any undertaking, prior to the approval of the expenditure of any Federal funds on the undertaking or prior to the issuance of any license, shall take into account the effect of the undertaking on any historic property. The head of the Federal agency shall afford the Council a reasonable opportunity to comment with regard to the undertaking.

54 U.S.C. § 306108. Several important legal points are immediately evident from the language of the statute:

- Section 106 imposes duties only on federal agencies.

- It does not directly regulate private property, or private or state actors, although the duties placed on federal agencies may have major consequences for any persons or entities that hope to work with a federal agency.

- Federal agencies have such duties only concerning "undertakings," whether their own or those of others receiving federal funds or requiring a federal license.

- Properties entitled to consideration include any that are listed or *eligible for* listing on the National Register.

- The Act does not require agencies to preserve any properties, but it only requires that they "take into account" the effects of undertakings on listed or eligible properties.

- The agencies also must allow the Advisory Council on Historic Preservation (ACHP) a reasonable opportunity to comment.

Beyond these clear and important propositions are numerous uncertainties that have been fleshed out through regulations and judicial interpretation. On the historic background to Section 106, see Jerry L. Rogers, *The National Historic Preservation Act: Fifty Years Young and Still Going Strong*, in THE NATIONAL HISTORIC PRESERVATION ACT: PAST, PRESENT, AND FUTURE (Kimball M. Banks & Ann M. Scott, eds., 2016).

Congress anticipated that such a mandatory process would prevent inadvertent destruction and promote a "productive harmony" between preservation and the achievement of other important goals of federal policy. A federal agency's duties are imposed directly on the "head" of the agency, indicating the importance Congress placed on this process and its hope that the NHPA would change the culture of each agency. At the same time, the regulations permit (with important exceptions discussed below) delegation of compliance to other responsible agency officials who may "use the services of applicants, consultants, or designees to prepare information, analyses and recommendations." 36 C.F.R. § 800.2(a)(3). The agency "remains legally responsible for all required findings and determinations." *Id.* However, as the First Circuit put it, "there is no specific requirement in the statute, the regulations or the [Administrative Procedure Act] that the [agency] provide detailed explanations for its decision or use any particular form of words signifying that it made an independent determination." *Neighborhood Ass'n of the Back Bay, Inc. v. Fed. Transit Admin.*, 463 F.3d 50, 60 (1st Cir. 2006). The statute and the implementing regulations confer important procedural rights on others, including on the state historic preservation officer, on any tribal historic preservation officer, and on members of the general public. Note that the provisions of Section 106 that relate to archaeological resources will be considered more fully in Chapter 8, and those relating to Native American groups will be considered more fully in Chapter 9.

B. THE ADVISORY COUNCIL ON HISTORIC PRESERVATION

Title II of the National Historic Preservation Act (NHPA) creates the Advisory Council on Historic Preservation (ACHP, or Council), an independent federal administrative agency. 54 U.S.C. § 304101(a). The ACHP is composed of twenty members, who represent various federal, state, and local constituencies. Two serve *ex officio*, but most are appointed by the President for four-year terms based upon criteria such as being a mayor, being a member of a tribe or of a Native Hawaiian organization, being an expert in preservation, or being a member of the general public. The ACHP meets only quarterly. Much of its work is carried out by a small professional staff, led by an Executive Director, and guided since 2018 by a full-time Chair.

Many of the powers of the ACHP are strictly advisory; it informs, recommends, comments, and encourages. Of these advisory powers, the most important is that the ACHP must have a "reasonable opportunity" to comment on an agency's compliance with Section 106 regarding any individual undertaking.

The ACHP's more important function is its express statutory authority to issue regulations "to govern the implementation of section 306108 of this title in its entirety." 54 U.S.C. § 304108. These regulations, found at 36 C.F.R. Part 800, provide detailed instructions on how agencies must fulfill their Section 106 obligations, including permitting the ACHP to comment. As interpretations of Section 106, the regulations "command substantial judicial deference." *McMillan Park Comm. v. Nat'l Capital Planning Comm'n*, 968 F.2d 1283, 1288 (D.C. Cir. 1992). Indeed, under the general approach mandated in *Chevron U.S.A., Inc. v. Nat. Res. Def. Council, Inc.*, 467 U.S. 837 (1984), courts must defer to reasonable interpretations of ambiguous provisions of Section 106 reflected in the ACHP regulations. *Neighborhood Ass'n of the Back Bay, Inc. v. Fed. Transit Admin.*, 463 F.3d 50, 59 (1st Cir. 2006).

Moreover, federal agencies can, themselves, rely on the ACHP's interpretation of the statute. In a recent case, a court rejected the wireless industry's challenge to the Federal Communications Commission's (FCC's) plan for addressing its preservation duties regarding new wireless towers. The plan incorporated the ACHP's regulatory specification of the scope of a federal agency's duties. The D.C. Circuit ruled that, "Given that we must defer * * * to the Council's reasonable interpretation of the meaning of section 106, we cannot see how it was arbitrary and capricious for the FCC to choose to do so as well." *CTIA-The Wireless Ass'n v. Fed. Commc'ns Comm'n*, 466 F.3d 105, 117 (D.C. Cir. 2006).

Federal agencies must act in accordance with the ACHP regulations. Section 110(a)(2)(E) of the NHPA provides that every federal agency must adopt procedures specifying how it will carry out its Section 106 duties, which must be "consistent with regulations promulgated by the Council." 54 U.S.C. § 306102(b)(5). The ACHP regulations interpret this provision to permit agencies to "develop procedures to implement section 106 and substitute them for all or part of subpart B of this part if they are consistent with the Council's regulations." 36 C.F.R. § 800.14(a). The ACHP reviews an agency's proposed regulations to determine if they are consistent and has approved several, including one for U.S. Army installations. *See* 69 Fed. Reg. 20,576 (Apr. 16, 2004).

The ACHP has revised its regulations several times to account for statutory amendments, executive orders, and enactment of other relevant statutes. The current regulations stem from a notice of proposed rulemaking originally published in 1994. Those proposed rules were controversial and prompted the ACHP to undertake several revisions until final rules were published in 2000. *See* 65 Fed. Reg. 77,698 (Dec. 12, 2000). Various trade associations then sought judicial review, which resulted in extensive and valuable judicial analysis of the ACHP's regulatory power. The D.C. District Court broadly affirmed the authority of the ACHP: "Under the plain meaning of the statute, therefore, the Council has the power to promulgate binding procedural regulations governing the section 106 process." *Nat'l Mining Ass'n v. Slater*, 167 F. Supp. 2d 265, 284 (D.D.C. 2001). The court, however, invalidated two elements of the ACHP's regulations which imposed substantive, rather than merely procedural, obligations on agencies. The court recognized the notorious difficulty of distinguishing legal substance from procedure in hard cases and articulated the following the standard: "[A] proposal is substantive only if it prevents the agency from acting at all or directly interferes with that agency's exercise of a right." *Id.* at 285. The court then specified what this standard meant for the NHPA:

> Under section 106, each federal agency is required to "take into account the effect" of that agency's undertaking on any property

that is included in or eligible for inclusion in the National Register. This, therefore, is both the duty and the right that Congress has explicitly delegated to each federal agency. Any regulation by the Council that directly interferes with that right, or prevents the agency from acting in furtherance of that duty, would be substantive and consequently invalid, because it violates the plain language of the statute. Other regulations are procedural and do not exceed the scope of authority granted to the Council under the NHPA.

Id. at 286.

Applying this formulation, the court upheld most of the challenged regulations as procedural. Even if regulatory "provisions contribute to the procedural complexity of the section 106 process * * * and may ultimately delay approval of an undertaking," such as by requiring the collection of additional information, consultation with interested parties, and documenting decision-making, they do not interfere with the agency's ability to finally make the determinations required by the NHPA. *Id.* The court did invalidate two rules as substantive and thus beyond the Council's authority. These had permitted the Council "to review and effectively reverse" agency determinations that there are no historic properties in an area, that an undertaking would not affect any historic properties, or that any effect would not be adverse, at least to the extent of requiring the agency to continue the 106 process. *Id* at 288. The distinction here is admittedly somewhat elusive; the invalidated rules merely permitted the ACHP to require the process to continue. The crucial point for the court seems to have been that the agency, not the ACHP, has the authority to make the crucial determination of whether the process should terminate or whether it should continue. The ACHP may specify which steps the agency should take in connection with such determinations and comment when it believes that the agency's actions have fallen short, but it cannot overrule the agency's decision.

In a subsequent appeal, the Court of Appeals set aside another element of the ACHP's definition of "undertaking" for conflicting with the "unambiguous" meaning of Section 106. *See Nat'l Mining Ass'n v. Fowler*, 324 F.3d 752 (D.C. Cir. 2003). This highlights an important check on the power of the ACHP, or on any federal agency, discussed above: While the ACHP's reasonable interpretation of its governing statute generally will receive deference from a court, it will be set aside if a court concludes that Congress, in the statute, has unambiguously given a different answer to "the precise question at issue." *Chevron, U.S.A., Inc.*, 467 U.S. at 842. We will examine the *National Mining Ass'n v. Fowler* case and the meaning of "undertaking" in detail in the next section.

The ACHP views itself as lacking authority to bring suit against agencies that fail to follow the regulations. It sees its enforcement role as limited to commenting on an agency's compliance; other parties can use these comments when litigating the agency's compliance with Section

106. This perspective is not surprising, since only federal agencies can be defendants in NHPA enforcement actions, and it is considered anomalous for federal agencies to sue each other, since this amounts to the federal government suing itself. The NHPA does not expressly authorize the ACHP to bring enforcement actions, as it does to comment and to issue "governing" regulations. Section 205(b) does provide that the General Counsel of the ACHP may:

> represent the Council in court when appropriate, including enforcement of agreements with Federal agencies to which the Council is a party; assist the Department of Justice in handling litigation concerning the Council in court; and perform such other legal duties and functions as the Executive Director and the Council may direct.

54 U.S.C. § 304105(b)(2)(B)–(D).

NOTES & QUESTIONS

1. The district court in *National Mining Ass'n v. Slater* relied on the ACHP's apparent lack of enforcement power to deflect a constitutional challenge to the agency's general authority. An industry group argued that the NHPA violated the Appointments Clause, U.S. CONST. art. II, § 2, cl. 2, which provides that the President shall appoint "officers of the United States" exercising substantial executive power. Two of the Council's twenty members serve *ex officio* and thus are not appointed by the President. The Court rejected this argument because the Council lacked "enforcement power, exemplified by [the] discretionary power to seek judicial relief." *Nat'l Mining Ass'n v. Slater*, 167 F. Supp. 2d 265, 297 (D.C. 2001) (quoting *Buckley v. Valeo*, 424 U.S. 1, 137–38 (1976)). Would it be better for the ACHP to be a more powerful agency subject to greater political control?

2. There have been many instances where the ACHP's official comments have been rejected by decision-makers. For example, the ACHP issued an official comment regarding the impact of the proposed installation of 130 offshore wind turbines in Nantucket Sound, off the coast of Massachusetts (known as the "Cape Wind" project). *See* Advisory Council on Historic Pres., Comments of the Advisory Council on Historic Preservation on the Proposed Authorization by the Minerals Management Service for Cape Wind Associates, LLC to Construct the Cape Wind Energy Project on Horseshoe Shoal in Nantucket Sound, Massachusetts (Apr. 2, 2010). The ACHP identified thirty-four historic properties on Cape Cod, Martha's Vineyard, and Nantucket Island that would be affected by the Cape Wind project. These properties included five properties with religious or cultural importance to area Native American tribes, as well as Nantucket Sound itself. At the time, the ACHP opined that "Adverse effects on historic properties will be direct and indirect, cannot be avoided, and cannot be satisfactorily mitigated." *Id.* at 1–2. In addition, the ACHP stated that the "steps to minimize and mitigate potential adverse effects * * * [were] insufficient given the number and importance of the resources at issue and the nature and scope of the Project's effects on them." *Id.* at 3.

Despite the ACHP's recommendation that the Secretary of the Interior not approve the project, the Secretary of the Interior approved it. Though the developers of Cape Wind went on to obtain most other necessary permits, the project ultimately failed, with developers bearing a $100 million loss after sixteen years. What does the initial approval of Cape Wind say about the relevance of the ACHP comments? What does it say about the Section 106 review process more generally? For another perspective on how Section 106 may be used to resolve conflicts between renewable energy and historic preservation, review the excerpt in Chapter 9 of *Quechan Tribe of Fort Yuma Reservation v. United States Department of the Interior*.

3.   In 2010, the National Trust for Historic Preservation published a report that suggested improvements to the way Section 106 is implemented. *See* LESLIE E. BARRAS, NATIONAL TRUST FOR HISTORIC PRESERVATION, SECTION 106 OF THE NATIONAL HISTORIC PRESERVATION ACT: BACK TO BASICS (2010). Among other things, it suggested that the ACHP take on several new roles, including: consulting with federal agencies on the adequacy of historic preservation staff capacity, becoming more active in commenting about National Environmental Policy Act matters, and issuing more and stronger opinion letters. What are the advantages of ACHP becoming more active in its approach to other federal agencies? Do you see any potential disadvantages?

C. UNDERTAKINGS: WHEN DOES SECTION 106 APPLY?

Section 106 of the National Historic Preservation Act (NHPA) imposes duties on a federal agency only in regard to an "undertaking." Identifying a proposed undertaking constitutes a necessary jurisdictional prerequisite for the application of preservation duties on an agency. Therefore, what Section 106 says about an undertaking requires close reading.

Unfortunately, Congress has done a poor job clarifying just what constitutes an undertaking, which poses difficult questions of interpretation. The term "undertaking" was not even part of the original proposal for the legislation that would eventually become Section 106. Originally, the proposed legislation would have applied only to a "project"—arguably a less ambiguous word than "undertaking." *See* H.R. REP. No. 1916 (1966), *reprinted in* 1966 U.S.C.C.A.N. 3307, 3310, 3319 (documenting this switch in terminology). One court suggested that "the change might simply suggest that § 106 applies to federal activities of any scope or kind." *CA 79-2516 WATCH (Waterbury Action to Conserve our Heritage Inc.) v. Harris*, 603 F.2d 310, 323 n.29 (2d Cir. 1979).

The NHPA itself did not, at least at first, shed much light on the new term. The NHPA originally defined "undertaking" only as any action described in Section 106. Congress later amended the NHPA in 1992 to define undertaking more specifically in 54 U.S.C. § 300320, the statutory provision at issue in the following case (decided during a time period in which the same provision was codified as 16 U.S.C. § 470w(7)). The first part of that provision indicates that the words "project," "activity," and "program" all are synonymous with "undertaking." Thus, an undertaking embraces any identifiable or discrete unit of action. Congress plainly intended the word "undertaking" to be read broadly, encompassing most specific agency activities. The second part of that provision limits undertakings to those carried out, funded, or licensed by the federal government. To impose a preservation duty on a federal agency, an undertaking also must be under the "direct or indirect jurisdiction" of the agency.

Not surprisingly, there has been much litigation over the scope of the undertaking requirement. Courts have held that activities that by their nature can have no effect on historic resources may not be undertakings. Thus, a federal taking of land through eminent domain has been held not to constitute an undertaking because subsequent federal decisions about how to use the land will be undertakings subject to Section 106. On the other hand, transactions that release land from federal control generally will be undertakings, because historic structures subsequently can be harmed outside the reach of the NHPA. *See* 36 C.F.R. § 800.5(a)(2)(vii). Renewal of a federal lease is also an undertaking, permitting the agency to seek lease terms avoiding adverse effects on historic properties. *See Pit River Tribe v. U.S. Forest Serv.*, 469 F.3d 768, 787 (9th Cir. 2006).

The following sections consider four types of potential undertakings: delegations of regulatory authority, neglect, federal licensing, and federal funding.

1. DELEGATIONS OF REGULATORY AUTHORITY

Is a federal agency's decision to delegate regulatory authority to a non-federal actor, which would not be bound by Section 106, an undertaking? Consider the following case.

National Mining Association v. Fowler
324 F.3d 752 (D.C. Cir. 2003)

[EDS.: All references to the National Historic Preservation Act have been recodified and often amended at title 54, Pub. L. No. 113–287, 128 Stat. 3094. We have tried to note below where specific provisions have moved.]

■ TATEL, CIRCUIT JUDGE.

The Advisory Council on Historic Preservation, an independent federal agency, is authorized by its organic statute to promulgate regulations ensuring that federally funded or federally licensed undertakings incorporate historic preservation values at the planning stage. Responding to Congress's expansion of the definition of "undertaking," the Council extended its regulation to projects licensed or permitted by state and local agencies "pursuant to a delegation or approval by a Federal agency." 36 C.F.R. § 800.16(y). Because this circuit has held that Congress's expanded definition of "undertaking" does not alter the statutory requirement that the Council regulate only *"federally funded* or *federally licensed* undertakings," *Sheridan Kalorama Historical Ass'n v. Christopher*, 49 F.3d 750, 755 (D.C. Cir. 1995) (emphases in original), we reverse the district court's decision to the contrary and remand the case for further proceedings consistent with this opinion.

I.

The National Historic Preservation Act, 16 U.S.C. § 470 *et seq.* [EDS.: moved to title 54, National Historic Preservation Act, Pub. L. No. 113–287, 128 Stat. 3094 *et seq.*], "requires each federal agency to take responsibility for the impact that its activities may have upon historic resources, and establishes the Advisory Council on Historic Preservation . . . to administer the Act." NHPA section 106 states:

> The head of any Federal agency having direct or indirect jurisdiction over a proposed *Federal or federally assisted* undertaking in any State and the head of any Federal department or independent agency having authority to *license* any undertaking shall, prior to the approval of the expenditure of any *Federal funds* on the undertaking or prior to the issuance of any *license*, as the case may be, take into account the effect of the undertaking on any district, site, building, structure, or object that is included in or eligible for inclusion in the National Register. The head of any such Federal agency shall afford the Advisory Council on Historic Preservation . . . a reasonable opportunity to comment with regard to such undertaking.

16 U.S.C. § 470f [EDS.: moved to 54 U.S.C. § 306108] (emphases added). An "essentially . . . procedural statute," *City of Alexandria v. Slater*, 198 F.3d 862, 871 (D.C. Cir. 1999), section 106 imposes no substantive standards on agencies, but it does require them to solicit the Council's comments and to "take into account the effect of [their] undertaking[s]." Section 211 adds that the Council may "promulgate such rules and regulations as it deems necessary to govern the implementation of [section 106] in its entirety." 16 U.S.C. § 470s [EDS.: moved to 54 U.S.C. § 304108].

This case involves a dispute over which projects trigger section 106's procedural requirements: (1) all statutory "undertakings" or (2) only "undertakings" that are "Federal or federally assisted" or licensed by a "Federal department or independent agency." Before 1992, this was a distinction without a difference, since section 301—the NHPA's definitional section—defined "undertaking" as "any action as described in [section 106]." 16 U.S.C. § 470w(7) (1988). In 1992, however, Congress amended section 301, replacing its cross-reference to section 106 with a specific definition:

"Undertaking" means a project, activity, or program funded in whole or in part under the direct or indirect jurisdiction of a Federal agency, including—

(A) those carried out by or on behalf of the agency;

(B) those carried out with Federal financial assistance;

(C) those requiring a Federal permit[,] license, or approval; and

(D) those subject to State or local regulation administered pursuant to a delegation or approval by a Federal agency.

16 U.S.C. § 470w(7) [EDS.: moved to 54 U.S.C. § 300320].

In 2000, following a seven-year rulemaking process, the Council promulgated a regulation (now codified at 36 C.F.R. § 800.1 *et seq.*) which "implemented the 1992 amendments to the . . . NHPA," 65 Fed. Reg. 77,698, 77,698 (Dec. 12, 2000), in order to "define how Federal agencies meet the[ir] statutory responsibilities" under section 106, 36 C.F.R. § 800.1(a). In a provision entitled "Initiation of the section 106 process," the Council's regulation specifies that agencies must first "determine whether the proposed Federal action is an undertaking as defined in § 800.16(y)." *Id.* § 800.3(a). In turn, section 800.16(y) defines "undertaking" in language virtually identical to NHPA section 301's, including its reference to undertakings "subject to State or local regulation administered pursuant to a delegation or approval by a Federal agency." The regulation goes on to establish a series of procedures—e.g., consultation with the Council, state historical preservation officers, and the public—with which agencies must comply if their actions qualify as "undertakings" with potential to affect historic properties. *See* 36 C.F.R. §§ 800.3–800.7.

Appellant National Mining Association (NMA), a non-profit trade organization, filed suit in the United States District Court for the District of Columbia, charging the Council with exceeding its statutory authority to promulgate regulations "govern[ing] the implementation" of section 106. 16 U.S.C. § 470s [EDS.: moved to 54 U.S.C. § 304108]. The NMA alleged that sections 800.3(a) and 800.16(y) of the regulation exceed the Council's statutory authority because they attach procedural requirements to undertakings "subject to State or local regulation administered pursuant to a delegation or approval by a Federal agency," even though such undertakings are neither funded nor licensed by the federal government as required by NHPA section 106. The NMA is concerned that the Council's regulation applies to state and local agencies that issue permits under so-called cooperative federalism statutes such as the Surface Mining Control and Reclamation Act (SMCRA), 30 U.S.C. § 1201 *et seq.*, the Clean Water Act, 33 U.S.C. § 1251 *et seq.*, and the Resource Conservation and Recovery Act, 42 U.S.C. § 6901 *et seq.* For example, although the NMA concedes that "[t]he federal government's approval of a State's *overall* SMCRA permitting program may arguably be an action subject to Section 106, because the federal government contributes funds to the general administration of state permitting programs and approves those programs," it contends that individual state mining permits do not fall within that section since "the federal government does not retain the authority to approve or reject any one mining project application."

On cross-motions for summary judgment, the district court rejected the NMA's argument that the Council lacks statutory authority to regulate state and local permitting agencies, holding that "section 106 applie[s] to the full range of undertakings defined in [section 301]." *Nat'l Mining Ass'n v. Slater*, 167 F. Supp. 2d 265, 290 (D.D.C. 2001). The NMA appeals. We review the district court's grant of summary judgment for the Council de novo. * * *

III.

Turning to the merits of the NMA's contention that the Council exceeded its statutory authority, we start, as always, by asking whether Congress has spoken to "the precise question at issue." *Chevron U.S.A., Inc. v. Nat. Res. Def. Council, Inc.*, 467 U.S. 837, 842 (1984). If it has, both we and the agency must give effect to Congress's unambiguously expressed intent. *Id.* at 842–43. Only if we find the statute either silent or ambiguous with respect to "the precise question at issue" do we proceed to *Chevron*'s second step, asking "whether the agency's answer is based on a permissible construction of the statute." *Id.* at 842–44.

In this case, our analysis begins and ends at *Chevron* step one. NHPA section 211 unambiguously limits the Council to promulgating regulations that "govern the implementation of [section 106]." 16 U.S.C. § 470s [EDS.: moved to 54 U.S.C. § 304108]. Not arguing otherwise, the Council contends that 36 C.F.R. § 800.3 lawfully implements section 106 because "the section 106 process applies to the full range of undertakings defined in section 301." That argument, however, is barred by *Sheridan Kalorama Historical Ass'n v. Christopher*, 49 F.3d 750 (D.C. Cir. 1995), which squarely holds that Congress's 1992 broadening of section 301 did not override section 106's requirement that the project be federally funded or licensed.

Sheridan Kalorama involved the Secretary of State's decision not to exercise his veto power under the Foreign Missions Act, 22 U.S.C. § 4301 *et seq.*, to halt the Republic of Turkey's plans to demolish its chancery. The Sheridan Kalorama Historical Association and others filed suit, alleging that NHPA section 106 required the Secretary to solicit Council comments on his decision *not* to veto Turkey's demolition. Because *Sheridan Kalorama*'s holding on this issue is dispositive here, we quote it in full:

> The plaintiffs—and indeed the [Council] and some other courts—proceed as if the review provision of § 106 automatically applies once a project is deemed an "undertaking." Such

confusion is understandable; for the 1992 amendment oddly appends the concepts of "licensing" and "approval" to the definition of "undertaking," even though the text of § 106 still applies by its terms only to *federally funded* or *federally licensed* undertakings. Thus however broadly the Congress or the [Council] define "undertaking," § 106 applies only to: 1) "any Federal agency having . . . jurisdiction over a proposed Federal or federally assisted undertaking"; and 2) "any Federal . . . agency having authority to license any undertaking." Such an agency is required, as the case may be, either to take certain actions "prior to the approval of the expenditure of any Federal funds on the undertaking," or "prior to the issuance of any license." Therefore, unless Turkey's efforts to replace its chancery are either federally funded or federally licensed, § 106 simply does not apply to its project.

Id. at 755–56 (internal citations omitted) (emphases in original). Concluding that the Secretary's inaction constituted neither federal funding nor federal licensing, the court ruled that section 106 did not apply. *Id.* at 756.

Nowhere does the Council's brief so much as mention this relevant discussion from *Sheridan Kalorama*. Instead, the Council points to a different section of the opinion discussing what the court viewed as a puzzling implication of section 301(7)'s introduction. According to the court, the phrase "funded in whole or in part under the direct or indirect jurisdiction of a federal agency, including . . ." seems to "confine the notion of an 'undertaking' " to federally funded projects "and thus by omission to exclude a federally licensed project from the coverage of the statute." *Id.* at 755. "That reading of the definition, however," the court explained, "would deprive the references to licensing in § 106 of any practical effect. We infer, therefore, that the amending Congress [in 1992] intended to expand the definition of an 'undertaking'—formerly limited to federally funded or licensed projects—to include projects requiring a federal 'permit' or merely federal 'approval.' " *Id.*

Contrary to the Council's contention, the last sentence of this passage does not hold that section 106 applies to the full range of section 301 "undertakings." Rather, it explains that Congress would not have amended section 301's definition of "undertaking" to exclude federally licensed projects, since doing so would rob section 106's application to "federally funded *or* licensed" undertakings of its full disjunctive scope. *Sheridan Kalorama* therefore concludes that amended section 301 must be interpreted as being at least as broad as section 106. In other words, the passage the Council relies on is entirely consistent with the one it ignores: The former explains that section 301, the definitional section, must be at least as broad as section 106, the jurisdictional section to which it applies; the latter explains that section 301 is in fact broader, since no matter how expansively Congress chooses to define the word "undertaking," section 106 confers on the Council jurisdiction over *"federally funded* or *federally licensed* undertakings" only. * * *

Because *Sheridan Kalorama* holds that "section 106 . . . applies by its terms only to *federally funded* or *federally licensed* undertakings," 49 F.3d at 755 (emphases in original), and not to undertakings that are merely "subject to State or local regulation administered pursuant to a delegation or approval by a Federal agency," 36 C.F.R. § 800.16(y), we reverse the judgment of the district court and remand the case for further proceedings consistent with this opinion.

NOTES & QUESTIONS

1. *National Mining Ass'n* is an entirely textual decision. Congress seems to have intended to impose the Section 106 process on undertakings conducted by state agencies exercising delegated federal authority, as the ACHP believed. The NHPA clearly does not impose preservation duties on state and local governments when they act under their own authority, such as when they change the zoning of land. But federal statutes sometimes permit or require delegation of federal regulatory authority to state and local government agencies. Under such "cooperative federalism," state or local agencies issue permits under the authority of federal law. For example, and not incidentally, Congress has provided that federal regulatory authority to issue mining permits under the Surface Mining Act may be delegated to states that meet federal standards, and it is entirely plausible that Congress would want the state agencies to consider the effects of granting mining permits on historic resources, just as the federal agency would if it were issuing permits under the same statute. The ACHP subsequently amended its regulatory definition of undertaking to eliminate any reference to state or local governments exercising delegated federal regulation. *See* 36 C.F.R. § 800.16(y).

2. The challenging industry group conceded that the Section 106 duties applied to the agency's initial decision to delegate permitting activity to a state, i.e., that the delegation itself is an undertaking. This makes sense. Federal decisions to release land from federal control generally will be undertakings because historic structures subsequently may be harmed outside the reach of NHPA. *See* 36 C.F.R. § 800.5(a)(2)(vii). Without such a process, delegation would merely deregulate adverse effects on historic properties. Although preservation issues might seem somewhat inchoate at the time of delegation, a programmatic agreement (discussed below) could provide a process by which more specific issues could be addressed as they come up.

This conclusion may be called into question by the Supreme Court's decision in *Nat'l Ass'n of Home Builders v. Defs. of Wildlife,* 551 U.S. 644 (2007). There, the Court held that section 7(a)(2) of the Endangered Species Act (ESA) does not apply to the delegation of permit authority to states under section 402(b) of the Clean Water Act (CWA). The ESA requires any federal agency to "insure that any action authorized, funded, or carried out by such agency * * * is not likely to jeopardize the continued existence of any endangered species or threatened species." 16 U.S.C. § 1536(a)(2). The Court held the ESA duty applies only to "discretionary" federal agency decisions, and that transferring permit authority to a state that meets the requirements of the CWA is mandatory. Such reasoning, however faulty, may also lead to some restriction on the applicability of the NHPA to some category of federal undertakings deemed "non-discretionary." *Cf. Ely v. Velde*, 451 F.2d 1130 (4th Cir. 1971) (holding that the NHPA applies to the federal decision that the Virginia prison plan conforms to the "block grant" provisions of the Safe Streets Act).

3. An additional, worrisome complexity is created by another infelicity in the language of section 301(7). It can be read to limit "undertaking" to projects receiving federal funds, thereby excluding projects that are subject to federal licensing but not receiving federal funds. How can that be? Section 301 defines undertaking to mean "a project, activity or program funded in whole or in part under the direct or indirect jurisdiction of a Federal agency, including * * * those requiring a Federal permit, license or approval." 36 C.F.R. § 800.16(y). Literally, section 301 limits undertakings to federally funded activities, and since Section 106 applies only to undertakings, its references to undertakings involving licensing would be rendered ineffective to create legal duties unless the licensed activity were federally funded as well.

Such a reading, however literally plausible, would plainly frustrate the purposes of the Act, as evinced in the long-standing, crucial language of Section 106. This was the conclusion reached by the *Sheridan Kalorama* court in the decision discussed in *Nat'l Mining Ass'n*, which held that an undertaking included activities subject to federal licensing. The literal reading could not be correct because it would "deprive the references to licensing in § 106 to any practical effect." *Sheridan Kalorama Historical Ass'n v. Christopher*, 49 F.3d 750, 755 (D.C. Cir. 1995). This seems right, especially as ambiguity in the statutory language requires a court to defer to the interpretation contained in the ACHP regulations.

But another court has taken a different view, dismissing a lawsuit after concluding, from a reading of section 301, that "the NHPA clearly contemplates a federal funding requirement." *W. Mohegan Tribe & Nation of N.Y. v. N.Y.*, 100 F. Supp. 2d 122, 127 (N.D.N.Y. 2000). The Second Circuit Court of Appeals affirmed on a different ground "without reaching the question of whether the district court properly construed the NHPA as applicable only to projects that are federally funded." *W. Mohegan Tribe & Nation of N.Y. v. New York*, 246 F.3d 230, 232 (2d Cir. 2001). *See also Fein v. Peltier*, 949 F. Supp. 374 (D.V.I. 1996) (an undertaking includes a project or activity which requires prior approval of a federal agency regardless of whether it is funded by the federal government).

4. In 2002, the Advisory Council on Historic Preservation permitted the Department of Defense to proceed with the maintenance, repair, renovation, demolition, and replacement of old military housing units, without having to conduct individual Section 106 analyses. This decision applied to 175,000 units and saved about $80 million in costs related to compliance. *See* Advisory Council on Historic Preservation, Capehart

Wherry Housing Challenge Spurred Innovative Solution (2006). What are the justifications for such a decision?

2. NEGLECT

Courts have found undertakings requiring initiation of the Section 106 process in a wide range of direct federal "projects, programs and activities." When the federal government itself proposes to demolish a building, build a dam, or fence rangeland, it seems obvious today that it engages in an undertaking subject to Section 106. Some activity may be more subtle, as the following case illustrates.

National Trust for Historic Preservation v. Blanck
938 F. Supp. 908 (D.D.C. 1996)

[EDS.: All references to the National Historic Preservation Act have been recodified and often amended at title 54, Pub. L. No. 113–287, 128 Stat. 3094. We have tried to note below where specific provisions have moved.]

■ FRIEDMAN, J.

This case concerns the extent of the federal government's obligation to spend scarce funds to preserve historic buildings under the National Historic Preservation Act ("NHPA"), 16 U.S.C. § 470 *et seq*. [EDS.: moved to title 54, National Historic Preservation Act, Pub. L. No. 113–287, 128 Stat. 3094 *et seq*.]. Plaintiffs, the National Trust for Historic Preservation and Save Our Seminary at Forest Glen, seek declaratory and injunctive relief to compel the Army to expend substantial sums of money in long-term preservation activities that, plaintiffs argue, are not only necessary to preserve the National Park Seminary Historic District, a community of historic buildings located at the Walter Reed Army Medical Center, but are statutorily mandated. The government asserts that it has in fact expended significant resources in order to preserve the Historic District consistent with the Department of the Army's spending priorities and mission, that it has complied with the requirements of the NHPA, and that the Act does not contemplate the kind of relief plaintiffs seek. * * *

I. Factual Background

Walter Reed Army Medical Center ("Walter Reed" or "WRAMC") is a medical care, research and teaching facility; Forest Glen, one of three geographically separate sections of Walter Reed, is an auxiliary service, support and research area in Silver Spring, Maryland. The National Park Seminary Historic District consists of 29 buildings spread over 23 acres of the Forest Glen section. The Maryland Historical Trust determined that twenty-four of those buildings contribute individually to the historic character of the Historic District while five other buildings do not. Walter Reed currently uses some of the 24 historic buildings for administrative purposes. The majority of the buildings, however, are not used at all.

A.   The Buildings of the Historic District

The National Park Seminary Historic District has been listed in the National Register of Historic Places since 1972. Built in the 1880s, Ye Forest Inne is the oldest building in the District. It was originally constructed as a resort and now serves as the Main Building (Building 101) of the National Park Seminary. The Odeon Theater (Building 104) was constructed in 1901, the Gymnasium (Building 118) in 1907, Aloha House (Building 116) in 1898, and the Villa (Building 199) in 1907. The Pergola Bridge spanned the glen and connected the Villa to the Practice House (Building 112). In the late 1890s and early 1900s, eight eclectic sorority houses were built, each in a different architectural style, which also are among the 29 buildings in the Historic District. In addition, the District contains formal gardens, foot bridges, retaining walls, walkways, trails, garden ornaments and statuary.

The parties agree that there has been significant damage to and deterioration of the buildings in the Historic District over the years, although they disagree about the extent of the damage and deterioration. At least the following facts are not in dispute. By 1989, Building 101, the largest building in the complex, showed some rotten wood joints, mortar loss and deterioration. The foundation walls of Senior House were badly deteriorated. The Pergola Bridge was "in a deteriorating condition and might well be considered unsafe. Maintenance [on the Bridge] has been stopped." Building 109 needed a new roof; Building 112 had water infiltration in all basement areas and serious wall damage; and Building 107 had a deteriorating structural condition. The Army subsequently reported in 1992 that the south wall of the dining room of Building 101 had partially collapsed and one of the columns in the west portico of the library wing had rotted and dropped eight to ten inches.

In 1990, KFS Historic Preservation Group, a paid consultant, prepared a "Section 106 Report" for the Army Corps of Engineers. The report found that the structures of the Historic District had "suffered serious and in some instances irreversible damage from long-term deferred maintenance. Several buildings have been condemned . . . [and] abandoned and are rapidly falling into ruinous condition." The report described a wide variety of damage and concluded that "[w]hile the appropriate mitigation measure would be to develop a Historic Preservation Plan, as specified by Army Regulation 420–40, at this time funds are not available for WRAMC to undertake such an action." The Army does not dispute that its failure to expend more resources to maintain the District caused at least some of the significant damage.

Figures 3-1 & 3-2:
The Main Building and the Porch of the Maidens at the
Aloha House at the National Park Seminary Site,
Silver Spring, MD

B.   Walter Reed's Efforts in the Historic District

Since acquiring the Historic District in 1942, the Army has made
some efforts to account for and preserve the historic value of the
buildings, primarily through the development of Master Plans and, in
1992, a Cultural Resource Management Plan. [EDS.: In addition, master

plans for the historic district were adopted in 1972, 1977, and 1992; a survey of historic buildings was completed in 1989; and a Cultural Resource Management Plan was completed in 1992. At various times, including 1979 and 1984, Walter Reed considered whether to excess the Historic District, each time opting to retain it. In 1991, Walter Reed consulted with various entities, including the National Capital Planning Commission and the Maryland State Historic Preservation Officer, about a decision to excess the district, but by the time this case was brought to trial, it reversed this decision, opting to retain the Historic District.] * * *

II.   Standard of Review * * *

In this case, the Army's actions are fully reviewable under the APA. The Court concludes that Congress did not create or intend to create an independent private right of action against the federal government under Section 305 of the NHPA. Accordingly, the Court will review the Army's actions under the arbitrary and capricious standard of the Administrative Procedure Act, 5 U.S.C. § 706, and based on the administrative record created by the agency.

III. The National Historic Preservation Act

[EDS.: The plaintiffs alleged that Walter Reed disregarded the consultation process of Section 106 of the NHPA and violated the substantive mandate on federal agencies under Section 110.] * * *

A.   The Section 106 Consultation Process

Section 106 of the NHPA requires that agencies give the Advisory Council on Historic Preservation a reasonable opportunity to comment on any "undertaking" that will "adversely affect" a listed property. The NHPA defines "undertaking," in relevant part, as "a project, activity, or program funded in whole or in part under the direct or indirect jurisdiction of a Federal agency" if carried out by a federal agency, with federal financial assistance or requiring a federal permit, license or approval. 16 U.S.C. § 470w(7) [EDS.: moved to 54 U.S.C. § 300320]. 36 C.F.R. § 800.2(o) defines an "undertaking" as

> any project, activity or program that can result in changes in the character or use of historic properties. . . . The project, activity or program must be under the direct or indirect jurisdiction of a Federal agency. Undertakings include new and continuing projects, activities, or programs and any of their elements not previously considered under section 106.

36 C.F.R. § 800.9(b)(4) defines an "adverse effect" of an undertaking as including but not limited to "[n]eglect of a property resulting in its deterioration or destruction."

Different circuits describe the Section 106 process as imposing more or less stringent or limited obligations upon agencies. *Compare United States v. 162.20 Acres of Land, More or Less, Etc.*, 639 F.2d 299, 302 (5th Cir. 1981) ("While the [NHPA] may seem to be no more than a 'command to consider,' it must be noted that the language is mandatory and the scope is broad.") *with Waterford Citizens' Ass'n v. Reilly*, 970 F.2d 1287, 1290–91 (4th Cir. 1992) ("[T]he scope of the obligations imposed upon federal agencies by the enactment of section 106 is quite narrow."). Nevertheless, Section 106 is universally interpreted as requiring agencies to consult and consider and not to engage in any particular preservation activities per se. The issue here is when the Army became obligated to consult with the Advisory Council on Historic Preservation and whether it did so at that time.

The Historic District was listed in the National Register in 1972. The Army decided not to excess the Historic District as early as 1979 and cemented that initial decision in 1984 despite having acquired additional information. Yet, no "Section 106 Report" was prepared until 1990, and that was done in connection with the preparation of a revised Master Plan in 1991.[12] Furthermore, there were no consultations with the relevant boards, commissions and historic trusts until 1991, and the revised Master Plan was not finally modified and approved until 1992. The question is whether any of these actions—or lack of action—violated the NHPA. The Army argues that until it affirmatively decided to excess the District in 1991 there was no "undertaking" on which to comment. Plaintiffs assert that the Army's failure to maintain the Historic District since at least 1984, when the Army made its decision not to excess the District, constitutes "demolition by neglect" that warrants relief.

It is clear that "an agency need not satisfy the § 106 process at all . . . unless it is engaged in an undertaking." *McMillan Park Comm. v. Nat'l Capital Planning Comm'n*, 968 F.2d 1283, 1289 (D.C. Cir. 1992). Although the regulations consider neglect of a property that results in deterioration or destruction to be a cognizable "adverse effect" of an undertaking, not every instance of neglect or destruction can be said to flow from a cognizable undertaking. As a general matter, the APA defines "agency action" to include "failure to act," 5 U.S.C. § 551(13), and, where an agency maintains a policy of inaction in the face of an explicit statutory mandate, generally a court may set that policy aside. The explicit terms of Section 106, however, require a finding not just of agency "action" but of an "undertaking"—that is, "a project, activity, or program." 16 U.S.C. § 470w(7) [EDS.: moved to 54 U.S.C. § 300320].

An agency's failure to act, without more, is not an "undertaking" under Section 106; indeed, if it were there would be a constant and ongoing requirement for ACHP comment and consultation. *See Sheridan Kalorama Historical Ass'n v. Christopher*, 49 F.3d 750, 754 (D.C. Cir. 1995) (State Department's failure to disapprove Turkish Embassy's plan to demolish building was not an undertaking where no federal funds or approval were involved). On the other hand, an undertaking includes any "activity . . . that can result in changes in the character or use of historic

---

[12] Master Plans are general planning documents and do not trigger the Section 106 consultation process. * * *

properties" and may include not only new but also "continuing" projects. 36 C.F.R. § 800.2(*o*). Thus, the NHPA contemplates a certain level of agency vigilance even in the absence of a specific new project. For example, Section 106 procedures must be "applied to ongoing Federal actions as long as a Federal agency has opportunity to exercise authority at any stage of an undertaking where alterations might be made to modify its impact on historic preservation goals." *Vieux Carre Prop. Owners, Residents & Assocs., Inc. v. Brown*, 948 F.2d 1436, 1444–45 (5th Cir. 1991). Even the Army recognizes that such ongoing and routine activities as maintenance and repair may rise to the level of undertakings. Accordingly, the analysis turns on the nature of the projects, activities and decisions that properly trigger Section 106 review.
* * *

In 1984, the Army decided not to excess the Historic District because the costs were too high and the process would take too long. This was not a mere failure to prevent another entity from taking action, *cf. Sheridan Kalorama Historical Ass'n*, 49 F.3d at 754, but a considered, affirmative decision by Walter Reed about how to allocate its limited resources. That decision had the sort of serious and long-term consequences for the Historic District that the NHPA requires be undertaken in consultation with the ACHP. Indeed, the record is replete with evidence attesting to the consideration given over the years to the decision whether to excess the District, and defendants acknowledge that an affirmative decision was made in 1984 not to do so. Yet there were no Section 106 consultations with the Advisory Council on Historic Preservation, the National Capital Planning Commission or the various Maryland state agencies about the overall disposition of the Historic District until 1991. The Court concludes that the 1984 decision not to excess the District was an undertaking under Section 106. It therefore should have been made in consultation with the Advisory Council on Historic Preservation.

B.   Section 110, The Secretary's Section 110 Guidelines and the Army's Regulations

Plaintiffs contend that Walter Reed not only disregarded the Section 106 consultation process but also violated the substantive mandate contained in Section 110 to repair and maintain the buildings in the District. Agency obligations under Section 110, however, are far less defined than those under Section 106, and the parties vigorously disagree as to their scope and effect.

1.   Section 110

The contested language of Section 110 reads as follows: "Each agency shall undertake, consistent with the preservation of such [historic] properties and the mission of the agency and the professional standards established pursuant to section 470a(g) of this title [EDS.: moved to 54 U.S.C. § 306101(b)], any preservation, as may be necessary to carry out this section." 16 U.S.C. § 470h–2(a)(1) [EDS.: moved to 54 U.S.C. § 306101(a)]. In addition, each agency "shall ensure" that properties listed in or eligible for the National Register of Historic Places "are managed and maintained in a way that considers the preservation of their historic [and] architectural . . . values in compliance with Section 470f [Section 106] of this title." 16 U.S.C. § 470h–2(a)(2)(B) [EDS.: moved to 54 U.S.C. § 306102(b)(2)]. In this case, the District was listed in the National Register in 1972 and the Army's most significant decision was taken in 1984 when the Army decided not to excess the District but rather to retain control over it. That 1984 decision, and the ongoing policy thereafter to treat the historic preservation of the District's buildings as a low priority, gave rise to much of the deterioration now complained of by plaintiffs.

The meaning of Section 110 is not clear on its face. On the one hand, the use of the word "shall" in Sections 110(a)(1) and (2) suggests that agencies have a mandatory obligation to engage in preservation, separate and apart from their obligations under Section 106. On the other hand, the section refers several times to the Section 106 consultation process and uses the word "consider" three times in describing an agency's responsibilities. 16 U.S.C. § 470h–2(a)(2)(B) & (C), (d) [EDS.: moved to 54 U.S.C. §§ 306102(b)(2) & (3), 306105]. It also provides that the agency must act consistent with its "missions and mandates." 16 U.S.C. § 470h–2(d) [EDS.: moved to 54 U.S.C. § 306105]. Reading the section as a whole, this suggests that Section 110 represents an elucidation and extension of the Section 106 process but not its replacement by new and independent substantive obligations of a different kind. * * *

The Court concludes that Section 110(a) cannot be read to create new substantive preservationist obligations separate and apart from the overwhelmingly procedural thrust of the NHPA as described by every court that has considered the Act. In interpreting other subsections of Section 110, the D.C. Circuit has reasoned that "the legislative history of § 110, though scant, supports [ ] reading [ ] that section in conjunction with § 106." *Lee v. Thornburgh*, 877 F.2d 1053, 1057 (D.C. Cir. 1989). The court pointed out that when Section 110 was added to the NHPA in 1980, Congress made clear that the new section "is not intended to change the preservation responsibilities of Federal agencies as required by any other laws, executive orders or regulations." *Id.* (quoting H.R. REP. NO. 1457, 97th Cong., 2d Sess. 36 (1980), *reprinted in* 1980 U.S.C.C.A.N. 6378, 6399). Plaintiffs' interpretation would create vast new preservationist responsibilities unrelated to the consultation provisions of Section 106 to which the rest of Section 110 constantly refers. Indeed, under plaintiffs' theory, Section 110 would replace Section 106 as the heart and soul of the NHPA, requiring an agency to spend money on historic preservation regardless of whether it was engaged in or contemplating an undertaking. Nothing in the statute or the legislative history suggests that Congress intended to alter the nature of the NHPA in such a fashion when it amended it in 1980, and the Court finds that Congress had no such intention.

2.   The Secretary's Guidelines and the Army's Regulations

The guidelines promulgated by the Secretary of the Interior support this interpretation. *See* Guidelines for Federal Agency Responsibilities Under Section 110 of the National Historic Preservation Act ("Section 110 Guidelines"), 53 Fed. Reg. 4728 (Feb. 17, 1988). * * *

The Section 110 Guidelines require the development by agencies of historic preservation plans and list a variety of factors that agencies "should consider" in establishing such plans and in managing historic properties. Nowhere, however, do they state that agencies have an affirmative obligation to spend money to preserve historic buildings. Rather, the entire thrust of the Guidelines is to channel agency decisionmaking in an informed preservationist direction consistent with the agency's mission. Since the NHPA expressly delegates the responsibility for promulgating such guidelines to the Secretary of the Department of the Interior, the Secretary's interpretation of Section 110 is entitled to substantial deference from the Court.

Walter Reed's obligations under Section 110 are further defined by the Army's own regulations. Army Regulation 420–40, promulgated in 1984 in compliance with the NHPA and various of the Secretary of the Interior's regulations and guidelines for historic preservation, provides in detail for the preparation of a Historic Preservation Plan ("HPP") as the main mechanism by which the Army is to comply with the requirements and implementing regulations of Sections 106 and 110 of the NHPA. * * *

The Court finds that the CRMP was the Historic Preservation Plan for the Historic District and that it satisfies the requirements of Army Regulation 420–40. The CRMP contains an extensive discussion of the history, condition and present needs of the Historic District. It proposes a detailed protection plan outlining the procedures for maintaining the historic properties, including the procedures to be followed under Section 106. Indeed, plaintiffs concede that the CRMP "provide[s] very specific and detailed guidance for the treatment and protection of the Historic District." Accordingly, the Court finds that the Army has been in compliance with the Section 110 Guidelines and its own regulations since 1992 when the CRMP was created and officially adopted. * * *

The Court concludes that since Walter Reed has formally complied with Army Regulation 420–40 by creating and adopting the CRMP, has spent substantial sums of money on repair, maintenance and preservation activities (although obviously not enough to avoid significant deterioration) and continues to make efforts to obtain additional funding to carry out its obligations under the CRMP, Walter Reed has complied with the Secretary's Guidelines and its own regulations. Its manner of doing so cannot be said to be arbitrary and capricious. It therefore has not violated Section 110 of the NHPA, at least since 1992.

From 1984 until 1992, however, Walter Reed was in compliance neither with Section 110 nor with its own regulations. Defendants have identified no documents in the administrative record that demonstrate that Walter Reed engaged in a deliberate, considered decisionmaking process to assess, consider and plan for the preservation needs of the Historic District during that period. Until the CRMP was adopted in 1992, the only planning document to make any reference to the historic needs of the District at all was the Master Plan of 1977, and between 1977 and 1992 no Master Plans were developed. It was not until 1991, when Major General Cameron proposed to excess the District and triggered a series of assessments by Walter Reed, that Walter Reed began seriously to assess its obligations under the NHPA. Accordingly, on this record, the Court finds that Walter Reed violated Section 110 and its own Army Regulation 420–40 beginning in 1984. These violations lasted until 1992 when the considered decisionmaking process finally produced the CRMP.

IV. Conclusion

From 1984, when Army Regulation 420–40 formalized the Army's obligations under Section 110 of the NHPA, until 1992, the Army violated Section 110 and its own regulations by neglecting the buildings in the Historic District without considering how to undertake, consistent with its mission, their preservation or alternative use. The Army also violated Section 106 of the NHPA in 1984 by failing to initiate consultation procedures with the Advisory Council on Historic Preservation when it decided not to excess the District, even though it was clear that the decision would cause further deterioration of the historic buildings.

Plaintiffs acknowledge that the Army undertook the proper Section 106 consultation procedures with respect to Major General Cameron's 1991 proposal to excess the District. The Army now represents to the Court that it is presently or is about to be engaged in further Section 106 consultation procedures because it has decided not to excess the District after all. The Court concludes that no purpose would be served by ordering the Army to engage in Section 106 consultation with respect to decisions made years ago. Similarly, Walter Reed's 1992 Cultural Resource Management Plan, while belated, rectifies the procedural and informational harm done by the Army's failure to prepare a Historic Preservation Plan between 1984 and 1992. Accordingly, the Court will not order the Army to undertake the consultations and assessments contemplated by Sections 106 and 110 of the NHPA and Army Regulation 420–40 since the Army has represented to the Court that it is in the process of doing so.

This leaves the very serious issue of the deterioration and damage that has resulted from the Army's neglect and failure to expend adequate resources on the preservation of the Historic District. Plaintiffs do not ask the Court, as in the typical NHPA case, to require the Army to halt a proposed undertaking such as the demolition or construction of a building, but rather to repair existing buildings to bring them back to a former level of integrity that pre-dates the Army's neglect. Plaintiffs argue that the Army's noncompliance with the NHPA and its own regulations caused significant harm to the buildings in the Historic District and that the Army is now obligated to make the District whole.

Plaintiffs are clearly correct that the Army's noncompliance has caused real harm. On the other hand, Walter Reed currently spends significant funds on repairing and maintaining the District and it is now in compliance with Sections 106 and 110 and its own regulations. The Court having concluded that Section 110 was not intended to create new substantive preservationist obligations, it follows that the NHPA does not give the Court the authority to order the Army to turn back the hands of time, or even to spend more money to halt further deterioration while the Army completes its plans for the Historic District.

This conclusion flows from the limited nature of Section 110 itself. The NHPA requires the Army to undertake the level of preservation necessary to carry out Section 110, consistent with its mission. 16 U.S.C. § 470h–2(a)(1) [EDS.: moved to 54 U.S.C. § 306101(a)]. Section 110 is to be read in conjunction with Section 106 which constitutes the main thrust of the NHPA. The case law in this and other circuits holds that an agency's duty to act under the NHPA is triggered only when there is an undertaking and that that obligation, once triggered, is procedural in nature. Section 110 itself does not require anything more, since the addition of Section 110 to the statute was not intended to expand the preservationist responsibilities of federal agencies beyond what the NHPA already required. Moreover, the Section 110 Guidelines demonstrate that the Secretary of the Interior has interpreted Section 110 to embody the requirement that agencies thoroughly consider preservationist goals in all aspects of agency decisionmaking but that Section 110 does not itself affirmatively mandate the preservation of historic buildings or other resources. The Court therefore concludes that Section 110, read in conjunction with Section 106, the statute as a whole and the case law, did not require Walter Reed to undertake any preservation beyond what was necessary to comply to the fullest extent possible with, and in the spirit of, the Section 106 consultation process and with its own Historic Preservation Plan.

While the Army could and, in a perfect world, should have done more to preserve the Historic District, the APA does not permit this Court to substitute its judgment for that of the agency with respect to resource allocations, so long as those allocations are not arbitrary or capricious, an abuse of discretion or contrary to law. *See Citizens to Pres. Overton Park, Inc. v. Volpe*, 401 U.S. 402, 415 (1971). While the Court may disagree with the Army's decisions—individual and cumulative—to permit the buildings of the Historic District to deteriorate, the Court finds that the Army's expenditure of nearly two million dollars in repairs and maintenance since 1992 was not insignificant, consistent with

Walter Reed's mission and mandate. The Court concludes that the Army's level of expenditure, although low in relation to the expensive preservation needs of the Historic District, did not constitute an abuse of discretion or an arbitrary and capricious response to the dictates of Section 110, the Secretary of the Interior's Guidelines and Army Regulation 420–40. The Army's course of conduct since 1992 therefore was permissible under the NHPA and the Court finds no basis in law on which to require the Army to invest any more funds in the District.

It may seem ironic for the Court to find that Walter Reed violated the NHPA and its own regulations for over eight years and nevertheless to conclude that the Army cannot now be ordered to fix what it undoubtedly broke. Congress has decided as a legislative matter, however, to institutionalize the national commitment to historic preservation by creating certain planning, consultation and decisionmaking procedures to assure adequate consideration of preservationist concerns and *not*, as plaintiffs would have it, by requiring federal agencies to spend the taxpayers' money on historic preservation when it is not earmarked for such purposes.

Lest this conclusion be misunderstood as somehow diminishing the Army's obligations under the NHPA or excusing its derelictions over the years, it should be emphasized that merely because a statutory requirement is described as "procedural" does not render it any less meaningful or mandatory. As the Fifth Circuit has observed, "[w]hile the [NHPA] may seem to be no more than a 'command to consider,' it must be noted that the language is mandatory and the scope is broad." *162.20 Acres of Land, More or Less, Etc.*, 639 F.2d at 302. Merely because "it is impossible for us to know with any degree of certainty just what the end result of the NHPA process would be[, it would be] inappropriate to pre-judge those results . . .," or to relieve an agency from its obligation to engage in the process. *Vieux Carré Prop. Owners, Residents & Assocs., Inc.*, 948 F.2d at 1446–47. Historic preservation by its very nature demands action to stem the otherwise inevitable wear and tear of time itself, and in obeying the NHPA's "command to consider," agencies necessarily will consider taking actions that they might not otherwise even have contemplated. While courts may not be authorized under the NHPA to order a recalcitrant agency to rebuild decaying historic treasures, it is their duty to declare what the agency's statutory obligations are and what the agency's procedural course should be. * * *

Accordingly, defendants' motion for summary judgment is granted and plaintiffs' motion for summary judgment is denied. The merits having been decided in this fashion, plaintiffs' motion for preliminary injunctive relief necessarily also is denied.

NOTES & QUESTIONS

1.   What exactly was the Army's action regarding National Seminary that constituted an undertaking? How was that different from simple

inactivity, however negligent it may have been? What should the Army have done to fulfill their Section 106 duties before commencing the undertaking? The ACHP now has adopted a regulation that specifies that "[n]eglect of a property which causes its deterioration" can be an "adverse effect." 36 C.F.R. § 800.5(a)(2)(vi). Does that mean that neglect alone will now constitute an undertaking?

2.   In what ways is Section 110 duplicative of Section 106? In what ways does Section 110 impose additional duties on federal agencies? Does Section 110 impose duties on agencies without any finding that the agency engaged in an undertaking?

3.   Other courts have, like this one, said that Section 110 obligations are not "substantive." The Ninth Circuit compared Section 110 to another law you will encounter in Chapter 5, Section 4(f) of the National Transportation Act, finding unpersuasive arguments that Section 110 was like Section 4(f). *See Presidio Historical Ass'n v. Presidio Tr.*, 811 F.3d 1154, 1170 (9th Cir. 2016) (noting that Congress declined to include language about "prudent and feasible alternatives," found in Section 4(f), in Section 110). *See also Neighborhood Ass'n of the Back Bay, Inc. v. Fed. Transit. Admin.*, 463 F.3d 50, 64 (1st Cir. 2006).

4.   In this case, the plaintiffs proved that the Army had violated both Section 106 and Section 110. As the court noted, a plaintiff who demonstrates there has been a violation of Section 106 is often entitled to an injunction preventing the agency from proceeding with the undertaking until it first complies with Section 106. What remedy did the plaintiffs receive for the proven violations in this case? Do you agree with Judge Friedman's decision about relief in this case? Do you think that the plaintiffs were satisfied?

5.   While the Council's regulations logically anticipate that a decision about whether an agency is engaged in an undertaking should occur before considering whether the undertaking will adversely affect historic properties, these questions cannot always be separate. The more likely it is that direct federal activity will harm a historic property, the more likely it will be considered an undertaking. If there is a real possibility that a federal activity will harm a historic resource, it should be considered an undertaking, so the agency can examine whether there will, in fact, be adverse effects and whether they can be mitigated.

6.   In material not included in the excerpt above, the *Blanck* court compared the NHPA to the National Environmental Policy Act (NEPA), 42 U.S.C. §§ 4321–4361, saying "their similarities shed light on the issue of agency action and inaction." *National Trust for Historic Pres. v. Blanck*, 938 F. Supp. 908, 919 (D.D.C. 1996). Like NHPA, NEPA is a procedural statute; it requires federal agencies to prepare statements regarding the environmental impact of any "major Federal action." The judge in *Blanck* likened Walter Reed's inaction to the inaction of the Secretary of the Interior in a NEPA case, *Defenders of Wildlife v. Andrus*, 627 F.2d 1238 (D.C. Cir. 1980). (The Secretary had failed to prevent the State of Alaska from killing 170 wolves.) The *Defenders of Wildlife* court found that under NEPA, the Secretary's inaction did not constitute a "federal action" requiring the preparation of an

environmental impact statement. In *Blanck*, the court's NEPA comparison did not determine the outcome. But the view that judicial interpretations of NEPA should inform interpretations of NHPA is misguided, given significant differences between the statutes. Further material involving judicial interpretations of NHPA and NEPA is included in Chapter 4.

Figures 3-3 & 3-4:
Continued Neglect at The National Seminary Site,
Silver Spring, MD

7.   Review Figures 3-3 and 3-4, photographs taken in 2011, documenting the continuing neglect at the National Seminary complex: the boarded-up Gymnasium (which once housed a bowling alley, solarium, and swimming pool) and another auxiliary building, adjacent to the main building. These portions of the historic district housed a finishing school for girls from 1894 to 1936. The Army purchased this portion of the property in 1942, and it was listed on the National Register of Historic Places in 1972, in an effort to protect the existing buildings from exterior and interior alterations and demolition. In 2001, after this case, the property came to be owned by Montgomery County, who in turn sold the property to the Alexander Company, which specializes in modernizing historic properties. Now, there are over 200 townhouses, apartments, and condominiums on the property, for rent or purchase. *See* Matt Blitz, *Explore the Strange, Fairy-Tale Landscape of National Park Seminary*, WASHINGTONIAN (Aug. 18, 2015).

3.   FEDERAL LICENSING OF UNDERTAKINGS

An important recurring legal issue is the meaning of the term "license" in Sections 106 and 301(7). How broad a range of federal oversights are included? This key jurisdictional term is not defined in the National Historic Preservation Act (NHPA). Section 301(7) includes within an undertaking "those requiring a Federal permit[,] license, or approval." This should probably be read as a syntactically awkward attempt to make clear that a license includes a permit or approval, even though the provision literally treats permits and approvals as actions in addition to a license. Because Section 106 duties apply to undertakings requiring federal "licenses," a literal-minded court might conclude that it does not apply to those requiring permits or approvals. The Advisory Council on Historic Preservation regulations, however, treat the terms as equivalents, extending 106 duties to all three. 36 C.F.R. § 800.16(y). This interpretation should receive judicial deference as a reasonable interpretation of ambiguous statutory language.

A decision handed down before enactment of Section 301 in 1992 gave "license" a narrow interpretation. In *Weintraub v. Rural Electrification Admin., U.S. Dep't of Agric.*, 457 F. Supp. 78 (M.D. Pa. 1978), a group of rural electric cooperatives planned to demolish a historic building to make way for a parking lot for their new headquarters building. Because they had borrowed money from the federal Rural Electrification Administration (REA), they needed approval from the REA for plans for construction of their headquarters buildings, including a parking lot. The court held that such an approval was not a license within the meaning of Section 106, stating:

> The Court believes that Congress intended the word "license" in that statute have its technical meaning; that is, that it refers to a written document constituting a permission or right to engage in some governmentally supervised activity. * * * The legislative history supports this interpretation. Originally, 16

U.S.C. § 470f [EDS.: moved to 54 U.S.C. § 306108] applied only to projects receiving federal funds. An amendment was added * * * to include federal licensing agencies. 1966 U.S.C.C.A.N. 3310. Certainly, the House Report strongly indicates that the amendment was designed to affect only federal agencies which engaged in licensing activities. Congress did not intend to affect every action which required federal approval. Consequently, the Court concludes that the regulation of REA which requires approval of headquarters buildings and their adjuncts does not provide for a license within the meaning of 16 U.S.C. § 470f [EDS.: moved to 54 U.S.C. § 306108].

Id. at 92. *Weintraub* may draw too strong an inference from ambiguous legislative history. In any event, its interpretation has to be seriously questioned after the enactment of Section 301(7) and its administrative interpretation.

Another good reason not to read "license" narrowly is the definition of the term in the Administrative Procedure Act, 5 U.S.C. § 551(8). That provision defines license to include "the whole or part of an agency permit, certificate, approval, registration, charter, membership, statutory exemption or other form of permission." Given the importance of the APA for agency action generally, the compatibility of the APA and of the NHPA definitions of license, and the desirability of construing the statutes congruently, courts should define license to mean any required affirmative approval by a federal agency necessary for some activity or project to go forward.

An agency's authority to disapprove or veto an action has not been equated with the requirement for a federal license or approval. In *Sheridan Kalorama Historical Ass'n*, 49 F.3d, the court held that the Secretary of State's decision not exercise his discretionary power under the Foreign Missions Act to veto Turkey's demolition of its historic embassy building in Washington, D.C., did not constitute federal licensing. The Court stated: "[B]y not requiring the Secretary's affirmative approval of chancery proposals, the Congress [in the Foreign Missions Act] specifically meant to avoid subjecting the Secretary to the procedures of the NHPA." *Id.* at 757. Similarly, when federal entities can only comment on a project but have no regulatory authority, the undertaking is not subject to licensing. *See Techworld Dev. Corp. v. D.C. Pres. League*, 648 F. Supp. 106 (D.D.C. 1986) (finding that a decision by the D.C. City Council to close a historic street was not a federal undertaking when the National Capital Planning Commission had authority to only comment on the decision).

Some courts decline to subject projects to Section 106 when federal approval is required only for a small, insignificant element of a complex project. In *Sugarloaf Citizens Ass'n v. Fed. Energy Regulatory Comm'n*, 959 F.2d 508 (4th Cir. 1992), petitioners sought to enjoin construction of a waste incinerator, which developers intended to qualify for federal benefits as a "small power production facility" under the Public Utility Regulatory Policies Act (PURPA). The Federal Energy Regulatory Commission had to certify that the ownership, size, and fuel use of the generator met the criteria of PURPA. The court held that certification did not amount to a licensing but was "merely a ministerial act" so that the agency had "no discretion to consider environmental values." *Id.* at 513. *See also Vieux Carré Prop. Owners, Residents & Assocs., Inc. v. Brown*, 875 F.2d 453, 465 (5th Cir. 1989) ("Congress clearly did not intend to require the Corps to subject such truly inconsequential projects to the procedural complexities of section [106]."); *Ringsred v. City of Duluth*, 828 F.2d 1305 (8th Cir. 1987) (the Secretary of the Interior's necessary approval of an Indian tribe's contract for construction of a parking ramp as not "improvident and unconscionable" does not subject a parking ramp project to federal licensing). While such a rule seems pragmatic, it is hard to justify within the language of the NHPA. By analogy to the funding cases below, an agency must conduct a Section 106 review before issuing a federal approval where it could deny approval based upon findings from the review. A federal agency's determination of the scope of an undertaking normally will be upheld if it is not arbitrary and capricious. *Harrison v. U.S. Dep't of the Army*, 2009 WL 3347109 (W.D. Ky. 2009) (upholding the Army determination that an undertaking involved only the 10.9 mile easement over Fort Knox and viewsheds but not the entire 40-mile long private electric transmission line).

One reason given for excluding incidental federal approvals from licensing seems clearly wrong. Several courts have fallaciously equated the threshold for finding an undertaking with that for finding a "major Federal action[ ] significantly affecting the quality of the human environment" under the National Environmental Policy Act (NEPA). 42 U.S.C. § 4332(2)(C). We compare these statutory standards in Chapter 4, explaining why "undertaking" applies to many more activities than does the NEPA threshold.

Agencies need to be careful when they reduce their licensing authority to avoid compliance with Section 106. In *United Keetoowah Band of Cherokee Indians in Okla. v. FCC*, 933 F.3d 728 (D.C. Cir 2019), the court set aside as arbitrary and capricious the agency's rule eliminating section 106 and NEPA review for construction of densely spaced small wireless facilities transmitting cellular signals. The agency sought to accomplish this deregulation by eliminating its authority to permit such installations. But the court held that the agency failed "to justify its determination that it is not in the public interest to require review of small cell deployments." *Id.* at 740.

4. FEDERAL FUNDING OF UNDERTAKINGS

A plain reading of Sections 106 and 301(7) of the National Historic Preservation Act (NHPA) could support the interpretation that any project using federal dollars, regardless of its supervision, should be considered an undertaking requiring initiation of the historic review process of 106. Section 106 requires review of any "federally assisted" undertaking prior to the "approval of the expenditure of any Federal funds." Section 301 defines an undertaking to include any "project, activity, or program funded in whole or in part under the direct or indirect jurisdiction of a Federal agency, including . . . those carried out with Federal financial assistance." 54 U.S.C. § 304111. These key provisions might seem to require a federal agency to consider historic resources whenever federal money of any amount supports an undertaking, even when the agency has only "indirect jurisdiction."

But the NHPA generally has not been read this way. Courts believe that the myriad paths along which federal funds may filter to projects, over which federal agencies have little or no control, make this literal reading implausible. Rather, the touchstone for a duty to begin the Section 106 review process has been an "approval of the expenditure" of federal funds through which the federal agency's consideration of the approval's effects on historic resources can influence the project. As one court has written: "[F]ederal financial assistance alone is insufficient to trigger the requirements of the NHPA. Instead, '[t]here must, in addition, be some form of federal approval, supervision, control, or at least a certain level of consultation, over the spending of federal funds.'" *Woodham v. Fed. Transit Admin.*, 125 F. Supp. 2d 1106, 1110 (N.D. Ga. 2000) (quoting *Maxwell St. Historic Pres. Coal. v. Bd. of Trs. of the Univ. of Ill.*, 2000 WL 1141439 (N.D. Ill. 2000)). Thus, courts look to the process for approval of federal funding, which generally equates federal agency control of the undertaking with that under the parallel federal licensing threshold.

Agencies and courts applying this vague and fact-sensitive approach sometimes reach prudent outcomes, although they sometimes unduly slight preservation goals. In *Lee*, 877 F.2d, the court held that Section 106 did not apply to construction of a local prison in Washington, D.C., adjacent to the historic Congressional Cemetery, even though Congress appropriated more than $50 million for the project. Neither Congress nor the District of Columbia are considered to be federal agencies, and Congress had directly appropriated the money to D.C. but delegated no approval functions to any federal agency. The court emphasized that the NHPA applies only to federal agencies and "only in relation to projects or programs they initiate or control through funding or approvals." *Id.* at 1058.

Even when funds pass through an agency, the agency may not have Section 106 duties when it cannot disapprove a project. In *Sac & Fox Nation of Mo. v. Norton,* 240 F.3d 1250 (10th Cir. 2001), a statute implementing settlement of a dispute between the United States and an Indian tribe required the Secretary of the Interior to expend federal funds for the purchase of land at the direction of the tribe. Because the federal agency had no discretion not to expend the funds, its consideration of the effects of doing so would have been ineffective to protect historic resources. *Id.* at 1263. The results in these cases seem defensible given that the NHPA directs its commands to federal agencies.

In *Woodham*, 125 F. Supp. 2d, the court found no federally assisted undertaking in a joint development project at a train station between a private developer and the Metropolitan Atlanta Rapid Transit Authority (MARTA). The Federal Transit Administration (FTA) had given MARTA nearly $4 million to buy the land for the station and another $1.6 million to buy additional land and to develop proposals for the joint project; the FTA later approved the ultimate development plan. The court stated conclusively that the FTA lacked discretion to disapprove the project if it "satisfied the statutory and regulatory requirements." *Id.* at 1110. This decision comes perilously close to requiring the applicable funding laws to expressly create discretion for the consideration of preservation interests mandated directly by the NHPA. It would frustrate the purposes of the NHPA to require that a statute authorizing approval of funding either itself incorporate preservation values or confer such broad discretion on the agency that it would be free to weigh preservation concerns in the absence of the NHPA.

A better approach was taken by the court in the early case of *Ely*, 451 F.2d. In that case, a Fourth Circuit panel considered the relationship between the NHPA and a federal statute that authorized a federal agency to disapprove grants to local police departments only on narrow grounds found within the agency's authorizing statute. The court stated the general statutory principle that "in the absence of unmistakable language to the contrary, we should hesitate to read the congressional solution to one problem—protection of local police autonomy—so broadly as unnecessarily to undercut solutions adopted by Congress to preserve and protect other social values, such as the natural and cultural environment." *Id.* at 1136. Courts should find that a statute providing criteria for approval of a federal grant precludes application of the NHPA only when the agency properly concludes that it lacks authority to deny funding based on preservation review.

Federal block grants to state and local governments create analogous problems regarding the applicability of Section 106. In *Business and Residents Alliance of East Harlem v. Jackson*, 430 F.3d 584 (2d Cir. 2005), the court considered whether a local government entity's approval of a loan, using a portion of the federal funds allocated to it to spur development in an "Empowerment Zone," triggered Section 106 review by the federal agencies, exercising limited oversight, primarily the Department of Housing and Urban Development (HUD). The court analyzed the complex relationships federal legislation created among HUD, New York State, New York City, and an alphabet soup of public corporations created to invest a large federal grant to revitalize an economically depressed area. The local development corporation had approved a $15 million loan, including $5 million from the federal block grant, to a developer proposing to build a large shopping center, which would require the demolition of an arguably historic factory building. A community group opposing the project sued, arguing that the federal agencies that had approved the block grant should have conducted a Section 106 review before the factory was demolished.

The court assumed that the use of federal funds in the development loan constituted an undertaking but held that Section 106 did not apply because the federal agencies had neither direct nor indirect jurisdiction over the shopping center project, which had been approved entirely by the local redevelopment agency. The local development agencies were authorized by the Empowerment Zone program to make their own decisions about what projects to fund subject only HUD cancelling the entire Empowerment Zone program for dramatic programmatic failures, none of which could be triggered by a Section 106 review. The court stated that "the process by which these funds were allocated took place entirely at the state and local level," concluding that the federal agencies had no "ability to block [a state agency] from proceeding to withdraw the $5 million in question from the [federal] draw down account that contains the federal block grants awarded to the New York City Empowerment Zone. . . . [W]e have concluded that no federal agency has jurisdiction over the . . . project, and that Section 106 of the NHPA is therefore inapplicable to the project."

Business & Residents Alliance of East Harlem provides a useful approach, grounded in the language of the NHPA, from which to determine whether there is sufficient federal involvement or control in a federally assisted undertaking. It asks whether the laws authorizing federal funding and agency approval leave room for the agency to withhold funds based on Section 106 review. The facts of the case limit the reach of this rule. The federal block grant had already been disbursed, and by the time of the trial, the proceeds were controlled by state and city officials. HUD oversight was limited to cataclysmic de-designation of the entire empowerment zone based on terms strictly limited by the relevant statute and by a memorandum of understanding among HUD, New York State, and New York City. HUD could reasonably interpret these binding legal provisions effectively to prohibit it from withdrawing funds based on a Section 106 review.

NOTES & QUESTIONS

1. One should be concerned that courts do not narrowly interpret the inclusive jurisdictional reach of federal, federally funded, or licensed undertakings. The language of Sections 106 and 301, as well as the ambitious Congressional findings in the original NHPA, suggest that agencies should engage in Section 106 review whenever they might be able to modify an activity to avoid or mitigate adverse effects on historic resources. It may well be that the ACHP should amend its regulations to specify further which forms of federal agency funding or licensing approvals subject programs and

projects to Section 106. Drawing the jurisdictional line in any case, however, requires good judgment exercised in sympathy with the purposes of the NHPA.

2.   Funding of minor projects may not subject a federal activity to Section 106 review. For example, federal funding of an optional environmental impact statement for a state bridge project amounts to "minimal" participation and does not trigger the NHPA. *Vill. of Los Ranchos de Albuquerque v. Barnhart*, 906 F.2d 1477, 1482 (10th Cir. 1990).

3.   The timing of federal expenditures matters. In *Vieux Carre Property Owners, Residents and Associates, Inc. v. Brown*, a historic preservation group brought suit against the U.S. Army Corps of Engineers under the NHPA and the Rivers and Harbors Act for the Corps's erection of an aquarium and the creation of a riverfront park without consideration of adverse effects. In that case, the appellate panel reversed the district court holding that the case was moot, finding that historic preservation review was necessary even if a federally licensed project was substantially complete. *Vieux Carre Prop. Owners, Residents & Assocs., Inc. v. Brown*, 948 F.2d 1436 (5th Cir. 1991).

However, in *Karst Environmental Education and Protection, Inc. v. Environmental Protection Agency*, environmental organizations sued the federal government over their failure to conduct the appropriate assessments under the National Environmental Policy Act and the NHPA in their approval of a transit park project. The court held that the claims were moot because the action was already funded and completed; the agencies lacked continuing authority over the project. *Karst Envtl. Educ. & Prot., Inc. v. Envtl. Prot. Agency*, 475 F.3d 1291 (D.C. Cir. 2007).

4.   Should a city be allowed to segment an activity to avoid triggering NHPA? The Seventh Circuit considered a lawsuit against a city with a pending road-widening project, which required demolition of historic buildings. City officials claimed that they would not seek federal funding. The panel held that the city could be enjoined from seeking or accepting federal reimbursement—holding city officials at their word, but allowing them to evade NHPA scrutiny. *See Old Town Neighborhood Assoc. v. Kauffman*, 333 F.3d 732, 735 (7th Cir. 2003). Does this decision protect historic assets? Are there other ways to do so?

D. THE SECTION 106 PROCESS

Having discussed whether an agency must conduct a Section 106 review, we now turn to the nature of that review. The process is specified in regulations adopted by the Advisory Council on Historic Preservation (ACHP), fleshing out the general duties of an agency in Section 106 to "take into account the effect of the undertaking" on historic properties and to "afford the Council a reasonable opportunity to comment with regard to the undertaking." 54 U.S.C. § 306108. The goals of the process are "to identify historic properties potentially affected by the undertaking, assess its effects and seek ways to avoid, minimize or mitigate any adverse effect on historic properties." 36 C.F.R. § 800.1(a).

The ACHP regulations provide detailed instructions on the elements of the process that agencies must follow. They provide for "programmatic agreements" that cover complex or often-occurring undertakings. They provide, alternatively, that agencies may adopt, subject to the approval of the ACHP, their own procedures to comply with Section 106. We will return to these alternatives after examining the process crafted by the ACHP which binds all other agencies.

1. WHEN MUST SECTION 106 REVIEW OCCUR?

When must an agency complete the review process required by the National Historic Preservation Act? Section 106 directs the federal agency to take into account the effect of its undertaking "prior to the approval of the expenditure of any Federal funds on the undertaking or prior to the issuance of any license." 54 U.S.C. § 306108. The regulations of the Advisory Council on Preservation reiterate this command, directing the agency to "ensure that the section 106 process is initiated early in the undertaking's planning, so that a broad range of alternatives may be considered during the planning process." 36 C.F.R. § 800.1(c). The same regulation also clarifies that an agency can plan or authorize "nondestructive project planning activities" for an undertaking before it complies with Section 106, "provided that such actions do not restrict the subsequent consideration of alternatives to avoid, minimize or mitigate the undertaking's adverse effects on historic properties." *Id.*

Changed circumstances may require additional Section 106 review. The scope or character of an undertaking may change, additional historic properties may be discovered, or previously unforeseen adverse effects may threaten historic properties. When an agency's initial compliance with Section 106 results in a memorandum of agreement or in a programmatic agreement specifying how such changes or new discoveries will be dealt with, these will govern if there is continuing jurisdiction. *Id.* § 800.13(a). When new discoveries are made without such prior planning, however, the regulations of the Advisory Council on Historic Preservation require the agency to make additional reasonable efforts to avoid, minimize, or mitigate adverse effects on historic properties. *Id.* § 800.13(b). Such efforts depend on the stage the undertaking has reached, the nature of the resources, and the degree of control that the agency can still exert. As such, these continuing agency duties reflect the court decisions applying Section 106 to ongoing federal actions. Courts have adhered to their repeated promise to "respect reasonable agency procedures for updating past reviews." *CA 79-2516 WATCH (Waterbury Action to Conserve our Heritage Inc.) v. Harris*, 603 F.2d 310, 324 n.30 (2d Cir. 1979).

A corollary to this continuing duty to consider new developments in an undertaking is that agencies may continue to rely on past Section 106 reviews as long as the project remains substantially the same. Moreover, when an agency has complied with Section 106 in regard to a project, another agency providing a subsequent additional approval for the project need not comply further with Section 106 if it finds that there are no new or additional facts not considered in the prior compliance. In *McMillan Park Commission v. National Capital Planning Commission*, 968 F.2d 1283 (D.C. Cir. 1992), the General Services Administration had considered the effects of transferring a historic site to the District of Columbia; when D.C. proposed subsequent amendments to its comprehensive plan regarding the site, citizens argued that the federal National Capital Planning Commission had to comply with Section 106 before it could approve the plan. The court rejected this view: "Where, as here, a project has been found by the Advisory Council to comply fully with the § 106 process, we * * * find that no undertaking occurs when that same project, with no new, unreviewed elements, comes before a second federal agency." *Id.* at 1289.

Section 106 does try to reach early actions by non-federal parties that can frustrate the protections of the statute. It directs that an agency "not grant a loan, loan guarantee, permit, license, or other assistance to an applicant that, with intent to avoid the requirements of section 306108 of this title, has intentionally significantly adversely affected a historic property to which the grant would relate, or having legal power to prevent it, has allowed the significant adverse effect to occur." 54 U.S.C. § 306113. But preservationists cannot use the provision to stop such "anticipatory demolition" before the federal agency becomes involved, since section 306113 creates only duties for the agency. When preservationists sought to stop a city demolishing a historic penitentiary before seeking federal money for a sports arena/highway project on the site, the court held that the claim was "simply not ripe." *Brewery Dist. Soc'y v. Fed. Highway Admin.*, 996 F. Supp. 750, 755 (S.D. Ohio 1998). The court added: "Section 470h–2(k) [EDS.: moved to 54 U.S.C. § 306113] requires, at a minimum, that the City be an 'applicant' for a 'loan, loan guarantee, permit, license, or other assistance' before the statute's obligations on federal agencies are triggered." *Id.*

2. PARTICIPANTS

Section 106 and the Advisory Council on Historic Preservation (ACHP) regulations place legal duties only on federal agencies with "direct or indirect jurisdiction" over an undertaking. Every federal agency with jurisdiction over an undertaking is responsible for carrying out the process. When several federal agencies are involved in an undertaking, they may designate a "lead federal agency" to act on their behalf. 36 C.F.R. § 800.2(a)(2).

Consultation is at the heart of the process. An agency's failure to consult with appropriate parties presents courts with the clearest basis for holding that an agency has failed to meet its Section 106 duties. For example, when an agency entered into contract to demolish a historic building without giving the ACHP an opportunity to comment, the court found a "clear violation" of Section 106. *Don't Tear It Down, Inc. v. Gen. Servs. Admin.*, 401 F. Supp. 1194, 1199 n.8 (D.D.C. 1975). The agency must involve consulting parties at all phases of the consultation and in specific steps. The agency must "involve" consulting parties in "findings and determinations." 36 C.F.R. § 800.2(a)(4). Failure to do so may violate Section 106, prompting judicial enjoining of an undertaking until full consultation is accomplished. Status as a consulting party is important also because consensus among consulting parties can smooth the way to an agency's determinations, but disagreements can extend the process and involve additional parties. Consulting parties thus can push the process in different directions by their agreement or disagreement with the agency.

The regulations specify who must and who may be "consulting parties." *Id.* § 800.2(c). The agency must consult with the relevant state historic preservation officers (SHPOs), tribal historic preservation officers (THPOs), local governments with jurisdiction over the areas an undertaking may affect, and the applicants for a relevant federal approval. Indian tribes also have rights to participate as consulting parties when an undertaking may have effects on tribal lands and where the tribe has not qualified a THPO. The agency may designate other individuals or organizations as consulting parties if they have a "demonstrated interest in the undertaking" or in its effects on historic properties. *Id.* § 800.2(c)(5). As will be seen, the SHPO or THPO has a special status in consultations, and her disagreement with the agency can imperil an agreement about the undertaking.

The key consulting party for any undertaking is the SHPO, who acts as the representative of the state in which potentially affected historic property is located. When more than one state is involved in an undertaking, the SHPOs can designate a lead SHPO to act on their behalf. When an Indian tribe has assumed the responsibilities of the SHPO for an undertaking on tribal land, the THPO acts in place of the SHPO. Failure to consult with the SHPO or with the THPO represents a clear violation of the regulations. In *Attakai v. United States*, 746 F. Supp. 1395, 1407 (D. Ariz. 1990), for example, the court found that the Bureau of Indian Affairs violated Section 106 when it performed its survey of possible historic resources without first consulting the SHPO. The court stated: "[T]he regulations clearly require consultation with the SHPO." *Id.* A case involving an allegation of failure to consult a THPO is studied in greater detail in Chapter 9. *See Quechan Tribe of Fort Yuma Indian Reservation v. United States Dep't of Interior*, 755 F. Supp. 2d 1104 (S.D. Cal. 2010) (finding that the tribe was likely to prevail on its claim that neither the tribe nor the THPO had been adequately consulted by the Bureau of Land Management before it decided to erect a large solar powered field).

The ACHP is the only entity with a statutory right to comment on an agency's meeting its 106 duties. An agency's failure to provide the

ACHP with a "reasonable opportunity to comment" is a major procedural fault that can render its undertaking unlawful. However, the ACHP can realistically only become involved in a small percentage of Section 106 processes. The regulations provide several points at which the ACHP must receive notice for it to decide whether to enter an individual review process, such as when an undertaking may affect a National Historic Landmark. The ACHP has established criteria for deciding whether to enter a particular process, such as the importance or the number of properties that may be affected and whether it involves important legal, policy, or procedural questions. 36 C.F.R. Part 800, Appendix A. The ACHP will not enter a process if no criterion is met, but it may elect not to do so even if one or more criteria are met. The ACHP must husband its resources because it has a small staff and because federal agencies engage in many undertakings. For example, federal agencies engaged in approximately 117,000 Section 106 processes in 2008, but the ACHP itself participated only in 862 of these cases. The ACHP issued formal comments in fewer than .01 percent of total projects undertaken by federal agencies or with their support. LESLIE E. BARRAS, NAT'L TRUST FOR HISTORIC PRES., SECTION 106 OF THE NATIONAL HISTORIC PRESERVATION ACT: BACK TO BASICS PART 2, TECHNICAL REPORT 22 & 41 (2010).

Other entities or persons must or may, depending on the circumstances, become consulting parties. When a tribe has not assumed the role of the SHPO, it still may designate a representative to be a consulting party for undertakings affecting tribal lands, along with the SHPO. An Indian tribe or a Native Hawaiian organization must be made a consulting party when an undertaking may affect historic properties to which it attaches "religious and cultural importance," within the meaning of Section 106(d)(6)(B). Local governments, where undertakings may have effects, may have a representative participate as a consulting party. Importantly, any applicant for federal assistance or license may be a consulting party. Finally, the agency may designate other interested parties as consulting parties, but it has discretion in consultation with the SHPO about whom to designate. Individuals and organizations wishing to be made consulting parties must formally request that the agency designate them. *Id.* § 800.3(f)(3). In *Neighborhood Association of the Back Bay, Inc. v. Federal Transit Administration,* 463 F.3d 50 (1st Cir. 2006), preservation groups attacked the Federal Transit Administration's compliance with Section 106 by arguing that they should have been made consulting parties because the agency knew that they were interested in the project at issue. The court rejected this claim, stating: "The regulations expressly require parties to make written request to become consulting parties, and give[ ] the agency and SHPO * * * the discretion to decide whether to grant the request." *Id.* at 61 n.5.

Interested organizations and individuals not made consulting parties may still participate, as members of the public. The regulations require the agency to "seek and consider" public views to a degree that reflects the nature of the undertaking and the public interest in it. 36 C.F.R. § 800.2(d). The agency, thus, must provide public information about the project and solicit public comment, although most aspects of how to involve the public are left to the discretion of the agency. The agency must publicize documentation for its decisions and provide an opportunity for the public to comment on resolving adverse effects. *Id.* § 800.6(a)(4). Agencies often provide notice through publishing an environmental assessment prepared to comply with the National Environmental Policy Act. The agency need not reach agreement with any public participant who has not been named a consulting party. However, members of the public sometimes can affect an agency's decision by influencing positions taken by the SHPO or by the THPO and eventually seek judicial review alleging that the agency's actions were "arbitrary and capricious" in violation of the Administrative Procedure Act standard used to review agency actions related to Section 106.

3.   HISTORIC PROPERTIES AFFECTED

The agency must next, in consultation with the state historic preservation officer (SHPO) or with the tribal historic preservation officer (THPO), identify historic properties that may be affected by the undertaking. The agency must first determine the "area of potential effects," defined as the "areas within which an undertaking may directly or indirectly cause alterations in the character or use of historic properties." 36 C.F.R. § 800.16(d). The agency, thus, must make a justified determination of the place where any foreseeable direct or indirect effects may occur. The areas within which such effects may occur should be delineated before historic properties are identified.

Agency determinations of the historic properties within the project area are subject to judicial review for compliance with the procedural requirements of Section 106 and the implementing regulations. *Friends of the Atglen-Susquehanna Trail, Inc. v. Surface Transp. Bd.*, 252 F.3d 246 (3d Cir. 2001). This delineation "requires a high level of agency expertise, and as such, the agency's determination is due a substantial amount of discretion." *Valley Cmt. Pres. Comm'n v. Mineta*, 373 F.3d 1078, 1092 (10th Cir. 2004); *see also Dine Citizens Against Ruining Our Env't v. Bernhardt*, 923 F.3d 831 (10th Cir. 2019) (finding the Bureau of Land Management under no obligation to include areas with potential indirect effects in the area of potential effects under NHPA). Where the consulting parties agree on the area that may be affected by an undertaking, an objecting party will have trouble persuading a court that the agency acted arbitrarily. *See Daingerfield Island Protective Soc'y v. Babbitt*, 40 F.3d 442 (D.C. Cir. 1994) (rejecting a citizens' association's challenge to the National Park Service's Section 106 review of design for an interchange on the George Washington Parkway because the ACHP had approved the design review).

The agency must also make "a reasonable and good faith effort" to identify historic properties within the areas. 36 C.F.R. § 800.4(b). Recall that Section 106 applies to any historic property "included on, or *eligible for* inclusion on, the National Register." 54 U.S.C. § 300308 (emphasis added). The ACHP regulations amplify this definition and clarify that properties "eligible for inclusion" include both those previously determined to be eligible (but not listed, for example, because of owner objection) and *all* other properties, public or private, that meet the criteria. 36 C.F.R. § 800.16(*l*)(2). A property's eligibility for listing on the National Register must be determined in accordance with National Park Service regulations, which provide a leading role for the SHPO and which incorporate the National Register criteria. *See* 36 C.F.R. § 63.2. To discover potential properties that meet these criteria, the agency must survey the area, review available records, and seek information from consulting parties. The agency must also take responsibility, again with consultation, to assess whether potential properties meet the criteria for inclusion on the National Register. The ACHP's amplified definition was upheld by the D.C. Circuit as a reasonable interpretation of the Act. *See CTIA-The Wireless Ass'n v. FCC*, 466 F.3d 105, 115–18 (D.C. Cir. 2006).

This duty on the agency to make a good faith effort to discover historic properties that may be affected by the undertaking constitutes an important protection, because only a fraction of the historic properties that could meet National Register criteria have been studied and documented. At the same time, it seriously expands the search efforts expected of an agency beyond reliance on the listings in the National Register. Section 106 of the NHPA originally required agencies only to consider the effects of their undertakings on properties included on the National Register, but it was amended in 1976 to include properties eligible for inclusion. By then, it had become clear that the process of expanding the Register would proceed more slowly than originally envisioned.

A provision added to the NHPA in 1992 further expands an agency's duties by providing that "[p]roperty of traditional religious and cultural importance to an Indian tribe or Native Hawaiian organization may be determined to be eligible for inclusion on the National Register." 54 U.S.C. § 302706(a). Such properties need not be tribal lands nor owned by an Indian tribe or by any of its members. Rather, traditional cultural properties are those associated "with cultural practices or beliefs of a living community that (a) are rooted in that community's history, and (b) are important in maintaining the continuing cultural identity of the community." Patricia L. Parker & Thomas King, *Guidelines for Evaluating and Documenting Traditional Cultural Properties* 1 (Nat'l Park Serv., Nat'l Register Bull. No. 38, 1998). Such properties may be sacred sites "where Native American religious practitioners have historically gone, and are known or thought to go today, to perform ceremonial activities in accordance with traditional cultural rules of practice." *Id.* The NHPA further requires the agency to consult with any Indian tribe or Native Hawaiian organization that attaches significance to such properties. 54 U.S.C. § 302706(b). The ACHP regulations specifically recognize that native people "may be reluctant to divulge specific information regarding the location, nature, and activities associated with such sites." 36 C.F.R. § 800.4(a)(4). The regulations recognize the challenges that this may pose in the process and also provide for confidentiality agreements to facilitate disclosure.

What constitutes a reasonable and good faith effort to identify historic properties will depend upon the circumstances of the undertaking. In determining the level of effort required, the regulations list many factors that the agency should consider, including past studies, the magnitude and nature of the undertaking, the degree of federal involvement, the nature and extent of the potential effects, other relevant professional and legal standards, and the confidentiality concerns of Native American groups. A court decision that illuminates aspects of an agency's duties to identify historic properties, generally, and sites of traditional cultural significance, specifically, is *Pueblo of Sandia v. United States*, 50 F.3d 856 (10th Cir. 1995). The court held that the Forest Service violated Section 106 by not conducting a reasonable and good faith effort to determine whether a canyon within a National Forest contained sites of cultural and religious significance to the Sandia Pueblo. The Forest Service had sent letters requesting information about such sites to potentially concerned tribes but did not receive specific information from them. Tribal members, however, had told the agency that they did not want to disclose specific details of site locations or activities. The court held that "a mere request for information is not necessarily sufficient to constitute the 'reasonable effort' section 106 requires." *Id.* at 860. The court went on to hold "that the information the tribes did communicate to the agency was sufficient to require the Forest Service to engage in further investigations, especially in light of regulations warning that tribes might be hesitant to divulge the type of information sought." *Id.* The court also held that the agency had not made a good faith effort to identify traditional cultural properties because it withheld, from the SHPO, affidavits asserting that such sites were present in the canyon. *Id.* at 862.

When the agency and the SHPO or THPO agree that a property meets the National Register criteria, the property is considered eligible for the purposes of Section 106. When they agree that a property is not eligible, it will normally be considered ineligible. When they disagree, the agency official must submit the issue of eligibility to the Keeper, pursuant to the process in 36 C.F.R. Part 63. The ACHP or the Secretary of the Interior can also request the agency to obtain a ruling from the Keeper, even if the agency and the SHPO have agreed that it is ineligible. The Keeper's decision on eligibility settles the matter administratively, although the parties may seek judicial review of the Keeper's decision under the Administrative Procedure Act. For more on this topic, refer to the note on "Agency Determination of Eligibility for the National Register" in Chapter 2.

When an agency determines either that there are no historic properties present or that they will not be affected by the undertaking, the agency must provide documentation to the SHPO and notice to all consulting parties. The agency must also make the documentation available to the public before approving the undertaking. The SHPO then has thirty days to object. If the SHPO does not object, the agency has completed its Section 106 responsibility. If the SHPO does object, and the parties then cannot resolve their disagreement, the agency official must forward the finding and documentation to the ACHP for its review. The decision and documentation should also be made public. The ACHP then has thirty days to give its opinion to the agency.

It is important to re-emphasize that the ACHP does not have authority at this point to make the agency follow its view or even to require further study of the matter. All it can do is give its opinion to the agency official in charge or to the head of the agency. The agency is free to adhere to its initial view and to give final notice to that effect. The ACHP will not seek judicial resolution of the difference. Other parties, however, may seek judicial review of the agency's decision, and the ACHP opinion and correspondence with the agency will be part of the record on review. When the agency and the SHPO agree that historic properties will be affected, the agency should give appropriate notice and the process moves to consideration of whether the effects are adverse.

4. ADVERSE EFFECTS

Once it has identified the historic properties that may be affected by an undertaking, the agency must evaluate whether the undertaking may impose *adverse effects* on the properties. The agency must act in consultation with the consulting parties and consider the view of both the consulting parties and the public. The regulatory definition of adverse effects is of crucial importance to the Section 106 process because a finding of adverse effects entails an agency duty to consider and to consult about measures to avoid, lessen, or mitigate such effects. As the regulations state: "An adverse effect is found when an undertaking may alter, directly or indirectly, any of the characteristics of a historic property that qualify the property for inclusion in the National Register in manner that would diminish the integrity of the property's location, design, setting, materials, workmanship, feeling, or association." 36 C.F.R. § 800.5(a)(1). Adverse effects are thus broadly defined but also limited to changes to those features that qualify a property for the Register. An adverse effect will be found when the relevant effects are only predictable or likely; certainty is not required. Thus, according to a longtime executive director of the Advisory Council on Historic Preservation (ACHP), adverse effects may include "long-term indirect impacts resulting from altered traffic patterns or growth-inducing activities that change the use or character of a significant property over time." John M. Fowler, *The Federal Preservation Program, in* A RICHER HERITAGE: HISTORIC PRESERVATION IN THE TWENTY-FIRST CENTURY 49 (Robert E. Stipe, ed. 2003).

The definition of adverse effects is amplified by the non-exclusive list of examples provided in the regulations. These are not so much specific examples as categories of actions that may constitute an adverse effect when they harm a significant characteristic of the property. They, too, deserve to be quoted:

(i) Physical destruction of or damage to all or part of the property;

(ii) Alteration of a property, including restoration, rehabilitation, repair, maintenance, stabilization, hazardous material remediation, and provision of handicapped access, that is not consistent with the Secretary's standards for the treatment of historic properties (36 C.F.R. Part 68) and applicable guidelines;

(iii) Removal of the property from its historic location;

(iv) Change of the character of the property's use or of physical features within the property's setting that contribute to its historic significance;

(v) Introduction of visual, atmospheric or audible elements that diminish the integrity of the property's significant historic features;

(vi) Neglect of a property which causes its deterioration, except where such neglect and deterioration are recognized qualities of a property of religious and cultural significance to an Indian tribe or Native Hawaiian organization; and

(vii) Transfer, lease, or sale of property out of Federal ownership or control without adequate and legally enforceable restrictions or conditions to ensure long-term preservation of the property's historic significance.

36 C.F.R. § 800.5(a)(2). Although some of the points made about adverse effects in the examples are obvious, such as the statement that destruction of the entire property will create an adverse effect, several deserve further comment. The third example in section 800.5(a)(2) makes moving a historic property a problematic solution for permitting an undertaking, except for properties whose settings do not contribute to their significance, which are primarily objects, such as locomotives. The fourth example may seem to have broader significance than it does because the use to which a property is put usually does not contribute to its significance. The concern with noise and visual clutter in the fifth example reaches new construction or projects in the environs of the

property to be protected, such as cell phone towers visible from the site. The sixth example seems to reach neglect by federal agencies of properties under their control, but applies only to undertakings, which may not include pure inaction.

If the agency finds no adverse effects, it must notify all consulting parties and provide them with documentation. *Id.*, § 800.5(c). An agency may rely on the reasonable analysis by its experts on whether a project will have adverse effects. *See Coliseum Square Assoc., Inc. v. Jackson,* 465 F.3d 215 (5th Cir. 2006). If, within thirty days, a consulting party notifies the agency that it disagrees, the agency must either resolve the disagreement or request the ACHP to review the finding. The ACHP then must review the finding and provide its opinion as to whether the agency has applied the criteria for adverse effects correctly. The agency must take into account any disagreement by the ACHP with its finding, although it can adhere to its original decision and terminate the process. Again, nothing in the National Historic Preservation Act requires the agency to reach any particular conclusion about adverse effects of the undertaking. A party with standing, however, may seek judicial review of the agency's decision and use the disagreement of the consulting party and the ACHP in support of its argument that the agency's action was arbitrary and capricious within the meaning of the Administrative Procedure Act. When the ACHP and the state historic preservation officer agree with the agency that the undertaking will cause no adverse effects, a complaining party will have a heavy burden of persuasion in court.

NOTES & QUESTIONS

1.   Cruise ships have been criticized for the environmental, cultural, and economic costs they impose on harbor towns. For background on their effects on historic properties, see Erica Avrami et al., Harboring Tourism: Cruise Ships in Historic Port Communities (2013). To end cruise ship activity in the historic port of Charleston, South Carolina, the Southern Preservation Law Center successfully brought a Section 106 challenge to permission granted by the U.S. Army Corps of Engineers, which allowed cruise ships to dock. A federal district court revoked the permit, stating: "[C]ourts have no obligation to stand aside and rubber-stamp their affirmance of administrative decisions that they deem inconsistent with a statutory mandate or that frustrate the congressional policy underlying a statute." *Pres. Soc'y of Charleston v. U.S. Army Corps of Eng'rs,* 2013 WL 6488282, at *1 (D.S.C. 2013).

In that case, there was a fundamental disagreement between the Advisory Council on Historic Preservation and the Army Corps about how the Army Corps should evaluate effects pursuant to Section 106. The Army Corps preferred the term "permit area," as it limited the affected area to the mere footprint of the pier that was needed to shore up new cruise line activity as opposed to the broader area of potential effects. The court held that "The Army Corps' determination to limit the 'scope of analysis' to the impact of the five concrete pile clusters, rather than the new passenger terminal, dramatically and improperly constricted the assessment of the potential environmental and historic landmark impacts of the proposed activity." *Id.* at *11.

2.   The question of Section 106 effects has also arisen in several cases involving the U.S. Postal Service (USPS), as its precarious fiscal situation has led it to attempt to monetize its real property assets, including its many historic post offices. It proposed to sell a historic post office in Berkeley, California, with a preservation restriction (similar to the kind covered in Chapter 10) as a way to achieve a determination that there would be no adverse effect. It proposed that the restriction be held by it, and that USPS would be able to approve demolition. The Advisory Council on Historic Preservation and the California State Historic Preservation Officer objected to the proposal, because the USPS is not an agency with the capacity and experience in managing such restrictions, and because the demolition-approval provision failed to actually protect the historic property. Meanwhile, the USPS sued the City of Berkeley to enjoin the City from applying a zoning ordinance that would have limited development potential on the site. *U.S. Postal Serv. v. City of Berkeley*, 228 F. Supp. 3d 963 (N.D. Cal. 2017) (denying the City's motion to dismiss).

Similarly, two organizations and their members brought suit, under both the National Environmental Policy Act (NEPA) and the National Historic Preservation Act (NHPA), against the USPS to enjoin the sale of a historic post office in Stamford, Connecticut. The district court held that the plaintiffs lacked standing to sue under NEPA because they did not suffer an injury (since they failed to produce evidence that showed that they directly benefitted from the historic features of the building), that the USPS had properly considered the environmental impacts of the sale under NEPA, and that there were no adverse effects under Section 106 of the NHPA because the agency had not acted arbitrarily and capriciously when it determined the adequacy of the preservation covenant. *See Nat'l Post Office Collaborate v. Donahoe*, 2014 WL 6686691 (D. Conn 2014). Do you anticipate additional litigation under the NHPA and other laws, as USPS finances are increasingly strained and it proposes more sell-offs of its historic real property assets? Why do ordinary people care so much about these structures?

3.   What is the standard for a finding of no adverse effects? In 1999, the Federal Aviation Administration (FAA) authorized a passenger shuttle service to operate approximately ten round trip flights between a small airport in a historic area near Boston and LaGuardia Airport. The FAA determined that these additional flights (an increase of 2.5 percent of overall flights) would have only de minimis effects on historic properties, and therefore cut short the Section 106 process before consultation occurred. The First Circuit upheld this decision against challenge, because the FAA had studied environmental impact, noise, air quality, and surface traffic, and the court concluded that no plausible doubts had been raised about this assessment. *See Save our Heritage, Inc. v. Fed. Aviation Admin.*, 269 F.3d 49 (1st Cir. 2001).

5. RESOLVING ADVERSE EFFECTS

If the agency finds that there are adverse effects, it must proceed to consult about alternatives and modifications to the undertaking with all consulting parties. The object is to develop and evaluate alternatives or modifications that can avoid, minimize, or mitigate the adverse effects. The agency also must notify the Advisory Council on Historic Preservation (ACHP) of its adverse effects finding and provide appropriate documentation. The agency *may* also invite the ACHP to participate in the consultation; it *must* do so if the undertaking will have an adverse effect on a National Historic Landmark. 36 C.F.R. § 800.6.

The agency must provide documentation about adverse effects to all consulting parties and to the general public. Members of the public must be given an opportunity to express their views on how to address adverse effects, for example by commenting on a draft environmental assessment. The decision about how to resolve the adverse effects, however, will be made by the agency in collaboration with the state historic preservation officer (SHPO) or with the tribal historic preservation officer (THPO), and with the ACHP if it participates. If the ACHP does not participate, and the agency and SHPO or THPO agree on how to avoid, minimize, or mitigate the adverse effects, they should execute a memorandum of agreement (MOA).

An MOA is a legally binding document that records the terms and conditions agreed upon to resolve adverse effects. *Id.* § 800.16(*o*). It specifies who will do what and when they will do it, how compliance will be monitored and reported, how the parties will deal with disputes and changed circumstances, and the duration and termination of the agreement itself. The agency and consulting parties essentially agree on what constitutes adequate avoidance or mitigation. Avoidance of adverse effects may be possible by changing the location, scope, or character of the undertaking. Typical mitigation measures include archeological data recovery, documentation, signage, moving of a resource, or provision of preservation funds. Obviously, an MOA can include measures of both avoidance and mitigation. The agency submits the MOA to the ACHP before approving the undertaking. That submission can terminate the Section 106 process. If the agency and the SHPO cannot agree on an MOA, the agency must invite the ACHP to enter. *Id.* § 800.6(b)(1)(v).

Once adverse effects have been identified, the process only ends with either an MOA or with termination by an agency head after review of the ACHP comments. Once the ACHP enters the case, it consults with other parties. If it, the agency, and the SHPO agree on how to resolve the adverse effects, they all will execute an MOA. Any one of the three can determine that further consultation will not be fruitful and terminate consultation. If the SHPO terminates consultation, the agency and the ACHP can execute an MOA without the SHPO. However, if a THPO terminates concerning an undertaking on tribal land, then the ACHP may only file comments. If the agency terminates, it must notify all consulting parties and request ACHP comments. In *Friends of the Atglen-Susquehanna Trail, Inc. v. Surface Transportation. Board,* 252 F.3d 246, 266–67 (3d Cir. 2001), the agency's order was vacated because it failed to submit its decision to terminate consultation to the ACHP for comment. The head of the agency can make a final decision to approve the undertaking, but only after considering the ACHP comments. Section 110(*l*) of the NHPA provides that the head of the agency must document the decision and may not delegate the responsibility. The final decision must be made public. Thus, the statute and the regulations leave the final substantive decision with the agency but make a decision in opposition to the SHPO or ACHP potentially painful as a matter of process, politics, or professional reputation.

An MOA must be signed by the agency, by the SHPO or THPO if it has agreed, and by the ACHP if it has participated. The agency may invite additional parties to sign and should invite any party that assumes responsibilities under the MOA, but the refusal of these additional parties to sign will not invalidate the MOA. The signatories can amend the MOA, and any signatory can terminate it after an attempt to amend. If a signatory terminates an MOA, the agency can execute a new agreement or request comments from the ACHP. Signatories and other beneficiaries can sue to enforce the MOA in case of a breach.

6. PROGRAMMATIC AGREEMENTS

The Section 106 process, structured for discrete projects, may seem cumbersome or inefficient for large-scale or long-term undertakings with several phases or applications. The Advisory Council on Historic Preservation (ACHP) regulations provide that a federal agency and the ACHP may "negotiate a programmatic agreement to govern the implementation of a particular program or the resolution of adverse effects from certain complex project situations or multiple undertakings." 36 C.F.R. § 800.14(b).

Programmatic agreements may be used for undertakings when warranted by circumstances, including when effects are "similar and repetitive" or "cannot be fully determined prior to approval" or result from "routine management activities." *Id.* § 800.14(b)(1). For example, the ACHP encourages creation of programmatic agreements to delegate review to local officials for federally assisted rehabilitation of historic properties for affordable housing. *See* Advisory Council on Historic Pres., Policy Statement on Affordable Housing and Historic Preservation, 72 Fed. Reg. 7387 (Feb. 15, 2007). A programmatic agreement resembles a memorandum of understanding in several ways, as it governs how the parties will address certain issues in the future, but it is premised on greater current ignorance and sets the terms as to how future consideration of effects will occur as information is gained.

The regulations seek to provide the same consultation process for adopting programmatic agreements as for considering discrete undertakings. Programmatic agreements must be negotiated among the agency, the ACHP, and the relevant State or Tribal Historic Preservation Officers. The National Conference of SHPOs and National Association of THPOs may also be consulted when a large-scale program will create effects across the nation. Consultation should also include other federal agencies, affected tribes, and the general public. The agency must provide public notice of the proposed agreement before it takes effect. The agreement will be binding and will satisfy the agency's Section 106 duties for activities to which it applies until it is terminated. It usually will require some specific preservation work for each instance of the undertaking.

An important example is the Federal Communications Commission's programmatic agreement for considering the historic effects of construction of cell phone towers across the nation. *See* Fed. Comm. Comm'n, Nationwide Programmatic Agreement for Review of Effects on Historic Properties for Certain Undertakings Approved by the Federal Communications Commission, F.C.C. 04–222 (2004). In effect, this programmatic agreement creates a process tailored specifically for the construction or rehabilitation of every cell phone tower. Among other things, it requires the FCC to notify tribes of proposed wireless construction in areas tribes have identified as containing religious or culturally significant properties. It was upheld against challenge by the cell phone trade association. *See CTIA-The Wireless Ass'n v. Fed. Commc'ns Comm'n*, 466 F.3d 105 (D.C. Cir. 2006). The D.C. Circuit has struck down at least one attempt by the FCC to ignore this programmatic agreement (and other Section 106 processes required under the National Historic Preservation Act (NHPA)) so the FCC could more rapidly construct 5G wireless facilities. United Keetoowah Band of Cherokee Indians in Okla. v. Fed. Commc'ns Comm'n, 933 F.3d 728 (D.C. Cir. 2019).

A decision that highlights the advantages of a programmatic agreement is *Mid States Coal. for Progress v. Surface Transp. Bd.*, 345 F.3d 520 (8th Cir. 2003), which is excerpted in Chapter 4. The Board approved a license for construction of a new 280-mile rail line. The panel held that the Board violated the NHPA by issuing the license before completing the Section 106 process. The Board admittedly did not identify all historic sites and adverse effects, nor did it consider specific mitigation measures. It simply required the license holder to comply with future mitigation measures, at the end of its review of the rail line's environmental impacts pursuant to the National Environmental Policy Act (NEPA). The court held: "The ACHP's regulations, when read in their entirety, thus permit an agency to defer completion of the NHPA process until after the NEPA process has run its course (and the environmentally preferred alternatives chosen), but require that NHPA issues be resolved by the time that the license is issued." *Id.* at 554. The court pointed out that the Board could have complied with Section 106 and deferred addressing specific sites, effects, and measures by employing a programmatic agreement: "If the programmatic agreement had been executed, the Board could have finalized the NHPA details at a future date according to the terms of the agreement, just as it wished." *Id.* at 555. Thus, a programmatic agreement gives an agency "flexibility" to issue a license or commence a complex project when it cannot immediately consider the effects in their entirety.

Courts consider that an agency's decision to use a programmatic agreement, when both the ACHP and the SHPO agree that the project is "complex," is entitled to substantial deference and will not be set aside unless it is arbitrary and capricious. In *Lesser v. City of Cape May*, 110 F. Supp. 2d 303 (D.N.J. 2000), on the advice of the SHPO and of the ACHP, the parties used a programmatic agreement to complete review for a Phase I rehabilitation of a historic hotel. They met the Secretary's Standards for the Treatment of Historic Properties, while federal project funding was available, but postponed serious consideration of the effects of Phase II new construction which was still only in the concept phase. The court found the use of the programmatic agreement reasonable given the specific approval of the ACHP, the need for immediate qualification for rehabilitation funds, and the promise to mitigate future adverse effects of Phase II in consultation with the SHPO and with the ACHP.

7. ALTERNATE PROCEDURES

The Advisory Council on Historic Preservation (ACHP) regulations also permit federal agencies to develop their own procedures to implement Section 106 in place of the process detailed in the ACHP regulations. *See* 36 C.F.R. § 800.14. Such alternate procedures permit an agency to tailor compliance with the peculiarities of its own mission. The ACHP must approve such alternate procedures as adequately implementing Section 106. These alternate procedures should be distinguished from the regulations that agencies adopt to comply with the Section 106 process as specified by the ACHP regulations. Section 110(a)(2)(E)(i) requires that an agency adopt procedures for compliance with Section 106 that are "consistent" with the ACHP regulations. 54 U.S.C. § 306102(b)(5)(A).

The legal effect of such approval is that the agency can satisfy Section 106 by following its published process. The United States Army, for example, which controls a vast number of historic properties, has adopted an alternate procedure, approved by the ACHP, which can be adopted by each installation commander. United States Army Command Unit Army Alternate Procedures to 36 C.F.R. Part 800. Under this process, the installation commander proposes for public comment a five-year "Historic Properties Component Plan" for maintenance, renovation, and possible demolition of historic properties under her command, which permits, after adoption, a streamlined process for treatment of each historic property. Refer to the court's treatment of the Army's alternate procedures in *National Trust for Historic Preservation v. Blanck*, excerpted earlier in this Chapter.

E. LITIGATING CLAIMS BASED ON SECTION 106

Actions to enforce Section 106 must always be brought against federal agencies or against federal officials in their official capacities. Only federal agencies or officials can be sued because only a federal agency can violate the National Historic Preservation Act (NHPA). Non-federal parties, such as local governments or private firms, may be joined as defendants with responsible federal agencies and enjoined if the federal defendants have given approvals to them, or required their participation in other ways, without complying with Section 106. *See, e.g.*, *Weintraub*, 457 F. Supp. at 87 (asserting jurisdiction and power to enjoin private parties seeking a permit to demolish a historic building). Sometimes a question arises as to whether a defendant is a federal agency. *Comm. to Save the Fox Bldg. v. Birmingham Branch of the Fed. Reserve Bank of Atlanta*, 497 F. Supp. 504, 509–10 (N.D. Ala. 1980) (finding that a Federal Reserve Branch is a federal agency subject to the NHPA, despite its structural independence from the federal government).

Agencies, not courts, carry out the NHPA. But, courts are the primary means to force agencies to adhere to the law. Because of the deference courts pay to "reasonable" agency decisions and interpretations of applicable law, the main benefits of the NHPA to historic preservation come from prodding agencies to improve their approaches to fulfilling their duties, not from routinely challenging them in court. Litigation, of course, can be part of an ongoing negotiation with, or effort to impose political pressure on, an agency.

1. STANDING

Litigation to test whether agencies have fulfilled their duties under the NHPA will be brought primarily by concerned citizens. As discussed above, the Advisory Council on Historic Preservation (ACHP) takes the view that it lacks authority to sue other federal agencies for violating the statute. State historic preservation officers (SHPOs) may sue, but rarely do, given political constraints and the influence they already exercise within the administrative process. Property owners sometimes challenge federal agencies for requiring them to take costly efforts to avoid harming historic properties in order to receive a federal approval, but the consensual nature of the Section 106 process militates against this. So the typical plaintiffs are individuals and organizations concerned that some historic property will be harmed by a federal undertaking.

To bring such actions, concerned citizens have to establish standing. Standing is the constitutional requirement that plaintiffs have a sufficient stake in the action so that that courts will conclude that they are deciding a real "case or controversy" within the meaning of Article III of the Constitution. In general, plaintiffs need to demonstrate that the agency's actions have injured them. Federal courts, including the Supreme Court, have actively questioned when citizens have standing to sue federal agencies for not carrying out their duties toward the public at large. Fortunately, as we will see, citizens generally have been permitted to bring actions to enforce Section 106 when they have been able to claim some particular interest in a historic property.

The "irreducible constitutional minimum of standing" consists of three elements: (1) injury in fact, (2) fairly traceable to the challenged action of the defendant, and (3) likely to be redressed by a favorable decision. *Lujan v. Defs. of Wildlife*, 504 U.S. 555, 560–61 (1992). Prospective litigants may also need to show that their harms are within the "zone of interests" that Congress intended the relevant statute to protect, the determination of which is a matter of statutory interpretation, rather than constitutional interpretation. *Ass'n of Data Processing Serv. Orgs., Inc. v. Camp*, 397 U.S. 150, 153 (1970).

The owner of a historic building damaged by a federal undertaking will have standing to contest compliance with the Section 106 process, because she has suffered direct physical and economic injury to her property. Parties seeking federal approval also may contest an agency's compliance when it denies or conditions approval on preservation grounds. Neighbors can establish standing by alleging injury to their property values or other economic interests from threatened damage to a nearby historic structure.

But the concept of injury is broader. The Supreme Court long ago recognized that injury to a wide range of non-economic interests also can establish standing. In 1972, it said: "We have held that environmental plaintiffs adequately allege injury in fact when they aver that they use the affected area and are persons 'for whom the aesthetic and recreational values of the area will be lessened' by the challenged activity." *Friends of the Earth, Inc. v. Laidlaw Envtl. Servs. (TOC), Inc.*, 528 U.S. 167, 183 (2000) (quoting *Sierra Club v. Morton*, 405 U.S. 727, 735 (1972)). These views have carried over unproblematically to historic preservation cases. Citizens who allege that a proposed undertaking endangers historic resources that they use or enjoy for their historic, aesthetic, or cultural values may establish standing for Section 106 challenges. Moreover, organizations representing such citizens may have standing if they can allege that their members will suffer such injuries. *See, e.g., Vieux Carre Prop. Owners, Residents & Assocs., Inc. v. Brown*, 875 F.2d 453, 458 (5th Cir. 1989) (holding that an organization of property owners within a historic district can challenge the Army Corps of Engineers' compliance with the NHPA in considering a permit for construction of an aquarium); *Neighborhood Dev. Corp. v. Advisory Council on Historic Pres., Dep't of Hous. & Urban Dev., City of Louisville,* 632 F.2d 21 (6th Cir. 1980) (holding that five organizations with individual members who enjoy and derive benefits from preservation and others who can be expected to use the affected properties can challenge a housing redevelopment project funded in part by a federal grant).

On the other hand, more general allegations regarding concern about historic resources, without current or imminent use or enjoyment of the particular resources in question, may be inadequate. In *Lujan v. Defenders of Wildlife,* for example, persons studying or interested in various endangered species were denied standing to contest agency inaction regarding those species because they had no present plan to see or work with the animals.

States and SHPOs have special standing to bring historic preservation actions. The D.C. District Court found standing for the State of Pennsylvania in *Commonwealth of Pa. v. Morton,* 381 F. Supp. 293 (D.D.C. 1974). The state had contested a land swap between the National Park Service and private parties, which enabled the private parties to build the infamous, now demolished, observation tower adjacent to the Gettysburg battlefield. The court observed that little actual harm needed to be shown "when the case involves a state suing as *parens patriae* for alleged environmental injury on behalf of its citizens." *Id.* at 300. (The court here anticipated the Supreme Court's decision permitting a state to sue the Environmental Protection Agency for failing to regulate carbon dioxide as a pollutant. *See Mass. v. Envtl. Prot. Agency,* 549 U.S. 497 (2007).)

A SHPO may be especially well-placed to bring suit, as the ACHP regulations provide that the SHPO "reflects the interests of the State and its citizens in the preservation of their cultural heritage." 36 C.F.R. § 800.2(c)(1)(i). *See, e.g., Weintraub v. Rural Electrification Admin.,* 457 F. Supp. 78, 88 (M.D. Pa. 1978) (finding that the Pennsylvania SHPO "can show that he would be injured * * * and his claim is arguably within the zone of interest to be protected or regulated by the National Historical Preservation Act" and that he "acts as *parens patriae* for the citizens of the Commonwealth of Pennsylvania"). Indian tribes enjoy broad rights to standing for any injury to resources on tribal lands or to sites having religious or cultural significance, whether or not they have assumed SHPO responsibilities. Environmental and historic preservation organizations also have standing to challenge the removal of a historic resource by the Keeper of the National Register's decision. *Sierra Club v. Jewell,* 764 F.3d 1 (D.C. Cir. 2014). Plaintiffs in these cases must join all indispensable parties, including the agency head and the permittee. *Id.*

2. CAUSE OF ACTION

For a statute to be enforceable by litigation, Congress must create a "cause of action," which is a form of lawsuit that a person may invoke in court. Congress may specify or limit the elements of such a suit. While it is clear that private persons with standing may sue federal officials to require compliance with Section 106, courts remain divided about the source of that cause of action. In the National Historic Preservation Act (NHPA), Congress did not expressly provide for cause of action. In the early years of the NHPA, many courts simply entertained NHPA suits without considering whether Congress had created a cause of action, which is a manifestation of the more freewheeling judicial approach to recognizing causes action that then existed.

Today, there are two schools of thought about what authorizes litigation to enforce Section 106. The choice between them may have consequences primarily for the timing of such suits. The older line of decisions maintains that Congress impliedly created a cause of action directly under the NHPA. At least two federal circuit courts of appeals have implied a cause of action from Section 305 of NHPA, which provides:

> In any civil action brought in any United States district court by any interested person to enforce this division, if the person substantially prevails in the action, the court may award attorney's fees, expert witness fees, and other costs of participating in the civil action, as the court considers reasonable.

54 U.S.C. § 307105. The court in *Boarhead Corp. v. Erickson*, 923 F.2d 1011 (3d Cir. 1991), for example, in addition to citing the long established judicial practice of entertaining suits to enforce Section 106, rather summarily interpreted Section 305 to mean that "Congress must have intended to establish a private right of action to interested parties * * * in these situations." *Id.* at 1017.

Certainly, the language of Section 305 is broad, referring to "any civil action brought * * * by any interested person." Even if it does not expressly authorize suits, it certainly promotes them by providing private litigants with a valuable right to request fees whenever they do prevail in a suit.

More recent decisions have considered the issue in greater depth and have held that private litigants must bring suits under the Administrative Procedure Act (APA), the important federal statute structuring judicial review of administrative actions, which makes any final agency action reviewable in court. *See* 5 U.S.C. §§ 701–06. The APA thus creates an explicit cause of action against federal agencies for actions that are contrary to law or that are "arbitrary and capricious." In *San Carlos Apache Tribe v. United States*, 417 F.3d 1091 (9th Cir. 2005), the court held that Congress did not create a private right of action under Section 106, but it did permit the plaintiffs to pursue their explicit statutory cause of action under the APA. Seeking to follow Supreme Court precedent, the appeals court noted that Section 106 provides only "directives to federal government actors," which can be enforced under the APA, rather than rights that could be enforced against some third party, like a state or a private entity. *Id.* at 1095. The court also quoted Justice Stephen Breyer, from an opinion issued when he was a court of appeals judge, arguing that courts generally should not infer that Congress creates implied rights of action against federal defendants because the availability of review under the APA eliminates the need for a new private right of action. *See N.A.A.C.P. v. Sec'y of Hous. & Urban Dev.*, 817 F.2d 149, 152 (1st Cir. 1987). The *San Carlos Apache Tribe* court also held that Section 305 "does not authorize suit against federal agencies" but does afford attorney's fees to parties that prevail in claims brought pursuant to the APA. *See San Carlos Apache Tribe*, 417 F.3d at 1099. *See also Nat'l Tr. for Historic Pres. v. Blanck*, 938 F. Supp. 908, 914–15 (D.D.C. 1996).

In most respects, it matters little whether a plaintiff's action lies under the NHPA directly or under the APA. Any court's evaluation of an agency's compliance with the requirements of the NHPA will be governed by the deferential standards of the APA, which directs courts to invalidate agency action that is "arbitrary, capricious, an abuse of discretion, or otherwise not in accordance with law." 5 U.S.C. § 706(2)(A). The crucial point is that a court does not substitute its views for those of the agency but evaluates on the basis of the record before the agency as to whether the agency followed legal requirements and made reasonable decisions. Courts have followed this substantive aspect of the APA even when they have viewed a plaintiff's suit as arising under the NHPA.

There might be a significant procedural difference about when litigation may be brought. Advocates pressing for a right of action under Section 106 are concerned about the provision of the APA limiting judicial review to "final agency action for which there is no other adequate remedy in a court." *See id.* § 704. Generally speaking, the APA does not permit courts to intervene in administrative processes until they are complete. Then, it authorizes a court to consider all aspects of the agency's decision. Plaintiffs must identify final agency action and not just complain broadly about federal involvement. *See Karst Envtl. Educ. & Prot., Inc. v. Envtl. Prot. Agency*, 475 F.3d 1291, 1297–98 (D.C. Cir. 2007). Nor can a plaintiff complain if the agency segments the project to avoid application of Section 106, or engages in anticipatory demolition or destruction of a historic resource prior to final agency action. Moreover, a complaining party must exhaust all administrative remedies before seeking judicial review under the APA. Thus, an agency's failure to consult with an affected party, for example, could be taken to court only at the conclusion of the Section 106 process in which the party had requested consultation. The court in *San Carlos Apache Tribe* articulated the opposite concern: "Were litigants able to sue directly under NHPA, they would be able to sidestep the traditional requirements of administrative review under the APA without express Congressional authorization." *San Carlos Apache Tribe*, 417 F.3d at 1096. There are both costs and benefits to holding off judicial intervention in agency action until the administrative process is complete.

Some federal activity may never result in final agency action. A student author argued that the federal activity at issue in the *San Carlos Apache Tribe* case—day-to-day operation of a federal dam—might never result in final agency action, thereby precluding any judicial review. *See* Timothy J. Famulare, Note, *Has* Sandoval *Doomed the Private Right of Action Under the National Historic Preservation Act?* 16 B.U. PUB. INT. L.J. 73, 91–92 (2006). Sophisticated parties may remedy this lacuna by formally requesting the agency to consider operation of the dam an undertaking subject to Section 106; a direct refusal by the agency then might well be considered final agency action on that point. The APA defines final agency action to include "failure to act." 5 U.S.C. § 551(13). Where an agency maintains a policy of inaction in the face of an explicit statutory mandate, a court may set that policy aside. Thus, parties may generally maneuver agencies into final action, although agencies may seek to avoid it.

Which side has the better of the legal argument? When federal courts of appeals are split, a party denied the right to sue under Section 106 might seek resolution of the question in the Supreme Court. For most lawyers, the question of which legal opinion is correct is inseparable from predicting how the Court would resolve the issue. Here, it seems likely that Congress, when the NHPA was passed in 1966, did expect that private parties could sue directly under Section 106. At that time, the Supreme Court took a liberal view to implying private rights of action under federal substantive standards. However, more recent Supreme Court decisions resist implying a right of action. In *Alexander v. Sandoval*, 532 U.S. 275 (2001), the Court expressly rejected giving "dispositive weight to the expectations that the enacting Congress had formed in light of the contemporary legal context." *Id.* at 287–88 (internal quotation marks omitted). In other words, the Court refused to interpret Congress's actions against the backdrop of how courts implied rights of action at the time Congress acted. Rather, the Court focused primarily on the text and structure of the statute. Given that approach, it seems unlikely that the Supreme Court would find an implied right of action under Section 106. The *San Carlos Apache Tribe* court sought to apply the Supreme Court's current approach, and there seems little reason to believe that it got that analysis wrong. This seems especially true given that Justice Breyer, who dissented in *Sandoval*, has written so forcefully against implying actions against federal agencies that can be brought under the APA. A party who wished courts to recognize a private right of action under Section 106 would be foolish to pursue the question in the current Supreme Court.

3. TIMING OF SUIT

When a suit may be brought is governed by several legal doctrines. Above, we discussed the need for final agency action before judicial review may be sought under the Administrative Procedures Act, which may result in a finding that a suit has been brought too soon. Here, we will discuss when a suit has been brought too late.

The National Historic Preservation Act contains no statute of limitations, which would bar the initiation of suit after some period after it could have first been brought, and courts have not sought to identify one to attach to it. Rather, they have used the equitable doctrine of laches, under which courts will bar suit when the plaintiff has indulged in unreasonable delay in bringing suit, which has exposed the defendant to undue prejudice. One court invoked laches to bar a Section 106 challenge by plaintiffs seeking to prevent the imminent demolition of a building because they had long known about the threat of demolition but had not sought judicial relief, while defendant in the meantime had expended large sums buying the building. *Comm. to Save the Fox Bldg. v. Birmingham Branch of the Fed. Reserve Bank*, 497 F. Supp. 504, 511, 513 (N.D. Ala. 1980). The court's application of laches to the facts of that case seems questionable, given the plaintiff's participation in many non-litigation efforts to save the building.

A more appropriate approach is shown in *CA 79-2516 WATCH (Waterbury Action to Conserve our Heritage Inc.) v. Harris*, 603 F.2d 310 (2d Cir. 1979), where the court rejected an argument for laches under broadly similar circumstances of a long-festering dispute about demolition. The court affirmed the trial court's view that laches did not bar the plaintiff's suit, "because the buildings about which they were concerned had not yet been demolished and because the plaintiffs could properly rely upon the federal agencies' performing their statutory duties." *Id.* at 315. The Second Circuit panel characterized the trial court's decision as "surely correct in view of the public interest in preserving the historic sites that remain and the continuing nature of HUD's supervision over acquisition, demolition, and other project activities." *Id.* at 315–16. It makes little sense to encourage preservationists to turn to the courts while there are ongoing discussions with the agency about the fate of a historic site.

Courts sometimes will dismiss suits in analogous circumstances using the doctrine of mootness, meaning that events have moved to the point where there is no longer a live dispute. In an early case, a court first had restrained an agency from demolition without engaging in the Section 106 process, but later dismissed the case as moot when the agency subsequently entered into consultation, reached agreements, and apologized for past failures. *Don't Tear It Down, Inc. v. Gen. Servs. Admin.*, 401 F. Supp. 1194, 1199 (D.D.C. 1975). Similarly, where the action that would have been subject to Section 106 review has already been completed, a claim will be dismissed as moot. *Caddo Nation of Okla. v. Wichita & Affiliated Tribes*, 786 Fed. Appx. 837 (10th Cir. 2019) (holding that NHPA and National Environmental Policy Act claims were moot to the extent that a history center was already completed).

More common are cases where an agency already has approved or provided funds for an undertaking by a non-federal party, but objectors complain that it did not comply with the NHPA. One example of such a case is *Gettysburg Battlefield Pres. Ass'n v. Gettysburg Coll.*, 799 F. Supp. 1571 (M.D. Pa. 1992), dealing with the National Park Service's swap of parcels of land with private developers who aimed to build an intrusive observation tower on the land they had obtained. When citizens sought to invoke Section 106 to prevent construction, the court held that the case was moot because the National Park Service no longer owned the property. In other words, as the court put it: "if the relevant federal agency retains no authority to terminate or significantly impact the project, a NHPA remedy similarly makes no sense." *Id.* at 1580–81. The Third Circuit, in a decision on which the *Gettysburg Battlefield Preservation Association* court relied, further clarified that the NHPA applies "to ongoing Federal actions as long as a Federal agency has opportunity to exercise authority at any stage of an undertaking where alterations might be made to modify its impact on historic preservation goals." *Morris Cty. Tr. for Historic Pres. v. Pierce*, 714 F.2d 271, 280 (3d Cir. 1983). The gist of these decisions is that cases are moot when the agency has acted so as to no longer have effective control over an undertaking.

4. REMEDIES

Here, it is important to recall that Section 106 imposes only procedural duties on federal agencies. When a court finds that an agency has failed to follow these procedures, it will order the agency to do so before proceeding with the undertaking. The court, itself, should not make any determinations about the eligibility of properties or about the effects of the undertakings, but it can require the agency to do so and to set aside agency findings that are arbitrary and capricious. *See generally Citizens to Pres. Overton Park, Inc. v. Volpe*, 401 U.S. 402 (1971). Although a court may require agencies to deliberate about historic buildings, it cannot order them expend funds to preserve the buildings. *Nat'l Tr. for Historic Pres. v. Blanck*, 938 F. Supp. 908, 925 (D.D.C. 1996).

If necessary, a court may enjoin demolition or alteration of a historic property until an agency fulfills its Section 106 duties. This is rarely necessary because agencies will readily comply with a court's determination of how the law applies to them. In *Merritt Parkway Conservancy v. Mineta*, 424 F. Supp. 2d 396, 425–26 (D. Conn. 2006), a case decided pursuant to Section 4(f) of the Department of Transportation Act (and excerpted in Chapter 5), the court indicated that it would enjoin any damage to the historic highway while the agency conducted its necessary study, unless the parties agreed to continue a voluntary moratorium on construction. Such an injunction can bind non-federal actors who have received federal funds or who are subject to federal approvals, so as to permit the federal agency's required consideration of preservation issues to have meaning.

Preliminary injunctions may also be issued to maintain the status quo while a court considers a complaint. To obtain such a preliminary injunction, a plaintiff must show that it is likely to succeed on the merits of its case, that it will suffer irreparable harm without the injunction, and that granting a preliminary injunction is in the public interest. Demolition of a building eligible for listing on the National Register constitutes the "irreparable harm" needed for a preliminary injunction. In other words: "[D]emolition is generally irreparable." *CA 79-2516 WATCH (Waterbury Action to Conserve our Heritage Inc.) v. Harris*, 603 F.2d 312 n.2 (2d Cir. 1979). That a judicial order preserving a building pending litigation generally will be in the public interest is shown by its eligibility for listing. *See Weintraub v. Rural Electrification Admin.*, 457 F. Supp. 78, 89 (M.D. Pa. 1978) (stating "the Court accepts the judgment of the Secretary of the Interior concerning this building's architectural and historic value").

5. ATTORNEY'S FEES

Section 305 of the National Historic Preservation Act (NHPA) expressly provides for payment of attorney's fees to plaintiffs' attorneys who win their cases. That provision states:

> In any civil action brought in any United States district court by any interested person to enforce this division, if the person substantially prevails in the action, the court may award attorney's fees, expert witness fees, and other costs of participating in the civil action, as the court considers reasonable.

54 U.S.C. § 307105. The NHPA provides attorney's fees more liberally than do other preservation statutes. In cases that combine claims under the NHPA, the National Environmental Policy Act, and Section 4(f) of the Department of Transportation Act, the plaintiffs cannot obtain fees under the NHPA unless the court has found that defendants have violated the NHPA, specifically. *Pres. Coal. of Erie Cty. v. Fed. Transit Admin.*, 356 F.3d 444, 456 (2d Cir. 2004).

NOTES & QUESTIONS

1. Based on what you know of the Section 106 processes, would you make any suggestions for improvements? For example, would you recommend expanding standing or limiting attorney's fees? In doing so, could you anticipate more or less public participation in the realization of the goals of Section 106?

2.   In 2010, the National Trust for Historic Preservation published a report that suggests improvements to the way Section 106 is implemented. *See* LESLIE E. BARRAS, NATIONAL TRUST FOR HISTORIC PRESERVATION, SECTION 106 OF THE NATIONAL HISTORIC PRESERVATION ACT: BACK TO BASICS (2010). Among other things, it suggested that federal agencies do more advance planning for historic properties and their treatment under federal laws (including the National Environmental Policy Act).

CHAPTER FOUR

ENVIRONMENTAL POLICY ACTS

Federal and state environmental protection statutes form an important part of the regulatory framework for historic preservation. Among these statutes, the most significant is the National Environmental Policy Act (NEPA). NEPA requires federal agencies to consider the impact of certain agency actions on the environment (including historic resources) and share their thinking with the public. Some of the state statutes modeled on NEPA—often called state environmental policy acts—go beyond study and require state agencies, or even private entities, to take reasonable action to protect historic resources. This Chapter considers the potential of both NEPA and state environmental policy acts to protect historic resources. It also discusses the complimentary, but complex, relationship between NEPA and the National Historic Preservation Act.

This Chapter is not intended to cover all legal issues at the intersection of historic preservation and the environment. In Chapter 1, we discuss the preservation of natural objects and introduce the modern challenge of climate change. In Chapter 12, we discuss international approaches to cultural heritage in the face of climate change. The law in those areas is rapidly evolving.

A. THE NATIONAL ENVIRONMENTAL POLICY ACT

The National Environmental Policy Act (NEPA), signed into law by President Nixon on New Year's Day in 1970, boldly declares it the policy of the federal government to use "all practicable means and measures" to promote "productive harmony" between environmental and other social values. NEPA embraces, within the "environment," historic and cultural resources. It provides that:

> [I]t is the continuing responsibility of the Federal Government to use all practicable means, consistent with other essential considerations of national policy, to improve and coordinate Federal plans, functions, programs, and resources to the end that the Nation may * * * (4) preserve important historic, cultural, and natural aspects of our national heritage.

42 U.S.C. § 4331(b). NEPA goes on to specifically require that federal agencies prepare, for "major Federal actions significantly affecting the quality of the human environment," detailed reports on the probable environmental impacts of such actions, and that they consider alternatives to such action. *Id.* § 4332(C). As a consequence, NEPA requires that agencies prepare environmental impact statements (EISs)

that address the adverse effects on historic resources and discuss alternatives to the proposed project.

In addition to setting out the requirement that agencies consider the impact of their actions on protected resources, NEPA created the Council on Environmental Quality (CEQ) in the executive office of the President. 42 U.S.C. § 4342. The NEPA process is now governed by detailed procedural requirements in the CEQ regulations. 40 C.F.R. Part 1500. The regulations are binding on federal agencies and are entitled to substantial deference from courts as interpretations of the statute. *See Andrus v. Sierra Club*, 442 U.S. 347, 357–58 (1979) ("CEQ's interpretation of NEPA is entitled to substantial deference"). They define all of NEPA's key terms. For example, they specify that environmental effects to be studied in an EIS include "aesthetic, historic, [and] cultural" effects. 40 C.F.R. § 1508.8(b). As another example, the regulations define a "major federal action" to include "projects and programs entirely or partly financed, assisted, conducted, regulated, or approved by federal agencies; new or revised agency rules, regulations, plans, policies, or procedures; and legislative proposals." *Id.* § 1508.18.

An agency can exclude from the NEPA process those actions that it has found, in a rulemaking, not to individually or cumulatively have a significant effect on the environment. *Id.* § 1508.4. If uncertain whether a specific action constitutes a major federal action, the agency may prepare an environmental assessment (EA), which provides a relatively short account of the project and explains whether an EIS is necessary. If the agency decides that it need not prepare an EIS, it issues a "finding of no significant impact" (FONSI). If the agency decides to prepare an EIS, it should first consult with other agencies and with the public to determine the scope of the EIS, including whether it needs to consider "connected actions." It then prepares a draft EIS, which is presented for public comment, followed by a final EIS. The CEQ regulations stress that the discussion of alternatives is "the heart of the environmental impact statement," and mandates that the agency "[r]igorously explore and objectively evaluate all reasonable alternatives." *Id.* § 1502.14. The agency's final decision on the project, including why it chose the course it did, rather than the alternatives, should be contained in a "record of decision" (ROD). This process has limited the frequency with which an EIS must be prepared. For example, between ninety and ninety-nine percent of federally funded highway projects proceed under a categorical exclusion, which involves only the preparation of an EA. *See* U.S. DEPARTMENT OF TRANSPORTATION, NATIONAL ENVIRONMENTAL POLICY ACT CATEGORICAL EXCLUSION SURVEY REVIEW (Nov. 27, 2012).

Judicial review may be invoked for the major decisions made by an agency in the NEPA process. The decision not to prepare an EIS will be reviewed under the "arbitrary and capricious" standard of the Administrative Procedure Act (APA), which establishes (among other things) how agencies must adopt regulations and how courts must review agency action. Under that statute, a reviewing court must "hold unlawful and set aside agency action, findings, and conclusions found to be—(A) arbitrary, capricious, an abuse of discretion, or otherwise not in accordance with law." 5 U.S.C. § 706(2); *see also Marsh v. Or. Nat. Res. Council*, 490 U.S. 360, 377 (1989) (finding that a court must uphold an agency decision not to prepare a supplemental EIS when it is not arbitrary). Courts will examine, under the same standard, the scope of the agency's EIS and the range of alternatives it considered. *See, e.g., Vt. Yankee Nuclear Power Corp. v. Nat. Res. Def. Council, Inc.*, 435 U.S. 519, 549–56 (1978) (finding that an agency decision not to study a proposed alternative violates NEPA only when it is arbitrary); *Kleppe v. Sierra Club*, 427 U.S. 390 (1976) (finding that an agency decision to prepare EISs only for individual coal leases, and not for regional effects, must be upheld if it is not arbitrary). Although the standards for judicial review of agency decisions in the NEPA process are now clear, court review will usually be unavailing. The Supreme Court has narrowly construed the general commands of NEPA, unless the agency has failed to follow the specific requirements of the CEQ regulations.

A substantial body of legal literature considers NEPA generally. We focus here on how NEPA applies to historic resources and on how it interfaces with the National Historic Preservation Act (NHPA). This topic includes both NEPA's own requirements for considering historic resources and the use of the NEPA process to satisfy the separate but overlapping requirements of Section 106 of the NHPA.

1. NEPA's CONSIDERATION REQUIREMENT

Recent Past Preservation Network v. Latschar
701 F. Supp. 2d 49 (D.D.C. 2010)

■ HOGAN, D.J.

I.   Background

The Recent Past Preservation Network ("RPPN"), Dion Neutra, and Christine Madrid French filed this lawsuit against the National Park Service and the named public officials in December 2006, seeking declaratory and injunctive relief "to ensure that the Park Service does not demolish the historic Gettysburg Cyclorama Center . . . ." The Gettysburg Cyclorama Center ("Cyclorama Center" or "the Center") was commissioned by the Park Service and designed by architect Richard Neutra to serve as a visitor center and to display a 356-foot long cylindrical painting by Paul Philippoteaux depicting "Pickett's Charge," a pivotal attack during the Battle of Gettysburg. The Center remains on Ziegler's Grove in Gettysburg National Park, but it no longer serves either of these functions.[1] In June 1999, the Park Service published a Final General Management Plan/Environmental Impact Statement (GMP/EIS) that included (as Alternative C) plans to remove the Center as part of an effort to rehabilitate the site to reflect conditions in 1863. On November 23, 1999, the Park Service issued a Record of Decision ("ROD") announcing its decision to implement Alternative C of the GMP/EIS. Based in part on the Center's eligibility for listing in the National Register of Historic Places, Plaintiffs contend that the Park Service has failed to comply with the requirements of the National Environmental Policy Act of 1969 ("NEPA"), 42 U.S.C. §§ 4231–4370f, and the National Historic Preservation Act ("NHPA"), 16 U.S.C. §§ 470 *et seq.* [EDS.: moved to title 54, National Historic Preservation Act, Pub. L. No. 113–287, 128 Stat. 3094 *et seq.*] * * *

[EDS.: The parties filed cross motions for summary judgment, which were referred to Magistrate Judge Kay, who issued a report recommending] that the Court grant summary judgment in favor of Plaintiffs on their NEPA claims and grant summary judgment in favor of Defendants on the NHPA claims. Defendants filed timely objections * * *. Plaintiffs filed a timely response, but raised no objections. They instead encourage the Court to adopt both Reports in full. The Court here considers *de novo* the portions of the Reports to which objections have been made.

II.   Analysis * * *

B.   Second Report and Recommendation: Cross-Motions for Summary Judgment

1.   NHPA Claims

Plaintiffs contend that the Park Service failed to properly consider the re-use and preservation of the Cyclorama Center as required by NHPA Section 110(a)(1). They also contend that the Park Service failed to prepare an adequate preservation program under NHPA § 110(a)(2). Magistrate Judge Kay determined the § 110(a)(1) claim to be time barred by 28 U.S.C. § 2401(a). Judge Kay also recommends granting summary judgment in favor of Defendants on the § 110(a)(2) claim based on evidence that an agency-wide preservation program exists and Plaintiffs' failure to demonstrate any deficiency in the program. The Plaintiffs filed no objections. The Court accordingly adopts the Second Report with regard to Plaintiffs' NHPA Claims, and will grant summary judgment in favor of Defendants on those claims.

---

[1]   The Center opened in 1962 but ceased to function as the visitor center and museum in 1971. The painting now resides in the Gettysburg National Military Park Museum and Visitor Center on Baltimore Pike.

2.   NEPA Claims

a.   Statutory Background

NEPA requires federal agencies to prepare, and make publicly available, an environmental impact statement ("EIS") before taking any major action "significantly affecting the quality of the human environment." *Citizens Against Burlington, Inc. v. Busey*, 938 F.2d 190, 193 (D.C. Cir. 1991). An EIS should "provide full and fair discussion of significant environmental impacts and inform decisionmakers and the public of the reasonable alternatives which would avoid or minimize adverse impacts or enhance the quality of the human environment." 40 C.F.R. § 1502.1. The EIS requirement obligates agencies to "take a 'hard look' at the environmental consequences before taking a major action." *Balt. Gas & Elec. Co. v. Nat. Res. Def. Council*, 462 U.S. 87, 97 (1983).

Council on Environmental Quality ("CEQ") regulations interpreting NEPA help agencies determine which actions require an EIS. *See* 40 C.F.R. § 1500.3 (2003). They permit an agency to prepare a more limited document (an Environmental Assessment or "EA"), if the agency's proposed action is neither categorically excluded from the requirement to produce an EIS nor would clearly require the production of an EIS. An EA is a "concise public document" that "[b]riefly provide[s] sufficient evidence and analysis for determining whether to prepare an [EIS]." 40 C.F.R. § 1508.9(a). If, pursuant to an EA, an agency determines that an EIS is not required, it must issue a "finding of no significant impact" ("FONSI"), which briefly presents the reasons why the proposed action will not have a significant impact on the human environment. CEQ regulations also impose a largely commonsense approach to paperwork and public notice.

NEPA imposes procedural requirements, but it does not divest agency decision makers of their authority to make professional decisions by compelling a particular result. Indeed, "[i]f the adverse environmental effects of the proposed action are adequately identified and evaluated, the agency is not constrained by NEPA from deciding that other values outweigh the environmental costs." *Robertson v. Methow Valley Citizens Council*, 490 U.S. 332, 350 (1989). In reviewing an EIS, the Court considers whether "the agency has made an adequate compilation of relevant information, has analyzed it reasonably, has not ignored pertinent data, and has made disclosures to the public." *Stewart Park & Reserve Coal. v. Slater*, 352 F.3d 545, 557 (2d Cir. 2003) (internal quotation marks omitted).

Figures 4-1 & 4-2:
Views of Richard Neutra's Cyclorama Center,
Gettysburg, PA

b.   Discussion

Plaintiffs contend that the Park Service failed to produce an adequate implementation level or site-specific environmental assessment or statement for the demolition of the Cyclorama Center in violation of NEPA.[7] Specifically, they claim that, with regard to the Center, the Park Service failed to prepare an EIS as required by 42 U.S.C. § 4332(2)(C) (Count I), failed to prepare an EA pursuant to 40 C.F.R. §§ 1501.3 and [EDS: 1501.4] (Count II), and failed to adequately analyze alternative methods of "restoring" Ziegler's Grove as required by 42 U.S.C. § 4332(2)(E) (Count III). They argue that these [EDS. sic] each of these omissions constitutes a failure to act under 5 U.S.C. § 706(1) and that the decision to destroy the Center without producing such assessments is an action that is arbitrary, capricious, or otherwise not in accordance with law under 5 U.S.C. § 706(2). Defendants claim that the Park Service's June 1999 Final General Management Plan/EIS ("GMP/EIS") satisfies NEPA's analytical requirements. Defendants also argue that the November 1999 Final Record of Decision ("ROD") constitutes notice of final agency action with regard to the Cyclorama Center. Plaintiffs dispute this, arguing that the Park Service contemplated, but never issued, a site-specific EIS.

Magistrate Judge Kay determined that the [EDS: sic] neither the 1999 GMP/EIS nor the ROD satisfied NEPA requirements with regard to the Center, noting that the 1999 GMP/EIS left the door open for "more detailed assessments of impacts . . . as part of necessary implementation planning."[8] Thus, the limitations clock did not begin ticking until some undetermined time after 1999. Judge Kay recommends that the Court grant summary judgment in favor of Plaintiffs on their NEPA claims because "the Park Service did not properly evaluate the site-specific environmental impacts of demolition of the Cyclorama Center and did not properly consider alternatives to demolition."

i.   Statute of Limitations

Defendants contend that Magistrate Judge Kay incorrectly determined that the 1999 ROD did not amount to notice of final agency action with regard to the Cyclorama Center. They accurately explain that NEPA requires agencies to evaluate environmental consequences before committing to any actions that might affect the quality of the human environment. Defendants then argue, without any supporting citation, that "an irreversible and irretrievable commitment of resources was

---

[7]   Agencies must make "diligent efforts to involve the public in preparing and implementing their NEPA procedures." 40 C.F.R. § 1506.6. Under Department of Interior regulations, the Park Service must, "to the extent practicable, provide for public notification and public involvement when an environmental assessment is being prepared. However, the methods for providing public notification and opportunities for public involvement are at the discretion of the Responsible Official." 43 C.F.R. § 46.305.

[8]   The Second Report cites internal Park Service guidance regarding site-specific analyses, including Director's Orders and the "DO-12 Handbook." To the extent the Report relies on these documents, Defendants object to its conclusion that the Park Service contemplated a future site-specific EIS on demolition of the Cyclorama Center on the grounds that the materials are not judicially enforceable. Defendants' argument is inapposite. Even without regard for these documents, Defendants have failed to show that the Park Service provided notice sufficient to trigger the limitations clock or to satisfy NEPA. Indeed, Judge Kay's analysis on this point is based primarily on the Park Service's description of the 1999 GMP/EIS as a "programmatic statement."

made, with the concomitant obligation to comply with NEPA." There is no support in the record for this notion.[10] Moreover, Defendants' argument conflates ripeness with final action for purposes of determining the limitations period. Even if a claim became ripe in 1999, Defendants bear the burden of demonstrating that Plaintiffs had sufficient notice to set the limitations clock running. *See, e.g., Sprint Commc'ns Co., L.P. v. Fed. Commc'ns Comm'n*, 76 F.3d 1221, 1226 (D.C. Cir. 1996) (noting that a court may deem a cause of action not to have accrued during a period of concealment). * * *

Defendants also contend that "the administrative record reflects a complete awareness by Plaintiffs and others that the Park Service intended the ROD to be the final agency action with regard to demolition of the Cyclorama Building." Defendants point to evidence indicating that, months prior to the publication of the Final GMP/EIS, Plaintiff Dion Neutra was informed that the preferred alternative would require demolition. Yet Defendants provide no authority suggesting that such awareness on the part of the individual plaintiffs would preclude the APA [EDS: Administrative Procedure Act] claims raised here. Rather than providing public notice of a final decision with regard to the Center, the ROD and GMP/EIS indicated a likelihood of a future, site-specific statement. * * *

ii.   Site-Specific Analysis

Defendants further suggest that the Second Report wrongly disregards the project-specific analyses referenced in the 1999 GMP/EIS. Specifically, they point to the 1995 and 1996 Draft Development Concept Plans/Environmental Assessments and the 1999 MOA between the Park Service, the Pennsylvania Historic Preservation Office, and the Advisory Council on Historic Preservation. The MOA does indicate that the decision to demolish was reached in August 1999, a few months before the ROD was issued. But as Judge Kay explained, neither the Draft EAs[11] nor the MOA was properly incorporated by reference into the Final EIS or ROD.[12] The Court cannot countenance disregard for NEPA's public notice requirements by considering unincorporated documents in its evaluation of the Park Service's actions here.

---

[10] Indeed, Defendants' counsel indicated that the Park Service had not solicited bids for demolition of the Center as of November 2008.

[11] Moreover, both the 1995 and 1996 Draft DCP/EAs were abandoned. Additionally, the 1996 DCP/EA did not invite comments, and the record does not reflect any response to the comments that the Park Service nevertheless received.

[12] The Final ROD does include, in an Appendix, a report that notes the "fatal" effect the Park Service's proposed action would have on the Center. Overall, however, the ROD discusses the effects of demolition and new construction only in general, park-wide terms (e.g., a loss of two acres of wetlands), and it is unclear about the fates of different facilities. *See, e.g.*, ROD at 13 ("Construction activities related to a *relocation* of the park's museum complex, visitor facilities and administrative facilities to a site removed from its prime resources have the potential to cause environmental harm." (emphasis added)).

iii. Alternatives to Demolition

Defendants also attack the Second Report's conclusion that the Park Service failed to properly consider alternatives to demolition of the Cyclorama Center. Magistrate Judge Kay's analysis properly focuses on the 1999 GMP/EIS, which provides a park-wide overview,[13] but does not provide the reader with an analysis of the Center's demolition and removal, either by way of discussion or adequate reference to another source. Consequently, Defendants' argument that any claim regarding alternatives to demolition not raised in comments before the agency was waived is unavailing. With regard to consideration of alternatives, the Court is careful not to treat the absence of evidence as evidence of absence. It may be that the Park Service conducted sufficient analyses yet failed to provide adequate notice,[14] but that would not change the result here.

iv. Scope of Remedies

Finally, Defendants object to the relief recommended by Judge Kay. They claim that an order requiring an EIS would "usurp" the agency's authority to decide whether a site-specific EIS is appropriate: "While a proposal contemplating the demolition of historic property certainly triggers NEPA obligations to undertake a review, as such a proposal is a 'major federal action,' it does [*sic*], on its own necessarily dictate the level of appropriate review." Defendants point to Section IV of the Second Report, which states, in pertinent part: "Because the Cyclorama Center was declared eligible for listing in the National Register of Historic Places . . . in 1998, any demolition of the building would itself be a significant impact, and therefore a major federal action affecting the environment and requiring an EIS under NEPA." This passage is incorrect. *See* 36 C.F.R. § 800.8 ("A finding of adverse effect on a historic property does not necessarily require an EIS under NEPA"). Accordingly, the Court will modify Section IV of the Report to ensure it is consistent with Judge Kay's concluding recommendation "that Defendants be ordered to undertake a full implementation-level and site-specific *environmental analysis* on the demolition of the Cyclorama Center and non-demolition alternatives before any implementing action is taken on the Center."[15]

---

[13] *See, e.g.*, Final GMP/EIS at 169–70 (A.R. 315–16) (noting that the park contains 148 historic buildings and that the "sheer number of buildings and structures places strain on the park's financial and staff resources").

[14] Scattered throughout the record are facts that support the Park Service's decision. The Section 106 Report describes the disrepair of the Center, the original plan to demolish the Center after seven years, mitigation measures, and reason for declining to rehabilitate the building ("Because the building is poured-in-place concrete, it cannot be jacked up"). *See also* Advisory Council Finding at 11 (The siting of the Center, "by today's standards, would be rejected out of hand.").

[15] Since Defendants concede this is a major federal action, they must determine whether it will "significantly affect[ ] the quality of the human environment." 42 U.S.C. § 4332(C). CEQ regulations provide options on how to make this determination, with the result being either (a) a categorical determination, or (b) an environmental assessment. 40 C.F.R. § 1501.4. After an

c.   Disposition of NEPA Claims

With regard to Section IV of the Second Report, the Court agrees that, with regard to the restoration of Ziegler's Grove and the demolition of the Cyclorama Center, the Park Service failed to produce an EIS sufficient to meet its obligations under NEPA. The Court does not agree that the Center's eligibility for listing in the National Register of Historic Places compels the conclusion that a site-specific EIS is required. * * * The upshot is that the Park Service must determine whether the proposed demolition and restoration constitutes a significant impact for purposes of 42 U.S.C. § 4332 and proceed accordingly. Whether that means a categorical determination or an environmental assessment followed by a FONSI or an EIS (or Supplemental EIS) is for the Park Service to determine.

Consistent with the other findings adopted here, the Court finds that the Park Service produced neither an adequate EIS, *see* 42 U.S.C. § 4332(C), nor any other assessment or determination consistent with 40 C.F.R. § 1501.4 covering the site of the Cyclorama Center. The Court agrees that by failing to take such action in satisfaction of NEPA before reaching a final decision to demolish the Center, the Park Service withheld or unreasonably delayed agency action under 5 U.S.C. § 706(1). The Court also agrees that the Park Service's final decision to destroy the Center and rehabilitate Ziegler's Grove without first satisfying NEPA constitutes an unlawful agency action under 5 U.S.C. § 706(2). Accordingly, the Court will grant summary judgment in favor of Plaintiffs on Counts I and II. The Court need not rule on the merits of Count III, as the Court's resolution of Counts I and II renders it moot, and the inadequate discussion of alternatives in the GMP/EIS has already been noted here.

III. Conclusion * * *

Proper, legally sufficient notice is a theme here—Plaintiffs must adequately explain the utility of extra-record evidence to the Court, and the Park Service must adequately describe its intentions to the public. As Magistrate Judge Kay noted, the Park Service may pursue the rehabilitation of the Ziegler's Grove cite [EDS.: sic] as its officials see fit in the exercise of their professional judgment. But that judgment must be informed, reached and announced in compliance with NEPA.

NOTES & QUESTIONS

1.   Richard Neutra (1892–1970) was an Austrian-born architect, who developed a modernist style that helped shape Southern California homes in the mid-twentieth century. His Visitor Center and Cyclorama Building at Gettysburg, shown in Figures 4-1 and 4-2, was one of his few public buildings in the East. It was one of the first "visitor centers" constructed by the Park

---

environmental assessment, the Park Service may prepare and issue either an EIS or a FONSI. *Id.; see also id.* § 1508.9.

Service, seeking to manage and instruct the large number of visitors who crowded national parks in the post-war era. The Park Service consciously chose to employ modern architecture for early visitor centers. *See* ETHAN CARR, MISSION 66: MODERNISM AND THE NATIONAL PARK DILEMMA (2007).

Opinions about the Neutra visitor center at Gettysburg were sharply divided. Architectural historians saw it as a major work of an important architect, gracefully expressing its period. The Park Service argued that it never functioned well as a visitor center and should never have been built on the actual battlefield, where it impairs interpretation of the battle. Is there a right answer as to what the Park Service should do with the Neutra building? How might preparation of an EIS help improve decision-making here?

In 2012, the National Park Service updated its EIS, finding that demolition was better overall than mothballing the building or moving it. In 2013, the Cyclorama Building was demolished. What does this result say about the impact of the NEPA process?

2.   The plaintiffs in *Latschar* did not argue that the Park Service's decision to demolish the Neutra building violated Section 106 of the NHPA, even though they believed that the Service had not adequately considered the effects of its actions on that historic structure. That seems to be because the Advisory Council on Historic Preservation and the SHPO had signed off on a Memorandum of Agreement completing the Section 106 process to the satisfaction of the consulting parties. What does NEPA add to the Section 106 process?

3.   Plaintiffs seeking to challenge an agency's determination about whether an EIS is required must take care to file their cases in a timely manner. Consider the facts behind *Gettysburg Battlefield Pres. Ass'n v. Gettysburg Coll.*, 799 F. Supp. 1571 (M.D. Pa. 1992), *aff'd*, 989 F.2d 487 (3d Cir. 1993). The story of that case began in 1987, when Congress directed the National Park Service to conduct a boundary study that would more clearly define the boundaries of the Gettysburg National Military Park. After the study was completed, the Park Service recommended that a 7.5 acre parcel be removed to make way for the rerouting of the Gettysburg Railroad from its location on the Gettysburg College campus. The Park Service conducted an environmental assessment of the proposed rerouting, which resulted in a "finding of no significant impact." Congress later adopted the recommended boundaries and gave the Secretary of the Interior the authority to acquire and convey park land, as well as exchange non-park federal land under certain circumstances. Using this authority, the Park Service deeded the 7.5 acre parcel to Gettysburg College in exchange for conservation easements over another Gettysburg College parcel and some money.

The most significant issue in the case appeared to be whether the exchange of the 7.5 acres was a major federal action subject to an environmental impact statement. However, the court never reached that question. It found that: "Given the lack of any showing or allegation of any *continuing control* by federal defendants over the challenged project, NEPA provides no jurisdiction to order an EIS or enjoin private parties here." *Id.* at

1577–78 (emphasis added). It thus considered the case moot and rejected the plaintiff nonprofit organization's NEPA claims. Does this case suggest to federal agencies that when they want to dispose of property, they should do so quickly?

4.   How should we evaluate the effectiveness of the NEPA process? Proponents and critics have debated this question since the statute was enacted. Some environmentalists have lamented that the protections of the statute are only procedural, not substantive. Professor Joseph Sax famously wrote: "[T]he emphasis on the redemptive quality of procedural reform is about nine parts myth and one part coconut oil." Joseph Sax, *The (Unhappy) Truth About NEPA*, 26 OKLA. L. REV. 239, 239 (1973). Supporters of government projects have lamented the time and effort devoted to creating voluminous reports, much of which consists of technical data of doubtful interest to anyone. NEPA also provides opportunities for inveterate opponents to delay a project by raising and litigating missing elements in the agency's NEPA analysis.

On the other hand, NEPA has promoted increased agency openness and public participation in major federal projects. Experience suggests that many federal agencies otherwise did not, and would not now, take environmental effects, including damage to historic resources, into account in planning and implementing projects. With NEPA, the most environmentally damaging projects never make it past the drawing board. Moreover, defenders of NEPA argue that the complaints about costs and delay greatly exaggerate the facts, especially since CEQ regulations have provided for tiering and categorical exclusions. *See* ROBERT G. DREHER, NEPA UNDER SIEGE: THE POLITICAL ASSAULT ON THE NATIONAL ENVIRONMENTAL POLICY ACT (2005). Do you think NEPA added value to agency decision-making in the above preservation cases commensurate with its costs?

5.   In some cases, a federal agency will determine that a full environmental impact statement is not necessary, and this determination will bring a legal challenge. Consider, for example, a suit brought by environmental advocacy groups to challenge the failure of the U.S. Forest Service to conduct an EIS when it permitted the vehicular retrieval of big game. The Ninth Circuit found that an EIS was not necessary, for four reasons: while retrieval might have a negative effect on the environment, the EAs did not raise substantial concerns; the project was neither highly controversial nor uncertain; and there did not appear to be precedential effect to this decision; and because the effects on threatened species would not be significant. *WildEarth Guardians v. Provencio*, 923 F.3d 655, 670–73 (9th Cir. 2019).

On the other hand, consider a suit brought by nonprofit conservation organizations against the Army Corps of Engineers, alleging that the Corps did not produce a required EIS. In that case, it was clear there would be adverse effects on significant sites, including Carter's Grove National Historic Landmark, and the Captain John Smith National Historic Trail (the only Congressionally-protected water trail). These adverse effects were sufficient to support a finding by the D.C. Circuit that an EIS was required under NEPA. *Nat'l Parks Conservation Assoc. v. Semonite*, 916 F.3d 1075 (D.C. Cir. 2019).

Do these decisions help to articulate a clear standard for federal agencies?

6. As the *Latschar* case suggests, courts are more used to taking a hard look at NEPA compliance than they are at Section 106 compliance, at least where the consulting parties have sanctioned the agency's efforts. Consider the relationship between the two statutes described in the following section.

2. NEPA AND NHPA

The relationship between the National Environmental Policy Act (NEPA) and the National Historic Preservation Act (NHPA) has significant implications on the way that historic resources are protected from potentially adverse federal government actions. As Chapter 3 described in greater detail, Section 106 of the NHPA requires that federal agencies "take into account the effect" of certain federal undertakings on any "district, site, building, structure, or object included on, or eligible for inclusion on, the National Register." 54 U.S.C. §§ 300308, 306108. Like Section 106 of the NHPA, NEPA imposes only procedural duties on agencies and not substantive outcomes. As the Ninth Circuit put it:

> Both Acts create obligations that are chiefly procedural in nature; both have the goal of generating information about the impact of federal actions on the environment; and both require that the relevant federal agency carefully consider the information produced. That is, both are designed to insure that the agency "stop, look, and listen" before moving ahead.

Pres. Coal., Inc. v. Pierce, 667 F.2d 851, 859 (9th Cir. 1982). Both acts require an agency to consider the significance of the resources that may be affected, as well as the nature and extent of the probable impact, and to develop and consider alternatives and mitigation measures. Under both statutes, the agency must share information with, and solicit comments from, the public before making a final decision.

While the two statutes were enacted to meet similar goals, there are real differences between them, and in general, the NHPA has been more restrictive on agency action than has NEPA. The most significant differences between NEPA and the NHPA are their scopes and their consultation requirements. NEPA, of course, requires consideration of a broad range of environmental effects, of which the effects on historic resources represent only one category. On the other hand, NEPA requires preparation of an EIS only for "major Federal actions significantly affecting the quality of the human environment," 42 U.S.C. § 4332(C), while the NHPA requires compliance with Section 106 for any "undertaking." As a prior executive director of the Advisory Council on Historic Preservation has explained:

By comparison, Section 106 obligates the agency not only to assess and disclose the effects of its actions, but also to consult with state and federal preservation agencies and other stakeholders to seek ways to avoid or reduce the harm. The agency ultimately retains final authority for the decision, but in reality consultation normally results in negotiated solutions. Thus, the protection afforded under Section 106 is significantly greater than under NEPA.

John M. Fowler, *The Federal Preservation Program*, *in* A RICHER HERITAGE: HISTORIC PRESERVATION IN THE TWENTY-FIRST CENTURY 52 (Robert E. Stipe, ed. 2003). For these reasons, NEPA will usually be less protective of historic properties than the NHPA will be.

In addition, NEPA contains quantitative measures which are absent from the NHPA. NEPA addresses "major" federal actions causing "significant" effects. *See* 40 C.F.R. § 1508.18. By contrast, the NHPA applies to any federal undertaking without regard to the scale of the probable effects. As Chapter 3 explains in greater detail, an undertaking includes "any project, activity, or program that can result in changes in the character or use of historic properties." *McMillan Park Comm. v. Nat'l Capital Planning Comm'n*, 968 F.2d 1283, 1285 (D.C. Cir. 1992) (quoting 36 C.F.R. § 800.2(*o*)). While any program or project significant enough to require NEPA review concerning historic or cultural resources will also require an NHPA process, many undertakings subject to the NHPA do not amount to "major Federal actions" under NEPA. The ACHP regulations provide for the differences in application, specifically stating that the finding of adverse effects (let alone a finding of an undertaking) under Section 106 does not necessarily require preparation of an EIS. Moreover, an agency's decision that a project is exempt from NEPA procedures does not mean that it is exempt from Section 106 review. 36 C.F.R. §§ 800.8(a)(1) & (b). The difference is reflected in the quantity of reviews: Only 543 EISs were filed with the Council on Environmental Quality (CEQ) in 2008, according to the CEQ website. The National Park Service reported for 2018 that State Historic Preservation Offices reviewed 130,500 Federal undertakings, compared to 101,500 in 2017, providing 95,200 National Register eligibility opinions (compared to 81,900 in 2017). Tribal Historic Preservation Offices reviewed 126,230 undertakings and made 7,000 eligibility opinions. NAT'L PARK SERV., HISTORIC PRESERVATION FUND ANNUAL REPORT 2018 2 (2019); NAT'L PARK SERV., HISTORIC PRESERVATION FUND ANNUAL REPORT 2017 2 (2018).

Despite these differences, the regulations for NEPA, the NHPA, and judicial interpretation of the two regimes have sought to construe them harmoniously. CEQ regulations require agencies to "[i]ntegrate the requirements of NEPA with other planning and environmental review procedures required by law * * * so that all such procedures run concurrently rather than consecutively." 40 C.F.R. § 1500.2(c). More specifically, these regulations require, where applicable, that the NEPA process incorporate the key elements of Section 106 review, as that review is set forth in the regulations promulgated by the Advisory Council on Historic Preservation (ACHP). In general, CEQ regulations direct that NEPA documents include "appropriate scoping, identification of historic properties, assessment of effects upon them, and consultation leading to resolution of any adverse effects." 36 C.F.R. § 800.8(a)(3). They require the agency to identify consulting parties and consult with them when preparing NEPA documents that identify historic resources, adverse effects upon them, and alternatives that may avoid, minimize, or mitigate such effects. *Id.* § 800.8(c)(1). Consulting parties possess special status to object to the adequacy of the treatment of historic resources in the documents, which require the agency to solicit ACHP comments and impose additional procedural duties upon the head of the agency to address ACHP comments agreeing with objections. *Id.* §§ 800.8(c)(2) & (3). The regulations go on to provide specific guidance for using the NEPA process to satisfy distinctive Section 106 requirements, including providing notice of intent to do so; full consultation with consulting parties (as determined by the ACHP regulations); development of alternatives to avoid, reduce, or mitigate adverse effects in consultation with those parties; and resolution of objections by consulting parties. *Id.* § 800.8(c).

Similarly, the ACHP regulations encourage federal agencies to "coordinate compliance with section 106 and the procedures in this part with any steps taken to meet the requirements of the National Environmental Policy Act." *Id.* § 800.8(a)(1). The ACHP regulations also create a process by which an agency can meet its NHPA duties while completing NEPA review. *See id.* § 800.8. The ACHP's authority to promulgate these regulations harmonizing NEPA and the NHPA was upheld in *Pres. Coal. of Erie Cty. v. Fed. Transit Admin.*, 356 F.3d 444, 454–55 (2d Cir. 2004) ("clearly a reasonable response to a situation involving the interplay of two federal statutes").

In construing the statutes and related regulations, some courts have gone too far in trying to harmonize judicial interpretation of statutes. A handful of courts have wrongly abrogated the threshold for application of Section 106 of the NHPA by tying it to the threshold criteria for requiring an EIS. Indeed, some courts have concluded that the threshold for finding an undertaking is the same as that for finding a major federal action. The Fourth Circuit, for example, has stated that: "The standard for triggering NHPA requirements is similar to that for the triggering of NEPA requirements." *Sugarloaf Citizens Ass'n v. Fed. Energy Regulatory Comm'n*, 959 F.2d 508, 515 (4th Cir. 1992). It is understandable that agencies and courts wish to harmonize the NHPA and NEPA because agencies simultaneously conduct reviews under the respective statutes concerning overlapping resources. Moreover, the implementing regulations for each statute take similar approaches to characterizing federal funding or permitting undertakings by non-federal entities. But such an equation ignores important differences in the language of the two statutes and in the regulations implementing them.

NEPA and the NHPA mandate separate, but overlapping, procedures, and requirements of both statutes must be observed when historic properties are affected by proposed federal actions. *Pres. Coal., Inc.*, 667 F.2d at 858. The independence of the two statutes is underscored by Section 110(a)(2)(i) of the NHPA, which provides: "Nothing in this Act shall be construed to require the preparation of an environmental impact statement where the statement would not otherwise be required under [NEPA]; or provide any exemption from any requirement respecting the preparation of an environmental impact statement under that Act." 54 U.S.C. § 306111. Moreover, the ACHP regulations harmonizing the two statutes provide: "If a project, activity or program is categorically excluded from NEPA review under an agency's NEPA procedures, the agency official shall determine if it still qualifies as an undertaking requiring review under section 106 pursuant to § 800.3(a)." 36 C.F.R. § 800.8(b). Agencies must take care to keep straight the distinctive requirements of both statutes, as is shown by the following case.

Mid States Coalition for Progress v. Surface Transportation Board

345 F.3d 520 (8th Cir. 2003)

■ MORRIS SHEPPARD ARNOLD, C.J.

Petitioners challenge the decision of the Surface Transportation Board issued January 30, 2002, giving final approval to the Dakota, Minnesota & Eastern Railroad Corporation's (DM & E) proposal to construct approximately 280 miles of new rail line to reach the coal mines of Wyoming's Powder River Basin (PRB) and to upgrade nearly 600 miles of existing rail line in Minnesota and South Dakota. They maintain that in giving its approval the Board violated 49 U.S.C. § 10901, the National Environmental Policy Act (NEPA) (42 U.S.C. §§ 4321–4370f), the National Historic Preservation Act (16 U.S.C. §§ 470 to 470w–6 [EDS.: moved to title 54, National Historic Preservation Act, Pub. L. No. 113–287, 128 Stat. 3094 *et seq.*]), and the Fort Laramie Treaty of 1868. Although we conclude that the Board should prevail on almost all of the issues raised by the petitioners, our rulings on a few issues require us to vacate the Board's decision and to remand for further proceedings not inconsistent with this opinion. * * *

[EDS.: The court examined, at length, the adequacy of the Draft Environmental Impact Statement (DEIS) and of the Final Environmental Impact Statement (FEIS) prepared by the Surface Transportation Board, finding them adequate in most respects but remanding them for further consideration of the effects of increased horn noise and coal consumption from additional trains.]

We next consider whether the Board has complied with § 106 of the National Historic Preservation Act (NHPA), 16 U.S.C. § 470f [EDS.: moved to 54 U.S.C. §§ 300308, 306108], which provides that a federal agency shall "take into account" the effect of its licensing decisions on properties "included in or eligible for inclusion in, the National Register [of Historic Places]." In order to carry out this broadly stated purpose, the Advisory Council on Historic Preservation (ACHP) has issued regulations implementing the NHPA, see 36 C.F.R. Part 800, which are binding on agencies. These regulations require that the relevant agency consult with a number of specified parties to identify historic properties, assess the adverse effects that the proposed project would have on those properties, and "seek ways to avoid, minimize or mitigate any adverse effects." 36 C.F.R. § 800.1(a). This process may be conducted separately, or, as in this case, in conjunction with an environmental review under NEPA. See 36 C.F.R. § 800.2(d)(3).

The Mid States Coalition first maintains that the Board failed to include all necessary parties in its consultation process. Under the regulations, an agency has a general duty to "provide the public with information about an undertaking and its effects on historic properties and [to] seek public comment and input." 36 C.F.R. § 800.2(d)(2). The regulations, however, specify that certain individuals and organizations, known as "consulting parties," are to be more formally involved in the agency's NHPA review. The agency must invite all relevant state historic preservation officers, tribal historic preservation officers, local government representatives, and the project applicant to participate in the NHPA process as consulting parties. Id. § 800.2(c). In addition to those who are consulting parties as a matter of right, other interested individuals or organizations "*may participate* as consulting parties due to the nature of their legal or economic relation to the undertaking . . . or their concern with the undertaking's effects on historic properties," id. § 800.2(c)(5) (emphasis added), if they request participation in writing and the agency determines that they should be granted consulting party status, id. § 800.3(f)(3).

The Mid States Coalition contends that the NHPA was violated because the Board failed to invite ranchers and farmers whose lands may contain historic properties to participate as consulting parties. The ACHP regulations make it apparent, however, that affected ranchers and farmers are not automatically entitled to be consulting parties. Because they have an economic interest in the proceeding, they may be added as consulting parties, but they must first make a request, in writing, to the Board. In this case, the Board has granted consulting party status to all individuals and organizations who made such a request. We believe, moreover, that the agency complied with its general duty to notify and allow comment from the public on matters of historic preservation during the environmental review process. *See* 36 C.F.R. §§ 800.3(e), 800.8(c)(1)(iv). The DEIS and the FEIS describe those sites along the proposed route that SEA initially identified as eligible for inclusion in the National Register of Historic Places. And since the public was encouraged to comment on all aspects of the DEIS, we cannot say that there was an insufficient opportunity for public comment under the NHPA.

The Mid States Coalition also asserts that the Board erred by issuing DM & E a license before it completed the NHPA process. The Board maintains that the NHPA's seemingly unambiguous directive to take effects into account "prior to the issuance of any license," 16 U.S.C. § 470f [EDS.: moved to 54 U.S.C. § 306108], is relaxed by the ACHP's implementing regulations.

As noted above, an NHPA analysis involves a three-step process of identification, assessment, and mitigation. The general expectation is that an agency will complete one step before moving on to the next, but the regulations permit an agency to use a "phased process" of identifying and evaluating properties where "alternatives under consideration consist of corridors or large land areas," 36 C.F.R. § 800.4(b)(2). The agency's phased process "should establish the likely presence of historic properties within the area of potential effects for each alternative . . . through background research, consultation and an appropriate level of field investigation, taking into account the number of alternatives under consideration, the magnitude of the undertaking and its likely effects, and the views of the [historic preservation officers] and any other consulting parties." *Id.*

We believe that SEA's analysis in the early stages adheres to this approach. During the period when there were still numerous alternatives under consideration, it was permissible for SEA to delay assessing the adverse effects of the project on specific sites. But as "specific aspects or locations of an alternative are refined," the regulation provides that the agency "shall proceed with the identification and evaluation of historic properties." *Id.* By requiring that agencies identify and assess individual properties as project alternatives become more concrete, the regulations assure that the agency will be in a position to proceed to the mitigation step.

Although the Board (through SEA) identified some potentially affected sites in the DEIS and FEIS, it has not made a final evaluation or adopted specific measures to avoid or mitigate any adverse effects, *see* 36 C.F.R. § 800.2(d)(3). It argues, however, that the ACHP's regulations permit it to defer these actions until after the license has been approved. We disagree. It is true that the regulations permit an agency to "defer final identification and evaluation of historic properties if it is specifically provided for in . . . the documents used by an agency official to comply with [NEPA] pursuant to [36 C.F.R.] § 800.8." *Id.* § 800.4(b)(2). But § 800.8, in turn, requires that an agency develop measures to "avoid, minimize, or mitigate" adverse effects and then bind itself to these measures in a record of decision. *Id.* § 800.8(c)(4). The ACHP's regulations, when read it their entirety, thus permit an agency to defer completion of the NHPA process until after the NEPA process has run its course (and the environmentally preferred alternatives chosen), but require that NHPA issues be resolved by the time that the license is issued. In this case, the Board's final decision contains a condition requiring DM & E to comply with whatever future mitigation requirements the Board finally arrives at. We do not think that this is the type of measure contemplated by the ACHP when it directed agencies to develop measures to "avoid, minimize, or mitigate" adverse effects.

We note that the ACHP's regulations offer agencies an alternative to the process described above. An agency may negotiate with consulting parties to develop "a programmatic agreement to govern the implementation of a particular program or the resolution of adverse effects from certain complex project situations." *Id.* § 800.14(b). While the programmatic agreement itself must be in place before the issuance of a license, it gives an agency flexibility when "effects on historic properties cannot be fully determined prior to approval of an undertaking," *id.* Indeed, the Board recognized this advantage, as evidenced by its continuing effort to negotiate an acceptable programmatic agreement before it issued its final decision.

We believe that the Board should have also recognized that it could not proceed without one. One month before the Board issued its final decision, the ACHP wrote a letter to the Board stating:

> As we understand it, [the Board] plans to make a decision on whether to approve or deny the proposed project at the end of the month. Given this short time frame and the critical need to coordinate the completion of Section 106 with any decision reached under [NEPA], we recommend you set up a conference call among the consulting parties in order to develop timely revisions to this [programmatic agreement], and that you circulate a revised final [programmatic agreement] as quickly as possible. Until these important issues are resolved, the Council will not be able to execute a [programmatic agreement] with [the Board] for this undertaking.

If the programmatic agreement had been executed, the Board could have finalized the NHPA details at a future date according to the terms of the agreement, just as it wished. Not willing to delay publication of its decision until after a consensus could be reached on the terms of the programmatic agreement, the Board instead issued the license having neither secured a programmatic agreement nor completed the alternate NHPA process. On remand, it must do one or the other. * * *

NOTES & QUESTIONS

1.   In *Recent Past Preservation Network v. Latschar*, excerpted in the prior section, the agency complied with Section 106 but failed to comply with NEPA. In *Mid States,* the agency substantially fulfilled its NEPA duties, but had not yet completed its Section 106 responsibilities. Is the compliance mandated in *Mid States* merely formal? What might it add to the NEPA analysis?

2.   Although NEPA is the better-known statute, the NHPA probably is more important for historic preservation law. The NHPA mandates more detailed consideration of the effects of more federal actions on historic properties, requires consultation with expert consulting parties independent of the responsible agency, and encourages agreements minimizing or mitigating harms. NEPA may provide preservation issues greater visibility because of the very public nature and reputation of the EIS process, but only in a context where the many environmental issues discussed do not obscure subtle preservation concerns.

3.   What if a local government destroys historic properties before receiving federal funding or applying for a federal permit, so as to avoid triggering either NEPA or NHPA? The city of Pittsburgh destroyed a historic civic arena, possibly with this in mind. *See Pres. Pittsburgh v. Conturo*, 477 Fed. Appx. 918 (3rd Cir. 2012) (dismissing an appeal from a local preservation group as moot, since the arena had already been destroyed and the group could therefore receive no relief). What is the remedy for such cases? Is there one?

4.   The issuance and receipt of federal grant funding can moot a case. In *Tyler v. Cisneros*, some homeowners near the site of a low-income housing project brought suit, seeking to enjoin construction of the project under both NEPA and the NHPA. Federal funding had already been disbursed for the project, and because objection was not brought during the funds' fifteen-day comment period, the NEPA claims were dismissed as moot. *Tyler v. Cisneros*, 136 F.3d 603 (9th Cir. 1998).

B. STATE ENVIRONMENTAL POLICY ACTS

Many states have adopted state environmental policy acts (SEPAs) that mirror NEPA. As the prior section in this Chapter described, NEPA requires detailed environmental impact statements (EISs) for "major Federal actions significantly affecting the quality of the human environment." 42 U.S.C. § 4332(C). Among other information, the EIS must identify the environmental impact of the proposed action, any unavoidable adverse environmental effects, and alternatives to the proposed action. *Id.* Through the EIS mandate, NEPA creates a process to ensure that agencies adequately consider the impact of their actions. It does not, however, mandate any substantive conclusions. Thus, even if the agency identifies an adverse effect on the environment, it may still proceed with the action. It is important to note that NEPA applies only to federal agencies' "major" "actions," which primarily include public programs and projects but may also include private projects and programs funded or permitted by the federal government. NEPA does not define "environment" and does not, by its terms, apply to historic preservation projects.

SEPAs that closely follow NEPA, such as Indiana's Environmental Policy Act, apply only to major state government actions significantly affecting the environment. IND. CODE §§ 13–12–4–1 to –10. Some states, however, have broadened the scope of their SEPAs to include local-level public projects as well as private projects and programs. SEPAs also differ with respect to whether they specifically list historic resources among those kinds of environmental resources they protect. Some follow the lead of NEPA and omit explicit reference to historic resources. Others, like the Connecticut Environmental Protection Act, explicitly include designated properties. The Connecticut statute, for example, covers:

> unreasonable destruction of historic structures and landmarks of the state, which shall be those properties (1) listed or under consideration for listing as individual units on the National Register of Historic Places * * * or (2) which are a part of a district listed or under consideration for listing on said national register and which have been determined by the State Historic Preservation Board to contribute to the historic significance of such district.

CONN. GEN. STAT. § 22a–19a. It applies to both public and private entities and entitles any person or entity to sue to prevent such destruction. *Id.* § 22a–16.

Like Connecticut, California has a particularly broad SEPA. Just eight months after Congress passed NEPA in 1969, California was the first state to pass its own Environmental Quality Act (CEQA). While many other states also enacted their own environmental legislation mirroring NEPA, not all state statutes have generated the high volume of litigation that CEQA has. CEQA has generated hundreds of lawsuits in California's trial and appellate level courts—perhaps more than any other single Californian law. The *Los Angeles Times* has criticized the way CEQA has been used, editorializing: "While CEQA is a vital tool that has made countless projects better since its inception, it is also too easily used to stop projects for reasons that have nothing to do with environmental protection." *Editorial: California's Signature Environmental Law Is Being Abused (Again) to Stop an Environmentally Friendly Project*, L.A. TIMES, July, 14, 2017. In contrast, Indiana's Environmental Policy Act has generated fewer than half a dozen cases. *See also* Jeffrey L. Carmichael, *The Indiana Environmental Policy Act: Casting a New Role for a Forgotten Statute*, 70 IND. L.J. 613 (1995) (noting that a prior Indiana SEPA had generated no litigation).

Several aspects of California's statutory scheme foster litigation, and it is important to point out differences between NEPA and CEQA. First,

California's threshold for when an environmental impact report of a given project is required is set much lower than the federal government's and that of other states. While NEPA only requires detailed environmental impact statements for "major Federal actions significantly affecting the quality of the human environment," California requires one whenever a project "*may* have a significant effect on the environment." CAL. PUB. RES. CODE § 21100(a) (emphasis added). Second, unlike NEPA and many states' environmental statutes, California's provides definitions of important terms, clarifying the situations to which CEQA applies. While NEPA does not define "environment," CEQA defines it as "the physical conditions which exist within the area which will be affected by a proposed project, including land, air, water, minerals, flora, fauna, noise, objects of historic or aesthetic significance." *Id.* § 21060.5. Historic preservation cases are thus explicitly covered by the CEQA statute.

In addition, unlike courts in many states, California courts interpret CEQA's environmental review procedures to apply to public projects undertaken by local, as well as by state agencies and includes the granting of approvals, licenses, or permits to private parties for projects. *See* Carmichael, 70 IND. L.J. at 640, *citing Friends of Mammoth v. Bd. of Supervisors*, 502 P.2d 1049, 1056 (Cal. 1972). Furthermore, while NEPA and statutes in states like Indiana require only that environmental impacts of projects be studied, CEQA actually requires agencies to "mitigate or avoid the significant effects on the environment of projects that it carries out or approves whenever it is feasible to do so." CAL. PUB. RES. CODE § 21002.1(b). So, a number of suits allege that the agency did not choose the least harmful option or adopt necessary, feasible mitigation measures. Finally, unlike NEPA, CEPA specifies the level of judicial review authorized for these cases, thus ensuring "administrative decisions would receive a certain amount of judicial scrutiny." Carmichael, 70 IND. L.J. at 626.

As you read the following case, consider the costs and benefits of California's approach in CEQA.

Architectural Heritage Association v. County of Monterey

19 Cal. Rptr. 3d 469 (Ct. App. 2004)

■ MCADAMS, J. * * *

This dispute involves Monterey County's Old Jail, located in Salinas, California. The County of Monterey (County) intends to demolish the Old Jail. Acting through its board of supervisors, the County decided to proceed under CEQA by way of a mitigated negative declaration. Plaintiffs Architectural Heritage Association and Mark Norris challenge that decision. According to plaintiffs, there is evidence supporting a fair argument that the planned demolition will result in loss of the jail's historic value and that the proposed mitigation measures are inadequate. Plaintiffs have pressed their claims both administratively and judicially.

To provide perspective for the procedural and substantive aspects of this dispute, we begin with an overview of CEQA.

Statutory Background

CEQA embodies our state's policy that "the long-term protection of the environment . . . shall be the guiding criterion in public decisions." CAL. PUB. RES. CODE § 21001, subd. (d). As this court recently noted, "the overriding purpose of CEQA is to ensure that agencies regulating activities that may affect the quality of the environment give primary consideration to preventing environmental damage." *Save Our Peninsula Comm. v. Monterey Cty. Bd. of Supervisors*, 104 Cal. Rptr. 2d 326 (Cal. Ct. App. 2001). As an aid to carrying out the statute, the State Resources Agency has issued a set of regulations, called Guidelines for the California Environmental Quality Act (Guidelines).[2] Together, CEQA and the Guidelines protect a variety of environmental values. Historic resources are among them.

Consistent with California's strong environmental policy, the statute and regulations "have established a three-tiered process to ensure that public agencies inform their decisions with environmental considerations." *Davidon Homes v. City of San Jose*, 62 Cal. Rptr. 2d 612, 612 (Cal. Ct. App. 1997).

"The first tier is jurisdictional, requiring that an agency conduct a preliminary review in order to determine whether CEQA applies to a proposed activity. (Guidelines §§ 15060, 15061.)" *Id.* at 614. "If the agency finds the project is exempt from CEQA under any of the stated exemptions, no further environmental review is necessary." *Id.* at 616. "If, however, the project does not fall within any exemption, the agency must proceed with the second tier and conduct an initial study. (Guidelines § 15063.)" *Id.*

The second tier of the process, the initial study, serves several purposes. Guidelines § 15063, subd. (c). One purpose is to inform the choice between a negative declaration and an environmental impact report (EIR). *Id.* subd. (c) (1). Another of the initial study's purposes is to eliminate unnecessary environmental impact reports. Guidelines § 15063, subd. (c)(7).

"CEQA excuses the preparation of an EIR and allows the use of a negative declaration when an initial study shows that there is no substantial evidence that the project may have a significant effect on the environment." *San Bernardino Valley Audubon Soc'y v. Metro. Water Dist.*, 83 Cal. Rptr. 2d 836 (Cal. Ct. App. 1999) (citing Guidelines § 15070).

---

[2] The Guidelines are located at title 14 of the California Code of Regulations, starting at section 15000. Further unspecified guideline references are to those regulations.

In certain situations where a straightforward negative declaration is not appropriate, the agency may permit use of a mitigated negative declaration (MND).

> If the initial study identifies potentially significant effects on the environment but revisions in the project plans 'would avoid the effects or mitigate the effects to a point where clearly no significant effect on the environment would occur' and there is no substantial evidence that the project as revised may have a significant effect on the environment, a mitigated negative declaration may be used.

Id. at 841; *see also, e.g.,* Guidelines § 15064, subd. (f)(2).

If the project does not qualify for a negative declaration of either type, "the third step in the process is to prepare a full environmental impact report." *Davidon Homes,* 62 Cal. Rptr. 2d at 616.

The California Supreme Court has "repeatedly recognized that the EIR is the 'heart of CEQA.'" *Laurel Heights Improvement Ass'n v. Regents of Univ. of Cal.,* 864 P.2d 502, 506 (Cal. 1993). As the court observed some three decades ago, "since the preparation of an EIR is the key to environmental protection under CEQA, accomplishment of the high objectives of that act requires the preparation of an EIR whenever it can be fairly argued on the basis of substantial evidence that the project may have significant environmental impact." *No Oil, Inc. v. City of L.A.,* 529 P.2d 66 (Cal. 1974). The court stressed "the importance of preparing an EIR in cases . . . in which the determination of a project's environmental effect turns upon the resolution of controverted issues of fact and forms the subject of intense public concern." *Id.* Other cases have since confirmed the statutory preference for resolving doubts in favor of an EIR.

With that overview of CEQA in mind, we now turn to the facts underlying this proceeding.

Factual and Procedural Background

At the heart of this dispute is the County's Old Jail, built in 1931 in the Gothic Revival style. The three-story structure was designed by Reed & Corlett, an architectural and engineering firm "responsible for numerous buildings in the San Francisco Bay Area from 1912 to 1933, many of which are still standing." The jail is located directly adjacent to the Monterey County courthouse, at 142 West Alisal Street in Salinas. The building is approximately 40 feet tall, with some 19,000 square feet of floor space. It consists of two primary wings, which are separated by a secured passageway. The original blueprints for the jail provided for a number of uses, some quite outmoded under current penal practices. The plans thus included a boys' department, vagrants' quarters, an insane cell, a padded cell, a delousing room, a darkroom, and a room for liquor storage. Some of the jail cells "contain detailed and artistic graffiti done by prisoners."

In December 1970, César Chávez was incarcerated in the Old Jail for approximately two weeks, for refusing to obey a court order to halt the United Farm Workers' lettuce boycott. His incarceration drew international attention, prompted visits from Coretta Scott King and Ethel Kennedy, and galvanized the burgeoning farm worker movement.

By the 1980s, the County had ceased using the structure as a jail. Since then, it has been used for records storage and as a temporary holding facility for prisoners appearing in court.

In December 1999, by unanimous vote of its Board of Supervisors, the County directed its staff "to take necessary actions to provide for demolition of [the] old jail facility in Salinas."

Various assessments of the jail preceded and followed the County's decision to demolish the structure.

Assessments of the Old Jail

1.   Physical Condition

Several reports commissioned by the County evaluated the jail's physical condition. A 1998 report noted the presence of asbestos and lead-based paint at the Old Jail. In August 2000, a property condition report on the Old Jail was prepared by Professional Service Industries, Inc. (PSI). Among other things, PSI's property condition report concluded that the roofs were in poor condition and that the building did not comply with the Americans with Disabilities Act. In September 2000, an indoor air quality evaluation revealed high levels of mold spores and lead dust in most locations in the building.

2.   Historic Status

The County also commissioned an assessment of the Old Jail as a cultural and historic resource. Dr. Robert Cartier of Archaeological Resource Management undertook that assessment, which was completed in July 2000. Cartier holds baccalaureate, graduate, and doctoral degrees in anthropology, and he has more than two decades of full-time experience in researching, interpreting, and writing about cultural and historical resources. In a section of the report detailing the jail's factual history, Cartier noted that it "was visited by some notable historical figures" and he specifically mentioned the 1970 jailing of César Chávez.

In his evaluation of the jail's cultural significance, Cartier stated: "A cultural resource is considered 'significant' if it qualifies as eligible for listing in the California Register of Historic Resources (CRHR). Properties that are eligible for listing in the CRHR must meet one or more" of four criteria, which he set forth in the report. The second factor (criterion 2) is particularly relevant here: "Association with the lives of persons important to local, California, or national history." Cartier observed that the Old Jail "is not currently listed on the California Register of Historic Resources. The jail structure does appear, however, to qualify as potentially eligible for listing on the CRHR under criterion 2."

The Cartier report also set forth the four parallel criteria for listing on the National Register of Historic Places (NRHP). Again, the second criterion is most pertinent here. That factor, criterion b, applies to places "associated with the lives of persons significant in our past." As with the state registry, Cartier observed, the Old Jail "is not currently listed on the National Register of Historic Places. However, this structure does appear to qualify as potentially eligible for listing on the National Register under criterion B." * * *

Administrative Proceedings Under CEQA * * *

1.   The Initial Study

On June 1, 2001, an initial study was completed.

The initial study identified several environmental factors potentially affected by demolition of the Old Jail, including cultural resources. * * * The initial study noted Cartier's conclusion that the Old Jail "qualifies as potentially eligible for listing on both the CRHR and the National Register." The initial study then concluded: "Consequently, the old jailhouse is a significant historical resource as defined by CEQA [Guidelines] Section 15064.5."

The initial study stated: "Without appropriate and extensive mitigation, the proposed demolition will cause a substantial adverse change to an historic resource." But it also noted that "the architectural integrity of the resource has been diminished by the deteriorated physical condition of the structure and the hazardous materials that are found extensively within" its components. Based on those factors, the initial study stated,

> renovation or reuse of the structure is not feasible. However, the demolition of the building represents an incremental loss of both the architectural style of 1930s jail construction and an historic resource potentially eligible for listing on both the California Register of Historic Resources and the National Register of Historic Places. Without appropriate mitigation, the demolition would have impacts that are cumulatively considerable when viewed in connection with the effects of past demolitions of architecturally significant and historically significant structures within the state. However, extensive mitigation measures have been developed to reduce these potential impacts to a less than significant level. * * *

Ultimately, the initial study concluded, with the proposed mitigations, the adverse environmental effects on cultural resources from demolition of the Old Jail will be less than significant. Based on that conclusion, the initial study called for preparation of a mitigated negative declaration.

2.   The Mitigated Negative Declaration

On June 14, 2001, the County gave notice of its intent to adopt a mitigated negative declaration.

Public comments were received in response. One was from the County's Historic Resources Review Board (Historic Board). The members of the Historic Board were "unanimous in their opinion that the draft Initial Study is insufficient upon which to address mitigation measures and recommend the County undertake a more extensive [EIR]." A memorandum from the Historic Board's jail subcommittee likewise recommended an EIR. In addition, Historic Board member Dorothy Steele Laage, acting in her personal capacity as a "concerned citizen of Monterey County," wrote in support of a full EIR. The comment period on the mitigated negative declaration ended on July 16, 2001.

A public hearing followed nearly a year later. It began on June 19, 2002. Those opposed to issuance of the demolition permit argued for preparation of an EIR, based on claims that the Old Jail is a cultural and historic resource. The hearing was continued to permit completion of an addendum to the historic monograph of the Old Jail, which had been prepared for the County by Carey & Company. At the continued hearing, held on July 3, 2002, the Department received additional testimony, further staff recommendations, and the third addendum to Carey & Company's monograph.

At the conclusion of the hearing, the Department adopted the mitigated negative declaration, together with a mitigation monitoring and reporting program, and it issued the demolition permit for the Old Jail. In order to mitigate the demolition's impact on the jail's value as an historic resource, the following conditions were imposed: photographic documentation to HABS standards; preparation of an historic monograph, including detailed descriptions of the jail's construction, the social environment in which it was built, its association with local, state, and national history, and jail culture; reuse or duplication of architectural elements from the building, with certain salvage details called out; and maintaining a complete set of the architectural and engineering blueprints at various agencies, including the local historical society. * * *

[EDS: An administrative appeal filed with the County's Board of Supervisors by plaintiff Architectural Heritage Association was denied on July 30, 2002. Plaintiffs Architectural Heritage Association and Mark Edwin Norris filed a petition for a writ of mandate in August 2002, which was denied in May 2003. This appeal followed.]

Discussion * * *

I.   Threshold Issues

Judicial review of an agency's efforts to comply with CEQA "shall extend only to whether there was a prejudicial abuse of discretion. Abuse of discretion is established if the agency has not proceeded in a manner required by law or if the determination is not supported by substantial evidence." *League for Prot. of Oakland's Architectural & Historic Res. v. City of Oakland*, 60 Cal.Rptr.2d 821, 826 (1997) (*City of Oakland*). When there is substantial evidence supporting a fair argument that the project will significantly impact the environment, an agency abuses its discretion in failing to require an EIR. *Id.* at 826. * * *

The "fair argument" test is very different from the usual measure of judicial deference given to agency decisions. *Cf., e.g., Fukuda v. City of Angels*, 977 P.2d 693 (Cal. 1999) (in administrative mandamus action, the trial court exercises its independent judgment but nevertheless "must afford a strong presumption of correctness" to administrative findings; appellate court reviews for substantial evidence). The fair argument test has limited application. It "was derived from an interpretation of the language of, and policies underlying, section 21151 itself. For this reason, the 'fair argument' test has been applied *only* to the decision whether to prepare an original EIR or a negative declaration." *Laurel Heights Improvement Ass'n*, 864 P.2d at 514.

"This test establishes a low threshold for initial preparation of an EIR, which reflects a preference for resolving doubts in favor of environmental review." *Santa Teresa Citizen Action Grp. v. City of San Jose*, 7 Cal.Rptr.3d 868, 879 (Cal. Ct. App. 868). * * *

Summarizing the three threshold issues, (A) we apply the fair argument standard to all three substantive issues presented—historicity, impact, and mitigation; (B) we limit our review to the administrative record; and (C) we consider whether plaintiffs have carried their burden. With the foregoing principles in mind, we turn to the substantive issues presented by this appeal.

II. Analysis

As we explain below, we conclude that plaintiffs have carried their burden of showing substantial evidence in the administrative record supporting a fair argument (A) that the Old Jail is an historic resource, (B) that its demolition will have a significant environmental impact, and (C) that the proposed mitigation measures are inadequate to reduce that impact to insignificance. * * *

A. Historic Status

According to plaintiffs, there is adequate evidence supporting a fair argument of historicity in the initial study alone. But they also cite other evidence, including the Cartier report, the Historic Board recommendation for a full EIR, and comments by speakers at the public hearings. The County discounts the substantiality of the cited evidence to support plaintiffs' historic status claim.

Our examination of the record persuades us that the "fair argument" test is satisfied here.

1.   The Initial Study

In the words of the initial study, "the old jailhouse is a significant historical resource as defined by CEQA [Guidelines] Section 15064.5."

The County attempts to discount that conclusion. It urges that "the sole basis" for the determination "is the same portion of the Cartier Report that places a heavy reliance on the Jail's association with César Chávez as a ground for deeming the Jail a historic resource." According to the County, "that part of the Cartier Report has very little evidentiary value" because of "its failure to discuss the federal criteria applicable to historic resources that may have gained significance within the last 50 years . . . ." On that basis, the County rejects the notion that the initial study constitutes substantial evidence supporting a fair argument that the Old Jail is an historic resource.

We are not persuaded by the County's attempts to minimize the evidentiary force of the initial study. Under the low threshold that governs our review, the initial study incorporates "enough relevant information and reasonable inferences from this information that a fair argument can be made" that the Old Jail is an historic resource. *Leonoff v. Monterey Cty. Bd. of Supervisors*, 272 Cal. Rptr. 372 (Cal. Ct. App. 1990). Here, that information includes the initial study's nod to "the architectural style of 1930s jail construction" as well as its adoption of Cartier's conclusion that the structure is "potentially eligible" for listing on both the NRHP and the CRHR based on its social or cultural significance. As the initial study confirms: "The old jail is known to be associated with important persons in local, regional, or national history, including César Chávez who was incarcerated at the jail between December 10–24, 1970, for refusing to obey a court order to stop a lettuce boycott. Mr. Chávez was a major contributor to the Mexican-American community in the Monterey and Santa Clara Valley areas. In addition, Ethel Kennedy, the widow of Robert Kennedy, and Coretta Scott King, the widow of Dr. Martin Luther King, Jr., reportedly visited Chávez during his incarceration in the jailhouse." Based on those observations alone, there is a fair argument that the Old Jail is historic.

Moreover, our determination that there is substantial evidence supporting a fair argument of the jail's historic status is bolstered by an examination of the administrative record as a whole. We therefore discuss some of the other evidence supporting plaintiffs' claim of historicity.

2.   The Cartier Report * * *

As noted above, the County challenges the evidentiary value of Cartier's assessment of NRHP eligibility to the extent it is based on association with César Chávez. As before, however, we find that challenge unavailing. Eligibility for inclusion on the National Register is not determinative. The governing statute "does not demand formal listing of a resource in a national, state or local register as a prerequisite to 'historical' status. The statutory language is more expansive and flexible." *City of Oakland*, 60 Cal. Rptr. 2d at 828.

The County also asserts: "From the standpoint of *architectural* or *physical* attributes, . . . the inescapable conclusion of the Cartier Report is that the Jail is *not* a historic resource." As the County correctly observes, Cartier did opine that the jail "does not display particularly rare or unique architecture" and that it "has a diminished architectural integrity" because of its physical deterioration. But those statements in the Cartier report do not rob it of its evidentiary value with respect to the *cultural* significance of the Old Jail.

In any event, other evidence in the administrative record supports a fair argument that the jail has architectural as well as cultural significance, including the initial study's reference to its style, submissions by the Historic Board, and comments by speakers at the public hearings.

3.   Historic Board * * *

In July 2001, by unanimous vote following a scheduled public meeting, the Historic Board [endorsed] * * * the view that the jail is an historic resource. In doing so, the Historic Board rejected the Department's recommendation that it adopt the mitigated negative declaration and approve the demolition permit.

The County attempts to minimize the finding of historic status by the Historic Board, employing a two-pronged attack. First, the County characterizes the Historic Board's finding as a "gratuitous conclusion" that carries no evidentiary weight, because it was made without conducting the specific type of public hearing envisioned by the Monterey County Code for the designation of historic resources. In addition, the County asserts, "conclusions reached by agency staff subordinate to agency decision makers on the ultimate issue of whether an impact is 'significant' do not constitute substantial evidence—they are merely inferences that may be disregarded."

We do not find either argument persuasive. As to the County's first point, we note that the Historic Board determination *was* made at a public hearing, at which review of the proposed MND was on the agenda—apparently at the request of the Department itself. Under the circumstances, we find nothing in the hearing process that diminishes the evidentiary force of the Historic Board's finding. As to its second point, the County supports its view that subordinate agency staff determinations lack evidentiary value by citing *Perley v. Bd. of Supervisors*, 187 Cal. Rptr. 53 (Cal. Ct. App. 1982). We do not read *Perley* so broadly. * * * *Perley* also predated the CEQA definition of substantial evidence codified in 1993, which logically includes the fact-based opinions of agency staff and commissioners within the codified parameters of "facts, reasonable assumptions predicated upon facts, and expert opinion supported by facts." (§ 21082.2, subd. (c).) Here, the record includes fact based evidence of historic status, which the Historic Board and its subcommittee had gained through meetings with County staff, a site view, and the review of pertinent documents.

In sum, we find the Historic Board's determination to be fact based and procedurally proper. It constitutes substantial evidence that the jail is historic.

4. Speakers

At the public hearing held by the Department in June and July 2002, a number of citizens voiced their opposition to the proposed mitigated negative declaration. Some stressed the social and cultural aspects of the jail's historic status; others spoke about its architectural significance; some addressed both features. * * *

We recognize that "substantial evidence" does not properly include argument, speculation, or unfounded opinions. § 21082.2, subd. (c); Guidelines § 15384, subd. (a). But we disagree with the County's characterization of the speakers' testimony as unsubstantiated opinion. For example, one of the speakers, Sales, is a certified historian; she linked the jail with "the perilous labor unrest in the Salinas Valley." Another speaker, Muñoz, is an architect; he noted that the jail is "a very rare style in Salinas and Monterey County." He also stated that the building exemplifies a "pioneering technique" in its use of integrated-color concrete. These and other speakers' remarks represent fact-based observations by people apparently qualified to speak to the question of the jail's historic status. That testimony constitutes substantial evidence, because it consists of "facts, reasonable assumptions predicated upon facts, and expert opinion supported by facts." § 21082.2, subd. (c).

Taken together, the following portions of the administrative record contain substantial evidence supporting a fair argument that the Old Jail is an historic resource, both culturally and architecturally: (1) the initial study, (2) the Cartier report, (3) the determination by the Historic Resources Review Board, and (4) the fact-based testimony of qualified speakers at the public hearing.

B. Demolition as a Significant Impact

Having concluded that there is a fair argument supporting the jail's status as an historic resource, we next consider the effect of its proposed demolition.

The pertinent legal question is whether demolition "may cause a substantial adverse change" to the jail's significance as an historical resource. § 21084.1. "A project that may cause a substantial adverse change in the significance of an historical resource is a project that may have a significant effect on the environment." *Id.*; *see* Guidelines § 15064.5, subd. (b). "Substantial adverse change in the significance of an historical resource means physical demolition" or other adverse effects, such that the significance of the historic resource "would be materially impaired." Guidelines § 15064.5, subd. (b)(1); *see also*

§ 5020.1, subd. (q) (same; CRHR definitions). Material impairment occurs when a project alters or destroys "those physical characteristics of an historical resource that convey its historical significance and that justify its inclusion" in a state or local historic registry. Guidelines § 15064.5, subd. (b)(2)(A).

Based on substantial evidence in the administrative record in this case, there can be little doubt that demolition will result in a substantial adverse impact on the jail. * * *

The County does not contend otherwise. Rather, it simply progresses to the next step in the analysis, the adequacy of the mitigation measures.

C.   Mitigation

As explained above, adoption of a mitigated negative declaration is proper only where the conditions imposed on the project reduce its adverse environmental impacts to a level of insignificance. § 21064.5; Guidelines § 15064, subd. (f)(2). By statutory definition, a mitigated negative declaration is one in which (1) the proposed conditions "avoid the effects or mitigate the effects to a point where *clearly* no significant effect on the environment would occur, *and* (2) there is *no substantial evidence* in light of the whole record before the public agency that the project, as revised, may have a significant effect on the environment." § 21064.5, italics added.

Here, to mitigate the impact of demolition on the jail's historic significance, the County imposed the following conditions: (1) photographic documentation; (2) preparation of an historic monograph; (3) salvage of certain architectural elements; and (4) maintenance of a set of blueprints.

Plaintiffs contend that the proposed mitigation measures are not adequate. They assert: "As drawing a chalk mark around a dead body is not mitigation, so archival documentation cannot normally reduce destruction of an historic resource to an insignificant level." As support for that assertion, plaintiffs rely on *City of Oakland*, 60 Cal. Rptr. 2d 821. The plaintiff in that case challenged a mitigated negative declaration adopted in connection with the planned demolition of Oakland's historic Montgomery Ward building. The mitigation measures in the Oakland MND included "documentation of the structure in a report and survey, display of a commemorative plaque, and a new shopping center with design features which reflect architectural elements of the demolished building." *Id.* at 829. The court found the proposed mitigations insufficient, concluding that they did "not reduce the effects of the demolition to less than a level of significance. [Citation.]" *Id.* The court explained:

Documentation of the historical features of the building and exhibition of a plaque do not reasonably begin to alleviate the impacts of its destruction. A large historical structure, once demolished, normally cannot be adequately replaced by reports and commemorative markers. Nor, we think, are the effects of the demolition reduced to a level of insignificance by a proposed new building with unspecified design elements which may incorporate features of the original architecture into an entirely different shopping center.

Id.

Countering plaintiffs' assertion of inadequate mitigation, the County cites three grounds for distinguishing *City of Oakland*. We are not persuaded by any of them.

The County's first ground for distinguishing *City of Oakland* rests on the fact that the Montgomery Ward building was listed as historic by the city itself in its own preexisting documentation. As we see it, however, that fact goes to the question of the building's historic status, not to the issue of mitigation. And in fact, the court mentioned that point under the heading "The Montgomery Ward Building as a Historic Resource" and not in connection with its discussion of "Mitigation Measures." *City of Oakland*, 60 Cal. Rptr. 2d at 828.

Second, according to the County, the Montgomery Ward building possessed structural architectural values while the Old Jail does not. As to that point, however, as we have explained above, we find substantial evidence in the administrative record to support a fair argument that the Old Jail has historic significance based on its architectural features, quite apart from its cultural associations. Furthermore, *City of Oakland* does not hold that historic status must always be based on architectural features. As discussed earlier, historic status may derive from other qualities as well. *See* § 5024.1, subd. (c); Guidelines § 15064.5, subd. (a)(3).

As a third ground of distinction, the County claims that in *City of Oakland* "demolition did not appear to be appropriate as the Montgomery Ward Building was apparently in good condition; it had suffered no structural degradation even if it sustained slight damage in the 1989 Loma Prieta earthquake." *See City of Oakland*, 60 Cal. Rptr. 2d at 823. While the court does mention the lack of structural degradation, it describes the Montgomery Ward building as having "fallen into severe disrepair, with peeling paint, broken windows, graffiti, and numerous code violations, including the presence of asbestos-containing materials." *Id.* Given that description, we find it difficult to accept the County's view that the court's decision was based in any way on the building's "good condition." In the same vein, we observe that the administrative record in this case does not support the County's determination that the Old Jail is in such poor condition that it requires demolition, a point we explore more fully below.

In short, we find no basis on which to distinguish *City of Oakland*. The analysis in that case is sound, and we apply it here.

On this record, we find substantial evidence supporting a fair argument that the proposed mitigation measures are inadequate, in that they fail to reduce the environmental detriment "to a point where clearly no significant effect" will result. § 21064.5.

D.   Need for an EIR

Without undertaking a full EIR, the County determined that the jail could not be saved, finding that "its preservation or adaptive reuse is impractical due to its age, design, and deteriorating condition, and opening up the building for more usable spaces would seriously degrade the structural integrity of the building and pose a safety hazard to its occupants and neighbors."

We find this determination insupportable, both factually and legally.

As a factual matter, the administrative record discloses mixed conclusions concerning the physical condition of the structure, as well as an incomplete investigation both of the jail's condition and of alternatives to demolition.

In the property condition report prepared by PSI in August 2000, limitations on access and the absence of detailed drawings prevented the evaluator from assessing some key areas of the structure. The unexplored areas include the foundations, the underside of the floor slabs, and the roof trusses. With respect to the roof, PSI stated: "No documentation was available for our review to determine the building's actual roof system. The type and quality of installation of underlying components of the roof membranes could not be determined without intrusive investigation and testing." Reporting on the accessible parts of the jail's superstructure, PSI did observe some evidence of water intrusion. By the same token, however, PSI "did not observe signs of visible distress" to the superstructure. Reporting on the exterior walls, PSI stated: "No major signs of concrete spalling or cracking could be seen during our site visit, except for a few isolated locations, such as at/and around concrete scuppers, at some eaves and soffits, and column capitals and architectural decorative stone features at the south elevation." PSI also acknowledged reports that "the building satisfactorily resisted the 1989 Loma Prieta earthquake without damage."

In determining that preservation of the jail was impractical, the County relied on Cartier's report for evidentiary support. Cartier's report mentions retention and adaptation as an alternative mitigation. But it notes that such a course for the jail "may be impractical due to its age and condition (e.g., its roof problems, deterioration of the concrete construction, specific design for secured incarceration, and its lack of compliance with current building codes)." The apparent basis for Cartier's assessment of the jail's condition is PSI's report. But as we explained above, that report is not definitive on the question of the jail's structural condition, much less on the need for demolition.

At the public hearings, several speakers urged the County to further explore alternatives to demolition, such as adaptive reuse. Muñoz argued for further study of "all the options that we could have on the building." Norris asserted that "a qualified historic architecture engineer needs to be brought in to assess the potential for remodeling the structural reinforcement." Sales observed that "an EIR will require that viable reuse be examined." That refrain is repeated in the final addendum to Carey & Company's historic monograph, which states:

> A question has arisen as to whether the existing building can be rehabilitated. It is Carey & Co.'s opinion that a study of this nature would involve reopening the environmental review process under . . . (CEQA). This kind of analysis under CEQA would probably be considered an alternatives analysis. Such an analysis would involve not only the feasibility of rehabilitating the existing building, but also other options such as moving the building, rehabilitating and adding on to the building, and doing nothing. One of the alternatives would probably have to be one that is environmentally superior to the proposed project. In this case that would be preserving and rehabilitating the building as a jail or for a new use, such as county offices.

The foregoing evidence discloses the need for further investigation of alternatives to demolition.

As a legal matter, the County erred in proceeding without benefit of a full environmental impact report. One function of an EIR is to address the adequacy of proposed mitigation measures. Guidelines § 15126.4. Another function is to consider alternatives to the project. Guidelines § 15126.4. Neither was fully explored here. In cases like this, an "EIR is required to identify and examine the full range of feasible mitigation measures and alternatives to demolition." *City of Oakland*, 60 Cal. Rptr. 2d at 829. By instead certifying the mitigated negative declaration, the County failed to proceed in the manner required by law.

Conclusion

Based on our independent review of the entire administrative record, we find that plaintiffs have carried their burden of citing to substantial evidence that supports a fair argument that the Old Jail is an historic resource, that its demolition will have a significant environmental impact, and that the proposed mitigation measures are inadequate to reduce that impact to insignificance. Based on that finding, and given the low threshold required for initial preparation of an EIR and the legislative preference for resolving doubts in favor of full environmental review, we conclude that this case must be remanded for preparation of an environmental impact report.

NOTES & QUESTIONS

1. In its decision, the court required the County to set aside its approvals for demolition and to prepare an environmental impact report that complied with CEQA before proceeding with any demolition. A lot has happened since then. In September 2004, the Old Jail and another building, along with the five acres upon which they sat, were listed on the National Register. County administrators appealed the listing to the Keeper of the National Register, but they have not been successful in delisting it. In 2009, the County unveiled a new plan that would have demolished most of the building and that would have added a historical display about César Chávez. This plan, too, has been fought by the Architectural Heritage Association and others.

The National Park Service conducted a César Chávez Special Resources Study, mandated by Congress, of sites around the country which were significant to Chávez and the farm labor movement. The Old Jail was one of the sites being considered under the Chávez program to be added to the national park system, though it was not one of the five selected assets. *See* NATIONAL PARK SERVICE, CESAR CHAVEZ SPECIAL RESOURCE STUDY (2013), https://parkplanning.nps.gov/projectHome.cfm?projectID=36145. What does this continuing regulatory drama suggest about the various kinds of protection for which historic resources may be eligible?

2. Are the rationales for preserving the Old Jail—that is, the cultural and architectural bases for its historic designation—convincing to you? Questions regarding designation are further considered in Chapter 2.

3. Are questions of the historical significance of buildings like the Old Jail in Monterey better resolved at the state or local levels? Did the CEQA litigation unduly interfere with the county's decision about what to preserve? Or, is the question of demolition of the jail one to be decided by a court insulated from politics, or should it be decided by a broader polity?

4. While California is a special case, some other states have interpreted their state NEPAs to provide vigorous protection to historic resources. For example, in *Conn. Historical Comm'n v. Town of Wallingford*, 2011 WL 1087088 (Conn. Super. Ct. 2011), the court permanently enjoined the town from demolishing a contributing building in a historic district listed in the National Register. The court relied on language in the Connecticut Environmental Protection Act that created a public trust in historic resources to find that the town had not shown that there were no feasible and prudent alternatives to demolition.

CHAPTER FIVE

SECTION 4(f) OF THE DEPARTMENT OF TRANSPORTATION ACT

Many federal laws that protect historic resources, such as the National Historic Preservation Act and the National Environmental Policy Act, provide procedural protections. In other words, they provide a process that decision-makers must follow prior to taking an action that might affect a historic resource. Only one major federal law provides substantive protection for historic resources: Section 4(f) of the Department of Transportation Act of 1966. The law was recodified (after a repeal and amendment) in 1983, but it remains known by its original statutory reference, Section 4(f).

Broadly put, Section 4(f) provides that a federal transportation program or project may adversely affect land of historic significance only if there is no prudent and feasible alternative to using the land, and only if the program or project maximizes planning to minimize harm to the protected historic site. If there are prudent and feasible alternatives, or if the program or project planning fails to minimize the harm to the historic site, then it may not proceed. These strong rules have saved individual buildings, tribal resources, and even whole neighborhoods from destruction. Moreover, they have inspired a handful of states to adopt similar language that provides the same substantive protection to sites of significance to the state. We turn first to the text, process, and interpretation of Section 4(f).

A. THE STATUTORY LANGUAGE

Section 4(f) of the Department of Transportation Act
49 U.S.C. § 303

(a) It is the policy of the United States Government that special effort should be made to preserve the natural beauty of the countryside and public park and recreation lands, wildlife and waterfowl refuges, and historic sites.

(b) The Secretary of Transportation shall cooperate and consult with the Secretaries of the Interior, Housing and Urban Development, and Agriculture, and with the States, in developing transportation plans and programs that include measures to maintain or enhance the natural beauty of lands crossed by transportation activities or facilities.

(c)   Approval of programs and projects.

Subject to subsection (d), the Secretary may approve a transportation program or project (other than any project for a park road or parkway under section 204 of title 23) requiring the use of publicly owned land of a public park, recreation area, or wildlife and waterfowl refuge of national, State, or local significance, or land of an historic site of national, State, or local significance (as determined by the Federal, State, or local officials having jurisdiction over the park, area, refuge, or site) only if—

(1)   there is no prudent and feasible alternative to using that land; and

(2)   the program or project includes all possible planning to minimize harm to the park, recreation area, wildlife and waterfowl refuge, or historic site resulting from the use.

(d)   De minimis impacts.

(1)   Requirements.

(A)   Requirements for historic sites. The requirements of this section shall be considered to be satisfied with respect to an area described in paragraph (2) if the Secretary determines, in accordance with this subsection, that a transportation program or project will have a de minimis impact on the area.

(B)   Requirements for parks, recreation areas, and wildlife or waterfowl refuges. The requirements of subsection (c)(1) shall be considered to be satisfied with respect to an area described in paragraph (3) if the Secretary determines, in accordance with this subsection, that a transportation program or project will have a de minimis impact on the area. The requirements of subsection (c)(2) with respect to an area described in paragraph (3) shall not include an alternatives analysis.

(C)   Criteria. In making any determination under this subsection, the Secretary shall consider to be part of a transportation program or project any avoidance, minimization, mitigation, or enhancement measures that are required to be implemented as a condition of approval of the transportation program or project.

(2)   Historic sites. With respect to historic sites, the Secretary may make a finding of de minimis impact only if—

(A)   the Secretary has determined, in accordance with the consultation process required under section 306108 of title 54, United States Code, that—

(i)   the transportation program or project will have no adverse effect on the historic site; or

(ii)   there will be no historic properties affected by the transportation program or project;

(B) the finding of the Secretary has received written concurrence from the applicable State historic preservation officer or tribal historic preservation officer (and from the Advisory Council on Historic Preservation if the Council is participating in the consultation process); and

(C) the finding of the Secretary has been developed in consultation with parties consulting as part of the process referred to in subparagraph (A).

(3) Parks, recreation areas, and wildlife or waterfowl refuges. With respect to parks, recreation areas, or wildlife or waterfowl refuges, the Secretary may make a finding of de minimis impact only if—

(A) the Secretary has determined, after public notice and opportunity for public review and comment, that the transportation program or project will not adversely affect the activities, features, and attributes of the park, recreation area, or wildlife or waterfowl refuge eligible for protection under this section; and

(B) the finding of the Secretary has received concurrence from the officials with jurisdiction over the park, recreation area, or wildlife or waterfowl refuge.

NOTES & QUESTIONS

1. What does it mean to "use" the land of a significant historic site? Demolition or dismantling of a historic site would certainly constitute a "use." Temporary occupancies of land that are adverse to the preservation purpose of Section 4(f) are also considered "uses." 23 C.F.R. § 774.17. What about uses that are less direct, such as noise or air pollution? Federal regulations have clarified that a "constructive use" occurs when the "proximity impacts" of a transportation program or project "are so severe that the protected activities, features, or attributes that qualify the property for protection under Section 4(f) are substantially impaired." 23 C.F.R. § 774.15. The Code of Federal Regulations provides examples of constructive uses, such as noise levels that impair sleeping in campgrounds, hearing a performance at an outdoor amphitheater, or enjoying a serene urban park.

Courts have articulated what kinds of proximity impacts are not constructive uses. Not all vibrations, for example, are constructive uses. *See Valley Cmty. Pres. Comm'n v. Mineta*, 373 F.3d 1078, 1092 (10th Cir. 2004) (citing the federal regulations and finding that vibrations could only constitute a constructive use under Section 4(f) if they substantially impaired the protected resource and were not mitigated by planning and monitoring).

In addition, a change in airport schedules or plane types is not necessarily subject to Section 4(f) review. *See Sierra Club v. Dep't of Transp.*, 753 F.2d 120, 130 (D.C. Cir. 1985) ("It can hardly be expected, once an airport has been in operation, that every change in flight scheduling or operations must be accompanied by a 303(c) statement."). One student commentator, however, has argued that courts should apply Section 4(f) to airports and to airplanes in the same way they apply Section 4(f) to highways and to cars. Matthew J. Christian, *Proliferation and Expansion of America's Airports at the Expense of its Treasured Parks and Preserves: Judicial Perversion of the Term "Use" in Section 4(f) of the Department of Transportation Act*, 3 NEV. L.J. 613 (2003). Courts have identified constructive use situations where highways border, restrict access, visually pollute, or heighten noise near protected resources. *Id.* at 624. What would happen if airports, including airport schedules, were subjected to the same treatment?

2. Can visual pollution ever constitute a constructive use? *See* 23 C.F.R. § 774.15(e)(2) for the regulators' perspective. A constructive use occurs when:

> The proximity of the proposed project substantially impairs esthetic features or attributes of a property protected by Section 4(f), where such features or attributes are considered important contributing elements to the value of the property. Examples of substantial impairment to visual or esthetic qualities would be the location of a proposed transportation facility in such proximity that it obstructs or eliminates the primary views of an architecturally significant historical building, or substantially detracts from the setting of a Section 4(f) property which derives its value in substantial part due to its setting.

Does this language go too far? Not far enough? Consider the result in *Citizen Advocates for Responsible Expansion v. Dole*, 770 F.2d 423 (5th Cir. 1985) (finding that a constructive use occurred when an overhead federal highway project interfered with the view of a historic building).

3. Notice that while parks, recreation areas, or wildlife refuges must be "publicly owned," there is no public ownership requirement in the statute for significant historic sites. Private land is protected by Section 4(f) as long as it has national, state, or local significance.

4. The "prudent and feasible" phrase is further articulated in the Code of Federal Regulations. The Code states, "An alternative is not feasible if it cannot be built as a matter of sound engineering judgment." 23 C.F.R. § 774.17. It adds:

(3) An alternative is not prudent if:

(i) It compromises the project to a degree that it is unreasonable to proceed with the project in light of its stated purpose and need;

(ii) It results in unacceptable safety or operational problems;

(iii) After reasonable mitigation, it still causes: (A) Severe social, economic, or environmental impacts; (B) Severe disruption to established communities; (C) Severe disproportionate impacts to minority or low income populations; or (D) Severe impacts to environmental resources protected under other Federal statutes;

(iv) It results in additional construction, maintenance, or operational costs of an extraordinary magnitude;

(v) It causes other unique problems or unusual factors; or

(vi) It involves multiple factors in paragraphs (3)(i) through (3)(v) of this definition, that while individually minor, cumulatively cause unique problems or impacts of extraordinary magnitude.

Id. Which of the two criteria—feasibility or prudency—is more likely to be the subject of a legal battle? Which is best left to the engineers?

5.   The "de minimis" test in Section 4(f) requires either that the program or the project has *no* adverse impact to the historic site, or that *no* historic properties are affected. Is this de minimis test mis-named? Consider its legislative history. It was added to Section 4(f) in 2005 to assuage the concerns of those who felt that Section 4(f) had been applied too broadly. Adding the provision silenced critics, who had advocated gutting the law entirely. *See* David Edward Kunz, *Section 4(f): Analyzing Differing Interpretations and Examining Proposals for Reform*, 31 J. LEGIS. 275, 315–25 (2005) (describing the legislative battles over the de minimis language).

6.   Note that the 2005 statutory amendment that added the de minimis exception to the Act also exempted the interstate highway system from protection as a historic property. The hugely significant system was authorized and many elements were built more than fifty years ago; Congress wanted to avoid subjecting improvements and repairs to Section 4(f) limitations. The exemption does not extend to historic properties that are not part of the interstate highway system but that happen to lie within or along the system rights of way, such as an aboriginal archeological site that is discovered beneath a highway median. The amendment also authorized the Federal Highway Administration to except from the exemption special elements of national or exceptional significance. The agency has excepted 132 features, including, for example, the George Washington Bridge. These excepted elements will not be automatically protected, but their significance can be addressed as issues arise despite the general exemption.

7.   In 2015, Section 4(f) was modified to eliminate the substantive mandate to conduct "all possible planning to minimize harm" if the Department of the Interior, the Advisory Council on Historic Preservation, and the applicable state and/or tribal historic preservation officers agree that a use of a historic property is not "feasible and prudent." *See* 23 U.S.C. § 138(c), 49 U.S.C. § 303(e). In addition, Congress changed the definition of "use" under Section 4(f) to state that "improvements to, or the maintenance, rehabilitation, or operation of" historic railroads or rail transit lines are not prohibited uses and do not need to be completely avoided, even if it is listed on the National Register of Historic Places. *See* 23 U.S.C. § 138(f) (exempting stations, abandoned railroad lines, unused bridges, and unused tunnels), 49 U.S.C. § 303(h) (same). Who benefits from these provisions? Is there a case to make that the public benefits from streamlined decision-making? Can you identify some of the advantages and disadvantages that such an action offers litigants in Section 4(f) disputes?

8.   Section 4(f) was first signed into law the same day as the National Historic Preservation Act (NHPA), on October 15, 1966. Both laws protect resources listed on or eligible for the National Register of Historic Places. *See*

23 C.F.R. § 774.17 (defining "historic site" for Section 4(f) purposes); 54 U.S.C. § 300308 (NHPA). There are, however, many differences in the ways that both laws protect historic resources. The key provision of the NHPA, Section 106, requires that federal agencies engaging in a federal or federally assisted undertaking "take into account the effect of the undertaking on any historic property." 54 U.S.C. § 306108. Does the duty to "take into account" impose substantive obligations on federal agencies? How does "use" in Section 4(f) differ from "effect" in Section 106? Consult Chapter 3 for more on this topic.

B. THE SECTION 4(f) PROCESS

Section 4(f) sets forth the rules for federal transportation programs and projects that impact historic sites and other resources. The process through which these rules are enforced merits further discussion, so in this Part, we will focus on key steps in the normal process, as well as the programmatic agreement process. The relevant regulations are codified at 23 C.F.R. §§ 774.1–.17.

1. KEY STEPS

a. DETERMINATION OF APPLICABILITY

The first step in the process is the determination, by the Secretary of the Department of Transportation, that Section 4(f) applies. Section 4(f) applies only to transportation programs or projects involving the divisions of the Department of Transportation, such the Federal Highway Administration, the Federal Transit Administration, the Federal Aviation Administration, the Federal Railroad Administration, and the National Highway Traffic Safety Administration. Planning for such programs or projects must be in the final stages. If no part of the Department of Transportation is involved in managing or funding the program or project, or if planning is not in the final stages, then Section 4(f) does not apply.

b. DETERMINATION OF A "USE"

The second step is determining whether a use of a protected resource has occurred. The program or project must "use" significant, publicly owned parkland, recreation areas, wildlife and waterfowl refuges, or land of a significant historic site. For the purposes of Section 4(f) review, a historic site may be significant if it is either placed on, or eligible for, a local register, state register, or the National Register. Eligibility for a register may be determined in consultation with the Keeper of the National Register, the state or tribal historic preservation officer, and/or local officials. (As the excerpt from *Stop H-3 v. Coleman* below indicates, the review of eligibility is not always straightforward.) If the site is not significant, or if a "use" has not occurred consistent with the regulatory criteria described in Note 1 of the preceding section, then the analysis ends.

c.   PRELIMINARY EVALUATION

If the analysis continues to the third stage, then the applicable division of the Department of Transportation must prepare, on behalf of the Secretary, a 4(f) evaluation. Often, this preparation involves a fairly lengthy series of drafts and comments before final approval occurs. Formal consultation with the Advisory Council on Historic Preservation and the state or tribal historic preservation officer occurs at this stage. Prior to completing a full evaluation, the division may consider whether the impact is merely de minimis. If the impact is determined to be de minimis, the evaluation ends, but if not, it continues.

d.   FULL EVALUATION (INCLUDING ALTERNATIVES)

The fourth stage, the full evaluation, involves a review of both the impact of the proposed program or project and a reasonable number of alternatives to the proposed program or project. The program or project may only proceed if it includes all possible planning to minimize harm to the protected resource and if there is no prudent and feasible alternative.

When it comes to evaluating alternatives, a reasonable number must be evaluated, or good reason must be shown, to indicate that the study of additional alternatives is not worthwhile. Section 4(f) duties on the agency vary depending on whether there are acceptable alternatives to using protected sites. If there exists a feasible and prudent alternative under Section 4(f)(1), then the agency categorically may not use the protected site. If no such alternative exists, the agency may use the site if it engages in adequate planning to reduce or mitigate harm under Section 4(f)(2). Thus, the identification and evaluation of alternatives are crucial to the process. Consideration of alternatives will often be presented in documents prepared for compliance with NEPA, in coordination with the Section 4(f) process.

Alternatives may be rejected if, consistent with the federal regulations described in Note 4 in the preceding section, they present extreme costs or extraordinary community disruption, among other things. If some feasible and prudent alternatives remain, then the alternative that would avoid the use of land from a Section 4(f) resource— the avoidance alternative—must be chosen.

Alternatives should be broadly understood to include both alternate routes and other approaches to an existing problem. Thus, in one case, a court found that the Secretary of Transportation violated Section 4(f)(1) when he approved funds to demolish a historic bridge without considering the availability of federal funds for rehabilitation. *Benton Franklin Riverfront Trailway & Bridge Comm. v. Lewis*, 701 F.2d 784, 789–90 (9th Cir. 1983). Under Section 4(f)(1), however, alternatives must not themselves "use" protected sites. As the Eleventh Circuit put it: "An alternate route that also impacts upon parks and historic sites is not an 'alternative to the use' of such property." *Druid Hills Civic Ass'n, Inc. v. Fed. Highway Admin.*, 772 F.2d 700, 715 (11th Cir. 1985).

To be feasible, an alternative should be physically practicable. The Supreme Court has made it clear that a judgment about feasibility "admits of little administrative discretion." *Citizens to Pres. Overton Park, Inc. v. Volpe*, 401 U.S. 402, 411 (1971). The Court clarified: "For this exemption to apply the Secretary must find as a matter of sound engineering it would not be feasible to build the highway along any other route." *Id.*

The agency's consideration of whether an alternative is prudent admits a wider range of factors, such as economics and aesthetics, but does not permit the agency to ignore the basic value choices made by Congress. The Supreme Court explained that while "cost" and "disruption of the community" were not to be ignored in weighing prudence: "protection of parkland was to be given paramount importance. The few green havens that are public parks were not to be lost unless there were truly unusual factors present in a particular case or the cost or community disruption resulting from alternate routes reached extraordinary magnitudes." *Id.* at 412–13. Although the Court's discussion was limited to the public parks at issue in *Overton Park*, subsequent lower court decisions have applied its precept to historic sites without question. *See, e.g., Concerned Citizens Alliance, Inc. v. Slater*, 176 F.3d 686, 702–03 (3d Cir. 1999) (holding that "the Secretary must consider every 'feasible and prudent' alternative that uses historically significant land when deciding which alternative will minimize harm, but that the Secretary has slightly greater leeway—compared to a 4(f)(1) inquiry—in using its expertise" for Section 4(f)(2) cases).

Adding to our understanding of alternatives is the following formulation, presented by the Ninth Circuit: "Alternatives that do not accomplish the purposes of the project may properly be rejected as imprudent." *Ariz. Past & Future Found., Inc. v. Lewis*, 722 F.2d 1423, 1428 (9th Cir. 1983). In that case, although another route satisfied some project objectives, the agency reasonably concluded that the alternate route would not relieve traffic congestion, which was a prime objective. Some courts have applied this test rather leniently. For example, one court of appeals held that that the agency need not consider a "no build" alternative, if it would not serve the project's purpose of building a new highway. *Druid Hills*, 772 F.2d at 715. The Ninth Circuit, however, properly requires a more detailed and specific agency justification for rejecting a no build option as imprudent. It has explained:

> The mere fact that a "need" for a highway has been "established" does not prove that not to build the highway would be "imprudent" under *Overton Park*. To the contrary, it must be shown that the implications of not building the highway pose an

"unusual situation," are "truly unusual factors," or represent cost or community disruption reaching "extraordinary magnitudes."

Stop H-3 Ass'n v. Dole, 740 F.2d 1442, 1455 n.21 (9th Cir. 1984). At the same time, "courts have held that an accumulation of smaller problems that, standing alone, would not individually constitute unique problems may together comprise sufficient reason for rejecting an alternative as imprudent." *Concerned Citizens*, 176 F.3d at 704.

If there is neither a prudent and feasible alternative nor an avoidance alternative, then the agency must proceed to the fifth stage of the Section 4(f) process. According to 23 C.F.R. § 774.3(c), the alternative that causes the least overall harm, and that includes all possible planning to minimize harm, may be selected. In determining what causes the least overall harm, the ability to mitigate adverse impacts, the severity of the harm remaining after mitigation, the relative significance of the protected resource, the views of the officials with jurisdiction, the degree to which the alternative meets the purposes and need of the project, and cost differences, among other things, may be considered.

NOTES & QUESTIONS

1.   How is Section 4(f) similar to the National Historic Preservation Act and the National Environmental Policy Act, covered in Chapters 3 and 4? How is it different?

Consultation, documentation, and careful consideration are required before a final decision may be made. But Section 4(f) goes further, in that it actually dictates the substance of the decision. The Department of Transportation and its affiliates may only proceed with projects that use significant historic land if there are no prudent and feasible alternatives to the project and if the project strives to minimize harm; otherwise, they may proceed if the impact is de minimis.

2.   What happens when a federal highway project begins and construction workers encounter an archaeological site that no one knew existed? Section 4(f) applies to all archaeological sites on or eligible for the National Register, even if such sites are discovered during construction, unless "the archeological resource is important chiefly because of what can be learned by data recovery and has minimal value for preservation in place [EDS.: and] * * * [t]he official(s) with jurisdiction over the Section 4(f) resource have been consulted and have not objected to" such a finding. 23 C.F.R. § 774.13(b). In other words, Section 4(f) applies to those historically significant archaeological sites that warrant preservation in place. In such circumstances, the Section 4(f) process is expedited, and the investment that has already been made in the federal transportation program or project is taken into account when determining whether any alternatives are prudent and feasible.

Does this regulatory framework hinder preservation of archaeological resources? The First Circuit has said that the adoption of special archaeological regulations by the Department of Transportation was a valid exercise of the Department's powers. *Town of Belmont v. Dole*, 766 F.2d 28 (1st Cir. 1985), *cert. denied*, 474 U.S. 1055 (1986). The First Circuit panel indicated that striking down these regulations would actually hinder Section 4(f)'s preservation purpose because if full Section 4(f) review applied, often times the discovered archaeological resource would be abandoned, rather than preserved in place or removed to a secure location. *Id.* at 33.

A student commentator rejected this perspective as being contrary to the legislative history and intent of Section 4(f). *See* Stanley D. Olesh, *The Roads Through Our Ruins: Archaeology and Section 4(f) of the Department of Transportation Act*, 28 WM. & MARY L. REV. 155 (1986). That author suggests that the Department should rescind its special archaeological regulations, and that Congress should amend not Section 4(f) but should rather amend one of the federal archaeological laws (such as the Archaeological Resources Protection Act, discussed in Chapter 8) to require any administrative agency, including the Department of Transportation, to treat any discovered archaeological resource as warranting preservation on site. Does this suggestion go too far?

2. THE PROGRAMMATIC AGREEMENT PROCESS

The impact of some programs and projects is greater than "de minimis" but not so great as to necessitate a full Section 4(f) review. These projects may undergo a special, time-saving evaluation called a "programmatic" Section 4(f) evaluation. Eligible projects include: those with a net benefit to a Section 4(f) property, those with only a minor impact on protected resources, those that involve the construction of bikeways or walkways, and those that involve historic bridges. 23 C.F.R. § 774.3(d). Programmatic Section 4(f) evaluations facilitate the processing of eligible projects.

Case Study: Programmatic Section 4(f) Evaluations: The Lake Keechelus Snowshed Bridge

A case study of a historic bridge may clarify how programmatic Section 4(f) evaluations work. In the case of bridges, programmatic Section 4(f) evaluations can be used by the Federal Highway Administration (FHWA) if: the bridge is to be replaced or rehabilitated with federal funds; the project will use a historic bridge on, or is eligible for, the National Register, but not for a National Historic Landmark; the facts are verified with FHWA documents; and the state historic preservation office and Advisory Council on Historic Preservation have been consulted and agree with the findings through Section 106 procedures. In a manner consistent with the other requirements of Section 4(f), the FHWA must evaluate: (1) a no-build alternative; (2) an alternative in which a new structure is built at a different location; and (3) an alternative that rehabilitates the historic bridge without affecting the bridge's historic integrity.

In the late 2000s, the FHWA and the Washington State Department of Transportation jointly planned to improve fifteen miles of federal interstate highway, I-90, in the mountainous central part of the state. The improvements were intended to enhance safety, reduce congestion, and reduce the risks of avalanches, among other things. Lake Keechelus Snowshed Bridge in central Washington State, a National Register of Historic Places-listed property that had fallen into disrepair, would have to be removed as a part of the larger improvement plan. According to the National Register nomination form, the Snowshed Bridge was the only remaining snowshed in the state, with a unique design that added to its significance.

Given these facts, it should be easy to understand why Section 4(f) review was required for the portion of the project that applied to the Snowshed Bridge, and therefore why the programmatic evaluation was triggered. In the programmatic evaluation, the no-build alternative was rejected because the bridge required repairs, whether or not the highway project proceeded, and because if the highway project proceeded, something would have to be done about the bridge, which no longer conformed to modern highway design standards. Similarly, the alternative requiring that a new structure be built at a different location was rejected because of the extraordinary cost, engineering problems, environmental impact, and disruption to established traffic patterns. Finally, rehabilitating the Snowshed Bridge was dismissed as being too expensive and too technically difficult, among other things. Therefore none of the three prudent and feasible alternatives to the removal of the Snowshed Bridge were accepted.

After these alternatives were rejected, federal and state authorities still had to determine that their proposed route minimized all harm. Admitting that the removal of the bridge would be harmful, the agencies suggested that a mitigating factor to such harm was that the bridge had been documented using photographs, surveys, and other means consistent with Historic American Engineering Record standards.

Demolition of the Keechelus Lake Snowshed Bridge was completed in April 2014, and, at the time of publication, construction is still underway on the I-90 Snoqualmie Pass East.

Figure 5-1:
The Lake Keechelus Snowshed Bridge,
Hyak, WA

NOTES & QUESTIONS

1.   As the preceding case study pointed out, even historic bridges on the National Register may be destroyed to make way for new roads, as long as Section 4(f) requirements are met. Does the programmatic Section 4(f) evaluation process make it too easy to destroy historic bridges without finding that there is no feasible and prudent alternative? Can you make an argument that the programmatic evaluation process, which is articulated only in the regulations and not in the statute, is contrary to law or at least creates a massive loophole in substantive protection?

2.   The description of the Lake Keechelus Snowshed Bridge story was taken from Chapter 5, entitled "Programmatic Section 4(f) Evaluation," of an environmental impact statement (EIS) required by the National Environmental Policy Act (NEPA), a statute examined in detail in Chapter 4. EISs are required when certain major federal actions significantly affect "the quality of the human environment." 42 U.S.C.§ 4332(C). The EIS was prepared by the Federal Highway Administration and the Washington State Department of Transportation. *See* FED. HIGHWAY ADMIN. & WASH. STATE DEP'T OF TRANSP., I-90 SNOQUALMIE PASS EAST: FINAL ENVIRONMENTAL IMPACT STATEMENT AND SECTION 4(F) EVALUATION (2008). The statute does not have a publication requirement, though Section 4(f) requires the publication of certain documents and requires that other assertions be obtained in writing (such as the written concurrence from officials with jurisdiction). In this case the authors were required to do an EIS and published their Section 4(f) analyses too. Are federal transportation

programs and projects that require Section 4(f) review likely to also be projects that require an EIS?

3. The authors of the EIS received approximately seven hundred unique comments on the overall plan to improve I-90 through the NEPA requirement that a draft EIS be subject to public input. Many comments were related to the Lake Keechelus Snowshed Bridge and the alternatives presented in the EIS. Should Section 4(f) evaluations have a public input component? Why or why not? Does it make a difference that NEPA requires that EIS authors provide a well-reasoned decision for their selection of a particular alternative, but it does not require that a certain result be achieved?

C. INTERPRETING SECTION 4(f)

Section 4(f) disputes often pit community activists—those who wish to preserve parks, historic sites, or ecologically significant areas—against transportation authorities who are trying to build multi-million dollar federal projects. Stakes are high, and litigation is fairly frequent. This section chronicles courts' responses to three major areas of dispute: first, the articulation of the standard by which courts review Section 4(f) decisions; second, the relationship between Section 4(f) and the National Historic Preservation Act; and third, the adequacy of Section 4(f) evaluations.

1. THE STANDARD FOR JUDICIAL REVIEW OF SECTION 4(f) DECISIONS

Section 4(f) of the Department of Transportation Act underlies the dispute in one of the most famous cases in administrative law, *Overton Park*. It articulated judicial review of agency decisions in light of the federal legislation in the late 1960s that required agencies to more carefully consider actions affecting the natural environment and historic resources.

Citizens to Preserve Overton Park, Inc. v. Volpe
401 U.S. 402 (1971)

■ Opinion of the Court by MR. JUSTICE MARSHALL, announced by MR. JUSTICE STEWART.

The growing public concern about the quality of our natural environment has prompted Congress in recent years to enact legislation designed to curb the accelerating destruction of our country's natural beauty. We are concerned in this case with § 4(f) of the Department of Transportation Act of 1966, as amended, and § 18(a) of the Federal-Aid Highway Act of 1968, 23 U.S.C. § 138 (1964 ed., Supp. V) (hereafter § 138). * * *

Petitioners, private citizens as well as local and national conservation organizations, contend that the Secretary has violated these statutes by authorizing the expenditure of federal funds for the construction of a six-lane interstate highway through a public park in Memphis, Tennessee. Their claim was rejected by the District Court, which granted the Secretary's motion for summary judgment, and the Court of Appeals for the Sixth Circuit affirmed. After oral argument, this Court granted a stay that halted construction and, treating the application for the stay as a petition for certiorari, granted review. We now reverse the judgment below and remand for further proceedings in the District Court.

Overton Park is 342-acre city park located near the center of Memphis. The park contains a zoo, a nine-hole municipal golf course, an outdoor theater, nature trails, a bridle path, an art academy, picnic areas, and 170 acres of forest. The proposed highway, which is to be a six lane, high-speed, expressway, will sever the zoo from the rest of the park. Although the roadway will be depressed below ground level except where it crosses a small creek, 26 acres of the park will be destroyed. The highway is to be a segment of Interstate Highway I-40, part of the National System of Interstate and Defense Highways. I-40 will provide Memphis with a major east-west expressway which will allow easier access to downtown Memphis from the residential areas on the eastern edge of the city.

Although the route through the park was approved by the Bureau of Public Roads in 1956 and by the Federal Highway Administrator in 1966, the enactment of § 4(f) of the Department of Transportation Act prevented distribution of federal funds for the section of the highway designated to go through Overton Park until the Secretary of Transportation determined whether the requirements of § 4(f) had been met. Federal funding for the rest of the project was, however, available; and the state acquired a right-of-way on both sides of the park. In April 1968, the Secretary announced that he concurred in the judgment of local officials that I-40 should be built through the park. And in September 1969 the State acquired the right-of-way inside Overton Park from the city.[15] Final approval for the project—the route as well as the design—was not announced until November 1969, after Congress had reiterated in § 138 of the Federal-Aid Highway Act that highway construction through public parks was to be restricted. * * *

Petitioners * * * also contend that it would be "feasible and prudent" to route I-40 around Overton Park either to the north or to the south. And they argue that if these alternative routes are not "feasible and prudent," the present plan does not include "all possible" methods for

---

[15] The State paid the City $2,000,000 for the 26-acre right-of-way and $206,000 to the Memphis Park Commission to replace park facilities that were to be destroyed by the highway. The city of Memphis has used $1,000,000 of these funds to pay for a new 160-acre park and it is anticipated that additional parkland will be acquired with the remaining money.

reducing harm to the park. Petitioners claim that I-40 could be built under the park by using either of two possible tunneling methods, and they claim that, at a minimum, by using advanced drainage techniques the expressway could be depressed below ground level along the entire route through the park including the section that crosses the small creek.
* * *

Section 4(f) of the Department of Transportation Act and § 138 of the Federal-Aid Highway Act are clear and specific directives. Both the Department of Transportation Act and the Federal-Aid to Highway Act provide that the Secretary "shall not approve any program or project" that requires the use of any public parkland "unless (1) there is no feasible and prudent alternative to the use of such land, and (2) such program includes all possible planning to minimize harm to such park * * *." 23 U.S.C. § 138 (1964 ed., Supp. V). This language is a plain and explicit bar to the use of federal funds for construction of highways through parks—only the most unusual situations are exempted.

Despite the clarity of the statutory language, respondents argue that the Secretary has wide discretion. They recognize that the requirement that there be no "feasible" alternative route admits of little administrative discretion. For this exemption to apply the Secretary must find that as a matter of sound engineering it would not be feasible to build the highway along any other route. Respondents argue, however, that the requirement that there be no other "prudent" route requires the Secretary to engage in a wide-ranging balancing of competing interests. They contend that the Secretary should weigh the detriment resulting from the destruction of parkland against the cost of other routes, safety considerations, and other factors, and determine on the basis of the importance that he attaches to these other factors whether, on balance, alternative feasible routes would be "prudent."

But no such wide-ranging endeavor was intended. It is obvious that in most cases considerations of cost, directness of route, and community disruption will indicate that parkland should be used for highway construction whenever possible. Although it may be necessary to transfer funds from one jurisdiction to another, there will always be a smaller outlay required from the public purse when parkland is used since the public already owns the land and there will be no need to pay for right-of-way. And since people do not live or work in parks, if a highway is built on parkland no one will have to leave his home or give up his business. Such factors are common to substantially all highway construction. Thus, if Congress intended these factors to be on an equal footing with preservation of parkland there would have been no need for the statutes.

Congress clearly did not intend that cost and disruption of the community were to be ignored by the Secretary. But the very existence of the statutes indicates that protection of parkland was to be given paramount importance. The few green havens that are public parks were not to be lost unless there were truly unusual factors present in a particular case or the cost or community disruption resulting from alternative routes reached extraordinary magnitudes. If the statutes are to have any meaning, the Secretary cannot approve the destruction of parkland unless he finds that alternative routes present unique problems.

Plainly, there is "law to apply" and thus the exemption for action "committed to agency discretion" is inapplicable. But the existence of judicial review is only the start: the standard for review must also be determined. For that we must look to § 706 of the Administrative Procedure Act, 5 U.S.C. § 706 (1964 ed., Supp. V), which provides that a "reviewing court shall * * * hold unlawful and set aside agency action, findings, and conclusions found" not to meet six separate standards. In all cases agency action must be set aside if the action was "arbitrary, capricious, an abuse of discretion, or otherwise not in accordance with law" or if the action failed to meet statutory, procedural, or constitutional requirements. 5 U.S.C. §§ 706(2) (A), (B), (C), (D) (1964 ed., Supp. V). In certain narrow, specifically limited situations, the agency action is to be set aside if the action was not supported by "substantial evidence." And in other equally narrow circumstances the reviewing court is to engage in a *de novo* review of the action and set it aside if it was "unwarranted by the facts." 5 U.S.C. §§ 706(2)(E), (F) (1964 ed., Supp. V).

Petitioners argue that the Secretary's approval of the construction of I-40 through Overton Park is subject to one or the other of these latter two standards of limited applicability. First, they contend that the "substantial evidence" standard of § 706(2)(E) must be applied. In the alternative, they claim that § 706(2)(F) applies and that there must be a *de novo* review to determine if the Secretary's action was "unwarranted by the facts." Neither of these standards is, however, applicable.

Review under the substantial-evidence test is authorized only when the agency action is taken pursuant to a rulemaking provision of the Administrative Procedure Act itself, 5 U.S.C. § 553 (1964 ed., Supp. V), or when the agency action is based on a public adjudicatory hearing. *See* 5 U.S.C. §§ 556, 557 (1964 ed., Supp. V). The Secretary's decision to allow the expenditure of federal funds to build I-40 through Overton Park was plainly not an exercise of a rulemaking function. And the only hearing that is required by either the Administrative Procedure Act or the statutes regulating the distribution of federal funds for highway construction is a public hearing conducted by local officials for the purpose of informing the community about the proposed project and eliciting community views on the design and route. 23 U.S.C. § 128 (1964 ed., Supp. V). The hearing is nonadjudicatory, quasi-legislative in nature. It is not designed to produce a record that is to be the basis of agency action—the basic requirement for substantial-evidence review. * * *

First, such *de novo* review is authorized when the action is adjudicatory in nature and the agency factfinding procedures are inadequate. And, there may be independent judicial factfinding when issues that were not before the agency are raised in a proceeding to enforce nonadjudicatory agency action. H.R. REP. No. 1980, 79th Cong., 2d Sess. Neither situation exists here.

Even though there is no *de novo* review in this case and the Secretary's approval of the route of I-40 does not have ultimately to meet the substantial-evidence test, the generally applicable standards of § 706 require the reviewing court to engage in a substantial inquiry. Certainly, the Secretary's decision is entitled to a presumption of regularity. But that presumption is not to shield his action from a thorough, probing, in-depth review.

The court is first required to decide whether the Secretary acted within the scope of his authority. *Schilling v. Rogers*, 363 U.S. 666, 676–77 (1960). This determination naturally begins with a delineation of the scope of the Secretary's authority and discretion. As has been shown, Congress has specified only a small range of choices that the Secretary can make. Also involved in this initial inquiry is a determination of whether on the facts the Secretary's decision can reasonably be said to be within that range. The reviewing court must consider whether the Secretary properly construed his authority to approve the use of parkland as limited to situations where there are no feasible alternative routes or where feasible alternative routes involve uniquely difficult problems. And the reviewing court must be able to find that the Secretary could have reasonably believed that in this case there are no feasible alternatives or that alternatives do involve unique problems.

Scrutiny of the facts does not end, however, with the determination that the Secretary has acted within the scope of his statutory authority. Section 706(2)(A) requires a finding that the actual choice made was not "arbitrary, capricious, an abuse of discretion, or otherwise not in accordance with law." 5 U.S.C. § 706(2)(A) (1964 ed., Supp. V). To make this finding the court must consider whether the decision was based on a consideration of the relevant factors and whether there has been a clear error of judgment. L. JAFFE, JUDICIAL CONTROL OF ADMINISTRATIVE ACTION 182 (1965). Although this inquiry into the facts is to be searching and careful, the ultimate standard of review is a narrow one. The court is not empowered to substitute its judgment for that of the agency.

The final inquiry is whether the Secretary's action followed the necessary procedural requirements. Here the only procedural error alleged is the failure of the Secretary to make formal findings and state his reason for allowing the highway to be built through the park.

Undoubtedly, review of the Secretary's action is hampered by his failure to make such findings, but the absence of formal findings does not necessarily require that the case be remanded to the Secretary. Neither the Department of Transportation Act nor the Federal-Aid Highway Act requires such formal findings. Moreover, the Administrative Procedure Act requirements that there be formal findings in certain rulemaking and adjudicatory proceedings do not apply to the Secretary's action here.

See 5 U.S.C. §§ 553(a)(2), 554(a) (1964 ed., Supp. V). And, although formal findings may be required in some cases in the absence of statutory directives when the nature of the agency action is ambiguous, those situations are rare. Plainly, there is no ambiguity here; the Secretary has approved the construction of I-40 through Overton Park and has approved a specific design for the project. * * *

Thus it is necessary to remand this case to the District Court for plenary review of the Secretary's decision. That review is to be based on the full administrative record that was before the Secretary at the time he made his decision. But since the bare record may not disclose the factors that were considered or the Secretary's construction of the evidence it may be necessary for the District Court to require some explanation in order to determine if the Secretary acted within the scope of his authority and if the Secretary's action was justifiable under the applicable standard.

The court may require the administrative officials who participated in the decision to give testimony explaining their action. Of course, such inquiry into the mental processes of administrative decisionmakers is usually to be avoided. *United States v. Morgan*, 313 U.S. 409, 422 (1941). And where there are administrative findings that were made at the same time as the decision, as was the case in *Morgan*, there must be a strong showing of bad faith or improper behavior before such inquiry may be made. But here there are no such formal findings and it may be that the only way there can be effective judicial review is by examining the decisionmakers themselves. *See Shaughnessy v. Accardi*, 349 U.S. 280 (1955).

The District Court is not, however, required to make such an inquiry. It may be that the Secretary can prepare formal findings including the information required by DOT Order 5610.1 that will provide an adequate explanation for his action. Such an explanation will, to some extent, be a "*post hoc* rationalization" and thus must be viewed critically. If the District Court decides that additional explanation is necessary, that court should consider which method will prove the most expeditious so that full review may be had as soon as possible.

Reversed and remanded.

NOTES & QUESTIONS

1.   When this case was decided, the Federal-Aid Highway Act of 1968 contained language that was virtually identical to the language in Section 4(f), codified at that time at 49 U.S.C. § 1653(f). Unlike Section 4(f), which applied to nearly all federal transportation projects, the Federal-Aid Highway Act applied only to projects within the Federal-Aid Highway Program, which coordinated the construction and siting of the federal interstate highway system. When Section 4(f) was recodified in 1983 at 49 U.S.C. § 303, the substance of the provisions diverged slightly. The

Congressional record indicates that the slight differences were not intended to produce different substantive results.

2.   Professor Peter Strauss has written a detailed account of the background of this case. He writes that in the 1950s, the city of Memphis was 60 percent white and 40 percent African-American. Overton Park was located in a predominantly white residential area, and in the 1950s the park was open to whites only, although black citizens could visit the Zoo on Tuesdays. *See* Peter L. Strauss, *Revisiting* Overton Park: *Political and Judicial Controls over Administrative Actions Affecting the Community*, 39 UCLA L. REV. 1251, 1290–91 (1992).

Professor Lucie White has also described the racial dimension of the *Overton Park* fight, imagining the perspective of an African-American schoolgirl visiting Overton Park one Tuesday:

> This girl's school bus would drive from a segregated school on the black fringes of the city—fringes that were already crossed by a freeway. It would pass the elegant homes where her own people, forty percent of the city's population, worked as maids and yardmen, until finally, in the center of this area, it would enter Overton Park. As I imagined this second girl taking that journey, I imagined mixed-up feelings of bitterness and awe. Although she loved the park, she also hated what its *preservation* would represent. Therefore, I imagined her spitefully, if also silently, allying with the bulldozers to fight those privileged groups who would suffer neither highways nor Negroes anywhere near their neighborhoods, and who knew how to work the system to get their way. I imagined her concluding that unless some of the freeways were built in the Overton Parks of the world—at least as a precedent—all of them would end up in her own back yard.

Lucie E. White, *Revaluing Politics: A Reply to Professor Strauss*, 39 UCLA L. REV. 1331, 1336 (1992).

3.   Although Section 4(f) and the *Overton Park* decision suggest that no formal, written findings are required, subsequent regulations require that the agency publish information about alternatives considered and mitigation measures used, in the environmental impact statement required by the National Environmental Policy Act, 23 C.F.R. § 771.125.

4.   As Footnote 15 mentions, the State of Tennessee purchased the twenty-six acres needed to construct I-40, as originally planned, for two million dollars from the City of Memphis in 1969. After this case was decided, the Department of Transportation proposed other plans, one of which went through an open trench in the park which was once a tunnel. Fights with neighbors continued. By 1981, the State of Tennessee asked that $300 million allocated for I-40 be freed up for other purposes. By 1987, the state had deeded the park back to the City of Memphis.

5.   In a portion of the *Overton Park* opinion omitted above, the Court held that it had jurisdiction to review the Secretary's Section 4(f) decision based on Section 10 of the Administrative Procedure Act, 5 U.S.C. § 701. Subsequently, the Court held that the APA did not confer subject matter

jurisdiction on courts to review agency action. *Califano v. Sanders,* 430 U.S. 99 (1977). However, in the same decision, the Court recognized that the then newly amended 28 U.S.C. § 1331(a) confers "jurisdiction on federal courts to review agency action, regardless of whether the APA of its own force may serve as a jurisdictional predicate." 430 U.S. at 105. *Overton Park's* interpretation of Section 4(f) remains good law.

2. INCORPORATING THE NATIONAL HISTORIC PRESERVATION ACT

The Secretary of the Department of Transportation is required to consult with the appropriate national, state, or local authorities through the Section 106 process of the National Historic Preservation Act when historic sites are the subject of a Section 4(f) review. The following case suggests that such consultation may not be seamless.

Stop H-3 Association v. Coleman

533 F.2d 434 (9th Cir. 1976), *cert. denied,* 429 U.S. 999 (1976)

■ Before KOELSCH, ELY and WALLACE, CIRCUIT JUDGES.

■ ELY, CIRCUIT JUDGE:

The Moanalua Valley, a beauteous natural wonder that many believe to be of great significance in Hawaiian history,[1] lies on Hawaii's Island of Oahu, directly in the path of a proposed Interstate Highway called H-3. The principal issue on this appeal is whether Moanalua qualifies for protection as an "historic site of ... State, or local significance" under section 4(f) of the Department of Transportation Act of 1966, as amended, 49 U.S.C. § 1653(f) (1970), and section 18 of the Federal-Aid Highway Act of 1968, 23 U.S.C. § 138 (1970). (Both statutes, which are essentially identical, are hereinafter referred to simply as "section 4(f)".) Relying on a published determination by the Secretary of the Interior that Moanalua is eligible for inclusion in the National Register of Historic Places, the appellants[3] contend that section 4(f)

---

[1]   According to the Advisory Council on Historic Preservation,

The historical and cultural significance of the (Moanalua) (V)alley stems from Hawaiian folklore and tradition and continues into the 20th century. The valley contains Kamanui, the valley of the great power, and Waolani, the valley of the spirits which was, in tradition, "the dwelling place of the gods." The forest of the valley retains a traditional natural state associated with the legend and history of the area.

The valley was the property of the royal house of Oahu, the scene of battles and other exploits which are extolled in the ancient Hawaiian chants, the Kahikilaulani. After King Kamehameha conquered the island of Oahu in 1796, the valley was the home of his supporters and eventually passed, in 1848, to his grandson, King Kamehameha V, then to Princess Ruth Keelikolani in 1872, and, upon her death, to her cousin, Princess Bernice Pauhi Bishop who willed it, in 1883, to her friend, Samuel Mills Damon.

[3]   The appellants are the Stop H-3 Ass'n, the Moanalua Valley Community Ass'n, the Kaiku Village Community Ass'n, Life of the Land, the Moanalua Garden Foundation, all of which are non-profit organizations chartered for the purposes of opposing the construction of H-3 or preserving the Moanalua Valley, and several named individuals.

applies. The appellees,[4] who rely primarily on a determination by Hawaii State officials that Moanalua is only of "marginal" historic significance, argue that section 4(f) is inapplicable to the routing of H-3 through the Valley. Agreeing with the appellees, the District Court dissolved the injunctions that it had previously entered against construction of the highway. *Stop H-3 Ass'n v. Brinegar*, 389 F. Supp. 1102 (D. Hawaii 1974). We reverse.

I.   Statutory Background

Public interest in preservation of the physical reminders of our Nation's past has prompted Congress to implement a strong national policy in favor of historic preservation. *See* 16 U.S.C. §§ 461, 470 [EDS.: moved to 54 U.S.C. §§ 320101, 300101]; 23 U.S.C. § 138; 49 U.S.C. § 1653(f) (1970). In section 4(f), Congress has determined that historic preservation should be given major consideration in connection with all proposed highway construction programs that are to receive financial aid from the federal government. The statute provides, in declaring national policy, that ". . . special effort should be made to preserve . . . historic sites." The statute further provides that before the Secretary of Transportation (hereinafter "the Secretary") may approve the use of Federal funds for a highway that will "use" land from ". . . an historic site of national, State, or local significance as so determined by (the Federal, State, or local officials having jurisdiction thereof)," he must determine that no "feasible and prudent" alternative route exists. If there is no "feasible and prudent" alternative, the Secretary may approve the project only if there has been ". . . all possible planning to minimize harm . . ." to the historic site. *See Citizens to Pres. Overton Park, Inc. v. Volpe*, 401 U.S. 402, 411–13 (1971). The requirements are stringent. Congress clearly reflected its intent that there shall no longer be reckless, ill-considered, wanton desecration of natural sites significantly related to our country's heritage. * * *

As defined in 36 C.F.R. § 800.3(f) (1975), the phrase "property eligible for inclusion in the National Register" means "any district, site, building, structure, or object which the Secretary of the Interior determines is likely to meet the National Register Criteria." For the purposes of NHPA, the regulations place property that is eligible for inclusion in the National Register on an equal footing with property that is actually listed in the Register.

II.   The Factual Setting

As planned, H-3 would constitute the third and final segment of Hawaii's Interstate Highway System. It would be a six-lane, controlled-access highway extending for approximately fifteen miles across the

---

The National Wildlife Federation has filed a brief as amicus curiae, supporting the appellants.

[4] Appellees are the Secretary of Transportation, the Hawaii Division Engineer for the Federal Highway Administration, and the Director of the Department of Transportation of the State of Hawaii.

southern half of Oahu, from near Pearl Harbor, on the Island's leeward side, across the Koolau Mountains, to the Kaneohe Marine Corps Air Station, on the windward side. Two conventional highways, the Pali and Likelike Highways, now provide trans-Koolau routes, but according to some official projections, these highways will soon be inadequate to serve the growing population on Oahu's windward side. The Moanalua Valley, which is privately owned, lies within Oahu's interior. H-3's projected route extends for approximately three miles along Moanalua's narrow floor. Within Moanalua, H-3 would pass from within 100 to 200 feet of a large petroglyph rock that is known as Pohaku ka Luahine.[6]

In March, 1973, the Moanalua Gardens Foundation, a private, non-profit organization that is interested in Moanalua's preservation, nominated both the Valley and Pohaku ka Luahine for inclusion in the National Register. On July 23, 1973, the Interior Secretary named Pohaku ka Luahine to the National Register. 39 Fed. Reg. 6402, 6422 (1974). In October of 1973, the Interior Secretary's Advisory Board on National Parks, Historic Sites, Buildings and Monuments considered the historic significance of Moanalua Valley. The Board noted that much of the information concerning Moanalua's importance existed only within the private notebooks of oral traditions about the Valley that had been kept by the Valley's former owner, Gertrude Damon, and that since the Damon notebooks had never been released by the Damon estate, they had never been subjected to rigorous scrutiny. Consequently, while the Board believed that Moanalua had not been conclusively demonstrated to be of national historic significance, it concluded that "[h]istorical, cultural, and natural values combined with outstanding potential for an environmental study area endow Moanalua Valley with an importance that makes its preservation clearly in the public interest."

On May 8, 1974, the Interior Secretary published a Notice in the *Federal Register* that Moanalua, along with a number of other properties,

> may be eligible for inclusion in the National Register of Historic Places and are therefore entitled to protection under section 1(3) and section 2(b) of Executive Order 11593 and other applicable Federal legislation.

---

[6]   The Advisory Council states that

Pohaku ka Luahine, a large boulder marked with petroglyphs, is located in the center of Moanalua Valley .... Pohaku ka Luahine is the largest free-standing petroglyph boulder on the island of Oahu and measures some 11' X 8' X 6'. There are only ten known petroglyph sites on the island of Oahu and only three such free-standing petroglyph boulders in the entire State.

The rock shows 22 carvings which have been identified as petroglyphs (rock carvings) of human figures and bird men which range in sizes up to approximately 20 inches. All these were carved or pecked into the boulder surface with crude stone tools and endless hours of labor. The rock carving is described by the State Historic Preservation Officer as a "superb artistic expression of form in a medium of hard rock, using the crudest of tools and an unknown duration of labor ... reason enough for ensuring the preservation of Pohaku ka Luahine." [T]he ancient Hawaiians believed that natural phenomena—both animate and inanimate—possess spiritual form and being. In tradition, the rock is sacred.

39 Fed. Reg. 16175–76 (1974). Explaining his decision, then Interior Secretary Morton wrote in a letter to the Governor of Hawaii that while Moanalua was not of national historic significance, the Valley "possessed historical and cultural values of at least local dimensions and, therefore, could meet the less stringent criteria of the National Register for sites of local significance."

Thereafter, however, on August 5, 1974, the Hawaii Historic Places Review Board, a State body responsible for evaluating and nominating Hawaiian properties for inclusion in the National Register and for maintaining the Hawaii Register of Historic Places, met concerning Moanalua and determined that the Valley was only of "marginal" local significance, a classification that affords the Valley no protection from destruction.

Since Pohaku ka Luahine had already been named to the National Register, the Federal Highway Administrator, in compliance with 36 C.F.R. § 800.4 (1975), requested the Advisory Council on Historic Preservation to comment concerning H-3's potential impact on the petroglyph rock. The Advisory Council met on August 6th and 7th, 1974. Because the Interior Secretary had recently determined that Moanalua was eligible for inclusion in the National Register, the Council broadened its review of H-3 from that requested by the Federal Highway Administrator to include the highway's potential impact on the Valley. The Advisory Council's report, copies of which were furnished to the Secretary of Transportation and to the Secretary of the Interior, concluded that both Pohaku ka Luahine and the Moanalua Valley possessed "historical, cultural, and archeological significance warranting their preservation."

Notwithstanding the Advisory Council's report and the Interior Secretary's published determination that Moanalua "may be eligible" for inclusion in the National Register, the Secretary of Transportation concluded, in September of 1974, that ". . . the Valley does not come under the provisions of Section 4(f)."

III. Discussion

The District Court did not dispute the significance attached by the regulations to property that is eligible for inclusion in the National Register. The court wrote: "(D)etermination by the secretary of interior that a property is eligible for inclusion in the National Register triggers all protections given to a property actually included until the eligibility is resolved." 389 F. Supp. at 1117. The court believed, however, that the Interior Secretary's May 8, 1974, *Federal Register* Notice, which stated that Moanalua "may be eligible" for inclusion in the Register, was not equivalent to a determination that the Valley "is eligible." We cannot accept this purported distinction.

As noted above, the regulations define "eligible for inclusion" in the National Register as meaning "likely to meet the National Register

Criteria." We are absolutely unable to perceive any meaningful distinction between "may be eligible" and "is likely to meet the criteria" for inclusion in the National Register. Furthermore, in his *Federal Register* Notice, the Interior Secretary specifically stated that the "may be eligible" designation entitled the listed properties to protection under the relevant Executive Order and "other applicable Federal legislation." This is the same protection that is provided under an "is eligible" determination. Finally, subsequent to the District Court's decision in this case, the Interior Secretary has resolved any remaining doubts by publishing a new *Federal Register* Notice concerning Moanalua. This Notice specifically states that the Valley has been determined "to be eligible for inclusion in the National Register." 40 Fed. Reg. 23906–07 (1975).

The District Court also concluded, and the appellees here contend, that since the Interior Secretary specifically determined Moanalua not to be of *national* historic significance, the question whether the Valley is significant in State or local history should be resolved solely by the Hawaii Historic Places Review Board. As previously noted, that Board has classified the Valley as being of only "marginal" historic significance. In our view, the District Court and the appellees have misconstrued section 4(f).

Section 4(f) applies to all properties that "the Federal, State, or local officials having jurisdiction thereof" determine to be of "national, State, or local significance." Under the NHPA, the Interior Secretary's "jurisdiction" to determine historic significance is not limited to properties of national importance.[13] In defining the National Register, the NHPA speaks in terms of properties "significant in American history, architecture, archeology, and culture," 16 U.S.C. § 470a(a)(1) (1970) [EDS.: moved to 54 U.S.C. §§ 302101, 302102]. To us, it appears beyond dispute that such significance can be found in properties that relate only to the history of a particular region, state, or locality. *See* 36 C.F.R. § 800.10 (1975); H.R. REP. No. 1916, 89th Cong., 2d Sess. (1966) *reproduced at* 1966 U.S.C.C.A.N. 3307. Since the Interior Secretary is the only official authorized to name properties to the National Register, we have no doubt that he has "jurisdiction" to determine whether properties have state or local historic significance.

---

[13] * * * If it should be held that the Interior Secretary has no power to determine that properties have state or local historic significance, there would, in our view, be a virtual nullification of the NHPA and Section 4(f). Only properties of "national" significance would have any lasting protection from destruction. Whenever a city or state preferred a Federally-funded highway to an historic site, the local body could simply declare the site insignificant. Such a holding would be without precedent and would completely defeat Congress's clear attempt to protect such properties by passing the NHPA and 4(f).

The Advisory Council's regulations, upon which the appellees have relied, undoubtedly support our interpretation of the Secretary's power under the NHPA. * * * The regulations do not require the concurrence of a state or local preservation official before the Secretary may conclude that a property is eligible for the Register. * * *

Under section 4(f)'s disjunctive language, if any of the officials having jurisdiction to determine that a site has national, State, or local historic significance, so decides then section 4(f) applies. Consequently, the Interior Secretary's determination that Moanalua is eligible for inclusion on the National Register as a site of local historic importance is not vitiated, and cannot be vitiated, by the State Review Board's finding that the Valley has only "marginal" significance. *See Named Individual Members v. Tex. Highway Dep't*, 446 F.2d 1013, 1025–27 (5th Cir. 1971), *cert. denied*, 406 U.S. 933 (1972) (section 4(f) applicable even though city officials had determined that city-owned parkland was of "secondary" importance to the construction of a freeway).[14]

In our court, the appellees have advanced three additional arguments which, if correct, might serve to validate the Transportation Secretary's decision that section 4(f) does not apply to the Moanalua Valley. First, taking a position different from that adopted by the District Court, the appellees assert that, even though the Secretary of the Interior may have determined Moanalua to be eligible for inclusion in the National Register, that determination does not constitute a finding of Moanalua's "historic significance" for the purposes of section 4(f). Appellees argue that section 4(f)'s application is narrowly restricted to properties that are actually included in the National Register or perhaps a similar state or local compilation of historic sites. We disagree.[15] In our

---

[14] Appellees contend that *Named Individual Members* is distinguishable from the instant appeal because there the city council did not find the park to be of no significance but only stated that the park was of "secondary" importance to the highway. We note that, somewhat similarly, the Hawaii Historic Places Review Board did not specifically find Moanalua to be of *no* historic significance. The Board classified the Valley as having "marginal" significance. As do the appellees here, the Highway Department in *Named Individual Members* argued that the local body's action constituted a finding of no significance. *Named Individual Members*, 446 F.2d at 1026. * * *

[15] * * * The legislative history of section 4(f) indicates that Congress inserted the language in question into the statute in order to broaden the statute's applicability. There is no hint in either the committee reports or the floor debates that Congress was seeking, by using the language, to give state and local officials power to vitiate Federal determinations that parklands or historic sites are significant. One of Congress's objectives was to require the Transportation Secretary to apply the statute whenever state or local officials declare a property significant, regardless of what Federal officials might think of the site. Congress's other goal was to guard against the situation wherein state or local officials decide that they would rather have a highway than a park or historic site and consequently declare the property to be insignificant. It is inconceivable that Congress intended that a local agency, by action or inaction, could disempower the Federal government, in a situation involving Federal funds, from preserving a site of historical American significance.

In the Senate's floor debate on the conference report pertaining to 4(f), Senator Yarborough asked Senator Randolph, who chaired the conference committee, the very question that concerns us:

(Senator Yarborough). The question has been raised that, if the local authorities said that a site had no historic significance, engineers could ram a highway through regardless of a site's being of historic significance. Is that correct?

MR. RANDOLPH. No; they could not ram it through, as the Senator has said.

MR. YARBOROUGH. Do the Secretary of Transportation and the highways officials of the Federal Government have the power to apply this provision of the bill as written even though the local officials say such a site has no significance?

MR. RANDOLPH. Under their power to approve plans, specifications, and estimates they can review such decisions.

view, the Interior Secretary's determination that Moanalua "is likely to meet" the established National Register Criteria constitutes a finding that the Valley has historic significance. A contrary conclusion would exalt form and ignore substance.

In making this argument, appellees rely on two paragraphs of a letter written by former Interior Secretary Morton concerning his determination that Moanalua is eligible for inclusion in the National Register. Secretary Morton wrote that his determination of Moanalua's eligibility for listing in the Register did not trigger the requirements of section 2(b) of Executive Order 11593 and that the Department of Transportation remained ". . . solely responsible for determining which provisions, if any, of the . . . Department of Transportation Act . . . are applicable" to H-3. We do not interpret Secretary Morton's letter as broadly as do the appellees. Section 2(b) of Executive Order 11593 establishes special requirements for the protection of historic sites that are located on lands owned by the United States. Since Moanalua is privately owned, the section, under its own terms, does not apply. Furthermore, there is no question that, as Secretary Morton stated, the Secretary of Transportation, not the Secretary of the Interior, is responsible for making the initial determination whether section 4(f) applies to a particular highway project. In making that determination, however, the Transportation Secretary must ascertain whether the project will use land from a site of historic significance, as determined by the Interior Secretary, or state or local historic preservation officials. Moreover, as here, the Transportation Secretary's decision is subject to judicial review.

Appellees next assert that the Interior Secretary's determination that Moanalua is eligible for inclusion in the National Register is invalid because the determination was not made in accordance with the procedures set forth in 36 C.F.R. § 800.4(a)(2) (1975). In pertinent part, that regulation reads:

MR. YARBOROUGH. * * * If you run a highway through a long, slender park . . . you do not have to pay any tax money for right-of-way. Thus the city council, hard pressed for money, is seeking to run a highway right through the center of one of the best parks in the State.

MR. RANDOLPH. We are not going to allow that. (Indicating that the Federal power is transcendent.)

114 Cong. Rec. 24036–37 (1968).

The only commentator to consider the question also agrees with our interpretation of section 4(f): * * *

It is inconceivable that a National Register property could be regarded as ineligible for protection under section 4(f), regardless of whether it was considered "significant" by the local or state governing bodies having political jurisdiction over the property. A similar triggering function may inhere in a local or state historic society, if it has official status to designate landmarks. It might also be found in a state parks or recreation commissioner with respect to local parks which he has the authority to classify for state purposes, although they may not be under his administrative control. (Emphasis added.)

Gray, *Section 4(f) of the Department of Transportation Act*, 32 MD. L. REV. 327, 386 (1973).

If (the Federal) Agency Official (responsible for a specific project) determines that a property (that will be adversely affected by the project) appears to meet the (National Register) Criteria, or if it is questionable whether the Criteria are met, the Agency Official shall request, in writing, an opinion from the Secretary of the Interior respecting the property's eligibility for inclusion in the National Register. The Secretary of the Interior's opinion . . . shall be conclusive for the purposes of these procedures.

Appellees contend that, since the Secretary of Transportation, who was the agency official responsible for H-3, did not request the Interior Secretary to determine whether Moanalua was eligible for inclusion in the National Register, the Interior Secretary had no authority to make such a determination.

Initially, we note that in making this argument appellees expose their own hands, some of which are not wholly clean. The regulation expressly and unambiguously provides that "if it is questionable" whether a property meets the National Register Criteria, the responsible agency official *shall* request the Interior Secretary's opinion. It is manifest that throughout 1974 it was at least "questionable" whether Moanalua was eligible for the National Register. The Valley had been nominated for the Register as early as March, 1973, and in 1974, the Valley was the subject of studies by the Advisory Council and the State's historic review board. On May 8, 1974, the Interior Secretary published an official notice that the Valley "may be eligible" for the National Register. The Transportation Secretary here seeks to avoid the effects of his own, wholly inexcusable, noncompliance with the regulation.

Furthermore, we find nothing in NHPA or the implementing regulations that would preclude the Interior Secretary from determining, on his own initiative, whether a property is eligible for inclusion in the National Register. Such could prove to be one of his most important and enduring contributions. The procedures set forth in 36 C.F.R. § 800.4 (1975) apply only to the special situation wherein a property not previously evaluated in the light of the National Register Criteria, is in imminent danger of alteration or destruction because of an on-going or proposed Federal project. Here, before the Interior Secretary acted, Moanalua had been nominated for inclusion in the Register by the Moanalua Gardens Foundation and had been studied by the Secretary's Advisory Board on National Parks, Historic Sites, Buildings, and Monuments. We believe that the Interior Secretary's determination was well within his power under the Congressional authorization conferred by the NHPA.

Finally, appellees have suggested that the Transportation Secretary's review and approval of the Environmental Impact Statement (EIS) pertaining to H-3, which includes some material concerning Moanalua's historic significance, as well as discussions of several alternatives to H-3's proposed route through the Moanalua Valley,[18] constitutes compliance with section 4(f). Section 4(f) does not require the Transportation Secretary to set forth specific findings and reasons for approving a project that will use land from parks or historic sites. *Citizens to Pres. Overton Park, Inc. v. Volpe*, 401 U.S. 402, 417–19 (1971). Nevertheless, a court reviewing the Secretary's 4(f) decision must satisfy itself that the Secretary evaluated the highway project with the mandates of section 4(f) clearly in mind. *Id.* at 416. On the administrative record, the Secretary's consistent position was not that he had complied with section 4(f) but that the statute was altogether inapplicable. In the light of that consistently recorded position, it is not possible, with factual accuracy, to conclude that the Secretary evaluated H-3 with the explicit directives of 4(f) firmly in mind. Furthermore, we note that the EIS provides no evidence that the Secretary complied with section 4(f). While the document does contain some discussion of the advantages and disadvantages of several alternatives to H-3, as the roadway is now planned, the analyses do not attempt to demonstrate, or purport to establish, that each of the alternatives is not "feasible or prudent," as those terms are defined within the context of section 4(f).

We conclude that the Secretary of the Interior has determined Moanalua to be eligible for inclusion in the National Register of Historic Places and that this determination entitles the Valley to the protections Congress has established for historic sites in section 4(f). We further conclude that the Secretary of Transportation did not comply with the requirements of section 4(f) before he approved Federal funding for H-3. * * *

The District Court's Order dissolving the injunctions against construction of H-3 is reversed. On remand, the District Court will enjoin construction of the highway until such time that the Secretary can demonstrate his full compliance with section 4(f) as the statute applies to Moanalua Valley and Pohaku ka Luahine and has made a determination in harmony with the statutory requirements.

Reversed and remanded.

■ WALLACE, CIRCUIT JUDGE (concurring and dissenting): * * *

I think it clear from an examination of the language of the statute itself and the legislative history that whatever authority the Secretary of the Interior may have with respect to the valley under the NHPA, he is not an official with jurisdiction of the valley within the meaning of this statute. * * *

---

[18] The alternatives discussed range from not building H-3 but instead improving, in various ways, the existing Pali and Likelike Highways, to placing H-3 along different routes across Oahu. Appellants contend that the City of Honolulu, containing a major portion of Oahu's population and undeniably having a vital interest in the trans-Koolua [EDS.: sic] traffic flow, supports an alternative to the construction of H-3 which would add to the Likelike Highway a single, reversible-flow lane, to be used exclusively for public bus transportation.

[T]he statute as amended in 1968 requires that a protected historic site have "national, State, or local significance" as determined by "the Federal, State, or local officials having jurisdiction thereof." While the language may not be crystal clear, I think that the determination of the state or local historic significance of a privately-owned site such as the valley must be made by the state or local officials in charge of state or local historic preservation activities.[3]

Appellants argue that the use by Congress of the plural "such officials" in section 4(f) demonstrates congressional recognition of the concurrent power of local and federal officials to determine the local significance of historic sites. However, the use of the plural could just as easily be an accommodation to state laws which may lodge historical preservation functions in more than one official. Further, a logical reading of that part of section 4(f) in the context of the question before us resolves the issue against appellants. The statute prohibits the Secretary of Transportation from approving any project "which requires the use of any publicly owned land from a public park, recreation area, or wildlife and waterfowl refuge (in three categories, i.e.) of national, State or local significance as determined by (three autonomous groups, i.e.) the Federal, State, or local officials having jurisdiction thereof, or any land from an historic site of national, State, or local significance as so determined by such officials unless. . . ." Applying logical canons of construction to this statute, it declares that each category of property is tied to its appropriate overseer insofar as jurisdiction and the rendering of at least the initial determination of significance are concerned. Each of the three categories is thus tied, respectively, to each of the designated officials; i.e., federal officials to property of "national" significance; property having state significance, to state officials; and property of local significance, to local officials. If this is true, the "as so determined by such officials" clause in section 4(f) would seem to me to require in this case a determination by the local (or perhaps state) officials as a condition precedent to bringing the section 4(f) protections into play.

However, whatever ambiguity may appear from the language of the statute is resolved by the legislative history. The committee report accompanying the Senate version of the Federal-Aid Highway Act of 1968 (which included the amendments under discussion here) noted: "The importance of the involvement of local officials in route selection, the

---

[3]   * * * [EDS.: *Named Individual Members* and similar] cases are distinguishable in that the sites involved were admittedly "of local significance"; the local officials nevertheless declared their preference for a highway. In this case, on the other hand, the local officials have not declared a preference for a highway through a locally significant site; they have determined that the site is not locally significant. The distinction is important because there are much greater local political constraints against declaring a locally important site "insignificant" than against declaring a preference for a highway. *See* Gray, *Section 4(f) of the Department of Transportation Act*, 32 MD. L. REV. 327, 384–85 (1973). Finally, it is noteworthy that the appellants here have not directly attacked the local officials' determination that the valley is not significant as an abuse of discretion or against the law. Their only contention is that the Secretary of the Interior's contrary determination is enough to trigger the section 4(f) protections, a contention which I would reject.

public hearing process, and the resolution and establishment of community goals and objectives cannot be overstated. . . With respect to a number of proposals contained in S. 3418, as reported, local authorities would be vital participants." S. REP. No. 1340, 90th Cong., 2d Sess. 11 (1968), *reprinted in* 3 U.S.C.C.A.N. 3482, 3492 (1968). While this passage of the report does not refer specifically to the role of local officials in determining the local historic significance of sites under section 4(f), the intent of Congress is made clear by an exchange on the floor of the Senate during discussion of the bill reported by the Conference Committee where the amendment of section 4(f) provoked one of the longest discussions. Senator Randolph, the leader of the Senate conferees, during a lengthy discussion provoked by the amendment of section 4(f) explained the theory thusly: "(I)t is important that the local people have a leadership. They can properly understand the importance of places that someone from afar may not realize. The importance of such places can *only* be understood by local people." 114 Cong. Rec. 24029 (1968) (emphasis added). * * *

Thus, there can be no reasonable doubt, in my judgment, that Congress did not intend the Secretary of the Interior to have authority to decide unilaterally whether local sites have historical significance. On the contrary, the legislative history of section 4(f) is clear: the protections extend to an historic site of state or local significance only if the state or local officials with authority to pass on historic values determine that a given site is significant. In this case, the state officials with such authority did not determine that the valley had historic significance, the Secretary of Transportation did not exercise his independent veto power and, therefore, no section 4(f) findings were required. * * *

NOTES & QUESTIONS

1.   The list of plaintiff-appellants in Footnote 3 of the majority opinion reveals the breadth of community organizations and individuals that might be gathered to object to federal transportation projects that proceed without a thorough Section 4(f) review. Why were so many organizations actually parties to the suit, rather than *amici curiae*?

The same standing rules apply here as apply to many other federal agency decisions. The U.S. Code states: "A person suffering legal wrong because of agency action, or adversely affected or aggrieved by agency action within the meaning of a relevant statute, is entitled to judicial review thereof." 5 U.S.C. § 702. The Supreme Court has articulated three elements a plaintiff must prove to establish standing: (1) an injury in fact; (2) an injury fairly traceable to the action of the defendant; and (3) the ability for the injury to be redressed by a favorable court decision. *Friends of the Earth, Inc. v. Laidlaw Envtl. Servs. (TOC), Inc.*, 528 U.S. 167, 180–81 (2000). Does allowing the organizations that were plaintiffs in *Stop H-3* to sue under liberal standing rules help to effectuate the purpose of Section 4(f)? Or, does it facilitate the filing of too many lawsuits?

2.   Consider the circumstances in which local officials may consider a historic site to be insignificant, while national officials consider the same site to be significant. Does the description of the *Maryland Law Review* article cited by the dissent in Footnote 3 shed some light on such circumstances? How did the majority, in Footnote 15, interpret the same article?

3.   This case presents another dimension of the relationship between Section 4(f) and the National Environmental Policy Act. The adoption of an environmental impact statement does not necessarily satisfy the requirements of Section 4(f). Such a statement would have to be drafted with specific reference to the requirements of Section 4(f)—for example, whether such alternatives were "feasible and prudent."

4.   Note that the finding of eligibility for local, state, or national designation should occur early enough in the process that review of alternatives can still occur in light of the historic resource. At what point should this be?

5.   Litigation over the H-3 highway in the *Stop H-3* case continued for many years. In 1984, a Ninth Circuit panel, with Judge Ely again presiding, considered, among other things, Interstate H-3's proposed route through public parkland. *Stop H-3 Ass'n v. Dole*, 740 F.2d 1442 (9th Cir. 1984), *cert. denied*, 471 U.S. 1108 (1985). One alternative that avoided using the park was rejected because "[i]t would require the dislocation of one church, four businesses and 31 residences * * *; [EDS.: and because it would] increase noise, air quality and visual impacts to residences in the general vicinity; require additional costs due to the need for the viaduct structure ($42 million additional); and require construction to lesser design geometric standards." *Id.* at 1451. The panel determined that "the Secretary could not have reasonably concluded that the increased cost of the [EDS.: avoidance alternative] was of the 'extraordinary magnitude' required by *Overton Park*." *Id.*

In 1986, Senator Daniel Inouye took the extraordinary step of inserting the following sentence into Section 114 of an appropriations bill:

> The Secretary of Transportation shall approve the construction of Interstate Highway H-3 between the Halawa interchange to, and including the Halekou interchange (a distance of approximately 10.7 miles), and such construction shall proceed to completion notwithstanding section 138 of title 23 and section 303 of title 49, United States Code. Pub. L. No. 99–500, 100 Stat. 1783–349 (later reenacted as Pub. L. No. 99–591, 100 Stat. 3341–349).

The anti-H-3 parties challenged Congress's ability to pass such a law, arguing that it violated the spending clause, the equal protection component of the due process clause, and the separation of powers principle. The Ninth Circuit rejected these challenges and lifted the injunction on construction. *Stop H-3 Ass'n v. Dole*, 870 F.2d 1419 (9th Cir. 1989). H-3 now travels east-west across the island of Oahu, with a final cost of approximately one million dollars per mile, making it one of the most expensive interstate highways to be built.

6.   You may be asking how a highway that is entirely contained within one state could be an "interstate" highway for the purpose of Section 4(f) review. An interstate highway may connect not only states, but also U.S. military sites. Highway H-3, numbered in the order of funding of interstate highways in the state of Hawaii, connects two military sites.

7.   Transportation projects are controversial in an island state. In 2005, the Federal Transit Administration (FTA) published a notice of intent to prepare an environmental impact statement and alternatives analysis for a rail line on the island of Oahu. The FTA went through its analysis required by the National Historic Preservation Act, the National Environmental Policy Act, and Section 4(f). A group of activists sued the FTA for violating all of these statutes, but two Section 4(f) claims are of interest. First, the plaintiffs claimed that the FTA violated Section 4(f) by failing to adopt either of two alternatives (managing traffic lanes or bus-rapid transit) to the rail line. The FTA successfully defended itself against this claim because the FTA had shown on the record that the two alternatives would not improve corridor mobility or travel reliability, would not reduce congestion, and would not substantially improve service. Second, the plaintiffs alleged that the FTA failed to identify all historic and cultural sites that might be affected. Again, the FTA prevailed, because it could show it made a "good faith and reasonable effort to identify" such sites. *Honolulutraffic.com v. Fed. Transit Admin.*, 742 F.3d 1222 (9th Cir. 2014). Who might be interested in stopping a rail line? What do you think the FTA did to show good faith efforts to identify historic sites?

8.   What do you think is the difference between traditional cultural properties and nontribal religious properties? Could it have to do with a responsibility for lands and properties held in trust? Could it have to do with the existence of tribal nations?

3.   The Adequacy of Section 4(f)(2) Planning to Minimize Harm

Section 4(f)(2) requires federal decision-makers to engage in "all possible planning to minimize harm" before moving forward with a federal transportation program or project that adversely affects historic sites. Individuals and organizations who wish to block such a program or project may challenge whether the decision-making process has been adequate. The following case is the most complete and probing judicial consideration of the agency's duties in this respect. The court's analysis of the detailed administrative record may present challenges to readers, but it accurately reflects the complexity of judicial review involving Section 4(f)(2).

Merritt Parkway Conservancy v. Mineta

424 F. Supp. 2d 396 (D. Conn. 2006)

MEMORANDUM OF DECISION

■ KRAVITZ, DISTRICT JUDGE.

In this lawsuit, Plaintiffs Merritt Parkway Conservancy, National Trust for Historic Preservation in the United States, Connecticut Trust for Historic Preservation, Norwalk Land Trust, Norwalk River Watershed Association, Norwalk Preservation Trust, and the Sierra Club challenge the decision of Defendants Secretary of Transportation and the Federal Highway Administration ("FHWA") to approve a highway construction project (the "Interchange Project") that was designed and will be managed by Defendant Commissioner of the Connecticut Department of Transportation ("ConnDOT"). The Interchange Project, which is expected to be completed in two phases over the next several years, will reconstruct and substantially enlarge the interchange between U.S. Route 7, Main Avenue, and the Merritt Parkway (U.S. Rt. 15) in Norwalk, Connecticut. * * *

It is clear that the Interchange Project, as currently designed, will have a significant impact on many of the aesthetic and historic features of the Merritt Parkway, including its historic bridges, ramps, ornamental parapets, and piers, as well as its park-like landscape and vistas. But it is equally clear that changes to the Merritt Parkway/Rt. 7 interchange to make it fully directional and to ease the significant traffic congestion in the Main Avenue area are needed. The difficulty is in reconciling the public interest in safety and convenience with the public interest in preservation of an important historic resource.

Congress undoubtedly thought it had provided an answer to this recurrent problem when it enacted Section 4(f) of the Department of Transportation Act * * *.

In enacting Section 4(f), Congress required FHWA to engage in planning and substantive analysis before FHWA approves a project so as to lessen the likelihood of disruption once a project is approved. Plaintiffs maintain that FHWA has failed to comply with this congressional mandate and, despite repeated encouragement from the Court, the parties have been unwilling or unable to reach a negotiated settlement of their differences. The Court is therefore confronted with a truly regrettable situation. The Interchange Project has already been approved by FHWA and, in reliance on that approval, ConnDOT has awarded costly bids for the project and has even begun preliminary construction. If the Interchange Project proceeds, Plaintiffs assert that irreparable harm to historic and natural resources will occur; if it does not proceed, taxpayers will foot the bill for increased costs in completing a highway project that is undoubtedly long overdue and important to the State of Connecticut. Either way, the citizenry is disserved. Moreover, as a result of the parties' intransigence, this Court is required to intervene in a complex dispute involving the public interest in an area in which the Court has absolutely no expertise or training—exactly the sort of matter that should be resolved by public officials and those whom they are charged with representing. Of course, the Court cannot know, and certainly should not decide, whether the current design for the Interchange Project is wise or unwise. That is for the public officials to determine consistent with the requirements of law. The Court's role is properly limited to assuring itself and the public, by means of what the Supreme Court has termed a "thorough, probing, in-depth review" of the administrative record, *Citizens To Pres. Overton Park, Inc. v. Volpe*, 401 U.S. 402, 415 (1971), that the Interchange Project was designed and approved by FHWA in accordance with Congress's substantive instruction that the FHWA engage in "all possible planning to minimize harm" to the Merritt Parkway.

Unfortunately, the administrative record, which this Court has reviewed in depth, does not adequately demonstrate that FHWA satisfied the requirements of Section 4(f)(2). The Court emphasizes that this conclusion does not mean that the current Interchange Project design fails to minimize harm to the Merritt Parkway. All it means is that the administrative record before this Court does not demonstrate that FHWA made such a finding or upon what reasoned basis it did so. With commendable candor, FHWA conceded as much at a hearing on Plaintiffs' request for preliminary injunction. But FHWA is not the only party at fault in this case. For their part, Plaintiffs appear to have been asleep at the switch as the designs for the Interchange Project made their way through the approval process in 2000 and 2001. Had Plaintiffs pressed their objections sooner, it is possible that disruption of the Interchange Project might have been avoided. ConnDOT is not blameless either. It has been well aware of Plaintiffs' concerns since at least 2004. Yet according to the Deputy Commissioner for Operations, Mr. Carl Bard, ConnDOT consciously chose to proceed without making changes to the Interchange Project, knowing full well that litigation would likely ensue and that the project might be delayed as a result. * * *

III. Findings of Fact * * *

A.   The Merritt Parkway

The Merritt Parkway is a thirty-eight mile stretch of scenic highway running east from the New York State line in Greenwich, Connecticut, to the Housatonic River. As a result of a variety of unique architectural, engineering, and historic features, including seventy-two bridges in a variety of modern architectural styles (sixty-five of which are formally listed as "contributing factors" to the historic significance of the Parkway), the Merritt Parkway was listed on the National Register of Historic Places in 1991. That designation brought the Merritt Parkway within the protective ambit of Section 106 of National Historic Preservation Act, 16 U.S.C. § 470f [EDS.: moved to 54 U.S.C. § 306108], and hence Section 4(f) of the Department of Transportation Act. Of the numerous bridges on the Merritt Parkway, three are located within the area of the Interchange Project: the Main Avenue Bridge, a classical revival, rustic design stone arch bridge over Main Avenue that was listed as a contributing element to the historic value of the Merritt Parkway in the 1991 nomination of the Parkway for the National Register; the Norwalk River Bridge, a triple-arched concrete bridge across the Norwalk River; and a concrete skew-span bridge over the Metro North right of way, west of the Norwalk River. All three of these bridges date to between 1936 and 1938. In addition, the Interchange Project will also affect the stone-arched Glover Avenue Bridge, which is not on the Parkway but is independently eligible for listing on the National Register of Historic Places and therefore is subject to the requirements of Section 4(f).

In 1994, ConnDOT developed comprehensive planning, maintenance, and landscaping specifications for the Parkway, namely the Merritt Parkway Landscape Master Plan and the Merritt Parkway Guidelines for General Maintenance and Transportation Improvements. These were followed at some point before 1999 by the Merritt Parkway Conservation and Restoration Plan: Bridge Restoration Guide. These three documents will be referred to collectively as the "Merritt Parkway Guidelines" or "Guidelines." Development of the Merritt Parkway Guidelines was integral to Commissioner Frankel's determination (previously quoted) that "the Merritt Parkway should receive special treatment, particularly in the areas of design, landscape, and maintenance procedures . . . based on [its] listing in the National register of Historic Places, its designation as a State Scenic Road, and its aesthetic value."

The Guidelines are comprehensive and set forth detailed objectives and specifications relating to all aspects of the Merritt Parkway. By their terms, the Guidelines, which do not always follow contemporary highway design standards, are intended to preserve and protect the unique features of the Parkway. * * *

In order to monitor compliance with the Merritt Parkway Guidelines, ConnDOT also created the Merritt Parkway Advisory Committee ("MPAC"), which currently includes representatives of the following entities: FHWA; ConnDOT; the Connecticut Historical Commission; the Connecticut Trust for Historic Preservation; the Connecticut Chapter of the American Society of Landscape Architects; the Connecticut Society of Architects; the Southwestern Regional Planning Agency; the Greater Bridgeport Regional Planning Agency; each town along the Merritt corridor; and the Merritt Parkway Conservancy, a Plaintiff in this action.

Figures 5-2 & 5-3:
The Main Avenue and Norwalk River Bridges
on the Merritt Parkway,
Norwalk, CT

B.   The Interchange Project

The current controversy arises from ConnDOT's plans to improve traffic flow and safety by reconstructing the interchange between the Merritt Parkway and Main Avenue in Norwalk, and by creating in the same area what the FHWA described at oral argument as a "massive interchange" providing full access from all directions between the Merritt Parkway and U.S. Route 7. The Interchange Project has a lengthy history dating back over thirty years, to a time when the Merritt Parkway was not listed on the National Register of Historic Places, and when design plans were not subject to review for compliance with Section 4(f) or the Guidelines. * * *

C.   The Purcell Report

In 1993, ConnDOT commissioned Purcell Associates Engineering to produce a report (the "Purcell Report") assessing options for constructing the Route 7/Merritt Parkway interchange. The Purcell Report examined six alternative designs for a fully directional interchange between Route 7 and the Merritt Parkway in Norwalk. * * * At oral argument, the parties agreed that Purcell could not have measured the alternative designs it studied against the Merritt Parkway Guidelines, because the Guidelines were not published until 1994, after the Purcell Report was completed. * * *

In recommending the second of the six alternative interchange designs for further study and development, the Purcell Report highlighted "its simplistic geometric features, less right-of-way impact and less intrusive vistas with the Merritt." However, there is no question that Purcell did not assess the design's impact on the historic features of the Merritt Parkway, or otherwise apply historic preservation considerations to the choice of design. Indeed, the record suggests that Purcell was informed by ConnDOT that the agency itself would take care of considering the environmental and historic issues raised by the alternative designs.

The record, as supplemented by the recently discovered ConnDOT documents, reflects that the interchange design recommended by Purcell in 1993 underwent at least one fairly radical revision with major implications for the historic fabric of the Merritt Parkway. In early 1995, ConnDOT apparently considered further design alternatives, one of which proposed to increase the width of Main Avenue from five lanes to six, and alter the location of Ramp C. The only information in the record about this decision to add a lane to Main Avenue is contained in the brief reports of three meetings in February and March 1995. The report of the March 6 meeting summarizes ConnDOT's findings with respect to the six-lane design as follows:

> The[e six-lane] alternative provides . . . better and safer traffic operation in the interchange area. The main disadvantage . . . is that it eliminates the possibility of replicating the existing structure type for Route 15 over Main Avenue.

> It was resolved that the six lane alternative be pursued in the preliminary design phase because of its superior traffic carrying capabilities and the fact that the Route 15 over Main Avenue

structure can be done with architectural treatments to resemble the existing structure.

Thus, the change from a five to six-lane alternative meant the demolition of the Merritt Parkway's Main Avenue Bridge.

The record does not reflect that during this time period ConnDOT or FHWA undertook any written assessments of the relative harm to the Merritt Parkway posed by the various design alternatives being considered by ConnDOT and Purcell. However, the additional documentation from 1995 provided by ConnDOT shows that during this early period ConnDOT and Purcell worked diligently and commendably to develop a design for the Interchange Project that was aesthetically appropriate for the Merritt Parkway. For example, Purcell drew up three designs for the structure that would replace the Main Avenue Bridge, expressly noting that "[i]n accordance with the Merritt Parkway Commission guidelines and in order to maintain the architectural significance of the existing bridge, the recommended alternate for the replacement of the bridge will have a similar shape and appearance." Similarly, the 1995 Structure Type Study for Glover Avenue Bridge over the Merritt Parkway discussed at some length the architectural concept behind the designs of the replacement bridges, namely "to 'replicate' the existing bridges as much as possible . . . by architectural massing and materials which are either identical or similar to the originally designed and constructed bridges." The study stated that "[t]he bridge abutments and arches of the newly designed bridges will be constructed of natural stone similar in size and color to the original bridges." With respect to the design of new bridges called for by the Project, the study noted that "each of the [ ] [new] bridges has been designed with a similar architectural vocabulary. . . with many of the architectural elements designed as variants of other existing Merritt Parkway Bridges."

D.   The 1998 Draft EA

Inexplicably, the administrative record is largely silent as to what transpired with respect to the Interchange Project between 1995 and 1998. However, in April 1998, ConnDOT and FHWA released a draft federal Environmental Assessment/Section 4(f) Evaluation ("Draft EA") evaluating the Freeway Extension and the Interchange Project. The Draft EA discussed several options for the Freeway Extension project, including Build, No-Build, TSM/Transit (improving the existing Route 7 infrastructure to improve traffic flow), and Widening (widening the exiting Route 7). The Freeway Extension was the option recommended by the Draft EA.

With respect to the Interchange Project, the Draft EA presented only a Build and a No-Build option. The document concluded that the No-Build option was infeasible because it would result in "continued use of a congested arterial . . . increased congestion and accidents." The Draft EA did not include discussion of any alternatives within the Build option, *see* File 126 at 324 ("[T]here is *one* build alternative for the interchange project and four build alternatives for the Route 7 freeway extension project.") (emphasis added). Thus, the Draft EA does not mention either the 1993 Purcell Report, with its six alternative build options, or ConnDOT's 1995 decision to select a six-lane alternative for Main Avenue (with the consequent demolition of the Main Avenue Bridge) over a five-lane option.

Yet, at the time the Draft EA was produced in 1998, ConnDOT had already known for three years that the Main Avenue Bridge would have to be removed, and that it would not be possible to replace it exactly "in kind" as required by the Merritt Parkway Guidelines. * * *

E.   Cooperation with Other Agencies, Section 106 Documentation and the MOA

Because the Glover Avenue Bridge was a National Register eligible property, Connecticut's State Historic Preservation Office, which is charged with monitoring compliance with the NHPA, expressed concerns about the fate of the bridge under the design of the Interchange Project proposed in the Draft EA. The State Historic Preservation Office also indicated that the Project had the potential adversely to affect the other historic bridges and the landscape of the Merritt Parkway.

Section 4(f) also requires FHWA to cooperate and consult with the Department of Interior (DOI) on transportation projects affecting natural and cultural resources. *See* 23 U.S.C. § 138. The DOI echoed the State Historic Preservation Officer's concern. * * *

In February 1999, FHWA and ConnDOT produced a report on the impacts of the Freeway Extension and Interchange Project on historic and archeological resources as required by Section 106 of the National Historic Preservation Act. The language of the Section 106 documentation is in large measure identical to that of the Draft EA. Thus, like the Draft EA, the Section 106 documentation acknowledged in generalized language that elements of the Merritt Parkway's historic fabric and features might be affected by the Interchange Project, and that the Glover Street Bridge would be removed, but the Section 106 documentation deferred providing any specifics as to the harm to historic properties pending final design detailing. The Section 106 documentation also did not mention that the Main Avenue Bridge would be demolished.

In November 1999, in accordance with the DOI's recommendation, FHWA and the State Historic Preservation Officer entered into a Memorandum of Understanding (MOA) that included the following undertaking, central to the current dispute. In the MOA, FHWA agreed to "*ensure the following measures are carried out*":

FHWA and/or ConnDOT shall provide the Merritt Parkway Advisory Committee with an opportunity to review and comment on the final design and landscape treatment for the Merritt Parkway-Route 7 interchange improvements. Modifications to the Merritt Parkway shall be consistent to the extent feasible with ConnDOT's Merritt Parkway Master Plan, the Merritt Parkway Guidelines for General Maintenance and Transportation Improvements and the Merritt Parkway Conservation and Restoration Plan: Bridge Restoration Guide.

([E]mphasis added). ConnDOT also signed the MOA under the word "Concur." As FHWA conceded at oral argument, by its express terms, the MOA commits FHWA and ConnDOT: (1) to provide MPAC an "opportunity to review and comment on the final design and landscape treatment" for the Interchange Project; and (2) to ensure that any modifications to the Parkway are "consistent to the extent feasible with" the Merritt Guidelines.

F.　The Final EA

In December 2000, two-and-a-half years after publication of the Draft EA, and one year after execution of the MOA, FHWA released its Final EA/Section 4(f) Evaluation for the Interchange Project ("Final EA"). The Final EA acknowledged ConnDOT's decision not to move forward with the Freeway Extension project. Instead, ConnDOT would proceed with a so-called Widening Alternative, which "represent[ed] a substantial reduction in environmental impacts compared with the Freeway [Extension] Alternative ... [and] the best balance of transportation service, protection of sensitive environmental resources, and cost."

With respect to the Interchange Project, the Final EA (like the Draft EA) stated that two alternatives, Build and No-Build, had been considered. * * *

The Final EA again explicitly pointed out that the Glover Avenue Bridge would be replaced. It also noted that "[i]mpacts to other bridges cannot be avoided under the Build Alternative, because the project includes the construction of new ramps at Bridge No. 530, which must extend to Bridges Nos. 720 and 721 to provide for adequate geometry." Final EA [doc. #7, ex. 1] Section 4(f) Evaluation at 23. However, as in the Draft EA and the Section 106 documentation, and by contrast with the discussion of the Glover Avenue Bridge, the Final EA never mentioned the fact that the plans for the Interchange Project required the demolition of the Main Avenue Bridge, that the Project had rejected a five-lane alternative in favor of a six-lane alternative for Main Street, or why.

Like the Draft EA and the Section 106 documentation, the Final EA contained no description of any efforts the parties had already undertaken to minimize or mitigate harm to the Merritt Parkway. Instead, the Final EA again deferred assessment of the likely impacts and the appropriate mitigation pending final design detailing. *Id.* at 21. * * *

On January 30, 2001, just six weeks after the Final EA had asserted that final design detailing had not been completed and had stated that "development of the build alternatives" would be "investigated," ConnDOT wrote to FHWA requesting approval for the design of the Interchange Project. During that six-week period there is nothing in the administrative record that shows that any build alternatives were being developed, let alone investigated for compliance with the Merritt Parkway Guidelines. Nevertheless, the Division Administrator of FHWA signed his concurrence to the design plan on February 1, 2001. * * *

G. MPAC Meetings Discussing the Interchange Project Prior to Final Approval

Since the MOA stipulates that MPAC would be given an opportunity to review and comment on the design for the Interchange Project, the Court reviewed the administrative record to determine what MPAC saw and when. * * *

From these documents it appears that MPAC discussed the Interchange Project in at least six meetings over the decade from 1995 to 2005. The minutes of the May 2, 1995, meeting reflect that it was announced that "the Route 15 structure over Main Ave would be replaced to allow for the widening of Main Ave to 6 lanes," and that "Glover Ave would also be widened on the approach to Main Ave which will require the replacement/widening of the structure over the Norwalk River." Thus, it is clear to the Court that, by May 1995, MPAC had been advised that both the Glover Avenue Bridge and the Main Avenue Bridge would be removed. The minutes of a meeting held in August 1995 demonstrate that MPAC was also aware of ConnDOT's intention to construct at least some ramps well above the grade of the Merritt Parkway, and that MPAC had voiced its concerns about the aesthetic implications of such a design choice. * * *

To summarize, by February 1995, the Interchange Project designs called for demolition of the Main Avenue Bridge, its replacement with a different kind of structure, and for the construction of certain ramps elevated 13–32 feet (4–10 meters) above the grade of the Merritt Parkway. However, although the record demonstrates that MPAC knew about these design decisions, none of the subsequently prepared statutory-compliance documentation—not the Draft EA, the Section 106 report, or the Final EA—ever mentioned these impacts on the Merritt Parkway, assessed any feasible alternatives to them or evaluated any means of minimizing the harm to the Merritt Parkway. * * *

H. Post-Approval Activity

FHWA asserts that it gave final approval to the Project in December 2001. In March and December of 2002 there were further MPAC meetings, but it does not appear that the Interchange Project was a subject of discussion at either of these meetings. In October 2003, FHWA wrote to the Advisory Council on Historic Preservation stating that FHWA had determined that the Interchange Project would have an adverse effect on the Merritt Parkway and the Glover Avenue Bridge, and that FHWA and the State Historic Preservation Officer had agreed that "there is no feasible and prudent alternative to avoid these impacts." The details of the analysis that led FHWA and the State Historic Preservation Officer to this conclusion are not disclosed in the record before the Court. FHWA informed the Advisory Council that the State Historic Preservation Officer, ConnDOT, and FHWA had agreed to execute a Memorandum of Agreement and invited the Advisory Council on Historic Preservation to "participate in the consultation to avoid the adverse impacts of this project."

In November 2003, the State Historic Preservation Officer wrote to ConnDOT expressing his sense that substantive design changes had occurred on the Interchange Project and that MOA should be revised accordingly. It does not appear from the record what substantive changes the State Historic Preservation Officer had in mind, and ConnDOT denied that there had been any such changes. Nonetheless, a revised MOA was negotiated to account for the discovery of archeological sites after the signing of the original MOA in 1999. The revised MOA was executed by ConnDOT on November 14, 2003, by the State Historic Preservation Officer on August 11, 2004, and by FHWA on May 31, 2005.

In June 2004, ConnDOT put the Interchange Project out to bid. In October 2004, Plaintiff Merritt Parkway Conservancy (the "Conservancy") purchased a copy of the final plans for the Interchange Project on file with ConnDOT. Even though it was a member of MPAC, the Conservancy asserts that it had not previously seen or received a copy of the final plans for the Interchange Project. Thereafter, the Conservancy sent an email to ConnDOT expressing its concerns about the final design, but was informed that "[s]ince the design is complete and construction bids have been received, changes to the layout of the improvements (e.g., ramp elevations) would not be possible, however variations in the landscape details could probably be accommodated."

In March 2005, the Interchange Project was featured on MPAC's agenda for the first time since July 2001, and the minutes reflect that the Conservancy again expressed its concerns about the final plans for the Project. Following this meeting, ConnDOT wrote to FHWA setting forth its understanding that it had fully complied with the requirements of the MOA. ConnDOT's letter discussed its efforts to satisfy the MOA requirement of coordination with MPAC, detailing the five MPAC meetings convened between May 1995 and March 2005. Notably, however, ConnDOT's letter did not address the MOA requirement that modifications to the Parkway be consistent to the extent feasible with the Merritt Parkway Guidelines. Indeed, at no point in the letter did ConnDOT affirmatively represent to FHWA that the final design was consistent to the extent feasible with the Merritt Parkway Guidelines, and nothing in the record indicates that FHWA itself ever undertook any inquiry or assessment into whether that requirement of the MOA had been satisfied.

On April 5, 2005, ConnDOT convened a public meeting at which the final plans for the Interchange Project were presented. ConnDOT proceeded to award a construction contract for the first phase of the Interchange Project on April 18, 2005. Construction, including blasting and other demolition work, began shortly thereafter.

IV. Summary Judgment

Plaintiffs have alleged violations of Section 4(f)(2) * * * and have moved for summary judgment on all counts. * * *

As explained below, because the record does not demonstrate that FHWA ever determined that the Interchange Project, as finally designed and approved, complied with Section 4(f), nor ever ensured that the commitments it had made in the MOA had been fulfilled, the Court concludes that a remand is appropriate on the Section 4(f) claim. * * *

A. * * *

Section 4(f)(2) itself does not elaborate on what constitutes "all possible planning to minimize harm." However, case law and FHWA publications indicate that the duty to minimize harm has two components. First, harm minimization requires FHWA to consider alternatives that result in less or less-drastic use of a Section 4(f) resource. This does not mean that FHWA must choose the alternative that does the least harm to protected areas using any means technically possible. "Although there is no express feasible and prudent exception to subsection (2), the act clearly implies that one is present." *La. Envtl. Soc'y, Inc. v. Coleman*, 537 F.2d 79, 86 (5th Cir. 1976). Thus, an alternative that minimizes harm can still be rejected if it is infeasible or imprudent. *Druid Hills Civic Ass'n v. Fed. Highway Admin.*, 772 F.2d 700, 716 (11th Cir. 1985).

Second, harm minimization requires "mitigation measures that compensate for residual impacts." FHWA Policy Paper at 7. In other words, whatever harm cannot be avoided by choosing between construction alternatives should be mitigated by design choices within the chosen construction option. Thus, if the only feasible construction plan requires removal of historic features, mitigation measures should be considered. Both aspects of FHWA's duty under Section 4(f)(2)— assessment of alternatives and consideration of minimization measures—are reflected in the commitments FHWA made in the MOA and the Final EA to investigate build alternatives to avoid impact to existing resources, to evaluate modifications for consistency with the Merritt Parkway Guidelines, and to ensure compliance with the Guidelines to the extent feasible. * * *

B.

Under the deferential standard of review and legal principles that guide this Court's review, FHWA needed only to present the Court with an administrative record tying its decision to approve the final design of the Interchange Project to facts indicating: (1) that the feasibility and prudence of alternative construction designs with less impact on the Merritt Parkway had been evaluated; and (2) that mitigation measures compensating for residual impacts had been complied with to the extent feasible. Unfortunately, the administrative record supplied to the Court does not show that FHWA complied with these requirements.

With respect to the requirement that alternative designs be considered as a means of minimizing harm, neither the Draft nor Final EA set forth any alternative ways of building the Interchange Project. To the contrary, the Draft and Final EA both candidly admit that, by contrast with the Freeway Extension, the only options considered for the Interchange Project were Build and No-Build. * * *

Recognizing this deficiency in its EA, FHWA has argued that the analysis of alternative construction designs included in the 1993 Purcell Report satisfied FHWA's obligation to consider and assess the feasibility of multiple designs to minimize harm. In supplementing the record, FHWA also supplied various plans and reports from 1995 which indicate that ConnDOT and Purcell were actively incorporating the aesthetic requirements of the Merritt Guidelines into the plans under development at that time. However, the 1993 Purcell Report and the 1995 plans and reports are inadequate to satisfy the minimization requirement of Section 4(f)(2) for at least two reasons.

First, although the 1995 plans reflect clear attention to historic and aesthetic considerations, the same is not true of the 1993 Purcell Report. As FHWA admitted at oral argument, there is simply no indication in the record that the 1993 Purcell Report embodies the kind of evaluation of harm minimization that Section 4(f)(2) requires. The Purcell Report does not purport to have analyzed the feasibility of the six design alternatives for their minimization of harm to historic resources. Rather, according to the Purcell Report, the "design criteria [were] . . . utilized to incorporate as much of the existing roadways and ramps as possible, minimize wetland impact, right-of-way acquisition and to meet the proposed plans of the communities served by this project." It is true that the Purcell Report apparently also considered something called the Merritt Parkway Commission Requirements, and FHWA speculated at the hearing that this may have been a reference to [EDS.: a] draft of the Merritt Guidelines published the following year. However, FHWA conceded that it was not in fact possible to determine from the administrative record what the "requirements" studied by Purcell really were.

Second, the Court notes that although Section 4(f) itself does not provide for written documentation of the basis for FHWA's conclusion that Section 4(f) has been satisfied, FHWA's Section 4(f) implementing regulations require that "evaluations of alternatives to avoid the use of section 4(f) land and of possible measures to minimize harm to such lands shall be developed by the applicant in cooperation with the Administration. . . [and] presented in the draft EIS [or] EA." 23 C.F.R. § 771.135(i) (emphasis added). Furthermore, "[w]hen adequate support exists for a section 4f determination, the discussion in the final EIS [or] FONSI. . . shall specifically address. . . [a]ll measures which will be taken to minimize harm to the section 4(f) property." *Id.* (j). If the 1993 and 1995 reports were sufficient to satisfy the harm minimization requirement of Section 4(f)(2), the Court is at a loss to understand why the Final EA not only makes no reference to these documents (contrary to the FHWA's own regulations), but instead states that "*[d]uring development of the build alternatives,* measures to avoid impacts to existing cultural and natural resources . . . *will be investigated,*" clearly indicating that the development of build alternatives was to occur *after* the publication of the EA because it could not have occurred previously.

The mere presence in the record of documents from which FHWA *might* have concluded that the requirements of Section 4(f)(2) had been met does not allow the Court to infer that FHWA in fact so concluded. Quite simply, this Court "is not empowered to substitute its judgment for that of the agency." *Stewart Park & Reserve Coal., Inc. (SPARC) v. Slater,* 352 F.3d 545, 558 (2d Cir. 2003). The Court understands that agency decisions are entitled to deference, and the Court is more than willing to accord that deference to the FHWA. But before the Court can defer to the agency, "the agency must provide an adequate explanation for its actions, . . . [and] the explanation must show a rational connection between the facts found and the choice made," and "the required explanation must be articulated by the agency at the time of its action." *Inova Alexandria Hosp. v. Shalala,* 244 F.3d 342, 350 (4th Cir. 2001). * * *

It may be that all such designs would have been extraordinarily expensive or utterly inadequate to meet traffic flow and safety needs, and thus infeasible and imprudent under Section 4(f)(1), but nothing in the record tells the Court whether FHWA in fact reached such a conclusion, or on what basis, and the Court may not scour the record to reach conclusions that FHWA itself may or may not have made.

The administrative record also fails to establish that FHWA ensured that the approved design appropriately mitigates any unavoidable harm to historic properties. The Draft and Final EA acknowledged likely harm to Merritt Parkway and other historic structures, but asserted that FHWA could not conduct any further analysis at the time of the publication of those documents (in 1998 and 2000) because final design detailing had not yet been completed. Instead, the Final EA relied on the commitments it undertook in the MOA to evaluate and take steps to mitigate harm on an ongoing basis in the future, in particular, to comply to "the extent feasible" with the Merritt Parkway Guidelines. Thus, the Final EA states that modifications to the Parkway "*will be evaluated* for consistency with" the Merritt Parkway Guidelines and that the "stipulations outlined in the MOA *will be followed*" during implementation of the project, ensuring that the impacts are properly mitigated." * * *

Contrary to the suggestion in Plaintiffs' briefs, FHWA's decision to rely on the future commitments the agency made in the Final EA and the MOA is not itself impermissible. * * *

Yet the administrative record does not reflect that FHWA took any steps to assure itself that the commitments to future compliance made in the MOA had been accomplished before finally approving the final design in December 2001. The centerpiece of the commitment to mitigation, upon which, for example, DOI conditioned its concurrence in the FHWA's decision to approve the Interchange Project, was compliance to the extent feasible with the Merritt Parkway Guidelines. But the FHWA conceded at oral argument that the final design for the Interchange Project, including demolition of the Main Avenue Bridge, and elevation of ramps up to 32 feet above the grade of the Merritt, does not fully comply with those Guidelines. Of course, that, in and of itself, is not fatal since the MOA stipulated only compliance "to the extent feasible." However, this Court could find nothing in the administrative record to indicate that, during the year between the issuance of the Final EA in December 2000 and the granting of final approval in December 2001, FHWA conducted any analysis or evaluation to confirm that compliance with the Guidelines was infeasible. The record is similarly bereft of any evidence that FHWA performed such an analysis after issuing its final design approval but before the Project was put out to bid in June 2004. * * *

As FHWA's own regulations recognize, FHWA had an obligation to circle back and ensure that the promises of future steps to minimize harm made in the Final EA and the MOA had been kept. * * * Yet, when asked by the Court where it should look in the record for confirmation that the future steps to mitigate harm promised by the Final EA and MOA were taken prior to final approval of the Interchange Project design in December 2001, counsel for FHWA stated "I didn't find anything. . . . That, to be further candid, is a gap." * * * In the absence of evidence in the record that FHWA made sure that the commitments undertaken in the Final EA and MOA had in fact been taken care of, FHWA cannot rely on the MOA to demonstrate that it complied with the substantive mandate of Section 4(f).

In the end, the best that can be said is that the administrative record demonstrates—as FHWA's counsel so commendably and candidly acknowledged at oral argument—"a not-so-good compliance" with Congress's directions in Section 4(f). While FHWA gamely suggested that even "not-so-good compliance" would satisfy its obligations, the Court cannot agree. Unlike the procedural focus of NEPA, Section 4(f) imposes important substantive requirements. * * *

Accordingly, the Court concludes that FHWA has not met its Section 4(f)(2) obligation to ensure that all possible planning was done to minimize harm prior to approving the Interchange Project. * * *

V. Remedy

Because it is not for the Court to substitute its judgment for that of FHWA, or "infring[e] upon the agency's decisions in areas where it has expertise," *Nat'l Audubon Soc'y v. Hoffman*, 132 F.3d 7, 19 (2d Cir. 1997), "the appropriate remedy is to remand the case to the agency to correct the deficiencies in the record and in its analysis," *id.* at 18. *See also SPARC*, 352 F.3d at 562; *D.C. Fed'n of Civic Ass'ns v. Volpe*, 459 F.2d 1231, 1239 (D.C. Cir. 1971). This matter is therefore remanded to FHWA with instructions to address the issues raised by Plaintiffs and to conduct further proceedings consistent with Section 4(f), during which Defendants can also consider Plaintiffs' related claims under NEPA and NHPA.

Plaintiffs have also sought injunctive relief halting further construction of the Interchange Project unless and until FHWA cures the defects in its compliance with Section 4(f)(2). * * *

[U]nless the parties agree among themselves to continue the voluntary moratorium that they have operated under for the past six months—and the Court urges the parties to do so—some form of injunctive relief would be appropriate in this case. The injunction, however, "should be tailored to restrain no more than what is reasonably required to accomplish its ends." *Nat'l Audubon Soc'y*, 422 F.3d at 201. The Court realizes that there may well be categories of construction work that could and should go forward without inevitably locking FHWA and ConnDOT into the current design for the Interchange Project or causing irreparable harm to the Merritt Parkway. In view of the voluntary moratorium to which ConnDOT has thus far submitted itself (and which it has not informed the Court that it intends immediately to terminate), the Court is willing to defer entry of an order on injunctive relief pending input from the parties as to the appropriate scope of such relief. Accordingly, the Court will order the parties jointly to report to the Court on whether the voluntary moratorium will be continued, and if not, to develop and submit to the Court a narrowly tailored form of injunctive relief that permits such work on the Interchange Project as can be undertaken without causing irreparable harm to the Merritt Parkway. * * *

FHWA is further ORDERED to conduct such further proceedings as necessary to cure the defects in its Section 4(f)(2) compliance (and at the same time consider Plaintiffs' concerns under NEPA and NHPA) and to advise the Court on a suitable deadline for the completion of such proceedings.

NOTES & QUESTIONS

1. Photos of two of the three bridges in question—the Main Avenue Bridge and the Norwalk River Bridge—are included in Figures 5-2 and 5-3. What do you think about their architectural merit as individual structures?

Can you picture how they would contribute to an ensemble effect on the Merritt Parkway?

Note that these photos are credited to the Historic American Engineering Record (HAER). The HAER, since 1969 a part of the National Park Service, fulfills the information-gathering function of governments in the preservation context. It documents individual sites and objects such as railroads, parkways, roads, canals, and bridges, among other engineering and industrial marvels. According to the Library of Congress, the HAER collection is among the most heavily used in the Prints and Photographs Division.

2.   What is the attitude taken by Judge Kravitz about the matter before him? Given the dueling studies and intricate technical details, do you sympathize with his perspective?

3.   Consider another case that criticized an inadequate record and a failure to consider a no-build alternative. Using the language of the Federal-Aid Highway Program statute that, at the time, was virtually identical to Section 4(f), the D.C. Circuit in 1972 found that the Secretary of Transportation should have considered whether the no-build alternative to the construction of a bridge in a historic neighborhood in Washington, D.C., was prudent and feasible. The panel stated:

> [T]he Secretary might determine that present and foreseeable traffic needs can be handled (perhaps by expansion of existing bridges) without construction of an additional river crossing. In that case, an entirely prudent and feasible alternative to the Three Sisters Bridge might be no bridge at all, and its construction would violate § 138.

D.C. Fed'n of Civic Ass'ns v. Volpe, 459 F.2d 1231, 1238 (D.C. Cir. 1971), *cert. denied*, 405 U.S. 1030 (1972). The proposed Three Sisters Bridge was never built. The defeat of the bridge was the climax of a long battle to prevent the construction of highways through Washington, D.C. and divert federal funds to the construction of mass transit. *See* ZACHARY M. SCHRAG, THE GREAT SOCIETY SUBWAY: A HISTORY OF THE WASHINGTON METRO 119–41 (2006).

4.   What about cases where the no-build option is the only evaluated alternative that does not affect historic sites? The court mentions *Druid Hills Civic Ass'n, Inc. v. Fed. Highway Admin.*, 772 F.2d 700 (11th Cir. 1985). In that case, a neighborhood association challenged the proposal of the Federal Highway Administration (FHWA) to build a highway through a historic neighborhood in Atlanta, Georgia. The FHWA evaluated five alternative designs for the parkway, including four "build" designs—each of which used or impacted protected areas—and one no-build design. Finding the record inadequate and the evaluation insufficient (particularly with respect to the degree of impact on the threatened parkland and historic sites), the court remanded the case to the Secretary for further review in accordance with Section 4(f). The court added that there are "no exceptions to the requirement that there be no prudent alternatives to the use of parks and historic sites before the Secretary can approve a project using protected properties." *Id.* at

716, n.19. Is the Eleventh Circuit's approach more favorable to environmental and preservation groups, or to federal highway officials?

Note that one of the plaintiffs in *Druid Hills* was the National Trust for Historic Preservation, who also joined as a plaintiff in *Merritt Parkway*. In both cases, as well as many other Section 4(f) cases, various state and local nonprofit organizations dedicated to preservation were engaged.

5.   This case illustrates a conflict between two public interests: (1) relieving traffic congestion, improving safety, and saving taxpayers cost overruns for contracts that have already been made, and (2) preserving an important historic resource. As we conclude this Chapter, consider whether Section 4(f) adequately balances both interests. If not, how should it be amended to better balance these interests? One attorney has chronicled various proposals to amend the law. David Edward Kunz, *Section 4(f): Analyzing Differing Interpretations and Examining Proposals for Reform*, 31 J. LEGIS. 275, 307–25 (2005).

6.   The Fifth Circuit, in the *Louisiana Environmental Society* case cited in *Merritt Parkway v. Mineta*, explains why Congress passed Section 4(f):

> It did so in recognition of the fact that it is always easier to build highways through publicly owned parks because people and their homes, businesses, schools and churches will not have to be displaced and its acquisition costs little or nothing. This thumb-on-the-scale approach is required whenever the parkland is to be used.

La. Envtl. Soc'y, Inc. v. Coleman, 537 F.2d 79, 84 (5th Cir. 1976). Does the same rationale underlie the Section 4(f) provisions for historic sites? If not, what does?

7.   In addition to being listed on the National Register, the Merritt Parkway is designated as a National Scenic Byway. Any person, group, or local government may nominate a road for Byway recognition. Included in the nomination must be: information about the road's significance, including particular archaeological, cultural, historic, natural, recreational, and scenic qualities; distinctive features of the byway corridor (points of interest, activities, events); and a corridor management plan, among other things. The Byways are not regulated, nor are they automatically funded. However, National Scenic Byways are promoted by the Department of Transportation as tourist designations and may be eligible for some grant funding. In 2019, $43 million of grants were given by the Federal Highway Administration for projects related to advanced transportation and congestion management technologies deployment, in only ten states. *See* U.S. Department of Transportation, *FY 2019 Advanced Transportation and Congestion Management Technologies Deployment (ATCMTD) Project Awards*, FEDERAL HIGHWAY ADMINISTRATION OFFICE OF OPERATIONS (June 17, 2020), https://ops.fhwa.dot.gov/fastact/atcmtd/2019/awards/index.htm.

As of 2020, the proposed interchange has not seen any significant construction.

D. STATE LAWS MODELED AFTER SECTION 4(f)

A small number of states have adopted key provisions of Section 4(f). State laws similar to Section 4(f) may apply to more types of historic resources than transportation projects. New Mexico, for example, passed the Prehistoric and Historic Sites Preservation Act in 1989. N.M. STAT. ANN. §§ 18–8–1 to 18–8–8. It provides, in relevant part:

> No public funds of the state or any of its agencies or political subdivisions shall be spent on any program or project that requires the use of any portion of or any land from a significant prehistoric or historic site unless there is no feasible and prudent alternative to such use, and unless the program or project includes all possible planning to preserve and protect and to minimize harm to the significant prehistoric or historic site resulting from such use.

Id. § 18–8–7. It protects properties listed on both the National Register of Historic Places and its New Mexico counterpart. *Id.* § 18–8–3(c).

Another state statute modeled after Section 4(f), the Kansas Historic Preservation Act, KAN. STAT. ANN. §§ 75–2715 to 75–2724, was enacted in 1977. It allowed the State Historic Preservation Officer (SHPO), to approve projects only if particular government officials concluded that "there is no feasible and prudent alternative * * * and that the program includes all possible planning to minimize harm to such historic property." *Id.* § 75–2724(a)(1). One interesting aspect about the Kansas statute was that at one point, it protected an area within five hundred feet around the designated property to the same extent as the landmark itself. In this regard, the Kansas law resembled France's preservation law, but not that of any other American jurisdiction. *See* Francois Quintard-Morenas, *Preservation of Historic Properties' Environs: American and French Approaches*, 36 URB. LAW. 137 (2004). This framework was controversial. While some applauded the preservation of historic context, others contended that the five hundred foot ring was arbitrary, or that it discouraged people from pursuing historic designation out of a fear that they would burden or upset their neighbors. In 2013, the Kansas legislature eliminated this so-called "environs" provision.

CHAPTER SIX

LOCAL REGULATION OF HISTORIC PROPERTY

Most public regulation of land use, including zoning, occurs at the level of local government. Thus, it is not surprising that public regulation of historic properties and the activities that may affect them primarily occurs locally. In Chapter 2, we considered the authority of local governments to designate historic properties that could be protected through local ordinances.

In this Chapter, we look at the powers and procedures by which local governments carry out such protection. Our introduction lays out the legal framework of local regulation, which derives wholly from state grants of authority to municipalities. The Chapter then provides examples of local approaches to regulating exterior changes to historic places, whether through demolition or alteration, and whether for buildings or landscapes. It turns next to three other kinds of local historic preservation laws: affirmative maintenance provisions, demolition delay provisions, and constraints on new construction in historic districts. We conclude with a section about the relationship between local historic preservation regulation and zoning. This discussion previews Chapter 7, in which we will examine the constitutional restraints on regulation of property for historic preservation.

A. INTRODUCTION TO LOCAL HISTORIC PROPERTY REGULATION

As of 2021, over 4,000 local governments across the United States had adopted historic district ordinances of some kind. *See* Sara C. Bronin, A Census of Local Historic District Legislation (unpublished manuscript on file with the author). The authority of local governments to regulate historic properties is established by state law, which varies from state to state. Some states grant broad powers to "home rule" communities, or to communities with the right to adopt their own charters. These communities can usually choose to regulate historic places within their broad power. In other cases, a state will provide specific authority for regulating historic properties.

Most states have adopted specific enabling authority for local governments to regulate historic places and create preservation commissions. In addition, all states grant local governments the power to enact zoning, and some expressly allow local governments to zone for historic preservation purposes. Local governments may regulate historic places through zoning in a variety of ways, but usually such regulation entails the creation of historic overlay zones with special rules embedded in a larger land use regulatory framework. More on the relationship between historic preservation and zoning follows in Part F.

For one example of a state that provides specific enabling authority, consider Connecticut, which allows property owners to vote to create both historic district commissions and historic districts. It provides:

> Any municipality may, by vote of its legislative body and in conformance with the standards and criteria formulated by the [State Historic Preservation Office], establish within its confines an historic district or districts to promote the educational, cultural, economic and general welfare of the public through the preservation and protection of the distinctive characteristics of buildings and places associated with the history of or indicative of a period or style of architecture of the municipality, of the state or of the nation.

CONN. GEN. STAT. § 7–147a(b). The legislative body appoints a "historic district study committee," which among other things develops a draft of the boundaries of the district and holds a public hearing on the establishment of the district. Every property owner in the district may vote as to whether the district should be created, using ballots modeled after one distributed by the SHPO. If two-thirds of property owners vote in favor, then the legislative body may—but does not have to—enact an ordinance to provide for the operation of the districts and the establishment of a historic commission. *Id.* § 7–147b. Once a district is formed, the study committee ceases to exist and a five-member historic district commission is created. *Id.* § 7–147c. Among other powers, such as the ability to issue certificates of appropriateness for historically compatible construction or rehabilitation, Connecticut historic district commissions may initiate planning and zoning proposals and may comment on all applications for zoning variances and special exceptions in historic districts. *Id.* § 7–147c–e. While Connecticut expressly prohibits commissions from regulating paint color, *id.* § 7–147d(c), about ten states expressly allow local governments to regulate paint color.

Some state laws specify the composition and size of local preservation commissions. Other times, local governments specify who may or must serve. Having people with some expertise in history, archaeology, architecture, and related fields can ensure good decision-making. It can also ensure that a local commission is eligible for federal funding through the certified local government program of the National Park Service. This program is offered to local governments that demonstrate a serious commitment to historic preservation, including having commissions with enough individuals with credible expertise.

With this context, peruse the following overview of the scope of local authority.

Julia H. Miller, National Trust for Historic Preservation, A Layperson's Guide to Historic Preservation Law
(2008)

Laws governing private actions affecting historic resources are primarily enacted at the local level pursuant to state enabling authority. Through historic preservation ordinances, local jurisdictions regulate changes to historic resources that would irreparably change or destroy their character. Projects reviewed range from window replacement or modification to plans for a new addition or even demolition. * * *

Local Preservation commissions or design review boards administer most local ordinances. Preservation commissions are administrative bodies of local governments and are typically established under the historic preservation ordinance. While the number of commission members and terms varies, depending on the size and needs of the community, individual members are generally required to have some expertise in certain areas, such as architecture, history, real estate and so forth, to ensure that informed decisions are made.

The scope of authority conferred on preservation commissions will vary considerably depending on state enabling authority, the relationship between the commission and other administrative agencies, and the support for historic resource protection. Historic preservation commissions may have either binding or advisory review authority over historic designations or changes to historic properties, and in some cases, they must be consulted regarding other land use actions affecting historic resources, such as a request for a variance or the subdivision of land. The historic preservation commission, however, is the governmental agency that grants or denies a permit to change historic property.

While variations exist from ordinance to ordinance, most include at least five major parts. Besides establishing a preservation commission, historic preservation ordinances generally set forth procedures and criteria for the designation of historic properties, along with procedures and criteria for reviewing requests to alter, move, or demolish such properties. Preservation ordinances also allow for consideration of hardship and other issues of special concern and establish a process for appeal and enforcement of its terms.

NOTES & QUESTIONS

1. In drafting historic preservation ordinances, where did the communities with ordinances begin? In the early 1980s, several commentators provided guidance on model provisions. *See* STEPHEN N. DENNIS, NAT'L TRUST FOR HISTORIC PRES., RECOMMENDED MODEL PROVISIONS FOR A PRESERVATION ORDINANCE, WITH ANNOTATIONS (1980); CHRISTOPHER J. DUERKSEN, A HANDBOOK ON HISTORIC PRESERVATION LAW (1983); RICHARD J. RODDEWIG, AM. PLANNING ASS'N, PREPARING A HISTORIC

PRESERVATION ORDINANCE (1983). Today, the National Alliance of Preservation Commissions maintains a website assembling historic preservation commission guidelines of selected localities, which can be used as models for other localities within the same state. It has also published model guidelines specific to the installation of solar energy systems in historic districts.

2.   How much civic involvement in historic preservation is desirable? Might it present some challenges for advocates of preservation? Professor Terry Tondro has criticized Connecticut's requirement that both the city government and two-thirds of property owners must consent to the designation, the length of time it takes to create a district, and the potential for the process to be subject to political pressure. See Terry Tondro, *An Historic Preservation Approach to Municipal Rehabilitation of Older Neighborhoods*, 8 CONN. L. REV. 248 (1975–76).

Houston takes a similar approach, requiring two-thirds of property owners to consent before an application for a historic district will be deemed final. Houston, Tex. Code § 33–222.1. However, in many large cities—including Chicago, New York, San Francisco, Washington, DC, and Philadelphia—property owners have no power to weigh in on the establishment of either commissions or districts.

3.   Although they all share the common purpose of historic preservation, local commissions vary broadly in their ability to facilitate this purpose. In 2009, the National Alliance of Preservation Commissions and the National Park Service surveyed about 550 local commissions across the country. The findings are fascinating but remain unpublished. Data sent to the authors of this book reveal some striking differences among commissions, particularly when it comes to funding, professional staff, and commission makeup. Half of the survey's respondents indicated having a budget of less than $10,000 and no professional staff to support the work of the commission. Only thirty-three of the respondents indicated having a budget over $50,000. In addition, half of the respondents stated that it was difficult to fill vacancies on the board itself, primarily because of lack of expertise or qualified candidates, but also because of lack of interest and insufficient staff/volunteer resources to conduct a search.

Another area of difference is the age of the commission. The number of respondents for each category of answer to the question "When was your commission created?" were:

Less than 1 year	5
1–5 years ago	45
6–10 years ago	64
11–15 years ago	53
16–20 years ago	75
21–25 years ago	63

26+ years ago	129
Don't know/Not sure	6

Nat'l Alliance of Pres. Comm'ns & Historic Pres. Fund, Nat'l Park Serv., Dep't of the Interior, 2009 Commission Data Project (unpublished data on file with authors).

4.   Should historic preservation commissioners be subject to conflict of interest rules? In *Barry v. Historic Dist. Comm'n of Borough of Litchfield*, 950 A.2d 1 (Conn. App. Ct. 2008), a property owner applied for a certificate of appropriateness for planned changes to the outside appearance of her home, which was located in a historic district. The historic district commission denied the application, after a commission member gave significant expert testimony against the property owner's application. The court found that the homeowner's right to fundamental fairness had been violated. Can you think of other ways in which local commission members might have difficulty maintaining neutrality?

B. REGULATING EXTERIOR CHANGES

The centerpiece of local historic preservation law is the power to control owner changes in the exterior of designated properties. Generally, the owner must obtain a permit from the local historic preservation board before demolishing, altering, or replacing any visible feature of a historic building. Typically, the board will grant such a permit only if it finds that the changes are "appropriate" or "compatible" with the historic character of the structure. In larger jurisdictions, this decision is usually made after recommendations from an expert staff.

Many jurisdictions that provide design guidelines to indicate which appearances are appropriate for predominant historic architectural styles also may categorically exclude from review certain features such as paint color or window materials. Localities may develop their own design guidelines, particularly for unique architectural styles or uses. They may draw from model guidelines from the National Alliance of Preservation Commissions or state-level organizations.

In addition to or in lieu of specific design guidelines, localities— either by law or in practice—often incorporate federal standards from the Secretary of Interior, published as the *Standards for the Treatment of Historic Properties* and known as "the Secretary's Standards." *See* 36 C.F.R. § 68. The Standards offer a set of principles, rather than technical or prescriptive mandates, which those parties interested in altering a designated property should take into account. The Standards, which are reproduced in part in Chapter 1, provide guidance for four treatment approaches: preservation, rehabilitation, restoration, and reconstruction. Historic preservation boards often consult with the Standards when making decisions about appropriateness or compatibility of projects that involve one of these four treatments.

It is important to note that some jurisdictions allow the regulation of interiors. Michigan, for example, expressly authorizes local governments to designate and regulate interiors. Mich. Comp. Laws Ann. § 399.205. New York City regulates interiors of places "customarily open and accessible to the public." *See* N.Y.C. Admin. Code §§ 301–322. These provisions regulating interiors have been upheld against challenge. *Matter of Teachers Insurance & Annuity Ass'n of America v. City of New York*, 623 N.E.2d 526 (1993) (finding that the interior of the Four Seasons restaurant satisfied criteria of the ordinance and could be regulated). Philadelphia added interiors to its ordinance, Philadelphia, Pa., Code § 14–1004(7), after the state supreme court found it lacked statutory authority to designate (and thus regulate) interiors absent explicit authorization. *United Artists' Theater Circuit, Inc. v. City of Philadelphia*, 635 A.2d 612 (1993). While historic interiors are important, we focus on exteriors in this Chapter, because they are by far more commonly regulated than interiors.

1. TWO LOCAL APPROACHES

Localities differ in how strictly they adhere to historic authenticity and permit adaptation for current use. The next two cases give some sense of the variety.

Gondelman v. District of Columbia Department of Consumer & Regulatory Affairs

789 A.2d 1238 (D.C. 2002)

■ REID, ASSOCIATE JUDGE.

In this case, the Mayor's Agent for Historic Preservation for the District of Columbia ("the Mayor's Agent") denied "the application for a curb cut and the related adjustments that would be made to the front of the real property located at 1924 Belmont Street, N.W., [in the Kalorama Historic District in] Washington, D.C." The application sought a preliminary permit, mainly to construct a garage on residential property and to excavate the berm and pave a portion of the front yard. Petitioners Larry S. Gondelman and Pauline Sobel ("the petitioners") challenge the Mayor's Agent's conclusion that their application does not meet the requirements of the District of Columbia Historic Landmark and Historic District Protection Act ("the Act"), D.C. CODE §§ 6–1101–6–1133 (2001). We affirm.

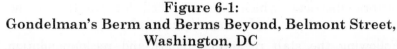

Figure 6-1:
Gondelman's Berm and Berms Beyond, Belmont Street,
Washington, DC

Factual Summary

The record on review shows that the area of the District known as Kalorama Triangle, and which encompasses the petitioners' residential property, was designated as part of the National Register of Historic Places in 1986. Subsequently, around March 2000, the petitioners sought a permit to make alterations to their residential property, including a curb cut and disturbance of the berm, to allow construction of a garage under the front of their attached row house.

A staff reviewer for the Historic Preservation Review Board ("the HPRB") recommended that the petitioners' application be denied "because the alterations are not consistent with the purposes of the preservation law." Specifically, the staff reviewer stated: * * *

> Typical of many houses in the Kalorama Triangle neighborhood, this early-20th-century Mission Style rowhouse is enhanced by the berm in its front yard, some of which is in public space. Historically, the front yards in Kalorama Triangle did not incorporate fences, nor paved areas, as fencing and paving were contrary to uninterrupted lawn aesthetic as defined by the suburban ideal.

> The proposals to excavate the berm, pave most of the front yard, and introduce a garage below the front porch are not compatible alterations with the character of this rowhouse nor the historic district in general. Moreover, the paving of public space in

historic districts, which was intended for planting is not consistent with the city's comprehensive plan.

Following the staff reviewer's report and recommendation, the HPRB held a public hearing on May 9, 2000, to consider the petitioners' application. * * * Mr. Gondelman explained how he intended to alter and enhance his property to meet the needs of the 21st Century in which the private vehicles play a major role; and why his proposed alteration would not lead others in the area to make the same request. He also mentioned other houses located near his property which have "front parking pads." Ms. Eig [his architectural historian expert witness] asserted that the "design [for petitioners' proposed alterations] works with the neighborhood. It is subtle, it is low-key, it is not trying to be something different than what it is, and it is not very dissimilar from houses that were designed with garages in similar neighborhoods." * * *

Mr. Charles Dynes, representing the Kalorama Citizens Association at the HPRB's May 2000 public hearing, testified against the petitioners' application. He maintained that, "the berm is terribly important." * * * "In the Kalorama Triangle . . . [the] berm is probably more important than the curb cut, although they're tied together." He added: "[T]he berms are a distinguishing feature, and on Belmont this particular set of berms is very important." * * *

In addition to his own testimony as a member of the Kalorama Citizens Association's Historic Committee, Mr. Dynes, who was a member of the HPRB when the Kalorama Triangle Historic District was approved for the National Register of Historic Places, read into the record a letter dated April 19, 2000, from the Historic Committee to the HPRB. The letter voiced opposition to the petitioners' proposed alterations on two grounds:

> One, introduction of a driveway would cause the loss of a significant section of the existing berm, which is an important feature in the continuity of [Belmont Road], as well as being an important unifying element in the Kalorama Triangle Historic District. Removal of a 7-foot width from the existing 14-foot-wide berm adjacent to the entry stair represents a 50 percent reduction and only leaves a 3-foot-wide planted area between the stair and the proposed driveway. This 3-foot-wide section is not wide enough to maintain the visual continuity of the berm.

> Number two, approval of this proposal would create an unwelcome precedent for other properties that have no alley access to seek the same remedy. We believe that the consequence of such a precedent would be negative for the integrity of the historic district, as there are numerous properties in this district that do not have alley access.

At the conclusion of Mr. Dynes' testimony, Mr. Gondelman took issue, asserting [that the berm was not visible from a prominent location]. * * *

Mr. Gondelman also urged the HPRB not to say, "because precedent is a concern, nobody can get it. You can't do that."

At the conclusion of its hearing, seven of the eight HPRB Board members present voted to adopt the staff report and to recommend rejection of the petitioners' preliminary permit application. Approximately four months after the HPRB's action, the Mayor's Agent held a public hearing in response to the HPRB's recommendation. * * *

Mr. Gondelman testified that 150 persons living within the Kalorama Historic District had signed a petition indicating no opposition to the petitioners' proposed alterations. He stated that he "knew that fear of precedent would be a concern. So [he] hired . . . Ms. Eig's firm to do a study." In his view, "[t]he fear of [setting] preceden[t] in this case is vastly overstated," because of the cost of attempting alterations for a front parking pad. Mr. Gondelman stressed that "[c]lose to 50 percent of the berm will be retained," and that a pergola would be erected over the proposed garage area.

Two months after the September 2000 public hearing, the Mayor's Agent issued his findings of fact, conclusions of law and order, and a month later, a clarifying amended order. The Mayor's Agent summarized the conclusion of the HPRB. In presenting his own determination, the Mayor's Agent recognized that some of the other properties in the area had curb cuts, but declared that there is "a significant difference between these properties and the [a]pplicants' landlocked rowhouse, which sits much closer to the curb." Continuing, the Mayor's Agent declared:

> Part of the rationale for adopting the Act was to stem the tide towards the diminution of the landscape features of historic districts in the District of Columbia, which would include the imposing of strict controls, which disfavors installing landscape reducing curb cuts, driveway installations, and berm removals in historic districts, as well as to bring some order and consistency to the architecture of the historic district. Once the Act and its enforcement became an integral part of legal enforcement in the District of Columbia, the fact that curb cuts and other related intrusions were made at a prior time, whether legally or illegally, cannot be used as a legal standard by which to evaluate this current [a]pplication, and authorize the granting of the relief sought.

> The granting of this [a]pplication would not only eliminate at least one on-street parking space, but would also reduce the green space which is an integral part of the Kalorama Triangle Historic District, and very likely create an atmosphere in which multiple petitions for additional curb cuts, driveways, and on-

site property parking will almost certainly follow, despite the applicants' self-effacing assertion that there appear to be no more than three (3) potential legally justifiable or sustainable additional petitions from among the other 24 landlocked homeowners in the historic district, due to zoning restrictions and other considerations as recited elsewhere in this record.

The *Comprehensive Plan for the National Capital*, adopted in 1985, recited in section 807(16)(f), that: "The landscaped green space on publicly owned, privately maintained front and side yards in Historic Districts and on Historic Landmarks should be preserved. Special care should be taken to protect these historic green areas from being paved over for vehicular access and parking."

In addition, the Mayor's Agent rejected the petitioners' "enhancement" and "adaptation to the 21st Century" arguments since "the applicants voluntarily elected to reside at the site, and thereby assumed the risk that future development might place some restriction or narrowing of the scope of their enjoyment."

Analysis

The petitioners contend that:

The Mayor's Agent overrode the uncontested evidence presented to him and relied on several factors that have no place in the [historic preservation] statutory scheme, i.e. the Petitioner's voluntary election to purchase a home in 1986 with no parking, the fear of setting a precedent for other such applications, the incompatibility of the removal of a portion of the berm with the character of the historical district, and the language of the Comprehensive Plan.

They argue that they presented unrefuted evidence that their proposed alterations would enhance their house and would be compatible with the character of the historic district. Generally, the respondent maintains that the decision of the Mayor's Agent is supported by substantial evidence in the record, and is in accordance with the Act. Specifically, the respondent argues that the petitioners' "proposed alteration is incompatible with the historic character of petitioners' home and the Kalorama historic district within which they reside."

We summarized our standard of review for this type of case in *Reneau v. District of Columbia*, 676 A.2d 913 (D.C. 1996):

Our review of this matter is limited and narrow. "We must uphold the Mayor's Agent's decision if the findings of fact are supported by substantial evidence in the record considered as a whole and the conclusions of law flow rationally from these findings." *Kalorama Heights Ltd. P'ship v. D.C. Dep't of Consumer & Regulatory Affairs*, 655 A.2d 865, 868 (D.C. 1995). "Moreover, when . . . the Mayor's Agent's [ ] decision is based on an 'interpretation of the statute and regulations it administers, that interpretation will be sustained unless shown to be unreasonable or in contravention of the language of the legislative history of the statute.' " *Id.* at 868. Furthermore, "[i]n making the necessary findings, a Mayor's Agent is 'not required to explain why [he or she] favored one witness' testimony over another, or one statistic over another." *Id.* at 868–69 (quoting *Don't Tear It Down, Inc. v. Department of Hous. and Cmty. Dev.*, 428 A.2d 369, 378 (D.C. 1981)). We have also said, however, that " 'some indication of the reason for rejecting expert, as opposed to lay, testimony is required.' " *Comm. for Washington's Riverfront Parks v. Thompson*, 451 A.2d 1177, 1193 (D.C. 1982).

Id. at 917. After reviewing the record in this matter and the arguments of the parties, we are satisfied that the Mayor's Agent's findings are based upon substantial evidence in the record, and that his conclusions flow rationally from the findings. Although, as an original matter, we might or might not agree with the Mayor's Agent's interpretation of the Act, we cannot say that his interpretation is unreasonable, nor inconsistent with the language of the Act. Nor can we say that the findings and conclusions of the Mayor's Agent provide no indication of his reason for not relying on the testimony of Ms. Eig, the architectural historian, that the petitioners' proposed alterations are compatible and consistent with the purposes of the Act.

We turn now to the applicable statutory provisions. Under § 6–1102 (1) of the Act, " 'Alter' or 'alteration' means a change in the exterior appearance of a building or structure or its site." Section 6–1105 (f) specifies that: "No permit shall be issued unless the Mayor finds that such issuance is necessary in the public interest." "Necessary in the public interest" is defined in § 6–1102 (10) to mean "consistent with the purposes of this subchapter as set forth in § 6–1101 (b)." Section 6–1101 (b)(1) summarizes the purposes of the subchapter "[w]ith respect to properties in historic districts" as:

(A) To retain and enhance those properties which contribute to the character of the historic district and to encourage their adaptation for current use;

(B) To assure that alterations of existing structures are compatible with the character of the historic district; and

(C) To assure that new construction and subdivision of lots in an historic district are compatible with the character of the historic district[.]

In contrast to § 6–1107 concerning new construction, both § 6–1104 pertaining to demolitions, and § 6–1105 relating to alterations, set forth the same standards for the issuance of a permit, that it be "necessary in the public interest" or that "failure to issue the permit will result in unreasonable economic hardship to the owner."[5] Only the "necessary in the public interest" standard is relevant to the case before us, since the petitioners do not argue "economic hardship."

The Act defines the "necessary in the public interest" standard to mean "consistent with the purposes . . . set forth in § 6–1101 (b)," that is, in relevant part, the retention and enhancement of "properties which contribute to the character of the historic district and [which] encourage their adaptation for current use," as well as the permitting of "alterations of existing structures [that] are compatible with the character of the historic district."

The petitioners rely on evidence, primarily the testimony of their architect, architectural historian, and one of the owners, maintaining that their proposed alterations adapt and enhance their house in a way that contributes to the character of the historic district, and urge that this evidence satisfies their burden under § 6–1101(b)(1)(A). Furthermore, they insist that § 6–1101(b)(1)(B) requires only a showing that the proposed alterations to their house alone, rather than the entire site of their home, "are compatible with the character of the historic district." They discount the Act's definition of "alteration" which means "a change in the exterior appearance of a building or structure *or its site*." D.C. CODE § 6–1102(1) (emphasis added).

Before beginning our examination of the parties' arguments, we set forth statutory interpretation principles that guide our analysis. "[W]e construe statutory provisions 'not in isolation, but together with other related provisions.'" *Olden v. United States*, 781 A.2d 740, 743 (D.C. 2001). "While statutory words are to be accorded their ordinary meaning absent indication of a contrary legislative intent[,] . . . statutory meaning is of course to be derived, not from the reading of a single sentence or section, but from consideration of an entire enactment against the backdrop of its policies and objectives." *Don't Tear It Down, Inc. v. Pennsylvania Ave. Dev. Corp.*, 642 F.2d 527, 533 (D.C. Cir. 1980). Thus, "[i]n construing [ ] two subsections . . ., we must at the same time give effect to the whole statute in light of its underlying objectives." *Baghini v. D.C. Dep't of Employment Servs.*, 525 A.2d 1027, 1029 (D.C. 1987).

In applying these statutory interpretation principles to this case, we are mindful that we give deference to the expertise of an agency, as well as its interpretation of its governing statute, unless that interpretation is unreasonable or inconsistent with the language of the statute, *see Reneau, supra*, 676 A.2d at 917. Here, we are satisfied that the Mayor's Agent's decision gives effect to the entire Act in light of its policies and

---

[5]   Section 6–1107 (f), involving new construction specifies that: "The permit shall be issued unless the Mayor . . . finds that the design of the building and the character of the historic district or historic landmark are incompatible; . . . ." The same standard of incompatibility also applies to the erection of an additional building or structure where there is currently a building or structure on the property.

objectives, and that concentration on a single provision, in isolation as the petitioners would have us do, is inappropriate.

The petitioners' burden under § 6–1105(f) is a heavy one. They must demonstrate that the issuance of a preliminary permit for their proposed alterations is "necessary in the public interest." To demonstrate necessity in the public interest, they must meet two statutory requirements. First, under § 6–1101(b)(1)(A), they must establish that their proposed alterations "retain and enhance . . . [historic] properties [in a manner] which contributes to the character of the historic district *and* [which] encourage[s] the[ ] adaptation [of historic properties] for current use." *Id.* (emphasis added). Under this subsection it is insufficient to emphasize only enhancement to adapt a property for current use. Rather, the applicant must also demonstrate that the proposed alterations will retain and enhance the historic property so that it contributes to the character of the historical district.

Second, under § 6–1101(b)(1)(B), they must demonstrate that their proposed "alterations of [the] existing structure[ ] are compatible with the character of the historic district." With respect to this requirement, the Mayor's Agent was not limited solely to a consideration of proposed changes to the structure, the petitioners' house. Rather, given the definition of "alterations" set forth in § 6–1102(1), the Mayor's Agent and the HPRB are authorized to consider the entire site on which the structure sits, that is, the petitioners' house as well as the land, including the berm.[6] At the HPRB's hearing, counsel for the petitioners told the HPRB: "Your authority on alterations is directed at the site and the exterior of historic landmarks, or the building or structure of a compatible building in a historic district, and not the site of the building within the historic district." In fact, under the plain meaning of the entire statutory scheme at issue here, the Mayor's Agent's and the HPRB's authority extends to the site and the structure which are the subject of the preliminary permit application, as well as to the question of whether the proposed alterations are "compatible with the character of the historic district." § 6–1101(b)(1)(B).

Therefore, in determining and interpreting its authority under § 6–1101(b), it was neither unreasonable nor legal error for the Mayor's Agent and the HPRB to reference the section of the District's Comprehensive Plan which mandates that "landscaped green space on publicly owned, privately maintained front and side yards in historic districts and on historic landmarks should be preserved," because that section reflects, in part, the policies and objectives of the District's historic preservation law.[7] We have previously said that District agencies

---

[6]   *See also* § 6–1105(a) ("Before the Mayor may issue a permit to alter the exterior or site of . . . a building or structure in an historic district, the Mayor shall review the permit application in accordance with this section").

[7]   The Comprehensive Plan Amendment Act of 1999, 46 D.C. Reg. 1441 (1999) includes Chapter 8, which contains policies governing preservation of historic properties and districts. Section 805.6 specifies:

may "look to the . . . elements [of the Comprehensive Plan] for general policy guidance." *National Cathedral Neighborhood Ass'n v. D.C. Bd. of Zoning Adjustment*, 753 A.2d 984, 987 (D.C. 2000). Similarly, it was neither unreasonable nor legal error for the Mayor's Agent to reference and decide this case in the context of the rationale for the historic preservation law. * * *

Nor was it unreasonable for the HPRB to consider the history of that district, including the construction of homes without garages due to the availability of public transportation; nor to take into account possible future similar requests for permits to construct parking under residences which would eliminate or decrease other berms, or the "stepped quality" of the 1900 block of Belmont Road. *See Foster v. Mayor's Agent for Historic Pres.*, 698 A.2d 411, 412 (D.C. 1997) (affirming the conclusion of the Mayor's Agent that the "permanent installation of [a particular structure] on public space [would be] inconsistent with preserving the sightliness and historic integrity of districts covered by the Act."); *Daro Realty, Inc. v. D.C. Zoning Comm'n*, 581 A.2d 295, 302 (D.C. 1990) (reliance upon the Comprehensive Plan to review the Zoning Commission and the HPRB's analysis under the Act).

Given the HPRB staff report, the recommendation of the HPRB to the Mayor's Agent, the Mayor's Agent's analysis, the testimony of Mr. Dynes before the HPRB, and the letter from the Historic Committee of the Kalorama Citizens Association, entities regarded as having expertise in the area of historic preservation and historic districts in Washington, D.C., we conclude that there is substantial evidence in the record on review to support the Mayor's Agent's decision. In addition, the record reveals some indication as to why the Mayor's Agent did not rely upon Ms. Eig's testimony, or that of Mr. Carroll, relating to "the other 24 landlocked homeowners in the historic district" who could or might file "legally justifiable or sustainable additional petitions." He characterized this testimony as "applicant's self-effacing assertion." Moreover, even Ms. Eig, in response to a question from Mr. Gondelman, acknowledged that one unique characteristic of the 1900 block of Belmont Road, N.W. is, "the stepped quality of it." The Mayor's Agent found that the "stepped quality" would be severely impacted by the applicants' proposed alterations and could serve as a precedent for other front parking pads that would reduce green space through berm removals. In short, the rationale and interpretation of the Act that is reflected in the Mayor's Agent's decision is neither unreasonable nor inconsistent with the Act;

The landscaped green space on publicly owned, privately maintained front and side yards in historic districts and on historic landmarks should be preserved. Special care should be taken to protect these historic green areas from being paved over for vehicular access and parking.

Chapter 12 of the document sets forth the Ward 1 plan; Ward 1 encompasses the Kalorama Triangle Historic District. Section 1225 of the Ward 1 plan sets forth objectives for preservation and historic features of the area. Section 1225.1 reads: "The objectives for preservation and historic features are to preserve the important historic features of Ward 1 while permitting new development that is compatible with those features."

hence, we owe deference to the agency's interpretation *See Reneau, supra,* 676 A.2d at 917 ("Although the decision is not a model of clarity, a close reading reveals that it contains a cogent analysis of the record evidence, flows rationally from the findings of fact, and contains no erroneous interpretations of law.").

Accordingly, for the foregoing reasons, we affirm the decision of the agency.

* * *

Turchi v. Philadelphia Board of License & Inspection Review
20 A.3d 586 (Pa. Commw. Ct. 2011)

■ JUBELIRER, J.

John J. Turchi, Jr. and Mary E. Turchi (Landowners) appeal from the May 19, 2010, Order of the Court of Common Pleas of Philadelphia County (trial court) affirming the November 9, 2008, decision of the Philadelphia Board of License and Inspection Review (Board) that reversed the November 19, 2007, decision of the Philadelphia Historical Commission (Historical Commission) approving a permit for the renovation and development of a historically designated building, the Dilworth House, located at 223–25 South Sixth Street within the City of Philadelphia's (City) Society Hill Historic District (the Project). Based on its interpretation of the Historic Preservation Ordinance, Philadelphia Code (Code) §§ 14–2007(1)–(10), the Historical Commission approved the Project and concluded that: (1) the renovations proposed in the Project were not a "demolition in significant part" and, therefore, the Project was an "alteration"[1] and not a "demolition"[2] under Section 2(f); and (2) the Project's renovations were "appropriate" under Section 7(k) of the Historic Preservation Ordinance. Concerned Citizens in Opposition to the Dilworth Development (Concerned Citizens) and the Society Hill Civic Association appealed to the Board. The Board disagreed with the Historical Commission's interpretations of "demolition in significant part" and "appropriateness" of the Project under the Historic Preservation Ordinance and disapproved the permit. Landowners appealed to the trial court, which affirmed the Board on the basis that neither the Philadelphia Home Rule Charter (Home Rule Charter), nor the Code, contains any language requiring that the Board grant

---

[1] An "alteration" is defined as "[a] change in the appearance of a building, structure, site or object which is not otherwise covered by the definition of demolition, or any other change for which a permit is required under The Philadelphia Code of General Ordinances." Section 2(a) of the HISTORIC PRESERVATION ORDINANCE, CODE § 14–2007(2)(a).

[2] A "demolition" is defined as "[t]he razing or destruction, whether entirely or *in significant part,* of a building, structure . . . . Demolition includes the removal of a building, structure . . . from its site or the removal or destruction of the façade or surface." Section 2(f) of the HISTORIC PRESERVATION ORDINANCE, CODE § 14–2007(2)(f) (emphasis added).

deference to the Historical Commission. Landowners now appeal to this Court.[3]

This appeal arises from Landowners' application to the Historical Commission for a permit to develop the Project pursuant to Section 7 of the Historic Preservation Ordinance, CODE § 14–2007(7) (establishing the procedures for obtaining a permit to alter or demolish an historically-designated building). The Project consists of the renovation and preservation of the brick-clad main portion of the Dilworth House and the removal of the side and rear wings, which would be replaced with a sixteen-story condominium structure that would connect to the Dilworth House. Because the Project requires the removal of the side and rear wings, along with integration of the condominiums into this historically-designated property, Landowners must comply with the permitting procedures of the Historic Preservation Ordinance. Additionally, because the Project requires the removal of a portion of an historically-designated property, the Historical Commission must first determine, pursuant to Section 2(f), whether this removal constitutes a "significant part" of the building because, and if it does, Section 7(j) prohibits the issuance of a permit unless the Historical Commission finds that the removal is in the public interest or that the building, structure, site, or object cannot be used for any purpose for which it may reasonably be adapted. CODE §§ 14–2007(2)(f), (7)(j). If the Project constitutes a removal *not* "in significant part," the removal is considered an "alteration," not a "demolition." CODE §§ 14–2007(2)(a), (f). The characterization of the Project as either an "alteration" or a "demolition" determines the factors that a permit applicant must satisfy to obtain a permit. Where the Historical Commission has no objection, the Board shall grant the permit subject to other applicable requirements, including, *inter alia*, those found in Section 7(k) regarding "appropriateness." CODE §§ 14–2007(7)(g), (k).

In this case, upon Landowners' application for a permit to renovate the Dilworth House,[5] the Historical Commission initially referred the application to its Architectural Committee. After hearing testimony that the wings, which Landowners sought to remove, were not a defining feature of the Dilworth House because they were service areas, were not architecturally significant portions of the Dilworth House, and were not visible parts of the Dilworth House, the Architectural Committee determined that the Project: (1) was not a "demolition in significant part"

---

[3]   We note that the Society Hill Civic Association was an original appellant to the Board, and in this appeal is an Amicus Curiae and did not file a brief. * * *

[5]   This was the fourth proposal submitted for the Project. The first application proposed a total demolition with construction of a 15-story residential building in its place, which was denied. Landowners withdrew the proposal. The second application proposed a total demolition with construction of a 15-story residential building with a portion of the front façade of the historic building to be rebuilt at the ground level of the new building, which was denied, followed by its withdrawal by Landowners. The third proposal, never officially submitted but distributed to the Historical Commission, proposed retaining most of the Dilworth House and constructing a residential building at the rear of the lot. No action was taken on this unofficial proposal.

pursuant to Section 2(f) of the Historic Preservation Ordinance and, therefore, was an "alteration" pursuant to Section 2(a); and (2) was "appropriate" pursuant to Section 7(k) of the Historic Preservation Ordinance.

Next, the full Historical Commission bifurcated its consideration of the Project. The Historical Commission first voted unanimously to approve the Project in concept, with one abstention. The Historical Commission granted final approval on November 9, 2007, after the Project was again discussed in an open public meeting, unanimously approving it as "*not* a 'demolition in significant part' " and, therefore, an alteration. Minutes of Meeting of the Historical Commission, November 9, 2007, at 14 (emphasis added).

Concerned Citizens appealed the Historical Commission's decision to the Board claiming, *inter alia*, that it committed errors of law: (1) in finding that the Project was not a "demolition" pursuant to the Historic Preservation Ordinance; (2) by not applying the proper Secretary of the Interior's "Standards for Rehabilitation and Guidelines for Rehabilitating Historic Buildings" (the Secretary's Standards), specifically Standards 1, 2, 9, and 10 of 36 C.F.R. § 67.7 (b); and (3) by not applying the Historic Preservation Ordinance to the Project. Additionally, the Society Hill Civic Association, Matthew DiJulio, and Benita Fair Langsdorf appealed the Historical Commission's decision on similar grounds and also claimed, *inter alia*, that the decision should be reversed because it was arbitrary and capricious. The Board held six full record hearings, issued findings of fact and conclusions of law, and reversed the Historical Commission. In doing so, the Board disagreed with the Historical Commission's interpretations of the terms "alteration" and "appropriateness" in the Historic Preservation Ordinance and determined that: (1) "the November [ ]9, 2007 approval by the Historical Commission that . . . [the] application 'is not a demolition in significant part' was in error,"; and (2) "the . . . approval [of] . . . [the] application to construct the [Project] was in error," because the Historical Commission did not define the Project as "appropriate" as the Board would have defined it.

Landowners appealed to the trial court, which affirmed the Board's determination, concluding that the Board "plays a supervising role over the [Historical] Commission subject to [the trial court's] review," and that the Board "has the authority to hear appeals directly from the [Historical] Commission and render a binding decision that affirms, modifies or reverses the [Historical] Commission." The trial court also concluded that "substantial evidence and testimony" taken by the Board "proved that the [Historical] Commission's decision conflicted with several factors under" the Historic Preservation Ordinance. The trial court reasoned that the Board has broad powers of review under Section 5–1005 of the Home Rule Charter. Concluding that the Home Rule Charter is clear and unambiguous, the trial court further explained that the Board's standard of review of the Historical Commission's decisions is *de novo*. The trial court rejected the argument that the Board must grant deference to the decisions of the Historical Commission because "[n]either the Code nor the [Home Rule] Charter has any language that the Board is required to give deference to the [Historical] Commission [ ]or any similar agency."

Landowners now appeal to this Court. A principal issue on appeal is whether the Board must give deference to the Historical Commission's determinations made pursuant to the Historic Preservation Ordinance, which the Historical Commission is charged with administering, and, if so, how the Board should apply this deference within its own proper scope and standard of review.

I.　The Historical Commission

Under the Historic Preservation Ordinance, the Historical Commission is the City agency empowered to designate buildings as historic and to approve or deny permit applications for alterations to and/or demolitions of historically-designated buildings. Sections 4(a), (b), and (d) of the Historic Preservation Ordinance, CODE §§ 14–2007(4)(a)–(b), (d). The composition of the Historical Commission is mandated by the Historic Preservation Ordinance and is very specific; it consists of various City government representatives and eight members appointed by the Mayor, including "an architect experienced in the field of historic preservation," a historian, an architectural historian, a real estate developer, "a representative of a Community Development Corporation," and "a representative of a community organization." Section 3 of the Historic Preservation Ordinance, CODE § 14–2007(3). The Historic Preservation Ordinance empowers the Historical Commission to exercise quasi-legislative discretion in designating buildings historic and administrative discretion in reviewing applications for alterations or demolitions of historically-designated properties. CODE § 14–2007(4). The administration of the Historic Preservation Ordinance requires reasoned applications of specialized knowledge and experience in the areas particularly affecting historic preservation in order to interpret the operative terms of the Historic Preservation Ordinance, such as those at issue in this case: "alteration," "demolition," "significant," and "appropriateness." *See generally* CODE §§ 14–2007(1)–(10). Thus, there are no bright-line standards or mechanical applications similar to those found in ordinary zoning or land use regulations, such as height restrictions or parking ratios; rather, the standards involved here, such as the "appropriateness" of a particular project, must take into consideration the historical importance of a particular property or structure and the design of a project. CODE § 14–2007(7)(k). To meet the specialized needs and requirements of administering a specialized ordinance, the Historic Preservation Ordinance empowers the Historical Commission to promulgate regulations and establish committees to assist in its administration of the Historic Preservation Ordinance and in setting the City's historic preservation policy. *See, e.g.*, CODE §§ 14–2007(4)(e)–(h).

II.   The Board of License and Inspection Review

Like the Historical Commission, the Board is a City agency. * * * In sum, the Board hears appeals involving all City permits and licenses, including those relating to building safety and sanitation, signs, zoning, plumbing and drainage facilities, sanitary facilities, sewage disposal systems, dumpsters, and handguns. Section 5–1002 of the HOME RULE CHARTER, PHILA. CHARTER § 5–1002.

Unlike the Historical Commission, the Board is empowered to hear appeals on many subject areas involving the issuance or denial of all permits and licenses in the City. The Board's members are not required to have specialized expertise in the area of historic preservation. Although Section 5–1005 of the Home Rule Charter gives the Board jurisdiction over City permit and license appeals generally, Section 10 of the Historic Preservation Ordinance specifically provides the right of appeal to the Board for "[a]ny person aggrieved by the issuance or denial of any permit reviewed by the [Historical] Commission." CODE § 14–2007(10).

III. The Principle of Administrative Agency Deference

It is a fundamental principle of administrative law that an administrative agency's interpretation of the statute it is charged to administer is entitled to deference on appellate review absent "fraud, bad faith, abuse of discretion, or clearly arbitrary action." *Winslow-Quattlebaum v. Md. Ins. Group*, 752 A.2d 878, 881 (Pa. 2000). Our Supreme Court has stated:

> It is well settled that when the courts of this Commonwealth are faced with interpreting statutory language, they afford great deference to the interpretation rendered by the administrative agency overseeing the implementation of such legislation.

Id. at 881. In another case in which our Supreme Court was confronted with an agency's interpretation of its own regulations, the Supreme Court cited the United States Supreme Court for the principle that:

> In reviewing an administrative agency's interpretation of its own regulations, courts are governed by a two step analysis. First, "[i]n construing administrative regulations, 'the ultimate criterion is the administrative interpretation, which becomes of controlling weight unless it is plainly erroneous or inconsistent with the regulation.' "

Dep't of Pub. Welfare v. Forbes Health Sys., 422 A.2d 480, 482 (Pa. 1980). In the instant case, the reviewing body is not a court, but a reviewing board found within the City's executive department that was created by the Home Rule Charter and granted adjudicatory authority to hear appeals on permit decisions from within its own Department of Licenses and Inspections. In addition, Section 10 of the Historic Preservation Ordinance specifically authorizes the Board to hear appeals by parties "aggrieved by the issuance or denial of any permit reviewed by the [Historical] Commission." CODE § 14–2007(10).

In examining the issue of competing interpretations of regulations by the quasi-judicial Environmental Hearing Board (EHB) and the Department of Environmental Protection (DEP), the agency charged with administering the Commonwealth of Pennsylvania's various environmental laws and regulations, this Court, in *Department of Environmental Protection v. North American Refractories Co.*, 791 A.2d 461, 465–66 (Pa. 2002), looked to the United States Supreme Court's analysis in *Martin v. Occupational Safety and Health Review Commission*, 499 U.S. 144 (1991), for guidance. "It is well established 'that an agency's construction of its own regulations is entitled to substantial deference.' " *Id.* at 150.

In *Martin*, the Supreme Court expressed the principle that, "[i]n situations in which 'the meaning of [regulatory] language is not free from doubt,' the reviewing court should give effect to the agency's interpretation so long as it is 'reasonable.' " *Id.* * * *

This principle of granting deference to administrative agency interpretations of the statutes or regulations they are charged with administering has been reaffirmed repeatedly by this and our Supreme Court. * * *

The Pennsylvania Supreme Court also has applied this principle to local administrative agencies as well. * * *

It is undisputed that the Historical Commission is the local administrative agency charged by City Council with administering the Historic Preservation Ordinance. It is also undisputed that City Council required that the Historical Commission be composed of members with specialized knowledge, background, and expertise in the area of historic preservation. Applying these facts to the principles of administrative law in this case where there are competing actors on the local level, i.e., the Historical Commission and the Board, we rely upon the analysis in *Martin*, as we did in *North American Refractories*, and apply that analysis to the case at bar.

We begin by applying *Martin*'s presumption against the adjudicative actor, i.e., the Board, because it is the administrative actor, i.e., the Historical Commission, that has numerous encounters with matters of historic preservation and those areas where the concern for historic preservation may conflict with the growth and development necessary to a large city. We also consider it important that the Historical Commission has greater expertise in this area and has been authorized to promulgate regulations and administer the Historic Preservation Ordinance. City Council invested the Historical Commission with the necessary authoritative interpretive powers to execute and interpret the Historic

Preservation Ordinance. From this, we conclude that City Council did not intend the Board to have the same authoritative interpretative powers. To permit the Board to reinterpret and reconsider the deliberative, purposeful, and carefully examined interpretations and policies of the Historical Commission would be beyond the Board's limited role as an appellate adjudicative entity, which must give deference to the Historical Commission's reasonable interpretations pursuant to *Martin* and *North American Refractories*. Therefore, we conclude that the Historical Commission's reasonable interpretations of the Historic Preservation Ordinance are entitled to deference and that these interpretations "become[ ] of controlling weight unless [they are] plainly erroneous or inconsistent" with the Historic Preservation Ordinance. *Forbes Health Sys.*, 422 A.2d at 482. Therefore, the Board must not substitute its own interpretation of a definition or term of the Historic Preservation Ordinance where the Historical Commission has already provided a reasonable interpretation of that definition or term.

IV. The Board's Decision

After holding public hearings and creating its own record in this case, the Board issued Findings of Fact and Conclusions of Law. The Board received evidence, as authorized by Section 5–1005 of the Home Rule Charter, and determined, *inter alia*, that the Historical Commission erroneously: (1) interpreted the Historic Preservation Ordinance's definition of a demolition; and (2) applied the Historic Preservation Ordinance's list of factors for assessing the "appropriateness" of an alteration in a historic district. In making these determinations and reversing those made by the Historical Commission, the Board gave no deference to the Historical Commission's interpretations of the relevant terms of the Historic Preservation Ordinance by limiting its review to determining whether the Historical Commission's interpretations were clearly erroneous or an abuse of discretion. * * *

We agree with the Historical Commission that the administrative interpretation and "[c]onstruction of the phrase 'in significant part' and the meaning of the statutory term 'demolition' are not matters of 'credibility,' " but are matters within the province of the administrative expertise of the Historical Commission. As such, the Historical Commission's interpretation of those phrases, as well as the Historic Preservation Ordinance in general, must be accorded deference under *Martin* * * * and *North American Refractories*. Where there are competing interpretations of the definitions of the operational terms in the Historic Preservation Ordinance, it is "within the province of the [Historical] Commission, not the Board," to interpret the Historic Preservation Ordinance and adopt a definition. When the Board replaced the Historical Commission's definitions with its own, transforming the interpretation of phrases into credibility determinations, the Board exceeded its appellate scope of review. When reviewing a decision of the Historical Commission, the Board's duty was to "determine if [the

Historical Commission's] actions can be sustained or supported by evidence taken by [the Board]." *North American Refractories*, 791 A.2d at 466. In reversing the Historical Commission's determinations, the Board erred in not giving the Historical Commission's interpretation of the definitions and phrases contained within the Historic Preservation Ordinance deference as required by, *inter alia*, *Martin* and *North American Refractories*.

The Board further exceeded its scope of review when it did not grant deference to the Historical Commission's interpretation of the meaning of "appropriateness" under the Historic Preservation Ordinance. The Board's findings of facts about structure height, neighboring properties, and the neighborhood's environment were within its province. However, the Historic Preservation Ordinance states in Section 7(k) that "[i]n making its determination as to the appropriateness of proposed alterations, demolition or construction, the [Historical] Commission *shall* consider the following:" and then continues by listing seven items. CODE, §§ 14–2007(7)(k) (emphasis added). The Board seemingly confined its examination of "appropriateness" to only some of the factors in the Historic Preservation Ordinance and did not review each of the factors set forth in the Historic Preservation Ordinance, and considered by the Historical Commission, in examining whether there was evidence in the record to support the Historical Commission's determination that the Project was appropriate for the neighborhood rather than explaining why the Historical Commission's interpretation of appropriateness was clearly erroneous under Section 7.

In sum, this Court concludes that the Board erred when it did not give deference to the Historical Commission's interpretations of the Historic Preservation Ordinance. * * *

For these reasons, the trial court's Order is vacated and this matter is remanded to the Board to issue a new determination in accordance with the foregoing opinion.

NOTES & QUESTIONS

1.   Decisions of historic preservation boards are sometimes subject to administrative appeal. The two cases above illustrate different approaches to such administrative review. The Washington, D.C., ordinance provides that the Mayor grants permits upon the recommendation of the Historic Preservation Review Board (HPRB). The Mayor always has delegated his or her authority to the Mayor's Agent, who may or may not have any expertise in preservation. While decisions by the Mayor would likely be highly political, the Mayor's Agent has tended toward legalistic decisions, a trend encouraged by D.C. administrative law, which requires formal trial-type procedures for such hearings. The Georgetown University Law Library electronically publishes and categorizes Mayor's Agents decisions, but Mayor's Agents have differed on whether prior decisions have any precedential value. The legislative history of the D.C. ordinance indicates

that developers pressed the Council not to allow the Board, which was expected to favor stringent preservation, to have the final administrative say on permits and exceptions. Should the Mayor's Agent defer to the HPRB?

The Philadelphia Board of License and Inspection Review hears appeals from many city agencies but has no expertise in historic preservation; the Pennsylvania Commonwealth Court refused to accord their decision any deference. In some jurisdictions, an appeal can go to the elected legislative body, such as the Oak Park Village Board of Trustees in the *Zaruba* case later in this Chapter. What kinds of factors would you expect an elected body to consider in deciding whether a property owner qualifies for a permit? Does such review raise constitutional or governance concerns?

2.   Consider the standards used by the preservation commissions in considering whether to grant the permits in the two cases above. Mr. Gondelman argued that building a garage under his house would "adapt and enhance" the historic structure by suiting it for modern transportation. The D.C. HPRB concluded that destruction of a characteristic landscape feature, the berm, would detract from the visual integrity of the row of intact houses, built to take advantage of public transportation. Do the purposes of the D.C. Act provide clear standards? Are they contradictory? What role does the District's Comprehensive Plan play in the decision? Is that appropriate?

By contrast, the Philadelphia Historical Commission permitted a far more radical alteration to the Dilworth House, including the demolition of rear and side wings and the construction of an attached sixteen-story building, because it did not involve "significant" demolition. By what standard did the Commission decide that the demolition was not significant? Is the Philadelphia ordinance less rigorous on its face than the D.C. ordinance? The Society Hill Historic District, in which the Dilworth House lies, was established in 1959 as part of an urban renewal project that pioneered the incorporation of preservation in large-scale redevelopment. In its "Guide for Property Owners," the Preservation Alliance for Greater Philadelphia describes the district as providing "a broad spectrum of architectural styles ranging from modest colonial dwellings and elegant Georgian, Federal, and Greek Revival houses to architecturally significant modern high-rises and contemporary rowhouses." How might that context play into the Commission's decision in this case? Note also that the Commission approved the project after rejecting two earlier proposals that would have demolished the entire Dilworth House.

3.   Front lawns in certain parts of Washington, D.C. are actually publicly, rather than privately, owned spaces. Did it matter to the court in *Gondelman* that the berm was legally public space versus private space? Should it?

4.   Figure 6-2 depicts the streetscape directly across the street from 1924 Belmont Street NW, the property at issue in *Gondelman*. These newer buildings, mentioned in the case, lack berms or other landscaping that characterize the Kalorama Historic District. Figure 6-1, which appears with the case, depicts the front lawn of 1924 Belmont Street in the foreground, and several berm-boasting neighbors just beyond. If the relatively new

construction across the street did not have to be compatibly landscaped, why did Gondelman's? Is the difference that Gondelman would have destroyed historic fabric, while the new construction did not necessarily do so? What might explain the neighbors' organizing against Gondelman's application to exchange the berm for a driveway? Would it help to know that parking is at a premium in the neighborhood?

Figure 6-2:
Across the Street from Gondelman's Home, Belmont Street,
Washington, DC

Is concern about setting a precedent a good reason for denying one owner permission?

5.   In 2015, the Pennsylvania Commonwealth Court found that the Board of License and Inspection Review, on remand, failed to give the historic commission deference required in the case excerpted above. The court reinstated the commission's approval. *See* Turchi v. Philadelphia Bd. of License & Inspection Review, No. 658 C.D. 2014, 2015 WL 5437160 (Pa. Commw. Ct. May 15, 2015). Nothing had been built by 2021, when the Turchis sold the Dilworth House property to another developer for $7.5 million—after twenty years of ownership.

6.   In 2019, a Historic Preservation Task Force appointed by the mayor of Philadelphia recommended replacing review of Historical Commission rulings by the Licenses and Inspections Review Board with appeals to an

administrative law judge knowledgeable about Philadelphia's preservation law and the Commission's powers and obligations.

2. REGULATING LANDSCAPES

Many local historic preservation laws regulate only "structures," such as buildings. Increasingly, however, these laws are being extended to include accessory structures, parking lots, and landscapes. As the *Gondelman* case illustrates, a landscape can be as important as a building in conveying the essential characteristics of a historic property. Neighbors in the Kalorama Triangle argued, and the Historic Preservation Review Board agreed, that the green berms provided an essential unifying character and reflected the centrality of public transportation to the original residents. Landscapes may gain protection through their inclusion in a historic district, as the landscape design often conveys different information than the associated structures.

Landscapes can also contribute to the significance of an individually designated landmark. Consider the Crane Estate, a National Historic Landmark in Ipswich, Massachusetts, which depends on the preservation of its formally designed grounds and gardens to convey the "Country Place Era." The mansion stands on a steep hill looking out to the Atlantic; maintaining the formal landscaping and the great lawn framing, designed by the sons of Frederick Law Olmsted, are essential to preserving the integrity of the entire site.

Historic landscapes convey a period of significant human interaction with the land. They are not always associated with a historic building or structure. Meridian Hill Park (also known as Malcolm X Park) in Washington, D.C., for example, is a public park that has been designated as a National Historic Landmark in part for its neo-classical landscaping, including water features such as a cascade and a pool. In addition to vernacular and designed landscapes, the National Park Service recognizes historic sites (natural landscapes where significant events took place) and ethnographic landscapes that carry traditional cultural or spiritual value. Consider the arguments surrounding the valuation of historic preservation discussed in Chapter 1. How can the value of a landscape site preserved independently of a historic structure be measured? Would a local ordinance restricting all future development on or requiring continuing care for a privately-owned landscape present an acute regulatory takings problem?

Figure 6-3:
Meridian Hill Park,
Washington, DC

The regulation and preservation of landscapes presents a number of unique challenges due to the changing and fragile nature of the living elements critical to a landscape's significance. Identification alone can be difficult: "Landscapes may go unrecognized because they are perceived as backdrops for other, more traditional resources, such as buildings or monuments. The organic quality of landscapes also contributes to their vulnerability; they change constantly but incrementally, and loss may not be apparent to the casual observer." Joanna M. Doherty, *An Introduction to Historic Landscape Preservation,* TERRA FIRMA: PUTTING HISTORIC LANDSCAPE PRES. ON SOLID GROUND (Mass. Dep't of Conservation & Recreation), 2005, at 6.

The difficulty of retaining the integrity of the design and original fabric of a historic landscape can also complicate the designation process: "If, for example, a property is primarily significant because of its internal road circulation, yet the historic road patterns are no longer discernable or have been badly damaged, then the landscape has suffered a loss of integrity that may make it ineligible for the National Register." J. Timothy Keller & Genevieve P. Keller, *How to Evaluate and Nominate Designated Historic Landscapes* 6 (Nat'l Park Serv., Nat'l Register Bull. No. 18, 1987).

Figure 6-4:
Landscape Preservation at Gettysburg Battlefield,
Gettysburg, PA

Historic battlefields present complex issues of landscape preservation. The terrain over which an important battle was fought should be preserved because of its crucial relation to the important event that occurred there. But over time, the terrain could develop independent appeal conveying the vernacular landscape of the era of the battle as such landscapes become more rare. Conservators seek to preserve or recreate the landscape that existed at the time of the battle, so visitors can perceive the movement of troops and locations of significant events. Battlefields also often are memorial sites to the fallen. The Gettysburg Battlefield—the subject of the *United States v. Gettysburg Electric Railway Co.* case in Chapter 1 and the *Recent Past Preservation Network v. Latschar* case in Chapter 4—presents an interesting example. A national park, the battlefield contains many memorials constructed in the nineteenth century. In recent years, the National Park Service has made it a priority to restore the landscape of the battlefield to its condition on the eve of the battle. To this end, existing trees have been cut down and new ones planted; grain fields and a peach orchard have been recreated. The National Park Service's proposal to demolish the 1962 Neutra Visitor Center, challenged in *Latschar*, was justified by the goal to provide visitors an experience of the terrain over which the battle was fought without distraction by modern intrusions.

Although beautiful, the recreated pastoral landscape at the battlefield provides a particular perspective on the events that occurred there. The landscape encountered by the troops in 1863 reflected the unselfconscious consequences of the agricultural practices of the time. But the reconstructed landscape today is a sophisticated reproduction. Restoring vernacular farmland to its historic appearance ironically requires employment of continuous professional management of dynamic natural processes. Such a managed landscape can foster an intensity of perception greater than that of any normal landscape, because the discordance of incompatible or contested spaces are eliminated to create a unified vision. Historian Jim Weeks complained about Gettysburg: "What visitors will see is not the 1863 battlefield, but a hyperreal version of it that conforms to their image of the original * * * [—] an 'airbrushed' improvement on the original without authentic blemishes or unpleasantness." JIM WEEKS, GETTYSBURG: MEMORY, MARKET, AND AN AMERICAN SHRINE 192 (2003). Moreover, this pastoral countryside frames the reality of the battle within a romantic context and distances the viewer from the horror of the slaughter. Should the NPS instead depict the ravaged land that the soldiers left? To what extent should the tastes of the more than one million tourists who visit Gettysburg every year weigh in such a decision? *See generally* J. Peter Byrne, *Hallowed Ground, The Gettysburg Battlefield in Historic Preservation Law*, 22 TUL. ENVTL. L. J. 203 (2009).

3. EXCEPTIONS TO REGULATION

a. ECONOMIC HARDSHIP

Most cities that restrict demolition or other changes in historic resources provide an exception for economic hardship. Generally, owners who can show that they cannot make some minimum economic return on a property because of preservation restrictions will receive a permit to demolish or substantially alter it. Note that the Takings Clause in the Fifth Amendment to the U.S. Constitution and state constitutional equivalents require that the government pay an owner just compensation when regulations, including preservation regulations, destroy the economic value of property, at least in some circumstances. Takings jurisprudence is discussed extensively in Chapter 7. In this section, we consider statutory provisions that permit destruction of historic structures based on some showing of economic loss.

Economic hardship provisions vary among cities. Usually such claims are brought before the historic preservation review board, but some localities employ another administrative officer to adjudicate such claims, such as the D.C. Mayor's Agent in the next case, and some permit appeal to the local legislature, as in the subsequent Illinois case. Some simply incorporate the constitutional standard for a regulatory taking, in which case the hardship exception operates like a variance in zoning law.

Others provide more detailed criteria for economic hardship, which may be easier to satisfy than the constitutional standard. Why would a preservation ordinance adopt a more specific or a more lenient standard?

900 G Street Associates v. Department of Housing & Community Development

430 A.2d 1387 (D.C. 1981)

■ KERN, J.

This is an appeal from an order entered by the so-called Mayor's Agent pursuant to the Historic Landmark and the Historic District Protective Act of 1978. D.C. Law 2–144, codified as D.C. CODE 1980 Supp., § 5–821 *et seq.* (The Act) [Eds.: now codified at D.C. CODE §§ 6–1101–6–1133], denying a permit to demolish the building now standing at 901 F St., N.W.

The property in question is located at 901 F St., N.W. on Lot 800, Square 376. The building on that property (the Building) was designed and built in 1867–69 by noted architects of the period in a modified French Renaissance style. It has historical importance for its use as the Masonic Temple from 1870 to 1908. Its location opposite the Old Patent Office (now designated the American Art Portrait Gallery) enhances its importance to the architectural and aesthetic integrity of the city.

The Building has long been recognized as of historic and architectural importance. It was placed on the National Register of Historic Places on May 8, 1974, and, as a Category II Landmark, on the District of Columbia Inventory of Historic Sites since the Inventory was first established in 1964. The building was subjected to substantial architectural changes in the 1920's to make it more suitable for commercial use, acquiring at that time the name "Lansburgh's" in reference to the store which occupied it. It is now unoccupied, structurally sound, and in a poor condition of maintenance and repair. These facts are uncontested by all parties.

Petitioner acquired the building on January 23, 1979, under an agreement entered into with the Young Women's Christian Association of the National Capital Area (YWCA) on September 15, 1978. That agreement provided for an exchange of land then held by petitioner for the property on which the Building is located plus additional sums of money. The YWCA held a lease and an option to purchase on the Building and its site. A fixed sum ($594,000) plus an additional sum of up to a maximum of $48,000, payment of which was contingent upon the speed and ultimate success of petitioner in obtaining the requisite authorization to demolish the Building, was to be paid by the YWCA to appellant in addition to the property exchange. The exchange was effected according to the agreement, except petitioner, and not the YWCA, made the purchase of the Building and its site directly from the then owner of record under the option to purchase.

Petitioner owns property separated by a public alley from the property on which the Building is located. It has applied for permission to close this alley and plans, upon demolition of the Building and the closing of the alley, to construct a major commercial office building upon its joint properties, including that property on which the Building now sits.

In late 1978 or early 1979, the Aaron Straus and Lillie Straus Foundation, Inc., a Maryland corporation and the then owner of record of the Building and the property on which it is located, applied under District of Columbia Council Regulation No. 73–25, which was the predecessor of the Act, to demolish the Building. As prescribed under that earlier Regulation, the Joint Committee on Landmarks considered the application for demolition and advised against it. The Mayor subsequently entered an order on March 2, 1979, delaying demolition pending negotiations with civic associations and public agencies with regard to ways in which the Building might be saved.

On July 12, 1979, petitioner applied for a demolition permit pursuant to the Act. A two-day hearing ensued, at which, by request of petitioner, the Mayor's Agent considered only testimony and arguments bearing on the issue of "unreasonable economic hardship" to the owner which would occur if the application to demolish the Building was denied. On December 21, 1979, the Mayor's Agent denied the application for a demolition permit. It is this denial which is before this court on appeal as a result of the petition for review.

The District of Columbia has protected historic landmarks to some degree since 1973. In doing so, the District of Columbia has followed the practice of many states and cities, which has been universally recognized as a legitimate exercise of governmental power. *See Penn Central Transp. Co. v. City of New York*, 438 U.S. 104, 129 (1978). The present Act was passed by the City Council on November 28, 1978, signed by the Mayor on December 27, 1978, and became effective on March 3, 1979. It increased the protection afforded historic landmarks and districts.

The Act requires, in pertinent part (§ 5–824(a)), that before the Mayor may issue a permit to demolish a building listed in the National Register of Historic Places or the District of Columbia Inventory of Historic Sites, the Mayor must review the application by seeking the recommendation of the Historic Preservation Review Board, § 5–824(b), and must find that "issuance of the permit is necessary in the public interest, or that failure to issue a permit will result in unreasonable economic hardship to the owner." § 5–824(e). In this case, the Joint Committee on Landmarks of the National Capital sat as the Historic Preservation Review Board and recommended against issuance of the permit. The Mayor was required, prior to determining to issue the demolition permit, to hold a public hearing. § 5–824(c). "Unreasonable economic hardship" is defined in the Act as amounting "to a taking of the owner's property without just compensation." § 5–822(n).

We point out that only the "unreasonable economic hardship" issue was considered in evaluating the application for demolition. At the hearing, an owner of a building is required to submit certain enumerated items of information, § 5–824(g)(1)(A) and (B), and any additional information which the Mayor may deem relevant. § 5–824(g)(2). Among the information to be supplied by the owner is "any consideration by the owner as to profitable adaptive uses for the property." § 5–824(g)(1)(A)(vii).

Final orders of the Mayor, entered on his behalf by the Mayor's agent, are reviewable in this court. D.C. CODE 1978 Supp., § 1–1510 and D.C. CODE 1980 Supp., § 5–832(b).

Petitioner has raised a number of issues and voiced a number of complaints regarding the manner in which the Mayor's Agent conducted the hearings and the content of the decision of the Mayor's Agent denying a permit to petitioner for demolition of the Building.

The relevance of some of these issues and complaints is directly contingent upon a determination by this court of preliminary questions of law and procedure in accordance with the position of appellant.

No party has claimed that the designation of the Building as a historic landmark worthy of preservation was made arbitrarily or improperly.

No party has challenged the legitimacy of the Act.

No party has challenged the conclusion of law of the Mayor's Agent that petitioner has the burden of proof in establishing "unreasonable economic hardship."

The basic question presented in this case is: at what juncture does the diminishment in value allegedly resulting from the governmental restriction on the use of property constitute an "unreasonable economic hardship" to the owner, which is here synonymous with an unconstitutional "taking"?

Preliminarily, we note there may be cases in which it is relevant to determine the reasonable expectations of profit which the owner or purchaser of a property entertained when purchasing the property before the government imposed restrictions. This is not such a case. The mere sale of a property does not expunge the rights of the prior owner, which become vested in the new owner, to compensation for taking its property. However, in this case, we must weigh in our calculations the listing of the Building on designated historical preservation rosters, the difficulties encountered by a prior owner in securing a permit for demolition of the Building, the terms of the agreement between the YWCA and appellant which contemplated the possibility that obtaining a permit to demolish the Building would be neither swift nor certain, and the publicized efforts of the City Council to enact a more stringent historical preservation statute.

Figures 6-5 & 6-6:
Two Views of 901 F Street NW,
Washington, DC

These all must have influenced the price which petitioner was willing to pay for the property, its realistic expectations for the uses which could be made of the property, and the profit that could be made from such uses or resale of the property. Purchases of land such as in the instant case are, by their very nature, speculative and profits on use of the land, if indeed there are any, or its appreciation in value, must necessarily be conjectural. If, as petitioner states in its brief, its transaction with the YWCA constituted, in part, a virtual charitable contribution, any analysis of the expectation of profit is necessarily even more unascertainable.

For the purpose of determining this case and without asserting that such assumptions are required by law, we will assume, as petitioner argues, the following: (1) that the property had been diminished in value by the inclusion of the Building within the protection of the Act; (2) that the value of the property to appellant would be greater if the demolition permit for the Building were issued; (3) that the Building and its site will be considered independently of any other property owned by petitioner; and (4) that no support or funding will be provided to petitioner for any renovation costs by governmental or private institutions. In our view, all this does not constitute a "taking."

We so conclude because, if there is a *reasonable* alternative economic use for the property after the imposition of the restriction on that property, there is no taking, and hence no unreasonable economic hardship to the owners, no matter how diminished the property may be in cash value and no matter if "higher" or "more beneficial" uses of the property have been proscribed.

We are persuaded to this conclusion by the Supreme Court's recent decision in *Penn Central Transportation Co. v. City of New York*. There, the Court held, *inter alia*, that the New York City Landmarks Preservation Law, in its application to Grand Central Terminal, did not constitute a "taking" of the owner's property. Despite *substantial* losses in revenue sustained by the owners due to the Terminal's designation as a landmark, the Court found that no "taking" could occur if a "reasonable return" on the property could still be obtained. Parenthetically, the New York City law explicitly guarantees a reasonable rate of return to owners of historic landmarks; the District of Columbia Act is silent on this point.
* * *

Although the Court approved the traditional, *albeit* difficult to apply, distinction in *Pennsylvania Coal Co. v. Mahon*, 260 U.S. 393 (1922), that legitimate statutes may become invalid if they "so frustrate distinct investment-backed expectations," *Penn Central*, 438 U.S. at 127, the Court stated that where the use of a landmark building remains "economically viable" and a "beneficial use" of the property is available, there is no "taking" merely because the owner's expectations of profits are not satisfied.

Where the historic preservation act to be applied does not specify an exact rate of return, or even any assured rate of return, as is true of the Act here, analogous principles of zoning and land use law may be applied. *See Hoboken Env't Comm., Inc. v. German Seaman's Mission of N.Y.*, 391 A.2d 577 (N.J. Super. 1978). Those principles establish that the "profitability" to an owner of restricted property is to be measured by whether *any* reasonable economic use exists for the property. [EDS.: emphasis added.]

In *Maher v. City of New Orleans*, 516 F.2d 1051 (5th Cir. 1975), *cert. denied*, 426 U.S. 905 (1976), * * * the circuit court, which had been asked to approve the grant of a demolition permit, found that a statutory provision requiring a permit before demolition, when applications for such permits could be discretionarily denied, did not *alone* establish a taking. The court observed that substantial diminution in value, although evidence of a taking, is not conclusive. *Id.* at 1066 n.83. The court further stated that: "In particular, Maher did not show that the sale of the property was impracticable, that commercial rental could not provide a reasonable rate of return, or that other potential use of the property was foreclosed." *Id.* at 1066.

Reflective of the degree to which the use of a restricted property may be diminished in value without constituting a taking is the case of *William C. Haas & Co. v. City & County of San Francisco*, 605 F.2d 1117 (9th Cir. 1979), *cert. denied*, 445 U.S. 928 (1980), where the value of the owner's property had been diminished by 95%, from $2 million to $100,000. The court in that case said, "nor can Haas transform a regulation into a taking by recharacterizing the diminution of the value of its property as an inability to obtain a favorable return on its investment." *Id.* at 1121.

We thus need only to consider in the instant case whether there is any other reasonable economic use for the Building. If there is, there has been neither a constitutional taking nor an unreasonable economic hardship imposed by the decision of the Mayor's Agent in this case. Petitioner had the burden of proof in the hearing to establish that no other reasonable economic use for the Building existed. Since the Act assigned the function of taking evidence and making determinations to the Mayor's Agent and she heard the testimony in the instant case and possessed the administrative expertise, the decision of the Mayor's Agent will be upheld by this court in resolving questions of fact unless it appears from the record that there is obvious and egregious error. *See Citizens Ass'n of Georgetown, Inc. v. D.C. Zoning Comm'n*, 402 A.2d 36 (D.C. 1979) (en banc); D.C. CODE 1973, § 1–1509(e).

The Mayor's Agent based her conclusion to deny the permit for demolition of the Building on findings that there were other reasonable economic uses for the Building. We must consider whether this conclusion was well founded on the record and whether the proceedings of the Mayor's Agent that established that record were properly conducted so as to permit the development of a full and credible record from which the conclusions expressed in the denial by the Mayor's Agent could be drawn. In our view, the record is more than adequate to establish that the Mayor's Agent could have reasonably concluded that an alternative economic use for the Building exists.

Specifically, there was evidence that supported the Mayor's Agent's conclusions that petitioner had not met its burden of proof to show that no reasonable economic alternative use for the Building existed. There was evidence to substantiate the claims that the Building could be rented "as is" or with minimal renovation and that the Building could be fully renovated at a cost of less than that claimed by petitioner and then rented.

Petitioner argues that the Mayor's Agent failed to accept its estimates for renovation; but, since its proposed renovation costs for the Building would total a per square floor foot cost of approximately three times that ever expended on any other renovation undertaken in the District of Columbia, the Mayor's Agent did not err in rejecting such estimate. Petitioner also argues that certain prescribed safety renovations were required by statute, or at least by concern for public safety, before other uses could be made of the Building. However, it was demonstrated on the record that similar buildings in the District of Columbia had complied with the same safety requirements without the need for such radical modifications.

Petitioner argues that admission of evidence of offers to purchase the Building were indications of a requirement that, because of the absence of an alternative use, it *must* sell the property; but as we view the findings, the presence of possible purchasers of the Building merely supported a conclusion by the Agent that there was an alternative economic use of the property.

Since the issue is whether there was an alternative economic use for the Building, without consideration of the cost of its acquisition or the profit petitioner anticipated from its operation, use, or sale, the determination by the Mayor's Agent upon this record that such an alternative existed must be upheld. There may be a case in which the alternative economic use of a property placed under restriction by the Act so diminishes the value of the property as to make it an unreasonable alternative, but this is not that case.

The denial of a permit for demolition by the Mayor's Agent of the Building is hereby upheld and petitioner's petition to reverse that denial is, in turn, denied.

NOTES & QUESTIONS

1.   901 F Street NW was eventually purchased, renovated, and adapted for modern office use in 2000. The project won awards from architects and realtors, as well as the D.C. Mayor's Award for Excellence in Historic Preservation. The project qualified for and received $1.5 million in federal historic tax credits. Two views of the project, provided in Figures 6-5 and 6-6, illustrate the building's relationship to the historic buildings on F Street and the newer buildings on 9th Street.

2.   What facts would a property owner need to prove to establish economic hardship in Washington, D.C.? How successful would such a showing likely be in a rising real estate market like Washington, D.C.? In a depressed real estate market? The owner negotiated the purchase price of 901 F Street NW before the Historic Landmark and Historic District

Protection Act was enacted and closed on the purchase of the building before it went into effect, although, as the court noted, deliberations on the proposed legislation in the District Council were widely publicized. How should these affect consideration of what constitutes an economic hardship?

3.   What are the benefits and the dangers of tying an economic hardship exception to a takings analysis involving the U.S. or state constitutions? Should expectations relating to potential returns on investments matter when local bodies are weighing hardship?

Zaruba v. Village of Oak Park
695 N.E.2d 510 (Ill. App. 1998)

■ ZWICK, J.

The issue in this case is whether the decision of the defendant, Village of Oak Park (the Village), to deny plaintiff, John Zaruba, a Certificate of Economic Hardship was made against the manifest weight of the evidence. The Certificate is required by a Village ordinance before a house located within an historic architectural district may be demolished. On administrative review, the circuit court reversed the Village. After reviewing the record, we find the Village's decision to deny the Certificate to have been supported by the evidence. We therefore affirm the Village's decision and reverse the circuit court.

The Village's Historic Preservation Ordinance (the Ordinance) became effective on January 1, 1994. The Ordinance prevents the demolition of landmark buildings or contributing architectural resources located within the Village's Frank Lloyd Wright Prairie School of Architecture Historic District (the District). Exceptions are made upon the granting of a Certificate of Appropriateness or Certificate of Economic Hardship.

Plaintiff purchased the property located at 616 N. Kenilworth Avenue, a lot within the District, on March 14, 1995. The property consisted of a 45-foot wide parcel containing an 86-year old single-family house. Plaintiff purchased the property for $227,500.

On June 23, 1995, plaintiff applied for a wrecking permit to demolish the building. At that time he was informed by Village staff that a wrecking permit could not be issued without the Village first issuing either a Certificate of Appropriateness or a Certificate of Economic Hardship.

Plaintiff subsequently applied for a Certificate of Appropriateness on grounds that the building was not a contributing resource to the District. The Historic Preservation Commission (the Commission) held a hearing and concluded that the building was a contributing resource. It therefore denied the plaintiff's request on July 13, 1995. Plaintiff was informed in writing of his right to challenge the decision at public hearing before the Village Board of Trustees, but elected not to pursue this remedy.

On August 1, 1995, plaintiff applied for a Certificate of Economic Hardship.

At the hearing before the Commission on September 14, 1995, plaintiff testified that he had lived for the preceding five years at 614 N. Kenilworth. For approximately 40 years prior to plaintiff's purchase of 616 N. Kenilworth, and for a short period thereafter, a man named John Glavin lived in the house at 616 N. Kenilworth. Glavin was in his early 90s at the time of the sale of his house to plaintiff.

Plaintiff testified that he had, over the years, "polite conversations" with Mr. Glavin about whether he would be willing to sell the property. In the fall prior to the hearing, the conversations became serious. Plaintiff offered Glavin $150,000 based upon a professional appraisal plaintiff commissioned showing the property was worth $165,000. Glavin was "somewhat insulted" by the offer and told plaintiff that he had already turned down a $200,000 bid for the property from a woman named Colleen Myra. Plaintiff spoke with Myra and verified her written offer to Glavin. Plaintiff eventually offered Glavin $227,500 for the property, which Glavin accepted.

Plaintiff testified that he was motivated to purchase the property because he wanted to protect his investment in his own home. He stated:

> I wanted to have some sort of control over what happened next door to me and I had the financial means to do so, so I made him an offer of $227,500 motivated by the desire to annex [his] property to mine to prevent somebody from, frankly, from adding a big addition on to the back of 616 and adding a big garage to the back and whatever that might have transpired which would have in a sense blocked my—blocked my view, filled up the backyard.

Plaintiff stated that he believed combining the two properties would increase the value of his home, but he could not offer an estimate of by how much the properties would be worth if joined together. He presented a detailed architectural drawing showing a proposed extension of his front porch over the existing driveway at 614 N. Kenilworth, as well as a proposed new side-facing garage which he planned to erect on the site where Glavin's house stood. The proposed garage was designed to carefully unify the two lots.

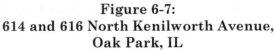

**Figure 6-7:
614 and 616 North Kenilworth Avenue,
Oak Park, IL**

It was established at the hearing that the Glavin house had substantially deteriorated over the course of the 40 years John Glavin had lived there. There were holes in the roof where a family of raccoons had taken up residence. The furnace was seriously damaged and several radiators had been disconnected. Water was leaking into the basement through a missing door and there was exposed wiring both inside and outside the house. Mortar in the chimney had eroded and the chimney was being held together by the supports of a television antennae. Siding on the southeast corner of the house was leaking. The house's foundation required tuckpointing in three or four locations. In addition, the garage was structurally unsound and in need of demolition. Plaintiff testified that when he purchased the house it was uninsurable due to the condition of the electrical and heating systems. Glavin did not have home owner's insurance on the property at the time of the sale to plaintiff.

After purchasing the property, plaintiff destroyed the garage and removed significant amounts of debris from the exterior of the home. He also had asbestos removed from the pipes around the furnace.

Plaintiff offered three separate and detailed estimates about what it would cost to renovate the property. He testified that any renovations would have to include tree removal, re-roofing, rebuilding of the chimney, extensive electrical work done to bring the wiring up to Village Code, interior and exterior painting, refurbishing of the leaded windows, sanding and cleaning of the wooden floors, installation of a new furnace and water heater, re-plumbing one of the bathrooms, replacement of several radiators, construction of a new garage, construction of new front stairs and railing, and basic kitchen renovations. One "top notch" estimate of the cost of renovation, not including non-essential work with the exception of the installation of central air conditioning, was $253,000. This estimate was made by Oak Park Design, a local rehabber. Plaintiff admitted that this estimate was high and stated that he was not relying upon it to make out his case of economic hardship.

Plaintiff reviewed the three estimates together and determined that a total "conservative estimate" of what it would cost to renovate the home would be $102,500. To this amount plaintiff added a general contractor's fee of 20% and the cost of work he had already done to the property. This brought his expected renovation sub-total to $126,997. When plaintiff added fees, taxes and the cost of borrowing, his "total estimate" for renovating the home was $141,500.

Plaintiff added his costs of purchasing the property from Glavin with his expected costs of refurbishing it, and concluded that he would have to sell the property without a real estate agent for a price of at least $369,000 ($227,500 plus $141,500) just to break even on his purchase. If an agent were used, a fee of approximately five percent would have to be added, bringing the total break-even sale price to $388,372.

To establish economic hardship under the Ordinance, plaintiff offered testimony as to what the real estate market would support in the area surrounding the Glavin house. He provided "real estate comps" showing houses of a similar size and style selling at prices between $200,000 and $330,000. He noted that these figures were for houses that each had features the renovated Glavin house would not have. For example, many of the houses had eat-in kitchens, central air conditioning or a den. One house, just five houses away from the Glavin house, was characterized as a particularly good comparison. It included a breakfast room, a fifth bedroom, foyer, completely new master bath, a finished third floor, basement and rec room—all features the Glavin house did not have—and was listed at a selling price of $330,000. Plaintiff testified that, based on the estimated costs of renovation and the real estate market in the area, it would simply not be possible to sell the Glavin house for anything approaching $388,000.

When asked about the market value of the Glavin property as a vacant lot, plaintiff testified that he had no opinion, except to say that he was willing to pay $227,500 for it. When asked about whether he knew of the existence of the Ordinance when he purchased the property, plaintiff testified that he knew there was an ordinance, but that he was unaware of its specifics.

Several neighbors testified in favor of plaintiff's application. Jean Brooks, Michael Gray, Robert Cimarusti, and Koster Van Gross all testified that the property had been steadily deteriorating over many years. Royce Cramton added that several of the homes in the neighborhood had double lots such as the one proposed by plaintiff. In addition to agreeing with the other neighbors, Barry Eisenberg testified that he was a professional economist and had reviewed the numbers that plaintiff had presented to the Commission. According to Eisenberg, "any reasonable assessment and compiling of the numbers [demonstrates] an economic hardship."

In opposition to the plaintiff's application, the Village presented the testimony of its Chief Building Inspector, Robert Borman. Borman testified that he had inspected the Glavin property and had given consideration to six specific areas. These were the overall condition of the building, the foundation, the heating plant, the electrical system, the plumbing system and the roof.

Borman found the exterior of the Glavin home to be in need of scraping, cleaning or painting and some stucco needed to be replaced. The front porch was structurally sound, although some windows and doors also needed replacement. In the front yard Borman found an abandoned oil tank of unknown size. The stone foundation was in good condition.

Borman stated the heating system was inoperable and in need of replacement. Only the radiators and some piping were salvageable. The electrical system needed to be totally reworked throughout the building and the plumbing system was outdated and in need of replacement. Borman also stated that the roofing material on the house was severely worn and there were visible holes in the roof. A "complete tear off of the roofing material and replacement of the sheathing" was required.

Borman concluded that, "[A]lthough the house is in need of a lot of rehabilitation, my findings show that the house is structurally sound." In Borman's experience, "the building should not be considered a candidate for demolition."

Ms. Lois Merrill testified that she was an experienced licensed real estate agent doing business in Oak Park since 1974. Although Merrill was not an appraiser, she testified that part of her job was to help sellers determine what an appropriate price would be for the sale of a given home. In that context, she had prepared a market value report which showed that one property near the Glavin home had been purchased for $137,500 in 1991 and then rehabbed and sold in 1993 for $268,000. Another property had been purchased for $176,500 in 1994 and then resold for $335,000 after rehabilitation. Merrill reviewed several local properties and noted that they had been selling for between $245,000 and $330,000.

Merrill testified that she had inspected the house and determined that, if it were to be sold "as is," it would sell between $160,000 and $180,000. She stated that if the property were rehabbed, it "might sell for a range between $280,000 and $300,000." She stated that there was evidence that the block could sustain a price over $300,000, but that would require the addition of more square footage to the structure of the house. She said that the house would not be a problem to sell and that, if Mr. Glavin had hired her, she might even have been able to sell it in the high 190s "that day." She testified, "It's that kind of marketplace where people would be very happy to get a hold of this kind of property." Although Merrill said she had heard the other witnesses, her view of the building was consistent with Borman's—i.e., that the house was structurally sound. She expressed surprise at the lack of damage to the inside of the home in light of the fact that the interior of the house had been partially exposed to the elements. In her written materials which Merrill presented to the Commission, Merrill described the property as "wonderful rehab opportunity. Location high demand."

A third witness for the Village was Mr. Mark Alger. He testified that he was the Construction Technologist for the Village's Single Family Homeowner Program. Mr. Alger had extensive experience in the construction and rehabilitation industry. Alger described the mission of the Single Family Home Program as bringing houses that are in the program up to Village Code and to what HUD refers to as "Housing Quality Standards." Alger used this same criteria in evaluating the Glavin home. He explained that, because of HUD's lower standards, there were disparities between what he would estimate a rehabilitation would cost and the costs plaintiff had estimated. For example, Alger said that he would not sand the hard-wood flooring in the house, although a home owner might prefer to have sanded flooring and such an improvement might make the home more marketable. He described the rehabilitation he considered necessary as that required to create a "medium quality home."

In Alger's view, the cost of rehabilitating the property would be $61,350, a figure which included both a 15% contingency and general contractor's fees. He admitted that one could "easily add another $25,000" to the renovations to make the home more marketable, but that these costs were not necessary to meet HUD's Home Quality Standards.

Following the testimony plaintiff made his closing argument and the Commissioners discussed the merits of both granting and denying plaintiff's application. The Commission then voted to deny the application. Subsequently, in a written decision, the Commission found that the plaintiff had failed to establish that the house was incapable of being put to any reasonable use or that he could not obtain a reasonable economic return from the property without first demolishing the building. The Commission also found that the building was structurally sound, although in need of extensive rehabilitation costing between $60,000 and $253,000. The Commission noted that there had been no substantial change in economic circumstances of the property since plaintiff purchased it and, therefore, any difficulty plaintiff encountered in obtaining a reasonable economic return on his purchase would be unaffected by the demolition of the building. The Commission concluded that any economic hardship placed upon the plaintiff had been brought about, at least in part, by his own actions.

The Village notified the plaintiff of the Commission's decision by letter dated September 26, 1995. The plaintiff timely appealed the decision to the Village Board of Trustees. Following a hearing on November 6, 1995, the Village Board adopted the Commission's findings.

On December 14, 1995, the plaintiff sought administrative review in the circuit court. On October 1, 1996, the circuit court reversed the Village and entered judgment in favor of the plaintiff. The court specifically noting that the building had been allowed to deteriorate for more than 30 years and determined that the rehabilitation of the building would cause plaintiff an economic hardship. The court also determined that the Commission should not have considered whether the plaintiff's economic hardship was self-imposed, at least absent a finding of an intent by him to circumvent the Ordinance. The Village brought this timely appeal.

As we have noted, the Ordinance precludes the issuance of a demolition permit until the issuance of a Certificate of Appropriateness or Certificate of Economic Hardship. VILL. OF OAK PARK, ILL. MUNICIPAL CODE, § 7–9–9 (eff. January 1, 1994). A Certificate of Economic Hardship is defined by the Ordinance as:

> A certificate issued by the Commission, after denying a certificate of appropriateness, which authorizes the performance of alterations, construction or relocation with regard to historic landmarks, or the removal or demolition of an historic landmark or a building, structure or improvement within an historic district when such historic landmarks, or properties within an historic district cannot be put to a reasonable beneficial use or the owner cannot obtain a reasonable economic return thereon without the proposed alteration, construction, relocation, removal or demolition.

We begin our analysis of the Ordinance by noting that it is the function of the appellate court to determine only whether the Commission's findings and decision which were adopted by the Board are against the manifest weight of the evidence. * * * Moreover, in reviewing the record, we are mindful that a Certificate of Economic Hardship is an exception to the general prohibition against demolishing contributing architectural resources located within the District. Thus, the burden at the hearing was squarely upon the plaintiff, the party seeking the certificate. In determining whether property is included within the scope of an exemption, all facts are to be construed and all debatable questions resolved against granting the exemption.

A decision is said to be contrary to the manifest weight of the evidence only when, after reviewing the evidence in a light most favorable to the administrative agency, the court determines that no rational trier of fact could have agreed with the agency's decision. In other words, reversal is appropriate only when the opposite conclusion of the one reached by the Commission is "clearly evident." If the record contains any evidence supporting the Commission's decision to deny the certificate, the decision must be sustained on review.

Plaintiff argues that, under the terms of the Ordinance and with regard to the Glavin property, he "cannot obtain a reasonable economic return thereon without the proposed * * * demolition." In our view, however, the evidence presented to the Commission was merely conflicting and therefore sufficient to support the Commission's ultimate determination.

The Ordinance lists five factors to be considered by the Commission * * * in determining whether a certificate should be issued. In the context of the facts presented, where the Commission did not make any specific recommendations to the plaintiff for changes which would allow the granting of a Certificate of Appropriateness, only the following four factors are relevant:[1] (1) a substantial decrease in the fair market value of the property as a result of the denial of the certificate of appropriateness; (2) the structural soundness of any structures on the property and their suitability for rehabilitation; (3) the economic feasibility of rehabilitation or reuse of the existing structure or improvement on the property in the case of proposed demolition; and (4) the cost of the proposed construction, alteration, relocation or demolition. *See* VILL. OF OAK PARK, ILL., MUNICIPAL ORDINANCE § 7–9–14 (eff. January 1, 1994).

Plaintiff failed to produce any evidence with regard to whether the denial of the Certificate of Appropriateness resulted in a substantial decrease in the property's fair market value. He stated repeatedly that he was not relying upon his purchase price to establish a fair market value for the Glavin property. Accordingly, this factor does not support his application.

With regard to the structural soundness of the Glavin house, all of the evidence supports the Village's decision. Robert Borman, the Village Chief Building Inspector, found that the building was deteriorating in many areas but he concluded that the building was structurally sound. The plaintiff's own evidence showed the building could be rehabilitated to Code requirements without work on the supporting structure of the house.

With regard to the feasibility of rehabilitation or use of the existing structure, we make several observations. First, plaintiff bases his entire case on a claim that the house was unmarketable at a reasonable price as a rehabilitation opportunity, yet we cannot help but note that plaintiff

---

[1]   The Ordinance also states that the Commission may consider "a substantial decrease in the pre-tax or after-tax return to owners of record or other investors in the property as a result of the denial of the certificate of appropriateness."

was unwilling to list the property so as to put his assertion of unmarketability to the test. The inference created by plaintiff's failure to list the property for sale is clearly one that must be held against his claim of unmarketability. Indeed, he admitted at the hearing that he purchased the property at what the market might consider an inflated price for rehabilitation precisely because he feared that the house would be purchased and that the new owner would expand it into the backyard. As the Village argues, if plaintiff can receive market value for the building in the same real estate market as when he purchased it, there can be no economic hardship as a result of the denial of his request to demolish the building.

Our second observation is that plaintiff only offered evidence as to what it would cost to renovate the house without adding square footage. Plaintiff's evidence leaves unresolved the question of whether the Village would have allowed a Certificate of Appropriateness for an addition to the house, as opposed to a complete tear-down. In such a situation, where an extension to the back of the Glavin house was proposed, it is quite possible that the plaintiff could recoup his investment.

Third, the evidence is far from clear that the house is incapable of being rehabbed and sold at a profit, at least if plaintiff had not deliberately overbid. In his brief plaintiff concedes that the property's fair market value was approximately $190,000 at the time he bought it for $227,500, but he insists that no one would willingly purchase the home as an investment at the $190,000 price. Although we agree that the evidence could have been interpreted by the Commission in this way, such an interpretation is not the only reasonable one. Mark Alger testified that the property could have been repaired and converted to a medium quality home for approximately $61,000, a price which included general contractor fees and a 15% contingency. The fact that Colleen Myra offered to purchase the house in its dilapidated state for $200,000 is particularly damaging to plaintiff's argument. Assuming a purchase price of $200,000, Myra could have lived in the home for under $265,000. Even if the property were resold, it is possible at these prices that Myra could have made a profit on the sale, even if a realtor's commission were added to her cost. This is because real estate agent Lois Merrill testified that the house could potentially sustain a price of from $280,000 to $300,000 if renovated.

Finally, with regard to the costs associated with the plaintiff's proposed renovation to the property, we note that he has failed to suggest the economic costs of leveling the Glavin house and building the new garage. These costs are important to consider because whether a Certificate of Economic Hardship should be granted under the Ordinance depends, in part, on whether demolishing the Glavin house will have the effect of lessening the economic burden of owning the property, a burden which may exist independently of whether demolition is allowed or denied. To this extent, the question is not so narrow as whether plaintiff can recover his out-of-pocket costs or make a profit by rehabilitating the Glavin property. Rather, the proper comparison must take into account all of the economic effects of plaintiff's proposal, including the net economic effect the proposed use of the Glavin lot will have on the value of plaintiff's existing home.

The question boils down to whether the demolition and proposed use of the combined properties will have a net economic benefit to plaintiff *vis a vis* renovating the Glavin property for resale. When all the costs are properly considered, it becomes clear that renovating the Glavin house for resale might be the best economic course for plaintiff *even if* a demolition permit were granted by the Commission, and *even if* renovating the property would mean plaintiff would suffer an out-of-pocket loss on his purchase of the Glavin property.

Assume, for example, that the Zaruba house has a fair market value of $350,000, and that the Glavin house has a fair market value of $200,000. Assume further that, after buying the Glavin property for $200,000 and spending $50,000 to tear it down and erect a new garage such as the one designed by plaintiff's architect, the fair market value of the combined properties would be $500,000. Under this scenario, plaintiff would be proposing to spend $250,000 to obtain a potential economic benefit of only $150,000, thus causing him to suffer a $100,000 loss in value on the transaction. If the evidence establishes that renovating the Glavin house and selling the property to a third party would cause a loss in value to plaintiff of $80,000, or even one of $90,000, renovating the Glavin house would still make economic sense over demolishing it and erecting a garage. This is because renovating and selling the Glavin property would produce a lesser economic loss than annexing the Glavin lot, tearing down the Glavin house and building a garage. Moreover, the resale of the renovated Glavin property would have the benefit to the Village of preserving one of the District's contributing architectural resources, the central purpose of the Village's Ordinance. In our view, the fact that plaintiff is willing to bear the more severe economic consequences of one course of action but not of the other is simply not relevant to an "economic" consideration of the hardship question.

In sum, we find evidence presented to the Commission to have been sufficient to sustain the decision of the Village Board. This being the case, the Commission's refusal to grant plaintiff a Certificate of Economic Hardship is affirmed.

NOTES & QUESTIONS

1.   The Frank Lloyd Wright Prairie School of Architecture Historic District protects an unparalleled collection of Prairie School style buildings designed by Frank Lloyd Wright and his followers. The block on which the Zaruba house is located is at the heart of both the local district, which protects about 1,500 properties, and the National Register district, which protects 80 of the most historic properties. The characteristics of the Prairie

School style include horizontal lines, overhanging eaves, natural materials, and open interior spaces. The Zaruba house is one block away from Frank Lloyd Wright's home and studio, shown in Figure 6-8 and the Wright-designed Hills-DeCaro House, which exemplifies the style and is shown in Figure 6-9 being renovated.

Figures 6-8 & 6-9:
Frank Lloyd Wright's Home and Studio and the Prairie
Style Hills-DeCaro House Being Rehabilitated,
Oak Park, IL

2. Now review Figure 6-7, a photo of the Kenilworth Avenue properties at issue in this case. 616 North Kenilworth Avenue is on the left; 614 is on the right. How does that photo compare with the photos mentioned in the preceding note? How would John Zaruba's proposals have resulted in a different appearance?

3. Should Mr. Zaruba have had any economic hardship case when he bought 616 after it already was subject to Oak Park's preservation ordinance? What is the relevance of the evidence that he paid more than fair market value for the house? The court states that the central question is whether Zaruba would suffer a larger economic loss from renovating the house than from demolishing it and concludes from the evidence in the record that he would not. Does such a test give sufficient weight to the value of the historic district?

Note that the testimony supports the prediction that a professional team could have purchased 616 from Mr. Glavin, renovated it, and turned a profit on resale while enhancing the value of Mr. Zaruba's house at 614. Indeed, that may have been what happened here. In 1999, Zaruba sold 616 North Kenilworth Avenue for $175,000, and in 2001, the new owners sold it for $650,000, presumably after a gut rehabilitation consistent with historic preservation laws.

4. Like most municipalities with economic hardship exceptions in the preservation ordinances, Oak Park declines to use numbers to specify what "a reasonable economic return" might be. New York City's law is unusual in providing a concrete definition of the "reasonable return" expected of a property: Less than a net annual return of 6 percent constitutes an "insufficient return" that triggers the issuance of a permit on hardship grounds. N.Y.C. ADMIN. CODE § 25–309. This criterion does not apply to tax exempt properties.

5. Here is a checklist of evidentiary issues offered by the National Trust for Historic Preservation as a tool for local preservation commissions considering economic hardship claims:

1. Current level of economic return

• Amount paid for the property, date of purchase, party from whom purchased, and relationship between the owner of record, the applicant, and person from whom property was purchased;

• Annual gross and net income from the property for the previous three years; itemized operating and maintenance expenses for the previous three years and depreciation deduction and annual cash flow before and after debt service, if any, during the same period;

• Remaining balance on the mortgage or other financing secured by the property and annual debt-service, if any, during the prior three years;

• Real estate taxes for the previous four years and assessed value of the property according to the two most recent assessed valuations;

- All appraisals obtained within the last two years by the owner or applicant in connection with the purchase, financing, or ownership of the property;

- Form of ownership or operation of the property, whether sole proprietorship, for-profit or not-for-profit corporation, limited partnership, joint venture, or other;

- Any state or federal income tax returns relating to the property for the last two years.

2.   Any listing of property for sale or rent; price asked, and offers received, if any, within the previous two years, including testimony and relevant documents regarding:

- Any real estate broker or firm engaged to sell or lease the property;

- Reasonableness of price or rent sought by the applicant;

- Any advertisements placed for the sale or rent of the property.

3.   Feasibility of alternative uses for the property that could earn a reasonable economic return:

- Report from a licensed engineer or architect with experience in rehabilitation as to the structural soundness of any buildings on the property and their suitability for rehabilitation;

- Cost estimates for the proposed construction, alteration, demolition, or removal, and an estimate of any additional cost that would be incurred to comply with the requirements for a certificate of appropriateness;

- Estimated market value of the property: (a) in its current condition; (b) after completion of the proposed alteration or demolition; and (c) after renovation of the existing property for continued use;

- Expert testimony or opinion on the feasibility of rehabilitation or reuse of the existing structure by an architect, developer, real estate consultant, appraiser, and/or other real estate professional experienced in historic properties and rehabilitation.

4.   Any evidence of self-created hardship through deliberate neglect or inadequate maintenance of the property.

5.   Knowledge of landmark designation or potential designation at time of acquisition.

6.   Economic incentives and/or funding available to the applicant through federal, state, city, or private programs.

Nat'l Trust for Historic Pres., *Assessing Economic Hardship Claims Under Historic Preservation Ordinances* 4–5 (2009).

b.   THE PUBLIC INTEREST EXCEPTION

Some jurisdictions permit the historic preservation board or other administrative officer to permit demolition on broad public interest grounds. Philadelphia's law provides, for example, that its Historical Commission can issue a demolition permit if it finds that "issuance of the building permit is necessary in the public interest." PHILADELPHIA, PA., HISTORIC PRESERVATION ORDINANCE, § 14–1005(6)(d); PHILADELPHIA HISTORICAL COMMISSION RULES AND REGULATIONS, § 6.3. The D.C. Special Merit provision is the most elaborate, and its interpretation has generated substantial litigation. As you read the next case, consider whether any jurisdiction should have a public interest exception and how any such exception should be cabined.

Committee of 100 on the Federal City v. District of Columbia Department of Consumer & Regulatory Affairs

571 A.2d 195 (D.C. 1990)

■ ROGERS, C.J.

Petitioner, the Committee of 100 on the Federal City (the Committee of 100), seeks review of an order of the Mayor's Agent under the Historic Landmark and Historic District Protection Act of 1978 (Preservation Act), D.C. CODE §§ 5–1001 *et seq.* (1988 Repl.) [EDS.: moved to D.C. CODE §§ 6–1101–6–1133], granting the applicant-intervenor S.J.G. Properties, Inc. (S.J.G.) a permit to demolish the Woodward Building, located within the Fifteenth Street Financial Historic District. The Committee of 100 contends that the amenities, consisting of approximately 30,000 square feet of residential space supplemented by a day care center for at least 57 persons, offered by the replacement building proposed by S.J.G., do not support a finding of special merit under the Preservation Act, D.C. CODE § 5–1002(11). The Committee also contends that the decision of the Mayor's Agent is not based on substantial evidence that the amenities are feasible, and that the Mayor's Agent erroneously factored into her special merit analysis the economic feasibility of the Woodward Building's renovation. Finally, the Committee of 100 contends that the Mayor's Agent may not use a covenant to bind a private owner on behalf of the District of Columbia. Even deferring to the Mayor's Agent's interpretation of the nature of the factors that would suffice for a project of special merit, and her conclusion that the residential and day care amenities were sufficiently special under the Preservation Act for a project of special merit, we conclude that the Mayor's Agent's order fails to address material issues relating to the feasibility of the proposed amenities and leaves undefined the nature of the covenant which was a central element of the special merit finding.

I

On September 24, 1986, S.J.G. applied for a permit to raze the Woodward Building and construct a new office building with underground parking at the site. The Historic Preservation Review Board unanimously voted to deny the application on the ground that demolition would be inconsistent with the purposes of the Preservation Act. D.C. CODE § 5–1003(c)(1).[1] Hearings were held before the Mayor's Agent at which the Committee of 100 and the Advisory Neighborhood Commission 2B joined as parties in opposition to the application for a demolition permit.

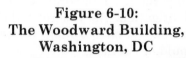

Figure 6-10:
The Woodward Building,
Washington, DC

By order of February 19, 1988, the Mayor's Agent found that S.J.G.'s proposal to demolish the Woodward Building is necessary in the public

---

[1]   The Staff Report and Recommendation, adopted by the Historic Preservation Review Board, explained that the Woodward Building is important as "an integral part of a historic district whose cohesiveness stems from common dates of construction, common history and the use of a common design vocabulary and philosophy." A new building, the report stated, "even one of high design quality, will inevitably reflect present-day technology and architectural style, and will disrupt the special sense of time and place represented by the Financial District."

As a result of this conclusion, the Review Board did not consider S.J.G.'s request to rule on the conceptual design of the proposed new building, as is required in most cases proposing new construction in a historic district. D.C. CODE § 5–1007(f). The review was unnecessary because the matter was referred to the Commission of Fine Arts (Commission), which is charged with reviewing proposed construction on this site under the Shipstead-Luce Act (D.C. CODE § 5–410). D.C. CODE § 5–1007(b).

The Commission on January 15, 1986, preliminarily approved the conceptual design of the new building, noting that if the District's preservation authorities had no objection to razing the Woodward building, then the Commission had no objection to the design for the proposed replacement building, subject to certain design changes if and when more detailed plans for the replacement building became available.

interest because it is consistent with the purposes of the Preservation Act and because it constitutes a project of special merit. The Mayor's Agent rejected S.J.G.'s claim that its project was of special merit by reason of exemplary architecture but accepted its claim of special merit based upon the special features of land planning that will promote the District's land planning objectives. In concluding that demolition of the Woodward building was necessary to construct a project of special merit, the Mayor's Agent "weighed the city's high priority for establishing a 'critical mass' of housing in the Downtown area" which market forces alone will not produce, the provision for day care services, and the absence of significant economic incentive for the owner of the building to renovate and maintain it.

The Mayor's Agent defined the special merit of the project in terms of the provisions of the new building for residential housing, day care, and parking. She therefore approved issuance of the demolition permit but made it subject to four conditions: (1) execution and recordation of a legally valid covenant between S.J.G. and the District of Columbia to run with the land and commit S.J.G. to use the top two floors of the proposed building for permanent residents, not transient business executives, and to use part of the building for a day care center capable of accommodating at least 57 children at a lease rate which will ensure its permanent operation; (2) submission of a day care feasibility study setting a proposed lease rate for the day care center; (3) a certificate of occupancy restricting the use of the top two floors for use by permanent residents and a portion of the square footage for use as a day care center; and (4) simultaneous issuance of a permit for new construction and demonstration by S.J.G. of its ability to complete the project.

The Committee of 100 seeks reversal of the February 19, 1988 order of the Mayor's Agent on three principal grounds: that the proposed project's amenities do not support a finding of special merit, that the Mayor's Agent's finding of special merit is not supported by substantial evidence of the feasibility of the amenities, and that her special merit analysis erroneously included consideration of the economic feasibility of renovation of the Woodward Building. Alternatively, the Committee seeks a remand for further proceedings relating to the feasibility requirements of the amenities and the covenant.

II

The Preservation Act provides that no permit shall issue to demolish a historic building or structure in a historic district "unless the Mayor finds that issuance of the permit is necessary in the public interest, or that failure to issue a permit will result in unreasonable economic hardship." D.C. CODE § 5–1004(e).[2] The Act defines "necessary in the public interest" as "consistent with the purposes of this [Act] as set forth

---

[2] S.J.G. does not contend it should be permitted to raze the Woodward Building on the basis of unreasonable economic hardship.

in § 5–1001(b)[3] or necessary to allow the construction of a project of special merit." D.C. CODE § 5–1002(10). A project of "special merit" is "a plan or building having significant benefits to the District of Columbia or to the community by virtue of exemplary architecture, special features of land planning, or social or other benefits having a high priority for community services." D.C. CODE § 5–1002(11).

The Committee of 100 contends that because the amenities relied on by the Mayor's Agent were not within the "special merit" project exception to preservation, the Mayor's Agent erred in applying a balancing test between the value of the historic structure and the merits of the proposed project. The Committee of 100 maintains that the Mayor's Agent may only engage in such a balancing test if the proposed amenities are sufficiently "special" to warrant inclusion on the special merit side of the equation.

This court "must uphold the Mayor's Agent's decision if her findings of fact are supported by substantial evidence in the record considered as a whole and the conclusions of law flow rationally from those findings." *MB Assocs. v. D.C. Dep't of Licenses, Investigation and Inspection*, 456 A.2d 344, 345 (D.C. 1982), and cases cited; D.C. CODE § 1–1510(a)(3)(E) (1987 Repl.). The findings of fact must be based on substantial evidence on each material contested issue, and the Mayor's Agent must reach rational conclusions based on these findings. In a demolition case, a determination by the Mayor's Agent that a project is of special merit implicitly includes the finding that issuance of a demolition permit is necessary in order for the proposed project to proceed. *Citizens Comm. to Save Rhodes Historic Tavern v. D.C. Dep't of Hous. and Cmty. Dev.*, 432 A.2d 710, 716 (D.C. 1981). Consequently, this court has held that the Mayor's Agent must balance the value of the community of the historic structure against the special merit of the proposed project. *Id.*

A.   Special Merit Project

The Preservation Act requires that a proposed amenity meet a high standard in order to qualify as a "special merit" project, the construction of which would warrant demolition of a building of historical significance. The social benefits to be included in a special merit project must have a "high priority" for community services. D.C. CODE § 5–1002(11). Thus, "factors which are common to all projects are not considered as special merits." REPORT OF THE COUNCIL OF THE DISTRICT OF COLUMBIA COMMITTEE ON HOUSING AND URBAN DEVELOPMENT ON BILL 2–367, "THE

---

[3] The purposes of the Preservation Act with respect to historic districts are:

(A)   To retain and enhance those properties which contribute to the character of the historic district and to encourage their adaptation for current use;

(B)   To assure that alterations of existing structures are compatible with the character of the historic district; and

(C)   To assure that new construction and subdivision of lots in a historic district are compatible with the character of the historic district.

D.C. CODE § 5–1001(b)(1).

HISTORIC LANDMARK AND HISTORIC DISTRICT PROTECTION ACT OF 1978"
6 (1978). *See MB Assoc., supra*, 456 A.2d at 346 (affirming denial of
demolition permit for Bond Building on ground proposed office building
was not a project of special merit since proposed contribution was
common to all downtown development).[4] The designation of a landmark
structure or historic district constitutes a formal determination that the
designated properties are worthy of "protection, enhancement and
perpetuation" as "distinctive elements of the city's cultural, social,
economic, political and architectural history." D.C. CODE § 5–1001(a)(1).
In order to justify the permanent loss and demolition of such a valuable
structure, therefore, the Preservation Act demands it be replaced with
something sufficiently "special." While the Preservation Act does not
require that a project of special merit be of epic proportions, the position
attributed to the Committee of 100 by S.J.G.,[5] the Preservation Act is not
standardless. A project of special merit must have "significant benefits to
the District of Columbia or to the community by virtue of exemplary
architecture, specific features of land planning, or social or other benefits
having a high priority for community services." D.C. CODE § 5–1002(11).

The Mayor's Agent noted S.J.G.'s claim that specific features of land
planning would further the goals and objectives of the District of
Columbia Comprehensive Plan and found the project to be one of special
merit because of its provision of social or other benefits having a high
priority for community service. S.J.G. maintained that its provision of
residential housing on the top two floors will "help promote the District
government's established goal of creating a 'Living Downtown' and will
help to extend activity in the area into the evening hours." The owner
further contended the day care services would meet "a clearly identified
need for day care that is located in close proximity to the work place and
will enhance the area's appeal to prospective tenants." He also stated
that S.J.G.'s participation in the D.C. Rideshare Program, and its
provision of parking in the building, would help to attract major
commercial tenants which would promote the economic vitality of the
historic district, and noted the proposed improvements in use of the
street and a pedestrian plaza. In our court, however, the District agrees
with the Committee of 100 that only the housing and day care proposals
are bases on which the special merit finding can properly rest.

---

[4] The proposed amenities in *MB Associates* involved economic revitalization, new open
spaces, infusion of private capital to an area, attraction of "first class" office and retail tenants,
parking facilities four grades below street level, and the addition of beauty and function to the
interior of the building.

[5] The Committee of 100 notes in its brief that past projects of special merit have included
the District of Columbia Convention Center (one-of-a-kind building), the PEPCO substation in
Georgetown (provision of electrical service conceded to be a project of special merit), an arts
exhibition center, and a block long structure consisting of a mix of land uses connected with the
Convention Center and ensuring activities downtown at different times of day and night. In
each of the approved special merit projects the amenities were designed to benefit more than
just a small group of people, and in the case of one of them, the Homer Building, the proposal
incorporated significant portions of the affected structure and was found to be exemplary
architecture.

The housing and day care components of S.J.G.'s proposal appear only in very general outline, and even if they could be found in a general sense under some circumstances to meet the high standards required for a project of "special merit," the Mayor's Agent failed to respond to material and relevant objections made at the hearing that such housing and day care amenities could be provided in a renovated Woodward Building and that the proposals were lacking any details to demonstrate their feasibility. To the extent that the Mayor's Agent relied on the District's Comprehensive Plan, the Committee of 100 argues persuasively that she relied on excerpts that were taken out of context. While she might properly reject objections about feasibility based on land costs, since S.J.G. owned the land, she avoided the other objections by deferring their resolution to the subsequent development of a covenant between S.J.G. and the District of Columbia. Consequently, consideration of whether there was any reasonable economic incentive for S.J.G. to provide the amenities in a renovated building was premature.

In her findings, the Mayor's Agent devoted considerable attention to the proposals relating to parking. Since parking must be considered with every downtown project, *see* 11 D.C. MUN. REGS. § 2101.1 (1987), it does not ordinarily qualify as an amenity of "special merit." By contrast, there is summary treatment of the proposals for residential and day care services on which S.J.G. and the Mayor's Agent place great emphasis in concluding that demolition of the Woodward Building was consistent with the public interest. S.J.G. proposed that approximately 30,000 square feet, or two of the twelve floors, of the new commercial building would be devoted to residential use. In its proposed findings of fact and conclusions of law, S.J.G. proposed that 2,000 square feet would be used for day care services. S.J.G. did not offer evidence on the nature and type of residential unit, and the Mayor's Agent did not explain how she arrived at day care services for at least 57 persons. We think that these findings are insufficient.

There also appears to be some confusion in the Mayor's Agent's reliance on the District's Comprehensive Plan as evidence of social policy. While day care is a priority for the greater District of Columbia community as a whole, the Comprehensive Plan focuses on indigent parents and does not direct that such programs be developed in the Downtown Area. The Mayor's Agent's findings on the high cost of Franklin Square properties, moreover, disclose that residents in the neighborhood are unlikely to be indigent parents, and that the cost of day care is unlikely to be within the means of working parents whom the Plan targets for assistance in the context of promoting economic self-support. The Mayor's Agent similarly misconstrues the Plan's concept for residential downtown housing in her reference to a "critical mass of housing." The reference in the Plan to the "city's high priority for establishing a 'critical mass' in the Downtown area," is used in a very different context for a different purpose. The Plan refers to a "critical mass of key land uses" and in view of the Plan's section targeting specific downtown areas for residential development, 10 D.C. MUN. REGS. § 903 (1987), which does not include the Financial District, it is more likely that the Plan envisions a mixture of commercial, cultural, retail and professional uses, rather than major housing development. Therefore, it is inappropriate in this case for the Mayor's Agent to factor in the Comprehensive Plan as though it supports S.J.G.'s proposal.

The Mayor's Agent could properly consider factors associated with alternatives to demolition such as cost, delay and technical feasibility. *Citizens Comm. to Save Historic Rhodes Tavern v. D.C. Dep't of Hous. & Cmty. Dev.*, 432 A.2d 710, 718 (D.C. 1981); *Don't Tear It Down, Inc. v. D.C. Dep't of Hous. & Cmty. Dev.*, 428 A.2d 369, 380 (D.C. 1981). The reasonableness of the proposed project must be considered in the context of whether "there are viable alternatives to demolition available, and the answer to this question determines necessity." *Don't Tear It Down, supra*, 428 A.2d at 380. Although the Mayor's Agent found that the renovation of the Woodward Building is not economically feasible, we conclude that her conclusion is not persuasively supported by her findings of fact. Moreover, economic feasibility is just one factor to be considered in determining whether to allow demolition.

The Mayor's Agent found that if S.J.G. were to renovate the Woodward, its return would be approximately 7.32 percent. The projected yield for typical downtown commercial-income producing properties is 7 to 9 percent. The Mayor's Agent found that in today's dollars, a renovated Woodward Building might command approximately $22.00–23.00 per square foot. Currently, S.J.G. receives approximately $15.00–16.00 per square foot. "Necessary" cannot be equated with "least expensive." *Id.* Where the economic burden of maintaining and preserving a historic building is onerous, the Preservation Act provides an owner with the opportunity to seek demolition on the separate ground of "unreasonable economic hardship." D.C. CODE § 5–1004(e). Although S.J.G.'s general partner testified that he had no incentive to borrow $30 million at 9 percent interest to renovate the Woodward Building, he admitted that the partnership was receiving a modest return on the building. He rested his claim that he should be permitted to demolish the building on his assertion that the proposed new construction is a special merit project in the public interest.

The weight accorded by the Mayor's Agent to her conclusion that renovation of the Woodward was not economically feasible is unclear. In her order she states that "[t]he issue is not whether a renovation can be done, but whether a Class 'B' building can command the level of rents necessary to justify the extraordinary expense of renovation," and concludes that renovation of the Woodward is not feasible. The issue is not whether a Class "B" building can command the level of rents necessary to justify the expense of renovation, but whether demolition of the Woodward Building and the historic values statutorily ascribed to buildings located within historic districts is justified by the cost of renovation and by the benefits which the new building would bring to the community. Although we agree with the Mayor's Agent that economic feasibility cannot reasonably be assessed in a vacuum, a petition based on the alleged special merits of the project cannot be granted on the basis of strikingly different consideration.

Moreover, as the Committee of 100 contends, the balancing of the historic value of the Woodward Building against the special merits of the project could not proceed until the Mayor's Agent found that the amenities proposed by S.J.G. were sufficient to constitute a project of special merit. In making the special merit determination, the feasibility of the amenities was a legitimate consideration.

B.   Feasibility of Amenities

The Committee of 100 contends that the Mayor's Agent's decision was not based on substantial evidence that the housing and day care proposals proposed by S.J.G. were feasible.[11] In this court the District states that, in view of the need for further proceedings in connection with the covenant, there should be an on-the-record examination of the economic feasibility of the residential and day care proposals. Indeed, the District maintains that the permanence of the housing and day care services is an integral part of the complete project and that a finding of economic feasibility "is appropriate, if not mandated," particularly since market forces alone are generally unlikely to produce such results. The Committee of 100 views this as a concession that the Mayor's Agent's decision is not supported by substantial evidence. For purposes of this proceeding so do we. As the Committee of 100 points out, while S.J.G. "tried in a general way to show that these amenities were *desirable*, . . . it submitted nothing to show that they could be successfully marketed or maintained in a way that would advance the goals attributed to them." The proposals for residential housing and day care were not a part of S.J.G.'s original proposal. S.J.G. presented no witnesses regarding the economic feasibility of housing at the site, which the Comprehensive Plan targets for "complete development . . . as the major center of office development in Downtown," In addition, S.J.G. presented no witnesses regarding the kind of housing that would be provided, although a goal of the Comprehensive Plan is to protect and enhance the historic quality of

---

[11] The Committee of 100 also contends that the Mayor's Agent erred in not requiring evidence on and making a finding as to S.J.G.'s ability to complete the new project. The Preservation Act does not require an evaluation of the applicant's ability to complete the proposed project until after a determination of special merit has been made. D.C. CODE § 5–1004(h) (where demolition necessary for construction of project of special merit, "no demolition permit shall be issued unless a permit for new construction is issued simultaneously under § 5–1007 and the owner demonstrates the ability to complete the project."). Here, in addition to the statutory requirements, the Mayor's Agent conditioned her approval of the demolition permit on a number of additional events taking place before the demolition permit will issue, namely satisfactory resolution by S.J.G. with the District government of matters to be included in the covenant. * * *

the 15th Street Financial District. 10 D.C. MUN. REGS. § 931.1 (1987). The Mayor's Agent's determination that demolition was necessary required findings in some greater detail as to the amenities that were said to be of special merit, *see MB Assocs., supra*, 456 A.2d at 346. These issues must be addressed as part of the contested case proceedings for determining whether to approve the application for demolition. D.C. CODE §§ 5–1004, 1–1509(a). * * *

Accordingly, because the Mayor's Agent's order of February 18, 1988 fails to address material issues raised by the Committee of 100 in opposition to the application, the case is remanded for further proceedings.

NOTES & QUESTIONS

1.   Note the approved projects of special merit mentioned in Footnote 5 in the *Committee of 100* case. Should every historic preservation ordinance permit demolition of listed buildings in order to construct such projects? Why? What are the probable effects of not having such an "escape hatch?" New York City's Landmarks Preservation Law does not contain a public interest exception for permits. The City's Landmarks Preservation Commission, however, has legal discretion not to designate historic properties, as discussed in Chapter 2. Is that another form of an "escape hatch"?

2.   Why did the services proposed for the Woodward Building not qualify for the special merit exception? How should opportunities for investment and employment in a depressed real estate market be balanced against preservation of a historic building?

3.   A ground for a finding of special merit in D.C. not discussed in the case above is "exemplary architecture" in the building that will replace the historic structure. What would be the criteria for such a finding? Note that the Mayor's Agent, the official entrusted with the finding, need have no expertise at all in architecture. In *Citizens Committee to Save Rhodes Historic Tavern v. District of Columbia Department of Housing and Community Development*, 432 A.2d 710 (D.C. 1981), the court upheld the Mayor Agent's finding of exemplary architecture in the incorporation of the facades of two historic buildings into a new office building. Few think that such a finding would be made or upheld today as preservationists have turned against saving only facades and plastering them on modern buildings.

Review, as an example of this trend, the hulking black glass building towering over a half-dozen or so retained historic facades, shown in Figure 6-11. Oddly, some faux historic stone or concrete bay windows have been incorporated into the façade of the new structure. On the other hand, sensitive additions that retain historic fabric can lead to successful preservation projects. Contrast the approach taken by the developers of the black glass building with the later approach taken by the developers of the International Spy Museum addition, nestled discreetly behind a row of historic buildings, shown in Figure 6-12.

Figure 6-11:
A Hulking Black Glass Building in Foggy Bottom,
Washington, DC

Figure 6-12:
The International Spy Museum Addition,
Washington, DC

4.   After this case was decided, S.J.G. Properties had a change of heart, and redeveloped the Woodward Building into a luxury residential apartment building—complete with a fitness center, a ground-floor wine shop and restaurant, and a roof deck with magnificent views of the nearby Washington Monument, the U.S. Treasury Building (a National Historic Landmark), and the National Mall. One block away from the White House, the Woodward commands some of the highest rents in D.C. Figure 6-10 shows the stately H Street façade, including dual wings.

C. AFFIRMATIVE MAINTENANCE LAWS

The preceding Section involved situations in which property owners seek permission from local governments to make alterations to exteriors of historic places, or demolish them altogether. The laws to which these property owners are subject do not always regulate situations in which owners allow their properties to undergo dramatic transformations as a result of neglect. Unfortunately, too many property owners neglect historic places—particularly historic buildings. In extreme cases, "demolition by neglect" will occur when a property owner neglects a historic resource until demolition has effectively occurred or becomes necessary.

Demolition by neglect is an environmental and sustainability issue, as it can take nearly two generations to offset the carbon impacts of demolition and new construction. Moreover, properties that fall victim to demolition by neglect become a public liability: they fail to generate needed tax revenue, and they depress surrounding property values. The less tangible effects of demolition by neglect include the erosion of community character and morale and, of course, the irreplaceable loss of historic craftsmanship and natural resources.

To counter this unfortunate circumstance, some jurisdictions have enacted affirmative maintenance provisions to require property owners to maintain their buildings to a standard of good repair. Affirmative maintenance provisions are distinct from the ordinances discussed in the preceding Section, because those ordinances typically exempt maintenance and minor repairs, so as not to overwhelm local historic preservation commissions.

The New York City Landmarks Law contains affirmative maintenance provisions. N.Y.C. ADMIN. CODE § 25–311. It states that people in charge of a designated historic place must keep in good repair "(1) all of the exterior portions of such improvement and (2) all interior portions thereof which, if not so maintained, may cause or tend to cause the exterior portions of such improvement to deteriorate, decay or become damaged or otherwise to fall into a state of disrepair." Under the Landmarks Law, the "person in charge" includes any person who possesses any part of the freehold, a vendee in possession, an executor, a trustee, a lessee, or an agent. *See* N.Y.C. ADMIN. CODE § 25–302(t). Local law creates penalties for failing to maintain properties in this manner, including "Type B" violations resulting in "significant deterioration" of a character-defining feature, for penalties up to $5,000 for a first offense and $250 day for later offenses. *Id.* §§ 25–302x(2), 25–317.1b(2)(a). If the building must be demolished, the City is entitled to its fair market value, defined as the value of the parcel with or without the improvement, whichever is greater. *Id.* § 25–317.1.

The City understands that simply having laws on the books is not sufficient. The City has established a procedure for dealing with these properties. It has created a system for early identification of buildings in disrepair, including monitoring building conditions through periodic documentation and liaising with the water board to know when the water is turned off in the building. It attempts to contact the property owner to repair the building. In some cases, a property owner is either unable or unwilling to make the necessary repairs. An owner may be experiencing some sort of trauma, whether it be mental illness, divorce, an estate battle, fraud, or bankruptcy; or she may have inherited a building she cannot afford to maintain. In those situations, it may prove necessary for the property owner to sell her historic building.

If a property owner is either unreachable or uncooperative, the Commission will bring suit to prevent the demolition of the property by neglect. For example, the owner of the once grand Windermere building in New York City was a Japanese person on life support in Tokyo. He was unable to participate, so litigation brought the desired result to protect and repair the building. *See City of N.Y. v. Toa Constr.*, No. 400584/08 (N.Y. Cty. Sup. Ct. May 14, 2009). We are indebted to Counsel Mark A. Silberman for an explanation of this approach.

When the Commission was formed in 1965, this type of litigation was not nearly as prevalent as it is today. Prior to 2002, the City's Landmarks Preservation Commission had only filed one lawsuit for demolition by neglect, which ended successfully after many years. *See City of N.Y. v. Goding*, No. 48530/1996 (N.Y. Sup. Ct. Feb. 6, 1998). Now, things are different. The deputy general counsel of the Commission has indicated that staff increasingly recognizes that "[t]ime is not on our side," so when property owners are unresponsive to the Commission's requests to repair properties, his office will not hesitate to bring demolition-by-neglect lawsuits. Frank St. Jacques, *Landmarks' John Weiss on Combating Demolition-by-Neglect*, CITY LAND: NEW YORK CITY LAND USE NEWS AND LEGAL RESEARCH (May 2, 2012).

Demolition by neglect may also be addressed by laws beyond historic preservation ordinances, and outside of enforcement by local preservation commissions. For example, some states allow for municipalities to adopt local regulation of blighted properties. Connecticut allows municipalities to establish local laws to prevent and remedy housing blight, giving them the power to establish fines of ten to one hundred dollars per day. CONN. GEN. STAT. § 7–148(c)(7)(H)(xv). States may also allow local governments to define, prohibit, and abate nuisances, which include the ability to deal with buildings that may be nuisances. *See, e.g.,* CONN. GEN. STAT. § 7–148(c)(7)(E).

Analyze the competing interests at stake in demolition-by-neglect cases. What would be some key arguments of preservation advocates in favor of preventing demolition by neglect? What about the private property owners?

D. DELAYS OF DEMOLITION

Many jurisdictions do not entirely prohibit demolition of historic structures, but only delay demolition to permit the purchase of the structure by a buyer willing to preserve it. Alexandria, Virginia, for example, provides that the owner of a contributing building within a historic district may receive a demolition permit if:

> the owner has for the period of time set forth in the time schedule hereinafter contained and at a price reasonably related to its fair market value made a bona fide offer to sell such building or structure and the land pertaining thereto to any person, government or agency thereof or political subdivision or agency thereof which gives reasonable assurance that it is willing to preserve and restore the building or structure and the land pertaining thereto.

ALEXANDRIA, VA., ZONING ORDINANCE art. 10, § 108(A)(2). The ordinance prescribes a listing period depending upon the price at which the property is being offered, under which nearly every building must be offered for a year. While undoubtedly helpful in preserving historic buildings, such delay provisions create games that allow determined owners to demolish properties, especially when the property is worth much more without the building. Consider the incentives and tactics suggested by the following case.

Pansini Custom Design Associates, LLC v. City of Ocean City

969 A.2d 1163 (N.J. Super. Ct. App. Div. 2009)

■ CARCHMAN, P.J.A.D.

The narrow issue that we address on this appeal is whether the use of averaging of comparable sales by the trial judge in fixing the fair market value of the real property in issue represents an appropriate evaluation methodology and whether it fulfills a judge's fact-finding responsibility. Here, the trial judge, after excluding the high and low comparable sales presented by the expert witnesses in competing appraisals, averaged the values of the remaining comparables to arrive at a fair market value. We disapprove of the practice of averaging and conclude that it does not represent a reasoned and considered valuation technique. We reverse and remand.

The facts underlying this appeal are not in significant dispute. Plaintiffs Pansini Custom Design Associates, LLC and Roger Parkin are the owners of the property in Ocean City known as 801 Fourth Street, Lot 49, Block 303, consisting of a 100 x 130 foot (13,000 square feet) parcel improved with a single-family residence with a detached garage. The parcel was acquired on May 27, 1999, for $710,000 from Elizabeth Sheehan, who had resided on the property as her home. The property had been a former United States Life Saving Service and United States Coast Guard Life Saving Station until its retirement in 1940. The 19th century building is one of the last four lifesaving stations on the East Coast built by the United States Life Saving Services, the predecessor to the United States Coast Guard. Thereafter, additions and alterations followed as the premises was converted to a single family residence.

The property was designated as a historic structure under historic-preservation provisions of the Ocean City Zoning Ordinance. Originally located on the beach, because of changing tides and land accretion, the property is now two and one-half blocks from the beach and ocean. It is located in a developed mixed area, primarily a two-family residential zone. The property has been vacant since the sale by Sheehan to plaintiffs.

Because of the designation of the property as a historic structure, a developer must comply with the procedures set forth in Ocean City's zoning ordinance, specifically, the requirements of the historic-preservation ordinance, which controls development and requires a series of steps before a property owner can demolish a historic building. OCEAN CITY, N.J. ORDINANCE §§ 25–1800.1 to –.15.3 [EDS: hereinafter O.C. ORD.]. The procedures under the ordinance require an owner to first apply to the City's Historic Preservation Commission for a demolition permit. O.C. ORD. § 25–1800.7.1. The Commission is charged with the responsibility of reviewing zoning applications that involve demolition, relocation or changes to historic buildings. O.C. ORD. § 25–1800.8.3. If the Commission denies the application, an applicant may appeal to the zoning board for review.

If the zoning board affirms the denial, an applicant may then obtain relief by adhering to a six-month waiting period during which it must try to sell the property for "fair market value" to "any person or organization, governmental agency thereof or political subdivision or agency thereof, which gives reasonable assurance that it is willing to preserve the building, place or structure and the land pertaining thereto." O.C. ORD. § 25–1800.10.1(d). In an earlier opinion, we interpreted that provision to mean fair market value of the property in its present use as a historic site. *Pansini Custom Design Assocs. v. City of Ocean City*, No. A–5635–99T5, 2002 WL 549413, slip op. at 6 (N.J. Super. Ct. App. Div. April 9, 2002), *certif. denied*, 803 A.2d 1161 (2002). If at the end of the waiting period the property remains unsold, the applicant may then develop the property "as a matter of right." O.C. ORD. § 25–1800.10.1.

These procedures have been followed, as before plaintiffs purchased the site, Sheehan applied to the Commission to demolish the life saving station and build three duplex units. That application was denied. The Board of Adjustment reversed and granted the application, and the Law Division sustained the Board's decision. We reversed. *See Citizens for Historic Pres., Inc. v. Sheehan*, Nos. A–5106–03T2 and A–5845–03T2, slip op. at 2 (N.J. Super. Ct. App. Div. July 26, 2005), *certif. denied*, 886 A.2d 660 (N.J. 2005). During that dispute, Pansini purchased the property from Sheehan and immediately began advertising its sale under the historic-preservation ordinance's notice provisions. *Citizens for Historic Pres.*, slip op. at 9.

Pansini advertised the property with a real estate broker for $1.1 million, which it deemed an appropriate price for a three-lot subdivision that could be developed with three duplexes. Defendant City of Ocean City disputed the price, claiming Pansini was required to advertise it for fair market value as a single-family home in a historic district. As noted earlier, we agreed with Ocean City, and in so doing, affirmed a trial court judgment concluding that Pansini did not comply with Ocean City's historic preservation ordinance. *Pansini Custom Design Assocs.*, slip op. at 5.

Plaintiffs then filed this declaratory judgment action in the Law Division and sought to establish fair market value so that it could advertise the property for sale consistent with the City's ordinance. The trial judge held a two-day trial and heard three witnesses: an appraiser hired by Pansini, an appraiser hired by Ocean City and an appraiser hired by defendant Saving Our Station Coalition (SOS), objectors to plaintiff's proposed development.

In his decision, the judge criticized the appraisal methods used by all of the parties. He found that Pansini's appraiser improperly considered potential development of the site's excess property beyond its current use when evaluating fair market value and adjusting comparative sales. He also criticized defendants' two appraisers, noting that the comparable sales they chose occurred during a time when the real estate market in Ocean City was "flat at best."

Despite these criticisms of the comparable sales and the appraiser's adjustments, the judge averaged them to establish fair market value. More specifically, he averaged the three highest comparable sales used by defendants' appraisers and the three lowest comparable sales used by Pansini's appraiser. Using this methodology, he declared the fair market value to be $1,072,500. This appeal by SOS followed.

As we noted, the judge considered three appraisal reports. First, plaintiffs' appraiser, Michael P. Hedden, offered five comparables. While the actual sales prices of the comparables ranged from $507,500 to $995,500, Hedden adjusted the sales upward in various amounts, including an adjustment of $843,744 for a property that sold for $507,500. Converting the adjustments to percentages, Hedden adjusted the five properties respectively by, 25%, 40%, 72%, 73% and 166%. Based on the adjusted comparable sales, Hedden opined that the fair market value of the subject property was $1,400,000.

Robert M. Sapio, Ocean City's appraiser, opined that the property's fair market value was $900,000. He reached this conclusion by utilizing four comparable sales that were priced in a range of $675,000 to $771,600 and were respectively adjusted by 17% in two instances and by 20% and 31% as to the other two sales.

Finally, SOS produced Michael J. Lange as its appraiser. Lange used three comparables, ranging in sales price from $950,000 to $1,100,000. He adjusted those sales downward by 10%, 15% and 20% and concluded that the fair market value was $850,000. Unlike the two prior appraisers, Lange did not use sales that were in the historic zone, concluding that those available sales were too old. He instead utilized sales closer to the beach and adjusted accordingly.

As we have previously noted, ultimately, the judge, in reaching his valuation, utilized the three highest comparable sales used by Sapio and the three lowest sales used by Hedden, averaged them and declared the result to be the fair market value.

A fact-finder's need for expert witnesses is well-defined. Expert testimony is required "where the fact[-]finder is not expected to have sufficient knowledge or experience and would have to speculate without the aid of expert testimony." *Torres v. Schripps, Inc.*, 776 A.2d 915 (N.J. Super. Ct. App. Div. 2001). Expert testimony is generally required to determine the fair market value of real property, but the "fact[-]finder is not bound to accept the testimony of an expert witness," and "may accept some of the expert's testimony and reject the rest." *Id.*

Where the judge has questioned or rejected the testimony of the expert, the judge, among other things, may appoint an independent expert.

Ultimately, the fact-finder, here the judge, must weigh and evaluate the experts' opinions, including their credibility, to fulfill the judge's responsibility in reaching a reasoned, just and factually supported conclusion. In our view, averaging cedes this unique responsibility to a simple mathematical formula and is an unacceptable methodology for fulfilling one's role as a fact-finder.

While there is limited authority for the proposition that averaging is an inappropriate appraisal technique, the majority of reasoned decisions addressing the subject support this view. * * *

We are of the view that averaging, whether of appraisals or comparable sales, is not an appropriate methodology for assessing divergent values. The reasoned weight of authority provides sound policy reasons for such a conclusion. Properties are not fungible. Even with adjustments during the appraisal process, there are sufficient differences that must be weighed and considered by the fact-finder in addressing the ultimate issue in dispute. Here, the properties offered by the three appraisers were disparate in a host of factors, including time of sale, location, amenities and virtually all of the elements that enter into the appraisal process.

Finally, we view with caution the danger foreseen by those courts that have addressed this issue. To allow averaging will result in appraisals slanted to the extreme. Averaging will generate appraisals that will intentionally distort and skew the values to insure a high or low number without concern that the fact finder must resolve the issue with a careful analysis of data that may result in adoption of one appraisal figure over another.

In sum, we conclude that the averaging engaged in by the trial judge here so flawed the process that his finding of fair market value cannot be sustained. * * *

Reversed and remanded for a new trial as to valuation.

NOTES & QUESTIONS

1. Note that Pansini's appraiser provided an appraisal of the property free for construction of a three-unit duplex, which assumes the demolition of the Lifesaving Station. Given Ocean City's demolition provision, why would the owner prefer a high appraisal? Why would the preservation organization prefer a lower appraisal?

2. To address concerns about listing property at inflated prices, the Alexandria, Virginia, code dictates that within fifteen days of a property being listed for sale, a written petition questioning the price, if signed by at least twenty-five owners of property in the Old and Historic Alexandria District, can be sent to the city manager. The city manager will then, at city expense, appoint three neutral real estate appraisers familiar with property values in the district, and they will file written reports with the city manager indicating whether they think the listed price is reasonably related to its fair market value. Whatever two of the three appraisers conclude will be a final determination. If they agree with the listing price, the process can proceed. If they do not, the offer to sell is voided and will have to be re-listed at a price reasonably related to the fair market value. Is that a better procedure than the averaging engaged in by the New Jersey trial judge?

3. How would you compare the fairness and efficacy of the delay of demolition pending sale provisions with the outright prohibition of demolition subject to an economic hardship exception?

4. Demolition delay ordinances may not be sufficient to protect historic places. In 1995, Houston adopted a historic preservation ordinance that amounted to a simple ninety-day delay provision for any demolition or renovation of structures within designated historic districts. Eighty percent of structures demolished in historic districts were demolished without the approval of the Houston Archaeological and Historical Commission (HAHC).

In 2010, the Houston City Council adopted significant changes to the ordinance to strengthen the ability of the city to protect and preserve designated historic properties. An owner who wants to demolish or significantly change a structure within a historic district now must apply for a certificate of appropriateness (COA) from the HAHC. A COA to demolish a contributing structure in a historic district may be granted in cases of unreasonable economic hardship or unusual or compelling circumstances. If the COA is denied, the owner can appeal to the planning commission and to the City Council. HOUS., TEX., HISTORIC PRESERVATION ORDINANCE ch.§ 33–243, art. VII (2010).

The amended ordinance gave owners of structures within already designated historic districts an opportunity to petition for that designation to be reconsidered, in light of the tougher restrictions on their property. To trigger that process, 10 percent of property owners within a historic district had to sign a reconsideration petition by a certain date. Six of the then-existing sixteen historic districts began the reconsideration process. Ultimately, none marshaled the 51 percent required to remove the historic designation. *See* Chris Moran, *Historic Districts See Few Changes*, HOUS. CHRON., Mar. 19, 2011. As of 2021, Houston has twenty-two historic districts.

E. NEW CONSTRUCTION

New construction within historic districts where no existing historic resources will be demolished or altered raises somewhat different issues than demolition or alteration of a contributing structure. No historic resources are lost, although the setting in which they are seen may be damaged by new structures that are jarring or unsympathetic. At the same time, duplication of existing architecture is anachronistic and often aesthetically deadening.

Sanchez v. Town of Beaufort

710 S.E.2d 350 (N.C. App. 2011)

■ CALABRIA, J.

Gerharda H. Sanchez ("petitioner") appeals the superior court's order affirming the decision of the Town of Beaufort ("the Town") Board of Adjustment ("the BOA"). The BOA reversed the decision of the Beaufort Historic Preservation Commission ("the BHPC") and ordered the BHPC to issue a Certificate of Appropriateness ("COA") to respondent Douglas E. Smith ("Smith"). We affirm.

I.   Background

Petitioner lives at 117 Front Street, in the historic district of Beaufort, North Carolina. Petitioner's home is located across the street from a property owned by Smith. Smith's property, located at 122 Front Street, contains a sixteen foot, two inch structure known as the "Carpenter Cottage." Smith purchased the property intending to demolish the Carpenter Cottage and construct a two-story structure in its place. In order to commence demolition and construction in the historic district, Smith was required by statute to submit applications for

COAs to the BHPC. The BHPC denied three of Smith's applications, and Smith appealed these denials to the BOA. The resulting BOA decisions were then appealed to the Carteret County Superior Court by either Smith or the Town, depending upon which party prevailed before the BOA.

The Carteret County Superior Court ordered Smith and the Town, including two members of the BHPC, to conduct mediation. The mediation was conducted in August 2008, and the parties reached a proposed settlement whereby Smith agreed to submit a new application for a one-and-one-half story structure with the condition that, if the new application was approved by the BHPC, all parties would dismiss any pending litigation. Smith submitted the new COA application, which proposed a one-and-one-half story structure that was twenty-nine feet tall, to the BHPC on 14 March 2009. The new application was considered and discussed at three separate public BHPC hearings, 7 April 2009, 5 May 2009, and 2 June 2009.

At the 7 April 2009 BHPC hearing, Smith explained his proposal to demolish the Carpenter Cottage as well as his construction plans for a new structure on the property. Smith's demolition plan was approved since the Carpenter Cottage was found to be beyond repair. However, petitioner, along with other members of the community, objected to the height of Smith's proposed new construction. Specifically, petitioner objected that the new structure would inhibit her view of Carrot Island and Taylor's Creek from her porch. Petitioner's husband testified that he estimated that the view added approximately $100,000–$150,000 of value to petitioner's home. At the conclusion of the hearing, the COA for new construction was tabled so that the BHPC could conduct further research regarding the possibility of building a one-and-one-half story structure at a reduced height.

At the 5 May 2009 hearing, Smith learned the BHPC would issue a COA for the construction of his proposed structure if he reduced the maximum height of the structure to twenty-four feet. On 2 June 2009, Smith presented additional drawings and explained his inability to reduce the height to twenty-four feet. Smith provided computer-aided design drawings that were professionally produced to demonstrate that a height of twenty-seven feet, three inches was the lowest height he would be able to build a structure that could be considered a reasonable use of the property. Smith explained to the BHPC the details regarding the proposed height of the ceilings on the first and second floor, as well as the requirements for the height of the foundation to comply with flood safety regulations. Nevertheless, the BHPC voted to deny Smith's application for a COA, because the twenty-seven foot, three inch height was considered non-conforming to the maximum height of twenty-four feet that had been approved at the conclusion of the 5 May 2009 hearing.

Smith appealed the BHPC's decision to the BOA. Smith's appeal was heard at a BOA hearing on 26 October 2009. At the hearing, Smith's counsel and the attorney for the Town addressed Smith's appeal. Petitioner's attorney also attempted to address the BOA, but the Town's attorney advised the BOA that the superior court was the proper forum for any appeals. Consequently, the BOA did not consider the arguments of petitioner's attorney. On 3 December 2009, the BOA entered an order which determined that the BHPC's twenty-four foot height requirement was arbitrary and capricious and remanded Smith's application to the BHPC with instructions to issue Smith a COA. On 15 December 2009, the BHPC voted to issue Smith the COA.

Petitioner filed a petition for a writ of *certiorari* in the Carteret County Superior Court, requesting that the court reverse the decision of the BOA and uphold the BHPC's denial of Smith's COA application. In response to the petition, the Town filed a response which asserted, *inter alia*, that petitioner did not have standing to challenge the BOA's decision. On 24 March 2010, the superior court entered an order affirming the BOA's decision. The superior court's order stated, "the height limitation for the proposed structure of 24 feet was arbitrary and not supported by evidence" and "the proposed structure height of 27 feet, 3 inches is congruous with the structures in the historic district as required by law." Petitioner appeals.

II. Standing

As an initial matter, we address the Town's argument that petitioner's appeal should be dismissed because petitioner lacks standing. While the Town raised this argument before the superior court, it was not explicitly addressed in the court's order affirming the decision of the BOA. Nevertheless, since "[s]tanding is a necessary prerequisite to a court's proper exercise of subject matter jurisdiction, ... issues pertaining to standing may be raised for the first time on appeal[.]" *Aubin v. Susi*, 560 S.E.2d 875, 878–79 (N.C. App. 2002).

"City ordinances creating historic districts, as other ordinances which limit the use of property, are zoning ordinances." *Unruh v. City of Asheville*, 388 S.E.2d 235, 236 (N.C. App. 1990). In the context of zoning ordinance disputes, our Supreme Court has stated:

> The mere fact that one's proposed lawful use of his own land will diminish the value of adjoining or nearby lands of another does not give to such other person a standing to maintain an action, or other legal proceeding, to prevent such use. If, however, the proposed use is unlawful, as where it is prohibited by a valid zoning ordinance, the owner of adjoining or nearby lands, who will sustain special damage from the proposed use through a reduction in the value of his own property, does have a standing to maintain such proceeding.

Jackson v. Board of Adjustment, 166 S.E.2d 78, 82 (N.C. 1969).

Pursuant to N.C. GEN. STAT. § 160A–400.9, a historic preservation commission "shall . . . prepare and adopt principles and guidelines . . . for new construction, alterations, additions, moving and demolition" in the historic district. N.C. GEN. STAT. § 160A–400.9 (c) (2009). Moreover,

> no exterior portion of any building or other structure (including masonry walls, fences, light fixtures, steps and pavement, or other appurtenant features) . . . shall be erected, altered, restored, moved, or demolished . . . within [a historic] district until after an application for a certificate of appropriateness as to exterior features has been submitted to and approved by the preservation commission.

N.C. GEN. STAT. § 160A–400.9 (a) (2009). There is no dispute that, pursuant to N.C. GEN. STAT. § 160A–400.9 (a), Smith must comply with established BHPC guidelines in order to obtain a COA from the BHPC and legally construct a new structure in place of the Carpenter Cottage. Although petitioner alleged that Smith's application did not comply with BHPC guidelines, in order to establish her standing, petitioner still has the burden of demonstrating that she would sustain " 'special damages' distinct from the rest of the community." *Heery v. Zoning Bd. of Adjustment*, 300 S.E.2d 869, 870 (N.C. App. 1983).

When making a standing determination, "we view the allegations as true and the supporting record in the light most favorable to the non-moving party." *Mangum v. Raleigh Bd. of Adjustment*, 669 S.E.2d 279, 283 (N.C. 2008). Petitioner alleged in her petition for writ of *certiorari* that her property was directly across the street from Smith's property. This allegation "in and of itself, is insufficient to grant standing, [but] it does bear some weight on the issue of whether the complaining party has suffered or will suffer special damages distinct from those damages to the public at large." *Id.*

Petitioner additionally alleged that the height of Smith's proposed structure did not conform with BHPC guidelines and thus should not have been granted a COA. She also alleged that at its proposed height, Smith's non-conforming structure would interfere with her use of her property by causing her to lose her private waterfront view. Both petitioner and her husband asserted during HPC hearings on Smith's application that the loss of this view would reduce the value of petitioner's property by at least $100,000. Treating petitioner's allegations as true and viewing the supporting record in the light most favorable to petitioner, she has established the special damages necessary to confer standing to challenge the BOA's decision. Accordingly, we address the merits of petitioner's appeal.

III. Standard of Review

Petitioner argues that the BOA erred by reversing the decision of the BHPC and ordering the BHPC to issue Smith a COA. The review of the BHPC's decision by the BOA, the superior court, and this Court is an appellate review in the nature of *certiorari*. *See* N.C. GEN. STAT. § 160A–400.9 (e) (2009). A proper *certiorari* review includes:

(1)   Reviewing the record for errors in law,

(2)   Insuring that procedures specified by law in both statute and ordinance are followed,

(3)   Insuring that appropriate due process rights of a petitioner are protected including the right to offer evidence, cross examine witnesses, and inspect documents,

(4)   Insuring that decisions of . . . boards are supported by competent, material and substantial evidence in the whole record, and

(5)   Insuring that decisions are not arbitrary and capricious.

Fantasy World, Inc. v. Greensboro Bd. of Adjustment, 496 S.E.2d 825, 827 (N.C. App. 1998).

III. Congruity

While N.C. GEN. STAT. § 160A–400.9(a) requires the issuance of a COA before construction can occur in a historic district, the statute also limits the discretion of a historic preservation commission in determining whether a COA should issue.

Under N.C. GEN. STAT. § 160A–400.9(a), the discretion of the preservation commission is limited: "the commission . . . shall take no action under this section except to prevent the construction . . . which would be *incongruous with the special character of the landmark or district.*" *Id.* (emphasis added). In *A-S-P Associates,* the Court interpreted this phrase to be "a contextual standard." *A-S-P Associates,* 258 S.E.2d at 454. "In this instance the standard of 'incongruity' must derive its meaning, if any, from the total physical environment of the Historic District." *Id.*

Meares v. Town of Beaufort, 667 S.E.2d 239, 242 (N.C. App. 2008). In the instant case, the BHPC determined that any structure on Smith's property over twenty-four feet in height would be incongruous with the historic district, and thus, denied Smith's application. On appeal, the BOA determined that this height requirement was arbitrary and capricious. We agree.

"An administrative ruling is deemed arbitrary and capricious when it is whimsical, willful, and an unreasonable action without consideration or in disregard of facts or law or without determining principle." *Ward v. Inscoe*, 603 S.E.2d 393, 399 (N.C. App. 2004). "[A] determination which is not supported by substantial evidence is an arbitrary decision. A decision which lacks a rational basis—where there is no substantial relationship between the facts disclosed by the record and conclusions reached by the board—is also termed 'arbitrary.' " *Godfrey v. Zoning Bd. of Adjustment*, 344 S.E.2d 272, 278 (N.C. 1986).

In the instant case, the whole record does not contain substantial evidence that would support the BHPC's determination that Smith's proposed new construction was not congruous with the rest of the historic district because it exceeded twenty-four feet. While there was evidence presented before the BHPC that there were other one-and-one-half story structures in the historic district that ranged between twenty and twenty-two feet in height, there was also evidence presented that the residences closest to the Smith property ranged from twenty-six to thirty-five feet in height. N.C. GEN. STAT. § 160A–400.9 does not permit the BHPC to "cherry pick" certain properties located within the historic district in order to determine the congruity of proposed construction; instead, the BHPC must determine congruity contextually, based upon "the total physical environment of the Historic District." *Meares*, 667 S.E.2d at 242 (internal quotation and citation omitted). Since a twenty-four foot maximum height requirement was not supported by the facts disclosed by the record, the decision of the BHPC to deny Smith's application was arbitrary and cannot stand.

Moreover, it is clear from the transcripts of the BHPC hearings that the BHPC's twenty-four foot height requirement was not reached on the basis of any particular determining principle. Rather, each BHPC member reached what he or she considered an appropriate height based on their own personal preferences. For example, BHPC member Fred McCune ("McCune") indicated that he reached the twenty-four foot requirement in the following manner:

> I think that five feet (5′) could be removed from the project without materially harming the internal design features, and I think that it is important to reduce the height on the south side of Ann Street. I mean Front Street. I think it is a unique area, and it does have a . . . there isn't much to compare it to, but I think that at twenty-nine foot (29′) structure . . .
>
> Chairman Wilson: What are you basing your reduction of five feet (5′) on?
>
> [McCune]: Well five feet (5′) would be if you had a . . . This is his determination, with a ten foot (10′) ceiling downstairs, and a nine foot (9′) ceiling upstairs, if you had eight foot (8′) ceilings, that's three feet (3′). . . .
>
> And then, if the duct work was to be relocated, that's two more feet. So that would be five feet (5′) without a lot of material changes. *Now it could be a different number, but I'm just throwing that out.*

(Emphasis added). Similarly, BHPC member Dan Krautheim ("Krautheim") made his own calculations on how the interior of Smith's structure could be configured so that it could reach a height of "twenty two and a half or twenty four" feet. BHPC member Les Sadler ("Sadler") simply stated that "twenty five feet (25′) is a reasonable height." When the twenty-four foot requirement was put to a vote by the BHPC, Krautheim explicitly admitted that none of the BHPC guidelines were used to determine that height. Since the twenty-four foot height requirement was established by each member of the BHPC without the use of any determining principle from the BHPC guidelines, it was clearly arbitrary. Petitioner's arguments to the contrary are overruled.

IV. Vista

Petitioner additionally argues that the BHPC's decision should have been upheld because Smith's application violated BHPC guidelines protecting the historic district's "vistas." However, the record clearly indicates that the BHPC did not reach its decision to deny Smith's application on the basis of any guidelines regulating vistas. During one of the meetings, BHPC members Krautheim and Sadler engaged in the following dialogue:

> [Krautheim]: We see the impact of the vista[3] on twenty two feet (22′). So you know you're going to lose that.
>
> [Sadler]: That vista is gone.
>
> [Krautheim]: It's gone, let's face it. The only way it's going to stay there is if he builds an eighteen foot (18′) structure. And you're still losing some of it.

As the BHPC continued to deliberate, BHPC Chairman Mamre Wilson reiterated that "anything above sixteen feet, two inches is going to obstruct the view." Thus, the BHPC believed that any protected vista would be obstructed once a structure over sixteen feet, two inches was constructed. Since the BHPC was willing to allow Smith to construct a structure that was twenty-four feet in height, which was almost eight feet higher than sixteen feet, two inches, it could not have denied Smith's subsequent COA application on the grounds of any vista protections. Consequently, the BHPC's decision cannot be upheld on this basis. This argument is overruled.

V. Conclusion

Treating petitioner's allegations as true and viewing the record in the light most favorable to petitioner, she established standing to challenge the decision of the BOA. The BHPC's twenty-four foot height requirement for Smith's COA application was not supported by the facts disclosed by the whole record and was made without the use of any determining principle. Therefore, the BOA correctly reversed the BHPC's arbitrary decision and ordered the BHPC to issue a COA to Smith. The decision of the superior court, affirming the decision of the BOA, is affirmed.

---

[3] The vista discussed by the BHPC members referred to the view of the general public from the street level on Front Street. The lost "vista" which petitioner alleged damaged the value of her property was a private vista from a porch located on her property.

NOTES & QUESTIONS

1.   The Design Guidelines for the Beaufort Historic District & Landmarks provides several principles that are supposed to guide decisions about the height of new construction:

Building Height/Scale

7.2.1.   New construction shall not exceed thirty-five feet in height.

7.2.2.   Make the scale of the proposed building compatible with the scale of contributing structures on the block or side of street.

7.2.3.   Design the proportion (the ratio of height to width) of the proposed new building and its architectural elements to be consistent with the proportion of contributing buildings and their associated architectural elements on the block or side of street.

7.2.4.   Use windows and doors in new construction that are compatible in proportion, shape, location, pattern, and size with windows and doors of contributing buildings on the block or side of street.

7.2.5.   If a contributing building was demolished or moved from the site, design the replacement building to be of similar height, scale, massing and location as the previously existing building. Applicants will have a heavy burden to demonstrate to the HPC that a replacement structure with different height, scale, and massing as the previously existing building is incongruous (sic) with the Historic District.

What arguments could the parties have made about the height of the proposed new house? What importance does height have more generally for assessing the appropriateness of new construction in a historic district?

2.   Beaufort's Design Guidelines also provide:

The vistas of Beaufort's waterfront play a crucial role in defining the character of Beaufort's Historic District. These include, but are not limited to: the sweeping vistas across Taylor's Creek, Gallant's Channel, and Town Creek; and views of the Historic District, particularly Front Street, from the water. An important factor in evaluating certificates of appropriateness for new construction and additions to existing structures will be the impact, from both the land and water on the vistas of Beaufort's waterfront. Generally, new construction, or additions to existing structures, that encroaches into the vistas of Beaufort's waterfront should be permitted only to the extent necessary to allow reasonable use of the property. In weighing the impact of new construction and additions to existing structures, the commission should consider the traditional setting or context of the subject property relating to the vistas of Beaufort's waterfront.

Did the court give adequate consideration to this guideline?

3.   The *Beaufort* court found that Mrs. Sanchez had standing to contest the Board's grant of a permit because she had suffered "special damage," in that the taller building would block her view. The general principles of standing to sue are discussed in Chapter 3.

4.   An aspect of standing theory, the special damage rule, mandates that an individual plaintiff's purported injury remain distinct from that suffered by the general public. Especially relevant in environmental litigation, this rule has historically frustrated citizen challenges to governmental inaction. In landmark preservation decisions, this rule remains a major obstacle, potentially thwarting citizens' efforts to preserve the cultural and historic character of a community. A student author has advocated for a broader reading of the special damage test in judicial landmark preservation decisions, to maintain local governmental motivations for historic preservation and avoid unnecessary litigation. *See* Matt Dulak, *What's it to You? Citizen Challenges to Landmark Preservation Decisions and the Special Damage Requirement*, 113 COLUM. L. REV. 447 (2013). Can you think of any justifications for maintaining a narrow reading of the special damage rule, or do you agree with Dulak that a broader reading would be more appropriate?

5.   Modern preservation theory rejects the idea that new construction in a historic district should copy the predominant historical style. The District of Columbia offers the following guidance:

> Compatibility does not mean exactly duplicating the existing buildings or environment. A new building should be seen as a product of its own time. To reproduce a historic building, or to copy exactly a style from the past, creates a false sense of history. By relating to the existing buildings and the environment, but being of its own time, a new building shows a district's evolution just as the existing buildings show its past. Perhaps the best way to think about a compatible new building is that it should be a good neighbor, enhancing the character of the district and respecting the context, rather than an exact clone.

New Construction in Historic Districts (Historic Preservation Guidelines, District of Columbia), 2010, at 2.

F. PRESERVATION AND ZONING

Historic preservation ordinances are sometimes integrated with a city's zoning code, but more often are created as separate but overlapping legal requirements and institutions. Zoning and historic preservation law have very different histories and constituencies. Zoning, which originated in the Progressive Era, governs the use, size, and placement of all buildings within a jurisdiction. While zoning ordinances often have restrictions for height, bulk, and setbacks, aesthetics are not a central focus. Zoning is most associated with suburban development of formerly open land.

Historic preservation, as we have seen, grew to prominence from grassroots movements in the 1960s and 1970s in opposition to the destruction of traditional buildings and communities, entirely legal under existing zoning laws. Preservation ordinances generally have nothing to say about the use of property and instead address changes in the publicly-visible appearance of historic buildings and districts.

While the differences between historic preservation and zoning law may seem obvious, in 2021, the Texas Supreme Court considered a claim by property owners in Houston that the city's historic preservation ordinance constituted zoning. Houston is the only large city in the United States without zoning, and zoning may not be adopted without several formal steps, including a citywide referendum. The court found for the City, holding that the historic preservation ordinance did not implement zoning as the term is commonly understood, and that the city had the power to adopt the ordinance under its home rule authority. *Powell v. City of Hous.*, No. 19–0689 (Tex. June 4, 2021). The court did find, however, that the ordinance satisfied a statutory term for "zoning regulations," requiring the city to undergo certain procedures before adoption. Because the City followed such procedures and was otherwise entitled to a presumption of validity, the ordinance withstood challenge. *See also* Brief for the City of Houston, with Historic Preservation Organizations and Legal Scholars as Amici Curiae, *Powell v. City of Hous.*, No. 19–0689 (Tex. Aug. 6, 2020). As you read the following cases, consider whether you agree that historic preservation regulation cannot be considered zoning. Identify similar and distinct features of zoning measures and historic preservation ordinances.

1. CONFLICTS WITH ZONING

While coordination of the policies and practices of zoning and historic preservation seems essential, conflicts often occur, particularly as regards the height of new construction, as the following case illustrates.

City of Tampa v. City National Bank of Florida
974 So.2d 408 (Fla. Dist. Ct. App. 2007)

■ PER CURIAM.

The City of Tampa has petitioned for certiorari relief from an order of the circuit court that effectively reverses the City's denial of a certificate of appropriateness (COA) for the respondents, City National Bank of Florida and Citivest Construction Corporation (hereinafter, Citivest), to build a multistory residential condominium tower on Bayshore Boulevard in Tampa. Bayshore Boulevard overlooks Tampa's Hillsborough Bay. Every day, hundreds of people enjoy its long, continuous sidewalk for walking, jogging, rollerblading, and bicycling. The homes on the inland side of the boulevard present a mix of stately older houses, low-rise apartments and condominiums, opulent new mansions, and high-rise condominiums. One section of Bayshore Boulevard, approximately three miles long, forms an outer edge of the Hyde Park Historic District.

The lots on which Citivest proposes to build are zoned to permit a high-rise multifamily structure, but they are located at the southern end of the Hyde Park Historic District, which consists predominantly of one- and two-story single-family homes and a few small low-rise apartment complexes. When Citivest appeared before the Architectural Review Commission (ARC) and then the City Council, the discussion focused almost entirely on the height of the proposed structure—a building twenty-four stories high, which would be located immediately adjacent to an eleven-story condominium built in the 1920s and a two-story apartment complex of similar vintage. Located across a side street from Citivest's corner lot is one of the oldest homes on Bayshore Boulevard—a two-story single-family house.

This case raises complex questions of statutory construction and asks whether the underlying zoning laws and the authority of the ARC over Citivest's buildable lots in the Hyde Park Historic District can be reconciled. In its review of the City's action, the circuit court concluded that the City departed from the essential requirements of law when it applied the Hyde Park ARC guidelines to conflict with and alter the building envelope that was contemplated by the applicable zoning ordinance and at least preliminarily approved by the zoning administrator. The COA was denied on the basis that the proposed structure violated the historic district guidelines. This case now comes to us on second-tier certiorari, and we deny the City's petition.

It is important to define what this case does not involve. This is not a takings case, nor does it involve a challenge to the zoning ordinances, the architectural review criteria, or the design guidelines. In fact, at this juncture, this court is powerless to comment upon or decide the validity of the ordinances involved. Nor is this court empowered to review the record to determine whether the City's decision was supported by competent, substantial evidence. The district court of appeal is simply the next step up the ladder of review—up from the ARC, to the City Council, and to the circuit court. Although the City Council apparently reviewed the ARC decision de novo, the circuit court's jurisdiction was through certiorari, and this court now must view this case through the very narrow lens of second-tier certiorari. "As a case travels up the judicial ladder, review should consistently become narrower, not broader." *Haines City Cmty. Dev. v. Heggs*, 658 So. 2d 523, 530 (Fla. 1995).

"As a practical matter, the circuit court's final ruling in most first-tier cases is conclusive, for second-tier review is extraordinarily limited." *Florida Power & Light Co. v. City of Dania*, 761 So. 2d 1089, 1092 (Fla. 2000). In a second-tier certiorari proceeding, the appellate court is limited to considering whether the circuit court afforded the parties due process and applied the correct law. *Id.* * * * [W]e are mindful that even though our scope of review is narrow, we are nevertheless charged with ascertaining whether the circuit court, by overlooking sources of established law or applying an incorrect analysis to those it considered, committed a serious error of fundamental dimensions. Our review convinces us that the circuit court's decision does not depart from the essential requirements of law.

The ARC, and subsequently the City, denied Citivest a COA for its proposed condominium project essentially on the basis that the structure was too tall for its historic-district location. As the circuit court found, the City departed from the essential requirements of law when it concluded that the Hyde Park Design Guidelines, as applied by the ARC, effectively "trump" the zoning administrator's review of the plans for compliance with the zoning dictates. The RM-75 zoning designation of the property determines the maximum height of the building. Section 27–77 (Table 4-2) of the City of Tampa's Zoning Code specifies that buildings in the RM-75 district are limited in height by a 4:1 ratio of height to setback from the lot line. In the simplest of terms, for each four feet of height, the setback must increase another foot, so the height is ultimately restricted by the size of the lot. The RM-75 zoning district for this site was created in 1987. Prior to that time—and well before the creation of the Hyde Park Historic District—the property carried a high-rise zoning designation under the City's comprehensive plan. Thus the City has never, through its zoning designations, suggested an intent to exclude a high-rise building from this site. When the current owner of the property purchased it in 1996, he did so on notice of both the zoning designation and the fact of the property's location within the Hyde Park Historic District. The converse is also true, however: when the Hyde Park Historic District was created, this property was placed into the district carrying its high-rise zoning designation.

Zoning is considered in chapter 27 of the Tampa City Code; subsumed within the zoning chapter are regulations governing the Architectural Review Commission. Zoning section 27–216, for instance, dictates that new construction in the Hyde Park Historic District cannot be undertaken before the ARC issues a COA. Section 27–216(*l*) requires the ARC to consider the effect of the construction on not only the building site but also on "the relationship between such work and other buildings, structures or objects on the landmark site or other property in the historic district." Obviously, in this case, the ARC, the City Council, neighbors, and other interested parties emphasized the size disparity between Citivest's proposed high-rise building and the predominantly one-and two-story houses in the historic district. But—and this is significant—the relationship consideration is qualified in the next sentence of that section: "In evaluating the effect and the relationship, the ARC shall consider historical and architectural significance, architectural style, design, arrangement, texture, materials and color."

Notably lacking is any mention of height or mass of the proposed structure relative to others in the neighborhood.

However, section 27–216(m) of the Code lists a number of additional considerations for new construction, and these were the focus of the ARC and City Council hearings.

> When the applicant wishes to undertake new construction within a historic district or on a landmark site, the ARC shall consider the compatibility of the new construction with the existing character of the district or the landmark, but the ARC shall not dictate the architectural style of the new construction. Compatible design shall mean architectural design and construction that will fit harmoniously into the district or the landmark site. New construction shall be *compatible in scale*, materials and quality of construction *with adjacent buildings and structures that have been designated.*

> The ARC shall include the following points in its consideration of an application for new construction:

> (1) *Scale: height and width*;

> (2) Setback;

> (3) Orientation and site coverage;

> (4) Alignment, rhythm and spacing of buildings;

> (5) Form and detail: Link between old and new;

> (6) Maintaining materials within the district or on the landmark site;

> (7) Maintaining quality within the district or on the landmark site;

> (8) Facade proportions and window patterns;

> (9) Entrances and porch projections;

> (10) Roof forms;

> (11) Horizontal, vertical or nondirectional emphasis.

(Emphasis added.)

The City argued at all stages in these proceedings that these criteria, particularly "scale: height and width," sanction the ARC's rejection of Citivest's proposed construction on the basis of height. In coming to that conclusion, both the City and the ARC rejected the theory that the term "scale: height and width" referred to the height-width ratio of the facades of a new building as compared with neighboring buildings within the historic district, which is essentially an aesthetic consideration. Instead, the ARC's and the City's focus converged on height alone, not the design aspects of scale.

Citivest, on the other hand, consistently contended that section 27–77 governs the parameters of its project and circumscribes the ARC's power to reject the building as too tall. Section 27–77(a)(2)(g) provides:

Schedule of statements of purpose and intent. The following array presents for the several districts the statements of purpose and intent applicable to each district. . . .

g.   RM-75 residential multiple-family. This district provides primarily for high density multiple-family residential development. Such high density residential structures shall be located in close proximity to regional shopping, employment and public transportation opportunities.

Section 27–77(c) additionally provides:

Schedule of area, height, bulk and placement regulations. Except as specifically provided in other sections of this chapter, regulations governing the minimum lot area and width, required front, side and rear yards, floor area ratio, *height of structures,* area of signs and related matters *shall be as shown in the schedule of area, height, bulk and placement regulations.*

(Emphasis added.) Thus section 27–77(c), particularly the accompanying Table 4–2 mentioned above, governs the permissible height of structures. In fact, the building height "shall be as shown in the schedule," unless conflicting regulations "specifically provide" otherwise. The design guidelines listed in section 27–216(m) are, on their face, not specific. That is because they are part of the larger context of aesthetic considerations appropriate for the historic district. Although they come within the City's zoning code, they are not specific zoning regulations.

Even if the design guidelines as set out in section 27–216(m) were specific regulations, they were never intended to conflict with or supersede the primary zoning designations. This is apparent from their original statutory enactment. The Hyde Park Historic District was created with reference to section 266.407, Florida Statutes (1995), later renumbered section 266.0057, titled "Powers of governing bodies in and of Hillsborough County; architectural review board." Section 27–213 of the City Code, titled "Architectural Review Commission-Powers and duties," refers to section 266.0057 and states:

The architectural review commission shall have the following responsibilities as authorized and empowered by the provisions of this chapter and by F.S. Ch. 266.0057, F.S.:

(1) Approval or disapproval of plans related to . . . new construction involving . . . historic districts. . .

(2) *Specific authorities and powers.* In addition to the powers and duties stated elsewhere, the ARC shall take action necessary and appropriate to accomplish the purposes of this division. These actions include:

a.   Approval or disapproval on applications for certificates of appropriateness . . .

The language of the enabling statute is a telling limitation on the powers of the ARC. Section 266.0057(2)(c)(1) authorizes the ARC to

[a]pprove or disapprove plans for buildings to be erected . . . within the historical district . . . [T]he control of the erection . . . of new . . . buildings or structures . . . is hereby designated to be a public purpose; *but no rule may be adopted which is in conflict with any zoning ordinance of the governing bodies applicable to such area.*

(Emphasis added.) Although the statute was sunsetted in 1997 when it became superfluous after the City had adopted its historic preservation ordinance, the continued inclusion of specific reference to the statute in the Code establishes a control and limitation upon the powers of the ARC.

Furthermore, section 27–216(*o*) of the Code states as follows:

The zoning administrator shall be the sole administrator of this Code as it pertains to landmark and historic district boundaries, the requirements for permitted or permissible special uses, the schedule of area, *height*, bulk and placement regulations, the parking requirements and any other item not dealing specifically with the procedure and review criteria for obtaining a certificate of appropriateness.

(Emphasis added.) The grammatical structure of that section reinforces its plain meaning that the zoning administrator, not the ARC, has the final word on height and "any other item not dealing specifically with the procedure and review criteria for obtaining" a COA. Thus, height—an item with which the COA review criteria are not concerned—is governed by the zoning administrator, not the ARC.

Our analysis of the applicable statutes, code sections, and case law convinces us that the circuit court correctly applied the law in this matter and did not overlook any other source that would assist in its review. This court has diligently combed every appendix, case, ordinance, and statute submitted on behalf of any party—and has searched many other resources—in an attempt to ascertain whether the ARC possesses the authority or power to require a reduction in height of the proposed building so that it will be "compatible" with the historic character of the neighborhood and the surrounding structures. Repeatedly, we have scoured the record and applicable law for the answer to this question: Can the ARC, based on the design criterion of "scale: height and width" alone, limit a proposed structure to any particular height? No such power granted by the appropriate sovereign has been identified.

The City could have solved this issue by rezoning this property or, alternatively, carving this land out of the historic district, or even defining an overlay district encompassing this property and others that would include height limitations. Section 27–458(a) of the City Code declares that "the purpose of an overlay district is to allow for the application of specific regulations to a distinct geographic area." And section 27–458(b) further declares: "The overlay district concept is discussed in the Comprehensive Plan as a method of preserving the character of an area. It will encourage development to occur that is compatible with the existing scale and pattern of surrounding properties." Section 27–523 defines a historic residential overlay district as follows:

> A special overlay district which recognizes and protects historic patterns of development including but not limited to the following physical elements: setback, height, site orientations and massing of buildings and accessory structures, placement of sidewalks, parking areas and infrastructure. Its purpose is to conserve existing neighborhood patterns of development by retaining historic structures that contribute to that pattern, while assuring that new construction will be consistent with it.

Thus, the City Code explicitly contemplates the creation of historic overlay districts in which building height can be limited in spite of underlying zoning. An example is the Seminole Heights Residential Historic Overlay District, which is separate and distinct from the historic district. The specific intent of the overlay district "is to ensure that infill residential development and additions thereto are *compatible* in building and structural orientation, *height*, lot dimensional requirements and other site spatial relationships to the precedent within the *established neighborhood*." TAMPA, FL., CITY CODE § 27–464(b) (emphasis added). Such extensive power was not granted to the Hyde Park Architectural Review Commission.

This is a true apples and oranges case. The historic guidelines do not envisage application to a lot zoned RM-75 for height and density as a vehicle to reduce the height of the building. They are design guidelines, not specific zoning regulations. Although this case does not present constitutional issues, this language from the Third District Court of Appeal is helpful: "Zoning as applied to the height of buildings is an exercise of the police power. The height limitation must be specific and must promote the health, welfare, safety, and morals of the public in order to be valid and withstand an attack upon it as an unwarranted exercise of that power." *Town of Bay Harbor Islands v. Burk*, 114 So. 2d 225, 227 (Fla. Dist. Ct. App.—3d Dist. 1959). A specific height restriction that could be generally applied to all properties in a historic district is permissible. *See Mandel v. City of Santa Fe*, 894 P.2d 1041 (N.M. App. 1995).

Unfortunately, the City has not undertaken legislative action that would avoid this conflict. The circuit court made this observation in its order denying the City's motion for clarification: "The City of Tampa has created this quagmire of competing and seemingly inconsistent building requirements." We fully concur with that opinion.

Having found no departure from the essential requirements of law in the circuit court's order denying the City's petition for certiorari, we deny this petition.

NOTES & QUESTIONS

1.   If there had been no zoning provision at all in the *Tampa* case, could the ARC have rejected an eighteen-story condominium building in the Hyde Park Historic District? If so, what difference does the zoning of the area for high-rise multi-family residences make? Note that the zoning ordinance did not require Citivest to build twenty-four stories, but only permitted buildings of that height.

2.   Cities seeking to create a historic district characterized by short buildings, such as nineteenth century mercantile buildings in a developing area of the downtown, where the zoning permits tall buildings, often seek to "downzone" the area, that is, reduce the heights or densities allowed by zoning. Whether the jurisdiction would treat a disparity between the zoning and what would be compatible with existing buildings to be a legal "quagmire," the disparity would expose the historic preservation ordinance to takings challenges and other protests based on the extent to which it restricts what otherwise would be the economic value of an open site. The *Penn Central* case itself, discussed in Chapter 7, presents a similar problem.

3.   Effective preservation of a district sometimes requires relaxation of zoning use restrictions. The SoHo neighborhood of New York City presents such a case. SoHo is characterized by graceful cast iron mercantile and industrial buildings of the nineteenth century, elegant examples of which are depicted in Figure 6-13. By the 1950s, the area was in decline, and the threat to demolish wide stretches to construct an eight-lane freeway loomed. Sensing an opportunity, artists, musicians, and other creative types began to utilize the buildings—often abandoned, dangerously ill-maintained, or poorly served by utilities—for live-work studios. To the extent that the studios were used as work spaces, they were illegal, because the area was zoned only for industrial uses. Moreover, tenants frequently lived in these "lofts" in further violation of zoning.

The New York City zoning ordinance gradually accommodated the demand to use these buildings lawfully for artistic, residential, and retail uses. The New York City Landmarks Preservation Commission designated the area a historic district in 1973, and subsequently expanded it.

Today, zoning rules require certified artists to live in much of the residential housing in SoHo. However, these rules are rarely enforced. As a result, much of SoHo is occupied by wealthy non-artists, and real estate prices are among the highest per square foot in the world. In 2021, Mayor Bill DeBlasio proposed sweeping changes to SoHo's zoning, which would allow greater residential density and mandatory set-asides of between 20 and 30 percent of housing units to be affordable housing. Local preservation groups have emerged to oppose the rezoning, suggesting that the rezoning is a giveaway to developers that will result only in luxury buildings towering over SoHo. Think back to the discussion in Chapter 1 about the growing concern of economic inequality. Does it hurt or help the preservation movement for preservationists to object to policies facilitating affordable housing? Is there a way for zoning to establish design guidelines that are consistent with the historic architectural character of the district?

Figure 6-13:
The Vibrant Wooster Street in the SoHo Neighborhood,
Manhattan, NY

4.   In an important opinion, the Supreme Court of Connecticut considered the ability of zoning boards to consider historic factors in their decision-making about whether to approve the subdivision of real property. In *Smith v. Zoning Board of Appeals of Town of Greenwich*, 629 A.2d 1089 (Conn. 1993), the town's zoning board of appeals rejected the proposed subdivision by a property owner seeking to divide a parcel in a historic district and build a home in an area that was then open space. The board explained that the proposal, if built, "would disrupt the 'sweeping front lawn' and, therefore, would not be consistent with the district's historic streetscape." *Id.* at 1093. In appealing this decision, the property owner argued that the zoning ordinance did not authorize the board to consider historic factors, but the court disagreed, finding that historic preservation fell within the board's mandate to consider factors affecting public health and safety. *Id.* at 1097–98. Alternately, the property owner argued, the board was not empowered to consider historic factors because the town's historic preservation commission was expressly granted that function. Again, the court disagreed, stating that the two bodies performed "different yet sometimes overlapping functions" and that both could consider historic

character. *Id.* at 1102–03. The *Smith* case not only illustrates the relationship between preservation and other land use regulations, but also reflects the growing importance of landscapes in the interpretation of historic preservation law.

5.   Projects may have to undergo review under both zoning laws and historic preservation laws. Consider, for example, a D.C. "planned unit development" project that received approvals from the local zoning commission and the Mayor's Agent for Historic Preservation to demolish underground storage cells and subdivide industrial open space. The land was part of a historic district, with landscape originally designed by noted landscape architect Frederick Law Olmsted, Jr. In separate decisions, the D.C. Court of Appeals upheld both approvals. First, it affirmed the Mayor's Agent's finding that the mixed-use project, featuring subsidized and market rate housing, retail, a public park and community center, and extensive restoration of historic features was a project of "special merit." *Friends of McMillan Park v. D.C. Mayor's Agent for Historic Preservation,* 209 A.3d 1155 (D.C. 2019). Subsequently the court also upheld the Commission's approval of the development as "not inconsistent" with the D.C. comprehensive plan. *Friends of McMillan Park v. D.C. Zoning Comm'n,* 211 A.3d 139, 149–51 (D.C. 2019). What do you think are the plusses and minuses of separating preservation decisions from all other land use decisions?

6.   In an unreported decision, the Colorado Court of Appeals held that a city charter provision requiring a supermajority vote on the Denver City Council for zoning district changes applied to the designation of a historic district. *O'Connell v. City Council of Denver,* 2019 WL 2108760 (Co. App. 2019). What are the differences and similarities between changing a zoning district and designating a historic district?

2.   FORM-BASED ZONING

Because preservation ordinances address only the appearance of existing buildings, they are highly compatible with form-based zoning, an emerging land use regulatory approach that may supplement or replace conventional zoning codes.

Form-based codes govern the *form* of new construction including fenestration, landscaping, façade articulation, and relationship with the street. Conventional zoning ordinances primarily govern the *use* of property by assigning zones within a locality within which particular uses are designated. While conventional zoning ordinances may govern heights, bulks, and lot setbacks, they rarely deal with design or physical relation to public space. In relaxing limitations on the uses of new buildings, a more vibrant mix of uses may be allowed than under a traditional code.

Form-based codes arose in the early 1980s out of the New Urbanism movement—a movement in architecture and planning that grew from dissatisfaction with urban development patterns required by conventional zoning ordinances. Conventional ordinances typically require wide streets, off-street parking, and separation of uses—which, combined, promote sprawl and dependence on automobiles. Conventional zoning thus frustrates architects and planners seeking to replicate the attractive features of traditional walkable, mixed use communities. Buildings in such communities are often oriented toward the sidewalk; it is their form, rather than their use, which facilitates vitality in public space.

How are form-based codes compatible with historic preservation rules? Most significantly, they have similar aims. Form-based codes, which apply to new construction, seek to replicate the vitality of walkable, mixed use, pedestrian-oriented neighborhoods. Many such traditional neighborhoods are protected by historic preservation ordinances. Hence while historic preservation ordinances preserve the character of historic neighborhoods, form-based codes allow for architecturally compatible new infill development in those neighborhoods, as well as provide guidelines for similarly-scaled new developments to be built from scratch.

In addition, both form-based codes and historic preservation ordinances have similar scopes. Both govern the outer envelope of buildings and their relationship to the street, without strictly governing use. A form-based code might, for example, mandate that any structures built within a certain neighborhood be two stories tall, provide a sidewalk, and include an ample porch within fifteen feet of the sidewalk. It also might have provisions that apply to buildings of different heights: Tall buildings may be required to be tiered or oriented in such a way as to preserve sunlight.

Finally, it may be important to note that although the neighborhoods that serve as models for New Urbanists were typically created prior to the implementation of conventional zoning, many have been preserved by historic preservation ordinances. So, in the interest of "preserving the prototype"—a concept introduced in Chapter 1—New Urbanists tend to support historic preservation ordinances.

The most famous town implementing form-based coding is Seaside, Florida, which was built from scratch using a set of simple rules governing both private and public space. (It was the filming location for the popular movie, *The Truman Show*.) Only a handful of communities, however, have adopted form-based codes, and none have eschewed provisions on land use entirely. Some form-based codes have replaced traditional zoning ordinances altogether, as is the case in Petaluma, California. Other communities, such as Arlington County, Virginia, have adopted optional form-based codes. Optional codes may exist alongside conventional zoning. As is the case in Denver, a developer may create tailor-made form-based coding for planned unit developments. *See* John M. Barry, *Form-Based Codes: Measured Success Through Both Mandatory and Optional Implementation*, 41 CONN. L. REV. 305 (2008) (describing the benefits and drawbacks of both mandatory and optional codes and suggesting optimal usage of each). *See also* H. William Freeman, *A New Legal Landscape for Planning and Zoning: Using Form-Based Codes to Promote New Urbanism and Sustainability*, 36 MICH. REAL PROP. REV. 117 (2009) (explaining the modern transition from traditional Euclidean zoning to form-based codes and explaining the related advantages). Although form-based codes have not yet been widely adopted, the compatibility with historic preservation ordinances suggests possibilities for future growth.

G. CONSERVATION DISTRICTS

Conservation districts are alternative devices to historic districts for preserving neighborhood character. Adopted under enabling legislation for historic preservation or for zoning, conservation districts display a wide range of provisions and applications, and are rather prevalent across the United Stated. They number nearly 3,000, with almost one in every county. *See About Districts*, NATIONAL ASSOCIATION OF CONSERVATION DISTRICTS, https://www.nacdnet.org/about-nacd/about-districts/. Such districts typically are older residential neighborhoods that lack sufficient historic significance or integrity, or in which there is less political support, for designation as a historic district. Conservation districts employ a permit system based upon specifically tailored neighborhood guidelines, which require new construction to be compatible with the scale and general design of existing houses. Some also contain guidelines for alterations, but these will be more lenient than those for a historic district. Demolition generally is not prohibited.

Conservation districts aim less to protect architectural integrity than overall neighborhood character from inappropriate development, such as "mansionization" (replacing small houses typical of a neighborhood with very large new houses) or condominium developments surrounded by parking lots. Homeowners in Dallas, Texas, had such motivations when they initiated the M Streets Conservation District, covering a neighborhood containing primarily 1920s and 1930s Tudor-style homes. *See* DALLAS, TEX. ORD. NO. 25116 (Nov. 13, 2002) (authorizing the creation of that district). The process of designation in Dallas is typical. A majority of property owners in the proposed district must initiate the process. Once the city receives a request to consider a new district, the city plan department must conduct a feasibility study. After that study is complete, the director of the city plan commission must decide whether a neighborhood is eligible for designation based on factors such as whether the neighborhood has significant architectural or cultural attributes, and whether it is stable or stabilizing. Upon a determination of eligibility, the planning department prepares a conceptual plan. After at least three rounds of public input, the city council may approve the conceptual plan. Eventually, the council may pass a full designation ordinance with specific regulations for the new conservation district. *See* DALLAS, TEX., DEV. CODE § 51A–4.505; *see also* Rebecca Lubens & Julia Miller, *Protecting Older Neighborhoods Through Conservation District Programs*, 21 PRES. L. REP. 1001 (2002–03) (describing the Dallas example and conservation districts more broadly).

Are conservation districts historic preservation "light," or do they perform a distinct function? Can you think of neighborhoods that would benefit from being designated as conservation districts? Why shouldn't that neighborhood become a historic district? How do conservation districts differ from zoning, including form-based zoning?

CHAPTER SEVEN

CONSTITUTIONAL ISSUES

Historic preservation laws—and, in particular, local ordinances—initiated new regulations of private property owners during a period of dynamic constitutional development. Many affected individuals and institutions have challenged the application of preservation laws as violating one or more federal constitutional provisions. Preservation laws largely have emerged intact from these challenges and have thrived after constitutional affirmation. At the same time, judicial opinions have drawn constitutional limits to preservation laws and have illuminated how such laws fit into our constitutional and regulatory structure.

This Chapter explores three bases for federal constitutional challenges of historic preservation ordinances: the takings clause, the First Amendment's free exercise and establishment of religion clauses, and the free speech clause. Each of these clauses may be applied to actions of the states (and by extension, localities) via incorporation of the Fourteenth Amendment. While this Chapter focuses on these three constitutional areas, related legal questions will also be considered. A discussion of the conflicts between historic preservation and religious liberty would not be complete, for example, without including information about an important federal statute—the Religious Land Use and Institutionalized Persons Act of 2000—which has since its passage been used in tandem with constitutional provisions to challenge historic preservation laws. Other constitutional issues have been considered in Chapter 1, including congressional power in *United States v. Gettysburg Electric Railway Co.*, 160 U.S. 668 (1896) and due process challenges in *Maher v. City of New Orleans*, 516 F.2d 1051 (5th Cir. 1975).

A. TAKINGS

The Fifth Amendment takings clause, which applies to the states (and by extension localities) via the Fourteenth Amendment, says "nor shall private property be taken for public use, without just compensation." U.S. CONST. amend. V. This Chapter focuses on federal law, but it is important to note that all fifty states have some version of a taking clause. The takings clause does not prohibit what are called "takings": acts of government appropriating property from private owners. However, the takings clause puts conditions on the exercise of that power, most importantly the obligation to pay the owner "just compensation"—essentially market value—for the property lost.

Government takings can occur in two primary ways. The first is for government to exercise eminent domain, which is the public power to condemn property for public use. In such cases, a government will affirmatively act to acquire title to property. This is a straightforward form of taking property.

In addition to eminent domain, the Supreme Court has long recognized "regulatory takings," which are more significant for historic preservation law. The Court first recognized the concept of regulatory takings in 1922, when it considered a law passed in Pennsylvania that, with only limited exceptions, forbade coal mining that would cause subsidence under land located beneath human habitations. *Pennsylvania Coal Co. v. Mahon*, 260 U.S. 393 (1922). The plaintiffs challenging this law owned rights to mine all of the coal under a private home and claimed that the statute effected an uncompensated taking of their right to mine their coal. The Supreme Court invalidated the regulation, saying that "to make it commercially impracticable to mine certain coal has very nearly the same effect for constitutional purposes as appropriating or destroying it." *Id.* at 414. Further, the Court noted that, "while property may be regulated to a certain extent, *if regulation goes too far* it will be recognized as a taking." *Id.* at 415 (emphasis added).

After *Pennsylvania Coal*, lower courts attempted to refine this vague standard. For one important example, we revisit *Maher v. City of New Orleans*, 516 F.2d 1051 (5th Cir. 1975), which was excerpted in Chapter 1. At issue was the Vieux Carré Ordinance, which regulated the preservation and maintenance of buildings in the French Quarter of New Orleans. The Ordinance requires owners to keep their properties in reasonable repair. In addition, it established a commission that issues (or denies) construction and demolition permits for owners of historic district properties. The *Maher* case was brought by a plaintiff whose request for a permit to replace a cottage located within the Vieux Carré historic district with a seven-apartment complex was denied by the Vieux Carré Commission.

The plaintiff argued that the Ordinance was an unconstitutional taking in two ways: First, it prevented him from pursuing "most profitable use to which his property may be put"; and second, it imposed affirmative maintenance obligations. *Id.* at 1065. The Fifth Circuit rejected both claims, stating:

> As the ordinance was applied to Maher, the denial of the permit to demolish and rebuild does not operate as a classic example of eminent domain, namely, a taking of Maher's property for government use. Nor did Maher demonstrate to the satisfaction of the district court that a taking occurred because the ordinance so diminished the property value as to leave Maher, in effect, nothing. In particular, Maher did not show that the sale of the property was impracticable, that commercial rental could not provide a reasonable rate of return, or that other potential use of the property was foreclosed. To the extent that such is the theory underlying Maher's claim, it fails for lack of proof. * * *

[EDS.: As to the second claim, t]he fact that an owner may incidentally be required to make out-of-pocket expenditures in order to remain in compliance with an ordinance does not per se render that ordinance a taking. In the interest of safety, it would seem that an ordinance might reasonably require buildings to have fire sprinklers or to provide emergency facilities for exits and light. In pursuit of health, provisions for plumbing or sewage disposal might be demanded. Compliance could well require owners to spend money. Yet, if the purpose be legitimate and the means reasonably consistent with the objective, the ordinance can withstand a frontal attack of invalidity.

Id. at 1066. The Fifth Circuit was careful to say that its decision was narrow, and that "in some set of circumstances, the expense of maintenance under the Ordinance were the city to exact compliance would be so unreasonable as to constitute a taking." *Id.* at 1067.

The court's reasoning in *Maher* illustrates one influential lower court's approach to takings jurisprudence after the Supreme Court decided *Pennsylvania Coal*. It is worth pointing out three key points before we move on to the Supreme Court's most important regulatory takings case, *Penn Central*. First, the *Maher* panel focused on the impact of the regulation on the claimant and suggests areas of inquiry—impracticability of a sale, failure to achieve reasonable rates of return, or foreclosure of certain uses—that a court might use to determine whether a plaintiff had been denied all economically viable use of her land. Second, the panel considered the extent of the government interests in enacting the ordinance, suggesting that health and public safety could well justify requirements on property owners to maintain their properties to a certain standard. Finally, in a passage not excerpted above, the panel referred to other ordinances that (unlike the Vieux Carré Ordinance) offered compensation—such as tax credits and transferable development rights—for parties whose requests to alter a historic building have been denied. *Id.* at 1065–66. All of the issues discussed by the *Maher* panel echo in the following landmark Supreme Court takings case.

1. *PENN CENTRAL*

Penn Central Transportation Company v. City of New York
438 U.S. 104 (1978)

■ MR. JUSTICE BRENNAN delivered the opinion of the Court.

The question presented is whether a city may, as part of a comprehensive program to preserve historic landmarks and historic districts, place restrictions on the development of individual historic landmarks—in addition to those imposed by applicable zoning ordinances—without effecting a "taking" requiring the payment of "just compensation." Specifically, we must decide whether the application of New York City's Landmarks Preservation Law to the parcel of land occupied by Grand Central Terminal has "taken" its owners' property in violation of the Fifth and Fourteenth Amendments.

I.A.

Over the past 50 years, all 50 States and over 500 municipalities have enacted laws to encourage or require the preservation of buildings and areas with historic or aesthetic importance. These nationwide legislative efforts have been precipitated by two concerns. The first is recognition that, in recent years, large numbers of historic structures, landmarks, and areas have been destroyed without adequate consideration of either the values represented therein or the possibility of preserving the destroyed properties for use in economically productive ways. The second is a widely shared belief that structures with special historic, cultural, or architectural significance enhance the quality of life for all. Not only do these buildings and their workmanship represent the lessons of the past and embody precious features of our heritage, they serve as examples of quality for today. "[H]istoric conservation is but one aspect of the much larger problem, basically an environmental one, of enhancing—or perhaps developing for the first time—the quality of life for people."

New York City, responding to similar concerns and acting pursuant to a New York State enabling Act, adopted its Landmarks Preservation Law in 1965.[5] The city acted from the conviction that "the standing of [New York City] as a world-wide tourist center and world capital of business, culture and government" would be threatened if legislation were not enacted to protect historic landmarks and neighborhoods from precipitate decisions to destroy or fundamentally alter their character. § 205–1.0(a). The city believed that comprehensive measures to safeguard desirable features of the existing urban fabric would benefit its citizens in a variety of ways: e. g., fostering "civic pride in the beauty and noble accomplishments of the past"; protecting and enhancing "the city's attractions to tourists and visitors"; "support[ing] and stimul[ating] business and industry"; "strengthen[ing] the economy of the city"; and promoting "the use of historic districts, landmarks, interior landmarks and scenic landmarks for the education, pleasure and welfare of the people of the city." § 205–1.0(b).

The New York City law is typical of many urban landmark laws in that its primary method of achieving its goals is not by acquisitions of historic properties, but rather by involving public entities in land-use decisions affecting these properties and providing services, standards,

---

[5] *See* N.Y. Gen. Mun. Law § 96–a (McKinney 1977). It declares that it is the public policy of the State of New York to preserve structures and areas with special historical or aesthetic interest or value and authorizes local governments to impose reasonable restrictions to perpetuate such structures and areas.

controls, and incentives that will encourage preservation by private owners and users. While the law does place special restrictions on landmark properties as a necessary feature to the attainment of its larger objectives, the major theme of the law is to ensure the owners of any such properties both a "reasonable return" on their investments and maximum latitude to use their parcels for purposes not inconsistent with the preservation goals.

The operation of the law can be briefly summarized. The primary responsibility for administering the law is vested in the Landmarks Preservation Commission (Commission), a broad based, 11-member agency assisted by a technical staff. The Commission first performs the function, critical to any landmark preservation effort, of identifying properties and areas that have "a special character or special historical or aesthetic interest or value as part of the development, heritage or cultural characteristics of the city, state or nation." § 207–1.0(n); *see* § 207–1.0(h). If the Commission determines, after giving all interested parties an opportunity to be heard, that a building or area satisfies the ordinance's criteria, it will designate a building to be a "landmark," § 207–1.0(n),[9] situated on a particular "landmark site," § 207–1.0(o), or will designate an area to be a "historic district," § 207–1.0(h). After the Commission makes a designation, New York City's Board of Estimate, after considering the relationship of the designated property "to the master plan, the zoning resolution, projected public improvements and any plans for the renewal of the area involved," § 207–2.0(g) (1), may modify or disapprove the designation, and the owner may seek judicial review of the final designation decision. Thus far, 31 historic districts and over 400 individual landmarks have been finally designated, and the process is a continuing one.

Final designation as a landmark results in restrictions upon the property owner's options concerning use of the landmark site. First, the law imposes a duty upon the owner to keep the exterior features of the building "in good repair" to assure that the law's objectives not be defeated by the landmark's falling into a state of irremediable disrepair. *See* § 207–10.0(a). Second, the Commission must approve in advance any proposal to alter the exterior architectural features of the landmark or to construct any exterior improvement on the landmark site, thus ensuring that decisions concerning construction on the landmark site are made with due consideration of both the public interest in the maintenance of the structure and the landowner's interest in use of the property. *See* §§ 207–4.0–207–9.0.

In the event an owner wishes to alter a landmark site, three separate procedures are available through which administrative approval may be

---

[9] " 'Landmark.' Any improvement, any part of which is thirty years old or older, which has a special character or special historical or aesthetic interest or value as part of the development, heritage or cultural characteristics of the city, state or nation and which has been designated as a landmark pursuant to the provisions of this chapter." § 207–1.0(n).

obtained. First, the owner may apply to the Commission for a "certificate of no effect on protected architectural features": that is, for an order approving the improvement or alteration on the ground that it will not change or affect any architectural feature of the landmark and will be in harmony therewith. *See* § 207–5.0. Denial of the certificate is subject to judicial review.

Second, the owner may apply to the Commission for a certificate of "appropriateness." *See* § 207–6.0. Such certificates will be granted if the Commission concludes—focusing upon aesthetic, historical, and architectural values—that the proposed construction on the landmark site would not unduly hinder the protection, enhancement, perpetuation, and use of the landmark. Again, denial of the certificate is subject to judicial review. Moreover, the owner who is denied either a certificate of no exterior effect or a certificate of appropriateness may submit an alternative or modified plan for approval. The final procedure—seeking a certificate of appropriateness on the ground of "insufficient return," *see* § 207–8.0—provides special mechanisms, which vary depending on whether or not the landmark enjoys a tax exemption, to ensure that designation does not cause economic hardship.

Although the designation of a landmark and landmark site restricts the owner's control over the parcel, designation also enhances the economic position of the landmark owner in one significant respect. Under New York City's zoning laws, owners of real property who have not developed their property to the full extent permitted by the applicable zoning laws are allowed to transfer development rights to contiguous parcels on the same city block. A 1968 ordinance gave the owners of landmark sites additional opportunities to transfer development rights to other parcels. Subject to a restriction that the floor area of the transferee lot may not be increased by more than 20% above its authorized level, the ordinance permitted transfers from a landmark parcel to property across the street or across a street intersection. In 1969, the law governing the conditions under which transfers from landmark parcels could occur was liberalized, *see* New York City Zoning Resolutions 74–79 to 74–793, apparently to ensure that the Landmarks Law would not unduly restrict the development options of the owners of Grand Central Terminal. The class of recipient lots was expanded to include lots "across a street and opposite to another lot or lots which except for the intervention of streets or street intersections f[or]m a series extending to the lot occupied by the landmark building [, provided that] all lots [are] in the same ownership." New York City Zoning Resolution 74–79 (emphasis deleted). In addition, the 1969 amendment permits, in highly commercialized areas like midtown Manhattan, the transfer of all unused development rights to a single parcel.

Figure 7-1:
Marcel Breuer's Proposal for the "Air Rights Building"
at Grand Central Terminal,
Manhattan, NY

B.

This case involves the application of New York City's Landmarks Preservation Law to Grand Central Terminal (Terminal). The Terminal, which is owned by the Penn Central Transportation Co. and its affiliates (Penn Central), is one of New York City's most famous buildings. Opened in 1913, it is regarded not only as providing an ingenious engineering solution to the problems presented by urban railroad stations, but also as a magnificent example of the French beaux-arts style.

The Terminal is located in midtown Manhattan. Its south facade faces 42d Street and that street's intersection with Park Avenue. At street level, the Terminal is bounded on the west by Vanderbilt Avenue, on the east by the Commodore Hotel, and on the north by the Pan-American Building. Although a 20-story office tower, to have been located above the Terminal, was part of the original design, the planned tower was never constructed. The Terminal itself is an eight-story structure which Penn Central uses as a railroad station and in which it rents space not needed for railroad purposes to a variety of commercial interests. * * *

On August 2, 1967, following a public hearing, the Commission designated the Terminal a "landmark" and designated the "city tax block" it occupies a "landmark site." The Board of Estimate confirmed this action on September 21, 1967. Although appellant Penn Central had opposed the designation before the Commission, it did not seek judicial review of the final designation decision. * * *

The Commission's reasons for rejecting [Penn Central's application to build a 55-story tower over the Terminal were as follows] * * *: "[We have] no fixed rule against making additions to designated buildings—it all depends on how they are done . . . But to balance a 55-story office tower above a flamboyant Beaux-Arts facade seems nothing more than an aesthetic joke. Quite simply, the tower would overwhelm the Terminal by its sheer mass. The 'addition' would be four times as high as the existing structure and would reduce the Landmark itself to the status of a curiosity." * * *

II.

The issues presented by appellants are (1) whether the restrictions imposed by New York City's law upon appellants' exploitation of the Terminal site effect a "taking" of appellants' property for a public use within the meaning of the Fifth Amendment, which of course is made applicable to the States through the Fourteenth Amendment, and, (2), if so, whether the transferable development rights afforded appellants constitute "just compensation" within the meaning of the Fifth Amendment. We need only address the question whether a "taking" has occurred.

A.

Before considering appellants' specific contentions, it will be useful to review the factors that have shaped the jurisprudence of the Fifth Amendment injunction "nor shall private property be taken for public use, without just compensation." The question of what constitutes a "taking" for purposes of the Fifth Amendment has proved to be a problem of considerable difficulty. While this Court has recognized that the "Fifth Amendment's guarantee . . . [is] designed to bar Government from forcing some people alone to bear public burdens which, in all fairness and justice, should be borne by the public as a whole," *Armstrong v. United States*, 364 U.S. 40, 49 (1960), this Court, quite simply, has been unable to develop any "set formula" for determining when "justice and fairness" require that economic injuries caused by public action be compensated by the government, rather than remain disproportionately concentrated on a few persons. Indeed, we have frequently observed that whether a particular restriction will be rendered invalid by the government's failure to pay for any losses proximately caused by it depends largely "upon the particular circumstances [in that] case." *United States v. Cent. Eureka Mining Co.*, 357 U.S. 155, 168 (1958). * * *

In engaging in these essentially ad hoc, factual inquiries, the Court's decisions have identified several factors that have particular significance. The economic impact of the regulation on the claimant and, particularly, the extent to which the regulation has interfered with distinct investment-backed expectations are, of course, relevant considerations. So, too, is the character of the governmental action. A "taking" may more readily be found when the interference with property can be characterized as a physical invasion by government, than when interference arises from some public program adjusting the benefits and burdens of economic life to promote the common good. * * *

Pennsylvania Coal Co. v. Mahon, 260 U.S. 393 (1922), is the leading case for the proposition that a state statute that substantially furthers important public policies may so frustrate distinct investment-backed expectations as to amount to a "taking." There the claimant had sold the surface rights to particular parcels of property, but expressly reserved the right to remove the coal thereunder. A Pennsylvania statute, enacted after the transactions, forbade any mining of coal that caused the subsidence of any house, unless the house was the property of the owner of the underlying coal and was more than 150 feet from the improved property of another. Because the statute made it commercially impracticable to mine the coal, *id.* at 414, and thus had nearly the same effect as the complete destruction of rights claimant had reserved from the owners of the surface land, *see id.* at 414–415, the Court held that the statute was invalid as effecting a "taking" without just compensation.

Finally, government actions that may be characterized as acquisitions of resources to permit or facilitate uniquely public functions have often been held to constitute "takings." * * *

B.

In contending that the New York City law has "taken" their property in violation of the Fifth and Fourteenth Amendments, appellants make a series of arguments, which, while tailored to the facts of this case, essentially urge that any substantial restriction imposed pursuant to a landmark law must be accompanied by just compensation if it is to be constitutional. Before considering these, we emphasize what is not in dispute. Because this Court has recognized, in a number of settings, that

States and cities may enact land-use restrictions or controls to enhance the quality of life by preserving the character and desirable aesthetic features of a city, appellants do not contest that New York City's objective of preserving structures and areas with special historic, architectural, or cultural significance is an entirely permissible governmental goal. They also do not dispute that the restrictions imposed on its parcel are appropriate means of securing the purposes of the New York City law. Finally, appellants do not challenge any of the specific factual premises of the decision below. They accept for present purposes both that the parcel of land occupied by Grand Central Terminal must, in its present state, be regarded as capable of earning a reasonable return, and that the transferable development rights afforded appellants by virtue of the Terminal's designation as a landmark are valuable, even if not as valuable as the rights to construct above the Terminal. In appellants' view none of these factors derogate from their claim that New York City's law has effected a "taking."

They first observe that the airspace above the Terminal is a valuable property interest, citing *United States v. Causby, supra.* They urge that the Landmarks Law has deprived them of any gainful use of their "air rights" above the Terminal and that, irrespective of the value of the remainder of their parcel, the city has "taken" their right to this superadjacent airspace, thus entitling them to "just compensation" measured by the fair market value of these air rights.

Apart from our own disagreement with appellants' characterization of the effect of the New York City law, the submission that appellants may establish a "taking" simply by showing that they have been denied the ability to exploit a property interest that they heretofore had believed was available for development is quite simply untenable. Were this the rule, this Court would have erred not only in upholding laws restricting the development of air rights, but also in approving those prohibiting both the subjacent, and the lateral, development of particular parcels. "Taking" jurisprudence does not divide a single parcel into discrete segments and attempt to determine whether rights in a particular segment have been entirely abrogated. In deciding whether a particular governmental action has effected a taking, this Court focuses rather both on the character of the action and on the nature and extent of the interference with rights in the parcel as a whole—here, the city tax block designated as the "landmark site."

Secondly, appellants, focusing on the character and impact of the New York City law, argue that it effects a "taking" because its operation has significantly diminished the value of the Terminal site. Appellants concede that the decisions sustaining other land-use regulations, which, like the New York City law, are reasonably related to the promotion of the general welfare, uniformly reject the proposition that diminution in property value, standing alone, can establish a "taking," and that the "taking" issue in these contexts is resolved by focusing on the uses the regulations permit. Appellants, moreover, also do not dispute that a showing of diminution in property value would not establish a taking if the restriction had been imposed as a result of historic-district legislation, *see generally Maher v. New Orleans*, 516 F.2d 1051 (5th Cir. 1975), but appellants argue that New York City's regulation of individual landmarks is fundamentally different from zoning or from historic-district legislation because the controls imposed by New York City's law apply only to individuals who own selected properties.

Stated baldly, appellants' position appears to be that the only means of ensuring that selected owners are not singled out to endure financial hardship for no reason is to hold that any restriction imposed on individual landmarks pursuant to the New York City scheme is a "taking" requiring the payment of "just compensation." Agreement with this argument would, of course, invalidate not just New York City's law, but all comparable landmark legislation in the Nation. We find no merit in it.

It is true, as appellants emphasize, that both historic-district legislation and zoning laws regulate all properties within given physical communities whereas landmark laws apply only to selected parcels. But, contrary to appellants' suggestions, landmark laws are not like discriminatory, or "reverse spot," zoning: that is, a land-use decision which arbitrarily singles out a particular parcel for different, less favorable treatment than the neighboring ones. In contrast to discriminatory zoning, which is the antithesis of land-use control as part of some comprehensive plan, the New York City law embodies a comprehensive plan to preserve structures of historic or aesthetic interest wherever they might be found in the city, and as noted, over 400 landmarks and 31 historic districts have been designated pursuant to this plan.

Equally without merit is the related argument that the decision to designate a structure as a landmark "is inevitably arbitrary or at least subjective, because it is basically a matter of taste," thus unavoidably singling out individual landowners for disparate and unfair treatment. The argument has a particularly hollow ring in this case. For appellants not only did not seek judicial review of either the designation or of the denials of the certificates of appropriateness and of no exterior effect, but do not even now suggest that the Commission's decisions concerning the Terminal were in any sense arbitrary or unprincipled. But, in any event, a landmark owner has a right to judicial review of any Commission decision, and, quite simply, there is no basis whatsoever for a conclusion that courts will have any greater difficulty identifying arbitrary or discriminatory action in the context of landmark regulation than in the context of classic zoning or indeed in any other context.

Next, appellants observe that New York City's law differs from zoning laws and historic-district ordinances in that the Landmarks Law does not impose identical or similar restrictions on all structures located in particular physical communities. It follows, they argue, that New York City's law is inherently incapable of producing the fair and equitable distribution of benefits and burdens of governmental action which is characteristic of zoning laws and historic-district legislation and which they maintain is a constitutional requirement if "just compensation" is not to be afforded. It is, of course, true that the Landmarks Law has a more severe impact on some landowners than on others, but that in itself does not mean that the law effects a "taking." Legislation designed to promote the general welfare commonly burdens some more than others. The owners of the brickyard in *Hadacheck*, of the cedar trees in *Miller v. Schoene*, and of the gravel and sand mine in *Goldblatt v. Hempstead*, were uniquely burdened by the legislation sustained in those cases. Similarly, zoning laws often affect some property owners more severely than others but have not been held to be invalid on that account. For example, the property owner in *Euclid* who wished to use its property for industrial purposes was affected far more severely by the ordinance than its neighbors who wished to use their land for residences.

In any event, appellants' repeated suggestions that they are solely burdened and unbenefited is factually inaccurate. This contention overlooks the fact that the New York City law applies to vast numbers of structures in the city in addition to the Terminal—all the structures contained in the 31 historic districts and over 400 individual landmarks, many of which are close to the Terminal. Unless we are to reject the judgment of the New York City Council that the preservation of landmarks benefits all New York citizens and all structures, both economically and by improving the quality of life in the city as a whole—which we are unwilling to do—we cannot conclude that the owners of the Terminal have in no sense been benefited by the Landmarks Law. Doubtless appellants believe they are more burdened than benefited by the law, but that must have been true, too, of the property owners in *Miller, Hadacheck, Euclid*, and *Goldblatt*.

Appellants' final broad-based attack would have us treat the law as an instance, like that in *United States v. Causby*, in which government, acting in an enterprise capacity, has appropriated part of their property for some strictly governmental purpose. Apart from the fact that *Causby* was a case of invasion of airspace that destroyed the use of the farm beneath and this New York City law has in nowise impaired the present use of the Terminal, the Landmarks Law neither exploits appellants' parcel for city purposes nor facilitates nor arises from any entrepreneurial operations of the city. The situation is not remotely like that in *Causby* where the airspace above the property was in the flight pattern for military aircraft. The Landmarks Law's effect is simply to prohibit appellants or anyone else from occupying portions of the airspace above the Terminal, while permitting appellants to use the remainder of the parcel in a gainful fashion. This is no more an appropriation of property by government for its own uses than is a zoning law prohibiting, for "aesthetic" reasons, two or more adult theaters within a specified area, *see Young v. American Mini Theatres, Inc.*, 427 U.S. 50 (1976), or a safety regulation prohibiting excavations below a certain level. *See Goldblatt v. Hempstead.*

C.

Rejection of appellants' broad arguments is not, however, the end of our inquiry, for all we thus far have established is that the New York City law is not rendered invalid by its failure to provide "just compensation" whenever a landmark owner is restricted in the exploitation of property interests, such as air rights, to a greater extent than provided for under applicable zoning laws. We now must consider whether the interference with appellants' property is of such a magnitude that "there must be an exercise of eminent domain and compensation to sustain [it]." *Pa. Coal*, 260 U.S. at 413. That inquiry may be narrowed to the question of the severity of the impact of the law on appellants' parcel, and its resolution in turn requires a careful assessment of the impact of the regulation on the Terminal site.

Unlike the governmental acts in *Goldblatt, Miller, Causby, Griggs,* and *Hadacheck*, the New York City law does not interfere in any way with the present uses of the Terminal. Its designation as a landmark not only permits but contemplates that appellants may continue to use the property precisely as it has been used for the past 65 years: as a railroad terminal containing office space and concessions. So the law does not interfere with what must be regarded as Penn Central's primary expectation concerning the use of the parcel. More importantly, on this record, we must regard the New York City law as permitting Penn Central not only to profit from the Terminal but also to obtain a "reasonable return" on its investment.

Appellants, moreover, exaggerate the effect of the law on their ability to make use of the air rights above the Terminal in two respects. First, it simply cannot be maintained, on this record, that appellants have been prohibited from occupying *any* portion of the airspace above the Terminal. While the Commission's actions in denying applications to construct an office building in excess of 50 stories above the Terminal may indicate that it will refuse to issue a certificate of appropriateness for any comparably sized structure, nothing the Commission has said or done suggests an intention to prohibit any construction above the Terminal. * * * Since appellants have not sought approval for the construction of a smaller structure, we do not know that appellants will be denied any use of any portion of the airspace above the Terminal.

Second, to the extent appellants have been denied the right to build above the Terminal, it is not literally accurate to say that they have been denied *all* use of even those pre-existing air rights. Their ability to use these rights has not been abrogated; they are made transferable to at least eight parcels in the vicinity of the Terminal, one or two of which have been found suitable for the construction of new office buildings.

Although appellants and others have argued that New York City's transferable development-rights program is far from ideal, the New York courts here supportably found that, at least in the case of the Terminal, the rights afforded are valuable. While these rights may well not have constituted "just compensation" if a "taking" had occurred, the rights nevertheless undoubtedly mitigate whatever financial burdens the law has imposed on appellants and, for that reason, are to be taken into account in considering the impact of regulation.

On this record, we conclude that the application of New York City's Landmarks Law has not effected a "taking" of appellants' property. The restrictions imposed are substantially related to the promotion of the general welfare and not only permit reasonable beneficial use of the landmark site but also afford appellants opportunities further to enhance not only the Terminal site proper but also other properties.[36] Affirmed.

■ MR. JUSTICE REHNQUIST, with whom THE CHIEF JUSTICE and MR. JUSTICE STEVENS join, dissenting.

* * * I.B.1.

Penn Central is prevented from further developing its property basically because too good a job was done in designing and building it. The city of New York, because of its unadorned admiration for the design, has decided that the owners of the building must preserve it unchanged for the benefit of sightseeing New Yorkers and tourists.

Unlike land-use regulations, appellees' actions do not merely *prohibit* Penn Central from using its property in a narrow set of noxious ways. Instead, appellees have placed an *affirmative* duty on Penn Central to maintain the Terminal in its present state and in "good repair." Appellants are not free to use their property as they see fit within broad outer boundaries but must strictly adhere to their past use except where appellees conclude that alternative uses would not detract from the landmark. While Penn Central may continue to use the Terminal as it is presently designed, appellees otherwise "exercise complete dominion and control over the surface of the land," *United States v. Causby*, 328 U.S. 256, 262 (1946), and must compensate the owner for his loss. * * *

Even where the government prohibits a noninjurious use, the Court has ruled that a taking does not take place if the prohibition applies over a broad cross section of land and thereby "secure[s] an average reciprocity of advantage." *Pennsylvania Coal Co. v. Mahon*, 260 U.S. 393, 415 (1922).[10] It is for this reason that zoning does not constitute a "taking." While zoning at times reduces *individual* property values, the burden is

---

[36] We emphasize that our holding today is on the present record, which in turn is based on Penn Central's present ability to use the Terminal for its intended purposes and in a gainful fashion. The city conceded at oral argument that if appellants can demonstrate at some point in the future that circumstances have so changed that the Terminal ceases to be "economically viable," appellants may obtain relief.

[10] * * * For the reasons noted in the text, historic zoning, as has been undertaken by cities, such as New Orleans, may well not require compensation under the Fifth Amendment.

shared relatively evenly and it is reasonable to conclude that on the whole an individual who is harmed by one aspect of the zoning will be benefited by another.

Here, however, a multimillion dollar loss has been imposed on appellants; it is uniquely felt and is not offset by any benefits flowing from the preservation of some 400 other "landmarks" in New York City. Appellees have imposed a substantial cost on less than one one-tenth of one percent of the buildings in New York City for the general benefit of all its people. It is exactly this imposition of general costs on a few individuals at which the "taking" protection is directed. * * *

The benefits that appellees believe will flow from preservation of the Grand Central Terminal will accrue to all the citizens of New York City. There is no reason to believe that appellants will enjoy a substantially greater share of these benefits. If the cost of preserving Grand Central Terminal were spread evenly across the entire population of the city of New York, the burden per person would be in cents per year—a minor cost appellees would surely concede for the benefit accrued. Instead, however, appellees would impose the entire cost of several million dollars per year on Penn Central. But it is precisely this sort of discrimination that the Fifth Amendment prohibits. * * *

C.

Appellees, apparently recognizing that the constraints imposed on a landmark site constitute a taking for Fifth Amendment purposes, do not leave the property owner empty-handed. As the Court notes, the property owner may theoretically "transfer" his previous right to develop the landmark property to adjacent properties if they are under his control. Appellees have coined this system "Transfer Development Rights," or TDR's. * * *

Appellees contend that, even if they have "taken" appellants' property, TDR's constitute "just compensation." Appellants, of course, argue that TDR's are highly imperfect compensation. Because the lower courts held that there was no "taking," they did not have to reach the question of whether or not just compensation has already been awarded. The New York Court of Appeals' discussion of TDR's gives some support to appellants: "The many defects in New York City's program for development rights transfers have been detailed elsewhere . . . . The area to which transfer is permitted is severely limited [and] complex procedures are required to obtain a transfer permit." * * * And in other cases the Court of Appeals has noted that TDR's have an "uncertain and contingent market value" and do "not adequately preserve" the value lost when a building is declared to be a landmark. * * * On the other hand, there is evidence in the record that Penn Central has been offered substantial amounts for its TDR's. Because the record on appeal is relatively slim, I would remand to the Court of Appeals for a determination of whether TDR's constitute a "full and perfect equivalent for the property taken."

NOTES & QUESTIONS

1.   Consider what changes in urban life and culture would lead the largest city in our country, with a famously dynamic real estate development market, to enact a preservation ordinance strong enough to prevent the changes to Grand Central Terminal challenged here.

A few blocks away from Grand Central Terminal sits the former site of the original Penn Station, built in 1910. About fifty years after the station opened, it began to fall into disrepair. When its owners decided to sell, a group of young architects banded together to form the Action Group for Better Architecture in New York, which organized a public protest against the station's demolition. Protesters' signs bore messages, including, "Shame" and "Don't Amputate—Renovate." Nevertheless, over the next three years, the historic station was completely demolished, including every decoration that adorned the outside of the edifice. The architecture critic Ada Louise Huxtable wrote, "The passing of Penn Station. . . confirms the demise of an age of opulent elegance, of conspicuous, magnificent spaces, rich and enduring materials, the monumental civic gesture, and extravagant expenditure for esthetic ends."

Preservation advocates and neighborhood defenders had sought a historic preservation ordinance for New York City for many years. The public reaction to the demolition of Penn Station became the catalyst for Mayor Robert Wagner to sign the Landmark Law on April 15, 1965, as a direct response to the Penn Station demolition. By the year 2020, the Landmarks Preservation Law had been invoked to protect more than 37,000 buildings and sites, including 1,439 individual landmarks, 120 interior landmarks, 11 scenic landmarks, and 149 historic districts and historic district extensions in all five boroughs. Moreover, the law inspired other historic preservation efforts, culminating in the enactment of the National Historic Preservation Act, covered in Chapter 3 of this book.

2.   *Penn Central* has become the seminal case regarding regulatory takings and historical preservation, inspiring decades of scholarship and analysis. Professor Byrne explored the framework created by *Penn Central* and the impact it has had on historic preservation laws, concluding that:

> The constitutional framework created by the decision has fostered a remarkable blossoming of historic preservation as a major tool of urban land use regulation. Preservation could never have played this role without the insulation from constitutional liability provided by the Penn Central Court, likewise, it could not have played this role if property owners had been denied all economic incentives to invest in the renovation and reuse of historic properties. Penn Central appears to have crafted a balance between local control and individual rights that has nourished preservation.

J. Peter Byrne, *Regulatory Takings Challenges to Historic Preservation Laws After Penn Central*, 15 FORDHAM ENVTL. L. REV. 313, 313–314 (2004).

3.   The *Penn Central* balancing test, now used in the vast majority of takings cases, considers both the economic impact of the regulation, particularly the extent to which the regulation has interfered with distinct

investment-backed expectations, and the character of the government action. *Penn Central* settled that historic preservation regulation generally and regulation of individual landmarks in particular are appropriate and important government action. Why was the large economic loss that the regulation imposed on the property insufficient to establish a taking? Note the Court's view that *Penn Central* had failed to show that it could not "use the Terminal for its intended purposes and in a gainful fashion."

Penn Central has endured because the opinion was written to hold together a Court with diverse views; the opinion protects the economic viability of a reasonable property investment while leaving much room for regulation. Close reading of the opinion must cope with the report by Justice Brennan's law clerk for this most important opinion for historic preservation that it "was basically written Memorial Day weekend in three consecutive near all-nighters." Transcript, *Looking Back on* Penn Central*: A Panel Discussion with the Supreme Court Litigators*, 15 FORDHAM ENVTL. L. REV. 287, 302 (2004).

4.   Does it matter who is bringing the claim? Recall the rule of thumb used in determining whether a historic resource will be designated historic: it usually must be at least fifty years old. Much can change in fifty years. If restrictions on historic resources usually come into effect only after fifty years have passed, how could any preservation restriction interfere with the original property owners' investment-backed expectations? Should subsequent owners' expectations be "tacked" onto the original owners' expectations? Why should expectations matter in the first place? Is the reasonable investment-backed expectations prong of the *Penn Central* balancing test just a distraction? Or is it a useful basis for the rejection of takings challenges of historic preservation rules, since no property owner can reasonably expect to be free from regulation?

5.   Much is made in *Penn Central* of the significance of transferable development rights (TDRs). TDRs represent the difference between the maximum development permissible under zoning ordinance and lesser amount of development under restrictions. They are assigned to properties subject to development restrictions, such as historic buildings. Once assigned, TDRs can then be transferred to other properties in a designated transferee area owned by the same property owner assigned the TDRs, or sold to owners of other properties in the receiving area. There are about 140 TDR programs in the United States; some attempt to preserve farmland and protect the environment, while others are used in the historic preservation context.

To which lots can TDRs be transferred? In New York, transferees must be "contiguous," meaning either across the street or across the intersection. The building to which the TDRs are transferred may be developed to a larger size than the zoning ordinance would otherwise permit. For example, a building that received five stories' worth of TDR credits would be allowed to build five stories higher than permitted by the zoning regulations. At the time of *Penn Central*, the transferee lot was only permitted a 20 percent increase in floor area through the transfer, reducing the value of the TDRs. In 1969, the Landmarks Commission changed the rule to allow for all the

TDRs at Penn Central to be transferred to one lot. Is this loosening of the TDR rules in 1969 significant? Is it significant that such rules were made only to benefit the Grand Central Terminal parcel—a "singling out" of benefits? If we ask the question that Justice Rehnquist does—that is, whether TDRs are enough compensation for a taking—does the change in the rules compensate enough for the taking Rehnquist believed occurred?

Ironically, Justice Powell wrote in his conference notes for the *Penn Central* case that Justice Blackmun thought that the Court need not consider TDRs and that Justice Stevens thought them irrelevant. Powell added "I think all of us agree to this."

Nearly twenty years after *Penn Central*, the Supreme Court determined that a property owner who received TDRs in lieu of a development approval could bring a regulatory takings claim, even if the owner did not try to sell the TDRs first. *Suitum v. Tahoe Regional Planning Agency*, 520 U.S. 725 (1997). The case was ripe for adjudication, the Court reasoned, because the valuation of the TDRs was "simply an issue of fact about possible market prices" and did not change the final decision issued by the agency. *Id.* at 741.

6. Why do we compensate takings, anyway? Scholars have suggested two primary reasons: fairness and efficiency. With respect to the first, fairness: Compensation ensures that one person or group is not singled out to bear all costs of governmental action. Government action is deliberate, and compensating "losers" helps to reduce demoralization costs—that is, the costs of losing economic decisions made by people unhappy about "unfair" government action.

With respect to the second, efficiency: Compensation ensures that government evaluates the cost of its actions and makes more efficient decisions. Frank Michelman's 1967 article on this topic remains a classic; he focuses on demoralization costs, efficiency gains, and settlement costs (the costs of settling to avoid demoralization costs) to explain why compensation is required. Frank I. Michelman, *Property, Utility, and Fairness: Comments on the Ethical Foundations of "Just Compensation" Law*, 80 HARV. L. REV. 1165 (1967). Joseph Sax, writing both before and after Michelman in two articles on the topic, takes a more limited approach to compensation. He first proposed that compensation be paid only when economic loss results from government's acting as an "enterpriser," that is, competing for various resources in private property. Later, he modified his position, arguing that compensation need only be required if the conduct being regulated produces no spillovers (external effects); in other words, if the government regulation protects neighbors or others from negative effects, the property owner regulated need not be compensated. *Takings, Private Property and Public Rights*, 81 YALE L. J. 149 (1971) & *Takings and the Police Power*, 74 YALE L. J. 36 (1964). Scholars favoring a broad compensation interpretation offer a variety of reasons. *See, e.g.,* Lawrence Blume & Daniel L. Rubinfeld, *Compensation for Takings: An Economic Analysis*, 72 CAL. L. REV. 569 (1984) (arguing that compensation is necessary because a private insurance market cannot function adequately to protect people against potential loss from governmental action). How might each of these scholars address historic preservation rules? What views do the majority and dissenting opinions of *Penn Central* take?

7.   Some photographs may provide context. Figure 7-2, which appears on the following page, shows the magnificent 42nd Street (southern) façade of Grand Central Terminal, in a canyon of tall structures all around. Figure 7-3 presents a view looking southward down Park Avenue, showing the stately 35-story Helmsley Building (built in 1929 and designated a landmark in 1987) and the 59-story Met Life Building just beyond. Although Grand Central Terminal is not visible in this photo, it sits directly behind the Met Life building. Does seeing these photographs of tall, dense skyscrapers crowding the fairly short Grand Central Terminal give you any pause about the alleged impact of the project at issue in *Penn Central*?

8.   One scholar has argued that, historically, regulations such as historic preservation rules were not part of the original understanding of the government actions restricted by the takings clause. According to Dean William Treanor, almost no pre-Fifth Amendment state charters or constitutions recognized a right to compensation when the government took private property. Only Massachusetts and Virginia's constitutions contained such a requirement, and Treanor asserts that such requirements were plainly limited to physical takings (not regulatory ones). He also explains that under the original understanding of the takings clause, courts were expected to defer to majoritarian decision-making (legislation) in most instances but defend those most likely to be the victims of a failure of process. *See* William Treanor, *The Original Understanding of the Takings Clause and the Political Process*, 95 COLUM. L. REV. 782 (1995). How far from the original understanding of the takings clause does *Penn Central* take us?

9.   Arguably, *Penn Central* treats historic preservation as constitutionally indistinguishable from zoning. But how do they compare practically? Zoning regulations may set standards, zone by zone, for building height, setbacks from lot lines, bulk, and uses. Within any given locality with both zoning and historic preservation restrictions, the number of properties subject to preservation restrictions is almost certainly fewer than the number subject to zoning restrictions. Often, review under both preservation and zoning ordinances is triggered by the same activities by property owners: construction, alteration, or demolition. A commission specially appointed to handle permission for such activities convenes to hear and decide individual cases. Going further, however, many local preservation ordinances impose affirmative duties on property owners to maintain their historic structures in good repair. Zoning ordinances do not impose such duties. At the same time, preservation ordinances generally do not regulate use of the property and preservation regulators arguably exercise less discretion than do zoning authorities. Do historic preservation laws impose burdens on fewer property owners than zoning ordinances do? Should that make them more constitutionally suspect? These issues are further explored in Chapter 6.

Figure 7-2:
42nd Street Façade of Grand Central Terminal,
Manhattan, NY

Figure 7-3:
Towering Skyscrapers North of Grand Central Terminal,
Manhattan, NY

10. Although *Penn Central* and the cases highlighted in this Chapter involve the takings clause of the U.S. Constitution, all fifty states have constitutional provisions that prohibit takings. Historic preservation laws have been tested by takings claims in several state courts. Back in 1955, the Massachusetts Supreme Judicial Court was asked whether a legislative proposal to allow Nantucket to regulate historic properties was an unconstitutional taking. The Court determined that the proposal was not an unconstitutional taking under Article 51 of the state constitution. *Opinion of the Justices*, 333 Mass. 773 (1955) (Opinion of the Justices to the Senate).

2. ECONOMIC IMPACT SINCE *PENN CENTRAL*

One of the biggest questions in *Penn Central* is how much of an economic impact the Landmarks Preservation Law had on the claimant. Indeed, this question dominates later historic preservation cases involving takings claims. Although the Supreme Court has not taken another takings case involving preservation regulations, several subsequent takings decisions have addressed the question of economic impact.

Perhaps most notable is the Court's decision in *Lucas v. South Carolina Coastal Council*, 505 U.S. 1003 (1992). In that case, the petitioner had purchased lots on the Atlantic Coast with the intention of building new structures on them. Two years after his purchase, the South Carolina Beachfront Management Act subsequently barred him from building as part of a statewide erosion prevention plan. The Court found that a regulation which denies all economically beneficial or productive use of land is a per se taking for which just compensation is required, unless the use proscribed was a nuisance at common law. *Lucas* provides one of the few bright-line rules in the murky sea of takings law dominated by *Penn Central*.

Can you see why many claimants would argue that their takings claims fall under *Lucas*? Is there any instance where a historic preservation regulation would deny all economically beneficial or productive use of land? Consider the following case, which considers both the *Lucas* per se rule and the *Penn Central* balancing test.

District Intown Properties Limited Partnership v. District of Columbia

198 F.3d 874 (D.C. Cir. 1999), *cert. denied*, 531 U.S. 812 (2000)

■ HARRY T. EDWARDS, CHIEF JUDGE:

In 1961, District Intown Limited Properties Partnership ("District Intown") purchased Cathedral Mansions South, an apartment building and landscaped lawn on Connecticut Avenue across from the National Zoo. District Intown subdivided this property into nine contiguous lots in 1988. In March 1989, all nine lots were declared historic landmarks. In July 1992, the Mayor of the District of Columbia denied District Intown's request for construction permits to build eight townhouses on eight of the nine lots, finding that the construction was incompatible with the property's landmark status. Alleging that the District of Columbia's denial constituted a taking, District Intown and its general partners sued under 42 U.S.C. § 1983 (1994) for just compensation under the Takings Clause of the Fifth Amendment.

Upon cross motions for summary judgment, the District Court granted summary judgment for the District of Columbia. *See District Intown Properties Ltd. P'ship v. District of Columbia*, 23 F.Supp.2d 30 (D. D.C. 1998). The District Court held that the relevant parcel for the purposes of determining whether a taking had occurred consisted of the entire property, including the apartment building, not the eight individual lots that District Intown sought to develop. *See id.* at 35–36. The court then analyzed the alleged taking under the Supreme Court's holdings in *Lucas v. South Carolina Coastal Council*, 505 U.S. 1003 (1992), and *Penn Central Transp. Co. v. City of New York*, 438 U.S. 104 (1978). The District Court found that there was no categorical taking under *Lucas*, because District Intown had not been deprived of all economic value in the relevant parcel. The trial court further held that District Intown could not make out a claim under *Penn Central*, because its reasonable investment-backed expectations had not been disappointed and it continued to receive economic benefits from the property.

We hold that the District Court correctly found that the relevant parcel for the takings analysis consisted of the entire property held by District Intown, *i.e.*, the property as it was originally purchased in 1961 and as it was held for 27 years prior to the 1988 subdivision. All relevant objective and subjective factors support this conclusion. When the property is viewed as a single parcel, there is no doubt that it has not been rendered valueless. Indeed, even if each subdivided parcel is considered separately, District Intown has not shown a "total taking" under Lucas. In addition, the record here does not show that District Intown's investment-backed expectations were disappointed. This is not surprising, because District Intown could not have had any reasonable investment-backed expectations of development given the background regulatory structure at the time of subdivision. Accordingly, we hold that District Intown did not present any genuine issue of material fact in support of a takings claim under *Penn Central* or *Lucas*. We therefore affirm the District Court's judgment.

I.   Background

In 1961, District Intown purchased in fee simple Lot 1 of Subdivision Square 2106 on Connecticut Avenue, across from the National Zoo. The property was known as Cathedral Mansions South and consisted of an apartment building and adjacent landscaped lawns. District Intown made no significant changes to the property until 1988, when it subdivided Cathedral Mansions South into nine lots, designated as Lots

106 through 114. The subdivisions were recorded on June 30, 1988. Lot 106 contains the apartment building, and Lots 107 through 114 are each portions of the landscaped lawn. The record indicates that District Intown spent $2,819 to survey the parcel and to record the subdivision. The record does not reflect any other expenses.

On December 30, 1988, District Intown applied for permits to build one townhouse on each of the eight landscaped lots. The zoning and structural engineering divisions of the Department of Consumer and Regulatory Affairs approved the permits on March 7, 1989. However, because the property is located across from the National Zoo, the permits were referred to the Commission on Fine Arts. *See* D.C. CODE ANN. § 5–410 (1994) ("Shipstead-Luce Act"). The Shipstead-Luce Act, in effect since the 1930s, empowers the Commission on Fine Arts to communicate to the Mayor "recommendations, including such changes, if any, as in its judgment are necessary to prevent reasonably avoidable impairment of the public values belonging" to various buildings and parks. *Id.* On March 31, 1989, the Commission on Fine Arts recommended against construction.

Figure 7-4:
The Lawns of Cathedral Mansions South,
Washington, DC

Beginning in 1987, before the property was subdivided, a movement developed in the Woodley Park community in support of designating the property a historic landmark. This culminated on March 2, 1989, when the group filed a landmark designation petition. This was five days before District Intown received zoning approval for the construction. The Historic Preservation Review Board ("Review Board") approved the landmark designation on May 17, 1989. Because the landmark designation petition was pending when District Intown's permits were approved for zoning, the permits were referred to the Review Board pursuant to the District of Columbia's landmark laws, *see* D.C. CODE ANN. § 5–1001 *et seq.* (1994 & Supp.1999), effective since 1979. On July 19, 1989, the Review Board recommended that the construction permits be denied. The permit applications were dismissed without prejudice on December 20, 1991.

On January 31, 1992, District Intown filed new permit applications identical in all respects to those previously dismissed. The permits were again referred to the Review Board, which recommended denial because construction on the lawn would be incompatible with its historic landmark status. Pursuant to D.C. CODE ANN. § 5–1007(e), District Intown requested a hearing before an agent designated by the Mayor. The hearing was held on July 22 and 24, 1992. The Mayor's agent agreed with the Review Board, stating that "any construction destroying the lawn" would be incompatible with its landmark status. * * *

Thereafter, on March 22, 1996, District Intown filed this § 1983 action. On cross motions for summary judgment, the District Court entered summary judgment for the District of Columbia on September 25, 1998. *See District Intown Properties Ltd. P'ship*, 23 F.Supp.2d at 39. * * * This appeal followed.

II. Analysis

A. Standard of Review

This court reviews a grant of summary judgment de novo. *See Aka v. Washington Hosp. Ctr.*, 156 F.3d 1284, 1288 (D.C. Cir. 1998) (en banc). A party is entitled to summary judgment if the record reveals that there is no genuine issue as to any material fact and that the moving party is entitled to judgment as a matter of law. *See* FED. R. CIV. P. 56(c). In deciding whether there is a genuine issue of material fact, the court must assume the truth of all statements proffered by the non-movant except for conclusory allegations lacking any factual basis in the record. *See Greene v. Dalton*, 164 F.3d 671, 675 (D.C. Cir. 1999). Summary judgment may be granted even if the movant has proffered no evidence, so long as the non-movant "fails to make a showing sufficient to establish the existence of an element essential to that party's case, and on which that party will bear the burden of proof at trial." *Celotex Corp. v. Catrett*, 477 U.S. 317, 322 (1986). As the "party challenging governmental action as an unconstitutional taking," District Intown bears a "substantial burden." *Eastern Enters. v. Apfel*, 524 U.S. 498, 523 (1998).

B. The Takings Analysis

The Takings Clause of the Fifth Amendment prohibits the government from taking "private property . . . for public use, without just compensation." U.S. CONST. amend. V. In a regulatory takings case, the principal focus of inquiry is whether a regulation "reaches a certain magnitude" in depriving an owner of the use of property. *Pennsylvania Coal Co. v. Mahon*, 260 U.S. 393, 413 (1922); *see also id.* at 415 (asking whether the regulation "goes too far"). The Supreme Court has indicated that most regulatory takings cases should be considered on an *ad hoc* basis, with three primary factors weighing in the balance: the regulation's economic impact on the claimant, the regulation's interference with the claimant's reasonable investment-backed expectations, and the character of the government action. *See Penn Central Transp. Co.*, 438 U.S. at 124.

The meaning of the three factors identified in *Penn Central* has been amplified by the Court, both in *Penn Central* and in later cases. The *regulation's economic effect* upon the claimant may be measured in several different ways. *See Hodel v. Irving*, 481 U.S. 704, 714 (1987) (looking to the market value of a property); *Keystone Bituminous Coal Ass'n v. DeBenedictis*, 480 U.S. 470, 495–96 (1987) (looking to whether the regulation makes property owner's coal operation "commercially impracticable"); *Andrus v. Allard*, 444 U.S. 51, 66 (1979) (looking to the possibility of other economic use besides sale, which was prohibited by the challenged regulation); *Penn Central Transp. Co.*, 438 U.S. at 136 (focusing on the ability to earn a reasonable rate of return). A *reasonable investment-backed expectation* "must be more than a 'unilateral expectation or an abstract need." *Ruckelshaus v. Monsanto Co.*, 467 U.S. 986, 1005–06 (1984) (quoting *Webb's Fabulous Pharmacies, Inc. v. Beckwith*, 449 U.S. 155, 161 (1980)). Claimants cannot establish a takings claim "simply by showing that they have been denied the ability to exploit a property interest that they heretofore had believed was available for development." *Penn Central Transp. Co.*, 438 U.S. at 130. And the *character of the governmental action* depends both on whether the government has legitimized a physical occupation of the property, *see Loretto v. Teleprompter Manhattan CATV Corp.*, 458 U.S. 419, 434–35 (1982), and whether the regulation has a legitimate public purpose, *see Keystone Bituminous Coal Ass'n*, 480 U.S. at 485. Finally, under all three of these factors, the effect of the regulation must be measured on the "parcel as a whole." *See Penn Central Transp. Co.*, 438 U.S. at 130–31.

The Supreme Court has indicated that it will find a "categorical" or *per se* taking in two circumstances. The first circumstance includes regulations that result in "permanent physical occupation of property." *Loretto*, 458 U.S. at 434–35. This circumstance is not at issue in this case. The second circumstance includes regulations pursuant to which the government denies *all* economically beneficial or productive use of property. *See Lucas*, 505 U.S. at 1015. This so-called "total taking" claim is at the heart of District Intown's complaint here. Unfortunately, the facial simplicity of the "total taking" standard belies the difficulty in its application. As the Court acknowledged in *Lucas*, its "rhetorical force . . . is greater than its precision, since the rule does not make clear the 'property interest' against which the loss of value is to be measured." 505 U.S. at 1016 n.7.

Under both *Lucas* and *Penn Central*, then, we must first define what constitutes the relevant parcel before we can evaluate the regulation's effect on that parcel. In the instant case the question is: Does the relevant parcel consist of the property as a whole or do the eight lots for which construction permits were denied constitute the relevant parcels? This has been referred to as the "denominator problem." *E.g., Loveladies Harbor, Inc. v. United States*, 28 F.3d 1171, 1179 (Fed. Cir. 1994). State law may offer some guidance on how to define the relevant parcel, but, as the Court has noted, state law is not always determinative. *Compare Lucas*, 505 U.S. at 1017 n.7 (suggesting that one may look to the influence of the State's property law—whether and to what extent the State has recognized and extended legal recognition to the particular interest alleged to have been deprived of all economic value—on the claimant's reasonable expectations), *with Keystone Bituminous Coal Ass'n*, 480 U.S. at 500 (refusing to treat the support estate as a separate parcel of property simply because Pennsylvania law recognizes it as such and noting that "our takings jurisprudence forecloses reliance on such legalistic distinctions within a bundle of property rights").

C.   The Relevant Parcel

The definition of the relevant parcel profoundly influences the outcome of a takings analysis. Above all, the parcel should be functionally coherent. In other words, more should unite the property than common ownership by the claimant. Thus, a court must also consider how both the property-owner and the government treat (and have treated) the property.

The District Court used several factors to determine the relevant parcel: the degree of contiguity, the dates of acquisition, the extent to which the parcel has been treated as a single unit, and the extent to which the restricted lots benefit the unregulated lot. *See District Intown*, 23 F.Supp.2d at 35 (citing *Ciampitti v. United States*, 22 Cl.Ct. 310, 318 (1991)). An analysis focused on these factors is eminently sound and it mirrors the approach taken by other courts in regulatory takings cases. * * *

Applying these factors, the District Court correctly determined that all nine lots should be treated as one parcel for the purpose of the court's takings analysis. The lots are spatially and functionally contiguous. District Intown purchased the property as a whole in 1961 and treated it as a single indivisible property for more than 25 years. District Intown presented no evidence that, even after subdivision, it treated the lawn lots separately from Lot 106, the lot that contains the apartment building, for the purposes of accounting or management. The intentional act of subdivision is the only evidence produced by District Intown that it has treated the lots as distinct units. In fact, before the Mayor's agent, District Intown did not come forward with evidence showing that it had, for accounting purposes, treated the lawn maintenance fees separately from expenses associated with maintaining the apartment building. While there is a dispute as to whether the adjacent landscaped lawn increases the apartment building's value, this is immaterial. Even if Lot 106 were deemed to have the same value with or without Lots 107 through 114, the application of the other three factors strongly suggests that Lots 106 through 114 are functionally part of the same property.

Appellants argue that the District Court was wrong to treat all the lots as a single parcel because it contradicts *Lucas* and two Federal Circuit cases. This argument falls flat. District Intown first argues that the *Lucas* Court termed "extreme" and "unsupportable" a similar decision by the state court in *Penn Central* to treat multiple holdings as a single parcel for takings analysis. This dictum, *see Lucas*, 505 U.S. at 1017 n.7, referred, however, only to the state court's decision to treat all of Penn Central's holdings *in the vicinity of Grand Central Station* as part of the denominator for the purposes of deciding whether plaintiffs could receive a reasonable return on their investment in Grand Central. *See Penn Central Transp. Co. v. City of New York*, 366 N.E.2d 1271, 1278 (N.Y. 1977). The *Penn Central* Court had no need to address this holding. The *Lucas* dictum casts aspersions on the state court's elevation of one factor, unity of ownership, over other factors in determining the relevant parcel. The District Court engaged in no such "extreme" conduct here; it did not look to all of District Intown's holdings in the vicinity of Cathedral Mansions South to evaluate the economic effect of the regulation at issue here; it looked to contiguous property that was purchased and treated as a single unit by appellants.

Similarly, the two Federal Circuit cases cited by District Intown do not undermine the District Court's definition of the relevant parcel. *See* Brief for Appellants at 16 (citing *Loveladies Harbor*, 28 F.3d at 1171 & *Fla. Rock Induss., Inc. v. United States*, 791 F.2d 893 (Fed. Cir. 1986)). Neither of these cases support appellants' position and, in fact, *Loveladies Harbor* supports the District Court's decision. In *Florida Rock Industries*, the court reviewed the Army Corps of Engineers' uncompensated rejection of the plaintiff's application to mine limestone on 98 acres of the plaintiff's wetland property. *See Florida Rock Induss.*, 791 F.2d at 896. The Federal Circuit affirmed the trial court's decision to consider the 98 acres as the relevant parcel separate from the adjacent 1,462 acres of wetland. *See id.* at 904. The Federal Circuit's justification for this decision, however, was that all the evidence and the findings indicated that the Army Corps of Engineers would have rejected mining on all of the property, so there was no point to including all 1,560 acres in the relevant parcel. *See id.* at 904–05. Thus, *Florida Rock Industries* is not analogous to the instant case; there is no indication that the District of Columbia will prevent District Intown from continuing to use its property to obtain income from its apartment building.

Loveladies Harbor lends support to the District Court's decision to treat Lots 106–114 as one parcel. The plaintiff in *Loveladies Harbor* sought to develop a total of 12.5 acres of land, consisting of 11.5 acres of wetlands and one acre of filled upland. *See Loveladies Harbor*, 28 F.3d at 1180. The Army Corps of Engineers refused to grant the permit required to fill the wetlands acreage. *See id.* at 1174. In reviewing whether this denial constituted a taking the Federal Circuit found that the trial court correctly concluded that the relevant parcel was the entire 12.5 acres, not just the 11.5 acres to which the permit denial applied. *See id.* at 1181. Thus, *Loveladies Harbor* argues against treating the property burdened by the regulation separately from contiguous property.

Moreover, the *Loveladies Harbor* Court emphasized that a "flexible approach, designed to account for factual nuances," guides its analysis of the denominator problem. *Id.* These factual nuances include "whether there remained substantial economically viable uses for plaintiff's property after the regulatory imposition," *id.* (citing *Deltona Corp. v. United States*, 228 Ct. Cl. 476 (1981)), and "the timing of transfers in light of the developing regulatory environment." *Id.* Both of these factors support our conclusion in the instant case that Cathedral Mansions South as a whole constitutes the relevant parcel.

Finally, *Penn Central* is instructive where, as here, appellants own a single piece of property that is divisible into several legally recognized entities. Indeed, the Court was rather blunt in saying that "'[t]aking' jurisprudence does not divide a single parcel into discrete segments and attempt to determine whether rights in a particular segment have been entirely abrogated." *Penn Central Transp. Co.*, 438 U.S. at 130. The Court also made it clear that a party may not "establish a 'taking' simply by showing that they have been denied the ability to exploit a property interest they heretofore had believed was available for development." *Id.* The Court found this suggestion to be "simply untenable." *Id.*

On the basis of the foregoing authority, it seems clear here that we must analyze District Intown's property not as separate, potentially divisible and transferable parcels, but as one contiguous parcel. Appellants note that the District of Columbia has taxed Lots 107 through 114 at a higher rate since subdivision, reflecting the District of Columbia's assessment that these lots are vacant developable land. They contend that it is inconsistent for the District of Columbia to speak from both sides of its mouth in this regard, claiming for tax purposes that the lots are developable, but refusing to permit development on the lots. We simply note that appellants retain the right to recombine the parcels and treat them as one property for the purposes of taxation, so no further disadvantage will befall them on this score. * * *

D.   Analysis Under *Lucas*

Given that Lots 106 through 114 should be treated as a single parcel, the District Court's denial of summary judgment on District Intown's *Lucas* claim is unremarkable. To come within *Lucas*, a claimant must show that its property is rendered "valueless" by a regulation. *Lucas*, 505 U.S. at 1009. District Intown presented no evidence to show that the regulation deprived the property as a whole of all economically beneficial use.

Even were we to view Lot 106 as distinct from Lots 107 through 114, it seems plain that the District Court should have granted appellees' motion for summary judgment. Drawing all inferences in favor of District Intown, the record does not support the conclusion that Lots 107 through 114 are rendered "valueless" by the regulation at issue. The record contains a finding by the Mayor's agent that any construction that destroyed the lawn would be incompatible with the lawn's status as a historic landmark. District Intown argues from this that its case fell on all fours within *Lucas*. District Intown seeks to extend *Lucas* beyond its reach. The *Lucas* Court consciously recognized that it was drawing an arbitrary line between total destruction of economic value and something marginally less than total destruction. *See* 505 U.S. at 1019 n.8 (pointing out that while the line establishing a categorical deprivation as requiring a complete diminution in value is arbitrary as it relates to someone who only suffers a 95% deprivation in value, the person whose deprivation is "one step short of complete" may still seek compensation under the Penn Central balancing test). District Intown propounded no evidence that the lawns' economic value was totally destroyed as is required by *Lucas*, nor did District Intown offer evidence of the plots' fair market value after its construction permits were denied. *Cf. Florida Rock Indus.*, 791 F.2d at 905 (reversing the trial court's finding that denial of permit constituted an uncompensated taking because the court failed to consider the property's fair market value after regulation). * * *

As noted in the foregoing discussion, we simply intend to highlight the limited nature of the *Lucas* inquiry, and note that there would be no "categorical" taking even were we to view the parcels as separate under *Lucas*. We do not pass on how the parcels would fare separately under *Penn Central*'s *ad hoc* analysis.

E.   Analysis under *Penn Central*

There are three main factors to be considered in *Penn Central*'s ad hoc inquiry: the character of the government action, the regulation's economic effect on the claimant, and the effect on investment-backed expectations. District Intown does not appear to argue that the character of the governmental action counsels finding a taking; this is not a permanent invasion, but rather a general regulation with a legitimate public purpose. As to the economic effects, District Intown offered no evidence that this regulation rendered Lots 106–114 unprofitable to maintain; there is nothing in the record to suggest that the apartment building does not bring in a sufficient return for District Intown, and a claimant must put forth striking evidence of economic effects to prevail even under the *ad hoc* inquiry. *See Penn Central Transp. Co.*, 438 U.S. at

131 (reviewing the Court's decisions upholding regulations despite diminution in a property's value of more than 75%).

Finally, District Intown did not present sufficient evidence that it had a reasonable investment-backed expectation to develop the lawns into apartment buildings. Here, as in *Penn Central*, the regulation does not interfere with District Intown's "primary expectation" concerning the use of the parcel, because it "not only permits but contemplates that appellants may continue to use the property precisely as it has been used" for the past 28 years. *Penn Central Transp. Co.*, 438 U.S. at 136.

District Intown suggested at oral argument that it has satisfied the requirement of demonstrating reasonable investment-backed expectations because it purchased property that, at the time of purchase, was subdividable. This is not sufficient to establish the existence of reasonable investment-backed expectations. In this case, where the development District Intown proposes departs from the property's traditional use, and the moment of purchase is so attenuated from the moment of subdivision, the claimant surely must point to some action beyond mere purchase to establish the reasonableness of its expectations.

Appellants also argue that their expectations of the property's use between the moment of purchase and the moment of subdivision could have reasonably changed. This may be, but when appellants subdivided they surely knew that the legal regime had changed since they first bought their property. Moreover, they knew that any subdivided parcel would be subject to that regime. Lucas teaches that a buyer's reasonable expectations must be put in the context of the underlying regulatory regime. *See* 505 U.S. at 1030 (stating that the Takings Clause does not require compensation when the restriction is proscribed by background state law rules or understandings). District Intown purchased and subdivided its property subject to an existing regulatory regime that establishes that District Intown could have had no reasonable expectations of development at the time it made its investments.

At the time of purchase, District Intown could have reasonably expected the Shipstead-Luce Act to affect its rights of development. For approximately 60 years, the Shipstead-Luce Act has restricted development on properties that, like Cathedral Mansions South, abut or border upon the National Zoo. *See* D.C. CODE ANN. § 5–410. Were that not sufficient, after 1979, D.C.'s historic landmark laws additionally limited expectations of development. *See id.* § 5–1001 *et seq.* Thus, at the time District Intown subdivided the property, it knew, or should have known, that the property was potentially subject to regulation under the landmark laws. *Cf.* Amicus Curiae Brief at 15 (pointing out that almost the entire length of Connecticut Avenue from M Street to almost a mile north of District Intown's property is either landmarked or within a historic district). Businesses that operate in an industry with a history of regulation have no reasonable expectation that regulation will not be strengthened to achieve established legislative ends. *See Concrete Pipe &*

Prods. v. Construction Laborers Pension Trust, 508 U.S. 602, 645 (1993). In this case, District Intown was in the real estate business, with a history of restriction of development for the purpose of preserving historic sites. Similarly, the Supreme Court rejected a company's claim of reasonable expectations that the Environmental Protection Agency would maintain trade secret confidentiality where the industry had long "been the focus of great public concern and significant government regulation" and the "possibility was substantial that the Federal Government . . . would find disclosure [of trade secrets] to be in the public interest." *Monsanto Co.*, 467 U.S. at 1008–09. Prior to and after subdivision, this particular property was the subject of increasing public activity devoted to restricting development through landmark designation. *See Good v. United States*, 189 F.3d 1355, 1361–63 (Fed. Cir. 1999) (finding the claimant had no reasonable expectations where he purchased the land subject to environmental regulation and watched as public concern for the environment increased and the applicable regulations became more stringent before seeking approval for development).

District Intown also argues that the District Court's finding that the regulation did not have a significant economic impact was erroneous. District Intown bases this argument on the assertion that they presented undisputed evidence that the lawns, absent development, add nothing to the value of the apartment building. This argument misunderstands the substantial burden District Intown faced in District Court. District Intown had to produce evidence showing that its entire property, including Lot 106, no longer provided a reasonable rate of return given the D.C. regulation. Whether the lawns add value to the apartment building is irrelevant to whether the property as a whole can be operated at a sufficient profit even with the regulation. In short, none of the *Penn Central* factors support District Intown's claim of a compensable deprivation of property.

III. Conclusion

For the reasons stated above, we affirm the District Court's grant of summary judgment in favor of the District of Columbia.

So ordered.

NOTES & QUESTIONS

1.   Why did the property owner in *District Intown* try to claim that the lawns were individual separate lots? Should their longtime ownership of the parcel as a whole and knowledge of potential restrictions have prevented them from having a successful *Lucas* claim?

2.   The *District Intown* result is not unusual. Only a handful of cases across the country have, since *Penn Central*, found that historic preservation laws were regulatory takings. Moreover, takings challenges against mere

designation under historic preservation ordinances have never been successful. Why not? Professor J. Peter Byrne explains:

> *Penn Central* has served to effectively insulate historic preservation from regulatory takings challenges for three principal reasons. First, *Penn Central* eliminated a variety of the concerns about coercive historic preservation regulations. Second, it directed attention to the value remaining in the property, and structures protected by preservation restrictions (as opposed to natural resources protected by environmental controls) nearly always have some economic value that a clever developer can exploit. Third, preservation ordinances have been drafted and administered in the light of *Penn Central* with sufficient flexibility to avoid constitutional confrontations. In general, the market has once again adapted to new land use restrictions.

J. Peter Byrne, *Regulatory Takings Challenges to Historic Preservation Laws After* Penn Central, 15 FORDHAM ENVTL. L. REV. 313, 316 (2004).

    3.   The Mayor's Agent is appointed by the mayor of the District of Columbia to act on his or her behalf to review and approve decisions made by the Historic Preservation Review Board. The Mayor's Agent need not have any particular qualifications or expertise. The Review Board acts in a merely advisory capacity to the Mayor and the Mayor's Agent. The Mayor's Agent, by contrast, is authorized to sign documents for applicants whose requests have been recommended for approval by the Review Board, and hears appeals from applicants whose requests have been recommended for denial. The Mayor's Agent need not accord decisive weight to the Review Board but must demonstrate that the Review Board's recommendations were considered to some extent. *Cf. Comm. for Washington's Riverfront Parks v. Thompson*, 451 A.2d 1177 (D.C. App. 1982) (discussing the Mayor's Agent's duties with respect to advisory opinions from the Commission on Fine Arts, an entity similar to the Review Board). Like many entities that hear reviews of preservation cases, the Mayor's Agent may consider the special merit of the project, the economic hardship on the applicant, and whether the project achieves the overall purposes of D.C.'s historic preservation law. What might be some potential areas of concern with respect to the powers of the Mayor's Agent? In the interest of full disclosure, note that one of the authors (Professor Byrne) is currently serving as D.C.'s Mayor's Agent Hearing Officer.

3. PHYSICAL TAKINGS

    The *District Intown* court mentions *Loretto v. Teleprompter Manhattan CATV Corp.*, 458 U.S. 419 (1982), as another per se takings rule from the Supreme Court. The subject of that case was a New York State law that required landlords to allow the cable company to install hardware on their property, without compensation, except some minimal amount of compensation determined by a board. The claimant was the owner of a mid-sized Manhattan apartment building. The Court held that any governmental regulation that resulted in a permanent physical occupation on private property could be considered a taking, to the extent of the occupation, because such an occupation was a governmental action of the most invasive character. Can you see why few historic preservation takings cases would invoke *Loretto*?

Consider one exception to this general rule. A Manhattan federal court found a *Loretto*-style physical taking when the New York City Landmarks Preservation Commission required a property owner to reinstall a large-scale structural sculpture (a grid of projecting steel beams) that it had removed for repairs. *See Bd. of Managers of Soho Int'l Arts Condo. v. City of New York*, 2005 WL 1153752 (S.D.N.Y. 2005). The artwork, shown in this photo, covered about seven stories' worth of wall space on the north side of a building that is designated as "contributing" to the SoHo-Cast Iron Historic District. The artwork was installed in 1973, around the same time the historic district was designated, and it was owned by a third party unrelated to the property owner. Note that the wall on which the sculpture is installed is otherwise window-less and feature-less, because the building's north side was "shaved off" as the result of the exercise of eminent domain during the widening of Houston Street.

In 1997, the property owner submitted an application to permanently remove the artwork, but it was denied a certificate of appropriateness by the Commission. The Commission found that the sculpture contributed to the architectural and historic character of the district because:

> [T]he sculpture * * * is a highly acclaimed work of art * * * by Forrest Myers, an important American artist; * * * Mr. Myers conceived of and installed the sculpture during this important time in the district's and city's history; * * * the sculpture became a symbol of Soho due to its presence at the prominent intersection of Broadway and Houston Street, and that during the intervening 28 years it has come to be known and experienced as the "gateway" to Soho; * * * the sculpture is evocative and representative of a significant era in the district's and city's history, when the cast iron buildings were being adaptively reused by artists and the area was being transformed into a world class center for contemporary and avant-garde art, and which era and transformation contributed significantly to the preservation of the cast iron buildings[.]

Bd. of Managers of Soho Int'l Arts Condo. v. City of New York, 2004 WL 1982520, at *4 (S.D.N.Y. 2004). The Commission later allowed the property owners to remove the sculpture for repairs, with the requirement that it reinstall the sculpture once the repairs were completed. Although the court acknowledged the Commission's desire to preserve the artwork, it nonetheless declared that a physical taking would occur if the artwork were actually to be reinstalled. *Bd. of Managers of Soho Int'l Arts Condo. v. City of New York*, 2005 WL

1153752, at *11–12. The court found that the Commission's decision prevented the property owner from using the wall "in any way other than as a mount for the Work; even if it could sell the property, 'the permanent occupation of that space by a stranger will . . . empty the right of any value, since the purchaser will also be unable to make any use of the property." ' *Id.* at *12 (quoting *Loretto*, 458 U.S. at 436). After the case was decided, the Landmarks Preservation Commission, the property owner, and the artist agreed that the sculpture could be installed several stories higher than its original location along the wall, so that the property owner could sell advertising space on the lower wall. That is precisely how the building appears today.

Figure 7-5:
Forrest Myers' Sculpture at 599 Broadway,
Manhattan, NY

This court found a taking in *Board of Managers* because the Commission's decision protected a modern addition that was not owned by the property owner. Can you think of any other possible instances where a board's decision or historic preservation ordinance may impose a physical taking?

B. RELIGIOUS LIBERTY

What happens when historic preservation regulations dictate one thing, but religious beliefs dictate another? Conflict occurs when a religious institution wishes to alter or replace a historic building it owns without having to comply fully with historic preservation rules, for religious reasons. The way courts have dealt with this conflict has changed over time as the Supreme Court and Congress have weighed in.

1. FIRST AMENDMENT ISSUES

Traditionally, zoning ordinances and the courts enforcing them were deferential to religious uses. *See* SARA C. BRONIN & DWIGHT H. MERRIAM, 2 RATHKOPF'S THE LAW OF ZONING AND PLANNING §§ 29:24 & 29:25 (4th ed. 2021). Over time, this level of deference eroded somewhat, as religious institutions grew in size, scope, and diversity of purpose and as land use regulations expanded beyond zoning to include historic preservation and other rules. Some religious institutions have brought lawsuits to challenge actions they view as discriminatory or infringing on the right to freely exercise their religion.

Until recently, these legal challenges have been based primarily on the First Amendment, which states in relevant part: "Congress shall make no law respecting an establishment of religion, or prohibiting the free exercise thereof." U.S. CONST. amend. I. The first part of this excerpted phrase is known as the establishment clause; the latter part, the free exercise clause. The Supreme Court has clarified that these two First Amendment religious liberty provisions prohibit governmental regulation of religious beliefs, punishment of individuals on the basis of their religious views, and involvement in settling content-based religious disputes. But there remain many legal gray areas with respect to both the establishment and free exercise clauses. This section necessarily condenses voluminous judicial material and academic commentary into a few pages, with the hope that even a brief treatment can highlight key issues.

We begin with some notes on the establishment clause. Challenges to historic preservation ordinances based on the establishment clause have primarily focused on whether religious institutions or religious users are treated differently by the ordinance, either as applied or as written. Depending on the circumstances, different treatment may be unconstitutional. A key case in this area of law is *Lemon v. Kurtzman*, 403 U.S. 602 (1971). *Lemon* set out a three-pronged test for the evaluation of the constitutionality of a statute being challenged under the establishment clause: "First, the statute must have a secular legislative purpose; second, its principal or primary effect must be one that neither advances nor inhibits religion; finally, the statute must not foster an excessive government entanglement with religion." *Id.* at 612–

13 (quotation marks omitted). The *Lemon* test is discussed in several of the cases below.

In addition to establishment clause challenges, free exercise challenges have been brought against historic preservation ordinances. A key question in such challenges is whether the free exercise clause has been violated as a result of an impermissibly high burden imposed by the ordinance. A 1963 First Amendment case, *Sherbert v. Verner*, 374 U.S. 398 (1963), established that the strict scrutiny test should be used for some free exercise claims. The facts that gave rise to *Sherbert* involved the State of South Carolina denying unemployment benefits to the plaintiff, who refused to work on Saturdays because doing so violated her religious beliefs. The Court held that the First Amendment is offended if government imposes a substantial burden on the free exercise of religion, unless a compelling interest justifies the burden. (It may be important to note that the Supreme Court decided a number of cases after *Sherbert* which further articulated its central holding, as some of the cases in this section will reveal; to limit the introductory material, we simply refer to *Sherbert* as the primary case on point.)

A second Supreme Court case involving free expression also played a role in lower courts' analysis of religious institutions' challenges of land use regulations. In *Schad v. Borough of Mount Ephraim*, 452 U.S. 61 (1981), the Court considered a case involving an operator of adult bookstore who had violated a zoning ordinance prohibiting all live entertainment. The Court held that if a zoning ordinance infringes on a protected liberty, it must be narrowly drawn and must further a sufficiently substantial government interest. This ruling gave lower courts an alternate ground on which to decide religious land use cases, as long as they decided that free exercise was a protected liberty.

The differences between *Sherbert* and *Schad*, even with these brief descriptions, should be clear. *Sherbert* addresses free exercise, while *Schad* addresses free expression. *Schad* involves land use regulations; *Sherbert* involves employment law. *Sherbert*'s scrutiny is stricter than *Schad*'s. Lower courts followed (and sometimes mixed) both.

The Supreme Court revisited the test for free exercise cases in *Employment Division, Department of Human Resources of the State of Oregon v. Smith.* 494 U.S. 872 (1990). The plaintiffs in that case were two individuals who had been dismissed from their jobs because they ingested peyote at a Native American religious ceremony. The Supreme Court noted that the conduct at issue in *Smith* (the ingestion of peyote) differed from the conduct at issue in *Sherbert* (refusing to work on Saturdays) because the conduct in *Smith* was illegal under state law. In addition, the Supreme Court differentiated the two laws at issue in the two cases, saying that the law in *Sherbert* required individual assessments, while the law in *Smith* was neutral and of general applicability. Stating that it had never previously ruled on a free exercise case involving a neutral, generally applicable rule, the Court departed from *Sherbert* to hold that: "[T]he right of free exercise does not relieve an individual of the obligation to comply with a valid and neutral law of general applicability on the ground that the law proscribes (or prescribes) conduct that his religion prescribes (or proscribes)." *Id.* at 879 (quotation marks omitted). Thus, according to the *Smith* court, a neutral law of general applicability need only meet the rational basis test to overcome a free exercise challenge. Consider the following Second Circuit case, which relies in part on *Smith* and also illuminates the way the takings clause may be applied to religious institutions.

Rector, Wardens, & Members of the Vestry of St. Bartholomew's Church v. City of New York

914 F.2d 348 (2d Cir. 1990), *cert. denied*, 499 U.S. 905 (1991)

■ WINTER, CIRCUIT JUDGE.

This appeal poses the question of whether a church may be prevented by New York City's Landmarks Law, now codified at New York City Administrative Code Sections 25–301 to 25–321 (1986), from replacing a church-owned building with an office tower. The question implicates both First and Fifth Amendment issues. Specifically, the Rector, Wardens, and Members of the Vestry of St. Bartholomew's Church ("the Church") appeal from Judge Sprizzo's decision that the New York City Landmarks Law, as applied to an auxiliary structure next to the Church's main house of worship, did not impose an unconstitutional burden on the free exercise of religion or effect a taking of property without just compensation.

The district court grounded its decision on its finding that the Church had failed to prove that the landmark regulation prevented the Church from carrying out its religious and charitable mission in its current buildings. We agree that this is the legal standard established by Supreme Court precedent governing both free exercise and takings claims. Moreover, we find no clear error in the district court's factual determinations. We therefore affirm. * * *

Background

St. Bartholomew's Church is a Protestant Episcopal Church organized in 1835 under the laws of the State of New York as a not-for-profit religious corporation. The main house of worship ("the Church building") stands on the east side of Park Avenue, between 50th and 51st Streets, in New York City. Constructed beginning in 1917 according to the plans of architect Bertram G. Goodhue, the Church building is a notable example of a Venetian adaptation of the Byzantine style, built on a Latin cross plan. Significant features include its polychromatic stone exterior, soaring octagonal dome, and large rose window. Perhaps most significantly, Goodhue incorporated into his building the Romanesque porch of St. Bartholomew's former Church building at Madison Avenue and 44th Street. Designed by the renowned architectural firm of McKim,

Mead & White, the porch is composed of a high arched central portal flanked by two lower arched doorways, all supported by slender columns. The doors themselves are richly decorated bronze, depicting Biblical themes.

Adjacent to the Church building, at the northeast corner of Park Avenue and 50th Street, is a terraced, seven-story building known as the Community House. It is the replacement of this building with an office tower that is at issue in the instant matter. Completed in 1928 by associates of Goodhue, the Community House complements the Church building in scale, materials and decoration. Together with the Church building, the Community House houses a variety of social and religious activities in which the Church is engaged. It contains a sixty-student preschool, a large theater, athletic facilities (including a pool, gymnasium, squash court, and weight and locker rooms), as well as several meeting rooms and offices for fellowship and counseling programs. A community ministry program, which provides food, clothing, and shelter to indigent persons, is operated mainly from the Church building. Meals are prepared in a small pantry on the first floor and served in the mortuary chapel. Ten homeless persons are housed nightly in the narthex.

Figure 7-6:
The St. Bartholomew's Church Complex,
Manhattan, NY

In 1967, finding that "St. Bartholomew's Church and Community House have a special character, special historical and aesthetic interest and value as part of the development, heritage and cultural aspects of New York City," the Landmarks Preservation Commission of the City of

New York (the "Commission") designated both buildings as "landmarks" pursuant to the Landmarks Law. This designation prohibits the alteration or demolition of the buildings without approval by the Commission. *See* N.Y.C. ADMIN. CODE § 25–305(a)(1) (1985).

The Church did not object to the landmarking of its property. In December 1983, pursuant to what is now New York City Administrative Code Section 25–307, the Church applied to the Commission for a "certificate of appropriateness" permitting it to replace the Community House with a fifty-nine story office tower. This request was denied as an inappropriate alteration. In December 1984, the Church filed a second application, scaling down the proposed tower to forty-seven stories. This application was also denied.

The Church thereafter filed a third application under a different procedure. Pursuant to Sections 207–4.0 and 207–8.0 of the New York City Administrative Code,[1] commonly known as the "hardship exception," it sought a certificate of appropriateness for the forty-seven story tower on the ground of the Community House's present inadequacy for church purposes. * * * [T]he Commission voted to deny the application because the Church had failed to prove the necessary hardship. Several months later the Commission issued a lengthy written determination detailing the reasons for its denial.

On April 8, 1986, the Church brought the instant action for declaratory and injunctive relief and damages pursuant to 42 U.S.C. § 1983. The complaint set forth a host of constitutional claims. It alleged that the Landmarks Law, facially and as applied to the Church, violates both the free exercise and establishment clauses of the First Amendment by excessively burdening the practice of religion and entangling the government in religious affairs. It also alleged that the Landmarks Law violates the equal protection and due process clauses of the Fourteenth Amendment because it applies different standards to charitable and commercial institutions respectively and constitutes a taking of property without just compensation. In addition, the Church alleged a variety of procedural due process violations and brought a pendent state law claim alleging that the Church should have been granted a certificate of appropriateness under New York law. * * *

In considering the Church's takings claim, the court adopted the standard articulated by New York State courts: An unconstitutional taking exists "where the landmark designation [of property owned by a charitable organization] would prevent or seriously interfere with the

---

[1] Now found at Section 25–309, the provision states that a certificate of appropriateness shall be granted to a not-for-profit applicant who shows, *inter alia*, that such

improvement has ceased to be adequate, suitable or appropriate for use for carrying out both (1) the purposes of such owner to which it is devoted and (2) those purposes to which it had been devoted when acquired unless such owner is not [sic] longer engaged in pursuing such purposes.

N.Y.C. ADMIN. CODE § 25–309(a)(2)(c) (1985).

carrying out of the charitable purpose of the institution." *St. Bartholomew's Church v. City of New York*, 728 F.Supp. 958, 966–67 (S.D.N.Y. 1989) (opinion and order). The district court applied the same test to the claim of an unconstitutional burden on religion. It thus stated, "[I]n this case, the First Amendment inquiry is identical in scope to the Fifth Amendment inquiry, since to prevail on either claim plaintiff must prove that it can no longer carry out its religious mission in its existing facilities." *Id.* at 966–67.

The district court then examined the record before the Commission in order to determine whether the Church had proved by a preponderance of the evidence that it can no longer carry out its charitable purpose in its existing facilities. * * * Having concluded that the Church had not carried its burden of demonstrating that the Landmarks Law precludes it from continuing its activities in its existing facilities, the district court rejected the Church's First and Fifth Amendment claims and entered judgment for defendants.

On appeal, the Church renews its free exercise and takings claims and argues that the district court's factual findings were clearly erroneous. * * *

Discussion

Sections 1 and 2 of this portion of the opinion reject the Church's free exercise and takings claims. Our discussion assumes the affirmance of the district court's factual findings as detailed in section 3.

1.   The Free Exercise Claim

The Church argues that the Landmarks Law substantially burdens religion in violation of the First Amendment as applied to the states through the Fourteenth Amendment. In particular, the Church contends that by denying its application to erect a commercial office tower on its property, the City of New York and the Landmarks Commission (collectively, "the City") have impaired the Church's ability to carry on and expand the ministerial and charitable activities that are central to its religious mission. It argues that the Community House is no longer a sufficient facility for its activities, and that the Church's financial base has eroded. The construction of an office tower similar to those that now surround St. Bartholomew's in midtown Manhattan, the Church asserts, is a means to provide better space for some of the Church's programs and income to support and expand its various ministerial and community activities. The Church thus argues that even if the proposed office tower will not house all of the Church's programs, the revenue generated by renting commercial office space will enable the Church to move some of its programs—such as sheltering the homeless—off-site. The Church concludes that the Landmarks Law unconstitutionally denies it the opportunity to exploit this means of carrying out its religious mission. Although the Landmarks Law substantially limits the options of the Church to raise revenue for purposes of expanding religious charitable activities, we believe the Church's claims are precluded by Supreme Court precedent.

As the Court recently stated in *Employment Division v. Smith*, 494 U.S. 872 (1990), the free exercise clause prohibits above all " 'governmental regulation of religious *beliefs* as such." ' *Id.* at 877 (quoting *Sherbert v. Verner*, 374 U.S. 398, 402 (1963) and citing cases). No one seriously contends that the Landmarks Law interferes with substantive religious views. However, apart from impinging on religious beliefs, governmental regulation may affect conduct or behavior associated with those beliefs. Supreme Court decisions indicate that while the government may not coerce an individual to adopt a certain belief or punish him for his religious views, it may restrict certain activities associated with the practice of religion pursuant to its general regulatory powers. For example, in *Smith* the Court held that the free exercise clause did not prohibit the State of Oregon from applying its drug laws to the religious use of peyote. *See* 494 U.S. 872. *Cf. United States v. Lee*, 455 U.S. 252 (1982).

The synthesis of this caselaw has been stated as follows: "[T]he right of free exercise does not relieve an individual of the obligation to comply with a 'valid and neutral law of general applicability on the ground that the law proscribes (or prescribes) conduct that his religion prescribes (or proscribes)." ' *Smith*, 494 U.S. at 879. The critical distinction is thus between a neutral, generally applicable law that happens to bear on religiously motivated action, and a regulation that restricts certain conduct because it is religiously oriented. *See id.* at 878.

The Landmarks Law is a facially neutral regulation of general applicability within the meaning of Supreme Court decisions. It thus applies to "[a]ny improvement, any part of which is thirty years old or older, which has a special character or special historical or aesthetic interest or value." N.Y.C. ADMIN. CODE § 25–302(n) (1986).

It is true that the Landmarks Law affects many religious buildings. The Church thus asserts that of the six hundred landmarked sites, over fifteen percent are religious properties and over five percent are Episcopal churches. Nevertheless, we do not understand those facts to demonstrate a lack of neutrality or general applicability. Because of the importance of religion, and of particular churches, in our social and cultural history, and because many churches are designed to be architecturally attractive, many religious structures are likely to fall within the neutral criteria—having "special character or special historical or aesthetic interest or value"—set forth by the Landmarks Law. N.Y.C. ADMIN. CODE § 25–302(n) (1986). This, however, is not evidence of an intent to discriminate against, or impinge on, religious belief in the designation of landmark sites.

The Church's brief cites commentators, including a former chair of the Commission, who are highly critical of the Landmarks Law on grounds that it accords great discretion to the Commission and that persons who have interests other than the preservation of historic sites or aesthetic structures may influence Commission decisions. Nevertheless, absent proof of the discriminatory exercise of discretion, there is no constitutional relevance to these observations. Zoning similarly regulates land use but it is hardly a process in which the exercise of discretion is constrained by scientific principles or unaffected by selfish or political interests, yet it passes constitutional muster. *See Euclid v. Ambler Realty Co.*, 272 U.S. 365 (1926).

The Church argues that landmarking and zoning differ in that landmarking targets only individual parcels while zoning affects larger segments. However, the Landmarks Law permits the designation of historic districts, *see* N.Y.C. ADMIN. CODE § 25–303(a) (4) (1986), while all zoning laws provide for variances for individual sites. Even if the two forms of regulation bear the different characteristics asserted by the Church, those differences are of no consequence in light of *Penn Central Transp. Co. v. City of New York*, 438 U.S. 104 (1978). There, the Court stated:

> [L]andmark laws are not like discriminatory, or "reverse spot," zoning: that is, a land-use decision which arbitrarily singles out a particular parcel for different, less favorable treatment than the neighboring ones. In contrast to discriminatory zoning, which is the antithesis of land-use control as part of some comprehensive plan, the New York City law embodies a comprehensive plan to preserve structures of historic or aesthetic interest wherever they might be found in the city.

Id. at 132 (citation omitted).

It is obvious that the Landmarks Law has drastically restricted the Church's ability to raise revenues to carry out its various charitable and ministerial programs. In this particular case, the revenues involved are very large because the Community House is on land that would be extremely valuable if put to commercial uses. Nevertheless, we understand Supreme Court decisions to indicate that neutral regulations that diminish the income of a religious organization do not implicate the free exercise clause. *See Jimmy Swaggart Ministries v. Bd. of Equalization*, 493 U.S. 378 (1990); *Hernandez v. Comm'r*, 490 U.S. 680 (1989). The central question in identifying an unconstitutional burden is whether the claimant has been denied the ability to practice his religion or coerced in the nature of those practices. In *Lyng v. Northwest Cemetery Protective Ass'n*, 485 U.S. 439 (1988), the Court explained,

> It is true that . . . indirect coercion or penalties on the free exercise of religion, not just outright prohibitions, are subject to scrutiny under the First Amendment. . . . This does not and cannot imply that incidental effects of government programs, which may make it more difficult to practice certain religions but which have no tendency to coerce individuals into acting contrary to their religious beliefs, require government to bring

forward a compelling justification for its otherwise lawful actions. The crucial word in the constitutional text is "prohibit". . .

We agree with the district court that no First Amendment violation has occurred absent a showing of discriminatory motive, coercion in religious practice or the Church's inability to carry out its religious mission in its existing facilities. *Cf. Yonkers Racing Corp. v. City of Yonkers*, 858 F.2d 855, 872 (2d Cir. 1988).

In sum, the Landmarks Law is a valid, neutral regulation of general applicability, and as explained below, we agree with the district court that the Church has failed to prove that it cannot continue its religious practice in its existing facilities.[4]

2. The Takings Claim

The Church also claims that the Landmarks Law so severely restricts its ability to use its property that it constitutes confiscation of property without just compensation in violation of the Fifth and Fourteenth Amendments.[5] However, the Supreme Court's decision in *Penn Central* compels us to hold otherwise.

In *Penn Central*, the Supreme Court held that the application of New York City's Landmarks Law to Grand Central Terminal did not effect an unconstitutional taking. *See* 438 U.S. at 138. That famous beaux arts style train station, located in midtown Manhattan (just eight blocks from St. Bartholomew's Church) was designated a landmark in 1967. *See id.* at 115–16. Shortly thereafter, Penn Central Transportation Company ("Penn Central"), principal owner of the Terminal, in order to increase its income, sought to build a high-rise office tower atop the Terminal. The Landmarks Commission, however, denied the proposal because " '[q]uite simply, the tower would overwhelm the Terminal by its sheer mass." ' *Id.* at 118 (quoting the record on appeal). The Supreme Court squarely rejected Penn Central's claim that the building restriction had unconstitutionally "taken" its property. Central to the Court's holding were the facts that the regulation did not interfere with the historical use of the property and that that use continued to be economically viable:

---

[4] The Church also argues that the Landmarks Law involves an excessive degree of entanglement between church and state in violation of the establishment clause. The district court dismissed this argument as irrelevant in the present context, reasoning that the entanglement doctrine applies only to instances of government funding of religious organizations. However, in *Jimmy Swaggart Ministries* the Supreme Court considered an entanglement claim in the context of government taxation of the sale of religious materials by a religious organization. The Court found no constitutional violation, as the regulation imposed only routine administrative and recordkeeping obligations, involved no continuing surveillance of the organization, and did not inquire into the religious doctrine or motives of the organization. *See* 493 U.S. at 391–95. These same factors are of course largely true of the Landmarks Law. The only scrutiny of the Church occurred in the proceedings for a certificate of appropriateness, and the matters scrutinized were exclusively financial and architectural. This degree of interaction does not rise to the level of unconstitutional entanglement.

[5] The Fifth Amendment provides in part, "nor shall private property be taken for public use, without just compensation," U.S. CONST. amend. V, and is applicable to the states through the Fourteenth Amendment.

[T]he New York City law does not interfere in any way with the present uses of the Terminal. Its designation as a landmark not only permits but contemplates that appellants may continue to use the property precisely as it has been used for the past 65 years: as a railroad terminal containing office space and concessions. So the law does not interfere with what must be regarded as Penn Central's primary expectation concerning the use of the parcel. More importantly, on this record, we must regard the New York City law as permitting Penn Central not only to profit from the Terminal but also to obtain a "reasonable return" on its investment.

Id. at 136.

Applying the *Penn Central* standard to property used for charitable purposes, the constitutional question is whether the land-use regulation impairs the continued operation of the property in its originally expected use. We conclude that the Landmarks Law does not effect an unconstitutional taking because the Church can continue its existing charitable and religious activities in its current facilities. Although the regulation may "freeze" the Church's property in its existing use and prevent the Church from expanding or altering its activities, *Penn Central* explicitly permits this. In that case, the Landmarks Law diminished the opportunity for Penn Central to earn what might have been substantial amounts by preventing it from building a skyscraper atop the Terminal. Here it prevents a similar development by the Church—one that, in contrast to the proposal to build an office tower over Grand Central Terminal, would involve the razing of a landmarked building—at least so long as the Church is able to continue its present activities in the existing buildings. In both cases, the deprivation of commercial value is palpable, but as we understand *Penn Central*, it does not constitute a taking so long as continued use for present activities is viable.

The Church offers several arguments to distinguish *Penn Central*, but we find them unavailing. First, it argues that while *Penn Central* stipulated that it was able to earn a "reasonable return" on the Terminal even under the regulation, *see* 438 U.S. at 129, in this case, the use of the Community House for commercial purposes would yield an estimated return of only six percent. Even if true, this fact is irrelevant. "Reasonable return" analysis was appropriate to determine the viability of the existing commercial use of the Terminal but has no bearing on the instant matter because the existing use of the Community House is for charitable rather than commercial purposes. So long as the Church can continue to use its property in the way that it has been using it—to house its charitable and religious activity—there is no unconstitutional taking.

Second, the Church notes that it presented a second proposal for a smaller building to the Commission, but *Penn Central* did not. This hardly makes any difference. Just as the Commission in *Penn Central* remained open to a building addition that " 'would harmonize in scale, material and character," ' 438 U.S. at 137 (quoting record on appeal), with the Terminal, it invited appellant to propose an addition to the Community House in the instant matter. Finally, we reject as unsupported appellant's argument that in *Penn Central* the property owner continued to enjoy valuable, transferrable rights to develop the airspace above the Terminal, *see* 438 U.S. at 137, while the Church's development rights have little value. *See* Section 3(a) *infra.*[6]

3.   Findings of the District Court

The principal factual finding of the district court—one central to its rejection of the Church's free exercise and takings claims—was that the Church "failed to show by a preponderance of the evidence that it can no longer conduct its charitable activities or carry out its religious mission in its existing facilities." *St. Bartholomew's Church v. City of New York,* 728 F.Supp. 958, 974–75 (S.D.N.Y. 1989) (opinion and order).

The Church claims that the Community House is an inadequate facility in which to carry out the various activities that presently comprise the Church's religious mission and charitable purpose. It further claims that it cannot afford to make the needed repairs and renovations to the Community House and Church building. It concludes that it must be allowed to replace the Community House with a revenue-generating office tower. The district court was unconvinced. It found that the Church failed to prove that the Community House is fundamentally unsuitable for its current use and that the cost of repair and rehabilitation is beyond the financial means of the Church. Appellant argues on appeal that these findings were clearly erroneous. Fed. R. Civ. P. 52(a). We disagree.

a.   Adequacy of the Community House

The Church claims that the amount and configuration of usable space in the Community House is insufficient to accommodate the Church's various programs. It relies principally upon an analysis of space in the Community House by Walker Associates, an interior design firm hired by the Church. Presented to the Commission in three written reports and related oral testimony (collectively, "the Walker Report"), this study concluded that the demands for space by the Church's various programs exceeded the capacity of the Community House. Additionally, the Walker Report stated that renovation or expansion was impractical due to the structural inflexibility of the building.

The district court discredited the Walker Report. With regard to space, there is no dispute that the Community House currently is too

---

[6]   Appellant urges further that application of the Landmarks Law to the Church does not substantially advance a legitimate state interest. While land use restrictions must be reviewed in the context of the individual property in question, the same government interest held to be valid in *Penn Central*—"preserving structures and areas with special historic, architectural or cultural significance," 438 U.S. at 129—is equally applicable here.

small. The Walker Report found that 8000 square feet of extra space is needed. The Commission placed the deficiency at about 4500 square feet.

Fatal, however, to the Church's claim is the absence of any showing that the space deficiency in the Community House cannot be remedied by a reconfiguration or expansion that is consistent with the purposes of the Landmarks Law. The Walker Report assumed that the Community House had an outmoded structure that precluded such an option. In fact, the building has a modern, light steel frame structure and was designed so that two additional floors could easily be added. Moreover, the Commission has indicated that it would be receptive to a proposal from the Church for such an addition. While expanding the amount of available space in the Community House may not provide ideal facilities for the Church's expanded programs, it does offer a means of continuing those programs in the existing building. Certainly the intermediate option of limited expansion must be thoroughly explored before jumping to replacement with a forty-seven story office building.

b.   Cost of Repair and Rehabilitation

The Church also argues that the necessary repairs to the physically deteriorating Church building and Community House would be prohibitively expensive. It relies on a study of the mechanical systems and exteriors of those buildings prepared by O'Brien, Krietzburg and Associates, a construction management firm, and submitted to the Commission through written reports and oral testimony (collectively, "the OKA Report"). The OKA Report estimated that it would cost approximately $11 million over two years to bring the buildings' mechanical, electrical, and plumbing systems into proper working order and to repair the buildings' exteriors.

The district court also rejected this conclusion, faulting the OKA Report for being biased in favor of replacement over rehabilitation, ignoring actual conditions at the property site, and using an inappropriate method of estimating costs. Further, the district court pointed to contradictory evidence presented to the Commission, both by persons opposing the proposed development and by neutral consultants. Based on this information, the court found $3 million "phased in over a period of several years" to be a reasonable estimate for repairs and replacement.

On appeal, the Church does not seriously defend the $11 million estimate contained in the OKA Report. Instead, it accepts the $3 million estimate for the work that it covers, but argues that this figure disregards certain "major elements of cost." In particular, the Church asserts that an additional $500,000 is necessary for life safety measures, $647,000 for repair of the church organ, and $360,000 for architectural and engineering fees. The City counters that the life safety additions would unnecessarily exceed building code requirements, that organ repair is not a proper expense for this proceeding, and that design fees would be negligible.

We need not rule on this dispute over approximately $1.5 million because it is not crucial to the district court's operative factual finding. As our discussion in the next section indicates, even if the potential cost of repairs totaled $4.5 million, the Church has not adequately demonstrated that it is unable to meet this expense. Thus, the district court's central finding that the Church had failed to prove that it cannot continue in its existing facilities does not hinge on whether any portion of this $1.5 million was excluded from its estimate of repair costs.

c. The Church's Finances

As a corollary to its claim that repair and rehabilitation of the Church building and Community House would be too costly, the Church argues that its financial condition does not allow it to make the necessary improvements and also continue its other programs. The district court, however, found that appellant had failed adequately to prove this assertion, a finding that is not clearly erroneous.

The Church has three primary sources of support and revenue: contributions in the form of pledges and offerings collected at worship services, income earned on investments, and fees charged for participation in activities conducted under its sponsorship. Investment income is derived from the Church's investment portfolio, known as the Consolidated Church Fund, the value of which stood at nearly $11 million at the end of 1984. The principal of this endowment consists of funds received as gifts or bequests. In addition, the Church's endowment includes a Properties Fund, representing resources in Church-owned property at acquired cost, net of depreciation, and a miscellaneous General Fund. Combined, these funds totalled just under $3.5 million at the end of 1984, giving the Church an overall endowment of about $14.3 million at that time. Over the decade preceding 1985, the Church's sources of revenue have sporadically kept pace with expenses, exceeding them in 1975, 1977, 1980, 1983 and 1984, and falling behind in 1976, 1978, 1979, 1981, and 1982. On the whole, the Church had only a slight net deficit over this period.

The Church's principal argument is that a major improvement expenditure of the type required to repair and renovate the Church building and Community House would severely damage this "precarious" balance of revenues and expenses. Because such an expenditure would come from endowment funds, the Church contends, future investment income will inevitably decline as the result of a depleted portfolio. Such a decrease in future revenues, it concludes, will produce "severe deficits."

While a reduced principal will yield less investment income, the Church has not demonstrated that its budget cannot withstand building improvement expenditures under a reasonable financing procedure. For example, as the district court noted, withdrawals from the endowment might be made gradually to minimize lost investment income, or the Church might borrow against its endowment, and repay the loan over an extended period of time. Appellant has offered no financial projections or cash flow analyses to prove that these financing methods are not feasible. Without such data, the district court's finding that the Church failed to prove prospective financial hardship is not clearly erroneous.

We also cannot ignore the paucity of evidence offered by the Church to show that other forms of revenue are not available. Its claim that a capital fundraising drive already has been exhausted as a financing possibility is undercut by evidence that longtime members of the congregation cannot recall any such drive. Also, evidence before the Commission indicated that the transferrable development rights for the airspace above the Church property are, contrary to the Church's claim, not worthless.

Finally, the Church argues that even if its endowment could withstand a building project, it is not at liberty to withdraw large sums for that purpose because of legal restrictions on the use of its investment funds. In particular, it urges that Section 717 of the New York Not-For-Profit Corporation Law prohibits the Church from expending the sums necessary to undergo a building project. That provision, however, does no more than impose upon the Church a fiduciary duty of care to manage the congregation's money in a prudent and responsible fashion, *see* N.Y. Not-for-Profit Corp. Law §§ 513, 717 (McKinney Supp.1990), and would be implicated only if the expenditures in question would unacceptably impair the Church's financial condition. * * *

Conclusion

For the reasons stated above, we affirm both the judgment of the district court in favor of the defendants-appellees. * * *

NOTES & QUESTIONS

1.   The district court opinion in the *St. Bartholomew's* case, 728 F.Supp. 958 (S.D.N.Y. 1989), was decided before the Supreme Court changed free exercise jurisprudence by handing down *Employment Division v. Smith*, 494 U.S. 872 (1990), on which the Second Circuit case relies. Instead, the district court relied on *Sherbert v. Verner*, 374 U.S. 398 (1963) and its progeny, finding that the burden on St. Bartholomew's Church was merely incidental, and not the substantial burden required to violate the free exercise clause. Based on the evidence described in the Second Circuit opinion above, do you agree?

2.   How does this court apply *Penn Central* to property used for charitable purposes? Is it fair for *Penn Central* to be applied differently to religious and other nonprofit institutions than to for-profit institutions such as Penn Central Railroad? Based on the evidence described in the opinion, do you agree with the court's assessment that the religious institution had other viable options to reconfigure or add to its space?

3.   Historic preservation ordinances may constrain religious organizations in various ways. Consider how the free exercise clause might apply if a city prohibited a church from changing its interior to facilitate

changes in liturgical practices. More cases resemble *St. Bartholomew's* in that the religious organization wants to sell or develop its valuable property to raise money for its mission. Is raising money from real estate development a fundamentally religious activity? Should it matter whether the religious organization needs the money to survive or simply wants funds to increase it religious activities? Should religious organizations have greater constitutional liberty to thrive than secular ones?

4.   The statutes of California grant nonprofit religious institutions veto power over designation of their property. *See* CAL. GOV'T CODE, §§ 25373 & 37361. To protest a designation, the religious institution must not only voice its objection, but must also "determine[ ] in a public forum that it will suffer substantial hardship, which is likely to deprive the association or corporation of economic return on its property, the reasonable use of its property, or the appropriate use of its property in the furtherance of its religious mission." *Id.* §§ 25373(d) & 37361(c).

In 2000, the California Supreme Court rejected constitutional challenges to this law from a nonprofit development corporation, several state and local architectural heritage and preservation organizations, the National Trust for Historic Preservation, thirty California cities, the American Planning Association, and the American Civil Liberties Union. *East Bay Asian Local Dev. Corp. v. State of California*, 13 P.3d 1122 (Cal. 2000), *cert. denied* 532 U.S. 1008 (2001). What interests might each of these plaintiffs have had in striking down this law? Citing *Lemon v. Kurtzman*, 403 U.S. 602 (1971), the state supreme court found that the statute did have a secular legislative purpose, did not advance religion, and "avoid[ed] any governmental entanglement with religion." *East Bay Asian*, 13 P.3d. at 1138. Which of these arguments is more convincing?

5.   Like local laws, federal statutes may be challenged on establishment clause grounds. Drafted to avoid such challenges, the regulations for the National Historic Preservation Act specifically state that the National Park Service may not consider religious significance when determining whether a property qualifies for the National Register. 36 C.F.R. § 60.4. Only religious properties "deriving primary significance from architectural or artistic distinction or historical importance" will be considered eligible. *Id.* This language is clearly drafted to avoid federal entanglement with religion by preventing the Park Service from evaluating the relative significance of religious beliefs. Are there any alternatives to this approach? As Chapter 9 discusses, federal law treats tribal sites differently, expressly allowing tribal properties of religious significance to be considered for the National Register. *See* 54 U.S.C. § 302706(a). What might explain this different treatment?

6.   At least one case was affected mid-stream by the Supreme Court's *Smith* decision. In 1990, the Supreme Court of Washington considered an as-applied challenge that two ordinances (Seattle's Landmarks Preservation Ordinance as well as a special ordinance designating a religious institution as a landmark) violated the federal and state free exercise clauses. *First Covenant Church v. City of Seattle*, 787 P.2d 1352 (Wash. 1990), *vacated and remanded by* 499 U.S. 901 (1991). The Landmarks Preservation Ordinance

included language that exempted religious institutions from certain historic preservation rules if the institution's requested alteration was "necessitated by changes in liturgy," provided that the institution and Seattle's preservation board work to find alternatives that would preserve the building's historic features. The state court found that even with this exemption, which it deemed "vague and unworkable," the ordinance failed the strict scrutiny of *Sherbert* and its progeny in part because historic preservation was not a compelling governmental interest. 787 P.2d at 1360.

The U.S. Supreme Court took certiorari. In 1991, it vacated the judgment and remanded the case back to the Washington Supreme Court for further proceedings consistent with *Smith*. Upon review, the Washington court reinstated its initial holding on the basis that *Smith* did not apply because the historic preservation laws at issue were neither neutral (because they mentioned religious institutions) nor generally applicable (because they individually assessed structures). *First Covenant Church v. City of Seattle*, 840 P.2d 174, 180–82 (Wash. 1992) (en banc).

7.   Figure 7-6, a photograph of the St. Bartholomew's complex from Park Avenue, shows the church on the left, the terraced Community House tucked in on the right (behind the temporary tent), and an active plaza between—all surrounded by tall skyscrapers. Although the Community House was added about a decade later, it was clearly done in a style meant to be compatible with architect Bertram Goodhue's original church building. How might a large-scale office tower replacement of the Community House have changed this scene?

8.   Are historic preservation laws neutral regarding religion? Are they generally applicable or do they involve individualized assessments? Does it depend, and if so, on what?

9.   Most courts, like the court in *St. Bartholomew's Church*, have upheld historic preservation ordinances against religious institutions' challenges based on the free exercise clause of the U.S. Constitution. *See, e.g.*, *First Church of Christ, Scientist v. Historic Dist. Comm'n of Town of Ridgefield*, 738 A.2d 224 (Conn. Super. 1998), *aff'd* 737 A.2d 989 (Conn. App. 1999) (rejecting a church's free exercise claims against a local historic commission prohibiting the church from installing vinyl siding).

A handful of state courts, however, have struck down historic preservation ordinances for violating *state* free exercise clauses. One example is *Society of Jesus v. Boston Landmarks Commission*, 564 N.E.2d 571 (Mass. 1990). In that case, the Supreme Judicial Court of Massachusetts considered a challenge to the Boston Landmarks Commission's designation of the interior of a church as historically significant, thus requiring the Commission's review before alterations could be made. Citing state precedents and Article 2 of the state's constitution, the court explained that:

> The designation restrains the Jesuits from worshiping "in the manner and season most agreeable to the dictates of [their] own conscience," contrary to art. 2. We are not persuaded by the commission's argument that the design and placement of, for example, the altar of the church is merely a secular question of

interior decoration. That argument misapprehends the central significance of the location and positioning of the altar to the Jesuits' religious practices. The configuration of the church interior is so freighted with religious meaning that it must be considered part and parcel of the Jesuits' religious worship. We conclude, therefore, that art. 2 protects the right freely to design interior spaces for religious worship, thus barring the government from regulating changes in such places, provided that no public safety question is presented.

Id. at 573. Ultimately, the court held that "historic preservation, though worthy, is not sufficiently compelling to justify restraints on the free exercise of religion, a right of primary importance. In short, under our hierarchy of constitutional values we must accept the possible loss of historically significant elements of the interior of this church as the price of safeguarding the right of religious freedom." *Id.* at 574. The Washington Supreme Court reached a similar result in *First Covenant Church v. City of Seattle*, 787 P.2d 1352 (Wash. 1990), *vacated and remanded*, 499 U.S. 901 (1991).

10. Do government decisions to fund or not fund historic preservation projects that aid religious buildings violate First Amendment religion clauses? During the Clinton administration, the Justice Department expressed the view that federal preservation grants to historic churches violate the Establishment Clause. This position was reversed during the George W. Bush administration in 2003, and a federal preservation grant was made to the Old North Church in Boston, the famous church from whose steeple lanterns were hung to signal Paul Revere in 1775 that the British were coming. Can churches have a secular cultural or historical significance such that government grants for their preservation do not violate the fundamental prohibition on government support for religion?

The New Jersey Supreme Court interpreted its state constitution to prohibit preservation grants by state and local governments to religious institutions; it further held that this prohibition does not violate the Establishment Clause. *Freedom From Religion Foundation v. Morris County Board of Chosen Freeholders*, 181 A.3d 992 (N.J. 2018). The U.S. Supreme Court denied certiorari. 139 S. Ct. 909 (2019). Justice Kavanaugh wrote separately for three justices to state that the New Jersey court's decision was "in serious tension with this Court's religious equality precedents." While agreeing that the case was inappropriate for granting certiorari, he stated: "At some point, this Court will need to decide whether governments that distribute historic preservation funds may deny funds to religious organizations simply because the organizations are religious." *Id.*

2. THE RELIGIOUS LAND USE AND INSTITUTIONALIZED PERSONS ACT OF 2000

After the Supreme Court decided *Smith*, strict scrutiny could not be used to evaluate the constitutionality of generally applicable land use laws. *See Employment Division, Department of Human Resources of the State of Oregon v. Smith.* 494 U.S. 872 (1990). Three years later,

Congress enacted a federal statute (the Religious Freedom Restoration Act, or RFRA) codifying strict scrutiny for a broad range of government actions affecting religious institutions. In 1997, the U.S. Supreme Court declared RFRA unconstitutional for violating the Fourteenth Amendment. 521 U.S. 507 (1997). Interestingly, the case originated as a challenge to the application of the preservation laws of Boerne, Texas. A Catholic congregation in Boerne sought to expand its tiny primary worship facility, which accommodated only about forty to sixty worshippers and was built in 1923 in the Mission architectural style of the region. *Id.* at 511. Citing the church's location within a historic district, city officials rejected the congregation's application for a building permit. The Archbishop of San Antonio, whose diocese included the small city of Boerne, filed the suit challenging the denial as a violation of RFRA. The city later advanced the argument that RFRA was unconstitutional.

The *Boerne* decision set off a political firestorm that resulted in pressure from advocates of religious institutions on Congress to restore strict scrutiny to laws of general applicability. In the wake of *Boerne*, these advocates understood that for a law like RFRA to survive constitutional scrutiny, they needed to present to Congress a body of evidence demonstrating discrimination against religious institutions. They decided to focus on two areas of law with enough cases to substantiate such allegations of discrimination: land use regulations and institutionalized persons (persons in prison and in state-run mental institutions). After holding hearings to gather evidence, Congress drafted and overwhelmingly voted in favor of the Religious Land Use and Institutionalized Persons Act (RLUIPA), which became law in 2000.

RLUIPA was more narrowly drafted than RFRA. RLUIPA applies only to cases involving religious land use and institutionalized persons (e.g., persons in prisons and state-run mental institutions). It applies to any law in which federal funding is involved (the Spending Power); any law in which interstate commerce is involved (the Commerce Power); and any land use regulation regarding which individualized assessments are made. In other words, Congress tried to overcome the defects of RFRA by (1) building a record of legislative history showing a need for remedial action ("religious discrimination"); and (2) designing the law to fall within Congressional powers authorized by the Constitution. The relevant land use regulations portions of RLUIPA are excerpted below.

Religious Land Use and Institutionalized Persons Act of 2000

42 U.S.C. § 2000cc et seq.

§ 2000cc.   Protection of land use as religious exercise

(a)   Substantial burdens

    (1)   General rule

No government shall impose or implement a land use regulation in a manner that imposes a substantial burden on the religious exercise of a person, including a religious assembly or institution, unless the government demonstrates that imposition of the burden on that person, assembly, or institution—

    (A) is in furtherance of a compelling governmental interest; and

    (B) is the least restrictive means of furthering that compelling governmental interest.

(2) Scope of application

This subsection applies in any case in which—

    (A) the substantial burden is imposed in a program or activity that receives Federal financial assistance, even if the burden results from a rule of general applicability;

    (B) the substantial burden affects, or removal of that substantial burden would affect, commerce with foreign nations, among the several States, or with Indian tribes, even if the burden results from a rule of general applicability; or

    (C) the substantial burden is imposed in the implementation of a land use regulation or system of land use regulations, under which a government makes, or has in place formal or informal procedures or practices that permit the government to make, individualized assessments of the proposed uses for the property involved.

(b) Discrimination and exclusion

(1) Equal terms

No government shall impose or implement a land use regulation in a manner that treats a religious assembly or institution on less than equal terms with a nonreligious assembly or institution.

(2) Nondiscrimination

No government shall impose or implement a land use regulation that discriminates against any assembly or institution on the basis of religion or religious denomination.

(3) Exclusions and limits

No government shall impose or implement a land use regulation that—

    (A) totally excludes religious assemblies from a jurisdiction; or

    (B) unreasonably limits religious assemblies, institutions, or structures within a jurisdiction. * * *

§ 2000cc–2. Judicial relief * * *

(b) Burden of persuasion

If a plaintiff produces prima facie evidence to support a claim alleging a violation of the Free Exercise Clause or a violation of section 2000cc of this title, the government shall bear the burden of persuasion on any element of the claim, except that the plaintiff shall bear the burden of persuasion on whether the law (including a regulation) or government practice that is challenged by the claim substantially burdens the plaintiff's exercise of religion. * * *

§ 2000cc–4. Establishment Clause unaffected

Nothing in this chapter shall be construed to affect, interpret, or in any way address that portion of the First Amendment to the Constitution prohibiting laws respecting an establishment of religion (referred to in this section as the "Establishment Clause"). Granting government funding, benefits, or exemptions, to the extent permissible under the Establishment Clause, shall not constitute a violation of this chapter. In this section, the term "granting", used with respect to government funding, benefits, or exemptions, does not include the denial of government funding, benefits, or exemptions.

§ 2000cc–5. Definitions

In this chapter: * * *

(4) Government

The term "government"—

    (A) means—

        (i)   a State, county, municipality, or other governmental entity created under the authority of a State;

        (ii) any branch, department, agency, instrumentality, or official of an entity listed in clause (i); and

        (iii) any other person acting under color of State law; and

    (B) for the purposes of sections 2000cc–2(b) and 2000cc–3 of this title, includes the United States, a branch, department, agency, instrumentality, or official of the United States, and any other person acting under color of Federal law.

(5) Land use regulation

The term "land use regulation" means a zoning or landmarking law, or the application of such a law, that limits or restricts a claimant's use or development of land (including a structure affixed to land), if the claimant has an ownership, leasehold, easement, servitude, or other property interest in the regulated land or a contract or option to acquire such an interest. * * *

(7) Religious exercise

    (A) In general

The term "religious exercise" includes any exercise of religion, whether or not compelled by, or central to, a system of religious belief.

(B) Rule

The use, building, or conversion of real property for the purpose of religious exercise shall be considered to be religious exercise of the person or entity that uses or intends to use the property for that purpose.

NOTES & QUESTIONS

1.   How does RLUIPA work? What is its scope? What must a governmental entity attempting to enforce a law challenged by RLUIPA show? Based on a reading of the statute alone, how often do you think that land use regulations survive RLUIPA challenges?

2.   Focus now on the definition of "religious exercise." The definition includes "any" exercise of religion, even if the exercise is not compelled by or central to one's religious beliefs. The drafters used this term because some prior free exercise jurisprudence required that the religious conduct for which a plaintiff was seeking protection be either compelled by or central to a religious belief. What effect did the drafters' departure from the centrality standard have on the applicability of RLUIPA?

3.   Many commentators have criticized the record created by Congress. Professor Marci A. Hamilton, for example, has written that the entire legislative history of alleged discrimination against religious institutions in land use cases included:

(1) two instances of unconstitutional state action; (2) two allegations of facts purporting to show unconstitutional government action; (3) two references to cases where the courts did not find constitutional violations and the religious entity criticized the result; (4) multiple references to garden variety zoning laws applied to churches; and (5) private, rather than governmental, expression that does not implicate constitutional violations.

Federalism and the Public Good: The True Story Behind the Religious Land Use and Institutionalized Persons Act, 78 IND. L.J. 311, 345 (2003). In fact, one of the studies presented to Congress showed that only 1 percent of religious institutions seeking a land use permit were denied. *Id.* at 351–52. If her summary is correct, does the record appear to reflect the kind of widespread, unconstitutional discrimination required to validate a broadly applicable law like RLUIPA?

4.   Should eminent domain—that is, the public power to condemn property for public use—be included in RLUIPA's definition of "land use regulation"? Senator Edward Kennedy apparently attempted to include language in RLUIPA specifically referring to eminent domain, but such language did not make it to the final bill. For contrasting opinions, see the following articles: Christopher Serkin & Nelson Tebbe, *Condemning Religion: RLUIPA and the Politics of Eminent Domain*, 85 NOTRE DAME L.

REV. 1 (2009) and Shelly Ross Saxer, *Eminent Domain Actions Targeting First Amendment Land Uses*, 69 MO. L. REV. 653 (2004).

5. Recall St. Bartholomew's Church's desire to demolish its community house to build a large office tower along with an expanded community facility including athletic facilities, pool, basketball court, theater, preschool, meeting rooms, kitchen and dining facilities. *See Rector, Wardens, & Members of the Vestry of St. Bartholomew's Church v. City of New York*, 728 F.Supp. 958 (S.D.N.Y. 1989), *aff'd*, 914 F.2d 348 (2d Cir. 1990), *cert. denied*, 499 U.S. 905 (1991). Would the Church have fared differently if it had been able to bring a claim against the City of New York based on RLUIPA?

6. RLUIPA's constitutionality has been challenged on a number of grounds. The Supreme Court has never ruled on the constitutionality of the land use provisions. However, it has upheld RLUIPA's institutionalized persons provisions against an establishment clause challenge. *See Cutter v. Wilkinson*, 544 U.S. 709 (2005). Consider how the court in the next case treats constitutional challenges made against RLUIPA's land use provisions.

7. Over the last decade, the Roman Catholic Church has sought to close underutilized churches. In Springfield, Massachusetts, the Church engaged in a battle with the city over a historic preservation ordinance creating a single property historic district that requires property owners to obtain approval before making exterior changes to the building. . The Church contended that the ordinance imposed a substantial burden in violation of RLUIPA. Is enactment of such an ordinance an individualized assessment that triggers scrutiny under RLUIPA? *See Roman Catholic Bishop of Springfield v. City of Springfield*, 724 F.3d 78 (1st Cir. 2013) (concluding that enactment itself was not an individualized assessment). Should it matter that in the *City of Springfield* case, the historic district was comprised of a single property—the church itself?

Denial of an application to modify a building in a historic district does constitute an individualized assessment, even if enactment or the ordinance does not. *See, e.g., Chabad Lubavitch of Litchfield County Inc. v. Litchfield Historic District Comm'n*, 768 F.3d 183 (2d Cir. 2014). After establishing that an individualized assessment has been made, the issue shifts to whether the denial constitutes a substantial burden. Such is the issue in the following case.

Episcopal Student Foundation v. City of Ann Arbor

341 F. Supp. 2d 691 (E. D. Mich. 2004)

■ BORMAN, DISTRICT JUDGE.

* * * Facts

The instant lawsuit involves a dispute between Plaintiff, Canterbury House, a non-profit corporation and instrumentality of the Episcopal Church, and the Defendants, the City of Ann Arbor and the Ann Arbor Historic District Commission (collectively, "Defendants"), over the proposed demolition of Canterbury House's current worship facility and construction of a new building in its place.

Canterbury House is a "religious organization serving students attending the University of Michigan in Ann Arbor, Michigan, and other Ann Arbor residents." It is currently located in a two-story building at 721 W. [EDS.: sic; should be East] Huron Street in Ann Arbor, Michigan. That address is located in the Old Fourth Ward Historic District, one of the oldest districts in the city.

Figure 7-7:
The Façade of the Canterbury House,
Ann Arbor, MI

Canterbury House contends that it offers an "unconventional approach to religion", emphasizing its spiritual community. It currently offers one weekly worship service at its West Huron facility (its "Jazz Mass"), and sponsors various social events to create a spiritual community for its members. Those social events include, amongst others, prayer and study groups, an alternative spring break, and a Saturday night concert series.

By offering these events, Canterbury House hopes to provide its members with an atmosphere that is free of drugs, alcohol, and sexual pressures, and thereby assemble a religiously based alternative to the "party scene" usually found on college campuses. Additionally, by opening its doors to others in the community who are not members of the church, the social activities allow Canterbury House to introduce those individuals to the church, and educate them in its religious mission. Thus, Canterbury House considers its social events to be "vital to the church's growth." * * *

Likewise, community outreach is central to Canterbury House's religious mission. As an example, Canterbury House's members participate in programs to feed the hungry in its community, and donate proceeds from its concert series to that cause. Finally, Canterbury House asserts that "having the congregation gather and worship as a whole" is central to its faith and its emphasis on the spiritual community.

In recent years, Canterbury House asserts it has experienced significant growth in its membership and has outgrown its current facility as a result. Due to the limited worship space in its current facility, Canterbury House contends it has been unable at times to accommodate all of the individuals who wish to attend worship services, and to seek growth. Similarly, because its current building only has a "small and outdated kitchen" and lacks a dining area, Canterbury House contends it is unable to fulfill its religious mission to help the hungry by preparing and serving meals at the church. Finally, Canterbury House asserts that the current building has no space for a student lounge, and no dedicated space for meditation. Thus, the church is unable to provide its members with an informal gathering place and an opportunity for individual worship, respectively. * * *

Canterbury House's desire to expand its current facility, coupled with its inability to find alternative property, led Canterbury House to apply for a building permit from the Ann Arbor Historic District Commission (the "Historic Commission") on March 1, 2002. Specifically, Canterbury House sought permission to demolish its current building, in order to construct a new building in its place that would enable it to fulfill its religious mission.

Canterbury House submitted detailed plans of its proposed new building in support of its application. The proposed church would have a larger meeting room to allow extended seating for worship services. In addition, the new church would have "space specifically devoted to meditation, a large dining area, a lounge, a library, an industrial size kitchen, an elevator, an 'all purpose room' that can be used for various programs, and other offices and work areas." * * *

[EDS. After the Historic Commission's denial of such permit and the State Historic Preservation Review Board's affirmation of such denial,] Canterbury House filed the instant lawsuit under 42 U.S.C. §§ 1983 and 1988. In its complaint, Canterbury House asserts that the Historic Commission's denial of its permit application to demolish its existing building and construct a new one in its place, violated Canterbury House's rights to free exercise of religion and freedom of assembly as guaranteed by * * * the Religious Land Use and Institutionalized Persons Act ("RLUIPA"), 42 U.S.C. § 2000cc. * * *

I.   The Instant Motion * * *

Plaintiff contends the Historic Commission's permit denial prevents it from engaging in its religious endeavors, and therefore, substantially burdens its free exercise of religion. * * *

Given this alleged substantial burden, Plaintiff asserts the Defendants must demonstrate that the land use regulation in question furthers a compelling government interest, and that the regulation is the least restrictive means of furthering that compelling interest. Plaintiff argues that the Defendants cannot overcome this hurdle because the Historic Preservation Ordinance, and the Historic Commission's denial thereunder, do not further a compelling government interest. Moreover, even if Defendants were able to advance a compelling interest, they cannot demonstrate that the ordinance is the least restrictive means of furthering that interest.

Defendants dispute each of Plaintiff's arguments, and, in fact, argue summary judgment is appropriate in their favor on Plaintiff's RLUIPA claim. Defendants contend that Plaintiff cannot establish that it has suffered a substantial burden on its free exercise of religion. In support, Defendants contend that the Historic Commission's denial of the demolition permit "has not caused Plaintiff to abandon the precepts of its religion nor has it put pressure on Plaintiff to modify its behavior or violate its beliefs." Moreover, Defendants assert that even if the ordinance constitutes a substantial burden, the ordinance furthers a compelling government interest—zoning—and is narrowly tailored to that interest.

Aside from these statutory arguments, Defendants contest Plaintiff's RLUIPA claim on constitutional grounds. Specifically, Defendants contend that the RLUIPA itself is unconstitutional as it (a) exceeds Congress's power under Section V of the Fourteenth Amendment, (b) exceeds Congress' powers under the Commerce Clause, and (c) violates the Establishment Clause of the First Amendment. Given these statutory and constitutional obstacles, Defendants contend summary judgment is warranted in their favor, not the Plaintiff's.

Analysis * * *

II. Religious Land Use and Institutionalized Persons Act Claim

Plaintiff argues that the Historic Commission's denial of its application to demolish its existing church violates the Religious Land Use and Institutionalized Persons Act ("RLUIPA") by imposing a substantial burden on its members' religious exercise. Defendants contest Plaintiff's argument, and assert the Commission's decision to deny Plaintiff's permit request did not substantially burden Plaintiff's religious free exercise, as contemplated under the RLUIPA. Even if it did, Defendants assert the RLUIPA is unconstitutional on multiple grounds.

At the outset, the Court observes the well-established principle that a court should defer addressing constitutional questions until it has resolved any statutory issues in the suit. If a case may be decided on statutory grounds, the court should refrain from addressing the constitutional issue. Thus, the Court begins its analysis by addressing Plaintiff's statutory claims under the RLUIPA. * * *

[A] plaintiff is entitled to protection under the RLUIPA if the plaintiff satisfies two separate tests. First, the plaintiff must establish one of three jurisdictional requirements listed under § 2000cc(a)(2)(A) through (C). After meeting the jurisdictional requirements, a plaintiff must satisfy the substantial burden test enunciated under § 2000cc(a)(1). With these prerequisites in mind, the Court turns to the arguments at hand.

A.   Jurisdictional Requirements

At the outset, Canterbury House contends that it satisfies two of the three jurisdictional requirements: interstate commerce pursuant to 42 U.S.C. § 2000cc(a)(2)(B), and an individualized assessment of plaintiff's proposed use of the property under 42 U.S.C. § 2000cc(a)(2)(C). The Court finds that Defendants' decision to deny Plaintiff's permit application constitutes an individualized assessment under a land use regulation regarding Plaintiff's proposed use of the property.

A "land use regulation" is defined by the Act as "a zoning or landmarking law, or the application of such a law, that limits or restricts a claimant's use or development of land (including a structure affixed to land), if the claimant has ownership, . . . or other property interest in the regulated land. . . [.]" (42 U.S.C. § 2000cc–5(5).) Ann Arbor's ordinance, which governs historical preservation, including the demolition of historical structures, certainly qualifies as a "land use regulation" within the Act's purview.

In addition, the Historic Commission's denial of Canterbury House's application to demolish its existing building constitutes an individualized assessment regarding the property's proposed use. Permit applications, like the one at bar, involving property situated in one of Ann Arbor's historic districts, are governed by Chapter 103 of Ann Arbor's City Code. Chapter 103 provides that applications for the alteration, removal, or demolition of a structure within an historic district must be referred to the Historic Commission, and reviewed on an individualized basis. In deciding whether to grant or deny a given application, the Historic Commission must consider each application individually in light of the five factors enumerated at § 8:409(4), and must disapprove applications "only on the basis of considerations specified" in that section. The Historic Commission's meeting minutes reveal that the commission did, in fact, review and deny Plaintiff's application based on the listed criteria.

It follows, therefore, that the Historic Commission's denial of Plaintiff's permit application constitutes an individualized assessment under a land use regulation. * * * Accordingly, the Court finds

Canterbury House has satisfied the jurisdictional requirements under 42 U.S.C. § 2000cc(a)(2)(C).

B. Substantial Burden

The Court now turns to the question of whether Defendants' denial of Plaintiff's application to demolish its existing building constitutes a "substantial burden" on Plaintiff's religious exercise within the meaning of the RLUIPA. As a preliminary issue, however, the Court must address Defendants' argument that Plaintiff has not adequately demonstrated that Defendants' actions burdened its "religious exercise".

(1) Religious Exercise

Defendants argue that the "religious" activities to which Plaintiff cites to justify demolishing its current facility are not, in fact, religious exercises. In support of this argument, Defendants point to Canterbury House's alleged religious needs to sponsor social events, including its "Saturday night concert series", feed its members and nonmembers, and provide a student lounge and meditation room. Defendants also question whether these activities are truly an integral part of Plaintiff's religious exercise, or simply designated as such for purposes of this lawsuit.

Although past cases involving religious free exercise claims under the First Amendment often analyzed whether the "religious exercise" implicated by a particular government action was central to the litigant's faith, the RLUIPA obviates the need for such an analysis by providing a statutory definition of "religious exercise". Under the RLUIPA, "religious exercise" includes "any exercise of religion, whether or not compelled by, or central to a system of religious belief." 42 U.S.C. § 2000cc–5(7)(A). The RLUIPA only requires that a claimant's beliefs are "sincerely held". *See, e.g., Westchester Day Sch. v. Vill. of Mamaroneck*, 280 F.Supp.2d 230, 239 (S.D.N.Y. 2003) (noting the government action at issue must compel action or inaction with respect to a sincerely held religious belief.) Taking the evidence in a light most favorable to the Plaintiff, the Court has no reason to doubt Plaintiff's religious beliefs are sincerely held, and will not delve further into those beliefs at this stage.

Similarly, the record supports a finding that Plaintiff's activities constitute "religious exercises", as defined by the RLUIPA. First, the RLUIPA specifically contemplates that religious exercise may include the "use, building, or conversion of real property" for religious purposes, as implicated in the case at bar. 42 U.S.C. § 2000cc–5(7)(B). Second, the religious exercises identified by Plaintiff qualify for RLUIPA's protections.

In this case, Plaintiff claims its religious mission and beliefs include: "providing a spiritual community for its members, creating a progressive and creative worship experience for its members, offering meditation, prayer and study groups for its members, and continually working to welcome new members into the congregation." Community outreach and regular worship as a whole are also "central to Canterbury House's faith and its emphasis on spiritual community."

The fact that many of these activities are not confined to religious worship does not mean, as Defendants suggest, that the acts themselves are not religious in nature. In fact, many religions offer services beyond traditional worship services as part of their religious offerings.

For example, churches often participate in charitable activities, or offer meditation and prayer groups to supplement their worship services. Likewise churches regularly hold fundraisers, such as Canterbury House's concert series, to support the church's religious endeavors. Stated differently, even Canterbury House's concert series has a religious purpose, in that it (a) enables the church to collect financial contributions to further the church's mission, and (b) provides members with an opportunity to meet and educate non-members in the community about Canterbury House's religion. In turn, such events enable Canterbury House to seek growth in its local community.

To summarize, the fact [sic] the Canterbury House's activities exceed its worship services makes them no less a part of Plaintiff's religious exercise. Given this holding, the Court must now determine whether Defendants' actions substantially burdened Plaintiff's religious exercise.

(2) Substantial Burden

As several courts have observed, the RLUIPA's history demonstrates that Congress intended to leave in tact the traditional "substantial burden" test, as defined by the Supreme Court's free exercise jurisprudence. Accordingly, this Court's analysis will be guided by cases applying the substantial burden standard in the free exercise context, as well as recent cases decided under the RLUIPA itself.

A review of such cases demonstrates that "substantial burden" has been described in myriad ways. *See, e.g., Sherbert*, 374 U.S. at 404 (occurs when a person is required to "choose between following the precepts of her religion and forfeiting [government] benefits, on the one hand, and abandoning the precepts of her religion . . . on the other."); *Thomas v. Review Bd. of the Ind. Empl. Sec. Div.*, 450 U.S. 707, 718 (1981) (exists where state "put[s] substantial pressure on an adherent to modify his religious behavior and to violate his beliefs"); *Murphy v. Zoning Comm'n of Town of New Milford*, 148 F.Supp.2d 173, 188–89 (D. Conn. 2001) (regulations must have a "chilling effect" on the exercise of religion to substantially burden religion). Conversely, a government regulation does not substantially burden one's religious exercise if it only has an incidental effect that makes it more expensive or difficult to practice the religion. *Braunfeld v. Brown*, 366 U.S. 599 (1961); *Lakewood, Ohio Congregation of Jehovah's Witnesses, Inc. v. City of Lakewood, Ohio*, 699 F.2d 303, 306 (6th Cir. 1983).

Along these lines, cases addressing alleged infringements of one's free exercise of religion may be loosely, but usefully, categorized into two camps. On the one hand, courts routinely find substantial burdens where compliance with the statute itself violates the individual's religious beliefs and noncompliance may subject him to criminal sanctions or the loss of a significant government privilege or benefit. *See Wisconsin v. Yoder*, 406 U.S. 205 (1972) (compulsory high school attendance law contrary to Amish religious beliefs); *Sherbert*, 374 U.S. 398 (denial of unemployment benefits to Seventh Day Adventist who refused to work on Saturday Sabbath). On the other hand, courts have been far more reluctant to find a violation where compliance with the challenged regulation makes the practice of one's religion more difficult or expensive, but the regulation is not inherently inconsistent with the litigant's beliefs. *See Braunfeld v. Brown*, 366 U.S. 599 (1961) (Sunday closing law made Orthodox Jewish merchants' religious observance more expensive.)

Given this split of authority, it is useful to review the landmark Supreme Court decisions that have shaped free exercise jurisprudence: *Sherbert*, 374 U.S. 398, *Yoder*, 406 U.S. 205, and *Braunfeld*, 366 U.S. 599. In *Sherbert*, the Supreme Court considered whether the denial of unemployment benefits to a Seventh Day Adventist whose employment was terminated for refusing to work on her Sabbath constituted a substantial burden on her religious free exercise. The Court concluded that it did because the state's denial "force[d] her to choose between following the precepts of her religion and forfeiting benefits, on the one hand, and abandoning the precepts of her religion in order to accept work, on the other[.]" *Sherbert*, 374 U.S. at 399–401. The Court went on to hold, "[to] condition the availability of benefits upon this applicant's willingness to violate a cardinal principle of her religious faith effectively penalizes the free exercise of her constitutional liberties." *Id.* at 404–06. The Sixth Circuit later characterized the infringement found in *Sherbert* as "severe, life-threatening economic sanctions." *Lakewood*, 699 F.2d at 306.

In *Yoder*, the Supreme Court faced the issue of whether a compulsory school attendance law which conflicted with Amish religious beliefs, and which imposed criminal sanctions for noncompliance, violated the free exercise clause. The Court held in the affirmative. In particular, the Supreme Court stated,

> The impact of the compulsory-attendance law on respondents' practice of the Amish religion is not only severe, but inescapable, for the Wisconsin law affirmatively compels them, under threat of criminal sanction, to perform acts undeniably at odds with fundamental tenets of their religious beliefs.

Yoder, 406 U.S. at 218.

Braunfeld, however, presents an insightful contrast to *Sherbert* and *Yoder*. *Braunfeld* involved a challenge to Pennsylvania's Sunday closing law by Orthodox Jewish merchants who argued that the law effectively required them to make a financial sacrifice to practice their religion. The

Supreme Court held that one's religion is not substantially burdened by a statute that makes one's religious observance more difficult or expensive. *Braunfeld*, 366 U.S. at 607.

More recently, the Supreme Court declined to find a substantial burden in *Lyng v. Northwest Indian Cemetery Protective Ass'n*, 485 U.S. 439 (1988), and *Locke v. Davey*, 540 U.S. 712 (2004). In the former, various Native American groups challenged the construction of a paved road through federal public land, asserting the construction would harm sacred areas traditionally used for religious rituals. Although the road "would interfere with [the plaintiffs'] ability to pursue spiritual fulfillment according to their own religious beliefs", the Court concluded it would neither coerce the plaintiffs into violating their religious beliefs, nor "penalize religious activity by denying any person an equal share of the rights, benefits, and privileges enjoyed by other citizens." *Lyng*, 485 U.S. at 449. In the latter case, the Supreme Court held that a state scholarship program that prohibited the use of scholarship funds for students pursuing theology degrees did not violate the Free Exercise Clause. In so holding, the Court noted that the program "imposed neither criminal sanctions or civil sanctions on any type of religious rite," and did not "require students to choose between their religious beliefs and receiving a government benefit." *Locke*, 540 U.S. at 720–21.

Also applying the standards set forth by the Supreme Court in *Sherbert*, *Yoder*, and *Braunfeld*, the Sixth Circuit addressed a congregation's challenge to its city's comprehensive zoning plan, which prohibited the congregation from constructing a place of worship on land owned by the congregation. See *Lakewood*, 699 F.2d at 305–08. Under the zoning plan, only ten percent of the city's property was designated as land on which a church could be built. The Sixth Circuit noted that the *Lakewood* ordinance did not prohibit the congregation, or any other faith, from worshiping in the city altogether. The congregation remained free to practice its faith through worship "whether the worship be in homes, schools, other churches, or meeting halls throughout the city." *Id.* at 307.

The Sixth Circuit also rejected the congregation's claim that the zoning ordinance imposed a substantial burden because land in commercial zoning districts (in which churches were permitted uses) was more expensive and less conducive to worship than the lot owned by the church. Although the "lots available to the Congregation may not meet its budget or satisfy its tastes", the Sixth Circuit held that the Free Exercise Clause "does not require the City to make all land or even the cheapest or most beautiful available to churches." *Id.*

The Sixth Circuit summarized its finding that the zoning ordinance did not impose a substantial burden of the congregation's free exercise by stating,

> [The ordinance] does not pressure the Congregation to abandon its religious beliefs through financial or criminal penalties. Neither does the ordinance tax the Congregation's exercise of its

religion. Despite the ordinance's financial and aesthetical imposition on the Congregation, we hold that the Congregation's freedom of religion . . . has not been infringed.

Id. at 307–08.

Against this background, the Court now turns to the arguments advanced by Canterbury House. Canterbury House asserts that Defendants' denial of its application to demolish its existing church constitutes a substantial burden on its religious free exercise. In particular, Canterbury House complains that because it cannot use its current building to fulfill all of its religious needs, the congregation must either be permitted to demolish its current facility and build a larger, "multi-faceted" facility, or purchase alternative property close to the University of Michigan's Ann Arbor campus (the "University"). According to Canterbury House, the latter alternative is not truly an option because there is "very little property that would suit Canterbury House's needs", and when such property becomes available, Canterbury House is outbid by "large developers" and the University. Thus, Canterbury House contends its only feasible choice is to demolish its current structure and build a new facility in its place. Because the Historic Commission denied Canterbury House's permit to do so, Canterbury House contends the Defendants have substantially burdened its religious exercise.

This Court, however, finds Canterbury House's argument to be inconsistent with the Supreme Court and Sixth Circuit precedent discussed in the preceding paragraphs. The Court finds that the burdens placed upon Canterbury House's religious exercise do not rise to level of severity contemplated by those courts' jurisprudence. * * * [T]his is not a case where Canterbury House must choose between exercising its religious beliefs and forgoing significant government benefits or incurring criminal or financial penalties. Nor does the denial of Canterbury House's permit prevent it from pursuing its religious beliefs, coerce its members into abandoning or violating those beliefs, or dissuade members from practicing their faith. In fact, the burdens imposed on Canterbury House pale in comparison to the infringing burdens found in *Sherbert* and *Yoder*. * * *

As a preliminary matter, the Court fails to understand how Defendants' permit denial substantially burdens Plaintiff's religious exercise when the solution to a majority of Plaintiff's myriad constraints appears to lie within Plaintiff's control. Plaintiff admitted at oral argument that its entire second floor—or *one half* of its current building space—is leased to commercial tenants. Given Plaintiff's alleged spacial [sic] limitations, it seems rather evident to the Court that rather than leasing that space to outsiders, the church could use its second floor to accommodate its own religious needs. At a minimum, it seems the second floor could be used (or renovated for use) as a meditation room, student lounge, and dining area, and could thereby satisfy many of Plaintiff's demands. Indeed, Plaintiff's counsel essentially conceded as much at oral argument.

Even putting aside the "second floor" option, Plaintiff's religious exercise has not been substantially burdened. First, there is no indication that Canterbury House is precluded from fulfilling its religious mission through worship as a whole, or through its various other activities, in other locations throughout the city. Nothing in the record suggests that Canterbury House could not lease or sublease an existing church or meeting hall to facilitate its worship as a whole, or its other religious endeavors. Although "[t]hese alternatives may be less appealing or more costly", neither the RLUIPA, nor the Constitution, requires Ann Arbor to subsidize the real estate market.[7]

On a side note, the Court notes that the University may open its facilities after hours to religious groups without running afoul of the Establishment Clause's prohibition on aiding or advancing religion. Indeed, banning religious use of a school facility after hours, while permitting non-religious use, violates the free speech clause of the First Amendment.

Equally important, the record demonstrates that Canterbury House presently offers or participates in many, if not all, of the religious activities which it cites in support of its substantial burden. For example, the record reveals that Canterbury House currently contributes financial assistance to the Ann Arbor Hunger Coalition, and its members currently prepare and serve meals "at many different local churches." Although it may be "incredibly beneficial" if Canterbury House were able to offer its own kitchen and dining room for such services, there is no indication that Canterbury House cannot continue to feed the hungry at such alternate locations, and thus fulfill its religious mission.

Likewise, the evidence in the record indicates that Canterbury House currently offers meditation, prayer, and study groups for its members. The Court is not convinced that the lack of a *designated* meditation space or student lounge imposes a substantial burden on Canterbury House or its members.

Finally, although Canterbury House may incur additional financial burdens, such as rental expenses to accommodate its entire congregation on occasion, or if it seeks additional growth, such financial burdens are not "substantial" under the RLUIPA. Similarly, although Canterbury House complains that other suitable land in the vicinity is too costly, or that others outbid Canterbury House when such land becomes available, those burdens do not render the City's permit denial actionable under the RLUIPA. * * *

---

[7] It also bears mentioning that there is no indication that the Historic Commission would not be receptive to requests to expand or renovate the existing facility, short of demolition. * * *

In sum, even accepting as true the burdens alleged by Canterbury House, and viewing them in a light most favorable to it, those burdens do not substantially burden Plaintiff's free exercise. * * *

For the foregoing reasons, the Court GRANTS Defendants' Motion for Summary Judgment and DENIES Plaintiff's Motion for Summary Judgment.

SO ORDERED.

NOTES & QUESTIONS

1.   Canterbury House's ability to demolish its facilities was subject to a local preservation ordinance that required prior approval of any demolition by the Ann Arbor Historic District Commission. Why did the Commission's decision to deny permission to demolish Canterbury House trigger RLUIPA?

2.   Consider Figure 7-7, a photograph of the Canterbury House, which includes part of a neighboring building. Interestingly, the entire first floor of the street-facing façade of the Canterbury House appears to have been altered with the addition of non-original plate glass doors and windows. The court did not mention these alterations in the case. In any event, the Ann Arbor Historic District Commission appeared to be primarily concerned with preserving the scale of the Old Fourth Ward Historic District, which is characterized by late nineteenth and early twentieth century two-story structures (originally residences and boarding houses) designed in the Greek Revival, Gothic Revival, Italianate, Shingle, and Queen Anne styles.

On another note, the Canterbury House is located at the outermost boundary of the historic district, just across the street from the University of Michigan campus. Should its transitional location have come into play in the court's reasoning?

3.   What activities does Canterbury House argue constitute its protectable "religious exercise"? Do you agree with the court's broad reading of this term, which expands the definition beyond activities directly involving worship or prayer?

At least some courts have protected auxiliary uses—that is, non-worship uses—of religious institutions bringing RLUIPA claims via the statute's definition of "religious exercise." Some scholars believe that expansive readings of "religious exercise" are problematic for local governments, especially in extreme cases, such as those involving megachurches that may include thousands of congregants and offer non-worship uses ranging from commercial fast food restaurants to basketball courts to retirement communities. *See* Sara C. Galvan, *Beyond Worship: the Religious Land Use and Institutionalized Persons Act of 2000 and Religious Institutions' Auxiliary Uses*, 24 YALE L. & POL'Y REV. 207 (2006). Others are less concerned with the broad reading of "religious exercise" because courts have limited RLUIPA's applicability by reading the "substantial burden" term narrowly. *See* Shelly Ross Saxer, *Faith in Action: Religious Accessory Uses and Land Use Regulation*, 2008 UTAH L. REV. 593. Professor Saxer's view appears to be supported by the court's analysis in *Episcopal Student Foundation*.

4. Why does the court find that Canterbury House had not suffered a "substantial burden"? Most involve zoning cases where a locality has prevented a religious group from locating within its borders. Some courts have held that zoning imposes a substantial burden when it renders religious exercise "effectively impracticable." *See, e.g., Civil Liberties for Urban Believers v. City of Chicago*, 342 F.3d 752, 761 (7th Cir. 2003). Others have developed a "bad faith" test that addresses grounds for denial that appear baseless. *See, e.g., Westchester Day Sch. v. Vill. of Mamaroneck*, 504 F.3d 338 (2d Cir. 2007) (finding RLUIPA violation from denial of a special permit for expansion of a religious school). Making sense of the substantial burden component has troubled courts in land use cases. But no court has found a preservation ordinance to impose a substantial burden under RLUIPA. The following case demonstrates what may follow if a court does find a substantial burden or, as occurs in the case, if the parties concede it.

5. If a court finds that the application of a historic preservation regulation does constitute a substantial burden, it might conclude that the regulation violates RLUIPA. In *Mount St. Scholastica, Inc. v. City of Atchison*, 482 F. Supp. 2d 1281 (D. Kan. 2007), the parties seem to have conceded that the denial of permission to a monastic community to demolish its "Administration Building" imposed a substantial burden on its religious practice. Although the case was brought under the free exercise clause rather than RLUIPA, the court held that *Smith* did not apply because the preservation ordinance, although neutral toward religion, required an individualized, case-by-case consideration of the grounds for demolition. As such, the court employed strict scrutiny, concluded that preservation did not constitute a compelling state interest, and granted summary judgment to the plaintiff. Arguably, the court made too much of the individualized determination of preservation permits in light of its neutrality toward religion. However, RLUIPA becomes applicable by its terms to land use regulations making "individualized assessments," and such regulations may fall outside *Smith's* lenient standard for statutes of general applicability. Can you identify situations in which a court would likely find that historic preservation advances a compelling state interest?

C. FREE SPEECH

The enforcement of historic preservation ordinances sometimes conflicts with the desires of property owners or others to express themselves. Aggrieved parties may appeal to the courts for relief through the free speech clause in the First Amendment of the U.S. Constitution: "Congress shall make no law * * * abridging the freedom of speech." U.S. CONST. amend. I. In general, the Supreme Court has interpreted this provision to require strict scrutiny when a governmental regulation singles out the press, takes aim at a small group of speakers, or engages in content-based discrimination. Strict scrutiny, however, is not required for regulations that aim to accomplish non-speech related goals, as long as the regulation passes some lesser scrutiny.

The Supreme Court has considered many free speech challenges to land use regulations such as zoning ordinances, although it has not considered free speech clause challenges to historic preservation ordinances specifically. Lower courts have handled free speech clause challenges to historic preservation ordinances by following the Supreme Court's decisions on land use regulations. This Chapter will cover two cases dealing with First Amendment based challenges.

1.   THE LEVEL OF SCRUTINY

Consider the following First Circuit case that outlines the considerations required to determine the appropriate level of constitutional scrutiny.

Globe Newspaper Company v. Beacon Hill Architectural Commission
100 F.3d 175 (1st Cir. 1996)

■ Before TORRUELLA, CHIEF JUDGE, CUMMINGS and CYR, CIRCUIT JUDGES.

■ TORRUELLA, CHIEF JUDGE. * * *

Defendant-Appellant Beacon Hill Architectural Commission (the "Commission") enacted a regulation, the Street Furniture Guideline, which effectively bans newspaper distribution boxes from the public streets of the Historic Beacon Hill District in Boston, Massachusetts (the "District"). The validity of this regulation was challenged in a suit filed in district court by Plaintiffs-Appellees, a group of newspaper publishers (the "Newspapers"). The district court held that the Commission lacked the authority to adopt the regulation and also that it violated rights guaranteed by the First Amendment.

In the ensuing appeal by the Commission, we concluded that the appropriate course of action was to certify the dispositive issue of state law to the Supreme Judicial Court of Massachusetts (the "SJC") and so proceeded. To the question

> Did the Beacon Hill Architectural Commission have the authority under 1955 Massachusetts Act Chapter 616 (as amended) to adopt the "Street Furniture Guideline"?

the SJC answered in the affirmative. *See Globe Newspaper Co. v. Beacon Hill Architectural Comm'n*, 659 N.E.2d 710 (Mass. 1996). In its response, the SJC held that the Commission had authority to regulate newsracks and other "street furniture" through rulemaking and to completely ban entire classes of structures such as newsracks. *Id.* at 590–91, 659 N.E.2d 710. Specifically, it said:

> As to streets and sidewalks, the [C]ommission's jurisdiction is concurrent with appropriate municipal agencies. Regulation of the sidewalks is rationally related to the goal of preserving the Historic Beacon Hill District. Section 4 of the enabling [A]ct provides the [C]ommission with the authority to issue rules that govern private conduct within its particular geographic area of responsibility. We conclude that, apart from constitutional considerations, outright bans on certain classes of structures are merely a practical consequence of the [C]ommission's ability to proscribe inappropriate exterior architectural features within the [D]istrict.

Id. We thus focus our attention on the constitutional issue, which requires us to determine whether the Street Furniture Guideline violates rights guaranteed by the First Amendment to the Newspapers. We conclude that it does not and reverse the decision of the district court.

Background

The Historic Beacon Hill District was created by an act of the Massachusetts General Court in 1955. [EDS: The "Massachusetts General Court" is not a court, but refers to a legislative session.] The Act is intended to

> promote the educational, cultural, economic and general welfare of the public through the preservation of the historic Beacon Hill district, and to maintain said district as a landmark in the history of architecture and as a tangible reminder of old Boston as it existed in the early days of the commonwealth.

1955 Mass. Acts ch. 616, § 2. The District's historical significance can hardly be doubted. Indeed, it was listed in the National Register of Historic Places and designated a National Historic Landmark on October 15, 1966 * * *.

The Commission was created to review proposed changes to the "exterior architectural feature[s]" of "structures" within the District. Anyone wishing to construct, reconstruct or alter an exterior architectural feature is required to apply to the Commission for a certificate of appropriateness. The Commission, "[i]n passing upon appropriateness," shall consider, *inter alia*, "the historical and architectural value and significance, architectural style, general design, arrangement, texture, material and color of the exterior architectural feature involved and the relationship thereof to the exterior architectural features of other structures in the immediate neighborhood." 1955 Mass. Acts ch. 616, § 7. Furthermore, the Commission must "spread upon its records the reasons for [its] determination" that a certificate of appropriateness should not issue. *Id.* An aggrieved party may appeal the Commission's decision to the Superior Court for Suffolk County, which "shall annul the determination of the [C]ommission" if it is "unwarranted by the evidence" or "insufficient in law." *Id.* § 10.

As previously noted it was not surprising that, "given the stream of applications for certificates of appropriateness, the Commission developed uniform policies toward certain recurring types of proposed alterations." *Globe Newspaper Co. v. Beacon Hill Architectural Comm'n,* 40 F.3d 18 (1st Cir. 1994). Specifically, in 1981, it formally adopted the policies as "guidelines." These guidelines regulate exterior architectural features such as masonry, roofs, windows, sash and shutters, doors, trim, paint, and ironwork. One of the guidelines states that "[f]reestanding signs are not permitted."

In the District, the Newspapers distribute their publications via home delivery, mail, store sales, street vendors, and "newsracks." Newsracks, we explained, are newspaper distribution boxes painted in various colors and featuring the name of the newspaper and other advertising logos, which are commonly anchored to lampposts, signposts, or fixtures on the sidewalk. The plaintiffs maintain a total of thirty-nine newsracks in the district.[2] Within the District, there are eleven stores that distribute, or are available to distribute, the Newspapers' publications. Outside the District, but within one block of the District's boundaries, the Newspapers' publications are sold through stores and newsracks. It is undisputed that no point within the District is more than 1,000 feet (approximately 1/5 of a mile) from a source of the Newspapers' publications.

Newsracks were first introduced to the District in the early 1980s, and by 1983, Beacon Hill residents had begun to complain of the "unsightliness, congestion and inconvenience associated with the vending machines." The Commission believed that the newsracks violated the guideline prohibiting free-standing signs. It took no enforcement action, however, because a city-wide regulation of newsracks was being discussed in the early 1980s.

In 1990, no regulation having been adopted, the Beacon Hill Civic Association petitioned the Commission for a guideline to exclude newsracks from the District. * * *

[In 1991, t]he Commission adopted a new guideline—the present Street Furniture Guideline—that bans all "street furniture," not just newsracks, from the District:

> Street furniture, as defined below, shall not be permitted in the Historic Beacon Hill District with the exception of approved store-front merchandise stands and those structures erected or placed by authorized public agencies for public safety and/or public welfare purposes. Street furniture is defined as any

---

[2]   The thirty-nine newsracks maintained by the Newspapers are broken down as follows: *Boston Globe* (9); *Boston Herald* (10); *The New York Times* (8); *The Wall Street Journal* (4); *USA Today* (3); and *TAB* (5). In addition to the Newspapers' newsracks, at least five other publishers maintain newsracks within the District.

structure erected or placed in the public or private ways on a temporary or permanent basis.

Authorized public safety/public welfare street furniture includes, but is not limited to, such structures as street lights, traffic lights, mail boxes, fire hydrants, street trees, and trash receptacles. Any such authorized public safety/public welfare street furniture or approved store-front merchandise stands shall be subject to Commission review and shall be in keeping with the architectural and historic character of the District and the criteria for exterior architectural features as specified in Chapter 616 of the Acts of 1955 as amended. * * *

Discussion

I.   The First Amendment and the Street Furniture Guideline * * *

B.   Legal Framework

The First Amendment states that "Congress shall make no law . . . abridging the freedom of speech, or of the press." U.S. CONST. amend. I. It is beyond dispute that the right to distribute newspapers is protected under the First Amendment. Here, the parties do not dispute that the Street Furniture Guideline effectively bans the use of newsracks as a method of distributing newspaper in the District. The issue, of course, is whether under the circumstances of the case, the Newspapers' First Amendment rights are impinged. We know that few constitutional rights, if any, are absolute, and in most constitutional litigation what courts are called upon to do is to balance competing fundamental rights. Such is the present situation.

It is by now axiomatic that the degree of protection provided by the Constitution depends "on the character of the property at issue." *Perry Educ. Ass'n v. Perry Local Educators' Ass'n*, 460 U.S. 37, 44 (1983). In the instant case, the "property at issue" is the District's streets and sidewalks. The Supreme Court has repeatedly recognized public streets "as the archetype of a traditional public forum." *Frisby v. Schultz*, 487 U.S. 474, 480 (1988) (noting that "[n]o particularized inquiry into the precise nature of a specific street is necessary" as all public streets are public fora). In these traditional public fora, "places which by long tradition or by government fiat have been devoted to assembly and debate," *Perry*, 460 U.S. at 45, government's authority to restrict speech is "sharply circumscribed." *Id.* As the Court in *Perry* explained,

> [f]or the state to enforce a content-based exclusion it must show that its regulation is necessary to serve a compelling state interest and that it is narrowly drawn to achieve that end.

Id. In traditional public fora, content-based restrictions are presumptively invalid and subject to "strict" scrutiny. The Court in *Perry* made clear, however, that in traditional public fora

[t]he state may also enforce regulations of the time, place, and manner of expression which are content-neutral, are narrowly tailored to serve a significant government interest, and leave open ample alternative channels of communication.

Perry, 460 U.S. at 45. Such time, place, and manner regulations are subject to "intermediate" scrutiny. *See, e.g., National Amusements, Inc. v. Town of Dedham*, 43 F. 3d 731, 736 (1st Cir. 1995).

Given the "differing analytic modalities, it is unsurprising that many First Amendment battles over the constitutionality of government regulations start with a debate about what level of scrutiny is appropriate." *Id.* at 737. The instant case is no exception. The key issue is thus determining whether the Street Furniture Guideline is content-based or otherwise has a content-based impact in which publications, particularly newspapers, are singled out for negative treatment, as is claimed by the Newspapers, or is content neutral on its face and application, as is alleged by the Commission. The answer to this inquiry will allow us to establish what level of scrutiny, strict or intermediate, is appropriate, a finding which will ultimately settle the outcome of this controversy.

C.   Content-Neutrality and Content-Based Impact

As this circuit has noted, "[t]he concept of what constitutes a content-based as opposed to a content-neutral regulation has proven protean in practice." *Id.* at 737. The Court's cases "teach that the 'principal inquiry in determining content neutrality, in speech cases generally and in time, place, or manner cases in particular, is whether the government has adopted a regulation of speech because of disagreement with the message it conveys.' " *Id.* "A regulation that serves purposes unrelated to the content of expression is deemed neutral, even if it has an incidental effect on some speakers or messages but not others." *Ward v. Rock Against Racism*, 491 U.S. 781, 791 (1989).

Under this test, the Street Furniture Guideline seems to be the very model of a content-neutral regulation. It does not make or otherwise demand reference to the content of the affected speech, either in its plain language or in its application. Indeed, as applied to newsracks, it operates as a complete ban without any reference to the content of a given publication whatsoever: uniquely concerned with the physical structure housing the speech, it restricts only the mode of distribution and would plainly apply even if they were empty. * * * [T]he Street Furniture Guideline is directed at aesthetic concerns and is unrelated to the suppression of ideas: indeed, nothing in the record suggests that the challenged regulation arose out of an effort to suppress any particular message communicated through the newsracks, nor do the Newspapers even contend as much.[9] That the Street Furniture Guideline results in a

---

[9]   We note further there is no suggestion, let alone argument, that the Street Furniture Guideline is content-based because it is "format-based," applying only to print media, or

total ban on newsracks is nothing more than an incidental effect of its stated aesthetic goal of enhancing the historic architecture of the District by reducing visual clutter: there is nothing in the record to contradict this. * * *

We note first that, to the extent the Newspapers' "targeting" and "differential treatment" arguments essentially rest upon the notion that strict scrutiny is always justified when the practical effect of a regulation is to regulate the First Amendment rights of a select group, this notion is misguided. *National Amusements*, 43 F.3d at 739. Simply put, this notion

> flies in the teeth of the secondary effects doctrine. Under [this] formulation, any regulation that has an effect on fewer than all First Amendment speakers or messages could be deemed to be a form of targeting and thus subjected to strict scrutiny. Yet the Supreme Court has recognized that a municipality lawfully may enact a regulation that "serves purposes unrelated to the content of expression . . . even if it has an incidental effect on some speakers or messages but not others."

Id. at 740 (quoting *Ward*, 491 U.S. at 791). More importantly,

> [i]n *Minneapolis Star*, the Court did not condemn all regulations that single out First Amendment speakers for differential treatment; rather, the Court acknowledged that certain forms of differential treatment may be "*justified by some special characteristic*" of the regulated speaker.

National Amusements, 43 F.3d at 740 (quoting *Minneapolis Star*, 460 U.S. at 585). Most relevant to the instant case, noting that "[s]econdary effects can comprise a special characteristic of a particular speaker or group of speakers," this court concluded that "the language . . . quoted from *Minneapolis Star* comfortably accommodates an exception to the prohibition on differential treatment for regulations aimed at secondary effects, so long as the disparity is reasonably related to a legitimate government interest." *National Amusements*, 43 F.3d at 740.

The Street Furniture Guideline falls within that exception. As an initial matter, we note that there is no indication that the Commission's alleged "targeting" or "differential treatment" was done in a purposeful attempt to interfere with the Newspapers' First Amendment activities: while it clearly takes away one method of distribution, other methods are left untouched.

More importantly, "street furniture" can obviously create or add to visual clutter in different ways such that solutions calling for differential treatment might be warranted. *Cf. Renton v. Playtime Theatres, Inc.*, 475 U.S. 41, 49 (1986) (noting that city treats certain movie theaters differently based on the markedly different effects upon their

---

"distribution-based," applying only to newsracks: in other words, no argument that the SFG is designed to suppress a particular message carried only through either of these two media. * * *

surroundings). *See Discovery Network*, 507 U.S. at 430 (noting that unlike speech in *Renton* "there [were] no secondary effects attributable to" the commercial-publication newsracks that distinguished them from the non-commercial publications newsracks). While the Newspapers complain that the Street Furniture Guideline "affects no other similarly situated object" in the District, the truth of the matter is that there simply is no other such object. Not only is there no record evidence that any other entity—public or private—uses newsracks or other objects that are similarly anchored to lampposts, signposts, or fixtures on the sidewalks to distribute its product to the public, but there is also no record evidence that such an entity would not be subject to the challenged regulation. In our view, that there is no such evidence, let alone a suggestion to that effect, only underscores the "uniqueness" of the newsracks and the way in which they impact upon the District. * * *

Finally, we are unpersuaded by the Newspapers claim that, because the regulation deprives publishers of an already significant and still growing percentage of their readers, its impact is hardly "incidental." While, as alleged by the Newspapers, newsracks may indeed be the "indisputable workhorse" of the daily press (a contention belied by the evidence regarding the District), nothing in the record suggests, let alone demonstrates, how the removal of the District's newsracks is so burdensome that it is not "incidental." As we see it, the Newspapers' complaint boils down to the potential reader passing through the District or the non-subscribing resident and, as we discuss later, ample alternative channels exist for the Newspapers to reach even these accidental transients passing through the District as well as those readers with more frequent ties to the District.

In sum, we find no cognizable basis for invoking strict scrutiny and, thus, apply an intermediate level of scrutiny.

D.   The Street Furniture Guideline Under Intermediate Scrutiny

Strict scrutiny aside, restrictions on the time, place and manner of protected expression in a public forum—and the Street Furniture Guideline's effective ban on newsracks upon the District's public and private ways certainly qualifies as such a restriction—should be upheld so long as they are "content-neutral, . . . narrowly tailored to serve a significant governmental interest, and allow for reasonable alternative channels of communication." *Perry*, 460 U.S. at 45. As we have already discussed, the Street Furniture Guideline is content-neutral. We turn, thus, to the remainder of the analysis.

Aesthetics: A Significant Government Interest?

Pointing to the fact that preservation of the District "as a landmark" is mandated by state law, see Acts of 1955, ch. 616, § 12, the Commission contends that its interest in preserving the District's historic and architectural character is a substantial government interest that justifies a narrowly tailored restriction. The Newspapers roundly disagree, arguing that the Commission's invocation of its statutory purpose cannot justify a ban of newsracks in a public forum. The district court did not decide either way. Instead, it took for granted that the Commission satisfied the significant government interest prong when it "assume[d] arguendo that the Commission's [a]esthetic interest is greater than that of the average community, because [the District] has been designated a special historic district." *Globe Newspaper*, 847 F.Supp. at 194.

The Commission has certainly met the "significant governmental interest" prong. On more than one occasion, the "Court has recognized aesthetics . . . as [a] significant government interest[ ] legitimately furthered through ordinances regulating First Amendment expression in various contexts." *Gold Coast*, 42 F.3d at 1345 (citing cases). Although there is no need to accord the Commission a greater than average interest in aesthetics, it would not be unreasonable to do so given its statutory mandate as well as the District's significance to both Massachusetts and the nation as a whole, as evidenced by its designation as a National Historic Landmark. *See* 36 C.F.R. § 65.2 (stating that such designations are reserved for "properties of exceptional value to the nation as a whole rather than to a particular State or locality").

We are not swayed by the Newspapers' claim that the Commission's aesthetic interests cannot constitute a significant government interest where a ban in a public forum is involved. Although it did not explicitly address, or otherwise test, the legitimacy of aesthetics through a public forum lens, the Court in *Discovery Network* acknowledged that the city's asserted interest in aesthetics was an "admittedly legitimate" interest justifying its regulation of sidewalk newsracks. *Discovery Network*, 507 U.S. at 424–25 (holding that newsrack regulation's distinction between commercial and non-commercial speech bore no relationship "whatsoever" to its asserted aesthetic interest). Indeed, the Newspapers' contentions to the contrary, there is abundant authority for the proposition that aesthetic interests constitute a significant government interest justifying content neutral, narrowly tailored regulations of a public forum that leave open ample alternative channels.

Our conclusion that the Commission's specified interests are "significant" does not end the inquiry. As "[i]n most cases, the outcome [of this prong] turns not on whether the specified interests are significant, but rather on whether the regulation is narrowly tailored to serve those interests." *Gold Coast*, 42 F.3d at 1345.

Is the Street Furniture Guideline Narrowly Tailored?

As the district court correctly set forth, the Court in *Ward* "explained that the narrow tailoring requirement does not mandate a least restrictive means analysis: '[r]ather, the requirement of narrow tailoring is satisfied so long as the . . . regulation promotes a substantial government interest that would be achieved less effectively absent the regulation.' " *National Amusements*, 43 F.3d at 744 (quoting *Ward*, 491 U.S. at 799). The regulation will be valid if it does not burden "substantially more" speech than is necessary to further the government interest. *Ward*, 491 U.S. at 799; see *Gold Coast*, 42 F.3d at 1345. Where aesthetic interests are at play, the challenged regulation must be judged by overall context: the government must show that the regulation of the feature at issue "would have more than a negligible impact on aesthetics," which generally requires that the government be making a *bona fide* or "comprehensive coordinated effort" to address aesthetic concerns in the affected community. *See Metromedia, Inc. v. San Diego*, 453 U.S. 490, 531 (1981). * * *

We * * * conclude that the regulation is narrowly tailored. First, and without a doubt, it promotes the Commission's significant or substantial government interest in preserving the District's aesthetics: as the SJC observed, "the [C]ommission has determined that [newsracks] are inappropriate, in part because they did not exist at the time with which the [C]ommission's preservation efforts are concerned." *Globe Newspaper*, 659 N.E.2d 710. Second, as the Report's review of the five available alternatives indicate, the Commission's aesthetic interest in preserving the District's historic and architectural character would not be achieved as effectively, absent the regulation: banning the newsracks would effectively, as the Commission's Report observed, most completely "reverse" their inappropriateness and "be most consistent with the purposes of the [D]istrict." Finally, it does so without burdening "substantially more" speech than is necessary: it does not burden, or otherwise adversely affect, any other means of distribution, including the use of street vendors in the public forum. * * *

In reaching our conclusion, we are mindful of the district court's "findings" that the Commission's interest could be met by, say, "subjecting newsracks and other street furniture to the same review process as store-front merchandise racks," and that it treats some "street furniture" with "preference." Unlike the district court, however, we do not conclude that such findings compel a determination—at least in this case—that the Street Furniture Guideline burdens "substantially more" speech than is necessary to accomplish its purpose and, thus, is not narrowly tailored. While the district court correctly considered the fact that less-burdensome alternatives exist, it gives too much weight to that fact alone. In so doing, it essentially discounts from the equation *Ward*'s inquiry into whether the Street Furniture Guideline "promotes [the Commission's interests such] that [they] would be *achieved less effectively absent the [Street Furniture Guideline]*." *Ward*, 491 U.S. at 799. * * *

Our conclusion is not swayed by the Newspapers' protestations that the Street Furniture Guideline, as applied to Charles Street (the most commercial in the District), is a "lost cause" and that the regulation does not remove all evidence of modern life. It is also not influenced by the district court's finding that there has been "no showing that newsracks are any more inherently out of keeping with the architectural character of the [D]istrict than other modern innovations." 847 F.Supp. at 194–95.

These contentions miss the point. As the SJC correctly observed, "the [C]ommission's charge is to preserve what it can of the . . . District as a tangible reminder of old Boston. That particular nonconforming uses predated that charge . . ., or that certain non-conforming uses have since been allowed to continue, has no effect on ongoing attempts the [C]ommission makes in preserving the [D]istrict." * * *

What is more, the Newspapers' argument, which is implicitly based on the notion that newsracks within the District may only be regulated as part of a comprehensive beautification or, better yet, "visual clutter reduction" plan, was rejected foursquare by the Court in *Members of City Council of City of Los Angeles v. Taxpayers for Vincent*, 466 U.S. 789, 807 n. 5 (1984) and *Metromedia*, 453 U.S. at 511–12. In any event, we dismiss as disingenuous the Newspapers' suggestion that the challenged regulation is not part of a "comprehensive" plan because it does not ban all "street furniture" or all evidence of modern life: not only is the Street Furniture Guideline consistent with its long-standing prohibition against freestanding signs, the Commission's guidelines, review process, decisions regarding cable television control boxes and traffic control boxes, not to mention its thorough approach regarding newsracks, all speak for themselves.

Last, but not least, contrary to the Newspapers' suggestion, that the Street Furniture Guideline operates as a complete ban does not, by itself, mean that it is not "narrowly tailored." While the Court has clearly "voiced particular concern with laws that foreclose an entire medium of expression," *City of Ladue v. Gilleo*, 512 U.S. 43, 55 (1994) (invalidating ordinance banning all residential signs), bans on the use of privately owned structures or displays on public property have been upheld. * * *

In sum, we conclude—contrary to the district court—that the Street Furniture Guideline is narrowly tailored.

The Final Hurdle: Ample Alternative Channels?

The district court did not reach this final prong, but we must before the full First Amendment analysis is completed.

Below, and on appeal, the Commission claims that ample alternative channels exist. The challenged regulation, it points out, leaves unaffected the Newspapers' primary means of distribution within the District: home delivery, sales by stores, street vendors, and mail. Even without newsracks, the Commission highlights, the Newspapers' publications are available within the District 24-hours a day, seven days a week, through private stores. Further still, it is undisputed that no point within the District is more than 1,000 feet (approximately 1/5 of a mile) from a source of publications and that adjacent to the District numerous additional sources exist, including newsracks: this, it emphasizes, is well within the 1/4 mile distance that the Sixth Circuit found sufficient in *Plain Dealer* when it upheld a ban on newsracks in a residential neighborhood. *See Plain Dealer Publ'g Co. v. City of Lakewood*, 794 F.2d 1139, 1147 (6th Cir. 1986). * * *

[T]he Newspapers counter with the argument that the availability of private sources is irrelevant to the inquiry. Accordingly, they claim that the only relevant available means of distribution is the use of street vendors in the public forum. While street vendors are unaffected by the Street Furniture Guideline, the Newspapers nonetheless contend that, because the cost of 24-hour street vending is substantially more burdensome than placing stationary newsracks, the regulation fails to leave available any practical or economical alternative to newsracks.

We are unpersuaded by the Newspapers' arguments regarding street vendors. * * *

In reaching this conclusion we reject as essentially irrelevant the contention that the cost of street vendors, let alone 24-hour street vending, is substantially more costly than placing a stationary newsrack. The First Amendment does not guarantee a right to the most cost-effective means of distribution or the rent-free use of public property. Moreover, the Newspapers' claim that street vendors are not a practical alternative is belied by the record, particularly with respect to the daily papers serving the Boston area: sales by street vendors for both the *Boston Herald* and the *Boston Globe* exceed those by newsracks. What is more, the record shows that newsracks come in either last or second-to-last place in terms of percentage of distribution. * * *

In addition, our conclusion is not swayed by the assertion that street vending may not be a viable alternative for all publications, particularly those that are free, such as the TAB. While we are aware that the Court, with good reason, "has shown special solicitude for forms of expression that are much less expensive than feasible alternatives and hence may be important to a large segment of the citizenry, . . . this solicitude has practical boundaries." *Vincent*, 466 U.S. at 812 n.30. Given that the regulation neither affects the TAB's primary means of distribution, the mail, which accounts for 79% of its distribution, nor prohibits the use of street vendors, such "practical boundaries" exist here. In any event, absent any record evidence regarding the feasibility or infeasibility of street vending for free publications, such as the *TAB*, we are particularly reluctant to treat free publications differently than those "for charge," or to otherwise alter our conclusion. * * *

Here, because the SFG leaves intact an alternative means of distribution within the public forum, and in the absence of any record evidence "call[ing] into legitimate question the adequacy of the alternate routes for [distribution]," *National Amusements*, 43 F.3d at 745, we conclude that the Street Furniture Guideline's effective ban on newsracks in no way runs afoul of the Newspapers' First Amendment right to distribute their publications. Accordingly, with this last prong satisfied, we find that the challenged guideline passes muster under the First Amendment: it is a reasonable, content-neutral time, place and manner restriction on the Newspapers' right to distribute their publications in the District. * * *

Conclusion

For the foregoing reasons, the * * * case is remanded to the district court for entry of judgment in favor of the Commission, and for such further necessary and appropriate proceedings and orders as are consistent with this decision.

NOTES & QUESTIONS

1.   The Beacon Hill neighborhood is one of the most well-preserved neighborhoods in the country. A National Historic Landmark District, it includes important historical sites, Federal-style rowhouses, and the Massachusetts State House (the state's seat of government), designed by renowned architect Charles Bulfinch. For further perspective on the district, see *Opinion of the Justices to the Senate*, 128 N.E.2d 563 (Mass. 1955) (upholding the creation of Historic Beacon Hill District).

Beacon Hill is also one of the most expensive neighborhoods in the city. Is there a correlation between well-preserved buildings and property values? If so, does this help explain why the Beacon Hill Architectural Commission was so concerned with newspaper racks? Is it appropriate for historic commissions to regulate "street furniture"?

2.   What powers did the Commission have? When the Commission made determinations, what standards did it use?

3.   The Supreme Court has never considered a total ban on newspaper racks. Neither has it considered a free speech case dealing with historic preservation regulations. The Supreme Court's free speech jurisprudence, as it intersects with land use law, has been primarily concerned with adult uses. One of the more significant cases in this area of law, *City of Renton v. Playtime Theaters*, 475 U.S. 41 (1986), is mentioned in *Globe Newspaper*. It involved a city zoning ordinance prohibiting the location of adult movie theaters within 1000 feet of residential zones, churches, or schools. There were no such theaters in the town prior to enactment of the ordinance. The ordinance left 520 acres, or 5 percent of the town open to adult sites. The Supreme Court held that the zoning ordinance did not impermissibly regulate speech because it was aimed at the secondary effects, such as crime and prostitution, associated with them. The Supreme Court analyzed the ordinance using intermediate scrutiny, determining that it was a content-neutral "time, place, and manner" regulation, meaning that it passed constitutional scrutiny if it advanced a substantial or significant government interest, was narrowly tailored, and allowed for reasonable alternative avenues for communication. Is the Beacon Hill Street Furniture Guideline directed at regulating content, any more than the Renton zoning ordinance was? Is the Street Furniture Guideline at issue in *Globe Newspaper* similarly aimed at secondary effects, and if so what are these effects?

Figures 7-8 & 7-9:
Scenes from the Back Bay,
Boston, MA

Often, localities regulate adult uses using a dispersion strategy (that is, prohibiting them from locating next to each other), barring them from residential areas, or limiting them to one zone. Would any of these solutions been workable for both the Beacon Hill Architectural Commission and the Newspapers?

4.   Beginning with *Erie Railroad Co. v. Tompkins*, 304 U.S. 64 (1938), the Supreme Court has required federal courts to apply state substantive law; they may not issue their own interpretations thereof. In many states, if a federal judge or panel hearing a case has a question about substantive state law that is determinative for its case, it may ask the highest state court to issue an advisory opinion on that particular issue. In other states, the state's highest court may be prohibited from issuing answers to certified questions, on the basis that opinions may only be issued when there is a ripe case or controversy. Before the First Circuit decided *Globe Newspaper*, it certified a question to the Supreme Judicial Court of Massachusetts, and the answer is included in the opinion.

5.   The Back Bay, a well-to-do neighborhood adjacent to Beacon Hill, also regulates street furniture. Review Figures 7-8 and 7-9: a photograph of Newbury Street (which serves as the commercial core of the Back Bay neighborhood) and another of a quieter residential street. In what ways would newsracks and other street furniture transform these streetscapes?

2. ARTISTS' RIGHTS

Perhaps the newspapers in *Globe Newspaper* were less sympathetic plaintiffs because they were commercial entities with other avenues of communication. How should court treat *individual* plaintiffs with free speech challenges against historic preservation laws? What if the aggrieved individuals are artists, whose life's work depends on the availability of avenues of expression?

Artists' moral rights are those personal rights attributed to an artist through the creative process under the theory that some products of human labor are so connected to individual self-expression their creator can never relinquish control over that product. In 1990, under international pressure, Congress passed a law, the Visual Artists Rights Act (VARA), 17 U.S.C. § 106A, that provided for artists' moral rights. More specifically, VARA protects artists who create certain kinds of visual artworks, including paintings, drawings, prints, sculpture, and still photographic images. If VARA applies, an artist may: claim exclusive authorship and prevent others from doing so; prevent use of their name in connection with any work which has been distorted, mutilated, or modified in some way which would hurt their reputation; prevent any intentional distortion, mutilation, or other modification which would hurt their reputation; and prevent destruction of a work "of recognized stature," and any intentional or grossly negligent destruction of that work. VARA does not apply to commercial artwork, including "any work made for hire." *See, e.g., Carter v. Helmsley-Spear*, 71 F.3d 77 (2d

Cir. 1995) (preventing three artists from claiming protection under VARA because the sculpture they designed for a Queens, New York, building was commissioned).

The Fourth Circuit considered a related question of artists' rights in *Burke v. City of Charleston*, 139 F.3d 401 (4th Cir. 1998). In that case, an artist (Burke) had painted a "garish" mural on the exterior wall of a restaurant in a large, nationally-known historic district in Charleston, South Carolina. The city's preservation program dates back to 1931, making it one of the oldest programs in the country. The local historic preservation review board, empowered to review exterior changes, ordered the property owner to cover the mural and eventually held it was inappropriate for the district. The artist—but not the property owner— appealed on First Amendment and other grounds. Finding that Burke failed to demonstrate an injury-in-fact, the Fourth Circuit found the artist lacked standing, because only the owner's free speech was regulated by the local board. Note that Burke's work was for hire, so it would not have fallen under the protection of VARA, but VARA and related state laws often provide an additional dimension to free speech claims involving artists.

Reflect back to the discussion in Part E of Chapter 3, regarding standing. That Chapter focused on the National Historic Preservation Act (NHPA), and it was noted that those who are entitled to enforce the NHPA generally had broad standing. As one example, the Sixth Circuit found that five neighborhood organizations in Louisville without legal control, leasehold interests, or ownership could sue to enforce the provisions of the NHPA. *See Neighborhood Dev. Corp. v. Advisory Council on Historic Pres.*, 632 F.2d 21 (6th Cir. 1980). As another, a federal court in Alabama determined that an unincorporated association of individuals and residents of Birmingham could sue to stop imminent demolition of National Register Building. *Comm. to Save the Fox Bldg. v. Birmingham Branch of Fed. Reserve Bank of Atlanta*, 497 F.Supp. 504 (N.D. Ala. 1980). Is the opposite true when it comes to standing to *challenge* historic preservation laws? Courts sometimes are accused of finding no standing when they do not want to reach the merits of a dispute.

CHAPTER EIGHT

Protections for Archaeological Sites

Most of this book deals with the dominant objective of modern historic preservation laws: the protection of designated historic buildings, which are, at most, a few hundred years old. But this country is filled with sites and artifacts—produced both by early European settlers and by Native American peoples—that are much older and do not necessarily take the form of habitable structures. Statutes, mostly federal, protect access to, and prohibit destruction of, these sites and artifacts. Chief among the reasons for these laws is their ability to reveal to researchers scientific or historical clues about our past. In addition, particularly with respect to Native American sites, there may be cultural or religious reasons for protection.

Archaeologically significant sites and artifacts require a different legal framework from the typical historic preservation statute. Archaeological protection statutes prohibit removal or alteration of key components, limit access, and even impose criminal penalties for violations—all in the name of material conservation. Historic preservation statutes, in addition to prohibiting or conditioning demolition, encourage rehabilitation, provide guidelines for repair and restoration, and establish processes for reviewing impacts on designated sites. Thus, archaeological protection statutes arrest unauthorized activities, while preservation statutes ultimately facilitate approved activities. In addition, it is important to note that the scope of archaeological protection statutes is often smaller than the scope of typical historic preservation statutes in that archaeological protection statutes (whether at the state or federal level) primarily protect resources found on public or Native American lands.

This Chapter focuses on the unique federal rules that apply to archaeologically significant sites and artifacts. It is not intended to be an exhaustive treatment of this issue; other scholars have covered this material in greater detail. *See generally* SHERRY HUTT ET AL., CULTURAL PROPERTY LAW: A PRACTITIONER'S GUIDE (2d ed. 2017). This Chapter does not cover the treatment of archeological resources on private land. These resources continue to be governed largely by the common law of lost and abandoned property, although states have enacted a patchwork of statutes providing additional restrictions. This Chapter also does not cover the vulnerability of archaeological resources to climate change, a topic addressed in Chapters 1 and 12. New laws must be drafted to address the challenge of sea level rise, wildfires, and other extreme weather conditions that may irrevocably destroy these resources.

This Chapter focuses on several key statutes that lay the foundation for a federal regulatory framework for the modern historic preservation movement. The next Chapter focuses on the federal rules that apply only to those sites and objects—some archaeologically significant, and some with contemporary significance—affiliated with Native American groups. As you read this Chapter, consider how and to what extent all of the statutes mentioned in this Chapter might work with federal statutes that explicitly apply to Native American resources, the subject of Chapter 9.

A. THE ANTIQUITIES ACT

At the dawn of the twentieth century, Congress passed one of the first federal laws protecting historic and prehistoric sites, the Antiquities Act of 1906. This Act, however, was limited in scope. While the law was recodified in recent years, fundamental elements remain, including provisions that follow.

Antiquities Act of 1906
54 U.S.C. §§ 320301–320302

§ 320301.   National monuments

(a) Presidential declaration.

The President may, in the President's discretion, declare by public proclamation historic landmarks, historic and prehistoric structures, and other objects of historic or scientific interest that are situated upon the lands owned or controlled by the Federal Government to be national monuments.

(b) Reservation of land.

The President may reserve parcels of land as a part of the national monuments. The limits of the parcels shall be confined to the smallest area compatible with the proper care and management of the objects to be protected.

(c) Relinquishment to Federal Government.

When an object is situated on a parcel covered by a bona fide unperfected claim or held in private ownership, the parcel, or so much of the parcel as may be necessary for the proper care and management of the object, may be relinquished to the Federal Government, and the Secretary may accept the relinquishment of the parcel on behalf of the Federal Government.

(d) Limitation on Extension or Establishment of National Monuments in Wyoming.

No extension or establishment of national monuments in Wyoming may be undertaken except by express authorization of Congress.

§ 320302.   Permits

(a) Authority to grant permit.

The Secretary, the Secretary of Agriculture, or the Secretary of the Army may grant a permit for the examination of ruins, the excavation of archeological sites, and the gathering of objects of antiquity on land under their respective jurisdictions to an institution that the Secretary concerned considers properly qualified to conduct the examination, excavation, or gathering, subject to such regulations as the Secretary concerned may prescribe.

(b) Purpose of examination, excavation, or gathering.

A permit may be granted only if—

(1) the examination, excavation, or gathering is undertaken for the benefit of a reputable museum, university, college, or other recognized scientific or educational institution, with a view to increasing the knowledge of the objects; and

(2) the gathering shall be made for permanent preservation in a public museum.

18 U.S.C. § 1866

§ 1866. Historic, archeologic, or prehistoric items and antiquities

(a) Violation of regulations authorized by chapter 3201 of title 54.

A person that violates any of the regulations authorized by chapter 3201 of title 54 shall be fined under this title and be adjudged to pay all cost of the proceedings.

(b) Appropriation of, injury to, or destruction of historic or prehistoric ruin or monument or object of antiquity.

A person that appropriates, excavates, injures, or destroys any historic or prehistoric ruin or monument or any other object of antiquity that is situated on land owned or controlled by the Federal Government without the permission of the head of the Federal agency having jurisdiction over the land on which the object is situated, shall be imprisoned not more than 90 days, fined under this title, or both.

NOTES & QUESTIONS

1.   What power does the Antiquities Act give the President? How is this power limited, if at all? What procedural requirements are laid out in the Act?

2.   To whom may permits for the "examination, excavation or gatherings" of objects of antiquity on federal lands be issued? Is this list too narrow? What does the permitting provision imply about the ownership of the antiquities covered in the statute?

3.   Under the Antiquities Act, what criminal fines and punishments may be imposed on those who destroy historic or prehistoric sites on federal

lands? Would these fines and punishments, as written, serve as a real deterrent?

4.   The Antiquities Act potentially applies to a large portion of the United States. The federal government owns about 30 percent, or 672 million acres, of land in this country. Its ownership is concentrated in the western states, where it owns, for example, 30 percent of land in Montana and 84 percent of land in Nevada. About 95 percent of federal lands are controlled by the Department of the Interior or the Department of Agriculture. Currently, there are 128 national monuments and about 70 former monuments. About half of the former national monuments have been converted to national parks, elevating their status and providing greater access to visitors.

5.   What do you make of the exception for Wyoming? Does it help to know that nearly half of Wyoming is owned by the federal government? Who do you think advocated for the inclusion of this provision?

One of the major questions in Antiquities Act jurisprudence is whether it is unconstitutionally vague. Consider the next case, which raises this issue, as well as evidentiary issues common in Antiquities Act cases.

United States v. Smyer
596 F.2d 939 (10th Cir. 1979), *cert. denied*, 444 U.S. 843 (1979)

[EDS.: All references to the Antiquities Act have been recodified and often amended at title 54 or title 18. We have noted below where specific provisions have moved.]

■ Before MCWILLIAMS, BREITENSTEIN and MCKAY, CIRCUIT JUDGES.

■ BREITENSTEIN, CIRCUIT JUDGE.

After trial to the court without a jury, the defendants-appellants were found guilty of each count of an eleven-count information charging violations of 16 U.S.C. § 433 [EDS.: moved to 18 U.S.C. § 1866] which relates to American antiquities. They received 90-day concurrent sentences on each count.

The offenses occurred in the Mimbres Ranger District, Gila National Forest, New Mexico. Count I charges that, without permission from the Secretary of Agriculture, the defendants excavated a prehistoric Mimbres ruin at an archaeological site, herein designated as 250, which was inhabited about 1000–1200 A.D. Count II charges excavation of a ruin at a site designated as 251. Counts III through XI charge the appropriation from the ruins of specified objects of antiquity, 800–900 years old.

The two sites are about 300 yards apart and may be approached either from the north or the south. Forest Rangers had observed "very wide, deep-lugged" tire tracks at the sites. On October 29, 1977, a Forest

Service Recreation Officer, Roybal, discovered that a vehicle with "wide, deep-lugged" tires had entered the northern road leading to the sites and had passed a Forest Service sign warning that the area was protected by the American Antiquities Act. Upon his request for assistance, Ranger Bradsby and Enforcement Officer Dresser came and the three followed the tire tracks to the ruins. They found freshly dug holes at each ruin, shovels, picks, a sifting screen, and a small pottery bowl. In an arroyo between the sites they found a four-wheel drive truck, the tires on which matched the earlier discovered tire marks. No one was present at the sites. The officers inventoried the contents of the truck and had it towed away. That evening defendant May came to Ranger Bradsby's home and said that "he had been scouting for deer and that his truck had been stolen." A few days later federal officers interviewed, and obtained statements from, both May and Smyer. The officers took some artifacts from Smyer's home without objection and later, on the execution of a search warrant, seized other pieces of Indian bowls.

Defendants urge that the Antiquities Act is unconstitutional because it is vague and uncertain. The Act, which was passed in 1906, provides:

> "Any person who shall appropriate, excavate, injure, or destroy any historic or prehistoric ruin or monument, or any object of antiquity, situated on lands owned or controlled by the Government of the United States, without the permission of the Secretary of the Department of the Government having jurisdiction over the lands on which said antiquities are situated, shall, upon conviction, be fined in a sum of not more than $500 or be imprisoned for a period of not more than ninety days, or shall suffer both fine and imprisonment, in the discretion of the court."

The claim of vagueness and uncertainty is based on the use in the statute of the words "ruin," and "object of antiquity." In *United States v. Diaz*, 499 F.2d 113, 114–15 (9th Cir. 1974), the Ninth Circuit held that "the statute, by use of undefined terms of uncommon usage, is fatally vague in violation of the due process clause of the Constitution." We respectfully disagree. In *Diaz* the charge was appropriation of objects of antiquity consisting of face masks found on an Indian Reservation. The masks had been made in 1969 or 1970. The government evidence was that " 'object of antiquity' could include something that was made just yesterday if related to religious or social traditions of long standing." *Id.* at 114. Those facts must be contrasted with the instant case where the evidence showed that objects 800–900 years old were taken from ancient sites for commercial motives. We do not have a case of hobbyists exploring the desert for arrow heads. *See id.* at 114. Defendants admitted visiting the sites on several occasions and May had sold Mimbres bowls to an archaeologist.

The charges here were the excavation of two ruins and the appropriation of several objects of antiquity. The defendants' attack can go only to "ruin" and "antiquity." A ruin is the remains of something which has been destroyed. WEBSTER'S NEW INTERNATIONAL DICTIONARY 2182 (2d ed. 1960). Antiquity refers to "times long since past." *Id.* at 119. When measured by common understanding and practice, the challenged language conveys a sufficiently definite warning as to the proscribed conduct. * * *

In assessing vagueness, a statute must be considered in the light of the conduct with which the defendant is charged. *See United States v. Nat'l Dairy Prods. Corp.*, 372 U.S. 29, 32–33 (1963). The Antiquities Act gives a person of ordinary intelligence a reasonable opportunity to know that excavating prehistoric Indian burial grounds and appropriating 800–900 year old artifacts is prohibited. We find no constitutional infirmity in § 433.

The Gila National Forest was established in 1899. *United States v. New Mexico*, 438 U.S. 696, 696–699 (1978). The Secretary of Agriculture has jurisdiction over historic sites within forest reserves. 43 C.F.R. § 3.1(a). To bolster their claim that they did not know they were in the National Forest, defendants argue that the Department gave inadequate notice that the two sites were on government land. The tire tracks of the vehicle went by an Antiquities Act sign. When the defendants saw the forest officers, one of whom was in uniform, they fled. Each defendant in his statement to officer Dresser admitted that he had been to the site several times. Mimbres bowls were found in Smyer's home. The trial court rejected the defendants' claim that they believed they were on private property. The overwhelming evidence shows violations of § 433. * * *

Defendants assert that the government did not comply with Rule 16, FED. R. CRIM. PRO., relating to discovery and inspection. At the trial much controversy arose over the government's compliance with a defense motion for discovery. One dispute related to a map of the area in which the antiquity sites were located. The defense claimed that they did not know that they were on government property. A land surveyor presented an area map. The defense claims that they did not receive an exact copy and that the evidence given by the surveyor included scientific tests or experiments within the purview of Rule 16(a)(1)(D). We are not impressed. We are convinced that the government complied with Rule 16. The record sustains the government's contention that the defendants knew they were on government land. If there was any misunderstanding about the map, the defendants were not prejudiced.

The defendants assert that the statements which they made to the officers should have been suppressed. The first complaint relates to statements of May to officer Bradsby on the evening that the officers impounded the truck. May came to Bradsby's home to inquire about the truck which, he said had been taken while he was "scouting for deer." Bradsby told him that the truck had been impounded. All the officer did was to answer defendant May's questions. Bradsby's testimony was properly received.

Officer Dresser separately interviewed Smyer and May. Neither was in custody at the time. Dresser gave each the required *Miranda* warnings and each signed a "Waiver of Rights." Each defendant was educated, intelligent, and under no compulsion. Dresser denied defendants' claims of threats and promises of leniency. Credibility is a matter for the trier of the facts. The court chose to believe Dresser. The defendants' statements were properly received.

The next objection goes to the receipt in evidence of the tangible objects which are the bases of Counts III to XI. During his interview with officer Dresser, May admitted digging at the ruins and selling two bowls. May offered to return the artifacts. At Smyer's home, May selected a number of artifacts from a collection and turned them over to the officer. Later the officer returned to Smyer's home with a search warrant and seized 31 bowls. A government expert testified that certain bowls were "all Mimbres classic or Mimbres Black on White Bowls." A shard found at the site fitted one of the bowls. A government expert placed the value of the artifacts taken by the defendants at about $4,000. The sites were prehistoric ruins inhabited by Mimbres Indians, a sub-group of the Mogollon culture, from about 1000 to 1200 A.D., and the bowls were made sometime during that period. The questioned evidence was either given voluntarily to the officer or obtained by a search warrant of unquestioned validity. The bowls were adequately identified with the site, both by physical evidence and the admissions of the defendants. The evidence was properly received.

Defendants object to the receipt in evidence of a photograph of defendant May, seized by the officers during an inventory search of the truck. The photo showed May standing with a skull on his head and on each shoulder. He was holding skeletal bones in his hands. The evidence showed the presence of skeletal bones at the sites. On cross-examination May said that the photo was of him.

After the officers found the truck, they investigated the surrounding area and found no one. They decided to impound the truck and made a routine inventory of its contents. While doing so, officer Roybal lowered a sun visor, and the questioned photo fell down. The routine inventory protected the owner's property while in police custody, protected the officers against claims and disputes and against potential danger. *South Dakota v. Opperman*, 428 U.S. 364 (1976), sustains the actions of the officers. They had reasonable cause to connect the truck with the excavations at the sites, and it had been abandoned. The seizure of the photo was proper. The evidence showed that the picture had been taken at site 250. The picture connected May with the site and was properly received in evidence.

Ranger Bradsby testified that the special-use permits, which authorized exploration of antiquity sites, were kept in his office and that neither May nor Smyer had a permit. The government introduced a computer print-out which named those who had the necessary permits. The introduction of the print-out is said to violate the Rules of Evidence, particularly Rule 802 (hearsay) and 602 (witnesses-lack of personal knowledge). The government says that the print-out is admissible under Rule 803(6) (Records of regularly conducted activity). The controversy need not be decided because other evidence showed that defendants did not have a permit, and they did not claim to have one. The government did not need to offer the print-out to prove its case, and the defendants were not prejudiced by its receipt.

Affirmed.

NOTES & QUESTIONS

1.   As the Tenth Circuit mentions, the Ninth Circuit takes a different view of the Antiquities Act's constitutionality. In *United States v. Diaz*, 499 F.2d 113 (9th Cir. 1974), the Ninth Circuit determined that the phrase "objects of antiquity" was so vague that it violated the due process clause of the Constitution. The panel stated:

> One must be able to know, with reasonable certainty, when he has happened on an area forbidden to his pick and shovel and what objects he must leave as he has found them. * * * Nowhere here do we find any definition of such terms as "ruin" or "monument" (whether historic or prehistoric) or "object of antiquity." The statute does not limit itself to Indian reservations or to Indian relics. Hobbyists who explore the desert and its ghost towns for arrowheads and antique bottles could arguably find themselves within the Act's proscriptions. * * * Here there was no notice whatsoever given by the statute that the word "antiquity" can have reference not only to the age of an object but also to the use for which the object was made and to which it was put, subjects not likely to be of common knowledge.

Id. at 114–115. It may be relevant to know that the defendant in *Diaz* was accused of wrongfully appropriating face masks that were used for sacred ceremonial purposes, and that had been made only three or four years prior to the alleged appropriation. Is the Ninth Circuit or Tenth Circuit view more convincing? Should a constitutional challenge to the Antiquities Act depend on the age or other characteristics of the objects at issue?

2.   The panel spends much of its discussion on evidentiary issues. Why would a focus on evidence be common in Antiquities Act cases?

3.   Why would these defendants spend so much money and time fighting the charges, in light of overwhelming evidence of their guilt and the light penalties imposed upon them? Perhaps they were concerned about the possible applicability of a related law, passed the same year that *Smyer* was decided: the Archaeological Resources Protection Act (ARPA). Compare the criminal and civil penalties imposed by ARPA with those of the Antiquities Act when the ARPA provisions are discussed in section C of this Chapter.

The following case considers the requirement in section 320301 that the structures or objects eligible to be declared national monuments under the Antiquities Act must be "situated upon the lands owned or controlled by the Federal Government."

Treasure Salvors, Inc. v. Unidentified Wrecked & Abandoned Sailing Vessel

569 F.2d 330 (5th Cir. 1978)

[EDS.: All references to the Antiquities Act have been recodified and often amended at title 54 or title 18. We have noted below where specific provisions have moved.]

■ GEWIN, CIRCUIT JUDGE:

Treasure Salvors, Inc., and Armada Research Corp., Florida corporations, sued for possession of and confirmation of title to an unidentified wrecked and abandoned vessel thought to be the Nuestra Senora de Atocha. The Atocha sank in the sea off the Marquesas Keys in 1622 while en route to Spain. The United States intervened, answered, and counterclaimed, asserting title to the vessel. Summary judgment was entered for the plaintiffs, 408 F.Supp. 907 (S.D. Fla. 1976), and the government appealed. We modify the district court's judgment, and affirm.

This action evokes all the romance and danger of the buccaneering days in the West Indies. It is rooted in an ancient tragedy of imperial Spain, and embraces a modern tragedy as well. The case also presents the story of a triumph, a story in which the daring and determination of the colonial settlers are mirrored by contemporary treasure seekers.

In late summer of 1622 a fleet of Spanish galleons, heavily laden with bullion exploited from the mines of the New World, set sail for Spain. Spain, at this period in her history, was embroiled in the vicious religious conflicts of the Thirty Years' War and desperately needed American bullion to finance her costly military adventures. As the fleet entered the Straits of Florida, seeking the strongest current of the Gulf Stream, it was met by a hurricane which drove it into the reef-laced waters off the Florida Keys. A number of vessels went down, including the richest galleon in the fleet, Nuestra Senora de Atocha. Five hundred fifty persons perished, and cargo with a contemporary value of perhaps $250 million was lost. A later hurricane shattered the Atocha and buried her beneath the sands.

For well over three centuries the wreck of the Atocha lay undisturbed beneath the wide shoal west of the Marquesas Keys, islets named after the reef where the Marquis of Cadereita camped while supervising unsuccessful salvage operations. Then, in 1971, after an arduous search aided by survivors' accounts of the 1622 wrecks, and an expenditure of more than $2 million, plaintiffs located the Atocha. Plaintiffs have retrieved gold, silver, artifacts, and armament valued at $6 million. Their costs have included four lives, among them the son and daughter-in-law of Melvin Fisher, plaintiffs' president and leader of the expedition. * * *

On this appeal the United States claims the treasure chiefly upon two grounds [EDS.: including]: (1) Application of the Antiquities Act to objects located on the outer continental shelf of the United States[.] * * *

The Antiquities Act

The Antiquities Act authorizes executive designation of historic landmarks, historic and prehistoric structures, and objects of historic or scientific interest situated upon lands owned or controlled by the United States as national monuments. Permission to examine ruins, excavate archaeological sites, and gather objects of antiquity must be sought from the secretary of the department exercising jurisdiction over such lands. As the district court noted, the Antiquities Act applies by its terms only to lands owned or controlled by the Government of the United States. The wreck of the Atocha rests on the continental shelf, outside the territorial waters of the United States.[14]

The government asserts that the Outer Continental Shelf Lands Act (OCSLA), 43 U.S.C. § 1331 et seq., demonstrates Congressional intent to extend the jurisdiction and control of the United States to the outer continental shelf. OCSLA was passed, along with the Submerged Lands Act, 43 U.S.C. § 1301 et seq., to clarify the respective interests of coastal states and the United States in the natural resources of the subsoil and seabed of the continental shelf. A look at the background and interpretation of OCSLA is necessary to determine its scope.

The Truman proclamation of September 28, 1945, spurred national and international interest in exploitation of the mineral wealth of the oceans. The proclamation asserted the jurisdiction and control of the United States over the mineral resources of the continental shelf, but was not intended to abridge the right of free and unimpeded navigation of waters above the shelf, nor to extend the limits of American territorial waters. See 13 Dep't State Bull. 485 (Sept. 30, 1945). The Convention on the Continental Shelf, written thirteen years later, assured to each coastal nation the exclusive right to explore and exploit the resources of

---

[14] The continental shelf is defined as the seabed and subsoil of the submarine areas adjacent to the coast but outside the area of the territorial sea, to a depth of 200 meters or, beyond that limit, to where the depth of the superjacent waters admits of the exploitation of the natural resources of the said areas. This is a legal, not a geological, definition. The territorial sea of the United States includes those waters lying not more than three miles (or three marine leagues in the Gulf of Mexico in the case of certain Gulf states) from the baseline (the artificial coast line). All parts of the sea not included in the territorial or internal waters of a nation constitute high seas. Nations maintain limited jurisdiction over waters lying not more than twelve miles from the baseline, in order to prevent or punish infringement of customs, fiscal, immigration or sanitary regulations within their territory or territorial sea. This belt of limited control is the contiguous zone. * * *

the seabed and subsoil, not only of its territorial sea, but also of the adjacent continental shelf beyond the territorial sea. * * *

In the Outer Continental Shelf Lands Act, "Congress emphatically implemented its view that the United States has paramount rights to the seabed beyond the three-mile limit." *United States v. Maine*, 420 U.S. 515, 526 (1975). * * *

43 U.S.C. § 1332(a) declares the policy of the United States to be "that the subsoil and seabed of the outer Continental Shelf appertain to the United States and are subject to its jurisdiction, control, and power of disposition as provided in this subchapter." Certain language in the Conference Committee report on the bill supports the view that Congress intended to extend the jurisdiction and control of the United States to both the seabed and subsoil. * * *

This court held in *Guess v. Read*, 290 F.2d 622, 625 (1961), *cert. denied*, 368 U.S. 957 (1962), that "(t)he Continental Shelf Act was enacted for the purpose, primarily, of asserting ownership of and jurisdiction over the minerals in and under the Continental Shelf." The structure of the Act itself, which is basically a guide to the administration and leasing of offshore mineral-producing properties, reinforces this conclusion. The Act consists almost exclusively of specific measures to facilitate exploitation of natural resources on the continental shelf. In addition, 43 U.S.C. § 1332(b) provides that the Act "shall be construed in such manner that the character as high seas of the waters above the outer Continental Shelf and the right to navigation and fishing therein shall not be affected." As the court below noted, an extension of jurisdiction for purposes of controlling the exploitation of the natural resources of the continental shelf is not necessarily an extension of sovereignty.

We believe that a limited construction of the Act comports with the primary purpose of resolving competing claims to ownership of the natural resources of the offshore seabed and subsoil. So read, the Act is consistent with Article 2 of the Convention on the Continental Shelf:

> 1.   The coastal state (nation) exercises over the continental shelf sovereign rights for the purpose of exploring it and exploiting its natural resources.

The Convention on the Continental Shelf was a product of the United Nations Conference on the Law of the Sea convened at Geneva in 1958. * * * [It] superseded any incompatible terminology in the domestic statute.

Interpretations of the Convention and the Act by legal scholars have, with remarkable accord, reached the same conclusion regarding the nature of control of the United States over the continental shelf. The most compelling explication of the Convention regarding national control over non-resource-related material in the shelf area is contained in the comments of the International Law Commission:

It is clearly understood that the rights in question do not cover objects such as wrecked ships and their cargoes (including bullion) lying on the seabed or covered by the sand of the subsoil.

This comment is consistent with the Commission's general perception of national jurisdiction over the continental shelf:

(The Commission) was unwilling to accept the sovereignty of the coastal State over the seabed and subsoil of the continental shelf ... the text as now adopted leaves no doubt that the rights conferred upon the coastal state cover all rights necessary for and connected with the exploration and exploitation of the natural resources of the continental shelf.

We have demonstrated the limited scope of American control over the wreck site. We conclude that the remains of the Atocha are not situated on lands owned or controlled by the United States under the provisions of the Antiquities Act. * * *

NOTES & QUESTIONS

1. Maritime and admiralty law are extremely specialized areas of law that depend on international treaties, state and federal laws, and custom. Footnote 14 provides background on the related issues considered in *Treasure Salvors*. On the international law of abandoned shipwrecks, *see* JANET BLAKE, INTERNATIONAL CULTURAL HERITAGE LAW (2015).

2. Other cases have dealt with how the Antiquities Act applies to abandoned shipwrecks. The Eleventh Circuit considered a case relating to the ownership of an eighteenth century English vessel that rested underwater, entirely within the confines of Biscayne National Park in Florida. The parties included the sport diver who "discovered" the sunken ship and the United States, which actually knew about the location of the ship at least a few years before the diver's discovery. In that case, a concurring Judge Kravitch agreed with the majority that the United States was the rightful owner. However, the judge felt that the majority opinion should have based its conclusion on the Antiquities Act, not common law. Judge Kravitch stated:

In the instant case, the shipwreck was found on submerged lands belonging in fee simple to the United States, and the vessel undoubtedly is an "antiquity." Therefore, the Antiquities Act's prohibition of "appropriat[ion]" and "excavat[ion]" supersedes the principles of maritime law on which plaintiff relies, and defeats plaintiff's claim of ownership of the vessel.

Klein v. Unidentified Wrecked & Abandoned Sailing Vessel, 758 F.2d 1511, 1515–16 (11th Cir. 1985). Judge Kravitch compared the facts in this case to *United States v. Smyer*, 596 F.2d 939 (10th Cir.), *cert. denied*, 444 U.S. 843 (1979). Consider this comparison when reading the next case.

Tulare County v. Bush

306 F.3d 1138 (D.C. Cir. 2002)

■ Before: EDWARDS and ROGERS, CIRCUIT JUDGES, and WILLIAMS, SENIOR CIRCUIT JUDGE.

■ ROGERS, CIRCUIT JUDGE:

This [case involves] a challenge to Presidential authority under the Antiquities Act of 1906 ("Act"), 16 U.S.C. § 431 (2000) [EDS.: moved to 54 U.S.C. § 320301]. * * * [W]e affirm the dismissal of the complaint for lack of subject matter jurisdiction and for failure to state a claim upon which relief may be granted pursuant to Federal Rules of Civil Procedure 12(b)(1) and 12(b)(6).

I.

In April 2000 President Clinton established by proclamation the Giant Sequoia National Monument pursuant to his authority under the Antiquities Act. Proclamation 7295, 65 Fed. Reg. 24,095 (Apr. 15, 2000). The Monument, which encompasses 327,769 acres of land in the Sequoia National Forest in south-central California, contains groves of giant sequoias, the world's largest trees, and their surrounding ecosystem. *Id.* at 24,095–97, 24,100.

Tulare County, which contains land near and within the Grand Sequoia National Monument ("Monument"), along with a number of other public and private entities that use the Monument area for business or recreational purposes (hereinafter "Tulare County"), filed a complaint seeking declaratory and injunctive relief. Tulare County alleged that the Proclamation violated various provisions of the Antiquities Act and the Property Clause of the Constitution, as well as the National Forest Management Act, the National Environmental Policy Act, and the parties' existing rights under a prior mediated settlement agreement. The district court, concluding that only facial review was appropriate, dismissed the complaint. *Tulare County v. Bush*, 185 F.Supp.2d 18 (D.D.C. 2001).

II.

On appeal, Tulare County contends that in dismissing its complaint prior to discovery, the district court erred in failing to accept as true the facts alleged in the complaint and in limiting its review to the face of the Proclamation rather than reviewing the President's discretionary factual determinations. Tulare County does not contend that the President lacks authority under the Antiquities Act to proclaim national monuments like Giant Sequoia, as the Supreme Court has long upheld such authority. *Cappaert v. United States*, 426 U.S. 128, 142 (1976); *Cameron v. United States*, 252 U.S. 450, 455 (1920). Rather, in Counts 1–4 of the complaint, Tulare County alleged that the Proclamation violated the Antiquities Act because it: (1) failed to identify the objects of historic or scientific interest with reasonable specificity; (2) designated as the basis for the Monument objects that do not qualify under the Act; (3) did not confine the size of the Monument "to the smallest area compatible with proper care and management of the objects to be protected," 16 U.S.C. § 431; and (4) increased the likelihood of harm by fires to any objects of alleged historic or scientific interest within the Monument rather than protecting those objects. * * *

The Antiquities Act provides, in relevant part, that the President, "in his discretion" may declare "historic landmarks . . . and other objects of historic or scientific interest . . . situated upon [federal] lands . . . to be national monuments, and may reserve . . . parcels of land . . . confined to the smallest area compatible with the proper care and management of the objects to be protected. . . ." 16 U.S.C. § 431. The court pointed out in *Mountain States Legal Foundation v. Bush*, 306 F.3d 1132 (2002), after reviewing Supreme Court authority discussing the scope of judicial review of discretionary Presidential decisionmaking, that the court "is necessarily sensitive to pleading requirements where, as here, it is asked to review the President's actions under a statute that confers very broad discretion on the President and separation of powers concerns are presented." *Mountain States*, 306 F.3d at 1137. Acknowledging that Congress has entrusted the courts with responsibility for determining the limits of statutory grants of authority, *id.* at 8, the court nonetheless declined to engage in *ultra vires* review in light of the absence of allegations or arguments in the record to indicate any infirmity in the challenged Proclamations. *Id.* at 9. Consequently, we review Tulare County's complaint to determine whether it contains factual allegations to support an *ultra vires* claim that would demonstrate the district court erred in declining to engage in a factual inquiry to ensure that the President complied with the statutory requirements.

Count 1 of Tulare County's complaint is premised on the assumption that the Antiquities Act requires the President to include a certain level of detail in the Proclamation. No such requirement exists. The Act authorizes the President, "in his discretion, to declare by public proclamation historic landmarks, historic and prehistoric structures, and other objects of historic or scientific interest." 16 U.S.C. § 431. The Presidential declaration at issue complies with that standard. The Proclamation lyrically describes "magnificent groves of towering giant sequoias," "bold granitic domes, spires, and plunging gorges," "an enormous number of habitats," "limestone caverns and . . . unique paleontological resources documenting tens of thousands of years of ecosystem change," as well as "many archaeological sites recording Native American occupation . . . and historic remnants of early Euroamerican settlement." Proclamation at 24,095. By identifying historic sites and objects of scientific interest located within the designated lands, the Proclamation adverts to the statutory standard. Hence, Count 1 fails as a matter of law.

Count 2 alleges that the President has designated nonqualifying objects for protection. The Antiquities Act provides that, in addition to historic landmarks and structures, "other objects of historic or scientific interest" may qualify, at the President's discretion, for protection as monuments. 16 U.S.C. § 431. Inclusion of such items as ecosystems and scenic vistas in the Proclamation did not contravene the terms of the statute by relying on nonqualifying features. In *Cappaert*, 426 U.S. at 141–42, the Supreme Court rejected a similar argument, holding that the President's Antiquities Act authority is not limited to protecting only archeological sites.

As relevant to Count 3 of the complaint, the Proclamation states that the Monument's 327,769-acre size "is the smallest area compatible with the proper care and management of the objects to be protected." Proclamation at 24,097. It also states that the sequoia groves are not contiguous but instead comprise part of a spectrum of interconnected ecosystems. *Id.* Tulare County alleges that no one in the Clinton Administration "made any meaningful investigation or determination of the smallest area necessary to protect any specifically identified objects of genuine historic or scientific interest." Instead, it alleges, President Clinton "bowed to political pressure . . . in designating a grossly oversized Monument unnecessary for the protection of any objects of genuine historic or scientific interest." This allegation is a legal conclusion couched as a factual allegation. "Although in reviewing the dismissal of a complaint the court must take 'all factual allegations in the complaint as true,' the court is 'not bound to accept as true a legal conclusion couched as a factual allegation.'" *Mountain States*, 306 F.3d at 1137 (quoting *Papasan v. Allain*, 478 U.S. 265, 286 (1986)).

Contrary to the assumption underlying Count 3, the Antiquities Act does not impose upon the President an obligation to make any particular investigation. And to the extent that Tulare County alleges that the Proclamation designates land that should not be included within the Monument, the complaint fails to identify the improperly designated lands with sufficient particularity to state a claim. *Id.* Insofar as Tulare County alleges that the Monument includes too much land, i.e., that the President abused his discretion by designating more land than is necessary to protect the specific objects of interest, Tulare County does not make the factual allegations sufficient to support its claims. This is particularly so as its claim that the Proclamation covered too much land is dependent on the proposition that parts of the Monument lack scientific or historical value, an issue on which Tulare County made no factual allegations.

Count 4 of the complaint alleges that the Monument designation actually increases the risk of harm from fires to many of the objects that the Proclamation aims to protect. However, the Proclamation expressly addresses the threat of wildfires and the need for forest restoration and protection. The Proclamation observes that forest renewal is needed because environmental change "has led to an unprecedented failure in sequoia reproduction," and that "a century of fire suppression and logging" has created "an increased hazard of wildfires of a severity that was rarely encountered in pre-Euroamerican times." Proclamation at 24,095. Count 4 contains no factual allegations, only conclusions, and it refers to current management rather than the designation under the Proclamation as the cause for likely increases in catastrophic fires. * * *

Accordingly, because "[a]t no point has [Tulare County] presented factual allegations that would occasion . . . *ultra vires* review of the Proclamation [ ]" *Mountain States*, 306 F.3d at 1136–37, we affirm the dismissal of the complaint.

NOTES & QUESTIONS

1.   Tulare County is located in the Central Valley, one of the most productive agricultural areas in the United States. Does the value of the surrounding land explain the opposition to the designation?

2.   As was the case with *United States v. Smyer*, *Tulare County* deals with whether the Antiquities Act is specific enough. *Tulare County*, however, deals with 54 U.S.C. § 320301 and not the penalties section, recodified at 18 U.S.C. § 1866. Is it surprising how few constraints are given to the President in section 320301?

As background, review the legislative history as chronicled by Professor Mark Squillace in *The Monumental Legacy of the Antiquities Act of 1906*, 37 GA. L. REV. 473 (2003). After painstakingly describing the evidence, he concludes that, contrary to popular wisdom, the drafters of the Antiquities Act intended for it to apply broadly: "Most commentators who have considered the Act and its legislative history have concluded that it was designed to protect only very small tracts of land around archaeological sites. The complex political history of the law, however, suggests that some of its promoters intended a much broader design." *Id.* at 477.

3.   Consider the first times section 320301 of the Antiquities Act (the former 16 U.S.C. § 431) was invoked by a sitting President. Almost immediately after the Antiquities Act was passed, President Theodore Roosevelt designated the Devil's Tower, Petrified Forest, Montezuma Castle, and El Morro as national monuments; all were sites of scenic but not necessarily scientific significance. In 1908 and 1909, President Roosevelt became bolder, designating 800,000 acres of the Grand Canyon of Arizona, then 600,000 acres of land surrounding Mount Olympus in Washington state as national monuments. Might these first uses of the Antiquities Act have been inconsistent with the requirement in section 320301(b) that monument designation "shall be confined to the smallest area compatible with the proper care and management of the objects to be protected"?

4.   President Clinton used the Antiquities Act at least twenty-two times to expand or create national monuments over five million acres. In one controversial proclamation, he set aside 1.7 million square miles in an economically depressed area of Utah as the Grand Staircase-Escalante

National Monument. This proclamation surprised many state and local leaders, who had been actively working to establish a mine in that area. They believed that the mine would stimulate economic development and create one thousand jobs. Opponents of the designation took the President to court, arguing that the monument designation violated the "smallest area" requirement in § 320301(b). The federal district court hearing the case determined that President Clinton had met that requirement because the proclamation declaring the Grand Staircase-Escalante National Monument specifically stated that he had considered the "smallest area" requirement. *Utah Ass'n of Counties v. Bush*, 316 F.Supp.2d 1172 (2004). The judge added, "Whether the President's designation best fulfilled the general congressional intention embodied in the Antiquities Act is not a matter for judicial inquiry." *Id.* at 1186. This result is consistent with *Tulare County*. But is it right?

5.   Many have criticized the executive branch for its expansive interpretation of the Antiquities Act. Professor Christine Klein explains that, for the critics, "perhaps the primary sin of the Antiquities Act is its unwitting synthesis of the human and natural realms, as it simultaneously protects large landscapes and the relics of ancient human civilizations under a single statutory scheme." In other words, it fails to clearly differentiate between the manner and nature of protections for natural resources versus human archaeological resources. *See* Christine A. Klein, *Preserving Monumental Landscapes Under the Antiquities Act*, 87 CORNELL L. REV. 1333, 1337 (2002). Why has the Antiquities Act endured nonetheless? Klein explains:

> the Act's longevity may be attributable to its ability to serve at least four core values identified by the public and by the courts: (1) the protection of land from development; (2) the recognition of "living landscapes"; (3) the ability to take emergency action to preserve the status quo of threatened lands; and (4) the vesting of political accountability directly in the President, rather than burying monument responsibility deep within a bureaucratic structure.

Id. at 1338.

6.   The relevant sections of the *Cappaert* case mentioned twice in the above excerpt are as follows:

> Devil's Hole is a deep limestone cavern in Nevada. Approximately 50 feet below the opening of the cavern is a pool 65 feet long, 10 feet wide, and at least 200 feet deep, although its actual depth is unknown. The pool is a remnant of the prehistoric Death Valley Lake System and is situated on land owned by the United States since the Treaty of Guadalupe Hidalgo in 1848, 9 Stat. 922. By the Proclamation of January 17, 1952 [and pursuant to the Antiquities Act], President Truman withdrew from the public domain a 40-acre tract of land surrounding Devil's Hole, making it a detached component of the Death Valley National Monument. * * *

> Petitioners in both cases argue that * * * the [Antiquities Act] did not give the President authority to reserve a pool. Under that Act, according to the *Cappaert* petitioners, the President may reserve

federal lands only to protect archeologic sites. However, the language of the Act which authorizes the President to proclaim as national monuments "historic landmarks, historic and prehistoric stctures [sic], and other objects of historic or scientific interest that are situated upon the lands owned or controlled by the Government" is not so limited. The pool in Devil's Hole and its rare inhabitants are "objects of historic or scientific interest."

Cappaert v. United States, 426 U.S. 128, 131, 141–42 (1976).

7.   President Trump in 2017 proclaimed that he was dramatically reducing the size of two national monuments in Utah. His proclamation aimed to reduce the size of Bears Ears National Monument by 85 percent and the Grand Staircase-Escalante National Monument by about half. He also directed the Secretary of the Interior to review other monument designations from previous Presidents to determine which monuments, if any, should be reduced in size or stripped of their designation. Needless to say, his actions were challenged in court and, at publication time, appear likely to be reversed by President Biden.

Look carefully again at the Antiquities Act. While it gives a President the power to create monuments, does it also give a President the power to reduce them? Even without the power to reduce explicitly stated, is there an argument that the reduction is implied in the power to create?

For one answer, see Mark Squillace et al, *Presidents Lack the Authority to Abolish or Diminish National Monuments*, 103 VA. L. REV. ONLINE 55 (2017).

B. THE HISTORIC SITES ACT

The Antiquities Act gave the President of the United States power to designate national monuments. About thirty years later, Congress passed another law, the Historic Sites Act of 1935, which expanded the executive branch's ability to preserve and maintain historic sites.

Historic Sites Act of 1935
54 U.S.C. §§ 320101–320102

§ 320101.   Declaration of national policy

It is declared that it is a national policy to preserve for public use historic sites, buildings, and objects of national significance for the inspiration and benefit of the people of the United States.

§ 320102.   Powers and duties of Secretary

(a) In general.

The Secretary, acting through the Director, for the purpose of effectuating the policy expressed in section 320101 of this title, has the powers and shall perform the duties set out in this section.

(b) Preservation of data.

The Secretary shall secure, collate, and preserve drawings, plans, photographs, and other data of historic and archaeologic sites, buildings, and objects.

(c) Survey.

The Secretary shall make a survey of historic and archaeologic sites, buildings, and objects for the purpose of determining which possess exceptional value as commemorating or illustrating the history of the United States.

(d) Investigations and researches.

The Secretary shall make necessary investigations and researches in the United States relating to particular sites, buildings, or objects to obtain accurate historical and archaeological facts and information concerning the sites, buildings, and objects.

(e) Acquisition of property.

The Secretary may, for the purpose of this chapter, acquire in the name of the United States by gift, purchase, or otherwise any property, personal or real, or any interest or estate in property, title to any real property to be satisfactory to the Secretary: Property that is owned by any religious or educational institution, or that is owned or administered for the benefit of the public shall not be acquired without the consent of the owner. No property shall be acquired or contract or agreement for the acquisition of the property made that will obligate the general fund of the Treasury for the payment of such property, unless or until Congress has appropriated money that is available for that purpose.

(f) Contracts and cooperative agreements.

The Secretary may contract and make cooperative agreements with States, municipal subdivisions, corporations, associations, or individuals, with proper bond where considered advisable, to protect, preserve, maintain, or operate any historic or archaeologic building, site, or object, or property used in connection with the building, site, or object, for public use, regardless whether the title to the building, site, object, or property is in the United States. No contract or cooperative agreement shall be made or entered into that will obligate the general fund of the Treasury unless or until Congress has appropriated money for such purpose.

(g) Protection of sites, buildings, objects, and property.

The Secretary shall restore, reconstruct, rehabilitate, preserve, and maintain historic or prehistoric sites, buildings, objects, and property of national historical or archaeological significance and where considered desirable establish and maintain museums in connection with the sites, buildings, objects, and property

(h) Tablets to mark or commemorate places and events.

The Secretary shall erect and maintain tablets to mark or commemorate historic or prehistoric places and events of national historical or archaeological significance.

(i) Operation for benefit of public.

The Secretary may operate and manage historic and archaeologic sites, buildings, and property acquired under this chapter together with lands and subordinate buildings for the benefit of the public, and may charge reasonable visitation fees and grant concessions, leases, or permits for the use of land, building space, roads, or trails when necessary or desirable either to accommodate the public or to facilitate administration. The Secretary may grant those concessions, leases, or permits and enter into contracts relating to the contracts, leases, or permits with responsible persons, firms, or corporations without advertising and without securing competitive bids.

(j) Corporation to carry out duties.

When the Secretary determines that it would be administratively burdensome to restore, reconstruct, operate, or maintain any particular historic or archaeologic site, building, or property donated to the United States through the Service, the Secretary may cause the restoration, reconstruction, operation, or maintenance to be done by organizing a corporation for that purpose under the laws of the District of Columbia or any State.

(k) Educational program and service.

The Secretary shall develop an educational program and service for the purpose of making available to the public facts and information pertaining to American historic and archaeologic sites, buildings, and properties of national significance. Reasonable charges may be made for the dissemination of any such information.

(*l*) Actions and regulations necessary to carry out chapter.

The Secretary shall perform any and all acts, and make regulations not inconsistent with this chapter that may be necessary and proper to carry out this chapter.

NOTES & QUESTIONS

1. What powers are granted to the Secretary of Interior under the Historic Sites Act? Look particularly at sections 320102(e) and (g). Section 320102(e) allows the Secretary to acquire property "by gift, purchase, or otherwise." What might "or otherwise" mean? Continue reading the following clause: "Property that is owned by any religious or educational institution, or that is owned or administered for the benefit of the public shall not be acquired without the consent of the owner." Now does one possible meaning of "or otherwise" become more clear?

The phrase is meant to include (among other things) the use of eminent domain—that is, the taking of land by government without the consent of the owner, for some public purpose. The Condemnation Act, 40 U.S.C. § 3113, first enacted in 1888, permits the use of condemnation by any federal officer having statutory power to acquire real property for public purposes unless specifically prohibited. The public purpose to be served by uses of eminent domain via the Historic Sites Act is included in the statute itself. Congress provided in section 320101 that national policy supported the preservation of historic sites, and further clarified in section 320101(g) that restoration, reconstruction, rehabilitation, preservation, and maintenance of historic or prehistoric sites and other properties could be a valid purpose of the acquisition provided for in section 320101(e). *See, e.g., Barnidge v. United States*, 101 F.2d 295 (8th Cir. 1939) (rejecting a challenge to the Historic Sites Act after the Secretary of the Interior condemned land on the banks of the Mississippi River in what is known as Old St. Louis to protect a significant site the Secretary deemed to be of national significance).

2. As referenced in Chapter 2, the Park Service began to consider the value of a list of historically significant buildings without regard to acquisition, and publicly announced the first list of National Historic Landmarks in 1960. Later, Congress enacted Section 106 protection for designated National Landmarks. Section 110(f) provides that the agency "shall to the maximum extent possible undertake such planning and actions as may be necessary to minimize harm to such the landmark." 54 U.S.C. § 306107. Could a private owner of a historic landmark face possible regulatory taking as well as eminent domain proceedings? Do you think that too little power is given to a private owner, or that it is appropriate given the objective of Historic Sites Act?

3. The Historic and Archaeological Data Protection Preservation Act of 1974 (HADPA), recodified at 54 U.S.C. §§ 312502–312508, expands the powers of the Secretary of the Interior beyond the Historic Sites Act of 1935. It aims to establish a policy of preserving historical and archaeological data that would otherwise be lost as a result of federal activities. If a federal agency finds or is notified in writing "that its activities in connection with any Federal construction project or federally licensed project, activity, or program may cause irreparable loss or destruction of significant scientific, prehistorical, historical, or archeological data," the agency must notify the Secretary of the Interior and describe the project, activity, or program and its effects. *Id.* § 312502(a). The Secretary of the Interior may also survey the affected site and is entitled to consult with appropriate federal or state agencies, or educational or cultural institutions, if any relics are found. *Id.* §§ 312503(a), 312506(2). HADPA also requires federal agencies to notify the Secretary of the Interior if they plan to build a dam. *Id.* § 302505. HADPA therefore protects archaeological resources during construction, not just at the planning stages.

What kinds of properties does the Historic Sites Act protect? How does its scope overlap with that of the National Historic Preservation Act? The following case explores these issues.

Historic Green Springs, Inc. v. Bergland
497 F.Supp. 839 (E.D. Va. 1980)

■ MERHIGE, JR., DISTRICT JUDGE.

MEMORANDUM

This case involves the controversy surrounding the designation of approximately 14,000 acres of land in Louisa County, Virginia, known as the Historic Green Springs District, as a National Historic Landmark, its listing in the National Register of Historic Places (hereinafter "National Register") * * *.

I.   Factual Background

The factual background that follows, regrettably, is necessarily detailed. The Historic Green Springs District comprises an area of approximately 14,000 acres, described as roughly the size of New York's Manhattan Island. The District lies within Louisa County, Virginia, about midway between Richmond and Charlottesville. While the national significance of the District's historic qualities is disputed, the area does constitute a beautiful and remarkably well-preserved concentration of eighteenth and nineteenth century buildings of architectural merit. Most of its land is used for agricultural purposes, although some commercial development may be found there, such as a lumber company, motel, meat processing plant, and used car dealership. Most importantly, two mining companies, VVL and W. R. Grace Co., Inc., have acquired mining rights over much of the land in and around the District for the mining and processing of vermiculite. Vermiculite is used in the production of plaster and lightweight concrete construction materials, fertilizers, paints, and insulation in both residential and commercial structures. The extent of the vermiculite deposits in the District has been termed significant.

The instant controversy over the district's historic value began as early as 1972, when the Commonwealth of Virginia proposed the construction of a new prison in the District. HGSI, with the support of the District's residents, organized a successful effort to block the construction. HGSI's efforts at promoting the District's historical qualities to state officials resulted in its recognition as a Virginia Historic Landmark by the Virginia Historic Landmarks Commission. This state commission in February, 1973, nominated the District to the National Register. On March 1, 1973, the Department of the Interior (hereinafter "the Department") approved the state nomination and listed the District on the National Register.[1] * * *

---

[1]   This listing on The National Register by state nomination was later found to have been defective for lack of adequate notice to the affected landowners.

In 1974, the Secretary considered designating the District a National Historic Landmark. In April, 1974, the Department's Advisory Board on National Parks, Historic Sites, Buildings & Monuments had presented to it a report on the District by Benjamin Levy, a Department historian. Levy's report, after noting a modicum of historical events and persons associated with the District, focused on the District's architectural qualities. Replete with photographs and diagrams, the report discussed in detail the characteristics of the various manor houses and outbuildings said to "constitute a textbook of Virginia architecture up to the period following the Civil War." Based upon this report, the Secretary designated the District a National Historic Landmark in 1974. * * *

Prompted, at least in part, by the protests of Green Springs landowners and by plaintiffs' counterclaim and third-party complaint in this action, the Department announced in the Federal Register on June 29, 1977, that it would reconsider the District's listing on the National Register as a state nomination and the District's designation as a National Historic Landmark. A public hearing was announced for the morning of July 27, 1977, for the purpose of receiving public comment on the reconsideration. By Federal Register announcement of July 18, 1977, the Department defined "reconsider" as to "determine anew, without any presumptions based on prior actions," the issues concerning the District. The Department, however, announced that the reconsideration process would not entail resubmission of the District's landmark status to the Department's Advisory Board. * * *

On July 27, 1977, the Department held public hearings concerning the District's listing on the National Register and its landmark designation * * *. A transcript of the morning hearing concerning the reconsideration of the District's landmark status reveals that great confusion existed over the scope of the hearing and over the action being proposed by the Department. Department officials at the hearing did not, for the most part, respond to the public's questions. By Federal Register notice of September 20, 1977, the Department announced the issuance of, and summarized, an environmental assessment and negative declaration concerning the redesignation of the District as a National Historic Landmark. The September 20 notice also clarified for the first time that the District could remain a National Historic Landmark despite a defective state nomination to the National Register. * * *

Finally, on December 13, 1977, the Secretary of the Interior decided to redesignate the District as a National Historic Landmark on his own authority * * *. The District's designation as a National Historic Landmark automatically placed it back on the National Register. 36 C.F.R. § 60.2(d)(2). These decisions were announced in the Federal Register on January 24, 1978.

Plaintiffs attacked the Secretary's decisions to designate the District as a National Historic Landmark * * * on several grounds. Initially, plaintiffs challenge the Secretary's authority to designate the District

* * * pursuant to the Historic Sites, Buildings and Antiquities Act of 1935. Plaintiffs contend that the Department of the Interior confused the standards for national significance under the Historic Sites Act of 1935 with the less strict standards of historic importance under the National Historic Preservation Act of 1966, 16 U.S.C. §§ 470 et seq [EDS.: moved to 54 U.S.C. § 300101 *et seq.*]. Arguing that the District's historical significance does not meet a level of national importance, the plaintiffs question the Secretary's authority under the Historic Sites Act of 1935 to take the administrative action challenged here. * * *

II. Scope of Review

This Court's scope of review of the administrative action challenged here is set out in *Citizens to Preserve Overton Park, Inc. v. Volpe*, 401 U.S. 402 (1971). The Court's inquiry is described therein as "substantial," to be based on a "thorough, probing, in-depth review" of the Secretary's decision. *Id.* at 415. This review is broken down into three steps. First, the Court is required to decide whether the Secretary acted within the scope of his authority. *Id.*; *Schilling v. Rogers*, 363 U.S. 666, 676–77 (1960). Second, the Court must decide, pursuant to § 706(2)(A) of the Administrative Procedure Act, that the Secretary's actual decision was not "arbitrary, capricious, an abuse of discretion, or otherwise not in accordance with law." *Citizens to Preserve Overton Park, supra* at 416. A corollary of this inquiry is a determination that the Secretary's action is not "contrary to constitutional right, power, privilege, or immunity" under § 706(2)(B). The third and final step is to determine whether the Secretary's action "followed the necessary procedural requirements." *Id.* at 417.

III. The Secretary's Scope of Authority * * *

The policy underlying the 1935 Act is contained in § 461 of the Act: "It is (hereby) declared that it is a national policy to preserve for public use historic sites, buildings and objects of national significance for the inspiration and benefit of the people of the United States." 16 U.S.C. § 461 [EDS.: moved to 54 U.S.C. § 320101]. In order to effectuate that policy, the Secretary of the Interior is empowered, inter alia, to acquire on behalf of the government any historic site, building, or object by gift, purchase, or otherwise. 16 U.S.C. § 462 [EDS.: moved to 54 U.S.C. § 320102(e)]. Further, the Secretary is authorized, in cooperation with state and local agencies and professional individuals, to recognize and study historic landmarks of national significance not owned by the federal government. To this end, the Secretary instituted the National Historic Landmark Program. * * * [T]he designation of the District as a National Landmark were accomplished pursuant to the 1935 Act.

In 1966, Congress passed the National Historic Preservation Act of 1966 (hereinafter "the 1966 Act"), 16 U.S.C. §§ 470 et seq., which provided for the recognition of historic places and objects of state and local importance in addition to those of national significance. The 1966 Act expanded the scope of the National Register to include not only

National Historic Landmarks and historic properties of the National Park System, but properties of state and local importance nominated by the states. For the first time in such legislation, allowance was made for the recognition of historic "districts" in addition to the previously recognized sites, buildings and objects. Further, the 1966 Act added "cultural" significance as a valid subject of federal protective measures. As part of this expanded concept of cultural and historical significance, the 1966 Act added architectural and archeological importance to social and political importance as worthy of recognition.

In summary, the 1935 Act restricted its scope to the few properties possessing truly national historical significance. The Secretary is empowered thereunder to acquire property on behalf of the United States and to designate as National Historic Landmarks those exceptional properties of national importance. The 1966 Act broadened the scope of federal historical preservation by recognizing properties of state and local importance and by adding "districts" and "cultural" values as subjects of federal protective measures. The 1966 Act did not authorize acquisition of such properties but, rather, provided for the listing on the National Register with the protection inherent in such listing.

Plaintiffs argue that designation of the District as a National Historic Landmark * * * though [an] authorized action[ ] under the 1935 Act, [was] accomplished by applying the standards of the 1966 Act. As a threshold matter, the Court finds that plaintiffs' contention that the District lacks national significance and is therefore not a proper subject of recognition under the 1935 Act is more appropriately an attack on the merits of the Secretary's decision rather than on his authority; the Court finds that the Secretary regarded the District's historic qualities as possessing national importance and did not misapply a state or local standard to the District. This attack on the merits will be addressed in a later section. However, plaintiffs do raise some apparent inconsistencies between the Secretary's actions under the 1935 Act and the language of that Act.

First, the Secretary appears to have based the findings of the District's historical significance on its architectural qualities, yet recognition of "architecture" and "cultural" values is only mentioned in the 1966 Act. Further, recognition of a historic "district," as opposed to sites, buildings and objects, is likewise mentioned only in the 1966 Act. * * *

The Court admittedly is troubled, however, by the Department's assertion that a "district" the size of Manhattan can be a historic "site," in spite of the absence of any significant commemorative event or historical person associated with it, and further that its architectural significance is covered by the term "historic" in the 1935 Act. A review of the legislative history of the 1935 Act and the 1966 Act reveals that the latter was necessitated by the narrow scope of the 1935 Act. In light of that fact, it strikes the Court as incongruous that the scope of the 1935

Act's protection should be expanded here so far beyond a literal reading of the Act's language.

In construing the extent of the Secretary's authority under the 1935 Act, the Court's task is made the more difficult by the absence of adequate substantive criteria for that which merits treatment as a National Historic Landmark or what constitutes national historic significance for purposes of acquiring property. Further, while the Court finds it possible that the Secretary's actions were authorized under the 1935 Act, the paltry statement of reasons for the Secretary's actions forces the Court to speculate about how the Secretary applied the Act's standards to the District. Because these and other procedural problems, in the Court's view, require a reversal and remand to the Secretary, as hereinafter discussed, the Court will not engage in speculation concerning the scope of the Secretary's authority. * * *

IV. Review of Secretary's Findings and Conclusions

As noted above, plaintiffs challenge the Secretary's decisions regarding the District as being arbitrary, capricious, and violative of the Fifth and Tenth Amendments. * * *

C.   Arbitrary or Capricious

Plaintiffs' chief attack on the merits of the Secretary's decisions is under the "arbitrary, capricious, (or) an abuse of discretion" standard of s 706(2) (A) of the Administrative Procedure Act (hereinafter "APA") as applied in *Citizens to Preserve Overton Park v. Volpe, supra.* Plaintiffs argue that the District has no historic value of national significance and that the Secretary's recognition of, and efforts towards preservation of such historic value are abuses of discretion under that standard.

Plaintiffs allege a total absence of historical events, persons, or structures of national importance associated with the District that could support the Secretary's findings and conclusions. They emphasize that the Department historian was able to find records of only a few Revolutionary War or Civil War skirmishes which took place in or near the District. One structure in the District was said to have been used briefly as a hospital during the Civil War. Some of the first of McCormick's reapers were said to have been used to harvest crops in the District-a slim basis indeed for the Secretary's conclusion.

Plaintiffs argue further that other factors apparently relied upon by the Department in addition to traditional historic values fail to explain or support the landmark designation of the entire District. The uniform soil type of District, which the Department perceived as a major factor contributing to the District's unbroken history of agrarian use, consists in fact of several soil types. The District's boundaries appear to be broader than either the underlying soil zone or the "visual unity" attributed to the District by Department officials. Finally, plaintiffs argue that the District's architectural significance in representing a rural community of the eighteenth and nineteenth centuries is of statewide importance at best, and, at worst, is merely a confusing array of contrasting architectural styles.

In reviewing the merits of the Secretary's decisions, the Court is required to consider whether the decisions were "based on a consideration of the relevant factors and whether there has been a clear error of judgment." *Citizens to Preserve Overton Park, supra* at 416, 91 S.Ct. at 824. As noted above, with regard to determining whether the Secretary acted within the scope of his authority, the absence of any detailed statement of reasons or of clear formal standards concerning national historic significance hinders the Court in ensuring that relevant factors were accurately considered. Cf. *Human Resources Management, Inc. v. Weaver*, 442 F.Supp. 241, 249 (D.D.C. 1978). Without them, the conclusory findings of national historic importance * * * offer provide little insight into whether the Secretary's discretion was properly exercised. However, rather than require the Secretary to submit post hoc rationalizations for his decisions, the Court must remand the case for proper compliance with procedural due process, as is set out below, of which a statement of reasons and promulgation of substantive standards are merely two of several components. * * *

VI. Conclusion

The Court thus finds the landmark designation invalid based on the Department's failure to promulgate substantive standards for national historic significance and its failure to prepare and publish rules of procedure to govern the designation process. The Court finds further that the administrative record provides an inadequate insight into the reasons underlying the landmark designation, including but not limited to the District's historic values of national importance and the justification for drawing the boundaries as they now exist. * * *

The Court must, therefore, remand this matter to the Department for promulgation of * * * substantive and procedural regulations consistent with the Court's opinion. On remand, the Court urges the Secretary not simply to codify the criteria and procedures developed informally in the instant case, but to articulate meaningful standards in as much detail as possible so that the Department's efforts are channeled efficiently, the public may make a meaningful response, and, in the event further judicial review is necessary, a court may determine that the proper standards have been applied. In articulating substantive standards, the Department should be careful to develop criteria for landmark designation that are consistent with the language of the 1935 Act. With regard to the standards to be applied to historic districts, the Department should address the question of a district's inclusion under the term "site" and provide for the criteria relevant to setting the boundaries of such a site. To the extent that other comments of the Court have suggested additional clarification, the Secretary should respond thereto in the subsequent promulgation of regulations.

In addition, the Secretary should ensure, by means of a clear statement of reasons, that the public and, if necessary, a reviewing court, can understand the grounds for his exercise of discretion. * * * No formal findings need be articulated, but the Secretary should indicate in as much detail as possible the reasoning supporting his ultimate decision.

ORDER

In accordance with the memorandum of the Court this day filed, and deeming it proper so to do, it is ADJUDGED and ORDERED that:

1.   The designation of the Historic Green Springs District as a National Historic Landmark and its placement on the National Register of Historic Places be, and the same are hereby set aside as violative of plaintiffs' due process rights under the Fifth Amendment, U.S. CONST. amend. V, and of the Administrative Procedure Act, 5 U.S.C. § 552(a)(1); * * *

3.   The Secretary shall remove the District from the National Register and any list of National Historic Landmarks; and

4.   The Secretary shall develop and promulgate regulations setting out substantive criteria and procedural guidelines for landmark designation under The Historic Sites Act of 1935, not inconsistent with the Court's memorandum. * * *

NOTES & QUESTIONS

1.   In the early 1970s, a prison was proposed in the area at issue in *Historic Green Springs, Inc.* As this case reveals, entities with interests in mining in the area played a more direct role in disputing the Secretary of the Interior's designation.

2.   Why did the Secretary of the Interior declare the historic district a landmark?

3.   By its terms, the Historic Sites Act was restricted in scope to the few properties possessing truly national historical significance. The National Historic Preservation Act of 1966, which is mentioned in this case and is the subject of Chapter 3 of this book, expanded the scope of federally protected historic properties to those of state and local significance. What does the court say about Congress's intent with respect to both laws?

4.   After this case was decided, Congress acted to restore the National Register status of this district. In addition, it commented on its intent with respect to the Historic Sites Act and included provisions that confirmed the authority of the Secretary of the Interior to designate National Historic Landmarks, in the 1980 amendments to the National Historic Preservation Act. *See* 54 U.S.C. § 302103. Federal regulations now establish the criteria and process the Secretary of the Interior must use prior to designating a National Historic Landmark. *See* 36 C.F.R. §§ 65.4–65.5.

5.   A wrinkle in the case, edited out of this excerpt, is that the Secretary of the Interior was also considering accepting preservation easements over the property in question. The Secretary now holds easements

over this property, much to the chagrin of some local property owners. One property owner, Peter F. Blackman, has been in disputes for years with the National Park Service (NPS) over its management of the easement over his property, the manor house at Eastern View Farm. Blackman had hoped to completely renovate the manor house. After the NPS rejected his plans, he commenced work on his own, arguing that the terms of the easement that had been conveyed to NPS were vague and contradictory. The NPS sued Blackman and obtained a preliminary injunction restraining him from conducting any further repairs on the property. Meanwhile, Blackman removed the front porch and much of the siding of the house, and he was found in criminal contempt of court for violating the preliminary injunction. *United States v. Blackman*, 2005 WL 2675095 (W.D. Va. 2005), *aff'd United States v. Blackman*, 2007 WL 1578278 (4th Cir. 2007). We will learn more about conservation and preservation restrictions in Chapter 10.

C. THE ARCHAEOLOGICAL RESOURCES PROTECTION ACT

In 1979, Congress passed the Archaeological Resources Protection Act to strengthen protections for archaeological resources found on public and Native American lands. It has since become one of the most important and effective tools for archaeological resource management and protection.

Archaeological Resources Protection Act of 1979
16 U.S.C. §§ 470aa–470*ll*

§ 470aa. Congressional findings and declaration of purpose

(a) The Congress finds that—

(1) archaeological resources on public lands and Indian lands are an accessible and irreplaceable part of the Nation's heritage;

(2) these resources are increasingly endangered because of their commercial attractiveness;

(3) existing Federal laws do not provide adequate protection to prevent the loss and destruction of these archaeological resources and sites resulting from uncontrolled excavations and pillage; and

(4) there is a wealth of archaeological information which has been legally obtained by private individuals for noncommercial purposes and which could voluntarily be made available to professional archaeologists and institutions.

(b) The purpose of this chapter is to secure, for the present and future benefit of the American people, the protection of archaeological resources and sites which are on public lands and Indian lands, and to foster increased cooperation and exchange of information between governmental authorities, the professional archaeological community, and private individuals having collections of archaeological resources and data which were obtained before October 31, 1979.

§ 470bb. Definitions

As used in this chapter—

(1) The term "archaeological resource" means any material remains of past human life or activities which are of archaeological interest, as determined under uniform regulations promulgated pursuant to this chapter. Such regulations containing such determination shall include, but not be limited to: pottery, basketry, bottles, weapons, weapon projectiles, tools, structures or portions of structures, pit houses, rock paintings, rock carvings, intaglios, graves, human skeletal materials, or any portion or piece of any of the foregoing items. Nonfossilized and fossilized paleontological specimens, or any portion or piece thereof, shall not be considered archaeological resources, under the regulations under this paragraph, unless found in an archaeological context. No item shall be treated as an archaeological resource under regulations under this paragraph unless such item is at least 100 years of age.

(2) The term "Federal land manager" means, with respect to any public lands, the Secretary of the department, or the head of any other agency or instrumentality of the United States, having primary management authority over such lands. * * *

(3) The term "public lands" means—

(A) lands which are owned and administered by the United States as part of—

(i) the national park system,

(ii) the national wildlife refuge system, or

(iii) the national forest system; and

(B) all other lands the fee title to which is held by the United States, other than lands on the Outer Continental Shelf and lands which are under the jurisdiction of the Smithsonian Institution.

(4) The term "Indian lands" means lands of Indian tribes, or Indian individuals, which are either held in trust by the United States or subject to a restriction against alienation imposed by the United States, except for any subsurface interests in lands not owned or controlled by an Indian tribe or an Indian individual.

(5) The term "Indian tribe" means any Indian tribe, band, nation, or other organized group or community, including any Alaska Native village or regional or village corporation as defined in, or established pursuant to, the Alaska Native Claims Settlement Act (85 Stat. 688) [43 U.S.C.A. § 1601 et seq.]. * * *

§ 470cc. Excavation and removal

(a) Application for permit

Any person may apply to the Federal land manager for a permit to excavate or remove any archaeological resource located on public lands or Indian lands and to carry out activities associated with such excavation or removal. The application shall be required, under uniform regulations under this chapter, to contain such information as the Federal land manager deems necessary, including information concerning the time, scope, and location and specific purpose of the proposed work.

(b) Determinations by Federal land manager prerequisite to issuance of permit

A permit may be issued pursuant to an application under subsection (a) of this section if the Federal land manager determines, pursuant to uniform regulations under this chapter, that—

    (1) the applicant is qualified, to carry out the permitted activity,

    (2) the activity is undertaken for the purpose of furthering archaeological knowledge in the public interest,

    (3) the archaeological resources which are excavated or removed from public lands will remain the property of the United States, and such resources and copies of associated archaeological records and data will be preserved by a suitable university, museum, or other scientific or educational institution, and

    (4) the activity pursuant to such permit is not inconsistent with any management plan applicable to the public lands concerned.

(c) Notification to Indian tribes of possible harm to or destruction of sites having religious or cultural importance

If a permit issued under this section may result in harm to, or destruction of, any religious or cultural site, as determined by the Federal land manager, before issuing such permit, the Federal land manager shall notify any Indian tribe which may consider the site as having religious or cultural importance. Such notice shall not be deemed a disclosure to the public for purposes of section 470hh of this title. * * *

(g) Excavation or removal by Indian tribes or tribe members; excavation or removal of resources located on Indian lands

    (1) No permit shall be required under this section or under the Act of June 8, 1906 (16 U.S.C. 431 [EDS.: moved to 54 U.S.C. § 320301]), for the excavation or removal by any Indian tribe or member thereof of any archaeological resource located on Indian lands of such Indian tribe, except that in the absence of tribal law regulating the excavation or removal of archaeological resources on Indian lands, an individual tribal member shall be required to obtain a permit under this section.

(2) In the case of any permits for the excavation or removal of any archaeological resource located on Indian lands, the permit may be granted only after obtaining the consent of the Indian or Indian tribe owning or having jurisdiction over such lands. The permit shall include such terms and conditions as may be requested by such Indian or Indian tribe. * * *

(i) Compliance with provisions relating to undertakings on property listed in the National Register not required

Issuance of a permit in accordance with this section and applicable regulations shall not require compliance with section 306108 of title 54. * * *

§ 470ee. Prohibited acts and criminal penalties

(a) Unauthorized excavation, removal, damage, alteration, or defacement of archaeological resources

No person may excavate, remove, damage, or otherwise alter or deface, or attempt to excavate, remove, damage, or otherwise alter or deface any archaeological resource located on public lands or Indian lands unless such activity is pursuant to a permit issued under section 470cc of this title, a permit referred to in section 470cc(h)(2) of this title, or the exemption contained in section 470cc(g)(1) of this title.

(b) Trafficking in archaeological resources the excavation or removal of which was wrongful under Federal law

No person may sell, purchase, exchange, transport, receive, or offer to sell, purchase, or exchange any archaeological resource if such resource was excavated or removed from public lands or Indian lands in violation of—

(1) the prohibition contained in subsection (a) of this section, or

(2) any provision, rule, regulation, ordinance, or permit in effect under any other provision of Federal law.

(c) Trafficking in interstate or foreign commerce in archaeological resources the excavation, removal, sale, purchase, exchange, transportation or receipt of which was wrongful under State or local law

No person may sell, purchase, exchange, transport, receive, or offer to sell, purchase, or exchange, in interstate or foreign commerce, any archaeological resource excavated, removed, sold, purchased, exchanged, transported, or received in violation of any provision, rule, regulation, ordinance, or permit in effect under State or local law.

(d) Penalties

Any person who knowingly violates, or counsels, procures, solicits, or employs any other person to violate, any prohibition contained in subsection (a), (b), or (c) of this section shall, upon conviction, be fined not more than $10,000 or imprisoned not more than one year, or both: Provided, however, That if the commercial or archaeological value of the archaeological resources involved and the cost of restoration and repair of such resources exceeds the sum of $500, such person shall be fined not more than $20,000 or imprisoned not more than two years, or both. In the case of a second or subsequent such violation upon conviction such person shall be fined not more than $100,000, or imprisoned not more than five years, or both. * * *

(g) Removal of arrowheads located on ground surface

Nothing in subsection (d) of this section shall be deemed applicable to any person with respect to the removal of arrowheads located on the surface of the ground.

§ 470ff. Civil penalties

(a) Assessment by Federal land manager

(1) Any person who violates any prohibition contained in an applicable regulation or permit issued under this chapter may be assessed a civil penalty by the Federal land manager concerned. * * *

§ 470hh. Confidentiality of information concerning nature and location of archaeological resources

(a) Disclosure of information

Information concerning the nature and location of any archaeological resource for which the excavation or removal requires a permit or other permission under this chapter or under any other provision of Federal law may not be made available to the public under subchapter II of chapter 5 of Title 5 or under any other provision of law unless the Federal land manager concerned determines that such disclosure would—

(1) further the purposes of this chapter or chapter 3125 of Title 54, and

(2) not create a risk of harm to such resources or to the site at which such resources are located. * * *

NOTES & QUESTIONS

1.   What is the purpose of the Archaeological Resources Protection Act of 1979 (ARPA)? How does ARPA accomplish this purpose? Explain the permitting regime established by the law.

2.   What, specifically, is prohibited by ARPA? What are the fines and penalties associated with violations of ARPA? Compare these with the specific penalty of imprisonment of not more than 90 days under the Antiquities Act, now codified at 18 U.S.C. § 1866.

3.   In *United States v. Austin*, 902 F.2d 743 (9th Cir. 1990), a defendant who had gathered some 2,800 Native American artifacts and had been convicted by a district court of violating ARPA appealed his conviction by arguing that ARPA was unconstitutionally overbroad. Among the artifacts that underlay the conviction were obsidian weapon projectiles and tools such as scrapers. The defendant argued that the words "tools" and

"weapons" in the definition of "archaeological resources" in section 470bb(1) of ARPA were too broad and did not give him fair notice that his excavation of the objects at issue was illegal. The panel dismissed Austin's "creative" argument in two paragraphs, stating that "[a]lthough he contends that 'weapons' and 'tools' are ambiguous terms, [t]he statute provided fair notice that it prohibited the activities for which Austin was convicted." *Austin*, 902 F.2d at 745.

4.   Section 470ee(d) of ARPA imposes penalties only if a defendant acted "knowingly." Courts have grappled with interesting questions interpreting this *mens rea* provision. In vacating the conviction of an individual with a high school education who took a skull from federal lands in Alaska, the Ninth Circuit held that the government must prove that the defendant knew that the object was an archeological resource. The court reasoned that since "removing objects that are not 'archaeological resources' from public land is not a violation of ARPA, the knowingly requirement should apply to the term 'archaeological resources' as well as the prohibited act of removing." *United States v. Lynch*, 233 F.3d 1139, 1144 (9th Cir. 2000). Is there any doubt that a skull is an archeological resource under ARPA? How may the government prove the defendant's knowledge? Why would the court require such proof?

The Tenth Circuit held that evidence of prior illegal activities involving an archeological site can establish knowledge and intent for the purposes of section 470ee(d). *United States v. Shumway*, 112 F.3d 1413, 1422 (10th Cir. 1997). Five years later, the same circuit faced a question about whether a defendant must "knowingly" be on federal land. It found:

> [E]xtending the *mens rea* requirement to the "located on public lands" element would frustrate the purpose of the Act. For example, it would often be difficult for the government to prove that a defendant knew he was on public land unless signs were posted at or near the archaeological site. Placing signs near sites, however, would draw the attention of potential looters.

United States v. Quarrell, 310 F.3d 664 (10th Cir. 2002). In *Quarrell*, the defendants (two brothers) admitted to knowing that the resources they had excavated from the Gila National Forest in New Mexico had significant historical value. *Id.* at 669. Should the identity of the finder matter in determining how to apply ARPA's *mens rea* provision? Was it that the defendant in *Lynch* was more sympathetic than the defendants in *Quarrell*? *See also* Roberto Iraola, *The Archaeological Resources Protection Act— Twenty Five Years Later*, 42 DUQ. L. REV. 221 (2004) (identifying these cases and addressing them in greater detail). Iraola suggests that while ARPA has withstood many constitutional challenges, *Lynch* represents "a setback of sorts, from the perspective of law enforcement." *Id.* at 245.

5.   Why does section 470hh require that managers responsible for the protection of archeological resources, in most cases, hold information about the locations and nature of these resources confidential? Is section 470hh consistent with the findings and declaration section of ARPA, and specifically the reference contained in section 470aa, which expresses a

desire that archaeological resources on public lands and Indian lands be accessible?

6. The provision referenced in section 470cc(i) is Section 106 of the National Historic Preservation Act, which is the subject of Chapter 3. That statutory provision requires federal agencies engaging in certain undertakings to "take into account the effect of the undertaking on any historic property." 54 U.S.C. § 306108. This provision may require federal agencies to undergo a lengthy process of evaluating the effects of their actions, as similar language appears in the regulations promulgated by the Departments of Agriculture, Defense, and the Interior, as well as the Tennessee Valley Authority—each with a federal land manager subject to the provisions of ARPA. In section 470cc(i), ARPA specifically states that the issuance of a permit does not, by itself, trigger Section 106 review requirements. As the regulations clarify, however "mere issuance of such a permit does not excuse the Federal land manager from compliance with section 106 where otherwise required." 43 C.F.R. § 7.12. In other words, if an agency issues an ARPA permit as part of a larger undertaking which would trigger Section 106 review, the agency cannot use section 470cc(i) of ARPA to excuse itself from complying with Section 106. Whom does this language most benefit? The application of Section 106 to archaeological resources is considered in greater length in the next section.

7. How does ARPA impact traditional rules relating to finds and salvage? Both the law of finds and the law of salvage are concepts originating in maritime law. The law of finds relates to the ability of an individual finding a lost or abandoned object to assert ownership of that object. The law of salvage grants the right of possession, or a reward, to a salvor who finds property still claimed or claimable by its rightful owner. Which of these traditional rules might apply to objects found on federal land with an ARPA permit? How does ARPA treat ownership of found objects differently than these traditional rules?

United States v. Gerber
999 F.2d 1112 (7th Cir. 1993), *cert. denied*, 510 U.S. 1071 (1994)

■ Before POSNER, RIPPLE, and ROVNER, CIRCUIT JUDGES.

■ POSNER, CIRCUIT JUDGE.

Arthur Joseph Gerber pleaded guilty to misdemeanor violations of the Archaeological Resources Protection Act of 1979, 16 U.S.C. §§ 470aa et seq., and was sentenced to twelve months in prison, reserving however his right to appeal on the ground that the Act is inapplicable to his offense. What he had done was to transport in interstate commerce Indian artifacts* that he had stolen from a burial mound on privately owned land in violation of Indiana's criminal laws of trespass and conversion. The section of the Archaeological Resources Protection Act

---

* We are mindful that "Native American" is the term preferred by most members of the American Indian community. Since, however, the statute and both of the parties use the term "Indian," we have decided to do likewise.

under which he was convicted provides that "no person may sell, purchase, exchange, transport, receive, or offer to sell, purchase, or exchange, in interstate or foreign commerce, any archaeological resource excavated, removed, sold, purchased, exchanged, transported, or received in violation of any provision, rule, regulation, ordinance, or permit in effect under State or local law." 16 U.S.C. § 470ee(c). Gerber argues that despite the references in this section to state and local law, the Act is inapplicable to archaeological objects removed from lands not owned either by the federal government or by Indian tribes. His back-up argument is that the provisions, rules, regulations, and so forth of state or local law to which the Act refers are limited to provisions expressly protecting archaeological objects or sites, as distinct from laws of general application such as those forbidding trespass and theft. The issues are novel because this is the first prosecution under the Act of someone who trafficked in archaeological objects removed from lands other than either federal or Indian lands.

More than fifteen hundred years ago in the American midwest Indians built a series of large earthen mounds over prepared mound floors containing human remains plus numerous ceremonial artifacts and grave goods made of silver, copper, wood, cloth, leather, obsidian, flint, mica, quartz, pearl, shells, and drilled, carved, or inlaid human and bear teeth. This mound culture, the product of a civilization that included the beginnings of settled agriculture, an elaborate ceremonialism, and far-flung trading networks, has been dubbed the "Hopewell phenomenon." N'OMI B. GREBER & KATHARINE C. RUHL, THE HOPEWELL SITE: A CONTEMPORARY ANALYSIS BASED ON THE WORK OF CHARLES C. WILLOUGHBY (1989); Warren K. Moorehead, *The Hopewell Mound Group of Ohio* (Field Museum of Natural History, Publication No. 211, 1922). In 1985 farmers sold General Electric a piece of untillable land in southwestern Indiana adjacent to one of its factories. The land contained a prominent knob on top of a ridge. Unbeknownst to anyone this knob was a Hopewell burial mound some 400 feet long, 175 feet wide, and 20 feet high. The mound and its contents (which included two human skeletons) were intact—even the perishable materials such as wood and leather artifacts were well preserved—and when discovered it would prove to be one of the five largest Hopewell burial mounds known.

A highway was planned to run through the ridge on which the knob was located. In the course of construction, in 1988, earth was removed from the knob to stabilize the roadbed. Workmen engaged in this removal discovered in the knob curious objects—turtleback-shaped rocks—which they showed to a heavy-equipment operator on the project, named Bill Way, who happened to be a collector of Indian artifacts. Recognizing the significance of the find, Way nosed his bulldozer into the knob and quickly discovered hundreds of artifacts, including copper axeheads, inlaid bear canines, and tooled leather. He loaded these items into his pickup truck and covered up the excavation he had made. An acquaintance put him in touch with Arthur Joseph Gerber, a well-known collector of Indian artifacts and promoter of annual Indian "relic shows." Gerber paid Way $6,000 for the artifacts and for revealing to Gerber the location of the mound. Way took Gerber to the site the same night, encountering other people digging for Indian artifacts. Gerber returned to the site several more times, excavating and removing hundreds of additional artifacts, including silver earspools, copper axeheads, pieces of worked leather, and rare silver musical instruments, some with the original reeds preserved. On Gerber's last visit to the site he was detected by a General Electric security guard and ejected. Shortly afterward Gerber sold some of the artifacts at his annual "Indian Relic Show of Shows" in Kentucky. He acknowledges that in entering upon General Electric's land without the company's permission and in removing, again without its permission, Indian artifacts buried there, he committed criminal trespass and conversion in violation of Indiana law. He also acknowledges having transported some of the stolen artifacts in interstate commerce.

The preamble of the Archaeological Resources Protection Act of 1979 states that "archaeological resources on public lands [defined elsewhere in the Act as *federal* public lands] and Indian lands are an accessible and irreplaceable part of the Nation's heritage" and that the purpose of the Act is "to secure, for the present and future benefit of the American people, the protection of archaeological resources and sites which are on public lands and Indian lands." 16 U.S.C. §§ 470aa(a)(1) & (b). Consistent with this preamble, most of the Act is given over to the regulation, in the form of civil and criminal penalties, permit requirements, forfeiture provisions, and other regulatory devices, of archaeological activities *on federal and Indian lands*. The criminal penalties are for archaeological activities conducted on those lands without a permit and for trafficking in archaeological objects that have been removed from them in violation either of the Act's permit requirements or of any other federal law. *Id.* §§ 470ee(a) & (b). Gerber did not remove Indian artifacts from federal or Indian lands, however, and was therefore prosecuted under the third criminal provision (§ 470ee(c), quoted earlier), which is not in terms limited to such lands.

The omission of any reference in subsection (c) to federal and Indian lands was, Gerber argues, inadvertent. Not only the preamble of the Act, but its legislative history, shows that all that Congress was concerned with was protecting archaeological sites and objects on federal and Indian lands. This is indeed all that the preamble mentions; and a principal sponsor of the Act said that "it does not affect any lands other than the public lands of the United States and [Indian] lands." 125 Cong.Rec. 17,394 (1979) (remarks of Congressman Udall). The legislative history contains no reference to archaeological sites or objects on state or private lands. The Act superseded the Antiquities Act of 1906, 16 U.S.C. §§ 431–33 [EDS.: moved to 54 U.S.C. §§ 320301–320303 & 18 U.S.C.

§ 1866], which had been expressly limited to federal lands. And if the Act applies to nonfederal, non-Indian lands, its provisions are at once overinclusive and underinclusive: overinclusive because the Act authorizes the federal court in which a defendant is prosecuted to order, in its discretion, the forfeiture of the archaeological objects involved in the violation to the United States (unless they were removed from Indian lands), *id.* § 470gg(b), (c); underinclusive because the provisions authorizing civil penalties and the payment of rewards to informers out of fines collected in criminal prosecutions under the Act are administered by officials who lack jurisdiction over nonfederal, non-Indian lands. *Id.* §§ 470bb(2), 470ff, 470gg(a). (The artifacts stolen by Gerber were recovered and are being held by the United States as evidence in this case, but they have not been ordered forfeited.) Most scholarly commentators on the Act assume that it is limited to federal and Indian lands. E.g., Kristine Olson Rogers, *Visigoths Revisited: The Prosecution of Archaeological Resource Thieves, Traffickers, and Vandals*, 2 J. ENVTL. L. & LITIG. 47, 72 (1987). Gerber reminds us of the rule of lenity in interpreting criminal statutes and of the implied constitutional prohibition against excessively vague criminal statutes. He adds that subsection (c) of section 470ee would not be a nullity if the Act were held to be limited to sites and objects on federal and Indian lands. A number of state laws prohibit trafficking in stolen Indian artifacts regardless of their origin, and it has not been suggested that these statutes are preempted by the federal Act even with respect to artifacts stolen from federal or Indian lands. A person who trafficked in Indian artifacts in violation of state law would be subject to federal prosecution only under subsection (c) even if the artifacts had been removed from federal or Indian lands, if the removal happened not to violate federal law.

We are not persuaded by these arguments. That the statute, the scholarly commentary, and the legislative history are all focused on federal and Indian lands may simply reflect the fact that the vast majority of Indian sites—and virtually all archaeological sites in the Western Hemisphere are Indian—are located either in Indian reservations or on the vast federal public lands of the West. Subsection (c) appears to be a catch-all provision designed to back up state and local laws protecting archaeological sites and objects wherever located. It resembles the Mann Act, the Lindbergh Law, the Hobbs Act, and a host of other federal statutes that affix federal criminal penalties to state crimes that, when committed in interstate commerce, are difficult for individual states to punish or prevent because coordinating the law enforcement efforts of different states is difficult. The reference to interstate commerce would be superfluous if the subsection were limited to artifacts taken from federal or Indian lands, since either source would establish federal jurisdiction with no need to require proof that the artifacts were transported in interstate commerce. Probably the subsection was added as an afterthought, so one is not surprised that it does not jibe perfectly with the surrounding provisions; but that does not make it invalid, and it certainly is not vague. And we cannot see how the purposes of the Act would be undermined by our giving subsection (c) the interpretation that its words invite.

An amicus brief filed by several associations of amateur archaeologists claims that such an interpretation will infringe their liberty to seek to enlarge archaeological knowledge by excavating private lands. But there is no right to go upon another person's land, without his permission, to look for valuable objects buried in the land and take them if you find them. At common law General Electric would have been the owner of the mound and its contents regardless of the fact that it was unaware of them. *Elwes v. Brigg Gas Co.*, 33 Ch. D. 562 (1886); *South Staffordshire Water Co. v. Sharman*, [1896] 2 Q.B. 44. The modern American law is the same. * * * *Allred* actually involved an Indian artifact. Although we have found no Indiana cases, we are given no reason to suppose that the Indiana courts would adopt a different rule. It would make no difference if they would. Whatever the rightful ownership of the mound and its contents under current American law, no one suggests that Way or Gerber obtained any rights to the artifacts in question. No doubt, theft is at the root of many titles; and priceless archaeological artifacts obtained in violation of local law are to be found in reputable museums all over the world. But it is almost inconceivable that Congress would have wanted to encourage amateur archaeologists to violate state laws in order to amass valuable collections of Indian artifacts, especially as many of these amateurs do not appreciate the importance to scholarship of leaving an archaeological site intact and undisturbed until the location of each object in it has been carefully mapped to enable inferences concerning the design, layout, size, and age of the site, and the practices and culture of the inhabitants, to be drawn. It is also unlikely that a Congress sufficiently interested in archaeology to impose substantial criminal penalties for the violation of archaeological regulations (the maximum criminal penalty under the Act is five years in prison plus a $100,000 fine, § 470ee(d)) would be so parochial as to confine its interests to archaeological sites and artifacts on federal and Indian lands merely because that is where most of them are.

We conclude that section 470ee(c) is not limited to objects removed from federal and Indian lands, but we must consider Gerber's alternative argument, that the section is limited to removals in violation of state and local laws explicitly concerned with the protection of archaeological sites or objects. Gerber argues that if it is not so limited all sorts of anomalies are created. Suppose he had bought an Indian artifact from its rightful owner but had failed to pay the applicable state sales tax, and had transported the artifact across state lines. Then he would, he tells us, be transporting in interstate commerce an archaeological object purchased in violation of state law. And likewise if he transported such an object in interstate commerce in a vehicle that exceeded the weight limitations imposed by state law.

These are poor examples. It is unlikely in either case that the state would consider the *transportation* of a good to be in violation of state law merely because sales tax had not been paid or an overweight vehicle had been used. But we agree with the general point, that the Act is limited to cases in which the violation of state law is related to the protection of archaeological sites or objects. A broader interpretation would carry the Act far beyond the objectives of its framers and create pitfalls for the unwary. But we do not think that to be deemed related to the protection of archaeological resources a state or local law must be *limited* to that protection. A law that forbade the theft of Indian artifacts "and any other objects having historical or artistic value" could not reasonably be thought a law unrelated to the protection of such artifacts merely because it had broader objectives. That is essentially what Indiana's laws forbidding trespass and conversion have: objectives that include but are not exhausted in the protection of Indian artifacts and other antiquities. A law that comprehensively protects the owner of land from unauthorized incursions, spoliations, and theft could well be thought to give all the protection to buried antiquities that they need, making the passage of a law specially protecting buried antiquities redundant—and the passage of new laws is never costless and rarely easy. The interpretation urged by Gerber would if accepted compel states desiring federal assistance in protecting Indian artifacts in nonfederal, non-Indian lands within their borders to pass laws that might duplicate protections already adequate conferred on landowners sitting atop undiscovered archaeological sites by existing laws of general applicability. Granted, all fifty states have laws expressly protecting their archaeological sites; and in 1989, too late for this case, Indiana amended its law to forbid—redundantly—what Gerber had done. So the interpretation for which he contends might not actually impose a significant burden on the states. But Indiana may not have amended its law earlier because it thought its general criminal laws of trespass and conversion adequate—for all we know, it amended the law in response to Gerber's contention that the federal Act contains a loophole through which he and others like him might be able to squeeze.

We conclude that Gerber's conduct was forbidden by the Act. We commend counsel, Harvey Silets for the defendant and Larry Mackey for the government, for the exceptional quality of their briefs and argument. We have not hesitated to criticize counsel who fall below minimum professional standards for lawyers practicing in this court; equally, counsel whose performance exceeds those standards by a generous margin deserve our public recognition and thanks.

Affirmed.

NOTES & QUESTIONS

1.   The Seventh Circuit found that Congress intended to include state and local laws that were not necessarily related to archaeological protections in the interstate trafficking provision, § 470ee(c), of the Archaeological Resources Protection Act (ARPA). How does this finding square with the Congressional statement of intent stated in section 470aa?

2.   Significantly, *Gerber* applies ARPA to archaeological resources that were found on private lands and moved across state lines. But why? Under basic principles of statutory construction, courts view any inserted or omitted language of a legislative body to be meaningful. The omission of the words "federal or public lands" in section 470ee(c) of ARPA was determinative for the Seventh Circuit, even if the legislative history might have suggested something else. What if Congress just made a mistake? If it did, it has not amended the provision at issue in *Gerber*, one of the very few cases that deal with ARPA.

3.   Should ARPA be applied not just to private lands, but also to foreign lands? Consider the case against, as argued by Andrew Adler, *An Unintended and Absurd Expansion: The Application of the Archaeological Resources Protection Act to Foreign Lands*, 38 N.M. L. REV. 133 (2008). Adler documents three antiquities-related investigations since 1996 in which federal prosecutors have applied section 470ee(c) to cases involving archaeological resources extracted from foreign lands. *Id.* at 143–145.

D. SECTION 106 PROVISIONS REGARDING ARCHAEOLOGICAL RESOURCES

Section 106 of the National Historic Preservation Act, the important federal statute discussed in greater detail in Chapter 3, applies to archaeological resources listed on or eligible for the National Register of Historic Places. Its key language is worth quoting again in full:

> The head of any Federal agency having direct or indirect jurisdiction over a proposed Federal or federally assisted undertaking in any State and the head of any Federal department or independent agency having authority to license any undertaking, prior to the approval of the expenditure of any Federal funds on the undertaking or prior to the issuance of any license, shall take into account the effect of the undertaking on any historic property. The head of any such Federal agency shall afford the Council a reasonable opportunity to comment with regard to such undertaking.

54 U.S.C. § 306108. Section 106 thus requires agencies engaging in certain undertakings to consider the effect of their actions on certain federally protected (or protectable) resources.

To be listed in the National Register, archaeological resources must meet certain criteria, which are further discussed in Chapter 2. Generally speaking, to be protectable, archaeological resources must be "districts, sites, buildings, structures, [or] objects" (the five types of protectable resources under Section 106) and must exhibit "integrity of location, design, setting, materials, workmanship, feeling, and association." 36 C.F.R. § 60.4. In addition, such resources must be significant in one of four ways: They must be associated with significant historical events, persons, or architectural characteristics, or they must "have yielded, or may be likely to yield, information important in prehistory or history." *Id.* § 60.4(d). Archaeological resources are most likely to be found significant for their information-providing qualities, the fourth measure of significance, also known as "Criterion D." Criterion D resources must, by implication of the word "history," be associated with human activity, and not be merely an unassociated natural feature.

The National Park Service has published detailed guidelines about Criterion D. Patrick W. Andrus, *How to Apply the National Register Criteria for Evaluation* (Nat'l Park Serv., Nat'l Register Bull. No. 15, 1990). The Bulletin explains that a Criterion D resource:

> must have characteristics suggesting the likelihood that it possesses configurations of artifacts, soil strata, structural remains, or other natural or cultural features that make it possible to do the following:
>
> > Test a hypothesis or hypotheses about events, groups, or processes in the past that bear on important research questions in the social or natural sciences or the humanities; or
> >
> > Corroborate or amplify currently available information suggesting that a hypothesis is either true or false; or
> >
> > Reconstruct the sequence of archeological cultures for the purpose of identifying and explaining continuities and discontinuities in the archeological record for a particular area.

Id. at 21. Bulletin 15 also clarifies what types of properties are ineligible for designation under Criterion D. These include properties which: cannot be identified with a particular time period or cultural group; fail to reveal enough information to determine if important research questions can be answered by its data; mix or superimpose artifact assemblages (e.g., a plowed site) that cannot be studied independently; have been reconstructed; or have been completely excavated. *Id.* at 21–24.

Examples of Criterion D resources listed on the National Register include:

- The 22-acre riparian Quinebaug River Prehistoric Archaeological District in Canterbury, Connecticut, which was previously used as a camp, a tool production site, an animal facility, an agricultural field, and a fishing site. The site contained evidence of Native American occupation as far back as 8,000 years ago and long-term seasonal occupations periodically since that time. The nomination suggests that three important research themes could be explored on the site: prehistoric exchange and communication routes, interior riverine adaptations, and interior settlement organization.

- The John W. Jones House in Elmira, New York, which was the home of a prominent African American (a formerly enslaved person) who helped fugitive enslaved people travel the Underground Railroad. The nineteenth-century home was constructed from parts of a nearby prison camp and was described as meeting Criterion D because the fabric of the structure (including fencing materials used in the interior of the house, impressions and remnants of posters, wallpaper, and old currency) had the potential to reveal information about the prison camp that was not contained in written sources.

- Minertown in Carter, Wisconsin, a 43.5-acre site occupied between 1892 to the 1930s that includes several residential and industrial structures once part of a productive European-American mill town. The site, which has maintained its integrity despite threats from Forest Service logging activity and vandalism, could possibly reveal information about the historic logging community, production technologies, and planning for "company towns."

As you can see from these examples, Criterion D sites encompass a range of human activities, types of archaeological and other resources, groups of people (both Native American and not), and periods in our history.

The completion of the National Register nomination for archaeological resources is extremely time-consuming and detail-intensive. The National Park Service has published a how-to-guide in Bulletin 16A, *How to Complete the National Register Registration Form* (Nat'l Park Serv., Nat'l Register Bull. No. 16a, 1997). That guide tells nominators to describe, among other characteristics: the environmental setting; the period of time when the resource is known or projected to have been used; the identity of any groups who might have had a role in creating the resource; the physical characteristics of the property; the appearance of the site during its significant use period; the impact of modern development; and a description of any archival or field work involving the resource. *Id.* at 32.

Formal listing on the National Register is not required for a site to be protected under Section 106. A site merely deemed eligible for listing will also receive Section 106 protection. To be deemed eligible for the National Register, archaeological sites and artifacts must be evaluated by a State Historic Preservation Officer or Tribal Historic Preservation

Officer, as applicable, using the designation criteria described above. Often discussions about eligibility occur when a possibly protectable site has been discovered during the course of preparing for an undertaking. For example, an agency constructing its new headquarters may unearth what appears to be the remains of human settlement in the course of excavation required to make room for a new foundation. At that point, the foundation work may be halted while the eligibility of the site for the National Register is evaluated by the relevant parties. The Keeper of the National Register of Historic Places, an official at the National Park Service, has final authority over both determinations of eligibility and listing.

In many instances, a federal agency will propose an undertaking in an area where no National Register listed properties exist. The agency still has a limited duty to identify significant properties in the area of potential effects. It must make "a reasonable and good faith effort to carry out appropriate identification efforts, which may include background research, consultation, oral history interviews, sample field investigation, and field survey." 36 C.F.R. § 800.4(b)(1). It does not need to perform a thorough review over the entire area of potential effects, especially where initial analysis has suggested that the likelihood of finding archaeological resources is low. Once a listed or eligible archaeological resource is discovered in an area affected by a proposed undertaking, however, Section 106 review is triggered.

The treatment of archaeological resources under Section 106 differs from the treatment of most other resources listed in or eligible for the National Register, including historic buildings. Protection for most of the resources listed on the National Register comes in the form of preservation, rehabilitation, restoration, or reconstruction. For archaeological resources whose primary value is informational, however, protection may be exhausted once the information has been obtained from those resources. Using the example given in the preceding paragraph, assume that the resources found on site during the foundation excavation were found to be eligible for the National Register because they had the potential to provide valuable archaeological and historical information under Criterion D. At that point, archaeologists may be called to the site to document, measure, categorize, photograph, and/or extract the resources to the extent that they provide such information. After this process ends, however, the construction work could resume unimpeded. In other words, Section 106 requirements normally are met once the archaeological dig is completed. Note, however, that other laws, such as the Archaeological Resources Protection Act, may govern disposition of extracted resources.

Archaeologists may have a formal role during the Section 106 consultation process in two instances. First, an archaeologist must be a party to the consultation process if she is an applicant for the federal assistance, permit, license, or other approval for the federal undertaking that triggers Section 106 review. 36 C.F.R. § 800.2(c)(4). Second, an archaeologist may be a consulting party if she is invited to participate by the federal agency, which has the authority to engage "[c]ertain individuals and organizations with a demonstrated interest in the undertaking * * * due to the nature of their legal or economic relation to the undertaking or affected properties, or their concern with the undertaking's effects on historic properties." 36 C.F.R. § 800.2(c)(5). Beyond these two means, archaeologists may participate in the consultation process as members of the general public.

On a practical level, Section 106 requirements have kept many archaeologists busy, while providing a mechanism for them to make a significant contribution to our collective knowledge of the European settlement period and of tribal activity.

NOTES & QUESTIONS

1.   The Freedom of Information Act, which provides public access to federal agency records, allows federal agencies to restrict disclosure of records "specifically exempted from disclosure by statute." 5 U.S.C. § 552(b)(3). Like the Archaeological Resources Protection Act (ARPA), the National Historic Preservation Act requires confidentiality about certain archaeological resources, thus providing a statutory exception to the Freedom of Information Act public disclosure rules. More specifically, Section 304 of statute provides that the federal agency and Secretary of the Department of the Interior may agree to:

> withhold from disclosure to the public information about the location, character, or ownership of a historic property if the Secretary and the agency determine that disclosure may—
>
> (1)   cause a significant invasion of privacy;
>
> (2)   risk harm to the historic property; or
>
> (3)   impede the use of a traditional religious site by practitioners.

54 U.S.C. § 307103. This provision applies only to properties listed in or eligible for the National Register, and only applies to certain types of information. What is the role of these confidentiality rules?

Compare and contrast this language with section 470hh of ARPA, excerpted earlier in this Chapter. Among other things, the National Historic Preservation Act adds a provision about impeding religious access, 54 U.S.C. § 307103(a)(3), which was not included in ARPA.

2.   The Advisory Council on Historic Preservation (ACHP), the independent federal agency that oversees Section 106 implementation and can influence agency behavior, has weighed in on the treatment of certain archaeological resources. In 2007, the ACHP published a policy regarding burial sites, human remains, and funerary objects. The policy stated that such sites and artifacts "should not be knowingly disturbed unless absolutely necessary, and only after the federal agency has consulted and fully

considered avoidance of impact and whether it is feasible to preserve them in place." Advisory Council on Historic Pres., Policy Statement Regarding Treatment of Burial Sites, Human Remains and Funerary Objects 4 (2007). The words "absolutely necessary" set a very high bar for agencies to overcome, uniquely high perhaps because of the nature of the resources.

The policy also stresses the importance of consultation with both Native American and Native Hawaiian groups, whose involvement is covered by ACHP regulations, and with "descendants" (defined as those with a biological or cultural relationship with the dead), whose involvement is not covered by ACHP regulations. *Id.* at 6. Finally, the policy specifically states that it is to be interpreted in accordance with the Native American Graves Protection and Repatriation Act, 25 U.S.C. § 3001–3013, discussed further in Chapter 9.

3.   How can fairly recent structures, such as the John W. Jones House in Elmira, New York, be listed on the National Register for meeting Criterion D? Why is the Jones House not listed solely as a result of its association to an important historical figure? Although Criterion D may be used to protect traditional archaeological resources (such as buried artifacts), building and structures can be eligible for Criterion D protection if study of them can yield important information about historical human activity. A building may not be protected under Criterion D, however, if the part that would have yielded such informational value has been destroyed, even if documentation of that part (such as photographs or drawings) still exists.

Case Study: African Burial Ground in New York City

One of the most high-profile disputes involving nationally significant archaeological resources related to the African Burial Ground, a National Historic Landmark in lower Manhattan. The 6.6-acre seventeenth- and eighteenth-century burial ground included over four hundred remains, of both enslaved and free blacks. About half were children. The diverse array of associated grave artifacts includes beads, shells, fasteners, coffins, clothing, coins, pipes, stoneware, and other items that reveal important facets of the lives of urban black populations.

Over time, layers of human development covered over the African Burial Ground. The remains were first re-discovered during the excavation of foundations for an office building and courthouse project coordinated by the General Services Administration (GSA), a federal agency, in 1991. The GSA had known about the possibility of discovering a burial ground on its construction site, in part from historical documents such as a 1755 map depicting the burial ground, located just beyond the borders of the developing city. Yet the GSA failed to adequately prepare for that possibility. During the initial excavation phase, an unknown number of remains were moved or destroyed. After acknowledging its discovery, the GSA originally announced its plans to quickly dispose of the remains and proceed with its building as planned.

After a national outcry, the GSA began to take the presence of the resources seriously. In 1991, the Advisory Council on Historic Preservation (ACHP), the New York City Landmarks Preservation Commission (LPC), and the GSA agreed on measures the GSA would use to mitigate the impact of its construction. These included: developing and implementing a research design for the cemetery and other impacted archaeological sites; sensitively removing all exposed human remains; analyzing the disturbed human remains and associated grave artifacts; reinterring the human remains and associated grave artifacts; developing a memorial, interpretative site, and public outreach program; and submitting quarterly reports to ACHP and the LPC. *See* Advisory Council on Historic Pres., New York: Construction of Foley Square U.S. Courthouse and Federal Building, New York (Closed Case Follow-up), Fall 2001. Despite agreeing to these mitigation measures, the GSA was publicly criticized by various parties for failing to meet the letter or the spirit of the agreement.

Figure 8-1:
The African Burial Ground,
Manhattan, NY

Years of contentious public engagement followed. Many groups, particularly the Caribbean and African-American community in New York City, felt marginalized by the process. Key Congressmen intervened on their behalf. In 1992, a federal statute was passed requiring the GSA to abandon its plans for a smaller, four-story building next to the larger office building that was being excavated, and to use that site for the memorial facility. In addition, a steering committee, primarily composed of African-Americans, was chartered by Congress to guide the disposition and commemoration of the remains. In 1993, the artifacts were placed on the National Register, thus formalizing their protected legal status.

By 2003, progress was being made. That year, the remains were reinterred in a thoughtful ceremony involving coffins handmade in Ghana. Around the same time, the GSA and the National Park Service entered into a memorandum of agreement that allowed the Park Service to have a say in the design of a memorial and interpretative center promised in the 1991 agreement. In 2006, President George W. Bush declared the site a national monument pursuant to his powers under the Antiquities Act. In 2007, a commemorative sculpture was installed on the site, and in 2010, the visitors' center finally opened—twenty years after the initial discovery.

In some ways, this site is unique. Not every site will receive national attention, Congressional involvement, or a multi-million-dollar visitors' center. Indeed, the efforts at the African Burial Ground have even been called "the single-most important, historic urban archaeological project undertaken in the United States." (This quote and much of the above-described historical information may be found on the website for the African Burial Ground.) Unfortunately, however, conflicts about similar archaeological resources will continue to occur. It is estimated that in Lower Manhattan alone, ten to twenty thousand bodies of enslaved and free black Americans still lie. Have federal agencies learned their lesson about early public engagement? Do urban sites present special challenges to be addressed by our laws? How might private developers not subject to the Section 106 process treat similar discoveries? Only time will tell.

CHAPTER NINE

PROTECTIONS FOR NATIVE AMERICAN SITES

Most of this book deals with the protection of historic structures that are, at most, a few hundred years old. But before Western Europeans and others came to the United States to develop such structures, Native Americans and the peoples of prehistory developed thriving civilizations here. Protecting their history poses distinctive challenges. This Chapter deals with the unique federal rules that apply to protections of sites and objects of antiquity, primarily those affiliated with Native American groups.

A. THE NATIVE AMERICAN GRAVES PROTECTION AND REPATRIATION ACT

Many of the laws discussed in this book mention, but do not exclusively address, Native American (including American Indian, Alaska Native, and Native Hawaiian) sites and artifacts. In 1990, Congress passed the Native American Graves Protection and Repatriation Act (NAGPRA), which exclusively addresses Native American artifacts. It protects and provides a process for the repatriation of human remains, funerary objects, and other cultural patrimony that are either (a) in the possession of federal agencies or museums, or (b) found on federal or tribal lands. NAGPRA also requires federal agencies and museums to create an inventory of Native American cultural items. Finally, it has a consultative function, requiring federal agencies to consult with Native American groups about permits to excavate on federal or tribal lands.

Although NAGPRA primarily governs objects and not structures or sites, careful analysis of the law exposes issues relating to identity, culture, and ownership that may inform our approach to traditional historic preservation laws. How might we determine when an object has special meaning to certain persons? When multiple individuals or groups conflict as to how to treat a historically significant object, what processes must be followed to determine which one should be the decision-maker? What role should government play in resolving such conflicts?

Since its enactment, NAGPRA has changed the way federal agencies, museums, Native American groups, and other institutions operate. NAGPRA is administered by an office at the Department of the Interior called the National NAGPRA program. It develops regulations and guidance for implementing NAGPRA; provides administrative and staff support for the NAGPRA Review Committee; assists Indian tribes,

Native Alaskan villages and corporations, Native Hawaiian organizations, museums, and Federal agencies with the NAGPRA process; maintains the Native American Consultation Database and other online databases; manages a grant program; and, makes program documents and publications available on the Internet.

1. THE TEXT OF NAGPRA

Native American Graves Protection and Repatriation Act of 1990
25 U.S.C. §§ 3001–3013

§ 3001. Definitions

For purposes of this chapter, the term—

(1) "burial site" means any natural or prepared physical location, whether originally below, on, or above the surface of the earth, into which as a part of the death rite or ceremony of a culture, individual human remains are deposited.

(2) "cultural affiliation" means that there is a relationship of shared group identity which can be reasonably traced historically or prehistorically between a present day Indian tribe or Native Hawaiian organization and an identifiable earlier group.

(3) "cultural items" means human remains and—

(A) "associated funerary objects" which shall mean objects that, as a part of the death rite or ceremony of a culture, are reasonably believed to have been placed with individual human remains either at the time of death or later, and both the human remains and associated funerary objects are presently in the possession or control of a Federal agency or museum, except that other items exclusively made for burial purposes or to contain human remains shall be considered as associated funerary objects.

(B) "unassociated funerary objects" which shall mean objects that, as a part of the death rite or ceremony of a culture, are reasonably believed to have been placed with individual human remains either at the time of death or later, where the remains are not in the possession or control of the Federal agency or museum and the objects can be identified by a preponderance of the evidence as related to specific individuals or families or to known human remains or, by a preponderance of the evidence, as having been removed from a specific burial site of an individual culturally affiliated with a particular Indian tribe,

(C) "sacred objects" which shall mean specific ceremonial objects which are needed by traditional Native American religious leaders for the practice of traditional Native American religions by their present day adherents, and

(D) "cultural patrimony" which shall mean an object having ongoing historical, traditional, or cultural importance central to the Native American group or culture itself, rather than property owned by an individual Native American, and which, therefore, cannot be alienated, appropriated, or conveyed by any individual regardless of whether or not the individual is a member of the Indian tribe or Native Hawaiian organization and such object shall have been considered inalienable by such Native American group at the time the object was separated from such group.

(4) "Federal agency" means any department, agency, or instrumentality of the United States. Such term does not include the Smithsonian Institution.

(5) "Federal lands" means any land other than tribal lands which are controlled or owned by the United States, including lands selected by but not yet conveyed to Alaska Native Corporations and groups organized pursuant to the Alaska Native Claims Settlement Act of 1971 [43 U.S.C. § 1601 et seq.].

(6) "Hui Malama I Na Kupuna O Hawai'i Nei" means the nonprofit, Native Hawaiian organization incorporated under the laws of the State of Hawaii by that name on April 17, 1989, for the purpose of providing guidance and expertise in decisions dealing with Native Hawaiian cultural issues, particularly burial issues.

(7) "Indian tribe" means any tribe, band, nation, or other organized group or community of Indians, including any Alaska Native village (as defined in, or established pursuant to, the Alaska Native Claims Settlement Act [43 U.S.C. § 1601 et seq.]) which is recognized as eligible for the special programs and services provided by the United States to Indians because of their status as Indians.

(8) "museum" means any institution or State or local government agency (including any institution of higher learning) that receives Federal funds and has possession of, or control over, Native American cultural items. Such term does not include the Smithsonian Institution or any other Federal agency.

(9) "Native American" means of, or relating to, a tribe, people, or culture that is indigenous to the United States.

(10) "Native Hawaiian" means any individual who is a descendant of the aboriginal people who, prior to 1778, occupied and exercised sovereignty in the area that now constitutes the State of Hawaii.

(11) "Native Hawaiian organization" means any organization which—

(A) serves and represents the interests of Native Hawaiians,

(B) has as a primary and stated purpose the provision of services to Native Hawaiians, and

(C) has expertise in Native Hawaiian Affairs, and shall include the Office of Hawaiian Affairs and Hui Malama I Na Kupuna O Hawai'i Nei.

(12) "Office of Hawaiian Affairs" means the Office of Hawaiian Affairs established by the constitution of the State of Hawaii.

(13) "right of possession" means possession obtained with the voluntary consent of an individual or group that had authority of alienation. The original acquisition of a Native American unassociated funerary object, sacred object or object of cultural patrimony from an Indian tribe or Native Hawaiian organization with the voluntary consent of an individual or group with authority to alienate such object is deemed to give right of possession of that object, unless the phrase so defined would, as applied in section 3005(c) of this title, result in a Fifth Amendment taking by the United States as determined by the United States Court of Federal Claims pursuant to 28 U.S.C. 1491 in which event the "right of possession" shall be as provided under otherwise applicable property law. The original acquisition of Native American human remains and associated funerary objects which were excavated, exhumed, or otherwise obtained with full knowledge and consent of the next of kin or the official governing body of the appropriate culturally affiliated Indian tribe or Native Hawaiian organization is deemed to give right of possession to those remains.

(14) "Secretary" means the Secretary of the Interior.

(15) "tribal land" means—

(A) all lands within the exterior boundaries of any Indian reservation;

(B) all dependent Indian communities;

(C) any lands administered for the benefit of Native Hawaiians pursuant to the Hawaiian Homes Commission Act, 1920, and section 4 of Public Law 86–3.

§ 3002. Ownership

(a) Native American human remains and objects

The ownership or control of Native American cultural items which are excavated or discovered on Federal or tribal lands after November 16, 1990, shall be (with priority given in the order listed)—

(1) in the case of Native American human remains and associated funerary objects, in the lineal descendants of the Native American; or

(2) in any case in which such lineal descendants cannot be ascertained, and in the case of unassociated funerary objects, sacred objects, and objects of cultural patrimony—

(A) in the Indian tribe or Native Hawaiian organization on whose tribal land such objects or remains were discovered;

(B) in the Indian tribe or Native Hawaiian organization which has the closest cultural affiliation with such remains or objects and which, upon notice, states a claim for such remains or objects; or

(C) if the cultural affiliation of the objects cannot be reasonably ascertained and if the objects were discovered on Federal land that is recognized by a final judgment of the Indian Claims Commission or the United States Court of Claims as the aboriginal land of some Indian tribe—

(1) in the Indian tribe that is recognized as aboriginally occupying the area in which the objects were discovered, if upon notice, such tribe states a claim for such remains or objects, or

(2) if it can be shown by a preponderance of the evidence that a different tribe has a stronger cultural relationship with the remains or objects than the tribe or organization specified in paragraph (1), in the Indian tribe that has the strongest demonstrated relationship, if upon notice, such tribe states a claim for such remains or objects.

(b) Unclaimed Native American human remains and objects

Native American cultural items not claimed under subsection (a) of this section shall be disposed of in accordance with regulations promulgated by the Secretary in consultation with the review committee established under section 3006 of this title, Native American groups, representatives of museums and the scientific community.

(c) Intentional excavation and removal of Native American human remains and objects

The intentional removal from or excavation of Native American cultural items from Federal or tribal lands for purposes of discovery, study, or removal of such items is permitted only if—

(1) such items are excavated or removed pursuant to a permit issued under section 470cc of Title 16 which shall be consistent with this Chapter;

(2) such items are excavated or removed after consultation with or, in the case of tribal lands, consent of the appropriate (if any) Indian tribe or Native Hawaiian organization;

(3) the ownership and right of control of the disposition of such items shall be as provided in subsections (a) and (b) of this section; and

(4) proof of consultation or consent under paragraph (2) is shown.

(d) Inadvertent discovery of Native American remains and objects

(1) Any person who knows, or has reason to know, that such person has discovered Native American cultural items on Federal or tribal

lands after November 16, 1990, shall notify, in writing, the Secretary of the Department, or head of any other agency or instrumentality of the United States, having primary management authority with respect to Federal lands and the appropriate Indian tribe or Native Hawaiian organization with respect to tribal lands, if known or readily ascertainable, and, in the case of lands that have been selected by an Alaska Native Corporation or group organized pursuant to the Alaska Native Claims Settlement Act of 1971 [43 U.S.C. § 1601 et seq.], the appropriate corporation or group. If the discovery occurred in connection with an activity, including (but not limited to) construction, mining, logging, and agriculture, the person shall cease the activity in the area of the discovery, make a reasonable effort to protect the items discovered before resuming such activity, and provide notice under this subsection. Following the notification under this subsection, and upon certification by the Secretary of the department or the head of any agency or instrumentality of the United States or the appropriate Indian tribe or Native Hawaiian organization that notification has been received, the activity may resume after 30 days of such certification.

(2)   The disposition of and control over any cultural items excavated or removed under this subsection shall be determined as provided for in this section. * * *

§ 3003.   Inventory for human remains and associated funerary objects

(a)   In general

Each Federal agency and each museum which has possession or control over holdings or collections of Native American human remains and associated funerary objects shall compile an inventory of such items and, to the extent possible based on information possessed by such museum or Federal agency, identify the geographical and cultural affiliation of such item. * * *

§ 3004.   Summary for unassociated funerary objects, sacred objects, and cultural patrimony

(a)   In general

Each Federal agency or museum which has possession or control over holdings or collections of Native American unassociated funerary objects, sacred objects, or objects of cultural patrimony shall provide a written summary of such objects based upon available information held by such agency or museum. The summary shall describe the scope of the collection, kinds of objects included, reference to geographical location, means and period of acquisition and cultural affiliation, where readily ascertainable. * * *

§ 3005.   Repatriation

(a) Repatriation of Native American human remains and objects possessed or controlled by Federal agencies and museums

(1) If, pursuant to section 3003 of this title, the cultural affiliation of Native American human remains and associated funerary objects with a particular Indian tribe or Native Hawaiian organization is established, then the Federal agency or museum, upon the request of a known lineal descendant of the Native American or of the tribe or organization and pursuant to subsections (b) and (e) of this section, shall expeditiously return such remains and associated funerary objects.

(2) If, pursuant to section 3004 of this title, the cultural affiliation with a particular Indian tribe or Native Hawaiian organization is shown with respect to unassociated funerary objects, sacred objects or objects of cultural patrimony, then the Federal agency or museum, upon the request of the Indian tribe or Native Hawaiian organization and pursuant to subsections (b), (c) and (e) of this section, shall expeditiously return such objects.

(3) The return of cultural items covered by this chapter shall be in consultation with the requesting lineal descendant or tribe or organization to determine the place and manner of delivery of such items.

(4) Where cultural affiliation of Native American human remains and funerary objects has not been established in an inventory prepared pursuant to section 3003 of this title, or the summary pursuant to section 3004 of this title, or where Native American human remains and funerary objects are not included upon any such inventory, then, upon request and pursuant to subsections (b) and (e) of this section and, in the case of unassociated funerary objects, subsection (c) of this section, such Native American human remains and funerary objects shall be expeditiously returned where the requesting Indian tribe or Native Hawaiian organization can show cultural affiliation by a preponderance of the evidence based upon geographical, kinship, biological, archaeological, anthropological, linguistic, folkloric, oral traditional, historical, or other relevant information or expert opinion.

(5) Upon request and pursuant to subsections (b), (c) and (e) of this section, sacred objects and objects of cultural patrimony shall be expeditiously returned where—

(A) the requesting party is the direct lineal descendant of an individual who owned the sacred object;

(B) the requesting Indian tribe or Native Hawaiian organization can show that the object was owned or controlled by the tribe or organization; or

(C) the requesting Indian tribe or Native Hawaiian organization can show that the sacred object was owned or controlled by a member thereof, provided that in the case where a sacred object was owned by a member thereof, there are no identifiable lineal descendants of said member or the lineal descendants, upon notice, have failed to make a claim for the object under this chapter.

(b)   Scientific study

If the lineal descendant, Indian tribe, or Native Hawaiian organization requests the return of culturally affiliated Native American cultural items, the Federal agency or museum shall expeditiously return such items unless such items are indispensable for completion of a specific scientific study, the outcome of which would be of major benefit to the United States. Such items shall be returned by no later than 90 days after the date on which the scientific study is completed.

(c)   Standard of repatriation

If a known lineal descendant or an Indian tribe or Native Hawaiian organization requests the return of Native American unassociated funerary objects, sacred objects or objects of cultural patrimony pursuant to this chapter and presents evidence which, if standing alone before the introduction of evidence to the contrary, would support a finding that the Federal agency or museum did not have the right of possession, then such agency or museum shall return such objects unless it can overcome such inference and prove that it has a right of possession to the objects.

(d)   Sharing of information by Federal agencies and museums

Any Federal agency or museum shall share what information it does possess regarding the object in question with the known lineal descendant, Indian tribe, or Native Hawaiian organization to assist in making a claim under this section.

(e)   Competing claims

Where there are multiple requests for repatriation of any cultural item and, after complying with the requirements of this chapter, the Federal agency or museum cannot clearly determine which requesting party is the most appropriate claimant, the agency or museum may retain such item until the requesting parties agree upon its disposition or the dispute is otherwise resolved pursuant to the provisions of this chapter or by a court of competent jurisdiction.

(f)   Museum obligation

Any museum which repatriates any item in good faith pursuant to this chapter shall not be liable for claims by an aggrieved party or for claims of breach of fiduciary duty, public trust, or violations of state law that are inconsistent with the provisions of this chapter. * * *

§ 3007.   Penalty

(a)   Penalty

Any museum that fails to comply with the requirements of this chapter may be assessed a civil penalty by the Secretary of the Interior pursuant to procedures established by the Secretary through regulation. A penalty assessed under this subsection shall be determined on the record after opportunity for an agency hearing. Each violation under this subsection shall be a separate offense.

(b) Amount of penalty

The amount of a penalty assessed under subsection (a) of this section shall be determined under regulations promulgated pursuant to this chapter, taking into account, in addition to other factors—

(1) the archaeological, historical, or commercial value of the item involved;

(2) the damages suffered, both economic and noneconomic, by an aggrieved party, and

(3) the number of violations that have occurred.

* * *

§ 3009. Savings provision

Nothing in this chapter shall be construed to—

(1) limit the authority of any Federal agency or museum to—

(A) return or repatriate Native American cultural items to Indian tribes, Native Hawaiian organizations, or individuals, and

(B) enter into any other agreement with the consent of the culturally affiliated tribe or organization as to the disposition of, or control over, items covered by this chapter;

(2) delay actions on repatriation requests that are pending on the date of enactment of this chapter;

(3) deny or otherwise affect access to any court;

(4) limit any procedural or substantive right which may otherwise be secured to individuals or Indian tribes or Native Hawaiian organizations; or

(5) limit the application of any State or Federal law pertaining to theft or stolen property. * * *

NOTES & QUESTIONS

1.   NAGPRA addresses issues at the core of the questions about cultural identity, memory, and historic preservation. For many Native American groups, it presents a welcome first step in the remedying of past wrongs relating to the appropriation of cultural items with lasting significance. Scholars have estimated that up to two million individual human remains may be subject to NAGPRA. *See* David J. Harris, *Respect for the Living and Respect for the Dead: Return of Indian and Other Native American Burial Remains*, 39 WASH. U. J. URB. & CONTEMP. L. 195, 195 n.3 (1991).

2.   How does NAGPRA define Native American cultural items? Should non-tangible items, such as songs or chants, be included?

3.   What happens when there are competing claims among tribes for cultural items that may be repatriated under NAGPRA? Who decides who will receive the items? Is the decision-making process set out under NAGPRA consistent with the law's intent?

4.   What do you make of section 3005(f) of NAGPRA? It was intended to address the possibility that museum trustees, in deciding to deaccession certain items pursuant to NAGPRA, could be exposed to liability for violating their fiduciary or other duties to their institutions under state law. As Patty Gerstenblith explains, one interpretation of section 3005(f) might be that "federal law preempts state law and so a museum that makes restitution pursuant to NAGPRA should be protected from the requirements of state fiduciary law." She suggests that, alternatively, § 3005(f) might prompt decision-makers at the affected museum to carefully weigh "whether it is better for the museum to engage in the repatriation process and receive federal funds or to opt out of the repatriation process and forego the benefits of federal funding and potentially be subject to fines and litigation." *See Acquisition and Deacquisition of Museum Collections and the Fiduciary Obligations of Museums to the Public*, 11 CARDOZO J. INT'L & COMP. L. 409, 431–32 (2003). Under what circumstances would museum trustees' deaccessioning under NAGPRA breach their fiduciary duties?

5.   NAGPRA defines "Native Hawaiians" and the term is used several times in the statute. How are Native Hawaiians treated by NAGPRA?

The Hawaii State Historic Preservation Division (the state's SHPO) is a museum subject to NAGPRA, according to the definition of "museum" in 25 U.S.C. § 3001(8), because it holds human remains and associated funerary objects subject to NAGPRA. In an employment lawsuit involving the Hawaii SHPO, a federal court reviewed a former employee's allegations that the SHPO violated NAGPRA's inventory requirement and determined that there was a genuine issue of material fact as to that claim. *See Brown v. Hawaii*, 679 F.Supp.2d 1188 (D. Haw. 2009) (dismissing the employee's request for summary judgment), *aff'd* 424 Fed. Appx. 642 (9th Cir. 2011). What challenges might state agencies have in complying with NAGPRA? Does NAGPRA provide any protection to government whistleblowers who identify deficiencies in compliance?

6.   Refer to the excerpts in Chapter 8 from the Antiquities Act of 1906, 54 U.S.C. § 320302, and Archaeological Resources Protection Act of 1979, 16 U.S.C. § 470cc. These provisions granted federal agencies broad authority to issue permits for the excavation and removal of Native American artifacts now covered by NAGPRA. Objects held by private entities that are not museums are not recoverable by tribes under NAGPRA. Why should the identity of the current holder subject objects obtained on federal land to different treatment?

7.   The U.S. General Accountability Office (GAO) released a report in 2010, mentioned in the Tribal Resolution, entitled *Native American Graves Protection and Repatriation Act: After Almost 20 Years, Key Federal Agencies Still Have Not Fully Complied with the Act*. It examined the extent to which eight key federal agencies with significant historical collections had complied

with the requirements of NAGPRA and found that none had fully satisfied the act's mandates with respect to either inventorying their cultural items or published notices of inventory completion in the Federal Register once inventories had been made. The GAO found that the U.S. Army Corps of Engineers, the U.S. Forest Service, and the National Park Service had done the best job of identifying their NAGPRA cultural items, while the Bureau of Indian Affairs and the Tennessee Valley Authority had done the worst. The Bureau of Land Management, Bureau of Reclamation, and the U.S. Fish and Wildlife Service (all at the Department of the Interior) fell somewhere in the middle.

NAGPRA compliance is not only a low priority for federal agencies, but it is likely a low priority for museums as well. What timelines are imposed on agencies and museums with respect to NAGPRA compliance? What penalties are imposed for federal agencies and museums that fail to comply with NAGPRA?

8.   Native American and Native Hawaiian groups, who have the most at stake in the way NAGPRA is implemented, have been particularly attuned to possible areas of improvement. A resolution adopted in 2010 by several tribal groups referenced the GAO report in the previous Note and raises important issues about the law's implementation. See Resolution of a Coalition of Authorized Representatives of Oklahoma and Southern Indian Tribes on the 20th Anniversary of the Native American Graves Protection and Repatriation Act (1990). Among other things, the tribes suggested increases in funding, improvements in the consultation process, and the appointment of an ombudsman.

2.   INTERPRETING NAGPRA

Most courts considering NAGPRA claims have focused on the statute's definitions. This section includes excerpts from two important cases that use different methods of statutory interpretation. The first examines NAGPRA's definition of cultural patrimony, while the second examines its definition of human remains.

United States v. Corrow
119 F.3d 796 (10th Cir. 1997)

■ Before PORFILIO, McWILLIAMS, and LUCERO, CIRCUIT JUDGES.

■ JOHN C. PORFILIO, CIRCUIT JUDGE.

This appeal raises issues of first impression in this Circuit under the Native American Graves Protection and Repatriation Act, 25 U.S.C. §§ 3001–3013 (NAGPRA). * * * Richard Nelson Corrow challenges the constitutionality of 25 U.S.C. § 3001(3)(D) of NAGPRA which defines "cultural patrimony," the basis for his conviction of trafficking in protected Native American cultural items in violation of 18 U.S.C. § 1170(b). First, he contends the definition is unconstitutionally vague, an argument the district court rejected in denying his motion to dismiss that count of the indictment and to reverse his conviction. * * * We affirm.

I.   Background

Until his death in 1991, Ray Winnie was a *hataali*, a Navajo religious singer. For more than twenty-five years Mr. Winnie chanted the Nightway and other Navajo ceremonies wearing Yei B'Chei originally owned by Hosteen Hataali Walker. Yei B'Chei or Yei B'Chei *jish* are ceremonial adornments, Native American artifacts whose English label, "masks," fails to connote the Navajo perception these cultural items embody living gods. Traditionally, a *hataali* passes the Yei B'Chei to a family or clan member who has studied the ceremonies or loans the Yei B'Chei to another Navajo clan, Mr. Winnie having acquired his Yei B'Chei from a different clan during his *hataali* apprenticeship. When Mr. Winnie died, he left no provision for the disposition of his Yei B'Chei, and no family or clan member requested them.

Richard Corrow, the owner of Artifacts Display Stands in Scottsdale, Arizona, is an afficionado of Navajo culture and religion, having, on occasion, participated in Navajo religious ceremonies. Some time after Mr. Winnie's death, Mr. Corrow traveled to Lukachukai, Arizona, to visit Mrs. Fannie Winnie, Mr. Winnie's 81-year-old widow, chatting with her; her granddaughter, Rose Bia; and other family members: a great granddaughter, Harriette Keyonnie; and a son-in-law. During one visit, Mrs. Winnie displayed some Navajo screens and robes, and Mr. Corrow inquired about the Yei B'Chei. By his third visit in August 1993, the Winnie family revealed the Yei B'Chei, twenty-two ceremonial masks, and permitted Mr. Corrow to photograph them. Mr. Corrow told Mrs. Winnie he wanted to buy them, suggesting he planned to deliver the Yei B'Chei to a young Navajo chanter in Utah to keep them sacred. Although Mr. Corrow initially offered $5,000, he readily agreed to the family's price of $10,000 for the Yei B'Chei, five headdresses, and other artifacts. Mr. Corrow drafted a receipt,[1] and Mrs. Winnie, who spoke no English, placed her thumbprint on the document after Ms. Bia read it to her in Navajo.

In November 1994, the owners of the East-West Trading Company in Santa Fe, New Mexico, contacted Mr. Corrow telling him that a wealthy Chicago surgeon was interested in purchasing a set of Yei B'Chei. In fact, the purported buyer was James Tanner, a National Park Service ranger operating undercover on information he had received about questionable trade at East-West. When Agent Tanner visited the business, its owners showed him photographs of seventeen of the twenty-

---

[1]   The receipt stated:

Sold to Richard N. Corrow on this date for cash paid in full, all of the medicine bundles for yei be chai [sic] and fire dance including masks owned by Hosteen Ray Winnie of Lukachucki [sic], AZ.

Selling these medicine bundles or jish is the wife of the late Mr. Winnie, Fanny [sic], and his granddaughter Rose, and his great granddaughter, Harriet, whose signatures are below.

The selling price is in cash of $10,000. Received by below this date.

two Yei B'Chei that Mr. Corrow purchased from Mrs. Winnie. In the photos, he noticed eagle and owl feathers in several of the large headdresses and ceremonial sticks bundled with small eagle feathers. After negotiations, Agent Tanner agreed to a purchase price of $70,000 for the Yei B'Chei, $50,000 for Mr. Corrow and a $20,000 commission to East-West's co-owners.

On December 9, 1994, Mr. Corrow arrived at the Albuquerque airport en route to Santa Fe carrying one large suitcase, one small suitcase, and a cardboard box. Yet once he was in Santa Fe, F.B.I. agents became worried East-West's owners had been alerted and abandoned their script for the planned buy, instead directly executing the search warrant. Agents found the two suitcases Mr. Corrow had carried to East-West, one holding Navajo religious objects, small bundles, herbs, mini prayer sticks, and other artifacts adorned with eagle feathers. Another suitcase contained eagle feathers rolled inside several cloth bundles, Yei B'Chei dance aprons, and five headdress pieces made of eagle and owl feathers. In the cardboard box was the set of twenty-two Yei B'Chei.

The government subsequently charged Mr. Corrow in a two-count indictment, Count one for trafficking in Native American cultural items in violation of 18 U.S.C. § 1170, 25 U.S.C. §§ 3001(3)(D), 3002(c), and 18 U.S.C. § 2[.] * * * The court rejected Mr. Corrow's pretrial motion to dismiss Count one based on its purported unconstitutional vagueness, and the trial proceeded comprised predominantly of the testimony of expert witnesses clashing over whether the Yei B'Chei constitute "cultural patrimony" protected by NAGPRA. Having concluded they do, the jury convicted Mr. Corrow of illegal trafficking in cultural items, Count one. * * * Post-trial, Mr. Corrow attacked his conviction renewing his challenge to the constitutionality of §§ 3001(3)(D) and 3002(c) of NAGPRA and to the sufficiency of the evidence underlying his conviction. *Corrow*, 941 F.Supp. at 1553. The district court denied the motion and sentenced him to two concurrent five-year probationary terms and one hundred hours of community service.

In this renewed challenge, Mr. Corrow asserts the court erred in failing to dismiss Count one on the ground the NAGPRA definition of cultural patrimony is unconstitutionally vague, trapping the unwary in its multitude of meanings and creating easy prey for the untrammeled discretion of law enforcement. Were NAGPRA's definitional bounds nevertheless discernible, Mr. Corrow then urges the evidence was insufficient to support his conviction on either count. Mr. Corrow acknowledges our de novo review of the legal question he raises, *United States v. Murphy*, 977 F.2d 503, 504 (10th Cir. 1992); and our task of deciding whether substantial evidence, both direct and circumstantial taken together, underpins the conviction to confirm a reasonable jury could find defendant guilty beyond a reasonable doubt. *United States v. Garcia-Emanuel*, 14 F.3d 1469, 1472 (10th Cir. 1994).

II. NAGPRA

Congress enacted NAGPRA in 1990 to achieve two principle objectives: to protect Native American human remains, funerary objects, sacred objects and objects of cultural patrimony presently on Federal or tribal lands; and to repatriate Native American human remains, associated funerary objects, sacred objects, and objects of cultural patrimony currently held or controlled by Federal agencies and museums. H.R. REP. No. 101–877 (1990), *reprinted in* 1990 U.S.C.C.A.N. 4367, 4368. The legislation and subsequent regulations, 43 C.F.R. §§ 10.1–10.17, provide a methodology for identifying objects; determining the rights of lineal descendants, Indian tribes and Native Hawaiian organizations; and retrieving and repatriating that property to Native American owners. NAGPRA's reach in protecting against further desecration of burial sites and restoring countless ancestral remains and cultural and sacred items to their tribal homes warrants its aspirational characterization as "human rights legislation." Jack F. Trope & Walter R. Echo-Hawk, *The Native American Graves Protection and Repatriation Act: Background and Legislative History*, 24 ARIZ. ST. L.J. 35, 37 (1992). Indeed, a Panel of National Dialogue on Museum-Native American Relations, which was convened to address the divergent interests of the museum and Native American communities, reported to Congress that "[r]espect for Native human rights is the paramount principle that should govern resolution of the issue when a claim is made." 1990 U.S.C.C.A.N. 4369–70.

Nonetheless to give teeth to this statutory mission, 18 U.S.C. § 1170 penalizes trafficking in Native American human remains and cultural items and creates a felony offense for a second or subsequent violation. Subsection 1170(b), the basis for prosecution here, states:

> Whoever knowingly sells, purchases, uses for profit, or transports for sale or profit any Native American cultural items obtained in violation of the Native American Grave Protection and Repatriation Act shall be fined in accordance with this title, imprisoned not more than one year, or both, and in the case of a second or subsequent violation, be fined in accordance with this title, imprisoned not more than 5 years, or both.

One must look to NAGPRA, 25 U.S.C. § 3001, for the definition of "cultural item." * * *

[T]o be judged "cultural patrimony" the object must have (1) ongoing historical, cultural or traditional importance; and (2) be considered inalienable by the tribe by virtue of the object's centrality in tribal culture. That is, the cultural item's essential function within the life and history of the tribe engenders its inalienability such that the property cannot constitute the personal property of an individual tribal member. "The key aspect of this definition is whether the property was of such central importance to the tribe or group that it was owned communally." Francis P. McManamon & Larry V. Nordby, *Implementing the Native*

American Graves Protection and Repatriation Act, 24 ARIZ. ST. L.J. 217, 233–34 (1992). The regulations mirror this definition and incorporate the Senate Report for its version of the bill which did not pass, S. REP. No. 473, at 1 (1990). 43 C.F.R. § 10.2(d)(4).[5]

In this prosecution, then, the definition of cultural patrimony divided into its three component parts required the government prove Mr. Corrow trafficked in an object that (1) was not owned by an individual Native American; (2) that could not be alienated, appropriated, or conveyed by an individual; and (3) had an ongoing historical, traditional, or cultural importance central to the Native American group. Mr. Corrow contends the first and second elements are unintelligible.[6] Thus, he argues, relying upon *United States v. Agnew*, 931 F.2d 1397, 1403 (10th Cir. 1991), the definition does not comport with the due process clause of the Fourteenth Amendment because it fails to give ordinary people fair notice about what conduct is prohibited in such a manner that discourages arbitrary and discriminatory law enforcement.

In support, Mr. Corrow arrays the conflicting expert testimony, characterized by the *amicus curiae*[7] as a conflict between orthodox and moderate Navajo religious views. For the government, Alfred Yazzie, an ordained *hataali* and Navajo Nation Historic Preservation representative, testified the Yei B'Chei must remain within the four sacred mountains of the Navajo for they represented the "heartbeat" of the Navajo people.[8] Also for the government, Harry Walters, a Navajo anthropologist, stated there is "no such thing as ownership of medicine bundles and that these are viewed as living entities." He equated

---

[5]   43 C.F.R. § 10.2(d)(4) states:

Objects of cultural patrimony means items having ongoing historical, traditional, or cultural importance central to the Indian tribe or Native Hawaiian organization itself, rather than property owned by an individual tribal or organization member. These objects are of such central importance that they may not be alienated, appropriated, or conveyed by any individual tribal or organization member. Such objects must have been considered inalienable by the culturally affiliated Indian tribe or Native Hawaiian organization at the time the object was separated from the group. Objects of cultural patrimony include items such as Zuni War Gods, the Confederacy Wampum Belts of the Iroquois, and other objects of similar character and significance to the Indian tribe or Native Hawaiian organization as a whole.

[6]   Before the district court, Mr. Corrow challenged the third element as well contending there was nothing unique about these Yei B'Chei. On appeal, he targets only the question of alienability.

[7]   The Antique Tribal Art Dealers Association, a trade organization promoting authenticity and ethical dealing in the sale of Native American artifacts, filed an amicus brief contending the government in this case "exploited a controversy between orthodox and moderate Navajo religious perspectives."

[8]   He stated, "This is my heartbeat, this is my life, this is my teaching. This causes me to behave right. It allows me to teach my children to behave. So it's a God-given gift to the Navajos and it has everything to do with the welfare and the health and wisdom." He explained the *hataali* is responsible for caring for the *jish*, restoring them in the event of exposure to the wrong people or places: "when they do come back we would have to use what we call a diagnosis to see what can be done and how we can treat them and bring them back to the respect that they should have." He explained the Navajo tradition of compensating a person who gives his Yei B'Chei to another chanter.

ownership with use, knowing the rituals, but acknowledged often cultural items are sold because of economic pressures. For Mr. Corrow, Jackson Gillis, a medicine man from Monument Valley, testified that if no claim is made by a clan relative or other singer, the *jish* pass to the widow who must care for them. If the widow feels uncomfortable keeping the *jish*, Mr. Gillis stated she has the right to sell them. Harrison Begay, another of Mr. Corrow's expert witnesses, agreed, explaining that because the masks themselves are "alive," a widow, uneasy about their remaining unused, may sell them. Billy Yellow, another *hataali* testifying for Mr. Corrow, reiterated the traditional disposition of a *hataali*'s Yei B'Chei to a spouse, the children, and grandchildren, although he stated nobody really owns the *jish* because they are living gods.

Given these conflicting views on the alienability of the Yei B'Chei, Mr. Corrow asks how an individual, even one educated in Navajo culture, indeed, one accepting the responsibility of inquiring further about the status of the item as the district court deduced from its reading of NAGPRA, can "ascertain ownership when the group itself cannot agree on that point?" The shadow cast by this question, he insists, sufficiently clouds the meaning of "cultural patrimony" to render it unconstitutional. Mr. Corrow's invocation of void-for-vagueness review, however, obfuscates both its doctrinal reach and its application to the facts of this case.

"[T]he void-for-vagueness doctrine requires that a penal statute define the criminal offense with sufficient definiteness that ordinary people can understand what conduct is prohibited and in a manner that does not encourage arbitrary and discriminatory enforcement." *Kolender v. Lawson*, 461 U.S. 352, 357 (1983). Although *Kolender* acknowledged a judicial shift from concern over deciding whether the statute provides actual notice to "the more important aspect of the vagueness doctrine . . . the requirement that a legislature establish minimal guidelines to govern law enforcement," *id.* at 358, the legality principle, no crime or punishment without law, is the essence of a Fifth Amendment due process challenge. See 1 W. LaFave & A. Scott, Substantive Criminal Law § 3.1, at 271 (1986). That is, given the limitations of language and syntax, a statute must convey to those individuals within its purview what it purports to prohibit and how it will punish an infraction. While the Court equates that requirement roughly with a notion of "fairness," it swathes it with the constitutional guarantees of the Fifth Amendment.[9]

A couple of applications of these principles are instructive to our review. In *Palmer v. City of Euclid*, 402 U.S. 544 (1971), the Court held a suspicious person municipal ordinance was "so vague and lacking in

---

[9]   When a federal statute is involved, the due process clause of the Fifth Amendment is implicated. However, a void-for-vagueness challenge to a state statute involves the Fourteenth Amendment's due process clause.

ascertainable standards of guilt that, as applied to Palmer, it failed to give 'a person of ordinary intelligence fair notice that his contemplated conduct is forbidden.' " *Id.* at 545 (quoting *United States v. Harriss*, 347 U.S. 612, 617 (1954)). The city ordinance defined a "suspicious person" as one wandering about the streets at late or unusual hours without visible or lawful business and a satisfactory explanation for his presence. The police had charged James Palmer with violating this ordinance after he had dropped a woman off late at night and then pulled onto the street, parked with his headlights on, and used a two-way radio. Mr. Palmer's imprecise explanation for his behavior coupled with the conduct itself, the police decided, violated the ordinance. The Court held, however, "in our view the ordinance gave insufficient notice to the average person that discharging a friend at an apartment house and then talking on a car radio while parked on the street was enough to show him to be 'without any visible or lawful business.' " *Id.* at 545–46.

In *Kolender*, the Court invalidated a California criminal statute which required persons loitering or wandering on the streets to provide "credible and reliable" identification. 461 U.S. at 353. Because the statute failed to describe with sufficient particularity "what a suspect must do to satisfy the statute," that is, what constitutes "credible and reliable" identification, the Court found it unconstitutional on its face "because it encourages arbitrary enforcement." *Id.* at 361. Hence, while *Kolender*'s focus is the potential for unrestrained police discretion, that concern remains rooted in the Court's predicate finding the statutory requirement of "credible and reliable" identification is unfair. In void-for-vagueness review "[t]he same facets of a statute usually raise concerns of both fair notice and adequate enforcement standards." *United States v. Gaudreau*, 860 F.2d 357, 359 (10th Cir. 1988). Consequently, under *Kolender*'s guidance, we "treat each as an element to be analyzed separately." *Id.* at 359–60.

However, the Court has made equally clear our analysis is not global. "[V]agueness challenges to statutes which do not involve First Amendment freedoms must be examined in the light of the facts of the case at hand." *United States v. Mazurie*, 419 U.S. 544, 550 (1975). Thus, to succeed, the proponent "who engages in some conduct that is clearly proscribed [by the challenged statute] cannot complain of the vagueness of the law as applied to the conduct of others." *Vill. of Hoffman Estates v. Flipside, Hoffman Estates, Inc.*, 455 U.S. 489, 495 (1982); *United States v. Austin*, 902 F.2d 743, 745 (9th Cir. 1990). Further, in a facial challenge raising no First Amendment or other claim that the act reaches constitutionally protected conduct, the complainant "must demonstrate that the law is impermissibly vague in *all* of its applications." *Id.* at 497 (emphasis added).

Mr. Corrow cannot meet that burden. First, deciding whether the statute gave him fair notice, the district court found, after reviewing all of the expert testimony, Mr. Corrow is knowledgeable about Navajo traditions and culture and "would have been aware that various tribal members viewed ownership of property differently." 941 F.Supp. at 1560. The court cited the testimony of Ms. Charlotte Frisbie, author of *Navajo Medicine Bundles or Jish: Acquisition, Transmission and Disposition in the Past and Present* (1987). Ms. Frisbie related several calls from Mr. Corrow inquiring about the prices of certain Navajo artifacts. *Id.* at 1562 n.13. Although she stated he did not specifically ask her about these Yei B'Chei, she expressed her objection to dealers and commercial handlers selling Native American cultural objects in the open market. *Id.* Ms. Frisbie also reminded him both of the Navajo Nation's implementing procedures to return cultural items and of the enactment of NAGPRA. *Id.* Most damning, Ms. Bia, Mrs. Winnie's granddaughter, recounted Mr. Corrow's representation that he wanted to buy the Yei B'Chei to pass on to another young chanter in Utah. Reasonably, a jury could infer from that representation that Mr. Corrow appreciated some dimension of the Yei B'Chei's inherent inalienability in Navajo culture. Although Mrs. Winnie stated she believed the Yei B'Chei belonged to her, she testified, "[t]here was another man that knew the ways and he had asked of [the Yei B'Chei] but I was the one that was stalling and ended up selling it." *Id.* at 1565. Although this man trained with her husband, he had not offered her any money. This is not a case of an unsuspecting tourist happening upon Mrs. Winnie's hogan and innocently purchasing the set of Yei B'Chei. Nor is it even close to *Palmer* or *Kolender* where the unwary had no means or ability to discern their conduct violated the acts in question.

Surely, this evidence establishes Mr. Corrow had some notice the Yei B'Chei he purchased were powerfully connected to Navajo religion and culture. While it may be true that even the experts in that culture differed in their views on alienability, *no* expert testified it was acceptable to sell Yei B'Chei to non-Navajos who planned to resell them for a profit, the very conduct § 1170(b) penalizes. All experts testified the Yei B'Chei resided within the Four Corners of the Navajo people and acknowledged the ritual cleansing and restoration required were the Yei B'Chei to be defiled in any way. Thus, while the parameters of the designation "cultural patrimony" might be unclear in some of its applications and at its edges, there is no doubt, in this case as applied to Mr. Corrow, the Yei B'Chei were cultural items which could not be purchased for a quick $40,000 turn of profit. Indeed, the Court observed in *Hoffman Estates*, 455 U.S. at 494 n.6, that "ambiguous meanings cause citizens to 'steer far wider of the unlawful zone' . . . than if the boundaries of the forbidden areas were clearly marked.' " *Baggett v. Bullitt*, 377 U.S. 360, 372 (1964) (quoting *Speiser v. Randall*, 357 U.S. 513, 526 (1958)) (internal quotation marks omitted). Consequently, even if the term cultural patrimony "might reflect some uncertainty as applied to extreme situations, the conduct for which [defendant] was prosecuted and convicted falls squarely within the core of the [Act]." *United States v. Amer*, 110 F.3d 873, 878 (2d Cir. 1997) (challenge to International

Parental Kidnapping Crime Act attacking such terms as "lawful exercise of parental rights" as unconstitutionally vague failed where defendant's retention of three children in Egypt when at least two of the children were born in New York and other child had stayed in New York for eight years was clearly proscribed by IPKCA).

Consequently, we believe Mr. Corrow had fair notice—if not of the precise words of NAGPRA—of their meaning that Native American objects "having ongoing historical, traditional, or cultural importance central to the Native American group . . . rather than property owned by an individual Native American" could not be bought and sold absent criminal consequences. Moreover, contrary to Mr. Corrow's assertion, § 3001(3)(D) is not infirm because it fails to list examples of cultural items. "In short, due process does not require that citizens be provided actual notice of all criminal rules and their meanings. The Constitution is satisfied if the necessary information is reasonably obtainable by the public." *United States v. Vasarajs*, 908 F.2d 443, 449 (9th Cir. 1990) (statute barring reentry onto military base was not unconstitutionally vague because it failed to inform individuals of the precise boundaries of the base).

While not dispositive, we would add § 1170(b) includes scienter as an element of the offense ("Whoever knowingly sells, purchases, uses for profit. . . ."). "A statutory requirement that an act must be willful or purposeful may not render certain, for all purposes, a statutory definition of the crime which is in some respects uncertain. But it does relieve the statute of the objection that it punishes without warning an offense of which the accused was unaware." *Screws v. United States*, 325 U.S. 91, 101–02 (1945) (Douglas, J., concurring). Here, the government was required to prove Mr. Corrow knowingly used the Yei B'Chei for profit assuring his understanding of the prohibited zone of conduct.[11] "[A] scienter requirement may mitigate a criminal law's vagueness by ensuring that it punishes only those who are aware their conduct is unlawful." *Gaudreau*, 860 F.2d at 360.

Our analysis of the fairness issue infuses our disposition of the second vagueness concern, the potential for arbitrary and discriminatory enforcement. Unlike the police in *Kolender* who had complete discretion to judge what "reliable and credible" identification might be, in this case,

---

[11] We do not say that a scienter requirement alone will rescue an otherwise vague statute, recognizing "it is possible willfully to bring about certain results and yet be without fair warning that such conduct is proscribed." 1 W. LaFave & A. Scott, Jr., Substantive Criminal Law § 2.3, at 131 (1986). We would add in Sherry Hutt, *Illegal Trafficking in Native American Human Remains and Cultural Items: A New Protection Tool*, 24 Ariz. St. L.J. 135, 146 (1992), the author states as a general-intent crime, "the prosecution must prove that the defendant knew he was engaging in a financial activity, but need not prove that the defendant knew that the item was protected. One who deals in Native American cultural items does so at the risk that an item may be protected by NAGPRA. Failure to realize an intended profit is not a defense to a section 4 violation. If the defendant bought, sold, used for profit, or transported for intended sale or profit a protected item, the law is violated, regardless of the actual beneficial outcome of the transaction." The discussion, of course, presumes the constitutionality of NAGPRA and its penalty provision.

as the district court found, the statute as applied caused law enforcement officers to inquire of tribal officials to determine whether the cultural item in question constituted cultural patrimony. 941 F.Supp. at 1564. Here, the Department of the Interior National Park Service officer, Mr. Young, examined a photograph of the Yei B'Chei and discussed their significance with other knowledgeable Park Service officers and representatives of the Navajo Nation before deciding the items constituted cultural patrimony. Mr. Young testified he participated in other NAGPRA investigations and was aware that law enforcement officers must first consult with tribal representatives to determine whether an item has ongoing historical, cultural, or traditional importance. We conclude, therefore, as applied to Mr. Corrow, § 1170(b) provides sufficient guidance to law enforcement to dispel the fear of subjective enforcement. We affirm the district court's denial of Mr. Corrow's motion to dismiss Count one.

Having failed in his constitutional challenge, Mr. Corrow urges we examine the same evidence which defeated the legal claim to support his contention the government failed to prove Mrs. Winnie was not the rightful owner of the Yei B'Chei. The evidence we detailed *infra* the expert and family members' testimony as well as that of Forest Service agents—viewed in the government's favor satisfies us that a rational jury could find beyond a reasonable doubt the Yei B'Chei are cultural patrimony which Mr. Corrow could not resell for profit. We therefore affirm the district court's denial of the motion for judgment of acquittal on Count one. * * *

We therefore AFFIRM the judgment of the district court.

NOTES & QUESTIONS

1. On appeal, Corrow disputed the issue of inalienability, arguing both that the Yei B'Chei were alienable and that, at a minimum, the alienability of the Yei B'Chei was in dispute among members of the tribe. How does the panel address Corrow's argument? What two-pronged due process analysis does it use instead?

2. How does the court's approach to vagueness compare to *United States v. Smyer*, 596 F.2d 939 (10th Cir. 1979), excerpted in Chapter 8?

Bonnichsen v. United States
367 F.3d 864 (9th. Cir. 2004)

■ Before ALDISERT, GRABER, and GOULD, CIRCUIT JUDGES.

■ GOULD, CIRCUIT JUDGE:

This is a case about the ancient human remains of a man who hunted and lived, or at least journeyed, in the Columbia Plateau an estimated 8340 to 9200 years ago, a time predating all recorded history from any place in the world, a time before the oldest cities of our world had been founded, a time so ancient that the pristine and untouched land and the primitive cultures that may have lived on it are not deeply understood by even the most well-informed men and women of our age. Seeking the opportunity of study, a group of scientists as Plaintiffs in this case brought an action against, *inter alia*, the United States Department of the Interior, challenging various Indian tribes' claim to one of the most important American anthropological and archaeological discoveries of the late twentieth century, and challenging the Interior Department's decision honoring the tribes' claim. The discovery that launched this contest was that of a human skeleton, estimated by carbon dating to be 8340 to 9200 years old, known popularly and commonly as "Kennewick Man," but known as "the Ancient One" to some American Indians[3] who now inhabit regions in Washington, Idaho, and Oregon, roughly proximate to the site on the Columbia River at Kennewick, Washington, where the bones were found. From the perspective of the scientists Plaintiffs, this skeleton is an irreplaceable source of information about early New World populations that warrants careful scientific inquiry to advance knowledge of distant times. Yet, from the perspective of the intervenor-Indian tribes the skeleton is that of an ancestor who, according to the tribes' religious and social traditions, should be buried immediately without further testing. * * *

I

In July 1996, teenagers going to a boat race discovered a human skull and bones near the shore of the Columbia River just outside Kennewick, Washington. The remains were found on federal property under the management of the United States Army Corps of Engineers ("Corps") and, at the request of the county coroner, were removed for analysis by an anthropologist, Dr. James Chatters, pursuant to an Archaeological Resources Protection Act of 1979 ("ARPA"), 16 U.S.C. §§ 470aa–470mm, permit. Because of physical features such as the shape of the skull and facial bones, anthropologists at first thought the remains were those of an early European settler. But the anthropologists then found a stone projectile point embedded in the skeleton's upper hip bone. The object's design, when viewed with x-rays and CT scans of the hip, resembled a style that was common before the documented arrival of Europeans in the region. Further study of the remains revealed characteristics unlike those of a European settler, yet also inconsistent with any American Indian remains previously documented in the region. A minute quantity of metacarpal bone was radiocarbon dated. The laboratory estimated the age of the bones to be between 8340 and 9200 years old.

The skeleton attracted attention because some of its physical features, such as the shape of the face and skull, differed from those of modern American Indians. Many scientists believed the discovery might

---

[3]   We use the term "American Indian" because the definition of "Native American," as used in Native American Graves Protection and Repatriation Act, is a disputed issue in this appeal.

shed light on the origins of humanity in the Americas. On August 31, 1996, Dr. Douglas Owsley, Division Head for Physical Anthropology at the Smithsonian Institution in Washington, D.C., made arrangements for Dr. Chatters to bring this important find to the Smithsonian's National Museum of Natural History for further study.

Indian tribes from the area of the Columbia River opposed scientific study of the remains on religious and social grounds. Four Indian groups (the "Tribal Claimants") demanded that the remains be turned over to them for immediate burial. The Tribal Claimants based their demand on the Native American Graves Protection and Repatriation Act ("NAGPRA"), 25 U.S.C. § 3001 et seq. The Corps agreed with the Tribal Claimants and, citing NAGPRA, seized the remains on September 10, 1996, shortly before they could be transported to the Smithsonian. The Corps also ordered an immediate halt to DNA testing, which was being done using the remainder of the bone sample that had been submitted earlier for radiocarbon dating. After investigation, the Corps decided to give the remains to the Tribal Claimants for burial. As required by NAGPRA, the Corps published a "Notice of Intent to Repatriate Human Remains" in a local newspaper on September 17, 1996, and September 24, 1996.

The scientists and others, including the Smithsonian Institution, objected to the Corps' decision, arguing that the remains were a rare discovery of national and international significance. In late September and early October 1996, several scientists asked Major General Ernest J. Herrell, Commander of the Corps' North Pacific Division, to allow qualified scientists to study the remains.

The scientists did not convince the Corps to permit them to study the remains, and commenced this litigation on October 16, 1996, in the United States District Court for the District of Oregon. * * *

On March 24, 1998, the Corps and the Secretary of the Interior entered into an agreement that effectively assigned to the Secretary responsibility to decide whether the remains were "Native American" under NAGPRA, and to determine their proper disposition. The Department of the Interior then assumed the role of lead agency on this case. * * *

Relying solely on the age of the remains and the fact that the remains were found within the United States, on January 13, 2000, the Secretary pronounced Kennewick Man's remains "Native American" within NAGPRA's meaning. And on September 25, 2000, the Secretary determined that a preponderance of the evidence supported the conclusion that the Kennewick remains were culturally affiliated with present-day Indian tribes. For this reason, the Secretary announced his final decision to award Kennewick Man's remains to a coalition of the Tribal Claimants. The Corps and the Secretary also denied Plaintiffs' request to study the remains.

Plaintiffs filed an amended complaint in the district court challenging the Secretary's decisions. The district court again ruled in Plaintiffs' favor. As pertinent to this appeal, the district court vacated the Secretary's decisions as contrary to the Administrative Procedure Act, 5 U.S.C. § 706(2)(A) ("APA"), on the ground that the Secretary improperly concluded that NAGPRA applies. *Bonnichsen v. United States*, 217 F.Supp.2d 1116, 1138–39 (2002). The district court also held that, because NAGPRA did not apply, Plaintiffs should have the opportunity to study Kennewick Man's remains under ARPA. Defendants and the Tribal Claimants appealed, and we stayed the district court's order granting Plaintiffs-scientists' study of the remains pending our decision herein. * * *

III

Our review of the Secretary's decision to transfer Kennewick Man to the Tribal Claimants is governed by the APA, which instructs courts to "hold unlawful and set aside agency action, findings, and conclusions found to be . . . arbitrary, capricious, an abuse of discretion, or otherwise not in accordance with law." 5 U.S.C. § 706(2)(A).

NAGPRA vests "ownership or control" of newly discovered Native American human remains in the decedent's lineal descendants or, if lineal descendants cannot be ascertained, in a tribe "affiliated" with the remains. 25 U.S.C. § 3002(a). NAGPRA mandates a two-part analysis. The first inquiry is whether human remains are Native American within the statute's meaning. If the remains are not Native American, then NAGPRA does not apply. However, if the remains are Native American, then NAGPRA applies, triggering the second inquiry of determining which persons or tribes are most closely affiliated with the remains.

The parties dispute whether the remains of Kennewick Man constitute Native American remains within NAGPRA's meaning. NAGPRA defines human remains as "Native American" if the remains are "of, or relating to, a tribe, people, or culture that is indigenous to the United States." 25 U.S.C. § 3001(9). The text of the relevant statutory clause is written in the present tense ("of, or relating to, a tribe, people, or culture that is indigenous"). Thus the statute unambiguously requires that human remains bear some relationship to a *presently existing* tribe, people, or culture to be considered Native American. * * *

Our conclusion that NAGPRA's language requires that human remains, to be considered Native American, bear some relationship to a presently existing tribe, people, or culture accords with NAGPRA's purposes. As regards newly discovered human remains, NAGPRA was enacted with two main goals: to respect the burial traditions of modern-day American Indians and to protect the dignity of the human body after death. NAGPRA was intended to benefit modern American Indians by sparing them the indignity and resentment that would be aroused by the despoiling of their ancestors' graves and the study or the display of their ancestors' remains. See H.R. REP. No. 101–877, at 4369 (1990) *reprinted in* 1990 U.S.C.C.A.N. 4367, 4368 ("For many years, Indian tribes have attempted to have the remains and funerary objects of *their ancestors returned to them*.") (emphasis added).

Congress's purposes would not be served by requiring the transfer to modern American Indians of human remains that bear no relationship to them. Yet, that would be the result under the Secretary's construction of the statute, which would give Native American status to any remains found within the United States regardless of age and regardless of lack of connection to existing indigenous tribes. The exhumation, study, and display of ancient human remains that are unrelated to modern American Indians was not a target of Congress's aim, nor was it precluded by NAGPRA.

NAGPRA was also intended to protect the dignity of the human body after death by ensuring that Native American graves and remains be treated with respect. *See* S. REP. No. 101–473, at 6 (1990) ("The Committee believes that human remains must at all times be treated with dignity and respect."); H.R. REP. No. 101–877, at 4372 (1990) ("Some Indian representatives testified that the spirits of *their* ancestors would not rest until they are returned to their homeland. . . ."). Congress's purpose is served by requiring the return to modern-day American Indians of human remains that bear some significant relationship to them.

Despite the statute's language and legislative history, the Secretary argues that the district court's interpretation "improperly collapses" NAGPRA's first inquiry (asking *whether* human remains are Native American) into NAGPRA's second inquiry (asking *which* American Indians or Indian tribe bears the closest relationship to Native American remains). The Secretary is mistaken. Though NAGPRA's two inquiries have some commonality in that both focus on the relationship between human remains and present-day Indians, the two inquiries differ significantly. The first inquiry requires only a general finding that remains have a significant relationship to a presently existing "tribe, people, or culture," a relationship that goes beyond features common to all humanity. The second inquiry requires a more specific finding that remains are most closely affiliated to specific lineal descendants or to a specific Indian tribe. The district court's interpretation of NAGPRA preserves the statute's two distinct inquiries. Because the record shows no relationship of Kennewick Man to the Tribal Claimants, the district court was correct in holding that NAGPRA has no application.

The Secretary finally argues that, under *Chevron U.S.A., Inc. v. Natural Resources Defense Council*, 467 U.S. 837 (1984), we must defer to the Secretary's interpretation of "Native American." The Secretary by regulation has defined "Native American" to mean "of, or relating to, a tribe, people, or culture indigenous to the United States." 43 C.F.R. § 10.2(d). The Secretary's regulation, enacted through notice and comment rulemaking, defines Native American exactly as NAGPRA defines it, with one critical exception: the regulation omits the present tense phrase "that is." *Compare* 25 U.S.C. § 3001(9) ("*a culture that is indigenous* to the United States") (emphasis added) *with* 43 C.F.R. § 10.2(d) ("a *culture indigenous* to the United States") (emphasis added). We hold, for the reasons discussed above, that NAGPRA's requirement that Native American remains bear some relationship to a *presently existing* tribe, people, or culture is unambiguous, and that the Secretary's contrary interpretation therefore is not owed Chevron deference. *See Chevron*, 467 U.S. at 842–43 ("If the intent of Congress is clear, that is the end of the matter; for the court, as well as the agency, must give effect to the unambiguously expressed intent of Congress."); *see also Wilderness Soc'y v. U.S. Fish & Wildlife Serv.*, 353 F.3d 1051, 1061 (9th Cir. 2003) (en banc) ("If, under these canons, or other traditional means of determining Congress's intentions, we are able to determine that Congress spoke clearly . . ., then we may not defer to the[agency's] contrary interpretation."). Moreover, the Secretary's regulation conflicts with NAGPRA's plain language and so is invalid for that reason. *See Whitman v. American Trucking Ass'ns*, 531 U.S. 457, 481, 121 (2001) (holding that *Chevron* deference is due only to a "*reasonable* interpretation made by the administrator of an agency") (emphasis added) (internal quotation marks omitted); *Public Employees Ret. Sys. of Ohio v. Betts*, 492 U.S. 158, 171 (1989) ("[N]o deference is due to agency interpretations at odds with the plain language of the statute itself."). Finally, the common maxim of statutory construction that we must give effect, if possible, to every word Congress used is fatal to the Secretary's attempt to amend NAGPRA by removing the phrase "that is." *See Bennett v. Spear*, 520 U.S. 154, 173 (1997), ("It is the 'cardinal principle of statutory construction' [that courts must] give effect, if possible, to every clause and word of a statute. . . ."). We hold that, notwithstanding 43 C.F.R. § 10.2(d), NAGPRA requires that human remains bear a significant relationship to a presently existing tribe, people, or culture to be considered Native American. The district court did not err in reaching that conclusion. * * *

Our conclusion that NAGPRA requires human remains to bear some relationship to a presently existing tribe, people, or culture to be considered "Native American" is also reinforced by how NAGPRA defines "sacred objects." NAGPRA defines "sacred objects" as "specific ceremonial objects which are needed by traditional Native American religious leaders for the practice of traditional Native American religions *by their present day adherents*." 25 U.S.C. § 3001(3)(C) (emphasis added). A literal reading of this definition reveals that any artifact to be deemed a "sacred object" must be connected to the practice of an American Indian religion by *present-day* peoples. This reading is consistent with our reading of "Native American"; that is, just as there must be a relationship between an artifact and a presently existing peoples for the artifact to be a "sacred object" under NAGPRA, there must be a relationship between a set of remains and a presently existing tribe, people, or culture for those remains to be "Native American" under NAGPRA.

Although NAGPRA does not specify precisely what kind of a relationship or precisely *how strong* a relationship ancient human remains must bear to modern Indian groups to qualify as Native American, NAGPRA's legislative history provides some guidance on what type of relationship may suffice. The House Committee on Interior and Insular Affairs emphasized in its report on NAGPRA that the statute was being enacted with modern-day American Indians' identifiable *ancestors* in mind. *See, e.g.,* H.R. REP. No. 101–877, at 4372 (1990) ("Indian representatives testified that the spirits of their ancestors would not rest until they are returned to their homeland. . ."); *id.* at 4369 ("For many years, Indian tribes have attempted to have the remains and funerary objects of *their ancestors* returned to them."). Human remains that are 8340 to 9200 years old and that bear only incidental genetic resemblance to modern-day American Indians, along with incidental genetic resemblance to other peoples, cannot be said to be the Indians' "ancestors" within Congress's meaning. Congress enacted NAGPRA to give American Indians control over the remains of their genetic and cultural forebearers, not over the remains of people bearing no special and significant genetic or cultural relationship to some presently existing indigenous tribe, people, or culture.

The age of Kennewick Man's remains, given the limited studies to date, makes it almost impossible to establish *any* relationship between the remains and presently existing American Indians. At least no significant relationship has yet been shown. We cannot give credence to an interpretation of NAGPRA advanced by the government and the Tribal Claimants that would apply its provisions to remains that have at most a tenuous, unknown, and unproven connection, asserted solely because of the geographical location of the find. * * *

We remand to the district court for further proceedings consistent with this opinion.

AFFIRMED.

NOTES & QUESTIONS

1. Scientists involved in NAGPRA cases can differ as to the underlying facts about disputed items. Both the Department of the Interior and the Society for American Archaeology determined that the Kennewick Man's remains were Native American for the purposes of NAGPRA. *See* Letter from Francis P. McManamon, U.S. Department of Interior Consulting Archaeologist, to Donald J. Barry, Assistant U.S. Secretary of the Interior for Fish and Wildlife and Parks (Jan. 11, 2000); Memorandum of Law in Support of the Society for American Archaeology's Amicus Curiae Submission at 1, *Bonnichsen v. United States,* 217 F. Supp.2d 1116 (D. Or. 2002) (CV 96–1481–JE). The plaintiff scientists in *Bonnichsen* thought otherwise.

In 2015, a team of scientists employing new techniques of genomic analysis determined that Kennewick Man's genetic makeup was Native American, and likely related to groups in the Pacific Northwest. The next year, federal legislation was enacted to allow the Kennewick Man to be returned to Native American tribes, which then buried him in a secret location in the Columbia River basin. Do you consider that a triumph for cultural values, science or both?

2.   Refer to the definition in NAGPRA of "cultural affiliation." 25 U.S.C. § 3001(2): "that there is a relationship of shared group identity which can be reasonably traced historically or prehistorically between a present day Indian tribe or Native Hawaiian organization and an identifiable earlier group." Is there a requirement that the relationship be "significant," as the court suggests? Does such a requirement exist elsewhere in the statute as excerpted above?

3.   At the close of fiscal year 2018, NAGPRA inventories of institutional holdings and collections revealed that 127,150 individual human remains and 967,031 funerary objects associated with such individuals had been deemed culturally unidentifiable and were not affiliated with a modern group. NAT'L PARK SERV., NATIONAL NAGPRA PROGRAM FISCAL YEAR 2018 REPORT 4 (2018). Does the number of unaffiliated remains indicate that NAGPRA's consultative function is not working? Or that the institutions applying NAGPRA's cultural affiliation definition are holding the bar too high? Or something else?

The Department of the Interior's NAGPRA Program has adopted regulations for culturally unaffiliated human remains, but not associated funerary objects. If no Native American group accepts control of human remains that have been identified as culturally unaffiliated, then the applicable agency or museum must re-inter them. 43 C.F.R. § 10.9(e) & 10.11. Is this the right resolution?

4.   The so-called Tribal Claimants in this case had another name for Kennewick Man: The Ancient One. Why do you think the court, who according to Footnote 3 was at least in part concerned with terminology, chose to call the remains Kennewick Man instead of The Ancient One? Is this choice consistent with its overall approach and its findings?

5.   Why did the Army Corps of Engineers transfer the power to determine whether the remains were Native American? Professor Allison Dussias explains that the Department of the Interior plays a key role in Indian affairs and policy:

> The Bureau of Indian Affairs is housed within the DOI, and the DOI thus has the most active role in carrying out the trust responsibility among the executive branch departments. Moreover, much of the federal land covered by NAGPRA on which Native American remains might be found is subject to the authority of the DOI and its sub-agencies, such as the National Park Service and the Bureau of Land Management.

See Allison M. Dussias, *Kennewick Man, Kinship, and the "Dying Race": The Ninth Circuit's Assimilationist Assault on the Native American Graves Protection and Repatriation Act*, 84 NEB. L. REV. 55, 77 (2005).

B. SECTION 106 PROVISIONS REGARDING TRIBAL RESOURCES

Although Chapter 3 discussed many aspects of Section 106 of the National Historic Preservation Act (NHPA), further discussion regarding its applicability to tribal resources is in order. Section 106 is the critical part of the key federal statute that protects a wide range of resources. The key language of Section 106, again, is as follows:

> The head of any Federal agency having direct or indirect jurisdiction over a proposed Federal or federally assisted undertaking in any State and the head of any Federal department or independent agency having authority to license any undertaking, prior to the approval of the expenditure of any Federal funds on the undertaking or prior to the issuance of any license, shall take into account the effect of the undertaking on any historic property. The head of any such Federal agency shall afford the Council a reasonable opportunity to comment with regard to such undertaking.

54 U.S.C. § 306108. Simply put, Section 106 imposes certain requirements on federal agencies to take the effect on historic resources into account when engaging in particular activities.

In addition, Section 106 requires agencies to "consult" appropriate stakeholders, including state historic preservation officers (SHPOs) and tribal historic preservation officers (THPOs). Federal regulations define consultation as "the process of seeking, discussing, and considering the views of other participants, and, where feasible, seeking agreement with them regarding matters arising in the section 106 process." 36 C.F.R. § 800.16(f). THPO is defined as "the tribal official appointed by the tribe's chief governing authority or designated by a tribal ordinance or preservation program who has assumed the responsibilities of the SHPO for purposes of section 106 compliance on tribal lands." *Id.* § 800.16(w). The following statutory excerpt further illuminates how the NHPA treats tribes and tribal property.

1. The Relevant NHPA Provisions

Historic Properties of Indian Tribes Provision of the National Historic Preservation Act
54 U.S.C. §§ 302701–302706

§ 302701.   Program to assist Indian tribes in preserving historic property

(a) Establishment of Program.—

The Secretary shall establish a program and promulgate regulations to assist Indian tribes in preserving their particular historic properties.

(b) Communication and Cooperation.—The Secretary shall foster communication and cooperation between Indian tribes and State Historic Preservation Officers in the administration of the national historic preservation program to—

(1) ensure that all types of historic properties and all public interests in such properties are given due consideration and

(2) encourage coordination among Indian tribes, State Historic Preservation Officers, and Federal agencies in historic preservation planning and in the identification, evaluation, protection, and interpretation of historic properties.

(c) Tribal Values.—

The program under subsection (a) shall be developed in such a manner as to ensure that tribal values are taken into account to the extent feasible. The Secretary may waive or modify requirements of this subdivision to conform to the cultural setting of tribal heritage preservation goals and objectives.

(d) Scope of Tribal Programs.—

The tribal programs implemented by specific tribal organizations may vary in scope, as determined by each Indian tribe's chief governing authority.

(e) Consultation.—

The Secretary shall consult with Indian tribes, other Federal agencies, State Historic Preservation Officers, and other interested parties concerning the program under subsection (a).

§ 302702.   Indian tribe to assume functions of State Historic Preservation Officer

An Indian tribe may assume all or any part of the functions of a State Historic Preservation Officer in accordance with sections 302302 and 302303 of this title, with respect to tribal land, as those responsibilities may be modified for tribal programs through regulations issued by the Secretary, if—

(1)   the Indian tribe's chief governing authority so requests;

(2)   the Indian tribe designates a tribal preservation official to administer the tribal historic preservation program, through appointment by the tribe's chief governing authority or as a tribal ordinance may otherwise provide;

(3)   the tribal preservation official provides the Secretary with a plan describing how the functions the tribal preservation official proposes to assume will be carried out;

(4)   the Secretary determines, after consulting with the Indian tribe, the appropriate State Historic Preservation Officer, the Council (if the Indian tribe proposes to assume the functions of the State Historic Preservation Officer with respect to review of undertakings under section 306108 of this title), and other Indian tribes, if any, whose tribal or aboriginal land may be affected by conduct of the tribal preservation program, that—

(A)   the tribal preservation program is fully capable of carrying out the functions specified in the plan provided under paragraph (3);

(B)   the plan defines the remaining responsibilities of the Secretary and the State Historic Preservation Officer; and

(C)   that the plan provides, with respect to properties neither owned by a member of the Indian tribe nor held in trust by the Secretary for the benefit of the Indian tribe, at the request of the owner of the properties, that the State Historic Preservation Officer, in addition to the tribal preservation official, may exercise the historic preservation responsibilities in accordance with subsections 302302 and 302303 of this title; and

(5)   based on satisfaction of the conditions stated in paragraphs (1), (2), (3), and (4), the Secretary approves the plan.

§ 302703.   Apportionment of grant funds

In consultation with interested Indian tribes, other Native American organizations and affected State Historic Preservation Officers, the Secretary shall establish and implement procedures for carrying out section 302902(c)(1)(A) of this title with respect to tribal programs that assume responsibilities under section 302702 of this title.

§ 302704.   Contracts and cooperative agreements

At the request of an Indian tribe whose preservation program has been approved to assume functions and responsibilities pursuant to section 302702 of this title, the Secretary shall enter into a contract or cooperative agreement with the Indian tribe permitting the assumption by the Indian tribe of any part of the responsibilities described in section 302304(b) of this title on tribal land, if—

(1)   the Secretary and the Indian tribe agree on additional financial assistance, if any, to the Indian tribe for the costs of carrying out those authorities;

(2)   the Secretary finds that the tribal historic preservation program has been demonstrated to be sufficient to carry out the contract or cooperative agreement and this division; and

(3)   the contract or cooperative agreement specifies the continuing responsibilities of the Secretary or of the appropriate State Historic Preservation Officers and provides for appropriate participation by—

(A)   the Indian tribe's traditional cultural authorities;

(B)   representatives of other Indian tribes whose traditional land is under the jurisdiction of the Indian tribe assuming responsibilities; and

(C)   the interested public.

§ 302705.   Agreement for review under tribal historic preservation regulations

The Council may enter into an agreement with an Indian tribe to permit undertakings on tribal land to be reviewed under tribal historic preservation regulations in place of review under regulations promulgated by the Council to govern compliance with section 306108 of this title, if the Council, after consultation with the Indian tribe and appropriate State Historic Preservation Officers, determines that the tribal preservation regulations will afford historic property consideration equivalent to that afforded by the Council's regulations.

§ 302706.   Eligibility for inclusion on National Register

(a)   In General.—

Properties of traditional religious and cultural importance to an Indian tribe or Native Hawaiian organization may be determined to be eligible for inclusion on the National Register.

(b)   Consultation.—

In carrying out its responsibilities under section 306108 of this title, a Federal agency shall consult with any Indian tribe or Native Hawaiian organization that attaches religious and cultural significance to a property described in subsection (a).

(c)   Hawaii.—In carrying out responsibilities under section 302303 of this title, the State Historic Preservation Officer for Hawaii shall—

(1)   consult with Native Hawaiian organizations in assessing the cultural significance of any property in determining whether to nominate the property to the National Register;

(2)   consult with Native Hawaiian organizations in developing the cultural component of a preservation program or plan for the property; and

(3)   enter into a memorandum of understanding or agreement with Native Hawaiian organizations for the assessment of the cultural significance of a property in determining whether to nominate the property to the National Register and to carry out the cultural component of such preservation program or plan.

NOTES & QUESTIONS

1. The National Historic Preservation Act has clearly defined SHPO obligations. Most importantly, the SHPO reviews National Register nominations and eligibility, and serves as the state's liaison to federal agencies engaging in the Section 106 consultation process. In addition, among other things, SHPOs must implement a statewide historic preservation plan, provide public education and technical assistance, and conduct a statewide survey of historic properties. *See* 54 U.S.C. § 302303. According to the above excerpt, under what circumstances may a THPO assume the obligations of a SHPO?

2. In several places, this excerpt mentions the capabilities of tribes or THPOs to carry out various duties, implying an assumption of insufficiency until the tribe proves otherwise. What does this assumption reveal about the relationship between the federal government and tribes, which is based on the legal construct that each are sovereign entities?

3. About 118 tribes currently have THPOs recognized by the Department of the Interior as being sufficiently capable of taking over SHPO duties as authorized by statute. SHPOs may nonetheless be involved in THPO affairs in certain circumstances. According to 54 U.S.C. § 302702, a THPO may only act in the place of the SHPO on "tribal lands." Tribal lands include "all lands within the exterior boundaries of any Indian reservation and all dependent Indian communities." 36 C.F.R. § 800.16(x). What about the millions of acres of non-Indian "islands" that are within reservation boundaries but neither owned by the tribes (or their members) nor held in trust for the tribes? According to 54 U.S.C. § 302702(4)(C), a non-Indian property owner owning land that meets this description may request that the SHPO and THPO share responsibilities. For background material on the creation of these islands and for a detailed description of the meaning of the term "dependent Indian communities," see COHEN'S HANDBOOK OF FEDERAL INDIAN LAW (Nell Jessup Newton et al. eds., 2005 ed.) or Judith V. Royster, *The Legacy of Allotment*, 27 ARIZ. ST. L. J. 1 (1995).

4. Look closely at 54 U.S.C. § 302706(c). Native Hawaiians do not have a THPO, but instead must consult through the state's SHPO. Does this arrangement have the potential to ignore the needs of Native Hawaiians? Note that 36 C.F.R. § 800.16 offers the following definitions:

(s)(1) *Native Hawaiian organization* means any organization which serves and represents the interests of Native Hawaiians; has as a primary and stated purpose the provision of services to Native Hawaiians; and has demonstrated expertise in aspects of historic preservation that are significant to Native Hawaiians.

(2) *Native Hawaiian means* any individual who is a descendant of the aboriginal people who, prior to 1778, occupied and exercised sovereignty in the area that now constitutes the State of Hawaii.

5. Some federal agency duties under Section 106 may be delegated to private consultants and contractors. Certain studies and analyses of complex projects, for example, may require competencies beyond those of agency staff. One duty which is nondelegable is the duty to consult directly with federally

recognized tribes. *See* 36 C.F.R. § 800.2(c)(2)(ii)(B) & (C). This duty reflects federal policy to treat tribal governments as sovereign nations and to interact with them on a government-to-government basis.

2. QUESTIONS ABOUT SIGNIFICANCE

For tribes to assert their rights under the National Historic Preservation Act, the property at issue must be listed on or eligible for the National Register. To achieve this status, the property must, first and foremost, have "significance." The National Historic Preservation Act and related regulations treat the evaluation of the significance of tribal sites differently from non-tribal sites in one key respect: They embrace religious significance as a criterion for tribal sites, while rejecting it for non-tribal sites. According to federal regulations:

> Ordinarily * * * properties owned by religious institutions or used for religious purposes * * * shall not be considered eligible for the National Register. However, such properties will qualify if they are integral parts of districts that do meet the criteria of [EDS.: sic] if they fall within the following categories:
>
> (a) A religious property deriving primary significance from architectural or artistic distinction or historical importance * * *

36 C.F.R. § 60.4(d)(a). One commentator has observed that this criterion "reflects the constitutional paradox of the separation of church and state" but frustrates religious leaders and imposes unneeded thematic and chronological constraints on National Park Service's designation process. John H. Sprinkle, *"History Is as History Was, and Cannot Be Changed": Origins of the National Register Criteria Consideration for Religious Properties*, 16 BLDGS. & LANDSCAPES: J. OF THE VERNACULAR ARCHITECTURE FORUM 1, 10–11 (Fall 2009).

Contrast the religious exception contained in 36 C.F.R. § 60.4 with the following language: "Properties of traditional religious and cultural importance to an Indian tribe or Native Hawaiian organization may be determined to be eligible for inclusion on the National Register." 54 U.S.C. § 302706(a). Should tribal sites be treated differently in this regard? If so, why?

Keep this different treatment in mind as you further explore the question of the significance of tribal sites. A few threshold issues are addressed in the next case: What constitutes a protectable tribal site under Section 106? How must a site's significance to a tribe be documented? How should courts treat tribal resources not on tribal lands?

Hoonah Indian Association v. Morrison

170 F.3d 1223 (9th Cir. 1999)

■ KLEINFELD, CIRCUIT JUDGE. * * *

The Forest Service gave notice of its intent to conduct timber sales in the Tongass National Forest in Southeast Alaska. 58 Fed. Reg. 21559–01, 37458–01 (1993). Two sales were proposed, called the Northwest Baranof and Eight Fathom, on Baranof Island north of Sitka, and on Chichagof Island around Hoonah.

The timber sales were planned pursuant to the Tongass Timber Reform Act, 16 U.S.C. § 539d. This federal law speaks not to all national forests but only to one, the Tongass National Forest in Southeast Alaska. It commands the Secretary of Agriculture to sell enough wood from the Tongass National Forest, subject to certain qualifications, to satisfy market demand:

> a.   Tongass National Forest timber supply; satisfaction of certain market demands. Subject to appropriations, other applicable law, and the requirements of the National Forest Management Act of 1976 (Public Law 94–588), except as provided in subsection (d) of this section, the Secretary shall, to the extent consistent with providing for the multiple use and sustained yield of all renewable forest resources, seek to provide a supply of timber from the Tongass National Forest which (1) meets the annual market demand for timber from such forest and (2) meets the market demand from such forest for each planning cycle.

16 U.S.C. § 539d(a). * * *

Hoonah Indian Association and Sitka Tribe brought this lawsuit and now appeal. Hoonah is among Alaska's larger villages, about 800 people, and Sitka is among its largest cities (by Alaska standards), close to 9,000 people. The Native community in each town has a tribal government. Both towns are in Southeast Alaska. Though the towns are distinct from the tribal governments (Sitka is largely non-Native, with a substantial Tlingit minority), the tribal governments are referred to herein for convenience as Hoonah and Sitka. Sitka and Hoonah both argue that the timber sales would violate 16 U.S.C. § 3120's limitation on dispositions affecting subsistence uses of public land. Sitka also argues that the Northwest Baranof sales would violate the National Historic Preservation Act, 16 U.S.C. § 470f.

The tribal governments moved for summary judgment, which was denied. They sought injunctions, which were denied as well. The United States moved for clarification, noting that the Tribes had moved for a permanent, not preliminary, injunction. The district court granted the clarification, stating that its order denying an injunction was a final decision. The Tribes appeal. Because there was no certification under

Federal Rule of Civil Procedure 54(b), we lack jurisdiction to review the denial of summary judgment. We have jurisdiction to review denial of the injunction under 28 U.S.C. § 1292(a)(1).

Analysis * * *

II.   National Historic Preservation Act.

This issue affects only the Northwest Baranof sale on Baranof Island outside of Sitka, not the Eight Fathom sale on Chichagof Island near Hoonah. From the time the Russians colonized what they called New Archangel, now Sitka, their relations with the Tlingits native to the area were hostile. American and British traders contributed to the hostility by trading with the Tlingits on better terms than the Russians, and supplying guns. In 1802, the Tlingits defeated the Russians and the Aleuts they forced to serve them, and took over the settlement. It took quite a while for the Russians to build up enough strength to try to take it back, but in 1804, Baranof assembled an entire fleet, and after a battle that lasted seven days, reconquered the fort. The Tlingits retreated north. * * *

The National Historic Preservation Act issue has to do with whether the route or routes one clan of the Tlingits, the Kiks.adi, took should have been designated a cultural site and the timber sale should have been enjoined while the process for listing it proceeded. The Tlingit fort is a historic site in present-day Sitka, but the route or routes of the march were not designated.

The applicable procedure under the Act, 16 U.S.C. §§ 470 et seq., is for State Historic Preservation Officers to identify and nominate properties for the National Register. 16 U.S.C. 470a(b)(3). The Act requires agencies, prior to undertaking projects on federal land, to "take into account the effect of the undertaking on any district, site, building, structure, or object that is included in or eligible for inclusion in the National Register." 16 U.S.C. § 470f. That language is carried over from the definitions section of the statute, defining "historic property" and "historic resource" as "any prehistoric or historic district, site, building, structure, or object included in, or eligible for inclusion on the National Register . . ." 16 U.S.C. § 470w(5).

In preparing the Environmental Impact Statement for the Northwest Baranof timber sales, Forest Service archaeologists identified 45 historic properties, and determined that 39 were eligible for inclusion in the National Register. The State Historic Preservation Office, charged with administering the NHPA, agreed with the Forest Service's findings. The Forest Service, with the Tribe's agreement, decided the 39 designated sites would not be affected by the timber sale. The route of the retreat after the Russian reconquest, called in the record the Kiks.adi Survival March, was not among the sites listed as eligible. The Sitka Tribe contends that the Forest Service's procedure regarding identification of the "Kiks.adi Survival March" violated the National Historic Preservation Act.

The Forest Service early in the process decided that the route of the survival march might be eligible for inclusion because of its cultural importance. The reason that it was ultimately not designated as a cultural site is that the Forest Service was unable to determine just where the Kiks.adi Survival March went. The Tribe argues that this was an arbitrary and capricious failure to designate, because oral history suggested multiple routes, at least one for the strong men and another for the women, children, and old people, and because it was arbitrary to require a site with observable physical identification.

The regulations say that if the relevant agency official and state historic preservation officer "agree that the criteria are not met, the property shall be considered not eligible." 36 C.F.R. § 800.4(c)(3). The Alaska State Historic Preservation Officer determined that the Survival March Trail was not eligible because it did not meet established criteria that "it have identified physical features" and that it be "a location where the people regularly returned to." Her determination was based upon review of the materials submitted to her by a panel of experts. The Tribe did not appeal the State Historic Preservation Officer's decision. It could have under 36 C.F.R. § 60.12. Failure to do so makes that decision unchallengeable for failure to exhaust administrative remedies, under 36 C.F.R. § 60.12(e).

The Tribe did challenge the Forest Service's environmental impact statement on the ground that the Forest Service did not recommend listing the Kiks.adi Survival March trail. Our review of that decision is limited to whether it was arbitrary or capricious. *See Natural Ress. Def. Council v. U. S. Dep't of Interior*, 113 F.3d 1121, 1123–24 (9th Cir. 1997).

The statute defines "historic property" and "historic resource" as "any prehistoric or historic district, site, building, structure, or object included in, or eligible for inclusion on the National Register . . ." 16 U.S.C. § 470w(5). The words "district, site, building, structure or object" all connote something more concretely bounded and defined than a general area over which a group of people passed.

The Tribe notes that 36 C.F.R. § 800.4(c)(1) requires agencies to "apply the National Register Criteria to properties that may be affected by the undertaking and have not been previously evaluated for National Register eligibility," and argues that the Forest Service never applied the National Register Criteria to the Survival March routes. But the record shows that it did. The Forest Service made extensive efforts for close to three years to identify the Kiks.adi Survival March routes, by consulting with experts and considering tribal traditions and individuals' recollections of what relatives had told them. There was no physical marking, no documentation, and no well established tribal consensus, to establish exactly what bear and deer trails, beaches, and other paths the retreating Kiks.adi had taken.

The regulations require the agency official to "[s]eek information in accordance with agency planning processes from . . . Indian tribes." 36 C.F.R. 800.4(a)(iii). He did. The tribe could not tell him just where the retreating Kiks.adi passed.

The Forest Service followed the regulations and used the National Register criteria, as the Tribe says it should have. Those criteria do not support the Tribe's position. The National Register Bulletin entitled "How To Apply the National Register Criteria for Evaluation" says in the explanation of "site" that "when the location of a prehistoric or historic event cannot be conclusively determined because no other cultural materials were present or survive, documentation must be carefully evaluated to determine whether the traditionally recognized or identified site is accurate." There was no original source documentation, and all the materials available were carefully evaluated, and did not confirm the accuracy of any suggested path. The criteria say that "[t]he actual location of a historic property, complemented by its setting, is particularly important in recapturing the sense of historic events and persons." *Id.* at 44. The "actual location" of the Kiks.adi route is unknown, and the Tribe's own submission called it a "symbolic" location as opposed to an "actual" one.

The Tribe places great emphasis on research by a Mr. Hope, a tribal member who had not grown up knowing where the march went, but after research, thought he had a good conclusion, supported by what his grandfather had told him and what he thought would be feasible, about the route. Mr. Hope appears to have coined the term, "Kiks.adi Survival March." The ages of the individuals are not in the record. But even if Mr. Hope's grandfather were 100 years old in 1987 when Mr. Hope became interested, and could remember geographical details back to when he was 10, that would go back only 90 years, to 1897, which would be 93 years after the Kiks.adi retreat. Other tribal members disagreed with Mr. Hope's theory, though eventually the Tribe decided to adopt it as its position.

Importantly, the Tribe's application says that the large number of people "would have necessitated being several routes taken so as to have enough food to eat along the way." That makes perfect sense. It would be hard to kill enough deer or catch enough fish for 1,000 people unless they spread out. But if they did, there would not be any particular path, just a general direction through a large wilderness.

That important things happened in a general area is not enough to make the area a "site." There has to be some good evidence of just where the site is and what its boundaries are, for it to qualify for federal designation as a historical site. The Historian of the National Register of Historic Places wrote, in opposition to listing the Kiks.adi route, that his staff consistently rejected "nominating such a wide swath of land with little if any identified physical features." The Historian noted that when trails had been designated, such as the Lewis and Clark Trail, only those particular rock formations, ruts, and other identified physical features where the trail was "confined to a very narrow corridor" were listed. That a general unbounded and imprecisely located area has important cultural significance is not enough. Abraham's tomb is an identifiable site, but the wanderings of the Jews in the Sinai Desert after the Exodus did not leave any accurately identifiable path that could be a "site."

The Forest Service did not act arbitrarily and capriciously, on this record, in concluding that it could not identify a "site" as the Kiks.adi Survival March.

Conclusion

The district judge correctly determined that because the Tribe could not prevail on the merits, and the Forest Service determinations were not arbitrary or capricious, the Tribe's prayer for an injunction against the timber sales should be denied. The judgment of the district court is AFFIRMED.

NOTES & QUESTIONS

1.   By what standard did the Ninth Circuit review the Forest Service determinations? On what basis did the Ninth Circuit find for the Forest Service?

2.   Oral history here was deemed to be insufficient to definitively establish the Kiks.adi Survival March route as a "site" meriting protection under the National Historic Preservation Act. The panel did not comment on whether more extensive oral history could have served as the basis for such protection. Should it? Why or why not? If a tribe's oral tradition treats an area as the place where significant events occurred, is it not a site having "traditional religious and cultural importance" regardless of whether there is objective evidence exactly where the events occurred? Does it matter whether the events occurred at all?

3.   Attorney Dean Suagee, a member of the Cherokee Nation of Oklahoma, has chronicled the back-and-forth between tribes, SHPOs, and the Advisory Council on Historic Preservation regarding the regulations dealing with tribal cultural property outside tribal lands. He reports that the tribes pushed to take over SHPO responsibility at two key points in the Section 106 consultation process: first, in determining whether effects on tribal cultural property would be adverse, and second, as a required signatory for any memorandum of agreement concluding the Section 106 process. One proposed compromise would have given the tribes the authority to bring the Advisory Council on Historic Preservation in at these key points. But the final rules gave tribes no authority to either bring in the Advisory Council or intervene themselves. *See* Dean B. Suagee, *The Cultural Heritage of American Indian Tribes and the Preservation of Biological Diversity*, 31 ARIZ. ST. L.J. 483, 524–27 (1999). Currently, 54 U.S.C. § 302706(b) sets forth the extent of tribal involvement in NHPA disputes involving tribal cultural property on non-tribal land. This involvement is limited to tribes (and Native Hawaiian organizations) serving as consulting authorities to federal

agencies where the subject property has some religious or cultural significance.

4. The environmental impact statement prepared by the Forest Service was required by the National Environmental Policy Act, 42 U.S.C. § 4332 (NEPA). NEPA requires that agencies prepare environmental impact statements when they undertake "major federal actions significantly affecting the quality of the human environment." *Id.* § 4332(C). Such statements must address the impact of a project and weigh alternatives to the agency's proposed action. *Id.* This important statute is covered more fully in Chapter 4.

3. THE CONSULTATION PROCESS

What does it mean to engage tribes in a meaningful consultation process under Section 106? Consider the following two cases.

Muckleshoot Indian Tribe v. United States Forest Service

177 F.3d 800 (9th Cir. 1999)

■ PER CURIAM.

Plaintiffs Muckleshoot Indian Tribe, Pilchuck Audubon Society, and Huckleberry Mountain Protection Society appeal the district court's grant of summary judgment on consolidated challenges to a land exchange between the United States Forest Service and Weyerhaeuser Company. Plaintiffs contend that the Forest Service violated * * * the National Historic Preservation Act ("NHPA"), 16 U.S.C. §§ 470–470w. We have jurisdiction pursuant to 28 U.S.C. § 1291, and we reverse.

I. Background

Huckleberry Mountain, the land subject to the dispute in this case, is located in the Green River watershed in the Mt. Baker-Snoqualmie National Forest ("the Forest") in the state of Washington. The Forest contains sixteen percent of the wilderness in the Pacific Northwest. Thirteen percent (259,545 acres) of the 1,983,774 acres within the National Forest boundary are privately owned, primarily by Weyerhaeuser and other large corporations. Most of the privately-owned lands are in the southern portion of the Forest, and are intermingled with federal lands in a checkerboard pattern of ownership that remains from the federal land grants to railroads a century ago.

Motivated in large part by a desire to unify land ownership, the United States Forest Service ("the Forest Service") and Weyerhaeuser Company ("Weyerhaeuser") began negotiations for a series of land exchanges pursuant to 43 U.S.C. § 1716, which authorizes the exchange of public lands within the National Forest system where "the public interest will be well served" by the exchange. In the 1980s, the Forest Service negotiated a land exchange with Weyerhaeuser and the

Burlington Northern Railroad Company involving lands near Huckleberry Mountain. Under the terms of the Alpine Lakes Exchange, as it became known, the United States conveyed a total of 21,676 acres of federally-owned Forest land to Weyerhaeuser and Burlington Northern in exchange for other property owned by the two companies. In the present appeal, plaintiffs challenge another land exchange between Weyerhaeuser and the Forest Service, the Huckleberry Mountain Exchange ("the Exchange"), in which the Forest Service again traded old growth forest lands in the Huckleberry Mountain area. Many of the parcels conveyed by the Forest Service in the Alpine Lakes Exchange are near or contiguous to federal lands that are part of the Exchange at issue in this appeal.

Although land within the Huckleberry Mountain Exchange Area had been tentatively identified during the Alpine Lakes Exchange negotiations between 1984 and 1987, negotiations began anew in 1988 with a revised list of federal land under consideration for exchange. In July 1991, Weyerhaeuser and the Forest Service signed a Statement of Intent to enter into an exchange, which identified the parcels to be included in the exchange. Between 1992 and 1994, the Forest Service conducted surveys regarding wetlands, wildlife, rare plants, hazardous waste, cultural resources and other matters, and subsequently reduced the federal acreage proposed for transfer.

The Forest Service initiated public consultation and comment and developed a list of six exchange alternatives. In July 1996, the Forest Service released a draft Environmental Impact Statement ("EIS"), pursuant to NEPA [the National Environmental Policy Act], 42 U.S.C. § 4332(2)(C), and mailed over 300 copies to interested parties. It then conducted three open meetings in communities near the Forest. Among those who provided comments on the Draft EIS was the Muckleshoot Indian Tribe (the "Tribe").

On November 26, 1996, the Forest Service issued a final EIS after receiving comments on the draft EIS. The EIS considered three alternatives: a "no action" alternative, and two closely related exchange alternatives. Concurrently, the Forest Service issued a Record of Decision that called for an implementation of the Exchange through a modification of "Alternative No. 3" as evaluated in the EIS.

The Pilchuck Audubon Society and the Huckleberry Mountain Protection Society (collectively "the Societies") and the Tribe lodged separate appeals of the EIS and the ROD with the Office of the Regional Forester. These appeals were denied on March 7, 1997. On March 28, 1997, pursuant to the ROD, Weyerhaeuser and the Forest Service executed an exchange agreement under which Weyerhaeuser conveyed to the United States 30,253 acres of land in and around Mt. Baker National Forest in return for 4,362 acres of land in the Huckleberry Mountain area. In addition, Weyerhaeuser donated to the United States 962 acres to the Alpine Lakes Wilderness and 1,034 acres for Forest

Service management. The National Forest lands that Weyerhaeuser received included old growth, commercial grade timber. The Forest Service also exchanged to Weyerhaeuser intact portions of the Huckleberry Divide Trail, a site important to the Tribe and that the Forest Service found eligible for inclusion in the National Register for Historic Preservation. Weyerhaeuser gave the Forest Service lands that were, for the most part, heavily logged and roaded. Weyerhaeuser intends to log the lands it received in the Exchange.

In the spring of 1997, the Tribe and the Societies commenced separate actions in the district court seeking declaratory and injunctive relief to halt the Huckleberry Mountain Exchange. The district court consolidated the two actions and granted Weyerhaeuser's motion to intervene because it was party to the Exchange. The combined action, brought pursuant to the Administrative Procedures Act, 5 U.S.C. §§ 701–06, alleged violations of the * * * NHPA, 16 U.S.C. § 470 et seq. * * * The district court denied all of these claims. * * *

II.   The National Historic Preservation Act Claims

The Muckleshoot Tribe is made up principally of descendants of tribes or bands that were parties to the Treaty of Point Elliott and the Treaty of Medicine Creek. The Tribe was organized pursuant to the Indian Reorganization Act of June 18, 1934. *See United States v. State of Washington*, 384 F.Supp. 312, 366 (W.D. Wash. 1974). The United States, acting by and through the Secretary of the Interior and his duly authorized delegates, has consistently recognized the Muckleshoot Tribe as the political successor in interest to certain of the Indian tribes, bands and villages that were parties to the Treaty of Point Elliott or the Treaty of Medicine Creek. *Id.*

The Indian ancestors to the present Muckleshoot Tribe included people from villages on the Green and White Rivers that form part of the drainage for Huckleberry Mountain. The Tribe alleges that for thousands of years, the ancestors of present tribal members used Huckleberry Mountain for cultural, religious, and resource purposes-uses that continue to the present day. The Forest Service lands exchanged to Weyerhaeuser were part of the Tribe's ancestral grounds.

Section 10 [sic: 106] of NHPA requires that, prior to any federal undertaking, the relevant federal agency "take into account the effect of the undertaking on any district, site, building, structure, or object that is included in or eligible for inclusion in the National Register" and "afford the Advisory Council on Historic Preservation ... a reasonable opportunity to comment with regard to such undertaking." 16 U.S.C. § 470f; *see also Hoonah Indian Ass'n v. Morrison*, 170 F.3d 1223, 1230 (9th Cir. 1999); 36 C.F.R. § 800. The Exchange was such an undertaking. 36 C.F.R. § 800.2(*o*).

We have held that Section 106 of NHPA is a "stop, look, and listen" provision that requires each federal agency to consider the effects of its programs. *See Apache Survival Coal. v. United States*, 21 F.3d 895, 906 (9th Cir. 1994). Under NHPA, a federal agency must make a reasonable and good faith effort to identify historic properties, 36 C.F.R. § 800.4(b); determine whether identified properties are eligible for listing on the National Register based on criteria in 36 C.F.R. § 60.4; assess the effects of the undertaking on any eligible historic properties found, 36 C.F.R. §§ 800.4(c), 800.5, 800.9(a); determine whether the effect will be adverse, 36 C.F.R. §§ 800.5(c), 800.9(b); and avoid or mitigate any adverse effects, 36 C.F.R. §§ 800.8(e), 800.9(c). The Forest Service must confer with the State Historic Preservation Officer ("SHPO") and seek the approval of the Advisory Council on Historic Preservation ("Council").

Additional NHPA provisions apply to Indian tribes.

(A) Properties of traditional religious and cultural importance to an Indian tribe ... may be determined to be eligible for inclusion in the National Register.

(B) In carrying out its responsibilities under Section 106, a Federal Agency shall consult with any Indian Tribe ... that attaches religious and cultural significance to properties described in Subparagraph (A).

16 U.S.C. § 470a(d)(6).

The Tribe's claims under NHPA can be divided into three categories. The Tribe first contends that the Forest Service failed to consult adequately with it regarding the identification of traditional cultural properties. The Tribe also contends that the Forest Service inadequately mitigated the harmful impact of the exchange on sites of cultural significance. Finally, the Tribe argues that the Forest Service violated NHPA by failing to nominate certain sites to the National Register. We conclude that the Forest Service has not satisfied NHPA's mitigation requirements.

A.   Identification of Traditional Cultural Properties

This Court has not yet had the opportunity to interpret the specific consultation requirements of NHPA. The regulations interpreting NHPA require that:

[T]he Agency official, the State Historic Preservation Officer and the [Advisory] Council [on Historic Preservation] should be sensitive to the special concerns of Indian tribes in historic preservation issues, which often extend beyond Indian lands to other historic properties. When an undertaking will affect Indian lands, the Agency Official shall invite the governing body of the responsible tribe to be a consulting party and to concur in any agreement. . . . When an undertaking may affect properties of historic value to an Indian tribe on non-Indian lands, the consulting parties shall afford such tribe the opportunity to participate as interested persons. Traditional cultural leaders and other Native Americans are considered to be interested person with respect to undertakings that may affect historic properties of significance to such persons.

36 C.F.R. § 800.1(c)(2)(iii).

Although we confront somewhat different issues, *Pueblo of Sandia v. United States*, 50 F.3d 856, 860 (10th Cir. 1995) is instructive. The Tenth Circuit concluded that the agency's mailing of form letters soliciting information from knowledgeable parties, combined with an address to the All Indian Pueblo Council requesting the same detailed information solicited by the form letter did not satisfy section 470f. In *Sandia*, the Forest Service did not find any of the properties eligible for inclusion and withheld relevant information from the SHPO during the consultation process. *Id.* at 862. The court found that although none of the tribes provided the information specifically solicited by the letters and presentation, the statements of the Governor of the Sandia Pueblo, a religious leader, and a highly qualified anthropologist, all indicating that the land was sacred, and that the tribes were unlikely to reveal information on the use of these lands, were sufficient to require the agency to evaluate the property for inclusion in the National Register. *Id.* at 861. The court also determined that the agency had failed to perform the required "good faith consultation" with the State Historic Preservation Office, and reversed the district court order approving the federal action. *Id.* at 862.

In the case before us, the record shows that the Forest Service researched historic sites in the Exchange area and communicated several times after the commencement of the public comment period with Tribal officials regarding the identification and protection of cultural resources that might be affected by the Exchange. The Forest Service initially identified only Mule Springs as eligible for listing in the National Register, and concluded that any adverse effect "may be negated through appropriately conducted data recovery." Two years later, after considering the concerns of the Tribe, the Forest Service excluded Mule Springs from the Exchange and retained the Forest Service access road in a cost-share status. Because this site was excluded from the Exchange, the district court correctly concluded that the Tribe suffered no injury. The Forest Service initially concluded that the Huckleberry Divide Trail ("Divide Trail") was ineligible for listing. After the SHPO suggested otherwise, the Forest Service reconsidered and found it eligible for listing but nonetheless included it in the lands exchanged to Weyerhaeuser. We discuss the Divide Trail in more detail below.

The Tribe also contends that the Forest Service ignored its claims that numerous other places of historical importance were situated on the portions of Huckleberry Mountain proposed for exchange. The Tribe requested a study of its historical places and trails, but in response, the Forest Service, which had already carried out research in the area, simply requested the immediate disclosure of any information the Tribe possessed about those sites. The Tribe was unable, or unwilling, to provide information sufficient to persuade the Agency that it should reconsider its decisions.

The Forest Service's action is in tension with the recommendations of the National Register Bulletin 38: *Guidelines for Evaluating and Documenting Traditional Cultural Properties* ("Bulletin 38"). Bulletin 38 provides the recognized criteria for the Forest Service's identification and assessment of places of cultural significance. In *Sandia*, the Tenth Circuit's finding that the agency had violated NHPA rested in part upon its finding that the agency failed to adhere to that document. 50 F.3d at 861. The Tribe urges us to find a comparable violation in this case.

While the deviations from Bulletin 38 policies in this case are similar to those in *Sandia*, they appear not to be as egregious, and probably do not provide sufficient grounds to conclude that the Forest Service failed to comply with NHPA identification and consultation requirements. First, Bulletin 38 does not impose a mandatory procedure, but merely establishes guidelines. Contravention of those recommendations, standing alone, probably does not constitute a violation of NHPA. Second, in this case, unlike *Sandia*, the Forest Service continued to seek the requested information over a period of time, *cf. Sandia*, 50 F.3d at 861–62, and the Forest Service had previously conducted research of its own to identify relevant traditional cultural properties.

Unlike in *Sandia*, there is no evidence that the Forest Service withheld information from the SHPO pertaining to historic sites, or failed to engage in good faith negotiations with SHPO. *Cf. Sandia*, 50 F.3d at 862. The record shows that the Forest Service resisted the Tribe's requests for a formal study of cultural properties because it would impede the finalization of the Exchange. Given more time or a more thorough exploration, the Forest Service might have discovered more eligible sites. However, the record also shows that the Tribe had many opportunities to reveal more information to the Forest Service. Although the Forest Service could have been more sensitive to the needs of the Tribe, we are unable to conclude that the Forest Service failed to make a reasonable and good faith effort to identify historic properties. Because we are reversing on other grounds, and because the record shows that the Forest Service's understanding and appreciation of the importance of the Huckleberry Mountain area to the Tribes grew over time, the Forest Service will have an opportunity to re-open its quest for and evaluation of historic sites on Huckleberry Mountain.

B.   The Effects of the Exchange

The Tribe also claims that the Forest Service's attempt to mitigate the adverse effect of transferring a portion of the Divide Trail, an important tribal ancestral transportation route, was inadequate. We agree.

When an agency determines that a property is eligible for listing, it must assess the effects of any proposed undertaking on the eligible property, 36 C.F.R. § 800.4(e), "giving consideration to the views . . . of interested persons." 36 C.F.R. § 800.5(a). Interested persons include tribes. 36 C.F.R. § 800.1(c)(2).

An undertaking has an "effect" when the undertaking "may alter characteristics of the property that may qualify the property for inclusion in the National Register . . . [including] alteration to features of a property's location, setting, or use. . . ." 36 C.F.R. § 800.9(a). An "effect" is "adverse" when it may "diminish the integrity of the property's location, . . . setting . . ., feeling, or association." 36 C.F.R. § 800.9(b). Examples of "adverse effects" include physical destruction, the introduction of visual, audible, or atmospheric elements that are out of character with the property or alter its setting, and transferring the property. *Id.*

In 1995, the Forest Service re-evaluated the eligibility of the Divide Trail for listing. The Divide Trail is a 17.5 mile historic aboriginal transportation route. The Forest Service found that portions of the trail possessed "adequate integrity of location, setting and feeling" to satisfy the eligibility criteria of 36 C.F.R. § 60.4. In the proposed Exchange, a portion of the intact trail would be transferred to Weyerhaeuser, where it would likely be logged and rendered ineligible for listing. Transfer and destruction of historic property are "adverse" effects. *See* 36 C.F.R. § 800.9(b).

The regulations offer three options to mitigate an otherwise adverse effect so that it is "considered as being not adverse," two of which are implicated here. 36 C.F.R. § 800.9(c). First, an agency may conduct appropriate research "[w]hen the historic property is of value *only for* its potential contribution to archeological, historical, or architectural research, *and* when such value can be substantially preserved through the conduct of appropriate research . . ." 36 C.F.R. § 800.9(c)(1) (emphasis added). Second, an adverse effect becomes "not adverse" when the undertaking is limited to the "transfer, lease, or sale of a historic property, *and adequate restrictions or conditions are included* to ensure preservation of the property's significant historic features." 36 C.F.R. § 800.9(c)(3) (emphasis added). The Tribe insists that the Forest Service elected the wrong remedy. We agree.

To mitigate the adverse effect of the Exchange, the Forest Service proposed to map the trail using a global positioning system and to photograph significant features along the trail. It rejected an easement or covenant because it concluded that it was too expensive and impractical to monitor Weyerhaeuser's land practices, and because "only" 25 percent of the eligible miles of trail would be transferred out of federal ownership. It also rejected the imposition of conditions to prevent logging and other degradation. Although the Forest Service purports to have acted under (c)(3), photographing and mapping the trail are not "adequate restrictions or conditions" that "ensure preservation of the property's significant historic features." *See* 36 C.F.R. § 800.9(c)(3). The parties agree that the trail is likely to be logged if it is transferred. The Forest Service has already concluded that previously logged and "obliterated" portions of the trail are ineligible for listing.

The district court determined erroneously that the Forest Service had proceeded under (c)(1) and concluded that the agency acted properly because any adverse effect may be "negated" if the historical and archeological value of the property can be preserved by conducting research on the site. The Forest Service did not, and could not, proceed under (c)(1). Under 36 C.F.R. § 800.9(c)(1), research is appropriate mitigation where the historic property is of value only for "its potential contribution to archeological, historical, or architectural research." The Muckleshoots value the Divide Trail for more than its "potential contribution to . . . research."

The Forest Service insists that it acted properly, because the SHPO concurred in its proposal to document the trail, provided that it document the entire intact portion, regardless of ownership, and maintain the portions of the trail not being transferred. These "conditions" do not preserve the trail's significant historic features. Moreover, in 1994, when SHPO first suggested that the Divide Trail probably was eligible for listing, it concluded that

> [i]n view of the unusual nature and remote location of the trail, documentation is probably not an effective mitigative measure. Rather, [SHPO] suggests execution of an easement or covenant attached to the transferring instrument. This easement would provide for the ongoing preservation of the Divide Trail and its setting after the land has been transferred.

While we do not decide whether the Forest Service's reasons for rejecting deed restrictions were valid, we note that it could have removed the trail from the Exchange as it did with Mule Springs. We conclude that documenting the trail did not satisfy the Forest Service's obligations to minimize the adverse effect of transferring the intact portions of the trail.

C.   Nomination of Historic Sites

Finally, the Tribe contends that the Forest Service violated the Preservation Act by failing to properly nominate the Divide Trail to the National Register. In light of our ruling, we need not address this issue. Upon remand, the Forest Service may wish to reconsider its treatment of the historic properties in the Exchange lands. * * *

V.   Conclusion * * *

We REVERSE and REMAND to the district court with directions that it remand to the Forest Service for further proceedings consistent with this opinion. Given Weyerhaeuser's representations that it has destroyed approximately ten percent of the property, and will continue to do so, we also enjoin any further activities on the land such as would be undertaken pursuant to the Huckleberry Mountain Exchange

Agreement as executed on March 28, 1997 until such time as the Forest Service satisfies its NHPA * * * obligations. The injunction shall take effect immediately by virtue of a separate order filed concomitantly with this opinion.

NOTES & QUESTIONS

1. In this case, the Ninth Circuit emphasizes the procedural nature of Section 106: that the National Historic Preservation Act requires only that agencies "stop, look, and listen." Does the court's analysis push the boundaries of this requirement? The court stated that the agency failed to "minimize the adverse effect" of its undertaking. The regulations, however, explicitly state that only consultation is required upon finding of an adverse effect: "If an adverse effect is found, the agency official shall consult further to resolve the adverse effect pursuant to § 800.6." 36 C.F.R. § 800.5(d)(2). The provision referenced in that quote, § 800.6, requires consultation with various parties, such as the Advisory Council on Historic Preservation, and State or Tribal Historic Preservation Officers. Moreover, it states that the effect of consultation is merely "to *seek ways* to avoid, minimize, *or* mitigate the adverse effects." § 800.6(b)(1)(i) & § 800.6(b)(2) (emphases added).

According to one student commentator, *Muckleshoot* confirmed that "judicial enforcement does not end with statutory consultation requirements: Courts will also enforce those regulations that require agencies to act on the information received from such consultations." Marcia Yablon, *Property Rights and Sacred Sites: Federal Regulatory Responses to American Indian Religious Claims on Public Land*, 113 YALE L.J. 1623, 1643 (2004). How far does this interpretation, enshrined in *Muckleshoot*, overstep the stated requirements of Section 106? What regulations required the Forest Service to mitigate adverse effects?

2. Why is the Muckleshoot Indian Tribe so concerned about tribal resources off reservation land? Although the Muckleshoots did not own the property at issue in this case, it is clear from the facts that they felt it was significant nonetheless. The Muckleshoots share, with almost every other tribe, the unfortunate history of allotment and loss of land significant to them. Between 1890 and 1910 alone, nearly 60 percent of the Muckleshoot reservation was transferred outside of tribal ownership as part of the Dawes General Allotment Act of 1887. The Dawes Act authorized the transfer of almost ninety million acres of tribal land to non-Indians such before transfers were abandoned in 1934. *See* 24 Stat. 388 (1887).

3. Two researchers at Arizona State University have published a postscript recording the immediate aftermath of the case. In the months following the Ninth Circuit decision, the Forest Service acknowledged that three areas of the Grass Mountain/Huckleberry Divide Trail were eligible for the National Register, but Weyerhaeuser (as owner) objected to their being listed. In late 2001, the Forest Service announced its intent to purchase 17 percent of the land previously traded to Weyerhaeuser for $6 million. Meanwhile, the Muckleshoot Tribe, Pilchuck Audubon Society, and Weyerhaeuser reached a settlement agreement that ended the litigation.

The property exchange proceeded roughly as anticipated by the case. *See* Randel Hanson & Giancarlo Panagiad, *Acts of Bureaucratic Dispossession: The Huckleberry Land Exchange, The Muckleshoot Indian Tribe, and Rational(ized) Forms of Contemporary Appropriation*, 7 GREAT PLAINS NAT. RESOURCES J. 169 (2002).

4.   What are "traditional cultural properties"? National Register Bulletin Number 38, referenced in the *Muckleshoot* case, defines a traditional cultural property as "one that is eligible for the National Register because of its association with cultural practices or beliefs of a living community that (a) are rooted in that community's history, and (b) are important in maintaining the continuing cultural identity of the community." Patricia L. Parker & Thomas F. King, *Guidelines for Evaluating and Documenting Traditional Cultural Properties* 1 (Nat'l Park Serv., Nat'l Register Bull. No. 38, 1992). The identification of a traditional cultural property must therefore originate from groups who may ascribe significance to the property. Background research, while essential in identifying appropriate groups, will not displace the need for direct consultation with such groups.

Sometimes a conflict may surface between collected research and the testimony of members of the group. When a conflict exists because documentation does not support a traditional cultural property designation, the National Park Service states that several other factors should be considered, including: the lack of uniform research that has been conducted across the country; the motivating interest of those who have conducted the research; and the possible reluctance of groups to disclose information regarding the property because of cultural beliefs. Consider these factors while reading the next case in this Chapter.

5.   The National Park Service has published several dozen Bulletins, which have no inherent legal authority. However, as you see in the *Muckleshoot* case, the Bulletins may be referenced by courts or otherwise incorporated into public and private review processes, and therefore do have a significant impact. According to the NPS website, the Bulletin series is intended to provide "guidance on evaluating, documenting, and listing different types of historic places." Bulletin 38, mentioned in the case, is among the most significant. Two other Bulletins have been essential to helping applicants assess properties before applying for designation: Bulletin 15, *How to Apply the National Register Criteria for Evaluation*, and Bulletin 16A, *How to Complete the National Register Registration Form*. Other Bulletins provide guidance for evaluating specific types of properties, such as residential suburbs, cemeteries, or shipwrecks. Still others, such as Bulletin 23, *How to Improve the Quality of Photographs for National Register Nominations*, provide technical assistance for preparing nominations. A full list appears on the NPS website.

6.   Through the end of 2024, an Interagency Memorandum of Understanding for the Protection of Indian Sacred Sites ensures that particular federal agencies work to "improve the protection of and tribal access to Indian sacred sites through enhanced and improved interdepartmental coordination and collaboration." The agencies who

entered into the agreement were: the Department of Defense, the Department of the Interior, the Department of Agriculture, the Department of Energy, and the Advisory Council on Historic Preservation. The memorandum defines a "sacred site" as "any specific, discrete, narrowly delineated location on Federal land that is identified by an Indian tribe. . . as sacred by virtue of its established religious significance to, or ceremonial use by, an Indian religion; provided that the tribe. . . has informed the agency of the existence of such a site." Sacred sites are also known as "traditional cultural properties." The memorandum also developed a draft policy statement on confidentiality for sensitive information regarding sacred sites that would be adopted by these Federal agencies.

What legal remedies does a tribe have when a consultation is required, but was not undertaken? Consider the following case, which weighs cultural values against the environmental values embodied in a proposed large renewable energy installation.

Quechan Tribe of Fort Yuma Reservation v. United States Department of the Interior

755 F.Supp.2d 1104 (S.D. Cal. 2010)

■ LARRY ALAN BURNS, D.J.

On October 29, 2010, Plaintiff (the "Tribe") filed its complaint, alleging Defendants' decision to approve a solar energy project violated various provisions of federal law. On November 12, the Tribe filed a motion for preliminary injunction, asking the Court to issue an order to preserve the status quo by enjoining proceeding with the project, pending the outcome of this litigation. After the motion was filed, Imperial Valley Solar LLC intervened as a Defendant. * * *

Background

The Quechan Tribe is a federally-recognized Indian tribe whose reservation is located mostly in Imperial County, California and partly in Arizona. A large solar energy project is planned on 6500 acres of federally-owned land known as the California Desert Conservation Area ("CDCA"). The Department of the Interior, as directed by Congress, developed a binding management plan for this area.

The project is being managed by a company called Tessera Solar, LLC. Tessera plans to install about 30,000 individual "suncatcher" solar collectors, expected to generate 709 megawatts when completed. The suncatchers will be about 40 feet high and 38 feet wide, and attached to pedestals about 18 feet high. Support buildings, roads, a pipeline, and a power line to support and service the network of collectors are also planned. Most of the project will be built on public lands. Tessera submitted an application to the state of California to develop the Imperial Valley Solar project. The project is planned in phases.

After communications among BLM, various agencies, the Tribe, and other Indian tribes, a series of agreements, decisions, and other documents was published. The final EIS was issued some time in July, 2010. At the same time, a Proposed Resource Management Plan-Amendment, amending the Department of the interior's CDCA was also published. On September 14 and 15, certain federal and state officials, including BLM's field manager, executed a programmatic agreement (the "Programmatic Agreement") for management of the project. The Tribe objected to this. On October 4, 2010, Director of the Bureau of Land Management Robert Abbey signed the Imperial Valley Record of Decision ("ROD") approving the project, and the next day Secretary of the Interior Ken Salazar signed the ROD. The ROD notice was published on October 13, 2010.

The area where the project would be located has a history of extensive use by Native American groups. The parties agree 459 cultural resources have been identified within the project area. These include over 300 locations of prehistoric use or settlement, and ancient trails that traverse the site. The tribes in this area cremated their dead and buried the remains, so the area also appears to contain archaeological sites and human remains. The draft environmental impact statement ("EIS") prepared by the BLM indicated the project "may wholly or partially destroy all archaeological sites on the surface of the project area."

The Tribe believes the project would destroy hundreds of their ancient cultural sites including burial sites, religious sites, ancient trails, and probably buried artifacts. Secondarily, it argues the project would endanger the habitat of the flat-tailed horned lizard, which is under consideration for listing under the Endangered Species Act and which is culturally important to the Tribe. The Tribe maintains Defendants were required to comply with * * * the National Historical Preservation Act (NHPA) * * * by making certain analyses and taking certain factors into account deciding to go ahead with the project. * * *

Preliminary Injunctive Relief

The four-factor test for issuance of injunctive relief is set forth in *Winter v. Natural Resources Defense Council, Inc.*, 555 U.S. 7 (2008):

> A plaintiff seeking a preliminary injunction must establish that he is likely to succeed on the merits, that he is likely to suffer irreparable harm in the absence of preliminary relief, that the balance of equities tips in his favor, and that an injunction is in the public interest. * * *

Here, the merits question is the most complex, and was the primary focus of briefing and argument. The Court considers this question first.

Merits Discussion * * *

The NHPA's purpose is to preserve historic resources, and early consultation with tribes is encouraged "to ensure that all types of historic properties and all public interests in such properties are given due consideration . . . ." *Te-Moak Tribe v. U. S. Dep't of Interior*, 608 F.3d 592, 609 (9th Cir. 2010) (quoting 16 U.S.C. § 470a(d)(1)(A)). The consultation process is governed by 36 C.F.R. § 800.2(c)(2), one of Section 106's implementing regulations. Under this regulation, "[c]onsultation should commence early in the planning process, in order to identify and discuss relevant preservation issues . . . ." *Id.* § 800.2(c)(2)(ii)(A). The Ninth Circuit has emphasized that the timing of required review processes can affect the outcome and [EDS: tardiness] is to be discouraged. The consultation requirement is not an empty formality; rather, it "must recognize the government-to-government relationship between the Federal Government and Indian tribes" and is to be "conducted in a manner sensitive to the concerns and needs of the Indian tribe." *Id.* § 800.2(c)(2)(ii)(C). A tribe may, if it wishes, designate representatives for the consultation. *Id.*

The Section 106 process is described in 36 C.F.R. §§ 800.2–800.6. After preliminary identification of the project and consulting parties, Section 106 requires identifying historic properties within a project's affected area, evaluating the project's potential effects on those properties, and resolving any adverse effects. The Tribe insists this consultation must be completed at least for Phase 1 of the project, before construction begins.

Throughout this process, the regulations require the agency to consult extensively with Indian tribes that fall within the definition of "consulting party," including here the Quechan Tribe. Section 800.4 alone requires at least seven issues about which the Tribe, as a consulting party, is entitled to be consulted before the project was approved. Under § 800.4(a)(3), BLM is required to consult with the Tribe [EDS.: to] identify issues relating to the project's potential effects on historic properties. Under § 800.4(a)(4), BLM is required to gather information from the Tribe to assist in identifying properties which may be of religious and cultural significance to it. Under § 800.4(b), BLM is required to consult with the Tribe to take steps necessary to identify historic properties within the area of potential effects. Under § 800.4(b)(1), BLM's official is required to take into account any confidentiality concerns raised by tribes during the identification process. Under § 800.4(c)(1), BLM must consult with the Tribe to apply National Register criteria to properties within the identified area, if they have not yet been evaluated for eligibility for listing in the National Register of Historic Places. Under § 800.4(c)(2), if the Tribe doesn't agree with the BLM's determination regarding National Register eligibility, it is entitled to ask for a determination. And under § 800.4(d)(1) and (2), if BLM determines no historic properties will be affected, it must give the Tribe a report and invite the Tribe to provide its views. Sections 800.5 and 800.6 require further consultation and review to resolve adverse effects and to deal with failure to resolve adverse effects.

Furthermore, under § 800.2, consulting parties that are Indian tribes are entitled to *special consideration* in the course of an agency's fulfillment of its consultation obligations. This is spelled out in extensive detail in § 800.2(c). Among other things, that section sets forth the following requirements:

(A) * * * *Consultation should commence early in the planning process, in order to identify and discuss relevant preservation issues and resolve concerns about the confidentiality of information on historic properties.*

* * *

36 C.F.R. § 800.2(c)(2)(ii)(A) (emphasis added). The Tribe points out the significance of the "confidentiality" provisions, citing *Pueblo of Sandia v. United States*, 50 F.3d 856, 861–62 (10th Cir. 1995) (noting that pueblo's reticence to share information about cultural and religious sites with outsiders was to be expected, and that federal government knew tribes would typically not answer general requests for information). * * *

Defendants, citing 36 C.F.R. § 800.14(b)(1)(ii), argue that "the execution of a Programmatic Agreement completes the Section 106 process" and is an acceptable way to resolve adverse effects from complex projects "[w]hen effects on historic properties cannot be fully determined prior to approval of an undertaking." But this is true only if "executing" means "carrying out;" merely entering into a programmatic agreement does not satisfy Section 106's consultation requirements. 36 C.F.R. § 800.14(b)(2)(iii) ("Compliance with the procedures established by an approved programmatic agreement satisfies the agency's section 106 responsibilities for all individual undertakings of the program covered by the agreement . . . .") The Tribe asks that consultation be completed at least for phase 1 before the project begins. That Defendants are resisting this suggests they are probably not prepared to do so.

The programmatic agreement must be negotiated in accordance with § 800.14(b), which itself requires an extensive consultation process. *Id.* § 800.14(f). The Tribe has also argued a programmatic agreement is not authorized for this type of project.

Defendants are correct that under § 800.4(b)(2), identification of historic properties can be deferred if "specifically provided for" in a programmatic agreement negotiated pursuant to § 800.14(b). But this deferral is not indefinite, and entering into an appropriately-negotiated programmatic agreement does not relieve the BLM of all responsibility. The second half of § 800.4(b)(2) contemplates consultation on historic properties as it becomes feasible:

The process should establish the likely presence of historic properties within the area of potential effects for each alternative or inaccessible area through background research, consultation and an appropriate level of field investigation, taking into account the number of alternatives under consideration, the magnitude of the undertaking and its likely effects, and the views of . . . any other consulting parties. As specific aspects or locations of an alternative are refined or access is gained, the agency official shall proceed with the identification and evaluation of historic properties in accordance with paragraphs (b)(1) and (c) of this section.

In short, entering into an appropriately-negotiated programmatic agreement can result in deferral of the consulting process, but it would only allow a temporary delay in consultation, until it is feasible to identify and consult with the Tribe about the historic properties. *Compare* Te-Moak, 608 F.3d at 610 (explaining that assessment of impact on environmental resources could be deferred where drilling locations in mineral exploration project could not reasonably be determined at the time of approval, but where plan required assessment as drilling locations became known).

Communications and Documentary Evidence

The Tribe's Evidence and Arguments

In support of its point that Defendants failed to adequately consult, the Tribe cites its letter to BLM's Field Manager on February 4, 2010, in which it expressed concern that the schedule for issuance of the ROD didn't allow enough time for adequate consultation, and that the required consultation was being inappropriate deferred. This letter says the Tribe had informally learned that a Programmatic Agreement was being developed, which BLM intended to approve by September, 2010. It also expressed the concern that, if the project were ultimately approved in spite of the presence of cultural resources, the quick schedule wouldn't allow enough time for BLM to consult with the tribe to develop a plan to avoid harming the sites.

By itself, this letter suggests the Tribe was consulted late in the planning process, wasn't being consulted when it wrote the letter, and was concerned about the lack of consultation. It also suggests the time frame for consultation was compressed. The Tribe also cites other later documents, showing that it expressed its dissatisfaction to the Department.

At oral argument, the Tribe admitted BLM engaged in some communication and did some consulting, but described the purported consulting as cursory and inadequate, consisting mostly of informational meetings where the Tribe's opinions were not sought, rather than government-to-government consultation.

Defendants' Evidence and Arguments

In response, Defendants provide string citations to materials in the record which they say document "extensive consultation with tribes, including Plaintiff." This description of the documents is general and cursory, and sheds little light on the degree to which BLM consulted with the Tribe, or whether the consultation was intended to comply with

NEPA or NHPA. First, the documentation includes consultations with other tribes, agencies, and with the public. While this other consultation appears to be required and serves other important purposes, it doesn't substitute for the mandatory consultation with the Quechan Tribe. In other words, that BLM did a lot of consulting in general doesn't show that its consultation with the Tribe was adequate under the regulations. Indeed, Defendants' grouping tribes together (referring to consultation with "tribes") is unhelpful: Indian tribes aren't interchangeable, and consultation with one tribe doesn't relieve the BLM of its obligation to consult with any other tribe that may be a consulting party under NHPA. At oral argument, the Court inquired of Defendants about consultation, but they were unable to be any more specific than they were in their briefing. * * *

Analysis of Documentary Evidence

Preliminarily, several points bear noting. First, the sheer volume of documents is not meaningful. The number of letters, reports, meetings, etc. and the size of the various documents doesn't in itself show the NHPA-required consultation occurred.

Second, the BLM's communications are replete with recitals of law (including Section 106), professions of good intent, and solicitations to consult with the Tribe. But mere *pro forma* recitals do not, by themselves, show BLM actually complied with the law. As discussed below, documentation that might support a finding that true government-to-government consultation occurred is painfully thin.

At oral argument, the Tribe described the meetings as cursory information sessions and the reports and other communications as inadequate. Its briefing also argues that Defendants have confused "contact" with required "consultation." * * * In response, Defendants argue that the Tribe "has been invited to government-to-government consultations since 2008" "BLM began informing the Tribe of proposed renewable energy projects within the California Desert District as early as 2007," and "[s]ince that time BLM has regularly updated the Tribe on the status of the [Imperial Valley Solar] project."

The Tribe's first document contact with BLM was the tribal historical preservation officer's letter of February 19, 2008. That letter put BLM on notice that the historical and cultural sites within the project area would be considered important to the Tribe. It also asked BLM to provide a survey of the area and to meet with the Tribe's government, which would have constituted government-to-government consultation. BLM could not have provided the survey at that time, and apparently also didn't comply with the meeting request, because the historic preservation officer re-sent the letter the next month. In fact, the documentary evidence doesn't show BLM ever met with the Tribe's government until October 16, 2010, well after the project was approved. All available evidence tends to show BLM repeatedly said it would be glad to meet with the Tribe, but never did so.

Although BLM invited the Tribe to attend public informational meetings about the project, the invitations do not appear to meet the requirements set forth in 36 C.F.R. § 800.2(c)(2)(ii). This is particularly true because the Tribe first requested a more private, closed meeting between BLM and its tribal council. In later communications, the Tribe continued to request that BLM meet with its tribal council on the Tribe's reservation. In addition, the Tribe repeatedly complained that the properties hadn't been identified, and asked for a map showing where the identified sites were, requests that apparently went unanswered at least as late as June, 2010. The Tribe's letter of August 4, 2010 apparently acknowledges receipt of maps, but asks for an extension of the deadline so it could review them before responding.

The documentary evidence also confirms the Tribe's contention that the number of identified sites continued to fluctuate. And Defendants have admitted the evaluation of sites eligible for inclusion in the National Register hasn't yet been completed.

BLM's invitation to "consult," then, amounted to little more than a general request for the Tribe to gather its own information about all sites within the area and disclose it at public meetings. Because of the lack of information, it was impossible for the Tribe to have been consulted meaningful [EDS: sic] as required in applicable regulations. The documentary evidence also discloses almost no "government-to-government" consultation. While public informational meetings, consultations with individual tribal members, meetings with government staff or contracted investigators, and written updates are obviously a helpful and necessary part of the process, they don't amount to the type of "government-to-government" consultation contemplated by the regulations. This is particularly true because the Tribe's government's requests for information and meetings were frequently rebuffed or responses were extremely delayed as BLM-imposed deadlines loomed or passed.

No letters from the BLM ever initiate government-to-government contact between the Tribe and the United States or its designated representatives, the BLM field managers Margaret Goodro, Vicki Wood, or acting field manager Daniel Steward. Rather, the Tribe was invited to attend public informational meetings or to consult with two members of her staff, an archaeologist and a person identified only as a "point of contact." The BLM in fact rebuffed the Tribe's August 4 request that the BLM meet with the tribal council on its reservation, proposing instead that the tribal council call BLM staff.

The Tribe also repeatedly protested it was not being given enough time or information to consider the Programmatic Agreement, a matter it was also entitled to be consulted about. The letters sent to the Tribe's president make clear BLM had determined a programmatic agreement would be used and would be entered into no later than September, 2010. The Tribe's letter of February 4, 2010 suggests the Tribe had discovered on its own that BLM was already drafting the Programmatic Agreement. Furthermore, BLM insisted that consulting parties send their suggestions in writing. The Tribe's requests to consult about the Programmatic Agreement were obviously not granted.

Defendants have emphasized the size, complexity, and expense of this project, as well as the time limits, and the facts are sympathetic. Tessera hoped to qualify for stimulus funds under the American Recovery and Reinvestment Act of 2009 by beginning construction no later than the end of this year, which is about two weeks away. To that end, BLM apparently imposed deadlines of its own choosing. Section 106's consulting requirements can be onerous, and would have been particularly so here. Because of the large number of consulting parties (including several tribes), the logistics and expense of consulting would have been incredibly difficult. None of this analysis is meant to suggest federal agencies must acquiesce to every tribal request.

That said, government agencies are not free to glide over requirements imposed by Congressionally-approved statutes and duly adopted regulations. The required consultation must at least meet the standards set forth in 36 C.F.R. § 800.2(c)(2)(ii), and should begin early. The Tribe was entitled to be provided with adequate information and time, consistent with its status as a government that is entitled to be consulted. The Tribe's consulting rights should have been respected. It is clear that did not happen here.

The Court therefore determines the Tribe is likely to prevail at least on its claim that it was not adequately consulted as required under NHPA before the project was approved. Because the project was approved "without observance of procedure required by law," the Tribe is entitled to have the BLM's actions set aside under 5 U.S.C. § 706(2)(D). * * *

Remaining Injunctive Relief Analysis

Having determined that the Tribe is likely to succeed on the merits, at least as to its claim that required NHPA consulting must be completed before phase 1 of the project begins, the Court turns to the remaining *Winter* factors.

Irreparable Harm

To obtain preliminary injunctive relief, the Tribe must show it is likely to suffer irreparable harm in the absence of preliminary relief. *Winter* emphasizes that the mere possibility of irreparable harm isn't enough; such harm must be likely. This is the easiest and most straightforward part of the inquiry, because the Court finds it is very likely the Tribe will suffer irreparable harm. * * *

Balance of Equities

To obtain injunctive relief under *Winter*, the Tribe must establish the balance of equities tips in its favor. *Winter* also refers to this as the "balance of hardships" inquiry. * * *

The Ninth Circuit has emphasized that consultation with tribes must begin early, and that if consultation begins after other parties may have invested a great deal of time and money, the other parties may become entrenched and inflexible, and the government agency may be inclined to tolerate degradation it would otherwise have insisted be avoided. *Te-Moak Tribe*, 608 F.3d at 609. This appears to be happening here. While the Court is sympathetic to the problems Defendants face, the fact that they are now pressed for time and somewhat desperate after having invested a great deal of effort and money is a problem of their own making and does not weigh in their favor. * * *

Congress and, to a lesser extent, the Department of the Interior could have made these consulting requirements less stringent, but they didn't. Congress could also have exempted renewable energy projects such as this from the Section 106 review process, but didn't. Congress could also extend ARRA project deadlines for this project but hasn't, though, it was conceded at argument, Congress still might do so.

The Court is mindful that Defendants face hardships as well. For example, Imperial Valley Solar has already spent millions of dollars preparing this project, and faces difficulties obtaining investment and financing if the project is held up. Even so, the Court finds the balance of equities tips heavily in the Tribe's favor.

Public Interest

The final step in the *Winter* analysis requires the Court to consider whether a preliminary injunction is in the public interest. Obviously there are many competing interests here. The interests the Tribe urges the Court to consider involve historic and cultural preservation, in this case of hundreds of prehistoric sites and other sites whose significance has yet to be completely evaluated. The Tribe itself is a sovereign, and both it and its members have an interest in protecting their cultural patrimony. The culture and history of the Tribe and its members are also part of the culture and history of the United States more generally.

The value of a renewal energy project of this magnitude to the public is also great. It provides the public with a significant amount of power while reducing pollution and dependence on fossil fuels. As Defendants point out, it is a goal of the federal government and the state of California to promote the development of such projects. Current federal policy as embodied in ARRA also favors the undertaking of projects of this time, as a way of creating jobs and stimulating the economy.

That being said, the Court looks to the statutes enacted by Congress rather than to its own analysis of desirable priorities in the first instance. *See, e.g., Marshall v. Barlow's, Inc.*, 436 U.S. 307, 331 (1978) (refusing to question Congress' weighing of interests when enacting statute); *Salazar v. Buono*, 130 S.Ct. 1803, 1828 (2010) (Scalia, J., concurring in the judgment) ("Federal courts have no warrant to revisit [Congress' decision about what is in the public interest]—and to risk replacing the people's judgment with their own . . . ."). Here, in enacting NHPA Congress has adjudged the preservation of historic properties and the rights of Indian tribes to consultation to be in the public interest. Congress could have, but didn't, include exemptions for renewable energy projects such as this one. And, as pointed out, Congress could determine this particular project is in the public interest and sweep aside ARRA deadlines as well as requirements under NHPA * * * to get it built. But because Congress didn't do that, and instead made the determination that preservation of historical properties takes priority here, the Court must adopt the same view.

Alternate Basis for Injunctive Relief

As an alternative basis for the Court's decision, *Alliance for Wild Rockies*, 622 F.3d at 1049–50 authorizes the granting of preliminary injunctive relief on a showing of " 'serious questions going to the merits' and a hardship balance that tips sharply toward the plaintiff . . ., assuming the other two elements of the *Winter* test are also met." The "likelihood of irreparable harm" factor is required, and is particularly emphasized. * * *

For the reasons just discussed, the Court also finds the hardship balance tips sharply towards the Tribe, and the other two *Winter* factors are also met. The most important of these factors, the likelihood of irreparable harm, is the clearest and most obvious. For these reasons, the Court holds either of these would also serve as an adequate basis for the grant of preliminary injunctive relief.

NOTES & QUESTIONS

1.   When a private investor begins to dig the foundations for a massive wind farm or solar panel field, she may find historic or cultural resources that require a project to be halted so that Section 106 review may take its course. Large-scale private projects will implicate Section 106 if they are considered to be "undertakings" under the National Historic Preservation Act. As Chapter 3 describes in greater detail, almost any project requiring a federal permit, license, or approval is an undertaking subject to Section 106 review. *See* 54 U.S.C. § 300320 (defining "undertaking"). Thus when private investors seek permission from the federal government to build a large-scale renewable energy facilities on public land, there is a near certainty that Section 106 will apply.

2.   *Quechan Tribe* is one of the first published cases involving a Section 106-based challenge to a large-scale renewable energy project. When you were reading the case, you probably imagined the visual and environmental impact of thirty thousand solar collectors, all fifty-eight feet tall, as was proposed in the Imperial Valley project. Historic preservation challenges will

become increasingly common as more investors seek to build renewable energy facilities on or near protected sites. How do we harmonize the need to address climate change (in part through renewable energy) with preservation and conservation values? The tension between historic preservation and climate change was introduced in Chapter 1.

3.   According to the court, what is the significance of a programmatic agreement? Is it appropriate in a case like this one?

4.   The confidentiality provisions in the Section 106 regulations echo those of the Archaeological Resources Protection Act of 1979, 16 U.S.C. § 470hh, discussed in Chapter 8. The Section 106 confidentiality provisions are further described in Bulletin No. 38, *Guidelines for Evaluating and Documenting Traditional Cultural Properties*. The Bulletin explains:

> Particularly where a property has supernatural connotations in the minds of those who ascribe significance to it, or where it is used in ongoing cultural activities that are not readily shared with outsiders, it may be strongly desired that both the nature and the precise location of the property be kept secret. Such a desire on the part of those who value a property should of course be respected, but it presents considerable problems for the use of National Register data in planning. In simplest terms, one cannot protect a property if one does not know that it is there.

> The need to reveal information about something that one's cultural system demands be kept secret can present agonizing problems for traditional groups and individuals. It is one reason that information on traditional cultural properties is not readily shared with Federal agencies and others during the planning and environmental review of construction and land use projects. However concerned one may be about the impacts of such a project on a traditional cultural property, it may be extremely difficult to express these concerns to an outsider if one's cultural system provides no acceptable mechanism for doing so. These difficulties are sometimes hard for outsiders to understand, but they should not be underrated. In some cultures it is sincerely believed that sharing information inappropriately with outsiders will lead to death or severe injury to one's family or group.

> As noted above, information on historic properties, including traditional cultural properties, may be kept confidential under the authority of Section 304 of the National Historic Preservation Act. This may not always be enough to satisfy the concerns of those who value, but fear the results of releasing information on, traditional cultural properties. In some cases these concerns may make it necessary not to nominate such properties formally at all, or not to seek formal determinations of eligibility, but simply to maintain some kind of minimal data in planning files. For example, in planning deployment of the MX missile system in Wyoming, the Air Force became aware that the Lakota Indian tribe in the area had concerns about the project's impacts on traditional cultural

properties, but was unwilling to identify and document the precise locations and significance of such properties. To resolve this problem, Air Force representatives met with the tribe's traditional cultural authorities and indicated where they wanted to construct the various facilities required by the deployment; the tribe's authorities indicated which of these locations were likely to present problems, without saying what the nature of the problems might be. The Air Force then designed the project to minimize use of such areas. In a narrow sense, obviously, the Air Force did not go through the process of evaluation recommended by this Bulletin; no specific properties were identified or evaluated to determine their eligibility for inclusion in the National Register. In a broader sense, however, the Air Force's approach represents excellent practice in the identification and treatment of traditional cultural properties. The Air Force consulted carefully and respectfully with those who ascribed traditional cultural significance to properties in the area, and sought to accommodate their concerns. The tribe responded favorably to this approach, and did not take undue advantage of it. Presumably, had the tribe expressed concern about such expansive or strategically located areas as to suggest that it was more interested in impeding the deployment than in protecting its valued properties the Air Force would have had to use a different approach.

Patricia L. Parker & Thomas King, *Guidelines for Evaluating and Documenting Traditional Cultural Properties* 19–20 (Nat'l Park Serv., Nat'l Register Bull. No. 38, 1998). Can the consultation between the Lakota tribe and the Air Force be replicated in every case involving sensitive sites? Why is confidentiality about tribal resources such an important issue? What barriers might be presented by each side (agency and tribe)?

5.   Do you agree with the court that Congress, and not the courts, should engage in balancing of public policy issues? How would you weigh the preservation of Native American resources against the installation of renewable energy production facilities? Should the scales be tipped in favor of the "good" that benefits more people?

CHAPTER TEN

CONSERVATION AND PRESERVATION RESTRICTIONS

Until this Chapter, this book has focused on *public* rules—including historic district regulations, zoning ordinances, and federal statutes—enacted through the legislative process and intended to be applied in a consistent way. We turn now to *private* real property interests created to protect historic properties through piecemeal agreements among neighbors, co-owners, current and subsequent owners, or owners and other third parties. These private agreements take the form of servitudes: tailored interests that run with the land and burden one property while benefiting other properties or persons. Servitudes subject certain parcels of land to special restrictions and may take the form of affirmative easements, negative easements, or restrictive covenants.

This Chapter focuses on two related types of servitudes: conservation restrictions and preservation restrictions. These restrictions, granted by a private property owner to a nonprofit organization or government agency, limit development or activity in order to protect important resources. "Conservation restrictions" generally protect scenic landscapes, wetlands, environmentally sensitive areas, and open space, while "preservation restrictions" generally protect historic structures (such as buildings). They typically last forever and often include provisions that require that a property owner preserve, affirmatively maintain, and/or allow third party access to all or some of her property. They may prohibit demolition, additions, changes to exteriors and sometimes interiors, subdivision, and/or certain uses. They may require an owner to keep insurance, indemnify any third party nonprofit organizations, and/or restore the protected portion of the property in case of casualty. In exchange for giving up certain rights, the property owner may receive money or other benefits, or qualify for a tax benefit for a charitable deduction or credit.

Some words on terminology are in order. Many—possibly most—of those who write about or work with conservation and preservation restrictions call them conservation and preservation "easements." This Chapter uses the term "restriction" instead of "easement" because the former term reduces doctrinal confusion. As the discussion below makes clear, restrictions are created by statute, and while some restrictions resemble common law easements, others resemble common law covenants. This Chapter's use of the term "restriction" stays above the easement-or-covenant debate and underscores the fact that conservation and preservation restrictions are creatures of state statutes, and not the common law. Seventeen states (about a third) actually use "conservation restriction" and/or "preservation restriction" in their statutes.

This Chapter has also declined to use the term "servitudes," which at least one scholar proposed in the 1980s as alternative "neutral" term. *See, e.g.,* Gerald Korngold, *Privately Held Conservation Servitudes: A Policy Analysis in the Context of Gross Real Covenants and Easements,* 63 TEX. L. REV. 433, 437 (1984) ("For clarity, conservation interests are referred to as conservation 'servitudes,' a neutral term that avoids the traditional categories."). Since 2000, the "servitudes" term has taken on a new dimension, with the Third Restatement of Property pushing for wider applicability. RESTATEMENT (THIRD) OF PROPERTY: SERVITUDES (2000). No state legislature has adopted the Restatement's approach so far.

This Chapter defines conservation and preservation restrictions and describes how they are created, altered, and terminated. In addition, it highlights how their growth has been influenced by federal and state tax rules.

A. CHARACTER AND CREATION

Understanding the character of conservation and preservation restrictions requires a brief background on servitudes, as property law traditionally defines them. These are private land use restrictions that have their origins in contract. Although they are consensual, in that they arise from an agreement, they bind subsequent owners of a burdened property simply by virtue of their acquisition of the property. Although they grew up slowly through the common law, they are extensively used in modern real estate development to give character to new developments.

There are many different types of servitudes, including equitable servitudes (sometimes called negative easements), restrictive covenants, and affirmative easements. In brief: equitable servitudes and restrictive covenants grant the right to enforce a restriction on someone else's land and also may require that a property owner perform certain acts, such as pay money for the upkeep of her property or common facilities. Affirmative easements grant the right to use someone else's land. Each of these types of servitudes has common law rules that courts have developed for their adoption and enforcement.

Conservation and preservation restrictions do not easily fit into any of these categories. They may have attributes of equitable servitudes, restrictive covenants, and affirmative easements—often all three at once. Thus, a provision that prevents a property owner from demolishing a structure or altering a scenic landscape most resembles an equitable servitude or restrictive covenant. A provision that requires a property owner to affirmatively maintain a protected portion of her property or pay an annual fee to a third party organization for preservation services also resembles a servitude or covenant. A provision that allows a third party nonprofit the right to access a property, so that the nonprofit might inspect it to ensure that the owner is in compliance with preservation restrictions, most resembles an affirmative easement.

Because conservation or preservation restrictions may include provisions that separately resemble different types of property interests, placing them into neat common law categories is difficult. For example, a restriction that resembles a restrictive covenant in one way might not meet the common law requirements for covenants' enforceability. The common law renders real covenants enforceable only if they meet certain requirements, which vary depending on the state but may include privity of estate, touching and concerning the land, and intent for the covenant to run with the land. If a court attempted to use traditional common law principles regarding covenants to evaluate a conservation or preservation restriction, the court may find that the restriction fails to meet some or all of these criteria and is therefore invalid. Most broadly, equitable servitudes and covenants can be enforced only by the owner of specifically benefitted land or her agent, but conservation and preservation restrictions typically are enforced by nonprofits or government agencies that usually do not own property benefited by the particular restriction ("in gross").

To avoid unintended invalidations, state statutes now govern how conservation and preservation restrictions can be created and enforced. These statutes provide the authority for private property owners to burden their properties with such restrictions and are drafted to avoid the application of common law principles that would render the restriction invalid. The earliest statutes allowing public bodies to obtain conservation and preservation restrictions for public use were passed by the Commonwealth of Massachusetts in the 1950s. Since then, statutes have expanded to allow private individuals and organizations the ability to obtain and manage conservation and preservation restrictions.

Although government agencies still hold such restrictions, private nonprofit organizations known as land trusts are now more readily identified with the land conservation movement. According to the Land Trust Alliance, approximately 1,723 national, statewide, and local nonprofit land trusts now operate in the United States. State and local trusts manage conservation and preservation restrictions covering nearly 9 million acres, and several million more acres of restrictions are managed by the two largest restriction-holding organizations, the Nature Conservancy and the Conservation Fund. All in all, such organizations have protected 56 million acres of land. The 56 million acre figure also includes acres owned in fee, as well as acres conserved during land trust negotiations on behalf of, and transfers to, governments or other entities with conservation purposes. *See* LAND TRUST ALLIANCE, 2015 NATIONAL LAND TRUST CENSUS REPORT 5 (2015). In addition, government agencies at all levels hold conservation and preservation restrictions and serve as stewards for several million more acres. Exact acreage figures are unknown because the number of restriction holders is so large and because restrictions are not generally required to be recorded centrally.

1. STATE STATUTES

About half of the states have unique, state-specific statutes dealing with conservation and preservation restrictions. The remaining states and the District of Columbia base their statutes on the Uniform Conservation Easement Act (UCEA), which was written by the National Conference of Commissioners on Uniform State Laws and approved by the American Bar Association in 1981. We provide the primary text of the UCEA, followed by the text of a statute in Connecticut, which has not adopted the UCEA.

a. UNIFORM CONSERVATION EASEMENT ACT

The UCEA aims to enable "durable restrictions and affirmative obligations to be attached to real property to protect natural and historic resources," to render those restrictions immune from "certain common law impediments which might otherwise be raised," and to maximize "the freedom of the creators of the transaction to impose restrictions on the use of land and improvements in order to protect them." UNIF. CONSERVATION EASEMENT ACT, prefatory note (1981).

Uniform Conservation Easement Act
(2007)

§ 1. [Definitions].

As used in this Act, unless the context otherwise requires:

(1) "Conservation easement" means a nonpossessory interest of a holder in real property imposing limitations or affirmative obligations the purposes of which include retaining or protecting natural, scenic, or open-space values of real property, assuring its availability for agricultural, forest, recreational, or open-space use, protecting natural resources, maintaining or enhancing air or water quality, or preserving the historical, architectural, archaeological, or cultural aspects of real property.

(2) "Holder" means:

(i) a governmental body empowered to hold an interest in real property under the laws of this State or the United States; or

(ii) a charitable corporation, charitable association, or charitable trust, the purposes or powers of which include retaining or protecting the natural, scenic, or open-space values of real property, assuring the availability of real property for agricultural, forest, recreational, or open-space use, protecting natural resources, maintaining or enhancing air or water quality, or preserving the historical, architectural, archaeological, or cultural aspects of real property.

(3) "Third-party right of enforcement" means a right provided in a conservation easement to enforce any of its terms granted to a governmental body, charitable corporation, charitable association, or charitable trust, which, although eligible to be a holder, is not a holder.

§ 2. [Creation, Conveyance, Acceptance, and Duration].

(a) Except as otherwise provided in this Act, a conservation easement may be created, conveyed, recorded, assigned, released, modified, terminated, or otherwise altered or affected in the same manner as other easements.

(b) No right or duty in favor of or against a holder and no right in favor of a person having a third-party right of enforcement arises under a conservation easement before its acceptance by the holder and a recordation of the acceptance.

(c) Except as provided in Section 3(b), a conservation easement is unlimited in duration unless the instrument creating it otherwise provides.

(d) An interest in real property in existence at the time a conservation easement is created is not impaired by it unless the owner of the interest is a party to the conservation easement or consents to it.

§ 3. [Judicial Actions].

(a) An action affecting a conservation easement may be brought by:

(1) an owner of an interest in the real property burdened by the easement;

(2) a holder of the easement;

(3) a person having a third-party right of enforcement; or

(4) a person authorized by other law.

(b) This Act does not affect the power of a court to modify or terminate a conservation easement in accordance with the principles of law and equity.

§ 4. [Validity].

A conservation easement is valid even though:

(1) it is not appurtenant to an interest in real property;

(2) it can be or has been assigned to another holder;

(3) it is not of a character that has been recognized traditionally at common law;

(4) it imposes a negative burden;

(5) it imposes affirmative obligations upon the owner of an interest in the burdened property or upon the holder;

(6) the benefit does not touch or concern real property; or

(7)   there is no privity of estate or of contract.

§ 5. [Applicability].

(a)   This Act applies to any interest created after its effective date which complies with this Act, whether designated as a conservation easement or as a covenant, equitable servitude, restriction, easement, or otherwise.

(b)   This Act applies to any interest created before its effective date if it would have been enforceable had it been created after its effective date unless retroactive application contravenes the constitution or laws of this State or the United States.

(c)   This Act does not invalidate any interest, whether designated as a conservation or preservation easement or as a covenant, equitable servitude, restriction, easement, or otherwise, that is enforceable under other law of this State.

§ 6. [Uniformity of Application and Construction].

This Act shall be applied and construed to effectuate its general purpose to make uniform the laws with respect to the subject of the Act among states enacting it.

NOTES & QUESTIONS

1.   Review the definition of "conservation easement" in section 1 of the UCEA. Does this term encompass both conservation and preservation restrictions as defined in this Chapter?

2.   Who may "hold" a conservation easement? Do holders have to agree to hold the conservation easement before any obligations are imposed on them?

3.   To what extent does the UCEA provide a role for governmental entities with respect to the creation and review of conservation easements? Some commentators say that government is not involved enough. Mary Ann King and Sally Fairfax, for example, have observed that the UCEA failed to include any role for government or the general public in the process of recording, monitoring, or enforcing easements. They argued that "the commissioners would have been justified in, and indeed the public nature of [conservation easements] now demands, establishing even more comprehensive requirements for recording" and ongoing review. *See* Mary Ann King & Sally K. Fairfax, *Public Accountability and Conservation Easements: Learning from the Uniform Conservation Easement Act Debates,* 46 NAT. RESOURCES J. 65, 96–98 (2006). What do they mean by "the public nature" of conservation easements? How would public review affect the rate of adoption of conservation easements?

4.   What is the intent behind section 2(a) of the UCEA? The Comment for that section explains that the UCEA encompasses state law requirements for easements except where otherwise explicitly stated:

> For example, the state's requirements concerning release of conventional easements apply as well to conservation easements because nothing in the Act provides otherwise. On the other hand,

if the state's existing law does not permit easements in gross to be assigned, it will not be applicable to conservation easements because Section 4(2) effectively authorizes their assignment.

5.   Who, other than holders, can bring actions to enforce, modify, terminate or otherwise affect conservation easements? Note that while section 3(a)(4) is intended to apply to those individuals who are given standing to sue by other state laws, it does not specifically include states' attorneys general. The National Conference of Commissioners on Uniform State Laws debated whether to specifically list states' attorneys general in this provision but ultimately declined to do so. Individual states thus have the flexibility under the UCEA to determine whether an attorney general may enforce a conservation easement.

In 2007, Maine, for example, clarified UCEA language to expressly authorize its attorney general to enforce conservation easements

> when the parties designated as having the right to do so under the terms of the conservation easement: (1) Are no longer in legal existence; (2) Are bankrupt or insolvent; (3) Cannot be contacted after reasonable diligence to do so; or (4) After 90 days' prior written notice by the Attorney General of the nature of the asserted failure, have failed to take reasonable actions to bring about compliance with the conservation easement.

ME. REV. STAT. ANN. tit. 33, § 478(1)(D). Although case law on point is minimal, commentators have suggested that attorneys review state rules on the charitable trust or public trust doctrines to find opportunities for attorney general involvement. *See* Jessica E. Jay, *Third-Party Enforcement of Conservation Easements,* 29 VT. L. REV. 757, 771–81 (2005) (identifying potential bases for such involvement as the UCEA and the common law, among other sources); Nancy A. McLaughlin & W. William Weeks, *In Defense of Conservation Easements: A Response to* The End of Perpetuity, 9 WYO. L. REV. 1, 63–65 (2009) (stating that "the state attorney general should have standing to sue to enforce a conservation easement on behalf of the public").

6.   Section 4 of the UCEA is one of its most important provisions. It targets potential challenges to conservation easements that might be raised without explicit statutory language regarding their validity. For example, one potential challenge relates to the limitation on development that all conservation easements include. This limitation might be characterized by a court as a negative easement because a third party can prevent the property owner from doing something on their property. At common law, courts were generally reluctant to enforce all but a handful of types of negative easements. The UCEA thus includes sections 4(3)–(4), which state that conservation easements are enforceable even if they are not traditionally recognized at common law and even if they impose a "negative burden."

7.   Should we standardize the form of conservation and preservation restrictions? Some commentators say yes. In a monograph for the Lincoln Institute of Land Policy, Jeff Pidot has argued that unlike (for example) leases—which he characterizes as "of limited duration, easily amended by the parties, and without public subsidy or interest"—restrictions are "of

unlimited duration, involve public subsidies and substantial public interest, and are not easily amended by the parties." *See* JEFF PIDOT, REINVENTING CONSERVATION EASEMENTS: A CRITICAL EXAMINATION AND IDEAS FOR REFORM 13–14 (2005). The differences, in his mind, are enough to justify the development of standard forms. Some standardization has been enforced by federal tax requirements for donation of conservation and preservation restrictions, which are discussed in Part C of this Chapter. Most significantly, although state law permits creation of temporary restrictions, federal tax law requires that such restrictions be perpetual to qualify for a charitable deduction. I.R.C. § 170(h)(2)(C); 26 C.F.R. § 1.170A–14(b)(2).

b.   A NON-UCEA EXAMPLE STATE STATUTE

Connecticut Statute on Conservation and Preservation Restrictions
CONN. GEN. STAT. ANN. §§ 47–42a—47–42d

§ 47–42a.   Definitions

For the purposes of sections 47–42b, 47–42c and 47–42d, the following definitions shall apply:

(a) "Conservation restriction" means a limitation, whether or not stated in the form of a restriction, easement, covenant or condition, in any deed, will or other instrument executed by or on behalf of the owner of the land described therein, including, but not limited to, the state or any political subdivision of the state, or in any order of taking such land whose purpose is to retain land or water areas predominantly in their natural, scenic or open condition or in agricultural, farming, forest or open space use.

(b) "Preservation restriction" means a limitation, whether or not stated in the form of a restriction, easement, covenant or condition, in any deed, will or other instrument executed by or on behalf of the owner of land, including, but not limited to, the state or any political subdivision of the state, or in any order of taking of such land whose purpose is to preserve historically significant structures or sites.

§ 47–42b.   Enforcement of conservation and preservation restrictions held by governmental body or charitable corporation

No conservation restriction held by any governmental body or by a charitable corporation or trust whose purposes include conservation of land or water areas and no preservation restriction held by any governmental body or by a charitable corporation or trust whose purposes include preservation of buildings or sites of historical significance shall be unenforceable on account of lack of privity of estate or contract or lack of benefit to particular land or on account of the benefit being assignable or being assigned to any other governmental body or to any charitable corporation or trust with like purposes.

§ 47–42c.   Acquisition of restrictions. Enforcement by Attorney General

Such conservation and preservation restrictions are interests in land and may be acquired by any governmental body or any charitable corporation or trust which has the power to acquire interests in land in the same manner as it may acquire other interests in land. Such restrictions may be enforced by injunction or proceedings in equity. The Attorney General may bring an action in the Superior Court to enforce the public interest in such restrictions.

§ 47–42d.   Permit applications filed with state or local land use agency, local building official or director of health. Appeals by party or state agency holding restriction. Civil penalty

(a) For purposes of this section, "state or local land use agency" includes, but is not limited to, a municipal planning commission, municipal zoning commission, combined municipal planning and zoning commission, a municipal zoning board of appeals, municipal inland wetlands and watercourses agency, a municipal historic district commission and any state agency that issues permits for the construction or improvement of real property.

(b) No person shall file a permit application with a state or local land use agency or a local building official or director of health, other than for interior work in an existing building or for exterior work on an existing building that does not expand or alter the footprint of such existing building, relating to property that is subject to a conservation restriction or a preservation restriction unless the applicant provides proof that the applicant has provided written notice of such application, by certified mail, return receipt requested, to the party holding such restriction, including, but not limited to, any state agency that holds such restriction, not later than sixty days prior to the filing of the permit application. In lieu of such notice, the applicant may submit a letter from the holder of such restriction or from the holder's authorized agent, verifying that the application is in compliance with the terms of the restriction. If the applicant has provided written notice pursuant to this subsection, the holder of the restriction may provide proof to the state or local land use agency or local building official or director of health that granting of the permit application will violate the terms of the restriction and such agency, official or director shall not grant the permit. Nothing in this section shall be construed to prohibit the filing of a permit application or to require such written notice when the activity that is the subject of such permit application will occur on a portion of property that is not restricted under the terms of such conservation or preservation restriction.

(c) If the applicant fails to comply with the provisions of subsection (b) of this section, (1) the party holding the conservation or preservation restriction, other than a state agency that holds such restriction, may, not later than fifteen days after receipt of actual notice of permit approval, file an appeal with the state or local land use agency or local building official or director of health, subject to any rules of such agency, official or director relating to appeals. The agency, official or director shall reverse the permit approval upon a finding that the requested land use violates the terms of such restriction; or (2) the state agency that holds such restriction may, not later than thirty days after receipt of actual notice of permit approval, file an appeal with the state or local land use agency or local building official or director of health, subject to any rules of such state or local land use agency, official or director relating to appeals. Such state or local land use agency, official or director shall immediately reverse such permit approval if the commissioner of the state agency that holds such restriction certifies that the land use authorized in such permit violates the terms of such conservation or preservation restriction. The commissioner of the state agency that holds such restriction may impose a civil penalty of not more than: (A) Five thousand dollars for a violation of subsection (b) of this section; and (B) one thousand dollars for each day that such violation continues after the applicant receives an order from such commissioner assessing a civil penalty pursuant to subparagraph (A) of this subsection.

NOTES & QUESTIONS

1. What are some key differences between the UCEA definition of "conservation easement" and the Connecticut definitions of "conservation restriction" and "preservation restriction"?

2. In section 47–42d, does the Connecticut statute fully address concerns regarding the lack of public review and oversight? Consider an excerpt from the older Massachusetts law on which the Connecticut statute was partially based, stating that conservation and preservation restrictions are enforceable only if:

> (a) [I]n case of a restriction held by a city or town or a commission, authority or other instrumentality thereof it is approved by the secretary of environmental affairs if a conservation restriction, * * * the Massachusetts historical commission if a preservation restriction, * * * and (b) in case of a restriction held by a charitable corporation or trust it is approved by the mayor, or in cities having a city manager the city manager, and the city council of the city, or selectmen or town meeting of the town, in which the land is situated, and the secretary of environmental affairs if a conservation restriction, * * * [or] the Massachusetts historical commission if a preservation restriction.

MASS. GEN. LAWS ch. 184, § 32. A handful of other states have also adopted more limited public review requirements. Nebraska requires local or county government approval for conservation easements not held by the state, and it provides a sixty-day comment period for planning commissions with jurisdiction. NEB. REV. ST. § 76–2,112(3). Virginia does not require a formal review process but does require that a conservation easement "conform in all respects to the comprehensive plan at the time the easement is granted for the area in which the real property is located." VA. CODE ANN., § 10.1–1010E.

3. State laws, such as the marketable record title acts, dictate whether and how real property interests must be recorded on land records. States require easements and covenants to be recorded, but only a handful specifically address the recordation of conservation and preservation restrictions (whether they take the form of easements or covenants). *See, e.g.,* CAL. CIV. CODE § 815.5 (requiring instruments creating or transferring conservation easements to "be recorded in the office of the county recorder of the county where the land is situated"). What characteristics of these restrictions make them prime candidates for recordation?

4. Unlike the UCEA, the Connecticut statute expressly authorizes its attorney general to enforce "the public interest" in the restriction. What do you think "the public interest" in conservation and preservation restrictions includes? What benefits has the legislature assumed about these restrictions?

5. Also unlike the UCEA, the Connecticut statute is silent regarding who can enforce a conservation or preservation restriction (except for the sentence in section 47–42c regarding enforcement by the Attorney General). In 1995, a state court considered a case in which a property owner, aware of a conservation restriction of an abutting piece of property, sued his neighbor to enforce the restriction in light of commercial logging activities engaged by the defendant. Using common law principles related to the enforceability of easements, the court found that only the easement holder (in that case, a nonprofit organization) was entitled to relief. *Burgess v. Breakell,* 1995 WL 476782 (Conn. Super. 1995).

Does blocking his suit defeat the purpose of conservation restriction regime? Consider that in Connecticut, anyone living within 100 feet of a historic district or abutting a designated wetland can sue to enforce certain protections of the district or wetland. Absent a separate statute authorizing neighbor actions, would the result in *Burgess* be the same under the UCEA? Should the UCEA and similar state laws be amended to allow neighbor suits?

6. California is another non-UCEA state. A 2015 federal district court case involved a historic post office building listed on the National Register of Historic Places, located on a piece of land being sold by the U.S. Postal Service to a developer. *City of Berkeley v. U.S. Postal Service,* 2015 WL 1737523 (N.D. Cal. 2015). The Postal Service proposed to sell the property subject to a preservation restriction that made it the holder and enforcer of the restriction and did not prohibit demolition of the building.

The proposed sale triggered the Section 106 review process discussed in greater detail in Chapter 3. After reviewing the draft restriction, the federal Advisory Council on Historic Preservation found it inadequate, stating that:

> the proposed covenant does not sufficiently ensure the long-term preservation of the property since the USPS, as covenant holder, has the unfettered authority to approve adverse effects to the property (including demolition) while having neither the

demonstrated experience in holding preservation covenants nor an apparent interest in the long term preservation of the property.

Compl. for Decl. and Inj. Relief ¶ 23. The National Trust for Historic Preservation sought an injunction to prevent the Postal Service from selling the building. Ultimately, the potential buyer backed out of the sale, and the lawsuit was dismissed as moot. *City of Berkeley v. U.S. Postal Service*, at *5. But it raises questions about the content of restrictions, which are usually agreed upon by private parties without any third party review.

2. EXACTED CONSERVATION AND PRESERVATION RESTRICTIONS

This Chapter has thus far considered conservation and preservation restrictions that are created using the familiar means of purchase and donation. Sometimes, restrictions are created when government agencies require developers to conserve land in exchange for public approvals of their projects. In such situations, a private property owner will make a promise to the public body that she will restrict the use of all or some of her land and devote it to conservation purposes. Professor Jessica Owley explains more about these "exacted conservation easements":

> Property owners seeking to change their land must often obtain federal, state, and local permits. Increasingly, these permits require mitigation measures when land changes result in environmental impacts like increased pollution or habitat destruction. At times, these mitigation measures take the form of conservation easements. Different than the traditionally studied conservation easements, these exacted conservation easements are not exactly voluntary. Exacted easements are secondary mitigation requirements for landowners seeking to fulfill goals other than land protection.

Jessica Owley Lippmann, *Exacted Conservation Easements: The Hard Case of Endangered Species Protection*, 19 J. ENVTL. L. & LITIG. 293, 295 (2004) (suggesting how conservation easements exacted as part of habitat conservation plans drafted pursuant to the Endangered Species Protection Act should be treated).

Elsewhere, Professor Owley has described how exacted conservation easements obtained as part of broader regulatory schemes differ from traditional conservation and preservation restrictions:

> First, they stem from very different justifications [in that traditional restrictions are voluntary and exacted conservation easements are not]. Second, exacted conservation easements always arise in a larger regulatory context. There is an undeniable intersection with exacted conservation easements and environmental and land-use laws. Traditional conservation easements may grow out of a regulatory framework also. Indeed, they may operate directly in support of environmental

law goals. However, they do not necessarily do so. It is a not a requirement for a traditional conservation easement as it is for exacted conservation easements. Finally, exacted conservation easements do not always adhere to state conservation easement laws. Drafters of exacted conservation easements may be more focused on meeting the goals of the underlying land-use regulation than satisfying state property law requirements. Further, where the underlying law is a federal one, there is a tenuous argument that the exacted conservation easements need not conform to state law in order to be enforceable. * * * When exacted conservation easements do not adhere either to state conservation easement laws or to other state property law, their enforceability is less certain. Even where based on federal law, the circumstances where exacted conservation easements can defy state law appear limited. Thus, these differences between traditional conservation easements and exacted conservation easements lead directly to significant concerns with the tool.

Jessica Owley Lippmann, *The Emergence of Exacted Conservation Easements*, 84 NEB. L. REV. 1043, 1111 (2006). *See also* Jessica Owley, *The Enforceability of Exacted Conservation Easements*, 36 VT. L. REV. 261 (2011) (describing problems with enforcing exacted conservation easements, including the difficulty in determining whether state statutes on conservation restrictions or other statutes on property law apply).

One case, *Smith v. Town of Mendon*, 822 N.E.2d 1214 (N.Y. 2004), illustrates the kinds of legal issues that exacted conservation easements may raise. In that case, the town sought, as a condition for a site plan approval, a conservation restriction from landowners seeking to construct a single-family home. The home would have been built on a lot with several environmentally sensitive areas, located next to a protected waterway. The town wanted the conservation restriction to restrict (among other things) building, removing vegetation, installing septic systems, and driving over certain parts of the lot. To determine the appropriate legal standard for the case, the court grappled with whether the proposed restriction was an exaction or a regulatory taking. It found that the proposed restriction was not an exaction because (according to its characterization of relevant Supreme Court jurisprudence) "there is no dedication of property to public use and the restriction merely places conditions on development." *Id.* at 1219. The court then analyzed the proposed exaction as a taking, concluding that, "a modest environmental advancement at a negligible cost to the landowner does not amount to a regulatory taking." *Id.* at 1221. The N.Y. Court of Appeals was split 4 to 3 in this case, making it a close decision. While *Smith v. Town of Mendon* deals with an exacted conservation restriction that limited development in environmentally sensitive areas, its logic may be extended to justify an exacted preservation restriction.

NOTES & QUESTIONS

1. The U.S. Supreme Court has rejected certain exactions as unconstitutional violations of the federal Takings Clause, which was explored in Chapter 7. In general, exactions are subject to higher scrutiny than other types of regulatory takings. See *Dolan v. City of Tigard*, 512 U.S. 374 (1994) (holding that exactions imposed on development should be "roughly proportional" to the costs imposed by the development); *Nollan v. California Coastal Commission*, 483 U.S. 825 (1987) (holding that exactions must have an "essential nexus" with the state's interest). What kinds of exacted restrictions would satisfy these tests? Consider the following:

- An exacted preservation restriction that preserves a façade in a historic district where such façades are not otherwise protected.

- An exacted conservation restriction that limits the use of a rural tract to agricultural or recreational uses, where the area has a master plan promoting preservation.

- An exacted preservation restriction that requires a developer to preserve in perpetuity facades of historic buildings, when the developer is demolishing everything behind the facades.

2. In most cases, exactions are voluntarily accepted by a property owner or developer who views the cost of paying the exaction as necessary to obtain a land use approval. Consider Professor Owley's contention that exacted conservation restrictions differ fundamentally from traditional restrictions. Does their genesis merit a completely different legal regime than the one applied to other restrictions?

3. Consider the real-world example of a property owner doing a large-scale redevelopment in the heart of a vibrant commercial neighborhood in Arlington, Virginia. Included in the overall development site were at least two extant historic buildings. Before the county would issue the final building permit, it required the developer to record preservation easements for the two buildings running to the benefit of the Northern Virginia Conservation Trust, the County Board, or another mutually agreeable entity. The easements would prevent changes to the exterior of the building, except: changes required to comply with laws such as the Americans with Disabilities Act; changes to signage, awnings, and similar physical features; and changes approved by the county landmark review board and county manager. *See* Arlington County, Va., County Board Regular Meeting of May 22, 2010, SP #397, Supplemental Report, May 19, 2010. Given the expense, hassle, and future restrictions associated with such a condition, why might a developer agree to it?

4. Do decisions like *Smith v. Town of Mendon* invite municipalities across the State of New York to engage in questionable behavior in requesting (or, some would say, extorting) concessions from property owners seeking permit approvals? Or are there other factors—perhaps political in nature—preventing a wave of exacted conservation restrictions?

5.   What happens if a property owner agrees to tender a conservation easement in exchange for a building permit, but changes her mind? In at least one state, she may be out of luck if she has already started construction. In 1989, a California state appeals court considered whether property owners could attack conditions for a building permit in a coastal zone after the property owners had complied with the conditions and started development. *See Rossco Holdings, Inc. v. State of Calif.*, 260 Cal.Rptr. 736 (Ct. App. 1989). The court determined that: "A landowner cannot challenge a condition imposed upon the granting of a permit after acquiescence in the condition by either specifically agreeing to the condition or failing to challenge its validity, and accepting the benefits afforded by the permit." *Id.* Although the *Rossco Holdings* case did not address a conservation easement exaction, it suggests that a property owner thinking of challenging a demand like the one imposed upon the Smiths in the above case should not proceed with development until their complaint has been formally lodged with the proper authorities.

6.   Recall that the U.S. Army was found to violate Section 106 of the National Historic Preservation Act for deciding not to maintain the historic but deteriorating National Park Seminary Historic District, located at the Silver Spring campus of the Walter Reed Army Medical Center, which was the subject of *National Trust for Historic Preservation v. Blanck*, 938 F.Supp. 908 (D.D.C. 1996), excerpted in Chapter 3. Subsequently, the Army discharged its responsibilities for the National Park Seminary buildings by transferring them to Montgomery County, Maryland, which then conveyed an interest to developers with attached preservation restrictions that required approval of all plans for alterations by the Maryland Historic Trust (the state preservation agency) and the Montgomery County Historic Preservation Commission. The property now has been successfully redeveloped into a large, remarkable residential community. This example illustrates that preservation restrictions may be created not just through exactions, but may result from a government transfer to satisfy Section 106.

7.   Conservation restrictions are often enacted to protect scenic landscapes, wetlands, environmentally sensitive areas, and open space. Do conservation restrictions play a role in combating climate change? Arguably, such restrictions could endanger efforts to halt climate change because of the "fixed terms" required by these restrictions. What changes can be made? The authors of one article suggest that the IRS release new guidelines regarding conservation restriction amendment and termination. *See* Adena R. Rissman et al., *Adapting Conservation Easements to Climate Change*, Conservation Letters (Mar. 25, 2014), at 15. Do you think this is good solution? Do you agree with the authors' comment that conservationists must rethink using these restrictions? *Id.* at 1.

3.   A CRITIQUE OF THE "DEAD HAND"

The most salient criticism of conservation and preservation restrictions is that they create "dead hand control" over future decisions despite limited present information. Professor Julia Mahoney presents this criticism as follows:

[W]idespread support for conservation servitudes is based upon two widely held but erroneous assumptions, each of which fails to justify the use of these instruments. The first assumption is that today's landowners, together with the institutions that purchase conservation servitudes and accept them for donation, are capable of making long-term land preservation decisions, and that they can and should identify particular parcels of land as deserving of perpetual protection. Acceptance of this assumption leads to the belief that the present generation has the right, or perhaps even the duty, to engage in long-range conservation planning through the imposition of conservation easements that spell out (often in considerable detail) permissible land uses. In other words, the ability of the present generation to predict the needs and preferences of future generations is so good that the present generation should save their descendants trouble and transaction costs by making a substantial number of land use decisions for them. All available evidence, however, indicates that our competence does not extend that far.

The second assumption is that the present generation represents nature's last or near-to-last chance, because once land is developed, it will never or almost never go back to being undeveloped. Under this supposition, the only way to ensure that future generations have a sufficient supply of undeveloped land is to preserve as much land as possible today, and to construct legal institutions to make it hard to reverse decisions not to develop. But this inference, too, appears to be incorrect, due both to the lack of long-term effects of much land development and to the instability of the categories of "development" and "preservation."

Julia D. Mahoney, *Perpetual Restrictions on Land and the Problem of the Future*, 88 VA. L. REV. 739, 744–75 (2002). Do you agree with Professor Mahoney that present generations lack enough information about the future to encumber land using restrictions? Are you disturbed that millions of acres have already been encumbered?

As the discussion later in this Chapter reveals, it may be difficult to extinguish a restriction. Could the Rule Against Perpetuities be used to terminate conservation and preservation restrictions? Not really. The Rule, with its origins in common law, limits restraints on the transferability of property and reduces the prospect of dead hand control. The Rule states that no interest in real property is valid unless the interest must vest, if it all, no later than 21 years (plus a period of gestation to cover a posthumous birth) after the death of some person alive when the interest was created. One could argue that perpetual conservation and preservation restrictions are precisely the kinds of arrangement that the Rule attempts to avoid. But the prohibition on perpetuity in the Rule is intended to address the problem of unbounded time for *vesting*. Vesting for conservation and preservation restrictions occurs when the restriction is created for some party's benefit. Regardless, the question is moot, since all fifty states have passed statutes enabling the creation of perpetual conservation and/or preservation restrictions, thus eliminating the possibility of challenges based on the common law Rule Against Perpetuities.

B. ALTERATION AND TERMINATION

As noted above, conservation and preservation restrictions—unique private agreements restricting private property and enforceable by a limited number of parties—are largely creatures of state statutes. While these statutes set forth how such restrictions may be created, they typically do not deal with two significant issues that may arise after creation: the alteration and termination of existing restrictions. Significantly, the Uniform Conservation Easement Act, which is excerpted in full in the prior section and serves as the basis for about half of the states' statutes on point, fails to address either issue.

With little to no statutory guidance, and because conservation and preservation restrictions are relatively new legal forms, there may be difficulties determining whether, or to what extent, to allow alteration or termination. Authorities and courts may draw on interpretations of traditional servitudes to fill in any gaps, or may look to other states' treatment of the issues. As you read the materials below, consider the big-picture policy rationales for greater or lesser flexibility in altering or terminating conservation and preservation restrictions.

1. ALTERATION

Conservation and preservation restrictions are, by and large, intended to last perpetually without amendment. There are some situations, however, which may require alteration: The nonprofit holder of the restriction may have been dissolved; the protected historic structure may require repairs prohibited by the restriction; or, public access may need to be curbed. Changes in the needs of parties holding the easement, the physical condition of the protected real property, or other circumstances could provoke a wide range of amendment proposals.

Prior to approving any amendment, each party involved should review key legal documents: the governing materials of all parties to the restriction; any tax-exemption approvals; laws regarding real property, tax, land use, and nonprofit issues; agreements involving third parties, such as tenants; and of course the language of the restriction itself. Some of these documents may expressly authorize amendments and describe the amendment process; others may be silent.

Whether such express language exists, if the parties agree, an amendment could take place in most jurisdictions without the interference of any public actors. Indeed, many believe that one of the most attractive features of conservation and preservation restrictions is their ability to be created or modified without governmental interference.

a.   AN EXAMPLE STATE STATUTE

Not all states take a laissez-faire approach to amendments. A growing number of states—including Louisiana, Maine, Massachusetts, and New Jersey—require the review and consent of a court, or certain public officials or entities, before a conservation or preservation restriction can be modified. Consider the following excerpt from the statutes of Maine, one of the few states that have specified how amendments (and terminations) must occur. Note that Maine's restriction-related statutes have been called "the most comprehensive in the nation." Jeff Pidot, *Conservation Easement Reform: As Maine Goes Should the Nation Follow?*, 74 LAW & CONTEMP. PROBLEMS 1, 21 (2011). Conservation restrictions cover about 10 percent of the state's land area, including the largest conservation easement area in the United States, which covers over 750,000 acres. *Id.* at 5. Because so much of its land has been conserved, the state may have a pressing need to address known problems, as the following statutory provisions attempt to do.

Maine's Conservation Easement Amendment and Termination Provisions

ME. REV. STAT. ANN. tit. 33, § 477–A & 478(3)

§ 477–A. Conservation Easement Standards.

1.   Conservation values.

A conservation easement executed on or after the effective date of this section must include a statement of the conservation purposes of the easement, the conservation attributes associated with the real property and the benefit to the general public intended to be served by the restriction on uses of the real property subject to the conservation easement.

2.   Amendment and termination.

Amendments and termination of a conservation easement may occur only pursuant to this subsection.

A.   A conservation easement executed on or after the effective date of this section must include a statement of the holder's power to agree to amendments to the terms of the conservation easement in a manner consistent with the limitations of paragraph B.

B.   A conservation easement may not be terminated or amended in such a manner as to materially detract from the conservation values intended for protection without the prior approval of the court in an action in which the Attorney General is made a party. In making this determination, the court shall consider, among other relevant factors, the purposes expressed by the parties in the easement and the public interest. If the value of the landowner's estate is increased by reason of the amendment or termination of a conservation easement, that increase must be paid over to the holder or to such nonprofit or governmental entity as the court may designate, to be used for the protection of conservation lands consistent, as nearly as possible, with the stated publicly beneficial conservation purposes of the easement. * * *

§ 478.   Judicial Actions. * * *

3.   Power of court.

The court may permit termination of a conservation easement or approve amendment to a conservation easement that materially detracts from the conservation values it serves, as provided in section 477–A, subsection 2, paragraph B, and may enforce a conservation easement by injunction or proceeding at law and in equity. A court may deny equitable enforcement of a conservation easement only when it finds that change of circumstances has rendered that easement no longer in the public interest or no longer serving the publicly beneficial conservation purposes identified in the conservation easement. If the court so finds, the court may allow damages as the only remedy in an action to enforce the easement.

NOTES & QUESTIONS

1.   How many parties must be involved in a judicial action to amend or terminate a conservation easement in Maine? What factors must a court consider in determining whether to approve an amendment or termination?

2.   According to the statute, what happens if the amendment or termination increases the value of the land governed by the conservation easement? Does this outcome seem fair?

3.   Maine's approach—which allows amendments of conservation easements within certain parameters—sits somewhere between two extremes: disallowing amendments altogether and allowing amendments at will. By what other parameters might a state limit the amendment process?

4.   Conservation and preservation restrictions are touted as being flexible tools that meet the needs of private parties, including property owners, nonprofit organizations, and the general public. This flexibility is clearly evidenced in the initial drafting process: Within a state's legal framework, the parties can otherwise agree amongst themselves to almost any initial terms. Should the fact that there is so much flexibility in drafting restrictions influence the level of flexibility during the term of the restriction? If so, should the level of flexibility during the term—in other words, the ability to alter an existing restriction—be greater or less?

5.   Courts in Maine and elsewhere have a number of traditional legal doctrines from which to draw in evaluating proposed amendments that come before them. One important doctrine is changed conditions (or changed

circumstances) doctrine, which applies to servitudes. The RESTATEMENT (THIRD) OF PROPERTY: SERVITUDES § 7.10(1) (2000) states the modern approach to this doctrine:

> When a change has taken place since the creation of a servitude that makes it impossible as a practical matter to accomplish the purpose for which the servitude was created, a court may modify the servitude to permit the purpose to be accomplished. If modification is not practicable, or would not be effective, a court may terminate the servitude. Compensation for resulting harm to the beneficiaries may be awarded as a condition of modifying or terminating the servitude.

Can you think of circumstances that would make a conservation or preservation restriction obsolete? How would a court apply the changed conditions doctrine to that situation?

A second traditional doctrine that has drawn much scholarly interest is the charitable trust approach. See the following note for a more thorough account of its relationship to conservation and preservation restrictions.

b.   THE CHARITABLE TRUST APPROACH TO CONSERVATION AND PRESERVATION RESTRICTIONS

The Maine statute requires that conservation easements must state "the benefit to the general public" and that a court must approve any amendments that "materially detract from the conservation values intended for protection." In using this language, the legislature seems to liken a conservation easement to a charitable trust, which is a trust established either by agreement or operation of law for charitable purposes with a public benefit. Conservation easements will often create a charitable trust type arrangement, with the organization holding the easement acting as a trustee, the public as beneficiary, and the property owner (the easement creator) as the grantor. Under common law, charitable trusts may not be amended to deviate from their charitable purposes without the approval of a court. More specifically, the *cy pres* doctrine and the related administrative deviation doctrine (which applies more narrowly, to administrative matters) allow a court to reform documents related to a charitable trust only if the court finds that the means of achieving the charitable purpose become "impossible or impracticable" as a result of changed conditions and such amendments would conform with the original intent of the trust.

Despite the similarities, neither the Maine legislature nor a Maine court has explicitly stated that there is a link between charitable trust rules and conservation restriction interpretation. In fact, to date, among all the states, no state legislature and only one state supreme court (Wyoming's) has found that charitable trust rules should apply to conservation restrictions. *See Hicks v. Dowd*, 157 P.3d 914, 919 (Wyo. 2007) ("Given the district court's unchallenged finding, we must agree that the Scenic Preserve Trust [a county wide land trust] is a charitable trust").

Despite the dearth of settled law on point, the call to treat amendments to conservation and preservation restrictions with the charitable trust rules has been growing. The leading proponent of this approach is Professor Nancy McLaughlin, who summarized her argument thus:

> [C]onservation easements donated to counties, cities, and other agencies of state government * * * or charitable organizations should be treated as restricted charitable gifts or charitable trusts, and the holders of such easements should be subject to the equitable rules governing a donee's use and disposition of charitable assets—including the well-settled rule that, except to the extent granted the power in the gift or trust instrument, the donee of a restricted charitable gift or charitable trust may not deviate from the administrative terms or charitable purpose thereof without receiving court approval therefor under the doctrine of administrative deviation or *cy pres* (sometimes referred to hereinafter as the "charitable trust rules"). Charitable trust rules are recommended as the framework within which to modify or terminate conservation easements because such rules were developed and refined over the centuries to deal precisely with the issue presented by conservation easements—how to appropriately balance: (i) the charitable donor's desire to exercise dead hand control over the use of his or her property and (ii) society's interest in ensuring that assets perpetually devoted to charitable purposes continue to provide benefits to the public.

Nancy A. McLaughlin, *Rethinking the Perpetual Nature of Conservation Easements*, 29 HARV. ENVTL. L. REV. 421, 428–29 (2005). From her perspective, the public has invested in the majority of conservation and preservation restrictions—most directly via tax subsidies such as income tax deduction allowances and property tax reductions.

Others disagree. In a 2006 paper entitled "Conservation Easement Amendments: A View From the Field," attorney Andrew C. Dana criticizes Professor McLaughlin's approach for being both legally problematic and contrary to public policy. Dana argues that conservation easements differ enough from charitable trusts that trust rules should not apply. Charitable trusts are often created by operation of law, not expressly like most conservation easements. Moreover, charitable trusts involve donations in which donors restrict the *trustee's* management of the property in trust, while donated conservation easements involve donations in which donors restrict *their own* use of the donated property. And while charitable trusts involve donations, many conservation easements—including those that arise through purchases, exactions, regulations, or eminent domain—do not.

In addition to the legal issues, Dana identifies public policy issues related to the application of charitable trust rules to conservation easements. For example, high transaction costs for both the parties and the public actors may be associated with obtaining judicial review required by *cy pres*. Such costs may be especially undesirable when an amendment is minor. When parties seeking amendments go to court, complex issues involving unique sets of facts would likely have to be litigated, since the individualized nature of conservation easements does not lend itself to standardized analysis remedies. When reviewing these complex issues, judges may be forced to weigh different policy goals (e.g., the benefits of preserving open space versus the benefits of new construction within formerly conserved lands) that are outside their areas of expertise. Finally, and perhaps most convincingly, Dana argues that the original parties to conservation easements may not want charitable trust rules to apply—preferring instead, for example, the doctrine of changed conditions that draws from the laws of servitudes (described in the above Notes & Questions).

The RESTATEMENT (THIRD) OF PROPERTY: SERVITUDES (2000) offers a position somewhere in the middle. It says that a conservation or preservation restriction held by a government agency or conservation organization may be modified or terminated in accordance with the *cy pres* doctrine of charitable trust law if the purpose for which it was created becomes impracticable. *Id.* § 7.11. Restrictions held by other private parties may be modified in accordance with the changed conditions doctrine. *Id.* § 7.10. The latter approach is more permissive than the former, in part because, in the view of the drafters of the Restatement, the public has a greater interest in restrictions held by government agencies and conservation organizations, so they should be more difficult to modify. In any case, the Restatement fails to directly address further application of charitable trust law to conservation and preservation restrictions.

Which of these three views is most convincing?

Case Study: The Problem of Myrtle Grove

Consider the following description of a real-world example of a proposed amendment to a conservation restriction that covers property in the eastern shore of Maryland, near the Chesapeake Bay. This description draws directly from, and would not be possible without, an article by Nancy A. McLaughlin. *Amending Perpetual Conservation Easements: A Case Study of the Myrtle Grove Controversy*, 40 U. RICH. L. REV. 1031 (2006).

In 1975, the National Trust for Historic Preservation (the "National Trust") accepted a conservation restriction encumbering the land and certain buildings of a 160-acre historic plantation, known as Myrtle Grove, located in Maryland and listed on the National Register. The donor, Margaret Donoho, was motivated in large part by the desire to preserve the property against subdivision and future development. The restriction prohibits not only subdivision (except for a single lot, of at least five acres, for a private residence for one of Donoho's heirs) and new construction, but also "any activities, actions, or uses detrimental or adverse to water conservation, erosion control, soil conservation, or fish and wildlife habitat preservation." *Id.* at 1044.

In 1988, thirteen years after delivering the restriction to the National Trust, Ms. Dohono passed away. Donoho's heirs subdivided the property in accordance with the original restriction, laying claim to a 45-acre portion of the lot. They sought after and received confirmation from the National Trust for Historic Preservation that all of the restrictions in Margaret Donoho's original grant would be fully in force after a sale of the remaining 115 acres. In 1989, they sold the 115 acres for $3 million to a trust established by a real estate developer, Herbert Miller, to benefit his wife (the "Miller Trust").

Over a period of three years, the Miller Trust completed an award-winning renovation to the site, including the buildings on it, in accordance with the original restriction. The renovations cost over $2.5 million. In 1992, the Miller Trust began to market the 115-acre property for sale for $6.5 million, and then reduced the price to $5.5 million, but it found no buyers. In 1993, citing financial hardship, the Miller Trust requested an amendment to the original restriction to allow the property to be subdivided into six additional residential lots. In 1994, the National Trust agreed to amend the restriction by limiting its applicability to a 47-acre "historic core," and permitting the remainder of the property to be divided into three residential lots upon which construction would be permitted subject to review by the National Trust. In exchange, the Trust would receive $68,700 from the Miller Trust, in part to offset the cost of enforcement and monitoring. This agreement was memorialized in a letter from the National Trust to the Miller Trust.

When Donoho's heirs found out about this arrangement, they were outraged because they believed that the amendment would directly contradict the intent and language of Margaret Donoho's restriction. Local historic preservation groups, too, became concerned, pressing the National Trust to change its mind and claiming that the National Trust's agreement to amend the restriction at Myrtle Grove would threaten the integrity of other restrictions. After initially defending its decision, the National Trust reversed course, notifying the Miller Trust that its approval of the amendment was withdrawn.

In 1997, the Miller Trust sued for breach of contract. The National Trust defended itself first on contractual grounds, and then by claiming that the restriction was a charitable trust and could not be amended under state law without a court's review. In 1998, the Attorney General of Maryland filed a suit also claiming that the restriction was a charitable trust. In December of that year, the parties settled. The National Trust paid the Miller Trust $225,000, and the parties agreed that subdivision of Myrtle Grove is prohibited, as is amending the restriction without consent of the Attorney General of Maryland.

NOTES & QUESTIONS

1.   Why did the National Trust agree to amend the conservation restriction in the first place? Perhaps the organization was sympathetic to the amount of money that the Miller Trust had invested in the site in terms of improvements and repairs. After all, the Miller Trust invested at least $5.5 million in the land and capital improvements and was unable to find a buyer that would help them break even. What other motivations might a land trust, nonprofit, or government agency have for agreeing to such a modification?

2.   Often, donors are motivated to make a conservation or preservation restriction perpetual for tax reasons. Many tax incentives, including the federal charitable income tax deduction for qualifying donations, require a perpetual term. Margaret Donoho received a tax deduction, but money did not appear to be the primary motivator in the case. What do she and her heirs appear to be most motivated by? What could Donoho have done if money were her primary motivation?

3.   The parties involved with the Myrtle Grove restriction initially agreed to the terms of the amendment. If Donoho's heirs had agreed also, the amendment may never have gone to court. In this case, the parties disagreed primarily about the prohibition on subdivision. Disagreements among parties might also occur if, for example, the proposed alteration would cause the grantor to lose certain tax benefits, or would jeopardize the tax exempt status of a nonprofit grantee. If one party wishes to amend against the wishes of another—or if a third party wishes to impose an amendment—a court or government agencies may become involved.

4.   Historic preservation can be an expensive proposition. At Myrtle Grove, what costs were imposed on the heirs? The Miller Trust? The National Trust? The general public?

5.   Few published cases involve conservation and preservation restrictions. Why not? Are they, by their nature, likely to settle, as was ultimately the case with the Myrtle Grove restriction? Or is standing to bring suits unduly limited?

Professor Carol Brown has criticized the limited standing to enforce or challenge conservation and preservation restrictions. She has argued that "members of the public—either individuals or public-private entities—who are not owners of an interest in real property affected by a conservation easement, holders of conservation easements, possessors of a third-party right of enforcement, or individuals authorized by some other law to bring an action affecting conservation easements" should have standing. Carol Necole Brown, *A Time to Preserve: A Call for Formal Private-Party Rights in Perpetual Conservation Easements*, 40 GA. L. REV. 85, 89 (2005).

What are the advantages and disadvantages of expanding standing? In the case of Myrtle Grove, Professor Brown's formulation would have allowed for one of the local preservation nonprofits who objected to the amendment to have brought suit and, for all practical purposes, to have influenced the settlement agreement. Expanding standing would therefore give certain individuals and organizations tremendous power.

2. TERMINATION

Once a conservation or preservation restriction is created, it may be difficult to extinguish. A court in law or equity may extinguish a restriction. A court is likely to do so if, for example, the structure being protected by the restriction has been destroyed. In addition, federal tax regulations allow for a restriction to be extinguished if, unexpectedly, using the restricted property for conservation purposes becomes impractical or impossible, and so long as any proceeds from the sale of the property absent the restriction is used for conservation purposes. *See* Treas. Reg. § 1.170A–14(c)(2) (2011).

Moreover, the vast majority of conservation and preservation restrictions are intended to last forever. In all but a handful of states, statutes make perpetual terms the default provision. For example, section 2 of the UCEA, adopted by about half of the states, says: "a conservation easement is unlimited in duration unless the instrument creating it otherwise provides." Going further, three states—California, Florida, and Hawaii—actually mandate perpetual terms. In addition, public tax incentive programs overwhelmingly require that restrictions be perpetual for property owners to receive the full benefit of donating restrictions. For similar reasons, many land trusts and governmental agencies which accept conservation and preservation restrictions require a perpetual term.

Are perpetual restrictions the best approach? Professor Barton Thompson urges state legislatures to consider supporting shorter-term easements. *See* Barton H. Thompson, Jr., *The Trouble with Time: Influencing the Conservation Choices of Future Generations*, 44 NAT. RES. J. 601 (2004). Going further, Professor Jessica Owley urges state legislatures to prohibit perpetual easements altogether. Instead, she urges the adoption of "renewable term conservation easements," which would require property owners and easement holders to reevaluate the restriction at periodic intervals determined by statute. She says, "Creating renewable conservation easements enables preservation of the land while enabling slight (or, if appropriate, major) modifications to account for changes in the natural or social environment." Jessica Owley, *Changing Property in a Changing World: A Call for the End of Perpetual Conservation Easements*, 30 STAN. ENVTL. L.J. 121, 165 (2011). Like Professor Thompson, she argues that shorter-term easements would enhance environmental protection because—when incorporated into holistic conservation planning efforts—they would provide a "more realistic sense of what is being preserved and what work is left to do." *Id.* at 170.

NOTES & QUESTIONS

1. Can termination of an easement occur by government condemnation (eminent domain)? Yes. Some states mandate that compensation must be given for a government action that condemns land burdened by a conservation restriction. *See, e.g.,* VA. CODE ANN. § 10.1–1010(F) (2011) (stating that in an eminent domain proceeding, "the holder of the conservation easement shall be compensated for the value of the easement"). In states that do not explicitly require compensation, how have donors avoided losing full compensation for their property? They have provided in the restriction that if the land is condemned the restriction will revert and the full value go back to the owner.

2. What should happen to a conservation or preservation restriction if the nonprofit organization holding it ceases to exist? Without careful drafting, such restrictions may automatically lapse or fall into legal limbo.

3. Empirical evidence related to termination and alteration of conservation and preservation restrictions is scant, but Professor Zachary Bray has made an important contribution. He conducted a survey of 113 restrictions held by local and regional private land trusts in the Commonwealth of Massachusetts, where restrictions had their legal start in this country. *See* Zachary Bray, *Reconciling Development and Natural Beauty: The Promise and Dilemma of Conservation Easements*, 34 HARV. ENVTL. L. REV. 119 (2010). Among other things, Bray found that only two of the restrictions addressed extinguishment by the property owner and holder, but that 88 percent of them addressed extinguishment via eminent domain or condemnation. *Id.* at 170. He also identified a handful of restrictions that were jointly held, either by more than one land trust or by a land trust and a government agency. Bray observes that while such arrangements may be cost-effective for the holders because they share in the costs of monitoring and enforcement, "jointly held restrictions may carry unintended consequences related to the problem of permanence: it is reasonable to assume that they will be even more difficult to amend or extinguish in the future than singly held restrictions." *Id.* at 171.

C. THE VALUE OF CONSERVATION AND PRESERVATION RESTRICTIONS

Some of the highest-profile legal issues involving conservation and preservation restrictions have related to the question of their value. This subsection first considers how the law calculates the worth of these restrictions, and then describes how tax law and policy have affected their development.

1. VALUATION

Determining the value of any interest in real property requires the special skills of an appraiser or other person well versed in real estate economics. Valuation of conservation and preservation restrictions may be more difficult than valuing other kinds of real property interests, due to the small number of market purchases and sales of such restrictions. Yet valuation may be sought for at least four reasons. First, the assessed value of a property may be reduced by the value of the restriction, meaning that the property owner would be allowed to pay lower property taxes. Second, the holder of the restriction may require an appraisal of the restriction's worth both for inventory purposes and to determine the extent of its expenses related to the administration and maintenance of the restricted parcel. Third, programs that purchase restrictions must assess their value prior to purchasing them. Fourth, the value of the restriction determines the extent of the tax advantages of a property owner who is donating it for charitable purposes.

In many cases, the value of a restriction is negative; that is, it diminishes the value of the property. It is important to recognize, however, that in certain instances, a restriction may have no effect, or may even increase the value of the subject property. Public and private entities, including Congress, have recognized the potential variety in valuations. *See, e.g.*, Treas. Reg. § 1.170A–14(h)(3)(ii) (2009) ("[T]here may be instances where the grant of a conservation restriction may have no material effect on the value of the property or may in fact serve to enhance, rather than reduce, the value of property. In such instances no deduction would be allowable.").

a. METHODS OF APPRAISALS

Methods of appraisals vary. One method of determining the value of real property is through comparable sales. An appraiser will review sales of conservation and preservation restrictions in roughly the same geographic area as the subject property, and adjust the average value, either upward or downward, on the basis of the subject property's unique characteristics. As noted above, this method has proven problematic for conservation and preservation restrictions because there is a lack of relevant market data. A second method of valuing real property, the replacement cost method, separates the value of the land from the value of any improvements. In the context of conservation and preservation restrictions, the replacement cost method is important because it has the potential to account for the costs imposed on property owners by restrictions that require the owner to replace or reproduce protected features. The replacement cost method may also be appropriate for restrictions that require direct expenditures on capital improvements, or that require the retention of obsolete or otherwise unfavorable improvements that impose future rehabilitation costs. The third method is based on income capitalization, a particularly appropriate method for commercial properties subject to conservation or preservation easements. The income capitalization approach would take into account a restriction's impact on income from tenant rents, operating expenses, insurance costs, repairs, additional reserves, and marketing costs, among others. See RICHARD J. RODDEWIG, APPRAISAL INST. & LAND TRUST ALLIANCE, APPRAISING CONSERVATION AND HISTORIC PRESERVATION EASEMENTS (2011). In addition, the Internal Revenue Service has published a guide on determining the value of donated property that validates the use of each of these three primary methods of valuing donated real estate, either individually or together, where appropriate. I.R.S., PUB. 561, DETERMINING THE VALUE OF DONATED PROPERTY 6–7 (2020).

Any of these methods of appraisals can be used to value restrictions, but care must be taken so that they stand up to judicial review. Regardless of the method chosen, public and private actors have come to accept a "before and after" approach. An appraiser determines the fair market value of the parcel overall, without taking the restriction into account (the "before" value) and the fair market value of the parcel after the restriction is imposed (the "after" value). The difference between the "before" and "after" values is the value of the restriction.

What approach is used by the following case, which involves a purchased conservation restriction in one of the few geographic areas in the country where there is a market, albeit small, for such restrictions?

Browning v. Commissioner
109 T.C. 303 (1997)

■ HALPERN, JUDGE.

[EDS.: The respondent Commissioner of the IRS determined that the married petitioners, Charles and Patricia Browning, had failed to pay $32,124 in federal income taxes between 1990 and 1993. The Brownings owned a 52.44-acre parcel in Howard County, Maryland which they used for agricultural purposes. The Browning parcel was bordered by parcels owned by William Barnes (the Barnes tract) and Gene Mullinix (the Mullinix tract).] * * *

By deed of easement dated December 14, 1990 (the conveyance date), petitioners conveyed to Howard County an easement restricting development of the land (the easement). In consideration thereof, petitioners received $30,000 in cash immediately and Howard County's agreement to make installment payments of an additional $279,000 over a period of approximately 30 years (for a total sales price of $309,000). The bulk of the sales price ($235,000) is to be paid at the end of the 30-year installment period. Interest on the unpaid balance of the sales price is payable at a minimum rate of 8 percent a year.

Land Preservation Program

Howard County acquired the easement pursuant to the county's Agricultural Land Preservation Program (the Program). The Program is the county's primary tool for preserving farmland. Pursuant to the Program, the county purchases development rights from landowners and holds those rights in perpetuity. The only permissible use of land in the Program is agricultural use. A landowner's participation in the Program is voluntary. The objective of the Program is to support the agricultural community by helping to keep the county's land base available for farming and by minimizing the impact of residential development in agricultural areas. * * *

[T]he county initially adopted a policy of paying no more than $6,500 an acre (later increased to $6,600) (the limitation). The maximum price was paid for the best qualified farmland as determined by a formula adopted by the county, and lesser amounts were paid for lesser qualified farmland. The limitation was adopted as a budgetary constraint because the county had limited funds to purchase development rights to the 20,000 to 30,000 acres it wished to encumber. Given Howard County's knowledge of the value of farmland in the county, the limitation was fixed so as to produce a price equal to only a portion (50 to 80 percent) of the maximum expected fair market value of development rights. In the case of each acquisition of development rights pursuant to the Program, before an offer was made by Howard County, the county obtained an appraisal of the value of the subject property both encumbered and unencumbered by the development restriction. The price offered by the county was always less than the reduction in fair market value indicated by the appraisal.

Market for Development Rights

During 1990, the only purchaser of development rights to farmland in Howard County was the county, under the Program.

[EDS.: The County's appraiser appraised the fair market value of the land at $771,600, the agricultural value at $173,052, and the value of the easement at $598,500. Because the Brownings received $309,000 from Howard County as the purchase price of the restriction, the Brownings claimed a charitable contribution on their federal income taxes of $289,500. Due to limitations on the annual amount that could be taken, the Brownings only actually claimed $172,547, spread out between 1990 and 1993.] * * *

Opinion

I.   Introduction

Petitioners assert that they made a bargain sale of the easement to Howard County and that they are entitled to claim a charitable contribution equal to the difference between the fair market value of the easement and the amount realized from the sale. Respondent contends that petitioners have failed to demonstrate that the fair market value of the easement exceeded the amount realized from the sale. There is no dispute regarding petitioners' satisfaction of any other requirements set forth in section 170 and the regulations thereunder, including whether the contributed property (if any) constitutes a "qualified conservation contribution" under section 170(h)(1). Therefore, the only issues we must address are the fair market value of the easement and the amount realized from the sale. * * *

III. Arguments of the Parties

Petitioners, relying principally on the testimony of their experts, contend that the fair market value of the easement on the conveyance date was $563,000. Petitioners argue that the amount realized on the sale of the easement is $309,000, and, therefore, the amount of the charitable contribution is $254,000.

Respondent argues that petitioners' conveyance of the easement to Howard County did not constitute a bargain sale because the amount paid by Howard County to petitioners was in line with the amount that the county paid generally for development rights under the Program and, thus, represented the fair market value of the easement. Respondent relies on section 1.170A–14(h)(3)(i), Income Tax Regs., which prescribes a methodology for determining the fair market value of donated easements of the type conveyed by petitioners to the county. Respondent argues that there is a universe of sales of development rights to the county under the Program, that that universe constitutes a substantial record of sales of comparable development rights, and that there were no other sales of development rights in the county during 1990. Relying on section 1.170A–14(h)(3)(i), Income Tax Regs., respondent denies the relevance of any appraisal evidence that would support any different (greater) fair market value. Thus, by, in effect, defining the fair market value of the property transferred by what the county paid for it, respondent denies that petitioners made a bargain sale to the county; denying that they made a bargain sale, respondent denies that they made a charitable contribution.

Alternatively, respondent argues that the fair market value of the easement is no greater than $367,000 and that the "valuable benefits" received by petitioners, including the $309,000 and the anticipated charitable contribution deductions, must be subtracted from that figure to determine properly the amount of the charitable contribution.

IV. Analysis of the Fair Market Value of the Easement

A.   Introduction

A bargain sale is a transfer of property that is in part a sale or exchange and in part a gift. See section 1.1001–1(e)(2) *Example (3)*, Income Tax Regs., which provides as follows:

> A transfers property to his son for $30,000. Such property in A's hands has an adjusted basis of $30,000 (and a fair market value of $60,000). A has no gain and has made a gift of $30,000, the

excess of $60,000, the fair market value, over the amount realized, $30,000.

Where the bargain sale is to a charitable organization, the gift generally constitutes a charitable contribution. * * *

B.   Section 1.170A–14(h)(3)(i), Income Tax Regs.

The general rule is that the amount of a charitable contribution made in property is the fair market value of the property at the time of the contribution. Sec. 1.170A–1(c)(1), Income Tax Regs. That is no less the general rule if the charitable contribution is of a partial interest in property, *id.* § 1.170A–7(c), including a perpetual conservation restriction such as the easement. *Id.* § 1.170A14(h)(3). The preferred way of determining fair market value is by applying the marketplace standard found in the regulations to the property contributed. *See id.* § 1.170A1(c)(2) ("fair market value is the price at which the property would change hands between a willing buyer and a willing seller, neither being under any compulsion to buy or sell and both having reasonable knowledge of relevant facts"). In the absence of a well-established market for property of the type contributed, however, the marketplace standard of the regulations may be difficult to apply. *See, e.g., Symington v. Commissioner,* 87 T.C. 892, 895 (1986) ("Unfortunately, since most open-space easements are granted by deed of gift there is rarely an established market from which to derive the fair market value.").

In the case of a perpetual conservation restriction, if the market for such restrictions is not well established, it is usually necessary to value the restriction by applying a "before and after" analysis; i.e., a comparison of the fair market value of the donor's property unencumbered by the restriction with the fair market value of the property after the conveyance of the restriction, with any diminution of value to be ascribed to the fair market value of the restriction. * * *

[W]e are not required to accept the substantial record of sales of development rights to Howard County under the Program as determinative of the fair market value of the easement when there is evidence to support a finding that those sales occur in an inhibited market.

D.   Uninhibited Markets

Notwithstanding the establishment of a market to which reference may be had for sales data, such data may not yield a demonstration of the fair market value of a particular property (or an interest in property) if general conditions or those affecting particularly the sales that have actually transpired do not "fairly" reflect the circumstances surrounding the specific property to be valued. * * *

We have found sales data not to be indicative of fair market value where property was sold to the highest bidder at an "unrestricted auction," with no minimum bid or number of bids required, and there was evidence that the property had an intrinsic value far in excess of the auction sales price and could have been sold under other circumstances at a considerably higher price. *McGuire v. Commissioner*, 44 T.C. 801, 809 (1965). In *Gillette Rubber Co. v. Commissioner*, 31 B.T.A. 483, 491 (1934), we rejected as determinative of the fair market value of certain common stock "a price known to be a low one, purposely made so to secure the good will of * * * [former] stockholders and give them a chance to recoup [their prior losses]."

On brief, respondent recites:

Petitioners contend that the cash paid by Howard County for the development rights to their property does not represent the fair market value of the development rights. This argument is largely based on two factors: 1. petitioners did not believe the cash payments represented the fair market value of the property conveyed; and 2. Howard County did not intend to pay them fair market value for their easement.

In response, respondent concedes that petitioners' evidence as to the subjective beliefs of the parties (petitioners and Howard County) is persuasive on the issue of donative intent. We take that response as a concession by respondent that petitioners and the county intended a bargain sale; i.e., a part sale part gift. Certainly, that conclusion is supported by the testimony of petitioner Charles Browning (the $6,000 an acre received for the easement "couldn't possibly represent the fair market value of the easement") and Donna Mennitto, administrator of the Program ("It was never the intention of the County to pay the full easement value and we do not believe that we ever did with the information that we had available."), and, thus, we accept respondent's concession and so find. Moreover, we believe that the record supports a finding that, under the Program generally, at the time petitioners conveyed the easement to the county and before, participants in the Program intended to make a gift to the county by way of a bargain sale of development rights. We have the testimony of two participants in the Program as to that point, petitioner Charles Browning and his neighbor, Gene Mullinix. In addition, Mr. Mullinix, who was a chairman of the board that supervised the Program and served on that board for 10 years, testified that the board that ran the Program never paid "full" fair market value for any easement that it purchased under the Program. Ms. Mennitto's testimony as to the procedures followed to implement the Program, including publication of the Program, public hearings at which properties offered to the Program were presented for comment, the limitations on what the county would pay, and the appraisal process designed to insure that the county did not pay the full amount of the value of the development rights indicated by that appraisal, all convince us that participants in the Program generally intended to make a gift to the county by way of a bargain sale of development rights, and we so find.

Of course, our finding that participants in the Program *intended* a bargain sale is not determinative that there was a bargain sale.

Nevertheless, it is determinative that the universe of sales to the county under the Program does not represent a universe populated with sellers all of whom (or, perhaps, even, *any* of whom) were looking for the best deal (highest price) possible. Sales data from that universe, thus, are not reflective of a market populated by buyers and sellers each trying to maximize profits by searching for the lowest (buyers) or highest (sellers) price possible. Any "market price" based on evidence from that market is not a market price fairly reflective of the price the easement would fetch in an uninhibited market. It is not a "fair" market price within the meaning of *Heiner v. Crosby*, 24 F.2d 191, 193 (1928) nor are the sales "market-place" sales within the meaning of section 1.170A14(h)(3)(i), Income Tax Regs., available to use as a "meaningful or valid" comparison to the sale of the easement.

E.   Before and After Valuation

1.   Introduction

The market for sales of development rights to the county under the Program was not an uninhibited market, but was a market characterized by sellers intending to make gifts to the county by way of bargain sales; therefore, petitioners are entitled to show the fair market value of the easement by evidence of the fair market value of the land before and after the conveyance of the easement. Sec. 1.170A–14(h)(3)(i), Income Tax Regs. (third substantive sentence). We shall now consider the expert testimony presented by both parties with respect to those values.

2.   After Value

The parties' expert appraisers, Messrs. Sapperstein (for petitioners) and Lipman (for respondent), agree that the highest and best use of the land after the conveyance of the easement to the county is as a farm. Both experts value the land subject to the easement at $157,000. Therefore, we find that the after value of the land subject to the easement on the conveyance date was $157,000.

3.   Before Value

Messrs. Sapperstein and Lipman also agree that the highest and best use of the land before the conveyance of the easement to the county was for development into single family residential lots. Both appraisers look to sales price data from sales of comparable properties sold for residential development purposes to determine the value of the land before conveyance of the easement. Mr. Lipman is of the opinion that the comparison should be made on both a "per acre" and "per raw lot" basis. He reports, however: "Unfortunately, at least from the standpoint of this appraisal, we do not have an engineer's estimate of lot yield for the subject property. Accordingly, we will depend primarily on value from a per acre perspective." Mr. Lipman is of the opinion that the value of the land before conveyance of the easement was $10,000 an acre (for a total value of $524,400).

Mr. Sapperstein did not think that a dollars-an-acre basis was a proper basis for reaching a conclusion as to the value of the land because, in his opinion:

> Knowledgeable buyers of the subject property type, are typically interested in the development potential of the property, and are concerned with the property's yield. By determining the number of lots that can be developed on the subject property, we remove from the appraisal problem any subjectivity related to the property's physical characteristics (i.e., shape, topography, wetlands, and other possible development constraints). Thus, a comparison can be made on a "value per lot" basis with the comparable sales, requiring adjustment for location, site orientation, and accessibility.

Mr. Sapperstein is of the opinion that the value of the land before conveyance of the easement to the county was $45,000 a lot. Based on the Benning report [EDS.: a report by a licensed landscape architect, which took site conditions into account], Mr. Sapperstein assumed that either 15 or 16 lots could be developed on the land and, accordingly, has the opinion that the value of the land before conveyance of the easement to the county is either $675,000 or $720,000.

Both Messrs. Lipman and Sapperstein are well qualified and provided us with helpful testimony. They both used sales of comparable properties to value the land before the conveyance of the easement to the county. Indeed, they relied on many of the same sales (of comparable properties) in reaching their respective conclusions. They agree that a dollar-a-lot basis is an appropriate basis for comparison. Because Mr. Lipman did not have an engineer's estimate of lot yield, he did not make a dollar-a-lot comparison, but, instead, relied on a dollar-an-acre comparison. Messrs. Lipman and Sapperstein reach different conclusions, which are difficult to reconcile because of the different basis of comparison adopted by each. We are not persuaded by Mr. Sapperstein that a dollar-a-lot basis is necessarily superior to a dollar-an-acre basis for making comparisons (we would have preferred to have each expert use both). Mr. Lipman, however, at trial, agreed that "a knowledgeable buyer of the property would buy this property based on a lot yield as opposed to an acreage basis" and, in his report, stated that a value of $43,700 a lot is "well supported by the market data."

Since the parties' experts appear to be in relative agreement as to the value of the lots that the land would yield (Sapperstein: $45,000 a lot; Lipman: $43,700 a lot), we shall derive the before value of the land by multiplying a dollar-a-lot value by the land's lot yield. In addition, we shall accept Mr. Sapperstein's value of $45,000 a lot because it was derived from his analysis using a dollar-a-lot comparison and not from a calculation derivative of a dollar-an-acre comparison, i.e., Mr. Lipman's dollar-a-lot value.

We shall now address the principal point of contention between the parties, the lot yield of the land. Based on the Benning report, Mr. Sapperstein assumes that the land could be developed into either 15 or 16 residential lots. Mr. Benning is of the opinion that, if the land were developed in conjunction with either or both of the adjacent tracts of land (the Barnes tract and the Mullinix tract), certain land exchanges would be undertaken that would increase lot yield and other efficiencies would be obtained, which would allow 16 lots to be developed on the land. In the absence of such joint development, Mr. Benning is of the opinion that only 15 lots could be developed on the land. Mr. Lipman opined that 12 lots could be developed on the land, but stated that the effective lot yield of the land is 13 lots (including the lot underlying the improvement).

In determining both the highest and best use of a parcel of land and the fair market value of the parcel resulting from such use, the use of the parcel in conjunction with other parcels may be taken into account. *See United States v. Fuller*, 409 U.S. 488, 490 (1973); *Dorsey v. Commissioner*, T.C.M. (RIA) 1990–242 (with respect to the charitable contribution of a facade easement: "The fair market value of the easement should be based on the highest and best use for the property on its valuation date, including potential development."). In *Olson v. United States*, 292 U.S. 246, 257 (1934), the Supreme Court noted, however:

> Elements affecting value that depend upon events or combinations of occurrences which, while within the realm of possibility, are not fairly shown to be reasonably probable, should be excluded from consideration, for that would be to allow mere speculation and conjecture to become a guide for the ascertainment of value—a thing to be condemned in business transactions as well as in judicial ascertainment of truth. * * *

Had petitioners not conveyed the easement to the county, certainly there was the potential for their developing the land together with either or both of Messrs. Barnes and Mullinix. Mr. Mullinix testified regarding joint action with petitioners; and the parties have stipulated that, although Mr. Barnes did not testify, his testimony would have been consistent with the testimony of Mr. Mullinix. Mr. Mullinix testified that there were benefits to either developing the properties jointly or jointly participating in the Program. He testified that there was no written or enforceable agreement for joint action and that there was "some talk" about Mr. Barnes and Mr. Browning's developing their tracts together and his not participating, although that would have put him "between a rock and a hard place." Mr. Mullinix testified that his preference was to participate in the Program and that, in fact, he, petitioners, and Mr. Barnes did do so in 1990. Petitioners have failed to convince us that, had they not participated in the Program, joint development was reasonably probable. Mr. Mullinix was a chairman of the board that supervised the Program and served on that board for 10 years. We think that he was strongly motivated to participate in the Program and would have borne some sacrifice to do so. From the stipulation that Mr. Barnes' testimony would have been consistent with that of Mr. Mullinix, we are unwilling to conclude that joint development between petitioners and Mr. Barnes was reasonably probable had petitioners decided to develop the land. We believe that, had petitioners decided against selling the easement to the county, the development of 16 lots on the land was not reasonably probable.

We have considered the testimony of all the experts and, although Mr. Lipman has raised some question in our mind as to the suitability of the land for 15 lots (on account of soil conditions and access), we have not been persuaded to disregard Mr. Benning's testimony, which we found competent and generally persuasive as to the 15 lot scenario. Accordingly, we find that the land was capable of being developed into 15 residential lots. At $45,000 a lot, the value of the land before conveyance of the easement to the county would be $675,000 on a dollar-a-lot basis, which is Mr. Sapperstein's opinion on the basis of the 15 lot scenario. Therefore, we find that the before value of the land on the conveyance date was $675,000.

4. Conclusion

Both of the parties' expert appraisers, Messrs. Lipman and Sapperstein, rejected the purchase prices paid by Howard County under the Program as evidence of the fair market value of any of the development rights conveyed to the county, including the easement conveyed by petitioners. We have considered the before and after valuation opinions of the parties' experts and conclude that the fair market value of the easement on the conveyance date was $518,000.

V. Analysis of the Amount Realized from the Sale of the Easement

Respondent argues that, in addition to the cash payments received and to be received by petitioners from Howard County, petitioners received other valuable consideration: "The record of this case makes clear that petitioners conveyed the development rights easement to Howard County with the expectation of receiving valuable benefits, including cash and anticipated charitable contributions." Respondent argues that the value of tax deferral received from the installment sale of the easement to the county, the tax-free nature of the interest on the county's debt, and the value of the charitable contribution deduction all must be subtracted from the fair market value of the easement in determining the amount of any gift to the county.

Respondent is mistaken. As stated, *supra*, section IV.A., the gift portion of a bargain sale is measured by the difference between the fair market value of the property and the amount realized from the sale. The tax consequences described are not part of the amount realized. Respondent's argument suggests that a taxpayer making a gift of stock worth $100 to a charitable organization may be entitled to a charitable contribution deduction of some lesser amount on account of the economic value of the deduction. That suggestion is untenable. The regulations provide explicitly that, if a charitable contribution is made in property, the amount of the contribution is the fair market value of the property. Sec. 1.170A–1(c)(1), Income Tax Regs.

Respondent's reliance on *DeJong v. Commissioner*, 309 F.2d 373 (9th Cir. 1962), is misplaced. In *DeJong*, this Court found that a portion of the claimed charitable contribution was made in anticipation of the charitable organization providing "free" schooling to the taxpayers' children. The cost of that education reduced the amount of the charitable contribution. In this case, Howard County and petitioners merely structured the easement conveyance in a manner that allowed petitioners to take advantage of certain tax benefits conferred by Congress. None of the tax consequences enjoyed by petitioners constitutes consideration that is to be taken into account in determining the amount realized by petitioners on the sale of the easement.

Respondent has not argued that, if we fail to find that any of the tax consequences constitutes consideration, the consideration received by petitioners in consideration of the conveyance of the easement to the county was other than $309,000. Accordingly, we find that, in consideration of conveying the easement to the county, petitioners received $309,000.

VI. Conclusion

On the conveyance date, petitioners made a charitable contribution to the county in the amount of $209,000 ($518,000–$309,000).

Decisions will be entered for petitioners.

NOTES & QUESTIONS

1.   Conservation restrictions may be deployed for many different purposes. In *Browning*, the easement was created as part of a county program to safeguard agricultural land. The program does not appear to require that properties encumbered by easements be maintained in any landscape configuration or be designated historic. Similar programs aim to foster local economic development or increase food security and do not necessarily have a historic preservation purpose in the strict sense. But they do have impacts that are fully compatible with historic preservation, particularly in places with historically active agricultural communities or in places with particularly distinctive agricultural landscapes.

2.   This case involved valuation for the purposes of receiving a federal income tax deduction. The process described herein has been adopted by states issuing tax incentives and by private entities requiring appraisals for conservation and preservation restrictions. According to the regulations and the Tax Court, what approach should be taken with respect to the methodology of appraisals? What is the significance of the bargain sale? And how does the Tax Court treat the IRS's argument that the tax benefits should be taken into account when evaluating the easement's fair market value?

Browning uses traditional "before and after" valuation to determine whether a tax deduction is appropriate. But what if there is no change in the valuation? If there is no change in valuation, then there is no deduction that can be taken as the restriction does not have a market impact. *See Chandler v. C.I.R.,* 142 T.C. 279 (2014).

3.   In *Browning,* to what extent, and for what purpose, did the court speculate as to the intent of the parties?

4.   A 1986 Tax Court opinion defined "highest and best use" as follows:

In determining the fair market value of property the realistic, objective potential uses for property control the valuation thereof. Thus, in determining the reasonable and probable use that supports the highest present value, we focus on the highest and most profitable use for which the property is adaptable and needed or likely to be needed in the reasonably near future. Moreover, the fair market value of property is not affected by whether the owner actually has put the property to its highest and best use; nor whether he ever intends to do so. Similarly, as long as the highest and best use is not prohibited by law, community opposition to such a use does not preclude us from valuing property as if it were so used.

Symington v. Commissioner, 87 T.C. 892, 896–97 (1986) (citations and quotation marks omitted). In *Browning,* there was no dispute about what constituted the "highest and best use" of the parcel. Can you imagine situations where the "highest and best use" of a parcel would be disputed?

Consider the case of Overlook Farm, a 59-acre site, with a historic manor house and other improvements, along the Potomac River in rural Loudon County, Virginia. The owners of Overlook Farm had granted to a nonprofit organization an "open space" easement which prohibited all new construction and prohibited subdivision. The IRS rejected the value of the easement on which the owners based their charitable contribution deduction. The Tax Court heard arguments from both parties' experts. While both experts agreed that the before-and-after approach should be used in determining the value of the easement and that the highest and best "after" use was a gentleman's country estate, they disagreed about the highest and best use "before" the easement was donated. The property owners' expert argued that the highest and best use of Overlook Farm was for a subdivided parcel containing five to eight luxury homesites. The IRS expert disagreed, concluding that the lack of water and sewage infrastructure, limited access, and political resistance to subdivision rendered any such use infeasible. After walking the site, the judge split the difference, ruling that the highest and best use of the property before the easement donation was for the development of two to four luxury homesites. The judge used this determination in calculating the value of the easement on a per-acre basis. *See Thayer v. Commissioner,* T.C.M. (P-H) 1977–370 (1977).

5.   The expert witnesses in *Browning* were both state-certified general real estate property appraisers. Although every state has licensing or certification programs for appraisals, not all require that a licensed or

certified appraiser be used in the particular case of conservation and preservation restriction appraisals. Just over half of the states, including Maryland, require licensure or certification for appraisals.

b.   THE "TEN TO FIFTEEN PERCENT" RULE

Given the complexity of appraisals, has the legal system developed any rules of thumb upon which property owners may rely? In certain geographic areas and for certain types of real property interests, possibly yes. For example, a 1985 Tax Court case, *Hilborn v. Commissioner*, evaluated competing claims by appraisers and found that a façade easement reduced by 10 percent the value of a historic property within the Vieux Carré (the French Quarter) of New Orleans. 85 T.C. 677, 698–99 (1985). Later courts have accepted the 10 percent figure for similar restrictions in the French Quarter without dispute. *See, e.g., Richmond v. United States*, 699 F.Supp. 578 (E.D. La. 1988) (evaluating the value of a façade easement within the French Quarter and applying the *Hilborn* 10 percent figure).

The Tax Court itself has rejected the notion of a "10 percent rule," however. In a case involving a property in New Orleans just outside the French Quarter, the Tax Court valued a façade easement as 10 percent of the property value but claimed:

> [W]e do not mean to imply that a general "10-percent rule" has been established with respect to facade donations. There was a fair amount of discussion by the parties at trial about whether the Court had established a "10-percent rule" in *Hilborn*. We did not there and do not here. *Hilborn* establishes as acceptable the before and after method of valuation, and while under the circumstances of that case a 10-percent figure was relied upon, valuation itself is still a question of facts and circumstances. Under the facts and circumstances of this case we find the value of the Property decreased 10 percent due to the encumbrance of the facade servitude.

Nicoladis v. Commissioner, T.C.M. (P-H) 1988–163 (1988).

Despite language in *Nicoladis* and other legal precedents, some have misinterpreted Tax Court and IRS decisions as establishing a 10 to 15 percent rule of thumb for the valuation of façade restriction donations. In particular, some land trusts and other easement-holding organizations aggressively advertised this supposed rule of thumb to single-family homeowners. Such advertisements suggested or explicitly stated that the IRS would accept without question valuations of façade restriction donations that fell within the 10 to 15 percent range. Homeowners persuaded to donate restrictions often paid thousands of dollars up front to these organizations, ostensibly to compensate the organizations for their future stewardship.

Such false claims have not gone unnoticed, or unprosecuted. As one recent example, the Trust for Architectural Easements recently settled a lawsuit brought by the Internal Revenue Service, which had audited three hundred owners of property involved with that organization and denied deductions in 70 percent of the cases. *See United States v. McClain*, No. 1:11–cv–01087–GK (D.D.C. 2011). Although it admitted no wrongdoing, the Trust for Architectural Easements was permanently enjoined from telling prospective donors that they may receive tax deductions in certain amounts for donating their façades to the organization and from accepting donations that lack a conservation purpose. *Id.* (July 15, 2011) (stipulated order of permanent injunction). Dealings of the Trust for Architectural Easements, formerly known as the National Architectural Trust, are examined further in the *Herman v. Commissioner*, T.C.M. (RIA) 2009–205, excerpted below.

Does standardization in courts' treatment of appraisals have more benefits than flaws, or vice versa? Consider whether uniform rules of thumb would prevent some of the abuses described in the following Notes.

c.   THE DIFFICULTIES AND ABUSES OF VALUATION

As the cases excerpted above clarify, it may be difficult to determine the value of conservation and preservation restrictions. They are unique legal entities—state-specific creations somewhere between the more popular property forms of easements and covenants. Statutory differences render analogies between restrictions and other forms of servitudes inapposite. At the same time, true market data for conservation and preservation restrictions is elusive because of the dearth of free market exchanges involving restrictions.

Moreover, conservation and preservation restrictions vary tremendously in scope and applicability. They range from a preservation restriction covering a single architectural element of a historic interior to a restriction covering a cluster of outbuildings to a conservation restriction covering hundreds of acres of virgin forest. They may apply to all of part of a single parcel or may extend across multiple parcels. They may (or may not) impose significant affirmative maintenance obligations, insurance provisions, and fees to the restriction holder. They may (or may not) allow subdivision, new construction, or rehabilitation. They may have a public access requirement. Almost any of these characteristics may be either absolute or conditional. Each must be weighed by a fact-finder evaluating a restriction.

As significant as the express language of the restriction itself are any pertinent land use, real estate, subdivision, and historic district regulations. The content of these regulations may overlap with the content of the restriction. If there is a lot of overlap, or if the restriction does not go farther than the regulations, then the restriction may have little effect on the value of the subject property. If the property is located in an area with few or no regulations—say, in a rural, unincorporated area—then a strict restriction may actually diminish the value of the subject property quite a bit.

Even where restrictions and regulations overlap, key differences may nonetheless affect valuation considerations. In general, restrictions may be more restrictive than ordinances. For example, a local historic district ordinance may prohibit changes in use or changes to architectural features, but, unlike a restriction, allow changes to be made subject to review and approval by a local governing body. An ordinance may delay demolition, while a restriction may prohibit it altogether. Ordinances may allow relief for economic hardship, while restrictions may not. The enforcement of ordinances may be affected by politics, just as the enforcement of restrictions may be affected by the level of funding for monitoring. Moreover, while local ordinances may be eliminated or revised, a restriction that runs with the property may be perpetual and may be difficult to amend. A good appraiser understands the regulatory context of the subject property and can evaluate its effects on the value of the restriction.

In part due to the difficulty of evaluating conservation and preservation restrictions, valuations have varied widely. And unfortunately, abuses that take advantage of the gray areas have abounded. A series of articles in 2003 in the *Washington Post* brought the issue of abuses to the fore. In one group of three articles, the authors focused on abuses at the Nature Conservancy, which holds a third of all conservation easements held by land trusts—more than any other single group. *See* Joseph M. Kiesecker et al., *Conservation Easements in Context: A Quantitative Analysis of Their Use by The Nature Conservancy*, 5 FRONTIERS IN ECOLOGY & ENV'T 125, 126 (2007). The *Post* articles described how the land trust had entered into business deals favorable to insiders and helped donors petition the IRS for questionable tax deductions. In one example, a donor gave $18,500,000 cash to the Nature Conservancy and took a charitable deduction for the full amount. The land trust used the $18,500,000 to purchase property to be conserved from the same donor. In this way, federal tax incentives were used to "close the gap" between the donor and the land trust. *See* Joe Stephens & David B. Ottaway, *Landing a Big One: Preservation, Private Development*, WASH. POST, May 6, 2003, at A9.

In another article dealing with broader issues, the authors revealed how property owners overestimated the value of restrictions they had donated to charitable organizations, which allowed them to benefit from huge federal tax breaks. In one instance, a developer placed a restriction over 220 acres, including a golf course shared by residents, of his new 450-acre subdivision. The same developer placed a second restriction over what he described as 131 "unusable acres" that included steep hillsides and floodplains. A town official interviewed for the story said that the developer would have had to keep 60 percent of the parcel as open space under existing regulations even without the restriction. *See* Joe Stephens & David B. Ottaway, *Developers Find Payoff in Preservation*, WASH. POST, Dec. 21, 2003, at A1.

Stories about this developer, the Nature Conservancy, and others inspired Congress, and some states, to make significant reforms to restriction-related tax incentives. In the next section, you will see how the law is now written to stem their abuses.

2. FEDERAL TAX DEDUCTIONS

The tax treatment of conservation and preservation restrictions has greatly impacted the number and scope of such restrictions. The single most significant rule has been Section 170(h) of the Internal Revenue Code, the federal tax deduction for qualified conservation contributions, and related provisions elsewhere in Section 170. This part of the Code establishes when taxpayers can receive an income tax deduction for making a gift of real property to a qualified organization. It is an exception to the general rule that partial interests in real estate may not be deducted. *See* I.R.C. § 170(f)(3)(A).

Tax deductions for conservation and preservation restrictions were initiated on a temporary basis in 1976 for certain restrictions that lasted at least thirty years. In 1980, Congress made the temporary program permanent and added the requirements that constitute the core of the tax credit program today, including that, to quality for a tax deduction, a restriction must last into perpetuity. In 2006, as part of the Pension Protection Act, revisions to Section 170 were made to combat some of the abuses of the deduction that had recently been widely publicized. Among other changes, the 2006 revisions and related regulations from the Department of the Treasury: clarified the type of property eligible for deductions, including property already in historic districts; required certified statements from both donors and donees regarding the capabilities of the donee to hold the conservation or preservation restriction; required other documentation regarding the value of the restriction; and imposed new, standardized qualifications for appraisers.

As the notes after the following excerpt suggest, judicial review of claimed tax deductions for conservation and preservation restrictions has been very active. Since 2006, more than a hundred tax court cases have involved conservation and preservation restrictions.

Qualified Conservation Contribution Provisions
I.R.C. § 170

(b) Percentage limitations.

(1) Individuals. * * *

(E) Contributions of qualified conservation contributions.

(i)   In general. Any qualified conservation contribution (as defined in subsection (h)(1)) shall be allowed to the extent the aggregate of such contributions does not exceed the excess of 50 percent of the taxpayer's contribution base over the amount of all other charitable contributions allowable under this paragraph.

(ii) Carryover. If the aggregate amount of contributions described in clause (i) exceeds the limitation of clause (i), such excess shall be treated (in a manner consistent with the rules of subsection (d)(1)) as a charitable contribution to which clause (i) applies in each of the 15 succeeding years in order of time. * * *

(f)   Disallowance of deduction in certain cases and special rules. * * *

(8)   Substantiation requirement for certain contributions.

(A)   General rule. No deduction shall be allowed under subsection (a) for any contribution of $250 or more unless the taxpayer substantiates the contribution by a contemporaneous written acknowledgment of the contribution by the donee organization that meets the requirements of subparagraph (B). * * *

(11) Qualified appraisal and other documentation for certain contributions. * * *

(C)   Qualified appraisal for contributions of more than $5,000. In the case of contributions of property for which a deduction of more than $5,000 is claimed, the requirements of this subparagraph are met if the individual, partnership, or corporation obtains a qualified appraisal of such property and attaches to the return for the taxable year in which such contribution is made such information regarding such property and such appraisal as the Secretary may require.

(D)   Substantiation for contributions of more than $500,000. In the case of contributions of property for which a deduction of more than $500,000 is claimed, the requirements of this subparagraph are met if the individual, partnership, or corporation attaches to the return for the taxable year a qualified appraisal of such property.

(E)   Qualified appraisal and appraiser. For purposes of this paragraph—

(i)   Qualified appraisal. The term "qualified appraisal" means, with respect to any property, an appraisal of such property which—

(I)   is treated for purposes of this paragraph as a qualified appraisal under regulations or other guidance prescribed by the Secretary, and

(II) is conducted by a qualified appraiser in accordance with generally accepted appraisal standards and any regulations or other guidance prescribed under subclause (I).

(ii) Qualified appraiser. Except as provided in clause (iii), the term "qualified appraiser" means an individual who—

(I) has earned an appraisal designation from a recognized professional appraiser organization or has otherwise met minimum education and experience requirements set forth in regulations prescribed by the Secretary,

(II) regularly performs appraisals for which the individual receives compensation, and

(III) meets such other requirements as may be prescribed by the Secretary in regulations or other guidance.

(iii) Specific appraisals. An individual shall not be treated as a qualified appraiser with respect to any specific appraisal unless—

(I) the individual demonstrates verifiable education and experience in valuing the type of property subject to the appraisal, and

(II) the individual has not been prohibited from practicing before the Internal Revenue Service by the Secretary under section 330(c) of Title 31, United States Code, at any time during the 3-year period ending on the date of the appraisal. * * *

(h) Qualified conservation contribution.

(1) In general. For purposes of subsection (f)(3)(B)(iii), the term "qualified conservation contribution" means a contribution—

(A) of a qualified real property interest,

(B) to a qualified organization,

(C) exclusively for conservation purposes.

(2) Qualified real property interest. For purposes of this subsection, the term "qualified real property interest" means any of the following interests in real property:

(A) the entire interest of the donor other than a qualified mineral interest,

(B) a remainder interest, and

(C) a restriction (granted in perpetuity) on the use which may be made of the real property.

(3) Qualified organization. For purposes of paragraph (1), the term "qualified organization" means an organization which—

(A) is described in clause (v) or (vi) of subsection (b)(1)(A), or

(B) is described in section 501(c)(3) and—

(i) meets the requirements of section 509(a)(2), or

(ii) meets the requirements of section 509(a)(3) and is controlled by an organization described in subparagraph (A) or in clause (i) of this subparagraph.

(4) Conservation purpose defined.

(A) In general. For purposes of this subsection, the term "conservation purpose" means—

(i)   the preservation of land areas for outdoor recreation by, or the education of, the general public,

(ii) the protection of a relatively natural habitat of fish, wildlife, or plants, or similar ecosystem,

(iii) the preservation of open space (including farmland and forest land) where such preservation is—

(I)   for the scenic enjoyment of the general public, or

(II) pursuant to a clearly delineated Federal, State, or local governmental conservation policy,

and will yield a significant public benefit, or

(iv) the preservation of an historically important land area or a certified historic structure.

(B) Special rules with respect to buildings in registered historic districts. In the case of any contribution of a qualified real property interest which is a restriction with respect to the exterior of a building described in subparagraph (C)(ii), such contribution shall not be considered to be exclusively for conservation purposes unless—

(i)   such interest—

(I)   includes a restriction which preserves the entire exterior of the building (including the front, sides, rear, and height of the building), and

(II) prohibits any change in the exterior of the building which is inconsistent with the historical character of such exterior,

(ii) the donor and donee enter into a written agreement certifying, under penalty of perjury, that the donee—

(I)   is a qualified organization (as defined in paragraph (3)) with a purpose of environmental protection, land conservation, open space preservation, or historic preservation, and

(II) has the resources to manage and enforce the restriction and a commitment to do so, and

(iii) in the case of any contribution made in a taxable year beginning after the date of the enactment of this subparagraph, the taxpayer includes with the taxpayer's return for the taxable year of the contribution—

(I)　a qualified appraisal (within the meaning of subsection (f)(11)(E)) of the qualified property interest,

(II)　photographs of the entire exterior of the building, and

(III) a description of all restrictions on the development of the building.

(C)　Certified historic structure. For purposes of subparagraph (A)(iv), the term "certified historic structure" means—

(i)　any building, structure, or land area which is listed in the National Register, or

(ii)　any building which is located in a registered historic district (as defined in section 47(c)(3)(B)) and is certified by the Secretary of the Interior to the Secretary as being of historic significance to the district. A building, structure, or land area satisfies the preceding sentence if it satisfies such sentence either at the time of the transfer or on the due date (including extensions) for filing the transferor's return under this chapter for the taxable year in which the transfer is made.

(5)　Exclusively for conservation purposes. For purposes of this subsection—

(A)　Conservation purpose must be protected. A contribution shall not be treated as exclusively for conservation purposes unless the conservation purpose is protected in perpetuity.

(B)　No surface mining permitted. * * *

NOTES & QUESTIONS

1.　What limitations are placed on a taxpayer's ability to take a qualified conservation contribution deduction in any given tax year? Over how many years can a taxpayer spread out a deduction? Note that section 170(b)(1)(E) had previously limited the annual deductible amount to thirty percent of a taxpayer's contribution base—defined in section 170(b)(1)(G)ᵧY as "adjusted gross income (computed without regard to any net operating loss carryback to the taxable year under section 172)"—and limited the carryover period to five years.

In some states, a qualified conservation contribution deduction can be limited by failing to record the restriction within the proper tax year. In *Zarlengo* v. C.I.R., T.C. Memo. 2014–161, a restriction created in 2004 but not recorded until 2005 was not a qualified contribution under New York state law. The failure to record also violated the perpetuity requirements of section 170(h)(2)(C) for the tax year before the recording of the restriction.

2.　Consider the substantiation requirements of section 170(f)(8). In a 2011 case, the Tax Court considered whether to grant the IRS's motion for summary judgment regarding a petition for reconsideration by married taxpayers claiming a deduction on their federal income tax for a charitable contribution of a façade easement to a nonprofit organization, the Alabama Historical Commission. The deduction had been disallowed by the IRS on the basis that the taxpayers failed to obtain a contemporaneous written acknowledgment of the contribution from the Commission, as is required by section 170(f)(8). The taxpayers argued that they had entered into a "Preservation and Conservation Easement Agreement" that met the requirements of section 170(f)(8). The agreement stated:

> for and in consideration of the sum of TEN DOLLARS, plus other good and valuable consideration, the receipt and sufficiency of which are hereby acknowledged, the Grantor [petitioner] does hereby irrevocably GRANT, BARGAIN, SELL, AND CONVEY unto the Grantee [the commission], its successors and assigns, a preservation and conservation easement to have and hold in perpetuity.

Schrimsher v. Commissioner, T.C.M. (RIA) 2011–71, *1 (2011). In addition, the agreement contained a merger clause indicating that it represented the full transaction and any prior discussions were reflected within it. The Tax Court was unsympathetic, granting the IRS's motion for summary judgment after finding that the recital of consideration, whether considered with the merger clause or not, was insufficient because it failed to explicitly state whether the Commission provided no, or some, services in exchange for the façade easement donation, as required by section 170(f)(8)(B)(ii).

3.   How do the "qualified appraisal" and "qualified appraiser" provisions excerpted from section 170(f)(11) work? Understanding the provisions can be incredibly important, as substantial compliance doctrine may not be enough to satisfy the provisions. *See Rothman v. C.I.R.*, T.C. Memo. 2012–218 (confirming *Rothman v. C.I.R.*, T.C. Memo. 2012–163 decision that multiple instances of the appraiser's failure to meet the provisions did not establish substantial compliance.)

4.   What does the "granted in perpetuity" requirement of section 170(h)(c)(2) mean? The Treasury Regulations state that, for a restriction to be considered enforceable in perpetuity, any mortgage encumbering it must include a subordination of rights by the mortgagee (the lender) to the qualified organization to preserve the restricted property in perpetuity. Treas. Reg. § 1.170A–14(g)(2). Similarly, if a restriction is extinguished by a judicial proceeding, all of the proceeds from a sale or exchange must be "used by the donee organization in a manner consistent with the conservation purposes of the original contribution." *Id.* § 1.170A–14(g)(6).

Consider two cases that have addressed the perpetuity requirement. The first case involved a façade easement donated to the National Architectural Trust, which was subject to a mortgage in which the mortgagee retained a "prior claim" to proceeds related to condemnation and insurance process in the event of any accident, hazard, or casualty. The First Circuit panel deciding the case found that the IRS's interpretation that the mortgagee's priority over such proceeds violated the perpetuity requirement was not reasonable and thus not entitled to deference. *Kaufman v. Shulman*,

687 F.3d 21, 28 (1st Cir. 2012). Subsequently, the court determined that the façade easement had no value and imposed penalties on the owner. *Kaufman v. C.I.R.*, 784 F.3d 56 (1st Cir. 2015).

The second case involved two façade easements donated to the D.C.-based L'Enfant Trust, which holds over 1,100 easements. Among other provisions, the deeds for these two easements allowed the L'Enfant Trust to consent to changes in the façade or to abandon its rights to the easements. The IRS argued that such provisions rendered the donation non-deductible because the easements were not given in perpetuity and thus were not "exclusively for conservation purposes" under section 170(h)(1)(C). The Court of Appeals for the D.C. Circuit disagreed, stating that the ability to approve changes allows for flexibility for the use of historic structures by future generations. The court added:

> The deeds impose an affirmative obligation upon Simmons "in perpetuity" to maintain the properties in a manner consistent with their historic character and grant L'Enfant the authority to inspect the properties and to enforce the easements. By their terms, the deeds will "survive any termination of Grantor's or the Grantee's existence." Although the deeds do not spell out precisely what would happen upon the dissolution of L'Enfant, D.C. law provides the easements would be transferred to another organization that engages in "activities substantially similar to those of" L'Enfant. D.C. CODE §§ 29–301.48, 29–301.56.

Commissioner v. Simmons, 646 F.3d 6, 10 (D.C. Cir. 2011). Preservation groups such as the National Trust for Historic Preservation cheered this decision for protecting organizations that hold conservation and preservation restrictions from what they termed the "IRS's assault." What does this conclusion suggest about the impact of state laws dealing on a court's review of the perpetuity requirement?

5.   Like other parts of section 170, section 170(h)(4)(A)(ii)—which establishes as a conservation purpose "the protection of a relatively natural habitat of fish, wildlife, or plants, or similar ecosystem"—has been further defined in regulations and in the court system. In *Glass v. Commissioner*, 471 F.3d 698 (6th Cir. 2006), the Sixth Circuit considered the donation of two discontinuous easements on a parcel bordering the Lake Michigan shoreline for approximately 460 feet. One easement constituted the northernmost 150 feet of shoreline and the other constituted the southernmost 260 feet of shoreline. Each extended just 120 feet landward from the ordinary high water mark. Experts testified that threatened species, including the Lake Huron tansy, pitcher's thistle, and bald eagles either used, or could use, the easement property as their habitat. Were these small parcels significant enough to satisfy the conservation purposes requirement for the tax deduction? The Sixth Circuit said yes. The court reviewed Treasury Regulations, which included "habitats for rare, endangered, or threatened species of animal, fish, or plants" among those types of properties satisfying the conservation purposes requirement. Treas. Reg. § 1.170A–14(d)(3). Should conservation restrictions covering habitat for threatened species

categorically be deemed to meet the conservation purposes requirement, regardless of size?

6.   Note that there are special provisions for buildings within historic districts. What is the purpose of section 170(h)(4)(B)? Is it overly prescriptive, or is such specificity necessary to stem potential abuses? The following case involved a tax return filed prior to Congress's addition of section 170(h)(4)(B) as part of the 2006 Pension Protection Act. It may shed light on Congress's rationale for including that section.

Herman v. Commissioner
T.C.M. (RIA) 2009–205

■ GUSTAFSON, JUDGE.

The Internal Revenue Service (IRS) determined a deficiency of $3,906,531 in petitioner J. Maurice Herman's 2003 Federal income tax and an accompanying accuracy-related penalty under section 6662(h) of $1,562,612.40. Mr. Herman petitioned this Court, pursuant to section 6213(a), to redetermine this deficiency and penalty. The case is now before the Court on respondent's motion for partial summary judgment pursuant to Rule 121. The issue for decision is whether Mr. Herman's contribution of a conservation easement with respect to unused development rights over property held by his wholly owned New York limited liability company, Windsor Plaza, L.L.C. (Windsor), preserves a "historically important land area" or a "certified historic structure" within the meaning of section 170(h)(4)(A)(iv) to meet the "conservation purpose" requirement of section 170(h)(1)(C) and (h)(4). For the reasons discussed below, we will grant respondent's motion. * * *

Title to the Fifth Avenue Property

Since 1975 Mr. Herman has owned directly or indirectly property on Fifth Avenue in New York, New York (the Fifth Avenue property). The Fifth Avenue property is improved with an eleven-story apartment building designed by the late Henry Otis Chapman in 1923 in the neo-Italianate Renaissance style of architecture. The building stands eight stories high at its front and eleven stories high at its rear, and stands within a row of taller buildings. Each building in that row stands immediately adjacent to the neighboring buildings on either side of it, and there is no undeveloped space between the building on the Fifth Avenue property and the taller buildings that abut it. These taller buildings are of approximately equal height to each other, and the building at issue is said to have the unfortunate appearance of a "chipped tooth"—first, because it is the only shorter building in the immediate vicinity, and second, because its front section stands only eight stories high, whereas its back section stands eleven stories high. Thus, when viewed from the street, the building's shorter front section appears to be chipped or incomplete.

On August 5, 1998, Mr. Herman transferred his rights, title, and interest in the Fifth Avenue property to Windsor, and a deed was recorded to reflect that transfer. Less than 5 months later, on December 31, 1998, by a document entitled "Assignment," Windsor transferred, assigned, and delivered to Mr. Herman all of its rights, title, and interest in and to all of its unused development rights with respect to the Fifth Avenue property, i.e., the rights to further develop the property by, among other things, adding additional floors to the preexisting building on the property. On the same day, by a document entitled "Agreement," Windsor agreed "along with its successors and assigns, to assist, and in no way withhold consent, the Assignee [i.e., Mr. Herman] his successors and assigns, in any manner the Assignee shall reasonably require in the development, improvement, sale, transfer, assignment or other disposition without limitation, of the aforementioned unused development rights." Neither the Assignment nor the Agreement was recorded.

Figure 10-1:
The "Chipped Tooth" at 952 Fifth Avenue,
Manhattan, NY

Historic Significance of the Fifth Avenue Property

The Fifth Avenue property is in the "Upper East Side Historic District," which is designated (i) a "registered historic district" within the meaning of section 47(c)(3)(B) by the Secretary of the Interior through the National Park Service (NPS), a bureau within the U.S. Department of the Interior; and (ii) a historic district by New York City and its Landmarks Preservation Commission.

The Landmarks Preservation Commission is the local government agency charged with "the protection, preservation, enhancement, perpetuation and use of landmarks, interior landmarks, scenic landmarks and historic districts" in New York City. N.Y.C. ADMIN. CODE § 25–303. It is responsible for designating landmarks and historic districts and regulating changes to those landmarks and historic districts. *Id.* In New York City it is unlawful to alter, reconstruct, or demolish a building in a historic district, like the building on the 5th Avenue property, without the prior consent of the Landmarks Preservation Commission. *Id.* § 25–305. In determining when to grant its consent to any change to a building, the Landmarks Preservation Commission must consider the effect of the proposed change on the exterior architectural features of the building and the relationship between the results of the proposed change on the building and the exterior architectural features of other neighboring buildings in the historic district. *Id.* § 25–307.

On August 27, 2003, Mr. Herman executed a form entitled "National Park Service Historic Preservation Certification Application Part 1— Evaluation of Significance," requesting the NPS to certify the historic significance of the Fifth Avenue property. Mr. Herman's request was reviewed by the NPS, and it determined that the Fifth Avenue property contributes to the significance of the Upper East Side Historic District and is a "certified historic structure" within the meaning of section 170(h)(4)(B)(ii). Neither Mr. Herman's request nor the NPS's determination specifies whether the apartment building, the underlying land, or the unused development rights are to be included in or excluded from the NPS's determination. However, neither party disputes that the apartment building was included in the NPS's determination and is a "certified historic structure."

Contribution of Conservation Easement on the Fifth Avenue Property

On December 15, 2003, Mr. Herman contributed the conservation easement at issue to the National Architectural Trust, Inc. (NAT), a nonprofit section 501(c)(3) organization (currently known as the Trust for Architectural Easements) by executing a document entitled "Declaration of Restrictive Covenant" (Covenant). On December 30, 2003, the Covenant was recorded in the Office of the City Register of the City of New York. The parties to the Covenant include Mr. Herman as the "Grantor," NAT as the Donee, and Windsor as the "Confirming Party." The term "Confirming Party" is not defined in the Covenant and has no defined meaning under New York law.

The Covenant restricts the development of 10,000 unspecified square feet of the 22,000 square feet of unused development right over the Fifth Avenue property:

WHEREAS, on December 31, 1998, Confirming Party owned the [Fifth Avenue property]:

WHEREAS, on December 31, 1998, Confirming Party transferred to Grantor all of Confirming Party's right, title and interest in and to all of Confirming Party's then unused development rights (the "Air Space") with respect to such [Fifth Avenue property];

WHEREAS, Confirming Party continues to own such [Fifth Avenue property], other than the Air Space (such property other than the Air Space is the "Property");

WHEREAS, *the Property's conservation and preservation values will be documented in the appraisal report of Jefferson Lee Appraisals, Inc., Pittsburgh, Pennsylvania* (the "Baseline Documentation"), *which will be incorporated herein by reference;*

WHEREAS, the grant of a conservation restriction by Grantor to Donee with respect to the Restricted Air Space *will assist in preserving and maintaining the Property and its architectural, historic and cultural features for the benefit of the people of the City of New York, the State of New York and the United States of America;*

1.   *Grantor, for the benefit of Donee (and its successors and assigns), does hereby agree that he will not build or otherwise improve 10,000 square feet of the Air Space* (the "Restricted Air Space"). The restrictive covenant imposed by the Paragraph 1 is the "Restrictive Covenant."

1.   *It is the purpose of the Restrictive Covenant to prevent development of the Restricted Air Space that would significantly diminish the Property's conservation and preservation values by removing the right to develop the additional housing and/or structures in the Restricted Air Space.*

3.   Grantor hereby agrees with Donee (and its successors and assigns) that he will not take any action with respect to the remaining Air Space (other than the Restricted Air Space) (such remaining Air Space other than the Restricted Air Space is the "Unrestricted Air Space") that is inconsistent with the applicable restrictions, if any, imposed by the New York City Landmarks Preservation Commission. Grantor agrees that any new construction work or rehabilitation work in the Unrestricted Air Space, whether or not Donee has given consent to undertake the same, will comply with the requirements of all applicable federal, state and local governmental law and regulations. *Confirming Party agrees that any new construction or rehabilitation work on the Property, whether or not Donee has given consent to undertake the same, will comply with the requirements of all applicable federal, state and local governmental law and regulations.* Grantor further agrees that, to the extent the height or density of the Unrestricted Air Space may be increased beyond that which exists as of the date of this Declaration by any action of the City of New York, such

additional height and/or density shall not be utilized for any construction over and above or adjacent to the Property.

16. *Confirming Party hereby agrees with Donee (and its successors and assigns) that it will not take any action that is inconsistent with the Restrictive Covenant* and that, at the request of Donee, it will deliver such instruments of further assurance relating to the Restrictive Covenant as may be requested by Donee. *Subject to the preceding sentence, nothing in this Declaration shall place a limit on the use of the Property.* (Emphasis added.)

Appraisal Report

Jefferson & Lee Appraisals, Inc. prepared an appraisal report for Mr. Herman that purports to calculate the diminution in value to the Fifth Avenue property resulting from the donation of the conservation easement. * * *

The appraisal report includes "[p]lans for building expansion" with respect to the apartment building on the Fifth Avenue property. These plans project hypothetical expansions to the existing apartment building "[i]n order to take potential maximum advantage of the allowable density" both before and after the donation of the conservation easement, and they include drawings of those hypothetical expansions. These drawings show a sixteen-story building (with sixteen stories at both the front and the rear of the building) before the donation, and a thirteen-story building (with thirteen stories at both front and rear) after the donation. Jefferson & Lee Appraisals, Inc., calculated the diminution in value to the Fifth Avenue property resulting from the donation of the conservation easement to be $21,850,000. * * *

Discussion

The question now before the Court is whether Mr. Herman's contribution of the easement had, as its exclusive purpose, "the *preservation* of an historically important *land area* or a certified historic *structure*" (emphasis added), within the meaning of section 170(h)(4)(A)(iv). Mr. Herman did not own, and did not contribute, any interest in either the existing structure at the Fifth Avenue property or the land on which it was built. The "air rights" easement that he did contribute did not oblige him to preserve—and he did not have the power to preserve—the structure of the existing building or the underlying land. Any undertaking that the structure would be preserved was made (if at all) by Windsor as the "Confirming Party" and not by Mr. Herman; and any assurance in the Covenant that the structure would be preserved was redundant of restrictions imposed by New York City's Administrative Code and the Landmarks Preservation Commission that implements those restrictions. Mr. Herman's easement did not, by its terms, specify which portion of the air space would not be developed, did not restrict him to the three-story proposal in the unrecorded appraisal report, and did not prohibit him or a subsequent bona fide purchaser from building six stories over any half (front, back, or side) of the existing building. Respondent contends that the conservation easement does not "preserv[e] * * * an historically important land area or a certified historic structure" within the meaning of section 170(h)(4)(A)(iv). We agree. * * *

III. Analysis of Mr. Herman's Easement

The historic preservation requirement of section 170(h)(4)(A)(iv) is met by showing the preservation of a "historically important land area" or "certified historic structure." Mr. Herman argues in the alternative that limiting the development of the apartment building on the Fifth Avenue property preserves either (i) a "certified historic structure," i.e., the apartment building, or (ii) a "historically important land area," i.e., the underlying property. Mr. Herman also argues that even if the conservation easement does not restrict the alteration or demolition of the apartment building, a restriction on "air rights" or "unused development rights" above that building is sufficient in and of itself to preserve the apartment building or the underlying land for purposes of section 170(h)(4)(A)(iv).

A.   Preservation of a Certified Historic Structure

The apartment building on the Fifth Avenue property is a "certified historic structure" within the meaning of section 170(h)(4)(B)(ii) because it was certified as such by the Secretary of the Interior through the NPS in response to Mr. Herman's request on August 27, 2003. Therefore, if the conservation easement at issue did in fact have the purpose of preserving the apartment building as a "certified historic structure," it would have been contributed "exclusively for conservation purposes" and Mr. Herman would be entitled to a deduction under section 170(a)(1). As a result, the determinative question is whether the conservation easement did in fact have the purpose of "preserv[ing]" the "structure" of the apartment building.

1.   Provisions of the Easement

The conservation easement restricts the development of 10,000 unspecified square feet of Mr. Herman's unused development rights over the apartment building on the Fifth Avenue property. The Covenant, which created the conservation easement, states that the donation of 10,000 square feet of the unused development rights "will assist in preserving and maintaining the Property and its architectural, historic and cultural features for the benefit of the people of the City of New York, the State of New York and the United States of America." However, by its own terms, the Covenant merely restricts the development of 10,000 square feet of the unused development rights over the existing apartment building. It does not preclude Mr. Herman, Windsor, or subsequent purchasers of the Fifth Avenue property from altering or even demolishing that existing building.

"[A] deduction will not be allowed if the contribution would accomplish one of the enumerated conservation purposes but would permit the destruction of other significant conservation interests." Sec. 1.170A–14(e)(2), Income Tax Regs. Assuming arguendo that limiting the development of the apartment building by 10,000 square feet does, in some way, preserve that building, the Covenant does not preclude the possibility that the building may be altered or even demolished. This allowance permits the destruction of what is clearly the most significant conservation purpose in the instant case—preserving the apartment building that was determined to be a "certified historic structure" by the NPS.

2.   Mr. Herman's Contentions

Mr. Herman contends that this analysis is flawed, because he, Windsor, and subsequent purchasers are restricted from altering or demolishing the apartment building under the terms of the Covenant and local law. Mr. Herman points to paragraph 16 of the Covenant, where Windsor, as the Confirming Party, agreed "that it will not take any action that is inconsistent with the Restrictive Covenant." He argues that demolishing the apartment building would be inconsistent with the stated purpose of the Covenant to "assist in preserving and maintaining the Property," which includes the apartment building.

Mr. Herman further argues that the appraisal report he commissioned from Jefferson & Lee Appraisals, Inc., including an attached drawing which illustrates a hypothetical expansion of the apartment building after the donation of the conservation easement, is incorporated in the Covenant by reference, because it was mentioned in the eleventh "WHEREAS" clause:

> WHEREAS, the Property's conservation and preservation values will be documented in the appraisal report of Jefferson Lee Appraisals, Inc., Pittsburgh, Pennsylvania (the "Baseline Documentation"), which will be incorporated herein by reference * * *.

He contends that the attached drawing illustrates the only permissible development of the apartment building after the donation of the conservation easement, and prevents him, Windsor, and subsequent purchasers from altering the building in a manner that is inconsistent with the attached drawing. Therefore, he argues, the only permissible alteration to the building would be the hypothetical expansion depicted in the drawing, i.e., to increase the height of the apartment building to thirteen stories, with the same number of stories at both the front and the rear. He correctly notes that this particular alteration would raise the apartment building's height to that of the other buildings on either side of it and heal its current "chipped tooth" appearance, arguably increasing the building's aesthetic and historical value.

However, Mr. Herman's contentions lack merit.

a.   Any Commitment To Preserve the Structure Under the Covenant Is Made by Windsor.

Paragraph 16 of the Covenant, on which Mr. Herman heavily relies, reflects undertakings by Windsor, not by Mr. Herman. Any preservation that results from Windsor's undertakings under this paragraph is not by way of a contribution from Mr. Herman and could not entitle him to the charitable contribution deduction that he claimed. Moreover, paragraph 16 merely provides that Windsor "will not take any action that is inconsistent with the Restrictive Covenant." That is, paragraph 16 arguably obliges Windsor to honor restrictions that are provided elsewhere in the Covenant and does not itself define what those restrictions are.

b.   The Covenant Does Not Preserve the Structure.

The Covenant restricts only the development of 10,000 unspecified square feet of unused development rights over the apartment building. In fact, the third sentence of paragraph 16 provides that "nothing in this Declaration shall place a limit on the use of the Property." In light of that provision, even demolishing the apartment building altogether would not be inconsistent with the Covenant. Building up only the front or only the rear of the apartment building above the neighboring buildings would likewise be consistent with the Covenant.

It might be argued that the appearance of a structure is "preserved" in an aesthetic sense by an easement that prevents vertical development above its existing height. Assuming arguendo that there can be circumstances in which an "air rights" easement accomplishes the preservation of a "structure," Mr. Herman's easement nonetheless fails to do so.

First, if Mr. Herman were to use his retained air rights to build up a full six stories, but only on the front half of the building, he would thereby create a facade that completely filled up the visible portion of the maximum height of the building. In that circumstance, the donated air rights held by the NAT as to the back half of the building would be totally hidden behind the developed front half of the building. The donated air rights would then have no function at all in preserving even the aesthetic values associated with preventing upward development.

Second, even if the retained air rights were used only to build three full stories, leaving three full stories' worth of space empty on top of the building, the original structure would not have been "preserved" at its original height. The donated air space would hover over an altered structure, not preserving the "certified historic structure" but instead preserving an unhistorical building consisting of the historic structure plus three newly developed stories. It could not fairly be said that the easement barring development of the top three stories somehow preserved the "certified historic structure" from which it was separated by three new stories. Moreover, the Covenant did not assure that the development would be three full stories, as we now show.

      c.   The Appraisal Report and the Attached Drawing Do Not Modify the Covenant To Limit the Development of the Building.

With respect to the appraisal report and the attached drawing, New York law provides that when a "contract is unambiguous on its face, there is no need to refer to its recitals, which are not part of the operative agreement." *Jones Apparel Group, Inc. v. Polo Ralph Lauren Corp.*, 791 N.Y.S.2d 409, 410 (App. Div. 2005). Since we hold that the Covenant is unambiguous on its face—stating that it restricts the development of 10,000 unspecified square feet of unused development rights without mention of other restrictions on the development or alteration of the apartment building—there is no need to refer to the recitals, including the eleventh "WHEREAS" clause in the Covenant, which incorporates the appraisal report and the attached drawing by reference. Even assuming arguendo that the attached drawing was part of the Covenant, the drawing was (the clause says) incorporated simply to "document [ ]" the "conservation and preservation *values*" (emphasis added) of the Fifth Avenue property—not to illustrate the only permissible development of the apartment building after the donation of the conservation easement.

Finally, even assuming arguendo that the attached drawing was part of the Covenant and was incorporated by reference to illustrate the only permissible development of the apartment building, that drawing and its mandate would not be binding on subsequent purchasers of the Fifth Avenue property because it was left unrecorded. For purposes of summary judgment, we assume that it was the intent of Mr. Herman as the owner of the retained development rights (and as the owner of Windsor, which owned the underlying building) to preserve the structure and appearance of the building and to limit development in a manner consistent with that preservation. However, the donation consisted not of Mr. Herman's intentions but of what he actually conveyed by the easement as written and recorded. To effect a contribution for a "conservation purpose * * * in perpetuity" (as required by section 170(h)(5)(A)), Mr. Herman needed to create a limitation that would survive the sale of the building and the sale of the remaining development rights to a bona fide purchaser who might not share Mr. Herman's subjective intentions. Unless that bona fide purchaser would be legally bound to the limitations depicted in the drawing, the easement failed to protect a conservation purpose in perpetuity.

Under N.Y. REAL PROP. LAW § 291–e (McKinney 2006), if an "exception, reservation or recital" refers to an unrecorded document, like the attached drawing, the reference does not affect the marketability of title or bind subsequent purchasers. *See also L.C. Stroh & Sons, Inc. v. Batavia Homes & Dev. Corp.*, 17 A.D.2d 385, 234 N.Y.S.2d 401, 405 (App.Div.1962) (N.Y. REAL PROP. LAW § 291–e "expressly relieves a prospective purchaser from the obligation of inquiring or examining into the facts and states that an exception, reservation or recital gives no notice beyond the recital itself. In other words, it rescinds the former rule that, upon notice of a recital such as that in question, one who was interested as a potential purchaser would have been charged with any knowledge that a reasonable inquiry would have produced"). Since the attached drawing could not bind subsequent purchasers, it did not protect the conservation purpose of preserving the apartment building "in perpetuity" and fails to meet the requirement of section 170(h)(5)(A).

d.   The Protections Afforded by Local Law Will Not Support a Deduction.

Mr. Herman contends that in addition to the terms of the Covenant, we must take into account local ordinances that could prohibit the alteration or demolition of the apartment building. We disagree. The protections afforded to the building by Federal, State, or local law, whatever they may be, are not part of the conservation easement that Mr. Herman contributed to NAT, and he is not entitled to a deduction under section 170(a)(1) for or because of them. In fact, it is local law and the rules of the Landmarks Preservation Commission that will preserve the building. Any right that the donee possesses under the Covenant to sue the donor to enforce the terms of the Covenant is, by definition, redundant of the Landmarks Preservation Commission's role of enforcing its regulations and preventing inappropriate alterations to the building.[5]

B.   Preservation of a Historically Important Land Area

Mr. Herman argues in the alternative that his contribution of the conservation easement preserves the land underlying the building, which he further contends is a historically important land area. The legislative history underlying section 170(h)(4)(A)(iv) describes a "historically important land area" as one that is important in its own right or in relation to "certified historic structures":

> The term "historically important land area" is intended to include independently significant land areas (for example, a civil war battlefield) and historic sites and related land areas, the physical or environmental features of which contribute to the historic or cultural importance and continuing integrity of certified historic structures such as Mount Vernon, or historic districts, such as Waterford, Virginia, or Harper's Ferry, West Virginia. For example, the integrity of a certified historic

---

[5]   As Mr. Herman's counsel explained at argument, the Covenant "say [s] that you [the donor] must do whatever the Landmarks Preservation Commission's rules require, and giving the NAT [the donee] the right of enforcement." He argued that the Landmarks Preservation Commission is an inadequate enforcer of its own rules and that the creation of a donee's private right to sue was an important contribution to preservation, but this argument has no evidentiary support in the record. In any event, it is difficult to justify a charitable contribution deduction for an owner's agreement to refrain from doing what he is already legally forbidden to do.

structure may be protected under this provision by perpetual restrictions on the development of such a related land area. * * *

S. REP. NO. 96–1007, at 12 (1980). The regulations under section 170(h)(4)(A)(iv) are consistent with the legislative history and provide a nonexclusive list of three categories of "historically important land area[s]":

(A) An independently significant land area including any related historic resources (for example, an archaeological site or a Civil War battlefield with related monuments, bridges, cannons, or houses) that meets the National Register Criteria for Evaluation in 36 C.F.R. 60.4 (Pub.L. 89–665, 80 Stat. 915);

(B) Any land area within a registered historic district including any buildings on the land area that can reasonably be considered as contributing to the significance of the district; and

(C) Any land area (including related historic resources) adjacent to a property listed individually in the National Register of Historic Places (but not within a registered historic district) in a case where the physical or environmental features of the land area contribute to the historic or cultural integrity of the property.

Sec. 1.170A–14(d)(5)(ii), Income Tax Regs. Assuming arguendo that the Fifth Avenue property is a "historically important land area" within the meaning of section 170(h)(4)(A)(iv), the undisputed facts in the record show that the conservation easement fails to preserve the underlying land.

Mr. Herman has not alleged, nor would the record support an inference, that the underlying land has independent historical significance, like a civil war battlefield. Thus, the underlying land could be a "historically important land area" only because of its proximity and relation to the apartment building on the Fifth Avenue property, which is a "certified historic structure." *See Turner v. Commissioner*, 126 T.C. 299, 316 (2006); S. REP. NO. 96–1007, at 12 (1980). The land's physical feature "which [contributes] to the historic or cultural importance" of the apartment building is simply its function as that building's foundation. *See* S. REP., *supra* at 12. As we discussed, *supra* section III.A.1, the conservation easement does not prevent the alteration or demolition of the apartment building. Therefore, it likewise does not protect the historic significance of the underlying land, which is simply to serve as the foundation of the apartment building.

C.   Restriction Solely on "Air Rights" or "Unused Development Rights"

Both parties acknowledge that there is no precedent that is directly on point, and we are aware of none. However, Mr. Herman cites *Dorsey v. Commissioner*, T.C.M. (P-H) 1990–242, as authority for the proposition that a conservation easement solely with respect to "air rights" or "unused development rights" may preserve a "historically important land area" or "certified historic structure." In *Dorsey*, however, the taxpayers donated to a charitable organization a conservation easement over a building that included (inter alia) a facade easement and air rights. Under the terms of the donation they (i) agreed to " 'preserve and maintain the roof, * * * exterior facade(s), the foundation, and structural support of the property' " and (ii) donated "all air development rights * * * to the Property." In *Dorsey* the parties had stipulated that the donation "qualifie[d] as a deductible 'qualified conservation contribution' * * *. Unresolved is the charitable contribution amount." In valuing the conservation easement, the Court assigned a value of $30,773.52 to the restriction on the building and $122,648.92 to the restriction on the air rights.

While the Court did thus assign a value to the restriction on the air rights in *Dorsey*, the Court addressed only a valuation question and did not address the conservation purpose of the donation, which purpose had been stipulated. In this case, on the other hand, the conservation purpose is disputed and is the very issue under consideration. *Dorsey* is simply not on point.

We have previously held that "proximity [to a 'certified historic structure'] alone does not provide a basis to support a claim of protection of a historical structure." *Turner, supra* at 316. In *Turner* the taxpayers purchased 29.3 acres of unimproved land and subsequently contributed to a charitable organization a conservation easement that limited to 30 the number of residences they could construct on the land. *Id.* at 301–309. The unimproved land was in close proximity to Mount Vernon and other "certified historic structures," but it was not independently significant. "[D]espite any ancillary benefit of limited development," we held that the conservation easement did not preserve Mt. Vernon or other nearby "certified historic structures." *Id.* at 315. Despite the unimproved land's close proximity to Mount Vernon—a quintessential "certified historic structure"—we still required the taxpayer to show "how his proposed limitation in the conservation easement preserved any historical structure." *Id.* at 316. On the undisputed facts of this case, the restriction on the unused development rights does not preclude the demolition of the apartment building. Thus, despite the "proximity" of the unused development rights to the apartment building and the underlying land, and despite the "ancillary benefit of limited development," we hold under the rationale of *Turner* that the conservation easement with respect to the unused development rights does not, in fact, preserve a "historically important land area" or "certified historic structure." *See id.* at 315–316. We decide only the case before us, and we therefore do not decide whether there might be some circumstances in which a restriction on "air rights" or "unused development rights" alone might preserve a "historically important land area" or "certified historic structure." On the undisputed facts before us, there is no such preservation.

Therefore, we hold that respondent has shown that he is entitled to partial summary judgment on his assertion that the contribution of the conservation easement was not "exclusively for conservation purposes" with respect to the historic preservation requirement under section 170(h)(4)(A)(iv). * * *

NOTES & QUESTIONS

1.   How would the enactment of section 170(h)(4)(B), which occurred after Herman's tax return was filed but before this case was decided, have affected the outcome of this case? Although this key aspect of the law has changed since *Herman* was decided, this case is nonetheless useful in that it recites terms of a real preservation restriction, engages the issue of overlapping local historic landmarking rules, and demonstrates taxpayer creativity.

2.   Although J. Maurice Herman and his company were not successful in making an arguably outlandish claim, other property owners have been luckier. In 2002, a real estate developer filed for a tax deduction of over $28 million for a conservation easement over a golf course. The Tax Court ruled against the IRS, which had rejected the deduction, in large part because of the expert testimony of the developer's appraiser. *See Kiva Dunes Conservation, LLC v. Commissioner*, T.C.M. (RIA) 2009–145.

3.   Note that the National Architectural Trust, which held the restriction in *Herman*, has also been involved with restrictions in other controversial cases. *See, e.g., Kaufman v. Shulman*, 687 F.3d 21, 28 (1st Cir. 2012); *1982 East, LLC v. Commissioner*, T.C.M. (RIA) 2011–84; *Graev v. C.I.R.*, 140 T.C 377 (2013). Even before these cases wound up in court, publicity about the questionable activities of the National Architectural Trust—including the peddling of preservation restrictions to property owners of houses in Washington, D.C., that were already governed by the city's strict preservation ordinance—raised concerns. *See, e.g.,* Joe Stephens & David B. Ottaway, *Developers Find Payoff in Preservation*, WASH. POST, Dec. 21, 2003, at A1. Does the organization's appearance in multiple cases and in the newspapers raise questions about its practices? Perhaps to distance itself from controversy, the organization has changed its name to the Trust for Architectural Easements. Its website indicates that it has accepted more than 825 preservation restrictions.

4.   Quid pro quo exchanges between an owner and a donee can negate a tax deduction if the owner is not forthright and does not include the exchange in the valuation. In *Seventeen Seventy Sherman, LLC., v. C.I.R.*, T.C. Memo. 2014–124 (2014), the Tax Court rejected a claim for deductions because the owner did not disclose that in exchange for a restriction on a property, he had received zoning changes on the property. Without including this in the valuation, the court held that it was impossible to determine whether the deduction was proper. Similarly, in *Graev v. C.I.R.*, 140 T.C 377 (2013), the Tax Court rejected a tax deduction claim, where a side agreement signed by the National Architectural Trust guaranteed the property owner a refund if the IRS failed to grant a deduction.

5.   Changes in 2006 to the federal tax code to reduce abuses by taxpayers claiming an income tax deduction have been largely successful. Through Form 990 Schedule D, the IRS is now tracking the number of new easements and number of easements that are modified, transferred, released, extinguished, or terminated by an organization. Both donors and donees have better guidance about the practices that the IRS. finds acceptable, while the number of donated restrictions continues to skyrocket. The following section may help explain why.

3.   OTHER FEDERAL AND STATE TAX INCENTIVES

In addition to the federal income tax deduction, other favorable tax rules encourage property owners to grant conservation and preservation restrictions. At the federal level, the estate tax may, in certain circumstances, be reduced by all or part of the value of a qualified conservation contribution. *See* I.R.C. § 2031. With this incentive, Congress intended to encourage contributions by land-rich, cash-poor individuals. It is applicable to estates of decedents who died after 1997, regardless of when the contribution was made.

Professor Nancy McLaughlin has criticized the inefficiency of this tax, observing that those contributions that occurred prior to 1997 were not stimulated by the tax and that heirs would receive a windfall. She argues: "Amending § 2031(c) to provide that the exclusion applies only with respect to land encumbered by a qualifying easement donated after the date of the enactment of § 2031(c) would improve the efficiency of the tax incentive program by reducing the cost of the program without affecting donation behavior." Nancy A. McLaughlin, *Increasing the Tax Incentives for Conservation Easement Donations—A Responsible Approach*, 31 ECOLOGY L. Q. 1, 94–95 (2004). It is important to note that there are times when a deduction in the estate tax may not influence donation behavior at all. In 2010, for example, Congress entirely eliminated the estate tax. Thus, the generous provisions of section 2031(c) likely had no effect.

In about a dozen states, conservation and preservation restrictions merit an income tax credit or deduction. Colorado is among the more generous states, offering a tax credit worth 50 percent of the fair market value of a qualifying charitable contribution, up to $375,000, which can be transferred to other taxpayers. *See* COLO. REV. STAT. § 39–22–522. Like other states, Colorado requires, among other certifications and information, a qualified appraisal submitted by a qualified appraiser, as defined in I.R.C. § 170(f)(11), excerpted above. Unlike most states, Colorado has established a regulatory agency, the Conservation Easement Oversight Commission, which reviews and implements administrative regulations and the state's easement program. Although the credit seems generous, the state legislature has imposed a cap on the aggregate amount of tax credits that the State may grant in any given year. (Between 2011 and 2013, the cap was $26 million, *id.* § 39–22–522(2.5).)

As another example, South Carolina offers a tax credit of 25 percent of the amount of a qualified charitable contribution (as defined by the I.R.C.), up to $250 per acre, with a maximum annual limit on each taxpayer's request of $52,500. It may be carried forward until it is used, or may be transferred to another taxpayer. *See* S.C. CODE ANN. §§ 12–6–3515 *et seq.* Virginia, likewise, gives qualifying taxpayers an income tax deduction of up to 40 percent of the value of a qualifying open-space easement, up to $50,000 for tax year 2011 or $100,000 for tax year 2012. Any excess amounts may be transferred (for a fee of 5 percent of the value of the credit) or carried forward for at least a decade. VA. CODE ANN. § 58.1–512. Beyond these three states, other state incentives vary as to size, transferability, carry-forward possibilities, and type of land qualifying for the incentive.

About a third of the states allow property owners who donate restrictions to deduct the value of the restriction from the assessed value of their property to reduce their property taxes. Therefore, in addition to any one-time credits or deductions on income tax, a property owner may continue to receive benefits on an ongoing basis. We do not include in these numbers programs that purchase restrictions outright, such as the Purchase of Agricultural Conservation Easement programs that have been developed by about twenty states and forty-five local governments.

NOTES & QUESTIONS

1.   Consider the circumstance of an individual possessing, as her primary asset, a large tract of agricultural land that directly borders a suburban development. The tract might have a large value by virtue of its location as a site to be subdivided for additional suburban development. If she dies leaving the tract of land and little cash, her descendants may be burdened with a significant estate tax that potentially forces them to sell the property to suburban real estate developers. What public policy rationales justify an estate tax benefit?

2.   What are the politics of restrictions? Can you think of any reasons why states that lean conservative, such as Colorado and Virginia, are among those most generous with tax breaks?

3.   Not surprisingly, conservation and preservation restrictions abound in areas where property owners are affluent. Are there tax incentives that could encourage conservation and preservation restrictions in low-income areas? Would transferability of such incentives to taxpayers who could take advantage of them be important?

4.   In 2017, the most recent year for which data is available, the IRS reported that 4,823 individuals seeking federal tax deductions claimed average easement donation values of $746,364. *See* Christopher Williams & Janette Wilson, *Individual Noncash Contributions 2017*, STATS. OF INCOME

BULL., Fall 2019, at 1. No doubt many claimants also took advantage of state incentives as well.

Professor Josh Eagle has suggested that favorable state and federal tax laws have encouraged this generosity—not that restriction donors are more generous than others. He hypothesizes:

> [E]asement values are high because many easement donors are giving away something that, while possibly valuable to someone else, is of little value to them. If [this hypothesis is] correct—and there does not appear to be another viable explanation for the data—it means that donors should be willing to accept an amount less than the current tax benefit in return for their donations. Thus, some amount of tax revenue foregone under the current approach represents waste.

Josh Eagle, *Notional Generosity: Explaining Charitable Donors' High Willingness to Part with Conservation Easements*, 35 HARV. ENVTL. L. REV. 47, 51–52 (2011). If Professor Eagle is correct, what does it mean for our tax policies favoring the donation of restrictions?

5.   Consider an alternative to tax incentives created in Minnesota, the Minnesota Multi-Faceted Approach to Prioritizing Land Easements (MMAPLE). Designed by the Minnesota Land Trust and Saint John's University, the MMAPLE program offers property owners compensation in exchange for the imposition of a conservation easements on their land. Property owners set the amount they wish to be paid for an easement during a reverse auction. Prior to running an auction, MMAPLE establishes a particular conservation goal in a region of the state and creates criteria by which to evaluate bids. While the property owner's price is an important factor, MMAPLE also evaluates the ecological benefits of the property and the rights reserved by the property owner. The program "rewards the owners of lands with the most valued ecological conditions and who are willing to be paid the least amount of compensation" through the reverse bidding process. *See* Kris Larson & Susan Steinwall, *"What Price Conservation? A New Model for Acquiring Conservation Easements,"* 30 Nat. Res. & Envtl., at 4 (Fall 2015). This program has many interesting features: it quantifies the environmental benefits of the easements, ensures effective expenditures of limited funds for easements, and attracts willing and enthusiastic property owners. How would one set up a similar program for preservation restrictions for buildings? Consider the issues in valuing restrictions on buildings for federal tax purposes, described above. How accurate would estimates of benefits for preservation restrictions be?

CHAPTER ELEVEN

PRESERVATION IN MODERN DEVELOPMENT

This Chapter considers four specific issues for real estate developers, property owners, architects, and neighbors involved with the rehabilitation or reuse of historic structures. It begins with an examination of historic rehabilitation tax credits, which provide public support for certain preservation projects. It then describes issues for owners of historic properties that are required to be accessible, as defined by a federal statute, the Americans with Disabilities Act. The Chapter turns next to the intersection of historic preservation and intellectual property law, an issue of particular concern to architects and others doing design work on historic sites. Finally, the Chapter returns to some of the fundamental questions considered in Chapter 1—what do we preserve, and why and how do we do it?—which are particularly salient in the context of the gentrification of neighborhoods that sometimes occurs when significant investments in the rehabilitation of older or historic properties are made.

Each of these four issues has been considered in recent years by legislatures, courts, and the public. Depending on whom you ask, they are seen as either opportunities or barriers to modern historic preservation development.

A. HISTORIC REHABILITATION TAX CREDITS

Federal and state tax laws have long given favorable treatment to investments in real estate, primarily to encourage private financing of construction, which can create jobs and improve property values.

Congress has provided tax benefits in the form of depreciation deductions allowed under the Accelerated Cost Recovery System and the Modified Accelerated Cost Recovery System of the Internal Revenue Code. 26 U.S.C. §§ 167–168. Federal tax law entitles investors in income-producing property to take annual "depreciation deduction[s]" from their taxable income. The policy goal of these deductions was to at least notionally reflect the gradual decline of an asset's value due to physical deterioration or "obsolescence." *Id.* § 167(a). In the Tax Reform Act of 1986, Congress offered an additional type of depreciation system, which applies only to non-personal use tangible property. *Id.* § 168(a). This provision allows "accelerated" depreciation, which is more beneficial to taxpayers, because it allows larger percentage depreciation deductions in the early years, when they are worth more because of the time value of money. Taken over the course of a property's "useful life," depreciation deductions enable taxpayers who are forced to capitalize their expenses to recover potentially the full amount of their original investment in the asset. The cost of capital improvements made to the property may also be recouped through separate depreciation deductions.

In addition, the federal Tax Code allows owners to benefit from a property's appreciation in value, but does not tax the gain during the period of ownership. For example, a property owner may qualify for a larger line of credit as the property increases in value, but no tax will be due on the property's appreciation until the owner sells it. Even then, any gain to the owner from the sale or transfer of the property is taxed at the favorable rate applied to long-term capital gains, which typically is lower than the rate at which ordinary income from sources such as salaries is taxed.

On top of these general advantages to investing in real estate, federal and state legislatures have developed programs to offer tax credits to certain taxpayers who plan to invest in qualifying historic rehabilitation projects. These programs make undertaking rehabilitation projects on old and historic buildings more affordable by refunding a portion of the cost to property owners in the form of tax credits. Credits offer taxpayers a reduction of their tax liability on a dollar-for-dollar basis, as compared with deductions, which are subtracted from taxable income upon which final tax liability is calculated and which are worth only the cost multiplied by the taxpayer's marginal tax rate. In this section, we examine tax credit programs designed to favor reinvestment in old and historic structures, which play a central role in financing the practice of preservation. For more background on the taxation of real property, refer to ALVIN L. ARNOLD & MYRON KOVE, REAL ESTATE PROFESSIONAL'S TAX GUIDE § 4:1 (2020).

1. THE FEDERAL REHABILITATION TAX CREDIT

The federal rehabilitation tax credit program represents the largest direct federal investment in historic preservation. Currently, the Tax Code allows a 20 percent credit for expenditures made during the rehabilitation of historic properties. This credit can be claimed against business income calculated for the purpose of either federal personal or corporate income tax. The amount of credit taxpayers can claim is limited to the excess over their specified minimum tax liability. 26 U.S.C. § 38(c)(4). However, the excess of any portion of the tax credit that cannot be used may be carried back one year and forward twenty. *Id.* § 49. The impact that the 20 percent credit has had on real estate development practices and historic preservation has come to define the program. Practitioners and advocates will often loosely refer to the rehabilitation tax credits, generally, as historic tax credits or HTCs. Before turning to the statutory language, some historical context may be helpful.

a.   HISTORICAL CONTEXT

In the decades following World War II, American cities suffered dramatic deterioration as a result of the mass migration of population and investment to suburban developments. Urban neighborhoods with historic buildings were among those most badly affected, with high rates of vacant and neglected structures across the country. The passage of the National Historic Preservation Act and the proliferation of state and local historic districts created regulations to protect designated properties from incompatible alteration and demolition. No doubt these regulations helped to focus attention on the importance of the historic built environment. But while they slowed destruction of historic places, they did not provide a positive incentive for property owners and developers to invest in rehabilitation projects.

Thus Congress began to look for ways to boost historic projects and to spur economic development in urban neighborhoods where historic properties were concentrated. The Tax Reform Act of 1976 was its first attempt to develop special incentives for rehabilitation projects. *See generally* TERSH BOASBERG, THOMAS A. COUGHLIN & JULIA H. MILLER, HISTORIC PRESERVATION LAW AND TAXATION § 10.01[2][b] (1989). That statute dramatically accelerated the depreciation deduction schedule for expenditures on renovations of "certified historic structures" defined as:

> a building or structure which is of a character subject to the allowance for depreciation * * * and which—
>
> (A) is listed in the National Register, or
>
> (B) is located in a registered historic district and is certified by the Secretary of the Interior * * * as being of historic significance to the district.

Id. § 10.01[1] (quoting the 1976 version of 26 U.S.C. § 191, which was repealed in 1981). It allowed for a five-year amortization for rehabilitation costs, allowing owners of historic properties to invest in rehabilitation projects and recoup all the cost of doing so in just sixty months. In addition, it made destruction of historic buildings less attractive by, among other things, prohibiting deductions for costs related to demolition or site clearing. Two years later, the Revenue Act of 1978 expanded the accelerated depreciation deduction period benefit to include any building older than twenty years, whether historic or not.

More significantly, the 1978 Act created the federal rehabilitation tax credit. The tax credit program rewarded owners for rehabilitating their old or historic properties, in part, by refunding to them a percentage of the project's cost in the form of tax credits that could be used to offset their federal income tax liability on a dollar-for-dollar basis. Providing this offset to tax liability created a strong incentive for property owners to reuse rather than tear down older buildings. In 1978, when the program began, the amount of the tax credit was set at 10 percent. In 1981, Congress passed the Economic Recovery Tax Act, which increased the portion of costs for which a credit was available. Investors could earn a 25 percent credit for certified historic rehabilitations, a 20 percent credit for commercial buildings at least 40 years old, and a 15 percent credit for non-historic buildings at least 30 years old. *Id.* § 10.01[2][c].

In 1986, Congress made sweeping changes to the Tax Code, including changes that affected the rehabilitation tax credit program. The two-tier system remained, but the value of the tax credits was reduced to 20 percent for the certified rehabilitation of a certified historic structure and 10 percent for the rehabilitation of non-historic buildings built before 1936. Importantly, the 1986 changes also ushered in passive activity loss rules, which limited the extent to which certain high-income individual investors could take advantage of the historic tax credit. In the mid-1990s, investors began to pair the rehabilitation tax credits with low-income housing tax credits and state historic tax credits.

Today, only the 20 percent credit remains, but its popularity has not diminished. The credit remains a very popular way to finance commercial historic projects, whether or not it is paired with another tax credit. Note that amidst these efforts to develop a tax credit program were other efforts to create financial incentives for preservation, including the creation of a tax deduction for qualifying conservation and preservation restrictions (the focus of Chapter 10).

b.   THE STATUTORY LANGUAGE

The following provisions of the Internal Revenue Code spell out the primary requirements of the federal rehabilitation tax credit.

Federal Rehabilitation Tax Credit Provisions
26 U.S.C. § 47

(a) General rule.

(1) In general. For purposes of section 46, for any taxable year during the 5-year period beginning in the taxable year in which a qualified rehabilitated building is placed in service, the rehabilitation credit for such year is an amount equal to the ratable share for such year.

(2) Ratable share. For purposes of paragraph (1), the ratable share for any taxable year during the period described in such paragraph is the amount equal to 20 percent of the qualified rehabilitation expenditures with respect to the qualified rehabilitated building, as allocated ratably to each year during such period.

(b) When expenditures taken into account.

(1) In general. Qualified rehabilitation expenditures with respect to any qualified rehabilitated building shall be taken into account for the taxable year in which such qualified rehabilitated building is placed in service. * * *

(c) Definitions. For purposes of this section—

(1) Qualified rehabilitated building.

(A) In general. The term "qualified rehabilitated building" means any building (and its structural components) if—

(i)   such building has been substantially rehabilitated,

(ii) such building was placed in service before the beginning of the rehabilitation,

(iii) such building is a certified historic structure, and

(iv) depreciation (or amortization in lieu of depreciation) is allowable with respect to such building.

(B) Substantially rehabilitated defined.

(i)   In general. For purposes of subparagraph (A)(i), a building shall be treated as having been substantially rehabilitated only if the qualified rehabilitation expenditures during the 24-month period selected by the taxpayer (at the time and in the manner prescribed by regulation) and ending with or within the taxable year exceed the greater of

(I)   the adjusted basis of such building (and its structural components), or

(II) $5,000.

The adjusted basis of the building (and its structural components) shall be determined as of the beginning of the 1st day of such 24-month period, or of the holding period of the building, whichever is later. For purposes of the preceding sentence, the determination of the beginning of the holding period shall be made without regard to any reconstruction by the taxpayer in connection with the rehabilitation.

(ii) Special rule for phased rehabilitation.—In the case of any rehabilitation which may reasonably be expected to be completed in phases set forth in architectural plans and specifications completed before the rehabilitation begins, clause (i) shall be applied by substituting "60-month period" for "24-month period".

(iii) Lessees. The Secretary shall prescribe by regulation rules for applying this subparagraph to lessees.

(C) Reconstruction. Rehabilitation includes reconstruction.

(2) Qualified rehabilitation expenditure defined.

(A) In general. The term "qualified rehabilitation expenditure" means any amount properly chargeable to capital account—

(i)   for property for which depreciation is allowable under section 168 and which is—

(I)   nonresidential real property,

(II) residential rental property,

(III) real property which has a class life of more than 12.5 years, or

(IV) an addition or improvement to property described in subclause (I), (II), or (III), and

(ii) in connection with the rehabilitation of a qualified rehabilitated building.

(B) Certain expenditures not included. The term "qualified rehabilitation expenditure" does not include—

(i) Straight line depreciation must be used. Any expenditure with respect to which the taxpayer does not use the straight line method over a recovery period determined under subsection (c) or (g) of section 168. * * *

(ii) Cost of acquisition. The cost of acquiring any building or interest therein.

(iii) Enlargements. Any expenditure attributable to the enlargement of an existing building. * * *

(v) Tax-exempt use property.

(I) In general. Any expenditure in connection with the rehabilitation of a building which is allocable to the portion of such property which is (or may reasonably be expected to be) tax-exempt use property[.] * * *

(vi) Expenditures of lessee. Any expenditure of a lessee of a building if, on the date the rehabilitation is completed, the remaining term of the lease (determined without regard to any renewal periods) is less than the recovery period determined under section 168(c). * * *

(3) Certified historic structure defined.

(A) In general. The term "certified historic structure" means any building (and its structural components) which—

(i) is listed in the National Register, or

(ii) is located in a registered historic district and is certified by the Secretary of the Interior to the Secretary as being of historic significance to the district.

(B) Registered historic district. The term "registered historic district" means—

(i) any district listed in the National Register, and

(ii) any district—

(I) which is designated under a statute of the appropriate State or local government, if such statute is certified by the Secretary of the Interior to the Secretary as containing criteria which will substantially achieve the purpose of preserving and rehabilitating buildings of historic significance to the district, and

(II) which is certified by the Secretary of the Interior to the Secretary as meeting substantially all of the requirements for the listing of districts in the National Register. * * *

(5) Election. This subsection shall apply to any taxpayer only if such taxpayer has made an election under this paragraph. Such an election shall apply to the taxable year for which made and all subsequent taxable years. Such an election, once made, may be revoked only with the consent of the Secretary.

NOTES & QUESTIONS

1. What are the two tax credits offered by these provisions, and to what kinds of properties might they be applied? There are some limitations on use of the 10 percent rehabilitation credit. For example, it must be used for non-residential rental purposes, 26 U.S.C. § 50(b)(2), and the building receiving the credit cannot have been moved, Treas. Reg. § 1.48–12(b)(5).

2. What does it mean to be a "substantial" renovation under 26 U.S.C. § 47(c)(1)(A)(i)? The cost of rehabilitation must exceed the adjusted basis in the building. The term "basis" has a specific and not necessarily intuitive meaning in the context of real estate transactions. For recordkeeping purposes, the Tax Code assigns the buyer a "basis" in the property equal to the purchase price. A property owner's basis in a building is automatically reduced by the annual depreciation deduction amounts they are allowed to take. Over the course of many years, the basis may depreciate to a zero value. In such cases, the statute requires a taxpayer to invest a minimum of $5,000 in qualified rehabilitation expenditures (QREs) to claim the credit. *Id.* § 47(c)(1)(B)(II).

Before basis was used to measure a "substantial" renovation under the statute, the Tax Court struggled to define the term based on the nature and scope of the rehabilitation work. *See, e.g., Webbe v. Commissioner*, 54 T.C.M. (P-H) 281 (T.C. 1987) (renovations were "substantial" where they were structural rather than merely cosmetic and the usefulness of the hotel building was upgraded significantly). The courts have upheld the IRS in rejecting the practice of measuring QREs against only the amount of basis allocable to the portion of the building that was renovated. Rather, for a building to be "substantially rehabilitated," the QREs must exceed the basis in the building as a whole. *Alexander v. Commissioner*, 97 T.C. 244, 247–49 (1991) (taxpayers denied rehabilitation credits when QREs made only for first floor rental apartment and did not exceed their basis in the entire house).

3. Though most state programs offer tax benefits to homeowners of historic properties, the federal historic rehabilitation tax credit program does not currently apply to owner-occupied residences. Since the mid-1990s, amending the Tax Code to extend tax benefits to historic homeowners has been a central lobbying effort of preservation advocates, led by the National

Trust for Historic Preservation. Multiple bills have been introduced on this issue, but none have made it to committee vote.

Some bills have imposed minimum investment requirements, meaning that a homeowner would have to spend a certain amount in order to be eligible for the credit. Congressmen who oppose minimum requirements argue that middle-class homeowners would be effectively precluded from benefiting from the policy, if they were unable to afford the initial investment in the rehabilitation work. Does removing the minimum investment requirement eliminate this criticism? It may be possible that a low-income homeowner cannot use a tax credit because she has insufficient taxable income. Instead, should there be a mechanism to transfer the credit? How about placing a cap on the amount of credit allowed? What economic and social arguments can be made in support of each of these provisions? Who benefits? What are the potential downsides?

4.   Qualified rehabilitation expenditures are further described in federal regulations (including the Secretary of the Interior's Standards for Rehabilitation, excerpted below) and other publications. The Technical Preservation Services division of the National Park Service offers an online guide for those interested in learning more about the tax credit programs. It lists items whose costs may be included as qualified rehabilitation expenditures: Walls, windows, stairs, and elevators are all eligible; cabinets, carpeting, financing fees, landscaping, sidewalks, and signage are not.

5.   What do you make of a provision including "reconstruction" within the meaning of rehabilitation? 26 U.S.C. § 47(c)(1)(C). Think back to our discussion in Chapter 1 about the four treatments of historic properties, as articulated by federal regulations. 36 C.F.R. § 68.3. As you may recall, reconstruction refers to rebuilding a historic structure that was removed, pursuant to documentation (including drawings and photographs) demonstrating the particulars of the removed structure. Is there any reason to distinguish the public benefit in rehabilitating a historic structure from the benefit in building a new replica from scratch?

6.   In 2020, Congress adopted changes affecting the historic tax credit in light of the economic downturn caused by the onset of COVID-19. The Coronavirus Aid, Relief and Economic Security (CARES) Act makes qualified improvement property eligible for one hundred percent bonus depreciation, retroactively applying to properties completed after 2017. Also in 2020, the Treasury Department issued emergency guidance extending the measuring period under the substantial rehabilitation test, to allow property owners with tax credit projects stalled during COVID-19 to complete their projects. INTERNAL REVENUE SERV., Notice 2020–58 (July 30, 2020).

c.   THE APPLICATION PROCESS

We turn now to the details of the application process for the percent federal rehabilitation tax credit. The program is jointly administered by the Secretary of the Interior and the Secretary of the Treasury, acting through the National Park Service (NPS) and the Internal Revenue Service (IRS), respectively. A taxpayer's project must satisfy the requirements of both federal agencies' regulations to qualify for the rehabilitation tax credit, but the IRS relies heavily on the professional expertise of the NPS staff and, in turn, its state historic preservation officer (SHPO) partners in the certification process. The Department of the Interior has thus taken the lead in promulgating regulations, 36 C.F.R. § 67.6, that set forth the procedure for the certification of projects that meet the credit requirements. Through this process, the Secretary of the Interior determines which projects it can certify to the Secretary of the Treasury as qualifying for the historic rehabilitation credit.

For taxpayers seeking the credit for a certified rehabilitation, the Historic Preservation Certification Application comes in three parts. Part 1 of the application determines whether the property qualifies as a certified historic structure. Buildings listed individually on the National Register automatically qualify. Otherwise, owners must submit Part 1 to provide information about the historical significance of the property to see if should be listed on the National Register, either as a "certified historic structure" individually or as a contributing building to a registered historic district. The SHPO, as the property owner's first contact with the certification process, reviews it first. It then recommends to NPS either to approve or deny the request. The Keeper makes the final determination using the designation criteria discussed in Chapter 2. If the Keeper chooses to list the building on the Register, the tax credit applicant may proceed to Part 2 of the application. Federal designation is a required step in the rehabilitation tax credit application process—even if ultimately the building never receives tax credits. As noted above, only properties rehabilitated for commercial, industrial, agricultural, or income-producing residential uses are eligible for the rehabilitation tax credit.

In Part 2 of the application for the tax credit, a taxpayer must provide a description of the proposed rehabilitation, including architectural plans and photographs. The SHPO works with the taxpayer, providing technical support and advice, to prepare the application for review. Along with the SHPO's recommendation, NPS reviews Part 2 of the application to determine whether it conforms to the Secretary's Standards for Rehabilitation (reproduced below), and issues a determination decision.

In Part 3 of the application, the taxpayer submits photographs of the completed rehabilitation work. A project is not approved as a certified rehabilitation until NPS verifies that the completed work complies with the Secretary's Standards for Rehabilitation and the description of rehabilitation from Part 2 of the application.

After awarding certified rehabilitation credits, the Secretary of the Interior and the Secretary of the Treasury both retain the right to revoke, or "recapture," the credits for violations of the procedure. Once the rehabilitation is complete, the taxpayer must hold the building for an additional five years, or else pay back the credit. During this five-year period, NPS and the SHPO also have the right to inspect the rehabilitated property for continued compliance with the approved description and scope of work. If they find a violation, NPS will revoke the certification and notify the IRS.

———————————

A key part of the application process for the federal rehabilitation tax credit is a demonstration that the project complies with the following Standards for Rehabilitation.

Secretary of the Interior's Standards for Rehabilitation
36 C.F.R. § 67.7

(a) The following Standards for Rehabilitation are the criteria used to determine if a rehabilitation project qualifies as a certified rehabilitation. The intent of the Standards is to assist the long-term preservation of a property's significance through the preservation of historic materials and features. The Standards pertain to historic buildings of all materials, construction types, sizes, and occupancy and encompass the exterior and the interior of historic buildings. The Standards also encompass related landscape features and the building's site and environment, as well as attached, adjacent, or related new construction. To be certified, a rehabilitation project must be determined by the Secretary to be consistent with the historic character of the structure(s) and, where applicable, the district in which it is located.

(b) The following Standards are to be applied to specific rehabilitation projects in a reasonable manner, taking into consideration economic and technical feasibility. * * *

(1) A property shall be used for its historic purpose or be placed in a new use that requires minimal change to the defining characteristics of the building and its site and environment.

(2) The historic character of a property shall be retained and preserved. The removal of historic materials or alteration of features and spaces that characterize a property shall be avoided.

(3) Each property shall be recognized as a physical record of its time, place, and use. Changes that create a false sense of historical development, such as adding conjectural features or architectural elements from other buildings, shall not be undertaken.

(4) Most properties change over time; those changes that have acquired historic significance in their own right shall be retained and preserved.

(5) Distinctive features, finishes, and construction techniques or examples of craftsmanship that characterize a historic property shall be preserved.

(6) Deteriorated historic features shall be repaired rather than replaced. Where the severity of deterioration requires replacement of a distinctive feature, the new feature shall match the old in design, color, texture, and other visual qualities and, where possible, materials. Replacement of missing features shall be substantiated by documentary, physical, or pictorial evidence.

(7) Chemical or physical treatments, such as sandblasting, that cause damage to historic materials shall not be used. The surface cleaning of structures, if appropriate, shall be undertaken using the gentlest means possible.

(8) Significant archeological resources affected by a project shall be protected and preserved. If such resources must be disturbed, mitigation measures shall be undertaken.

(9) New additions, exterior alterations, or related new construction shall not destroy historic materials that characterize the property. The new work shall be differentiated from the old and shall be compatible with the massing, size, scale, and architectural features to protect the historic integrity of the property and its environment.

(10) New additions and adjacent or related new construction shall be undertaken in such a manner that if removed in the future, the essential form and integrity of the historic property and its environment would be unimpaired.

(c) The quality of materials and craftsmanship used in a rehabilitation project must be commensurate with the quality of materials and craftsmanship of the historic building in question. * * * Inappropriate physical treatments include, but are not limited to: improper repointing techniques; improper exterior masonry cleaning methods; or improper introduction of insulation where damage to historic fabric would result. In almost all situations, use of these materials and treatments will result in denial of certification. Similarly, exterior additions that duplicate the form, material, and detailing of the structure to the extent that they compromise the historic character of the structure will result in denial of certification. For further information on appropriate and inappropriate rehabilitation treatments, owners are to consult the Guidelines for Rehabilitating Historic Buildings published by the NPS. * * *

(e) Prior approval of a project by Federal, State, and local agencies and organizations does not ensure certification by the Secretary for Federal tax purposes. The Secretary's Standards for Rehabilitation take precedence over other regulations and codes in determining whether the rehabilitation project is consistent with the historic character of the property and, where applicable, the district in which it is located. * * *

NOTES & QUESTIONS

1. The Secretary of the Interior's Standards for Rehabilitation contained in 36 C.F.R. § 67.7 differ slightly (though not much) from the

Secretary of the Interior's Standards for the Treatment of Historic Properties, *id.* § 68.3, excerpted in Chapter 1. The regulations in Part 67 focus on "certified historic structures" as they are defined in the federal rehabilitation tax credit. The regulations in Part 68 apply more broadly to projects of all kinds. Despite the minor differences, persons seeking federal tax benefits should not rely on the language of Part 68 to guide its physical rehabilitation efforts. *See id.* § 68.1 (stating the intent of both Parts).

2.　　Physical integrity of designated structures is a central concept in historic preservation law. As we saw in Chapter 2, a property may be listed on the National Register only if it possesses "integrity of location, design, setting, materials, workmanship, feeling, and association." 36 C.F.R. § 60.4. And as we learned in Chapter 3, the National Historic Preservation Act protects the integrity of designated structures against adverse effects of certain federal undertakings. *See* 36 C.F.R. § 800.5(a)(1) (finding an adverse effect when an undertaking altered important characteristics of a National Register property "in a manner that would diminish [its] integrity"). Regulations for the tax credit also take integrity into account, requiring that there be enough historic material to preserve at the outset, and that the rehabilitation process not disturb existing integrity. As one example, moving a designated structure may jeopardize its eligibility for tax credits.

3.　　Consider the application of the Standards for Rehabilitation to The Octagon on Roosevelt Island, a mixed-use development that centers on a nineteenth-century octagonal-shaped tower that once formed the main entry hall of New York City's now-defunct Metropolitan Hospital. The tower had fallen into disrepair, and the roof had caved in, while the wings of the hospital had been demolished. Figure 11-1 and 11-2 show the pre-development state of the tower, both inside and out. With so little historic fabric remaining, what parts of the Standards might have been critical in assessing the historic compatibility of the tower's redevelopment?

With the assistance of federal rehabilitation tax credits and a state tax credit for green buildings, the developer, Becker + Becker Associates, restored and reconstructed the tower and added the new wings in 2006. To gain approval for the project, the developer had to present architectural plans that satisfied not only the New York City preservation board, but also the State Historic Preservation Office and the Roosevelt Island Operating Corporation. The project has been a commercial success and won awards from the New York Landmarks Conservancy and the Environmental Protection Agency for its historic and sustainable building elements. The "after" photograph in Figure 11-3 shows the two new wings, which approximate the volume of lost elements of the historic building.

4.　　To the extent that a project being proposed for the tax credit is proposed as a reconstruction pursuant to 26 U.S.C. § 47(c)(1)(C), the project would follow the Secretary of the Interior's Standards for Reconstruction. *See* 36 C.F.R. § 68.3.

Figures 11-1, 11-2, 11-3:
The Octagon: Before and After Rehabilitation,
Roosevelt Island, NY

The following case demonstrates the crucial role compliance with the Secretary's Standards for Rehabilitation plays in the certification process. Note that the case involves tax credits in pre-1986 amounts, and that as of 2017, the 10 percent credit referenced in the case has been repealed.

Amoco Production Company v. United States Department of the Interior
763 F.Supp. 514 (N.D. Okla. 1990)

■ VAN SICKLE, SENIOR DISTRICT JUDGE.

Amoco Production Company appeals from the final decision of the Chief Appeals Officer for the Department of the Interior denying Amoco's request for certification of the Philcade Building in Tulsa, Oklahoma as a "certified historic structure" as required for income tax credit under the Internal Revenue Code, 26 U.S.C. § 48(g), and the denial by the Keeper of the National Register to retroactively remove from the Register the Philcade as an historic building.

After a thorough review of the final administrative decision of the National Park Service of the Department of the Interior, the Court finds that the decision was not violative of the Administrative Procedure Act, 5 U.S.C. Sections 706(2)(A), (D), (E), and neither declaratory nor equitable relief will be granted. Therefore, the Court finds in favor of the defendants, National Park Service and Department of the Interior, and against the plaintiff, Amoco.

Background

This action centers on the rehabilitation by Amoco of the 13-story Philcade Building located in downtown Tulsa, Oklahoma. Original construction of the Philcade began in 1929 by Waite Phillips, a prominent Tulsa philanthropist and industrialist, and was completed in 1931. The Philcade was designed by Oklahoma architect Leon Senter, and is considered one of his most important works.

The building houses commercial activities on its ground floor, mezzanine and second floor areas. Marble pilasters, ornamental plaster frieze and ceiling comprise the Philcade's ground floor interior, with its corridors containing terrazzo floors, marble wainscot, and solid mahogany office doors. The shape of the building's exterior third through thirteenth floors originally formed a deep "U" or "H" shape, with two tower wings forming a light well and allowing natural ventilation for interior spaces. Terra cotta and cast iron cover the building's exterior and the wings contain light colored brick, double-hung steel windows and brick chevron pilasters.

Figures 11-4 & 11-5:
The Philcade Building in 1962 and 2011,
Tulsa, OK

In the early 1980's, the Philcade was in need of rehabilitation in order to make it compliant with modern safety requirements. Amoco sought to make the required structural safety changes while maintaining the historical character of the building. After drawing plans containing a number of different options for renovating the building, Amoco met with the Oklahoma State Historic Preservation Office in July, 1984 to advise them of the rehabilitation plans and to seek the federal income tax credits provided under statute.

Amoco's decision to rehabilitate and modernize the Philcade was guided, in part, by the tax incentive provisions of the Economic Recovery Tax Act of 1981. Under that Act, two modes of tax incentives allowed a building owner to obtain either (1) a 20 percent tax credit for rehabilitation of structures at least 40 years old or (2) a 25 percent tax credit for the rehabilitation of a "certified historic structure." 26 U.S.C. Section 46(a)(2)(F)(i).

To qualify for the 20 percent tax credit, a building owner need not seek National Park Service approval; the only substantive requirement was that the building be at least 40 years old. Consistent with the two methods of seeking federal tax subsidies, the 20 percent tax credit was not available if expenditures were "attributable to the rehabilitation of a certified historic structure." Id. § 48(g)(2)(B)(iv).

Qualification for the 25 percent tax credit is a much more complicated procedure and requires two part certifications by the Secretary of the Interior, acting through the National Park Service. Part I requires that the property be certified as a historic structure through nomination for inclusion on the National Register of Historic Places. Part II dictates that the rehabilitation project must be certified by the National Park Service as consistent with the historic character of the building. Id. § 48(g). The certification process begins through the State Historic Preservation Officer who makes recommendations to the National Park Service as to both parts of the certification process. These recommendations by state historic officers are generally followed by the National Park Service, but the final decision by law must be made by the Secretary upon review of the application and related information. 36 C.F.R. § 67.4(b)(3), (5). Part II certification, through state historic officer recommendation, may be sought at any point after Part I certification, even after actual rehabilitation work has begun, but the regulations encourage certification prior to building rehabilitation. Id. § 67.6(a)(1). Undertaking rehabilitation prior to National Park Service approval subjects the building owner to the risks of non-certification. Id. * * *

In July 1986, the Oklahoma Preservation Review Committee considered the request by Amoco for Part I certification, i.e. the nomination of the Philcade for listing on the National Register of Historic Places. The parties dispute whether rehabilitation plans were presented; but evidence exists in the administrative record which shows that construction had already begun on the Philcade and Amoco had been informed of the risks therein. Nonetheless, the Committee decided to nominate the Philcade for Part I certification. On September 18, 1986, the Keeper of the National Register approved the nomination and the Philcade was placed on the National Register.

On November 25, 1986, Amoco sought Part II certification for the Philcade from the State Historic Preservation Officer. The State Historic Preservation Officer recommended certification, subject to certain conditions * * *. Evidence in the administrative record reveals that the State Historic Preservation Officer recommended that the Park Service further review the application because of a perceived lack of information concerning demolition, substantial interior alterations and construction of the new addition to the Philcade.

On April 21, 1987, the National Park Service denied Amoco's Part II application by determining that the rehabilitation was not "consistent with the historic character of the property or the district in which it is located and the project does not meet the Secretary of the Interior's 'Standards for Rehabilitation.' " Specifically, the Park Service found that the proposed construction of a connecting link between the building's two wings, proposed changes to the Philcade's interior, and the proposed replacement of the building's steel double-hung windows with bronze aluminum sash, each and of themselves constituted a failure of the Secretary's standards and necessitated certification denial. The National Park Service considered the proposed connecting link a critical flaw in the rehabilitation plans:

> If constructed as proposed, major character defining features of the building will be destroyed. The most damaging work item is the addition of a connecting link between the east and west wings. The connector changes the historic appearance of the building by "filling in" the deep space created by the two wings. The architectural detailing of the two wings and the "U" shape of the building with its decorative friezes and chevron pilasters make a strong statement that would be destroyed if filled in by the connector as is proposed. * * *

Amoco appealed the certification denial by the National Park Service to Ernest Allen Connally, the Park Service's Chief Appeals Officer in Washington, D.C. After a *de novo* review, the Appeals Officer on March 31, 1988 dismissed the objections of the regional office to the building interior alterations * * *. The Appeals Officer nonetheless denied the appeal based on the addition of the connecting link, holding that Amoco's decision to construct the link was a matter of preference, among available approaches to the safety code problems, which "radically impair[ed] the essential character of the Philcade." * * *

Amoco thereafter filed a Petition for Reconsideration on March 31, 1988 and asserted that: (1) The Philcade's most important historic and architectural feature was its lobby/arcade and not its external form; (2) the decision to construct the connecting link, and not internal stairs, was not a "matter of preference" but was made to prevent damage to the lobby/arcade and the exterior street-level facade; (3) the placement of the connecting link, slightly set-back into the building, and the addition's design and materials preserves the original historic form and architectural style and character; (4) the National Park Service had previously certified other rehabilitation projects involving similar "infill" additions.

On October 12, 1988, the Chief Appeals Officer, after analyzing voluminous additional material submitted by Amoco, determined that the previous decisions of the National Park Service denying certification were proper. * * *

On December 4, 1989, Amoco petitioned the State Historic Preservation Officer requesting the delisting of the Philcade from the National Register pursuant to 36 C.F.R. § 60.15(a)(4), which authorizes the Keeper to remove properties from the National Register where there has been prejudicial procedural error in the nomination and listing process. The State Historic Preservation Officer responded by maintaining that no procedural error occurred during the nomination of the Philcade, and that photographs and other documentation provided during the procedure established the building's eligibility for placement on the National Register. The decision to nominate the Philcade to the National Register, according to the Preservation Officer, was not based on proposed additions to the building, nor tax considerations.

The Keeper of the National Register on February 2, 1990 determined that no procedural error had occurred in the nomination and listing of the Philcade, and that removal based on equitable considerations was not allowed. * * * Despite the construction by Amoco of the connecting link, the Keeper determined that the Philcade, considered as a whole, retained "sufficient integrity of location, design, setting, materials, workmanship, feeling, and association within the meaning of 26 C.F.R. § 60.4 to continue to qualify it for listing within the National Register as a significant example of the Art Deco style as developed in Tulsa, Oklahoma."

On March 16, 1989, Amoco commenced this action for judicial review of the National Park Service's denial of certification. Amoco alleged that the certification denial was violative of the Administrative Procedure Act, 5 U.S.C. §§ 706(2)(A), (D), (E) as it was allegedly arbitrary, capricious, an abuse of discretion, not in accordance with law, and was unsupported by substantial evidence. * * * A motion for summary judgment was filed by Amoco on September 25, 1990 and by the National Park Service on September 17, 1990. * * * On November 30, 1990, this Court heard oral arguments in the matter which included an on-site viewing of the Philcade Building. * * *

Discussion

I.   Whether the decision by the National Park Service denying certification for the Philcade Building as a "Certified Historic Structure" was arbitrary or capricious or otherwise violative of the Administrative Procedure Act.

The scope of review with regard to administrative decisions of an agency is governed by the provisions of the Administrative Procedure Act. This court must strike down the findings and conclusions of an agency that are, *inter alia,* "arbitrary, capricious, an abuse of discretion, or otherwise not in accordance with the law," or are "unsupported by substantial evidence in the case." 5 U.S.C. § 706(2); *Citizens to Preserve Overton Park v. Volpe,* 401 U.S. 402 (1971). The Court's review is narrow, but it does not substitute its judgment for that of the agency, nor does it merely "rubber stamp" the Secretary's action. *Volpe, supra* * * *.

Amoco argues that the National Park Service ignored evidence in the record supporting the position that the most significant feature of the Philcade was its lobby/arcade and not its external form, and that the rehabilitation work was consistent with the building's historic character. According to Amoco, the record contains expert evidence that construction of the connecting link did not adversely affect the building's character. Amoco contends the National Park Service failed to present contrary evidence, and never viewed the building; thus, statements by the Park Service concerning the importance of the external form were conclusory and not reasoned from the facts.

The National Park Service argues that under the Secretary's Standards for Rehabilitation the agency is granted discretionary authority in certification after a consideration of all relevant factors. The Chief Appeals Officer evaluated the project based on "before" photographs, and information and history contained in the official documentation furnished by Amoco in its application for nomination to be placed on the National Register. Each of Philcade project's shortcomings were fully identified and explained in the Appeals Officer's decisions and each holding had a rational basis under the Secretary's Standards.

The National Park Service also vigorously defends the charge that it failed to make a reasoned decision because it did not conduct an on-site inspection of the Philcade. Initially, the Park Service notes that inspections are authorized under 36 C.F.R. § 67.6(e) but are not required; a site visit in most cases is not necessary or practical as complete documentation, including photographs, as recommended under the regulations. The administrative record is replete with photographs of the Philcade both prior to and after rehabilitation, and the building's interior and exterior portions are clearly evident. Combined with architectural drawings of the building, the National Park Service argues that there are no grounds whatsoever to suggest that it was unable to make a reasoned decision based on the record before it.

The Court finds the National Park Service's arguments persuasive and rejects Amoco's contention that the Park Service provided an unreasoned or conclusory certification denial. The National Park Service is necessarily bound by regulatory standards defining certification of historic structures, but it also is vested with discretionary authority upon evaluation of all relevant evidence. Evidence in this case included the aforementioned photographs and architectural drawings, the statement of Professor Wilson, and all other information contained in the Part I and Part II applications (in addition to information supplied by Amoco on appeal and reconsideration).

A site visit by the National Park Service to the Philcade certainly would not have been detrimental to its consideration of Amoco's application. Ample evidence existed from these applications, however, to make a reasoned analysis and decision, and a finding that evidence supports the decision of the National Park Service.

Essentially, Amoco's contention boils down to a question concerning the architectural significance of the two wings, which it claims is overshadowed by the interior lobby. On numerous occasions, however, Amoco referred to the exterior architecture in its description of the historic nature of the Philcade. It commented in Part I of its application: "The wing and well configuration of the office floors together with the large windows offered each tenant reasonable comfort in an era before modern air conditioning." Combined with information concerning the history of such structures in the 1920s and 1930s, it was not unreasonable for the National Park Service to determine that the characteristic historic nature of the Philcade was its exterior form. Moreover, the National Park Service determination included an evaluation of all relevant evidence regarding the Philcade including the interior and exterior. It simply does not follow that, because the Park Service differed with Amoco in what it considered the Philcade's chief historic characteristic, its determination was unreasonable.

Amoco argues further that evidence of other rehabilitations where the National Park Service granted certification compels it to make a similar ruling in this case. It is not necessary for the Court to elaborate on each of the case examples provided by Amoco, as the Court rejects the attempt to bind the National Park Service's discretionary authority to precedent. Each application must be viewed individually, and a reasoned decision must be made with certification only upon a project's consistency with the Secretary's Standards for Rehabilitation. Having considered and rejected these other projects, the Chief Appeals Officer went beyond what was necessary in order to make his reasoned decision. That decision denying certification will not be disturbed.

II.   Whether the Court, on the basis of equitable considerations, should direct the Keeper of the National Register to delist the Philcade Building from the National Register.

Amoco seeks to enlist the equitable powers of the Court to direct the Keeper of the National Register to retroactively delist the Philcade Building from the National Register and thereby remedy what it considers the unfair result caused by the National Park Service's certification denial. Without retroactive delisting, Amoco will not have available federal tax credits for the Philcade's rehabilitation expenditures. These tax credits were initially made unavailable by the failure of the Park Service to certify the Philcade as a "certified historic structure." This so-called "Catch-22" situation should be remedied, according to Amoco, by placing it in the position it would have been in had the Philcade not been listed on the National Register. * * *

Amoco's rights are governed by law, according to the National Park Service, because Congress intended that a flawed rehabilitation of a certified historic structure would lead to the same result Amoco is faced with. * * * Amoco seeks a remedy, however, which does not rest in law. The National Park Service could not grant, under the regulations, the relief Amoco seeks in this case since the delisting of a historic structure cannot be done retroactively. 36 C.F.R. § 67.6(f). Review under the Administrative Procedures Act standards by a Court would clearly have no remedial effect in this situation. Thus, the Court must consider the issue based on equitable principles.

Although Amoco can seek the Court's equity jurisdiction, the equities of this particular scenario do not favor retroactive delisting of the Philcade from the National Register. Amoco was aware of the modes of obtaining federal tax credits prior to its attempt to have the Philcade listed on the National Register. The choice to have it nominated for listing, and the completion of Part I of the two part certification process, necessarily requires that it fulfill the Secretary's Standards for Rehabilitation. The attendant risk of pursuing such a course involves potential denial of certification, as was seen in this case. The risks involved necessitate that a building owner seek approval prior to, or in the early stages, of rehabilitation. Preliminary approval of projects is allowed and suggested by the regulations. Having been informed of such risks by both the State Historic Preservation Officer and the National Park Service, Amoco cannot now claim that it was unaware of the consequences of certification denial.

Furthermore, to allow the retroactive delisting of the Philcade and thus make Amoco's expenditures available for tax credits at the 20 percent level would permit a building owner to improperly rehabilitate a certified historic structure, obtain a retroactive decertification, and then claim the federal tax credit for the non-historic rehabilitation. While Congress sought to provide incentive for historic rehabilitation, it also sought "to provide a strong disincentive for failing to properly rehabilitate a certified structure." *Id.* Therefore, the Court finds that such a retroactive delisting would not further the Congressional intent with regard to rehabilitation of historic structures.

Finally, the Court notes that Amoco has expended substantial sums in its rehabilitation of the Philcade. Through a series of questionable judgments in its approach to the certification process, and in analyzing the potential risks which necessarily are involved in administrative procedures, Amoco has placed itself in the present unfavorable situation. The National Park Service acted reasonably and within its discretion in making its decisions regarding the Philcade project, and gave thoughtful and thorough review upon appeal and reconsideration of its certification denial. Having observed no arbitrary or capricious abuse of discretion, the Court finds that the actions of the National Park Service were proper and its decisions are hereby affirmed.

NOTES & QUESTIONS

1.   What role does precedent play in the National Park Service's evaluation of applications in making certification decisions? The court in *Amoco* refuses to "bind the National Park Service's discretionary authority to precedent." *Amoco Prod. Co. v. U.S. Dep't of the Interior*, 763 F.Supp. 514, 522 (N.D. Okla. 1990). In addition to encouraging courts to uphold certifications, is there reason for the NPS to consider prior decisions in evaluating new applications?

2.   Was the NPS too strict in rejecting the Philcade rehabilitation? What duty, if any, does the state historic preservation officer (SHPO) have to communicate to the taxpayer the specific risks of denial when sending an application with a recommendation "subject to certain conditions" for NPS review? In the *Amoco* case, if the reservations about the application were due to a lack of information, should the SHPO have recommended the application without having seen that determinative information? Consider the following statistical data of NPS application denials and appeals in fiscal year 2016:

- NPS denied 33 of the 1,553 Part 1 "certification of significance" applications it reviewed.

- NPS denied certification to 41 rehabilitation projects of the 2,338 Part 2 and 3 "certification of rehabilitation" applications it received.

- Of the 41 denials, 32 were appealed. The NPS's Chief Appeals Officer heard 22 appeals in 2016; however, an appeal is not necessarily heard in the same fiscal year in which a project was denied.

- Of the 26 appeals decided during the year, 4 were overturned, and 22 were upheld, in whole or in part. Fourteen projects were with conditions. When the Chief Appeals Officer decides to uphold a denial decision with conditions, the owner is given an opportunity to resubmit an application for further consideration after changing the plans to bring the project into conformance with the Secretary of the Interior's Standards.

See TECHNICAL PRES. SERVS. NAT'L PARK SERV. FEDERAL TAX INCENTIVES FOR REHABILITATING HISTORIC BUILDINGS: STATISTICAL REPORT AND ANALYSIS FOR FISCAL YEAR 2016 9–10 (2016).

In your opinion, do the outcomes of the appeals decisions suggest that the entire process is fair and predictable? Or is the original denial of an application inconclusive and unreliable? Navigating the application process quickly can represent significant value to property owners. Not surprisingly, a niche market of architecture and consulting firms specializing in historic renovations has developed in response to the demand for expertise that the rehabilitation tax credit program creates.

3.   Consider the following excerpt:

Another issue pertaining to the size of the credits and their impact is the concern that "more and more buildings of marginal historical significance [will be] proposed for listing on the National Register." The Senate Budget Committee has estimated that nearly one million buildings are potentially eligible for special tax treatment; there is no doubt that a portion of them are less historically significant. Because of the competition among potentially certifiable buildings for tax credit qualification, however, this fear of marginal significance seems overstated in that it is much less risky to try to certify an assuredly historic structure than a marginal one. Thus, at least in the near term, the worry about too many marginally significant buildings is precluded by the large number of good historic buildings available.

The Impact of ERTA and TEFRA on Tax Credits for Historic Preservation, 48 LAW & CONTEMP. PROBS. 259, 268 (1985). As you can see, the above article was written in 1985. Arguably, the "near term" has passed, and the relevant sections of the code remain intact. Is this still a concern? What are the economic problems presented by listing more buildings of marginal historical significance to the National Register? To a state or local register? When might we reach a tipping point, and what should be done?

4.   Courts have recognized that the federal historic tax credit program allows officials to review interiors, like the ones at issue in the Philcade. *See, e.g.*, Schneider P'ship v. Dep't of Interior, 693 F. Supp. 223 (D.N.J. 1988) (rejecting the taxpayer's claim that the review of interior spaces was impermissible, reasoning that the term "buildings" in federal laws establishing the historic tax credit program includes interiors). Given the purpose of historic preservation regulation discussed in Chapter 1, should the federal government be regulating interior spaces?

d.   TRANSFERS OF THE CREDIT

The Tax Code allows property owners to use the credit to offset their own tax payments, and they may apply the credits back one year and forward for up to twenty years. 26 U.S.C. § 39(a). However, some technicalities in how the Tax Code operates can make benefitting from the historic preservation credit tricky. Often, in the early years of a development, deductions taken for interest payments on the debt, depreciation, and operation expenses more than offset taxable income from the property, so there is no tax liability for the credits to offset.

In limited instances, property owners can share the benefit of their excess credits with other individuals and entities seeking to reduce their tax burden. The Tax Code does not permit property owners to transfer the benefits of tax credits simply through a direct sale to an investor. Although owners cannot transfer federal tax credits under current law, investors can participate in the project and earn tax credits under complex rules. But to claim the benefits of the tax credits on their tax returns, investors must prove to the IRS that they maintain a sufficient level of participation in the investment. To determine the validity of the participation level, the IRS looks to such factors as the investor's percent of ownership interest, the length of the term of investment, and the proportionality of the benefit received to the amount invested. Why are such restrictions employed to limit the purchase of tax credits from otherwise qualifying projects? In some cases, complex investment structures that have attempted to allow property owners to benefit from tax credits have faced scrutiny. For example, the Third Circuit heard a case concerning a developer's creation of a limited liability company to attract an investor to use the federal historic tax credit. *Historic Boardwalk Hall, LLC v. Commissioner*, 694 F.3d 425 (3rd Cir. 2012). The investor was to be given a 3 percent priority return with put and call arrangements and had a 99.9 percent interest in the federal historic rehabilitation credits. The court determined that the investor did not share in the developer's business purpose of "rehabilitat[ing] and operat[ing]" the historic property. *Id.* at 458. In short, an investor who "lack[s] a meaningful stake in either the success or failure" of the rehabilitation is "not a bona fide partner." *Id.* at 463. Is this decision consistent with the general principle in tax law that transactions are respected only if they have economic substance? Are we making it too hard for people to invest in historic properties?

e.   COMBINING TAX CREDITS

Developers have come to rely on their ability to combine rehabilitation tax credits with funds from other public incentive programs, such as brownfield redevelopment funds and low-income housing tax credits. This has proven to be a powerful financing mechanism for socially desirable developments, as it provides sufficient incentive for developers to undertake projects that otherwise would be financially infeasible.

The federal Tax Code allows developers of affordable housing to utilize rehabilitation tax credits in tandem with the Low-Income Housing Tax Credits program, and this option has enabled the creation of tens of thousands of affordable housing units. In many cases, like the St.

Joseph's project, combining tax credits has been essential to the financial feasibility of the development. Additional examples of affordable housing projects financed with rehabilitation tax credits can be found on the National Park Service website.

How much do tax credits offset development costs? The following example illustrates the tax benefits to a taxpayer whose rehabilitation project qualifies for both the Historic Rehabilitation Tax Credit (HRTC) and the Low-Income Housing Tax Credit (LIHTC) programs:

> A taxpayer purchases an apartment building that has been designated a certified historic structure for $3,000,000. Of the total price, $500,000 is allocated to land. The taxpayer decides to rehabilitate the building and spends $4,000,000 on qualified rehabilitation expenditures and claims the 20 percent rehabilitation tax credit. If the taxpayer rents 40 percent of the building to low-income tenants and qualifies the project for the low income housing tax credit, the tax benefits for this project are as follows:

Amount of HRTC =	**$4,000,000 × 20% = $800,000**
Amount of LIHTC =	**Acquisition $2,500,000 × 40% × 4% = $40,000** [where Acquisition = $3,000,000 purchase price − $500,000 land]
Rehabilitation =	**$3,200,000 × 40% × 9% = $115,200** [where $3,200,000 = $4,000,000 − $800,000 tax credit]
Total Annual Credit =	**$155,200**
Amount of Annual Depreciation =	**$6,500,000 − $800,000 = $5,700,000 divided by 27.5 years = $207,273** [where $6,500,000 = $2,500,000 acquisition + $4,000,000 improvements, and where 27.5 years = depreciation period, or the building's "useful life"]
Annual Depreciation Tax Benefit =	**$207,273 × 0.28 = $58,036** [assuming tax bracket of 28%]
Total Annual Tax Benefit =	**$58,036 + $155,200 = $213,236**

INTERNAL REVENUE SERV., MARKET SEGMENT SPECIALIZATION PROGRAM GUIDELINE: REHABILITATION TAX CREDIT 23–26 (2002).

Case Study: St. Joseph's Senior Apartments

Consider the following description of a real-world example of a tax credit project in Oakland, California. This description is adapted from an article by the California Housing Partnership Corporation. *See* Ca. Hsg. Pship Corp., *St. Joseph's Senior Apartments Groundbreaking: Historic Rehabilitation Through Tax Credit Financing*, HSG. PRES. NEWS, Apr./May 2010, at 1–3.

In May 2010, advocates for affordable housing development celebrated the groundbreaking on the St. Joseph's Senior Apartments development. Completed in the summer of 2011, the first phase of the development rehabilitated a five-story Georgian Revival style brick building to create 84 units of affordable housing for low-income seniors and 3,200 square feet of ground floor commercial space within its historic shell.

Built in 1912, the Little Sisters of the Poor opened their new building at 2647 International Boulevard as a convalescent home for the elderly. The nuns operated St. Joseph's Home for the Aged until 1979, when they were forced to close the facility due to a lack of funds needed to bring the building up to modern building code standards. Subsequently, 2647 International Boulevard changed use and ownership several times. Despite suffering deferred maintenance, the building and site retained its historic character.

In 2006, the nonprofit affordable housing developer BRIDGE Housing acquired the building, intending to rehabilitate it to take advantage of incentives offered to developers of affordable housing in Oakland's Coliseum Redevelopment Area. BRIDGE Housing had structured the financing of the St. Joseph's renovation project as a combination of 4 percent Low-Income Housing Tax Credits and a loan from a state program. By 2008, however, the onset of the financial crisis caused the state to stop issuing bonds. With no willing lenders in the market, the project was put on hold.

Not long before, the developer had discovered that the unreinforced brick building required an expensive seismic retrofit, which was not accounted for in the original scope of work. The increase in construction costs from the major improvements to the historic building's structural system prompted the developer to seek rehabilitation tax credits. As described elsewhere in this Chapter, this process involves National Park Service (NPS) approval at three stages: Part 1, the certification of the project as a historic structure; Part 2, the determination that the rehabilitation proposal conforms with the Secretary's Standards for Rehabilitation; and Part 3, that the completed work complies with the Secretary's Standards.

While the project was on hold, BRIDGE Housing pursued the 3-part application process for rehabilitation tax credits to cover the financing gap. In late 2008, the NPS approved the Part 1 Application, which earned St. Joseph's a spot on the National Register of Historic Places.

The developer's rehabilitation plans preserved completely the exterior of the Georgian revival building and most of the associated buildings on the complex. The plans also retained distinctive site features including an iron picket fence and six heritage palm trees. The local preservation review board found that the renovation would have "no adverse impacts" on the historic character of the building. The NPS affirmed this decision, determining that the plans were in accordance with the Secretary's Standards for Rehabilitation. Thus, in January 2009, the Part 2 Application was approved and the project qualified for 20 percent historic tax credits, to be calculated based upon an estimated $19,000,000 of qualifying rehabilitation work.

The timing of the approval was fortuitous. Less than one month later, in February 2009, Congress passed the American Recovery and Reinvestment Act, which included a new Tax Credit Assistance Program and Tax Credit Exchange Program. Under these programs, the St. Joseph's project received preference from the California Tax Credit Allocation Committee for being "shovel ready" and was awarded the remaining necessary funds in August 2009. With the allocation of the 4 percent Low-Income Housing Tax Credits in place, and supported by a strong price from the project's tax credit investor, BRIDGE Housing was able to attract a bank to provide a tax-exempt construction loan.

The May 2010 groundbreaking event marked the symbolic end to the protracted struggle to finance the ambitious adaptive reuse project. In the end, the St. Joseph's project earned nearly six million dollars of historic tax credit equity from the sale of its rehabilitation tax credits to an investor.

The Oakland community has praised the project for the dual public interests it serves: preserving a beloved historic landmark and providing much-needed services to the area's low income elderly population. In addition, the development is expected to revitalize the neighborhood by eliminating blight and reducing crime. With its location on major public transit bus routes, residents of St. Joseph's Senior Apartments will benefit from the several markets, pharmacies, restaurants, and senior center all within a mile radius of the development. As a testament to the overwhelming demand for senior affordable housing in the area, the project had a full waitlist even before it opened.

NOTES & QUESTIONS

1.   From the outset, the plan for St. Joseph's Senior Apartments had been to adaptively reuse the historic structure. Why then was applying for historic rehabilitation tax credits not also in the developer's initial financing plan?

2.   The cost of renovating a historic property is higher for some projects than it is for others. For example, rehabilitations of places of public accommodation demand particularly skillful and creative design solutions that will both comply with the requirements of the Americans with Disabilities Act, a statute considered in the next section, and gain approval under historic preservation review. How might a developer go about determining the costs and benefits of applying for historic rehabilitation tax credits? What factors would weigh in favor of entering into the program's regulatory scheme, and which against?

f.   THE IMPACT OF THE CREDIT

The federal rehabilitation tax credit program offers the largest and most effective stimulus for private investment in historic preservation and urban revitalization. Between the years 1976 and 2001, approximately $25 billion was invested in the rehabilitation of over 29,000 historic properties. By 2010, the total investment under the program (including the years 1976–78, when the federal government offered the sixty-month amortization period but did not yet offer tax credits) more than doubled, growing to $58 billion. By 2020, the program had invested over $102 billion in 45,383 properties. Projects qualifying for rehabilitation credits range in size from minor repairs to a building's roof and other exterior elements to full-scale renovations of interior structural and mechanical systems.

Regardless of the scale of a project, the tax credit program serves the interests of preservation by extending the physical life of a building, but also its economic life: "Rehabilitation investment gives old and historic buildings a more viable place in the contemporary real estate market, thereby guaranteeing their continued use and contribution to an area's economic vitality." JAYNE F. BOYLE ET AL., A GUIDE TO TAX-ADVANTAGED REHABILITATION 1–2 (4th ed. 2002).

Some of the millions spent in qualified certified rehabilitations have gone into traditional preservation projects, such as those that maintain all historic features of the building without changes, and those that allow the building to be used as it was used historically. Most developers, however, have used the federal rehabilitation tax credit as a key project finance tool to repurpose historic buildings for new uses. They have renovated abandoned buildings to meet the current demands for housing or commercial services in the surrounding neighborhood. Projects across the country have successfully provided the pioneering development necessary to attract further economic investment and bring new vibrancy to abandoned urban areas.

2.   STATE REHABILITATION TAX CREDITS

As of 2021, thirty-six states operate their own historic rehabilitation tax credit programs. Most state tax credits are modeled after the federal program, and thus function to enhance the incentive to invest in the certification process. States stand to gain substantially from the spillover benefits of the policy, by bringing in more federal investment that work to increase property values.

As one example, Virginia's Historic Rehabilitation Tax Credit program has played an essential role in the preservation of thousands of historic properties since its inception in 1997. Between 1997 and 2017, the program issued $1.2 billion in tax credits, reimbursing 25 percent of eligible rehabilitation expenses. Those tax credits have stimulated $4.5 billion in private investment since 1997. Although the $1.2 billion in tax credits issued represents revenue not immediately realized by the Commonwealth, much of the $4.5 billion of private investment may not have otherwise occurred, according to a 2018 economic impact study by Virginia Commonwealth University. The study found that the Commonwealth's investment in historic preservation tax credits is repaid in five to nine years.

Not all state tax credits are created equal. The public policy division of the National Trust for Historic Preservation has observed that two key components characterize the most effective state tax credit programs: no limit on credit amounts awarded and the transferability of credits. *See* HARRY K. SCHWARTZ, NAT'L TRUST FOR HISTORIC PRES., STATE TAX CREDITS FOR HISTORIC PRESERVATION: A PUBLIC POLICY REPORT 1–3 (2011).

Some states place an annual aggregate cap on the total amount of credits the state is permitted to grant applicants. Kentucky, for example, limits the entire program to five million dollars per year. In states with aggregate caps, applicants must compete for credits or win them through a lottery system. How would you expect these caps to affect the size and makeup of the applicant pool? The size and type of projects? Other states simply limit the amount of credit allowed for a single project. Either form of cap dampens the participation rates and effectiveness of the policy.

The transferability, or not, of a credit also greatly impacts its popularity. If a tax credit is not transferable in any way, individuals without a high enough tax burden will have no use for them. In some states, such as Kansas and Missouri, taxpayers have the option of selling the credits. Other states allow the credits to be carried back or carried forward to count against taxes paid in previous or future years. A few state programs make the credit refundable, including Maryland, Iowa, and Louisiana. *See* SCHWARTZ, *supra* at 3. Several state historic preservation tax incentive programs include rehabilitation credits to historic homeowners, along with other benefits.

NOTES & QUESTIONS

1.   When "success" is measured in hundreds of millions of tax dollars foregone by the state, the most expensive programs become the most vulnerable targets in debates over balancing the budget. In 2011, the

Missouri legislature, aiming to address a budget deficit, sharply constricted the state's historic tax credit program. At its peak in the mid-2000s, Missouri was granting over $250 million in historic tax credits per year, as developers used them to transform great swaths of abandoned warehouses in downtown St. Louis. Under the current legislation, an aggregate annual cap limits the total amount available to large projects to $90 million, with no cap set for projects receiving less than $270,000 in tax credits. The legislation also prohibits developers from combining historic tax credits with certain low-income housing credits, to prevent developers from receiving too many subsidies. In nearly every state, demand outpaces supply. Rhode Island, for example, allocated its fiscal year 2021 credits in one day, disappointing thirty-four of the fifty-three applicants that submitted applications the day the state began taking applications.

Fortunately, states are continuing to introduce new programs. In 2019, California enacted a state historic tax credit. California has set an annual state cap of $50 million, and allocated $2 million specifically for residences, and another $8 million for projects that have qualified rehabilitation expenditures of less than $1 million. Currently, the program is set to allow a 20 percent credit on personal income and corporation taxes; the credit can rise to 25 percent for certain structures, including those that are affordable housing for lower income households.

2.   The courts have addressed the issue of sufficient levels of investor participation in a variety of transactional contexts. As was mentioned in the discussion of the practical application of federal historic tax credits above, developers have responded by creating complex investment structures. Entering a business enterprise partnership with the developer or holding a partnership role in an investment fund has generally been considered an acceptable level of participation for an investor to claim historic tax credits.

The Fourth Circuit struck down the validity of allocating the benefits of state preservation tax credits to individual investors through a partnership arrangement. *Virginia Historic Tax Credit Fund v. Commissioner*, 639 F.3d 129 (4th Cir. 2011). The level of partnership participation was not at issue in this case, but the court determined that the credit allocation amounted to a gain of property acquired through a disguised sale because the developers did not face sufficient entrepreneurial risk. The court ruled that such gain must be taxed as ordinary income, thus offsetting the credits and stripping the deal of any tax benefit. The case dealt specifically with a fund set up to aggregate investments in Virginia's strong Historic Tax Credit program, which requires allocation through partnership and prohibits the transfer of tax credits. *Id.* at 145; *see also* VA. CODE ANN. § 58.1–339.2 (2011). The case may have ramifications beyond Virginia, however, because it brings into question the validity of the practice in any state program. Practitioners are continuing to assess the magnitude of the impacts from the ruling, but it seems certain to deter investment.

B. THE AMERICANS WITH DISABILITIES ACT

1. THE STATUTORY STRUCTURE

The Americans with Disabilities Act of 1990 (ADA) prohibits discrimination against persons on the basis of disability in several important areas. 42 U.S.C. §§ 12101–12213. The ADA differs from more traditional civil rights statutes, such as the Civil Rights Act of 1964: Although both prohibit discrimination, the ADA also imposes affirmative duties on various entities to reasonably accommodate persons with disabilities. Thus, a building owner must not only admit a person with a disability, but she must also in some circumstances reconfigure her building to allow the disabled person to use and enjoy it.

Titles II and III of the ADA have important consequences for historic preservation law. Title III has broader implications for preservation than Title II because Title III applies to all private buildings considered to be "public accommodations." The ADA defines a place of "public accommodation" broadly by categories to include nearly all facilities open to the public, such as restaurants, retail stores, and schools, but not places of worship. 42 U.S.C. § 12187. Under Title III, all new construction and alterations to existing commercial facilities and public accommodations must be designed to be "readily accessible to and usable by individuals with disabilities." *Id.* § 12183. Moreover, owners of such existing buildings must "remove architectural barriers . . . where such removal is readily achievable." *Id.* § 12182 (b)(2)(iv). These requirements create tension with historic preservation goals because older buildings generally were not designed with disabled access in mind. Widening doorways or constructing ramps to provide access can destroy historically significant features of a property. Congress acknowledged the tension while drafting the ADA. *Id.* § 12204(c); *see* 136 CONG. REC. H2421–02 (daily ed. May 17, 1990) (statement of Rep. Hoyer).

Title II imposes duties on public entities to provide access to services, programs, and activities to all persons, regardless of disability status. *See id.* §§ 12131–12165. One public entity on which Title II imposes duties is the Advisory Council on Historic Preservation, a federal agency that oversees federal historic preservation law. The approach of the Advisory Council to meeting its obligations under Title II is discussed below.

Compliance with ADA rules can be complicated, and the Department of Justice (DOJ) has a special program—the ADA Technical Assistance Program—that provides free information regarding compliance to businesses, nonprofits, state and local governments, and the public. In addition, the DOJ has the authority to file lawsuits in federal court to ensure compliance with the ADA. Finally, the DOJ has primary responsibility for drafting ADA regulations. The following regulatory provisions demonstrate the approach taken by the DOJ regulations to reconciling the competing interests of the federal policies favoring historic preservation and disability access.

ADA Compliance Standards for Historic Properties: Federal Regulations Provisions
28 C.F.R. § 36.402

(a) General.

(1) Any alteration to a place of public accommodation or a commercial facility, after January 26, 1992, shall be made so as to ensure that, to the maximum extent feasible, the altered portions of the facility are readily accessible to and usable by individuals with disabilities, including individuals who use wheelchairs.

(2) An alteration is deemed to be undertaken after January 26, 1992, if the physical alteration of the property begins after that date.

(b) Alteration. For the purposes of this part, an alteration is a change to a place of public accommodation or a commercial facility that affects or could affect the usability of the building or facility or any part thereof.

(1) Alterations include, but are not limited to, remodeling, renovation, rehabilitation, reconstruction, historic restoration, changes or rearrangement in structural parts or elements, and changes or rearrangement in the plan configuration of walls and full-height partitions. Normal maintenance, reroofing, painting or wallpapering, asbestos removal, or changes to mechanical and electrical systems are not alterations unless they affect the usability of the building or facility. * * *

28 C.F.R. § 36.304

(a) General. A public accommodation shall remove architectural barriers in existing facilities, including communication barriers that are structural in nature, where such removal is readily achievable, i.e., easily accomplishable and able to be carried out without much difficulty or expense. * * *

28 C.F.R. § 36.405

(a) Alterations to buildings or facilities that are eligible for listing in the National Register of Historic Places under the National Historic Preservation Act, 16 U.S.C. 470 et seq., or are designated as historic under State or local law, shall comply to the maximum extent feasible with this part.

(b) If it is determined that it is not feasible to provide physical access to an historic property that is a place of public accommodation in a manner that will not threaten or destroy the historic significance of the building or the facility, alternative methods of access shall be provided pursuant to the requirements of subpart C of this part. [EDS.: 28 C.F.R. §§ 36.301–36.311.]

NOTES & QUESTIONS

1. There is a misconception that the Americans with Disabilities Act is a building code. While it does provide some examples of compliant buildings, the ADA is not a building code. Building codes set forth particular technical details about dimensions, materials, and techniques and are adopted primarily at the state level to govern all construction activity regarding buildings. For many years, building codes focused on new construction, and failed to fully account for the unique characteristics and challenges of historic properties. The International Code Council, a professional body that develops building codes through a peer review process, has created the International Existing Building Code, which has been adopted in forty-two states. Previously, rehabilitation subcodes, such as Article 32 from New Jersey, proved to have a catalytic effect on development in historic urban neighborhoods. *See* Sara C. Galvan, *Rehabilitating Rehab through State Building Codes*, 115 YALE L.J. 1744 (2006).

2. Imagine that you have a legal client who plans to convert a warehouse, considered to be a contributing building to a locally designated historic district, to a brew pub. Your client plans extensive changes to the interior of the building but none to the sole pedestrian entrance up three wide concrete steps. Would replacing the steps with a ramp damage the building's historic significance? Would you advise your client to resist replacing the steps with an accessible ramp on the ground that he is not altering them?

3. The ADA also deals with accessibility to certain public programs, and it treats historic preservation programs differently from other public programs. Historic preservation programs are defined as "programs conducted by a public entity that have preservation of historic properties as a primary purpose." 28 C.F.R. § 35.104; 41 C.F.R. § 101–8.311(b). What kinds of public programs fitting this description come to mind? Tours of a publicly-owned historic house museum is one common example. Federal regulations state that where physical changes to a building are excused, entities must offer audio-visual methods, special guides, or other innovative means to approximate the experience of the program for those who cannot physically access it.

2. ACCESS TO BUILDINGS OPEN TO THE PUBLIC

a. THE "READILY ACHIEVABLE" STANDARD

The above regulations give historic properties that serve as places of public accommodation special treatment under the Americans with Disabilities Act. The following case demonstrates the balance that must be struck to satisfy the conflicting laws and serve the competing public interests of universal access and historic preservation.

Gathright-Dietrich v. Atlanta Landmarks, Inc.
452 F.3d 1269 (11th Cir. 2006)

■ DUBINA, CIRCUIT JUDGE.

Appellants, Margo Gathright-Dietrich and Bonnie Bonham, appeal the district court's order granting summary judgment to appellee, Atlanta Landmarks, Inc., on their claim pursuant to Title III of the Americans with Disabilities Act ("ADA"), 42 U.S.C. § 12182, *et seq.* For the reasons that follow, we affirm.

I.   Background

The venue at issue in this appeal is The Fox Theatre ("The Fox") in Atlanta, Georgia, which was designed in the late 1920's. The Fox serves the Atlanta area as an unique and opulent entertainment center. The Fox is owned and operated by Atlanta Landmarks, Inc., a non-profit organization that led a successful community-wide effort to "Save The Fox" in the 1970's. The Fox contains significant historic features ranging from its seating configuration, to its simulated night-sky ceiling, to its faux painting techniques, to its original DC current-run elevators with AC converters. Because of these unique features, in 1974, the National Register of Historic Places added The Fox to its list. In 1976, the United States Department of the Interior designated The Fox a National Historic Landmark. Additionally, in 1991, due to its architectural and historical significance, The Fox became one of only nine buildings in the State of Georgia to be designated a Landmark Museum Building by the State Historic Preservation Officer of the Georgia Department of Natural Resources.

Prior to the passage of the ADA, The Fox installed removable theater seats to accommodate individuals in wheelchairs and created wheelchair-accessible restrooms. From the mid-1980's and throughout the 1990's, The Fox continued its efforts to make the theater more disabled-accessible, including (1) the installation of an elevator to give disabled patrons access to the theater's ballrooms; (2) the installation of a wheelchair-accessible box office; (3) the installation of a wheelchair-accessible telephone; (4) the addition of four new wheelchair-accessible restrooms; (5) the addition of a wheelchair-accessible concession area on the mezzanine level of the theater; and (6) the installation of a ramp to give performers, patrons, and visitors in wheelchairs access to the stage.
* * *

Appellants, undisputed patrons of the arts, have attended numerous events at The Fox. They filed suit under Title III of the ADA alleging that they and other wheelchair patrons are denied access to events at The Fox comparable to the access given to non-wheelchair patrons. Specifically, the appellants asserted that certain areas designated for wheelchair patrons are physically inaccessible to them; that the quality of their access is inferior; and that barriers exist in connection with ticket pricing and sales at The Fox. Following discovery, The Fox filed a motion for summary judgment, contending that the ADA did not mandate removal of any alleged architectural barriers. The district court granted The Fox's motion, finding that although the appellants proved that there were seating barriers, they failed to meet their burden of production to demonstrate that removal of those barriers was "readily achievable." In so ruling, the district court adopted the approach followed by the Tenth Circuit in *Colorado Cross Disability Coalition v. Hermanson Family Limited Partnership I*, 264 F.3d 999 (10th Cir. 2001), the only appellate decision addressing the issue. The district court also found that the changes that The Fox had already made to accommodate wheelchair patrons at the theater were sufficient to satisfy the ADA. Appellants filed a timely appeal.

II. Issue

Whether the district court erred in granting summary judgment to The Fox because it determined that appellants could not meet their burden of production on the issue of whether their proposed modifications relating to wheelchair seating at The Fox were "readily achievable" under Title III of the ADA.

III. Standard of Review

This court reviews the district court's order granting summary judgment *de novo*, viewing the evidence in the light most favorable to the non-moving party. *Wilson v. B/E Aerospace, Inc.*, 376 F.3d 1079, 1085 (11th Cir. 2004).

IV. Discussion

A. Title III of the ADA

The ADA is comprehensive legislation that addresses discrimination against disabled individuals. The ADA has three sections: Title I regulates discrimination in the workplace; Title II prohibits discrimination by public entities; and Title III prohibits discrimination by private entities in places of public accommodation. Title III applies to the present case and provides:

> No individual shall be discriminated against on the basis of disability in the full and equal enjoyment of the goods, services, facilities, privileges, advantages, or accommodations of any place of public accommodation by any person who owns, leases (or leases to), or operates a place of public accommodation.

42 U.S.C. § 12182(a). * * * After this date, facilities have to meet exacting design and implementation standards to be in compliance with the ADA. The ADA imposes different requirements on the owners and operators of facilities that existed prior to its enactment date. For those facilities, the ADA states that discrimination includes a private entity's "failure to remove architectural barriers ... where such removal is readily achievable." 42 U.S.C. § 12182(b)(2)(A)(iv). Where removal is not "readily achievable," failure of the entity to make goods, services and facilities

"available through alternative methods if such methods are readily achievable," may constitute discrimination under the ADA. 42 U.S.C. § 12182(b)(2)(A)(v).

The ADA defines "readily achievable" as "easily accomplishable and able to be carried out without much difficulty or expense." 42 U.S.C. § 12181(9). Congress included in the ADA factors to be considered in evaluating whether removal of a barrier is "readily achievable." These factors are (1) nature and cost of the action; (2) overall financial resources of the facility or facilities involved; (3) number of persons employed at such facility; (4) effect on expenses and resources; (5) impact of such action upon the operation of the facility; (6) overall financial resources of the covered entity; (7) overall size of the business of a covered entity; (8) the number, type, and location of its facilities; (9) type of operation or operations of the covered entity, including composition, structure, and functions of the workforce of such entity; and (10) geographic separateness, administrative or fiscal relationship of the facility or facilities in question to the covered entity. *Id.*

"The Department of Justice [ ] has interpreted the ADA's barrier removal and alteration requirements in accordance with the Congressional desire to take into account the national interest in preserving significant historical buildings." *Speciner v. NationsBank, N.A.*, 215 F.Supp.2d 622, 628–29 (D. Md. 2002). Thus, in the context of an historic building, "barrier removal would not be considered 'readily achievable' if it would threaten or destroy the historic significance of [the] building." *Id.* at 629 (quoting ADA Title III DOJ Technical Assistance Manual § III-4.4200). The alterations to the historic building need only comply with the accessibility standards "to the maximum extent feasible." 28 C.F.R. § 36.405(a). The ADA's implementing regulations provide specific procedures for determining feasibility, and the regulations state that "[i]f it is determined . . . that it is not feasible to provide physical access to an historic property . . . in a manner that will not threaten or destroy the historic significance of the building or facility, alternative methods of access shall be provided. . . ." *Id.* § 36.405(b).

B.   Application of Standard

Appellants argue on appeal that the district court erred in applying the burden of proof established in *Colorado Cross*. Under this approach, the plaintiff has the initial burden of production to show (1) that an architectural barrier exists; and (2) that the proposed method of architectural barrier removal is "readily achievable," i.e., "easily accomplishable and able to be carried out without much difficulty or expense" under the particular circumstances of the case. *Colorado Cross*, 264 F.3d at 1007. If the plaintiff meets this burden, the defendant then bears the ultimate burden of persuasion that barrier removal is not "readily achievable." *Id.* at 1002–03.

Appellants do not object to the general burden-shifting framework articulated by these cases, but instead, object to the amount and specificity of evidence required to meet their burden of showing that barrier removal was "readily achievable." Appellants contend that in order to meet their burden of production on this issue, the district court held that they must present evidence of "(1) a specific design to remove the barriers alleged; (2) the cost of removal or of the proposed remedy; and (3) the effect on the finances and operation of the facility." [R. Vol. 7, Doc. 107, p. 21]. Because of the expense involved in drafting what amounts to a "pre-approved construction contract for a sum certain which includes detailed plans, impact statements, engineering studies, and permits," the appellants argue that this standard guarantees that "virtually no plaintiff could afford to bring an architectural barrier removal claim." *Colorado Cross,* 264 F.3d at 1011 (Lucero, J., dissenting). We disagree.

The district court did not err in following the burden of proof enunciated in *Colorado Cross,* and we adopt that burden shifting framework for the reasons articulated by the *Colorado Cross* court. Moreover, the district court did not impose too heavy a burden on appellants to show that barrier removal was "readily achievable." The appellants did not satisfy their burden of production to show that a vast majority of the alleged conditions they cited, ranging from ticket pricing and sales policies, to restrooms and concession areas, constituted barriers to access for wheelchair patrons under the ADA. As for the alleged seat-number barrier, the appellants could not meet their burden of showing that the barrier removal was "readily achievable." Under the standard enunciated in *Colorado Cross,* a plaintiff must present sufficient evidence so that a defendant can evaluate the proposed solution to a barrier, the difficulty of accomplishing it, the cost implementation, and the economic operation of the facility. Without evidence on these issues, a defendant cannot determine if it can meet its subsequent burden of persuasion.

In this case, appellants submitted three proposed options relating to wheelchair seating, but they failed to produce any reliable evidence that those proposals were "readily achievable." Appellants' seating proposals involved the addition of at least 27 wheelchair seating positions, as well as modification of the existing wheelchair locations. Appellants' expert proposed three options: (1) The Fox could provide additional seating in existing level areas; (2) The Fox could remove rows of existing seats and modify the floor slab to create new inset sections on the orchestra level; and (3) The Fox could add raised platforms at various locations throughout the theater. However, these proposals were non-specific, conceptual proposals that did not provide any detailed cost analysis. Appellants did not provide any evidence of the number of seats lost, the number of wheelchair and companion seats gained, where they could be located, what it would cost to implement them, or what effect they could have economically or operationally on the theater. Appellants also failed to provide expert testimony to assure the feasibility of their proposed seating modifications and did not, in any meaningful way, address the engineering and structural concerns associated with their proposals or the effect that those proposals would have on the historic features of the theater. * * *

Assuming *arguendo* that the evidence proffered by appellants did satisfy their burden of production for barrier removal, we conclude that the district court's grant of summary judgment would still be appropriate because The Fox rebutted any showing by establishing that removal of the alleged barriers could not be accomplished without much difficulty or expense. The Fox presented undisputed evidence that lowering a portion of the floor, as appellants proposed, would directly affect the historic nature of the theater; the actual seating configuration in the theater is a character-defining feature of The Fox, and the permanent removal of seats would require the approval of the State Historic Preservation Officer; the floor that would be affected by appellants' proposals is historically significant; the implementation of certain of appellants' proposals would involve closing the theater for a period of time; the appellants' proposals would result in the elimination of seats belonging to season ticket holders; and a decrease in the number of regular theater seats would directly impact The Fox's ability to compete with other venues, possibly resulting in lost revenue. Therefore, The Fox satisfied its burden of persuasion, proving that barrier removal was not "readily achievable."

V.   Conclusion

Because we conclude that the district court properly applied the burden-shifting standard enunciated in *Colorado Cross* to the particular facts of this case, we affirm the district court's order granting summary judgment to The Fox.

Affirmed.

NOTES & QUESTIONS

1.   Why did the court in the above case find that the plaintiffs failed to prove that the alterations they proposed were "readily achievable"? According to a footnote in the district court decision, the only acknowledgement that the plaintiffs made of the impacts their proposals would have on the historic character of the theater were "occasional broad, unspecific comment[s]" made by their architectural expert. *Gathright-Dietrich v. Atlanta Landmarks, Inc.*, 435 F.Supp.2d 1217, 1233 n.26 (N.D. Ga. 2005). What evidence does the court of appeals suggest plaintiffs could have supplied to meet their burden of proof?

2.   What factors did the court consider persuasive in accepting the Fox Theater's argument that it need not adopt the plaintiffs' suggestions for improving access? What role does cost play in this analysis? Are the impacts on historic preservation considered separately from the general factors that determine "readily achievable" in non-historic buildings? Based on your interpretation of the regulations, should they be? The ADA Title III Technical Assistance Manual advises that barrier removal is not considered

readily achievable "if it would threaten or destroy the historic significance of a building or facility that is eligible for listing in the National Register of Historic Places under the [National Historic Preservation Act] or is designated as historic under State or local law." DEP'T OF JUSTICE, ADA TITLE III TECHNICAL ASSISTANCE MANUAL COVERING PUBLIC ACCOMMODATIONS AND COMMERCIAL FACILITIES III-4.3600 (1993). Does this language encompass the Fox Theater's concern, accepted by the court, that reducing the number of seats to accommodate more wheelchair access would reduce theater revenues?

3.   Included in the allegations that the Fox Theater violated Title III due to issues of physical inaccessibility were charges that the Appellants' "quality of access" was also inferior. To what does this refer? In the instant case, the district court decision explained that it was "the absence of shoulder-to-shoulder companion seats and the fact [that] wheelchair-designated restrooms lack the decor and ambiance of restrooms available to the public generally" that degraded their experience at the theater. *Gathright-Dietrich v. Atlanta Landmarks, Inc.*, 435 F.Supp.2d 1217, 1221 (N.D. Ga. 2005). Such claims of violation of the "full and equal enjoyment" clause of Title III highlight an additional layer of tension between disability law and historic preservation law. 42 U.S.C. § 12182. The tension is especially uncomfortable for managers of buildings open to the public specifically for the purpose of making available the benefits of historic preservation. In these cases, the most stringent preservation choices—deciding not to install an elevator to a second floor, for example—would exclude a segment of historic house enthusiasts from full enjoyment of a visit. How does this comport with the basic premise that historic preservation law is justified in terms of the "public benefit" it confers? The district court was concerned with this tension, and at the end of its opinion included this admonition of the Fox Theater:

> While the Court finds Defendant has done enough to comply with the ADA, it is disappointing that this grand and unique theater is satisfied in meeting its minimum obligations under the ADA. The Fox exists today because the public undertook to ensure its survival. It was the citizens of Atlanta who saved The Fox because they wanted to preserve a precious city treasure. The Atlanta community comes to the Fox in many ways, including by wheelchairs. All citizens would hope that The Fox will look carefully at the special role it plays in the Atlanta community and work hard to ensure that all Atlantans, the able bodied and the disabled, those who walk and those who wheel, can enjoy comparable entertainment experiences in this remarkable facility. It is what this community expects from the stewards of this historically special venue.

Gathright-Dietrich, 435 F.Supp.2d at 1236.

4.   When can historic properties provide "alternative methods of access" to comply with the ADA? In *Molski v. Foley Estates Vineyard & Winery*, 531 F.3d 1043 (9th Cir. 2008), the court considered a claim by a person with paraplegia against Foley Estates Vineyard under the ADA for

failing to make readily achievable alterations to its historic tasting room. The plaintiff argued that Foley's construction of a wheelchair-accessible gazebo with a "big bell" to summon for service did not provide an adequate "alternative accommodation" for visitors with disabilities. The court upheld the injunction ordering the "readily achievable" removal of barriers on the interior of the building, and remanded the question of the exterior ramp back to the district court. The court emphasized that Foley had an obligation under the ADA "to make readily available changes to enable the *maximum* participation *possible* for those who are able to access the interior of the wine-tasting room." *Id.* at 1050 (emphasis added). This was despite the fact that the steep exterior ramp would remain as a barrier and exclude visitors with certain disabilities. The opinion stressed the limited role of the alternative accommodation provision:

> Although we find the gazebo inadequate for those who could otherwise access the wine-tasting room, the gazebo provides an important avenue of participation for those who cannot traverse the steps or ramp to the wine-tasting room. * * * The gazebo places those who could otherwise access the wine-tasting room at a disadvantage that the ADA seeks to remove. Thus, the Gazebo is not an appropriate alternative accommodation.

Id., at 1050.

b.   THE "THREATEN OR DESTROY" STANDARD

The Department of Justice ADA Compliance Standards provide an exception when providing disability access would "threaten or destroy" the historic significance of a building under 28 C.F.R. § 36.405. How is it determined if alterations will cause this level of harm? Guidelines implementing the Standards set out a procedure by which the entity undertaking the alterations consults with the appropriate authority or authorities, generally the state historic preservation officer (SHPO), to make the final determination. *See* U.S. ARCHITECTURAL & TRANSPORTATION BARRIERS COMPLIANCE BOARD (ACCESS BOARD), ADA ACCESSIBILITY GUIDELINES FOR BUILDINGS AND FACILITIES (ADAAG) 4.1.7(2) (2002). If the authority confirms that compliance with accessibility requirements would cross the "threaten or destroy" threshold, then an alternative set of accessibility design requirements will be used. Alterations to buildings subject to Section 106 of the National Historic Preservation Act require the entity to follow the Section 106 review process, and either the SHPO or the Advisory Council on Historic Preservation (ACHP) can make the "threaten or destroy" determination. When the consultation takes place outside of the Section 106 review process, the SHPO is the sole authority. The ADAAG also state minimum requirements for a public historic building in matters of access, information displays, and toilets. *Id.* at 4.1.7(3).

One commentator, attorney Grant Fondo, has provided a critical analysis of the historic preservation exception to the ADA. He outlines the ways in which the "threaten and destroy" standards might function to limit the exception's application as follows:

> The most significant aspect of [the historic preservation exception] provision is the interpretation of the phrase "threaten or destroy the historic significance of historic buildings." Prior to the DOJ's final publication of rules, there was extensive debate about the standard to be applied. Some commentators criticized the proposed DOJ standard [because it] would not exempt the site from accessibility requirements unless the alteration substantially impaired the historic features of a property. * * * Commentators representing the National Trust and the Advisory Council on Historic Preservation advocated application of the "adverse effect" standard currently used under the NHPA. Preservationists preferred the adverse effect standard because they were familiar with it, and because it was less stringent than the "threaten or destroy" standard contained in the ADA. Others argued that stronger language was needed to ensure access to historic buildings. These groups argued that if historic buildings could be modified to include plumbing and electricity, they could similarly be renovated to make the building accessible. The DOJ rejected the adverse effect interpretation advocated by preservationists as inconsistent with Congressional intent and language under section 12204(c), and instead adopted the more stringent "threaten or destroy" standard.

> The threshold to meet the "threaten or destroy" standard was intended to be very high. The DOJ stated in its preamble to the final regulations that section 12204(c) is to "be applied only in those very rare situations in which it is not possible to provide access to an historic property using the . . . access provisions in the ADAAG."

Grant P. Fondo, *Access Reigns Supreme: Title III of the Americans with Disabilities Act and Historic Preservation*, 9 B.Y.U. J. PUB. L. 99, 122–23 (1994).

Fondo's critique goes on to conclude that the difficult qualification standard and limited protections of the historic preservation exception result in the goals of the ADA superseding those of the NHPA. One of his key concerns was that even after it has been determined that ADA alterations will "threaten or destroy," historic properties are still not exempt from certain minimum compliance requirements. *Id.* at 123. The requirements of the alternative accessibility standards for historic properties include providing an accessible entrance and an accessible route to all publicly used spaces on the level where the accessible entrance is located. *See* ADAAG at 4.1.7(3).

NOTES & QUESTIONS

1.   Do you agree with Fondo's view that Congress offered little to preservationists in drafting the ADA's preservation exception as a compromise? Does it matter that ACHP must be consulted if it is determined the application of these alternative standards would still threaten or destroy historic significance?

2.   Somewhat surprisingly, the "threaten or destroy" standard is not heavily litigated. In fact, on the whole, very few lawsuits have arisen out of the inherent tensions in increasing access to historic properties. Why might that be? One analysis attributes this fact to the apparent success of the consultation process set out in the ADAAG. *See* Christopher Parkin, *A Comparative Analysis of the Tension Created by Disability Access and Historic Preservation Laws in the United States and England*, 22 CONN. J. INT'L L. 379, 381 (2007) (finding willingness to work with the access needs of the disabled in correspondence from historic building operators to Department of Justice). In addition, the analysis notes a general willingness among business owners to make accommodations and comply with the law. The author goes on to discuss the fear service providers are likely to feel in contemplating defending a lawsuit based on their ability to prove their buildings qualify for the exception under the "threaten or destroy" standard. *Id.* at 402. The pressure this creates for property owners to settle claims may also help to explain the dearth of lawsuits. Can you think of other reasons?

3.   Would you expect local preservation boards to be more lenient in granting applications for alterations providing disabled access? Why? Is that appropriate? Your answer may depend on your conceptualization of the "public benefit" value of historic preservation. Is the source of the value of historic properties simply that they exist, or is the true benefit realized when people can see and experience them? *See* 41 C.F.R. § 101–8.311(b)(iv) ("Because the primary benefit of an Historic Preservation Program is the experience of the historic property itself, in taking steps to achieve accessibility, recipients shall give priority to those means which make the historic property, or portions thereof, physically accessible to handicapped individuals.").

4.   What kinds of alterations are typically necessary to make historic buildings accessible? Which alterations would you expect are the most likely to affect historically significant features and trigger the "threaten and destroy" standard? In what ways could alterations for accessibility compliance be designed to mitigate harm? The National Park Service's Technical Preservation Services division published Preservation Brief 32 to provide guidance on this issue. *See* Thomas C. Jester & Sharon C. Park, *Making Historic Properties Accessible* (Nat'l Park Serv., Pres. Assistance Div., Brief No. 32 1993).

3. ACCESS TO PUBLIC PROGRAMS

Public entities—federal, state, regional, and local governments, as well as school districts and other special purpose districts—have an additional responsibility under the ADA to make government services and programs accessible. Title II states that no person shall "be excluded from participation in or be denied the benefits of the services, programs, or activities of a public entity" by reason of disability. 42 U.S.C. § 12132. One obvious implication of this rule is that public buildings where people go to receive government services, such as courthouses and schools, must be made accessible.

The easiest way to comply with Title II would be to fully renovate public buildings, but in some cases renovation would conflict with another important public goal: historic preservation. How should a public entity comply with its duties under Title II when the property qualifies for the Title III exemption from making physical alterations? In these instances, Title II requires all branches of state and local government to remove accessibility barriers by either relocating public services to an accessible facility or by making the services available through "alternative methods," as suggested by 28 C.F.R. § 36.305. Physical access is preferred when the public service provided is the historic preservation itself, as in the example of the historic house museum below.

Although all public entities must comply with Title II, it may be worth highlighting two special cases for illustrative purposes. The first is the Advisory Council on Historic Preservation (ACHP), established by the National Historic Preservation Act (NHPA) in 1966. The ACHP is a key player in federal historic preservation policy, charged with advising the President and Congress. In addition, it consults with federal agencies to confirm that their activities comply with Section 106 of the NHPA, further discussed in Chapter 3. In both its consultative and policy roles, the ACHP provides public "services, programs, or activities" that implicate Title II. In response to Title II, the Advisory Council on Historic Preservation has enacted regulations to define the scope of its duty to comply with the ADA while serving the purposes of the NHPA. Although the regulations provide that ACHP will not exclude from participation or discriminate against any person with a disability, 36 C.F.R. § 812.130, the regulations state that the general obligation does not "require the agency to take any action that would result in a substantial impairment of significant historic features of an historic property." *Id.* § 812.150(a)(2).

A second set of public entities on which Title II has significant impact are public transit authorities receiving federal funding. Title II requires that public transit authorities identify "key stations" in their system and ensure that those stations are accessible. *See* 42 U.S.C. § 12147. Department of Transportation regulations further specify the duties of transit authorities to provide accessible transportation services. *See* 49 C.F.R. §§ 37.41–61. The regulations apply differently to new construction projects than to retrofits of existing transit facilities. Among other things, the regulations require that new transit facilities be fully accessible, unless unique features of the terrain make accessibility "structurally impracticable." *Id.* § 37.41. Alterations affecting usability must merely incorporate accessibility "to the maximum extent feasible." *Id.* § 37.43.

NOTES & QUESTIONS

1. The following hypothetical illustrates acceptable methods and levels of alternative access for public entities with historic properties that provide public services implicating Title II:

> A town-operated two story historic house museum, which dates from 1885, provides tours and public programs focused on the exhibition of a typical 19th century Victorian house.

> A self-evaluation determines that the house is not accessible. After considering the options for providing access to the programs and services, the town decides that it is not possible to move the museum programs to other accessible locations because the historic house itself is a critical part of the historic house program. The town develops plans to alter the facility to provide physical access to the first floor. These alterations are planned in compliance with the historic preservation requirements of the ADA Standards.

> After reviewing the alterations with the State historic preservation office, the town determines that the second floor cannot be made accessible without threatening the unique features and historic significance of the house. Because the town must consider alternatives to structural changes in these instances, the town establishes a policy to locate all temporary programs on the first floor. In addition, the town documents the second floor spaces and content using video or other innovative solutions and provides an accessible viewing area on the first floor.

DISABILITY RIGHTS SECTION, DEP'T OF JUSTICE, ADA GUIDE FOR SMALL TOWNS 3 (2000). What differentiates these acceptable suggestions by the DOJ from the unacceptable practices employed at Foley Estate Vineyard, described a few pages ago, in the note on *Molski v. Foley Estates Vineyard & Winery*, 531 F.3d 1043 (9th Cir. 2008)?

Consider a second hypothetical: a town library is listed on the state historic register and it is determined the exterior cannot be modified to provide an accessible entrance in a way that would not threaten or destroy the historic significance of the library building. What options are available for the staff to provide library services in an alternative manner to patrons with disabilities who cannot access the library? *See* DISABILITY RIGHTS SECTION, DEP'T OF JUSTICE, ADA GUIDE FOR SMALL TOWNS 2–3 (2000). Note that the *ADA Guide for Small Towns* is one of several publications that the DOJ uses to clarify ADA compliance requirements. Other guides address issues specific to small businesses, operators of polling places, gas station owners, and hotels.

2. How do the ACHP's regulations mirror the historic preservation exceptions included in Title III of the ADA? How do they differ? In what ways do the ACHP regulations specifically address its obligations under Title II?

What about its duties under National Historic Preservation Act? Do the regulations strike a fair balance?

3. The process of renovating a historic building to make it compliant with the ADA can be done quite successfully, while meeting several public goals. A 2009 renovation to Washington, D.C.'s historic (1820) city hall and courthouse, shown in Figure 11-6, provided a new home for the D.C. Court of Appeals. Hidden behind the walls in this photograph are graceful ramps that provide access to the level grade entrance. The modern transparent entry pavilion allows viewers to enjoy the historic elements of the building's façade. The design of the entrance complements the building's historic features in scale and geometry without imitating them, while housing modern security equipment. The project has won numerous awards for excellence in architecture, historic preservation, and construction.

Figure 11-6:
A Modern, ADA-Compliant Addition to the
D.C. Court of Appeals, Washington, DC

4. ADA AND NHPA

The following decision provides a rare judicial analysis of the interplay between the requirements of the Americans with Disabilities Act and Section 106 of the National Historic Preservation Act (covered in Chapter 3). The key question the court considered was whether the Federal Transit Administration's proposal to alter a transit station to, among other things, provide elevator access and improve accessibility to public transportation had impermissible effects on nearby historic properties.

Neighborhood Association of the Back Bay, Inc. v. Federal Transit Administration

463 F.3d 50 (1st Cir. 2006)

[EDS.: All references to the National Historic Preservation Act have been recodified and often amended at title 54, Pub. L. No. 113–287, 128 Stat. 3094. We have tried to note below where specific provisions have moved.]

■ DYK, C.J.

The Neighborhood Association of the Back Bay, Inc. ("NABB") and the Boston Preservation Alliance ("BPA") (collectively "Plaintiffs") brought suit against the Federal Transit Authority [EDS.: sic] ("FTA") and Massachusetts Bay Transportation Authority ("MBTA"), asserting that planned modifications to the Copley Square transit station violated historical preservation statutes. The United States District Court for the District of Massachusetts denied preliminary and final injunctive relief. Because we conclude that the plaintiffs have not established a violation of applicable federal or state statutes, we affirm.

This case primarily presents questions as to whether the FTA, in providing funding to the MBTA to make the Copley Square station compliant with the Americans with Disabilities Act ("ADA"), 42 U.S.C. §§ 12101–12213 (2000), has violated various federal statutes designed to preserve historic properties.

I.

Under Title II of the ADA, 42 U.S.C. §§ 12131–12165 (2000), and its implementing regulations, 49 C.F.R. §§ 37.47–51, public transit authorities receiving federal funds are required to identify "key stations" in their transit stations and then make those stations accessible to wheelchair users. 42 U.S.C. § 12147.

In 1992 the Copley Square station was identified by the MBTA as a key station, and plans were made to modify the station to make it wheelchair accessible. To make the station wheelchair accessible would require installation of new inbound and outbound elevators to transport wheelchair users.

Under 49 U.S.C. § 5310, the FTA provides federal funds to state entities such as the MBTA to assist them in achieving compliance with the ADA. However, in providing funding, the FTA, like other federal agencies, must ensure that the funded projects comply with various federal statutes dealing with historic preservation, including two sections of the National Historic Preservation Act ("NHPA")—16 U.S.C. § 470f [EDS.: moved to 54 U.S.C. § 306108] ("section 106"), and 16 U.S.C. § 470h–2(f) [EDS.: moved to 54 U.S.C. § 306107] ("section 110(f)"). * * *

The problem with the planned modifications to the Copley Square station lies in the fact that the station is adjacent to the Boston Public Library ("the Library") and the Old South Church ("the Church"), both of which are designated as National Landmarks and are listed on the National Register of Historic Places. The Library and Church are located within the Back Bay Historic District, which is itself on the National Register of Historic Places, as is the existing inbound entrance headhouse to Copley station. The proposed modifications to the station would require use of part of the Library steps for the inbound elevator and construction of an outbound elevator adjacent to the Church. * * *

Figure 11-7:
The Copley Square Façade of the Boston Public Library,
Boston, MA

To comply with these statutes, the FTA must find that the state entity complies with each statute before disbursing federal funds for any transportation project, including an ADA accessibility project. But the FTA need not undertake separate reviews under each statute. 36 C.F.R. § 800.3(b). Furthermore, in determining compliance with these statutes a federal agency such as the FTA can rely on state agencies such as the MBTA, and on consultants. *Id.* § 800.2(a)(3). Here, the FTA, in concluding that the Copley Station project complied with all these statutes, relied on "information, analyses and recommendations" prepared by the MBTA. The MBTA, in turn, relied on consultants.

II.

The MBTA initially addressed the requirements of the ADA in 1995. The MBTA commissioned a consultant to perform a study, the "Schematic Design Report" (the "1995 Report"), that explored options for making these key stations accessible. The 1995 Report identified several options for locating elevators at the Copley Square station, and listed advantages and disadvantages of each. It identified four options for locating the outbound elevator: option A located the elevator in front of the Church, and options B, C, and D located it across the street from the Church. The report noted that option A "has the most serious historic adjacency issues" with respect to the Church, but that it created "[n]o major impacts on streetscape elements and infrastructure," required little construction work, and was "[l]ocate[d] along the main path of access."

The report identified two potential locations for the inbound elevator: option E located the elevator adjacent to the existing historic wrought iron subway entrance on the Library steps, and option F located it about 150 feet away from the existing entrance without using the Library steps. Option E called for the construction of a matching structure on the other side of the existing entrance. The 1995 Report concluded that failure to build this matching structure would "seriously compromise the explicit symmetry of the [historic landmark] composition." It also stated that option E "is problematic because it not only creates the very difficult task of imposing new structures along side the intricately detailed wrought iron headhouse, but also creates many interface problems with the Boston Public Library." As for option F, the report noted that it had a lesser "streetscape and urban impact" than option E, "but place[d] the entrance in a remote location from the main entry to the station," which raised questions of ADA compliance and also posed a number of engineering difficulties.

At some point before May 28, 2002, the MBTA settled on option E (library steps), minus the matching structure, for the inbound elevator, and option A for the outbound elevator, locating the elevator in front of the Church. The matching structure for the inbound elevator was rejected because it would have been positioned above the Library's basement, making it impractical to anchor. Meetings were held with representatives of the Library and the Church; no objection was raised to the locations of the elevators. However, on August 22, 2003, plaintiff NABB by letter requested various changes to the project, including the locations for both inbound and outbound elevators. The letter requested that the inbound elevator be placed 150 feet away from the existing Library entrance (option F), rather than on the Library steps, and that the outbound elevator be placed across the street from the Church rather than directly in front of it. NABB did not then assert that the placement of the elevators violated federal statutory requirements.

The MBTA first addressed the requirements of the various federal historical preservation statutes when it requested that its preservation consultant prepare a report (the "Carolan Report"). Though entitled "Section 106 and 4(f) Review," the Carolan Report only discussed Section 106 and did not mention section 4(f) at all. Nor did the report address the requirements of section 110(f). The report described the project, including the planned elevator locations, and explained the effects of the project. The report concluded that "the primary effect of [the project] would be a visual one," and that the selected designs "will not interfere with existing historic architectural structures." The report did not discuss the alternative locations, but concluded that the planned locations and designs for the inbound and outbound elevators would not have an "adverse effect" within the meaning of section 106.

On August 29, 2003, based on the Carolan Report, the MBTA sent a letter to the FTA stating that "[i]n view of these facts, it is our opinion that the project will have 'No Adverse Effect' on any historic resources." The MBTA "request[ed] a determination of No Adverse Effect by FTA."

As the regulations require,[1] the FTA by letter formally advised the Massachusetts Historic Commission ("MHC") of the Copley Station improvement on January 23, 2004, and requested "[the MHC's] concurrence in [the FTA's] determination that this project will have no adverse effect on historic resources." The parties appear to agree that this letter constitutes the FTA's finding of "no adverse effect" under section 106. The MHC concurred in the FTA's finding of "no adverse effect" on January 29, 2004. * * *

III.

Plaintiffs NABB and BPA filed suit under the APA on June 9, 2005, alleging that the FTA and MBTA violated sections 106 and 110(f) of NHPA, and section 4(f) of DOTA in approving the project. * * *

Following a hearing, the district court denied plaintiffs' request for injunctive relief. * * *

[T]he district court rejected the plaintiffs' argument that the FTA violated the procedural requirements of the section 106 regulations by failing adequately to document its "no adverse effect" finding, by failing to independently review the project, or by failing to consult with the requisite "consulting parties" in reaching the conclusion that there would be no adverse effect. The district court also concluded that plaintiffs had not established that the no adverse effect finding was arbitrary and capricious. * * *

Discussion

Judicial review here is governed by the Administrative Procedure Act, 5 U.S.C. § 706, which requires that agency action be set aside if the action was "arbitrary, capricious, an abuse of discretion, or otherwise not in accordance with law" or if the action failed to meet statutory, procedural, or constitutional requirements.

Precision of expression is not the hallmark of either the historic preservation statutes involved here or the regulations promulgated to implement those statutes. In view of this ambiguity, we defer, where appropriate, to the various agency views as to the applicable requirements. Under the *Chevron* doctrine, an agency's interpretation of a statute is entitled to weight when the statute is silent or ambiguous.

---

[1]   The regulations promulgated under section 106 provide that "[i]f the agency official proposes a finding of no adverse effect, the agency official shall notify all consulting parties [here including the MHC] . . . [and] the [MHC] shall have 30 days from receipt to review the finding." 36 C.F.R. § 800.5(c). If the MHC disagrees, further consultation is required. *Id.* § 800.5(c)(2).

See Chevron U.S.A., Inc. v. Nat. Res. Def. Council, Inc., 467 U.S. 837, 842–43 (1984). We also owe deference to an agency's interpretation of its own regulations.

Here, we owe *Chevron* deference to the statutory interpretations reflected in the regulations promulgated by the Advisory Council on Historic Preservation ("ACHP") under sections 106 and 110, and promulgated by DOTA under section 4f. * * * We do not owe deference to the FTA's interpretation of the regulations promulgated by other agencies, such as the section 106 and 110(f) regulations. Nonetheless, we owe deference to the FTA's no adverse effect finding under sections 106 and 110, since the FTA has jurisdiction to make the finding, even though it does not have interpretive authority.

Underlying deference to agency action are assumptions that the agencies are better able to articulate the pertinent policies, and to reconcile the policies of potentially conflicting statutes. An equally important assumption is that the agencies will, in fact, carefully consider the policy issues and articulate their resolution with clarity. Here the goals of the historic preservation statutes potentially conflict with the mandates of the ADA. As we will see, the FTA, while adequately performing its assigned task, has fallen short of distinction in doing so, giving little more than the bare minimum attention to historic preservation issues. Of even greater concern, the agencies * * * charged with promulgating regulations interpreting the historic preservation statutes and reconciling them with the ADA have issued regulations that are in some respects cryptic and confusing. While we have been able to construe those regulations in the present case so as to resolve the matter at hand, the deficiencies in the existing regulations likely invite further litigation as to future projects.

I.   Compliance with Section 106 of NHPA

The National Historic Preservation Act of 1966, 16 U.S.C. § 470 *et seq.* [EDS.: moved to Pub. L. 96–515, Title I, § 101(a) *et seq.*], "requires each federal agency to take responsibility for the impact that its activities may have upon historic resources, and establishes the Advisory Council on Historic Preservation ['ACHP'] . . . to administer the Act." *City of Grapevine v. Dep't of Transp.*, 17 F.3d 1502, 1508 (D.C. Cir. 1994).

Section 106 of the NHPA requires that the FTA or any other federal agency, in funding a project,

> take into account the effect of the undertaking [project] on any district, site, building, structure, or object that is included in or eligible for inclusion in the National Register. The head of any such Federal agency shall afford the Advisory Council on Historic Preservation established under part B of this subchapter a reasonable opportunity to comment with regard to such undertaking.

The Library and Church are included in the National Register. Under such circumstances, the ACHP regulations require the FTA to determine whether the project will have an "adverse effect" on the historic properties. 36 C.F.R. § 800.5. If the agency finds an adverse effect, then the agency must follow procedures under section 800.6 designed to avoid or mitigate the adverse effects. *Id.* §§ 800.5(d)(2); 800.6(a),(b); 800.7 ("failure to resolve adverse effects"). *See id.* § 800.8 (coordination with NEPA, including early 106 review).

Section 106 is a procedural statute that requires agency decisionmakers to "stop, look, and listen," but not to reach particular outcomes. *Narragansett Indian Tribe v. Warwick Sewer Auth.*, 334 F.3d 161, 166 (1st Cir. 2003).

Plaintiffs argue that for various reasons the requirements of section 106 were not met. Plaintiffs first contend that the FTA committed procedural error during the process leading up to the "no adverse effect" finding. Plaintiffs complain that the FTA did not conduct an independent analysis of historical impacts of the undertaking and instead improperly relied on the determination of the Carolan Report and the MBTA. However, the regulations expressly permit an agency to "use the services of applicants, consultants, or designees to prepare information, analysis and recommendations," 36 C.F.R. § 800.2(a)(3); *see also Narragansett Indian Tribe*, 334 F.3d at 168 ("The regulations themselves explicitly contemplate the use of consultants to provide analyses for use in the § 106 process.").

Although the plaintiffs urge that there is no indication that the FTA made the required independent determination, there is no specific requirement in the statute, the regulations or the APA that the FTA provide detailed explanations for its decision or use any particular form of words signifying that it made an independent determination. Moreover, we are required to presume that the FTA abided by the statutory requirements in the absence of any showing that it did not do so. As the district court found here, "[p]laintiffs offer no credible evidence indicating that the FTA did not conduct an independent review, or that it 'rubber stamped' the MBTA's conclusion of 'no adverse effects.' "

We also see no merit in plaintiffs' contention that the documentation provided to the MHC by the FTA did not adequately explain the basis of the no adverse effect finding. They rely on regulations that require that the documentation "enable" reviewing parties "to understand [the] basis" of the adverse effect finding as required by the regulations. 36 C.F.R. § 800.11(a); *see also id.* § 800.11(e) (requiring documentation to support an adverse effect finding). The plaintiffs' primary contention is that the underlying documentation did not address alternative locations for the elevators, but there is nothing in the statute or regulations that requires the consideration of alternatives in making the no adverse effect determination. Plaintiffs' fallback position is that the document did not consider elevator location at all in reaching the no adverse effects finding.

This is not correct. The documents, including the Carolan Report, described in detail the basis for the finding and considered the location of the elevators in making the finding.[5]

Turning to the merits, the plaintiffs also contend that the no adverse effect finding is not sustainable. Again, we disagree.

Plaintiffs argue that the regulations promulgated under section 106 compel a finding of "adverse effect." Their principal contention is that locating the inbound elevator on the Library steps will have an adverse effect on the Library.

The section 106 regulations, 36 C.F.R. § 800.5 ("Assessment of adverse effects"), set forth the criteria for determining whether an action will have an adverse effect. Section 800.5(a) provides that the "agency official shall apply the criteria of adverse effect to historic properties within the area of potential adverse effects." Section 800.5(a)(1) ("Criteria of adverse effect") provides:

> An adverse effect is found when an undertaking may alter, directly or indirectly, any of the characteristics of a historic property that qualify the property for inclusion in the National Register in a manner that would *diminish the integrity* of the property's location, design, setting, materials, workmanship, feeling or association . . . . (emphasis added).

The FTA relied on various documents to support its no adverse effect finding, including its implicit conclusion that the integrity of the Library was not compromised. The plaintiffs argue that the 1995 Report would only support a finding of no diminishment if the original option E had been adopted (using matching headhouses on either side of the library) and that the report did not support such a finding with respect to the final plan that eliminated the matching headhouse. Plaintiffs correctly point out that the 1995 Report concluded that the elimination of the matching headhouse would *"seriously compromise the explicit symmetry of the composition."* (Emphasis added.) However, the 1995 Report was not addressed to federal statutory requirements, and the FTA primarily relied on the later Carolan report, which was prepared after the elimination of the matching headhouse, for this purpose. The Carolan Report described the historic setting of Copley Station at length, and concluded that the selected designs "will not interfere with existing historic architectural structures." This report amply supports the agency's conclusion that the inbound elevator would not have an adverse effect, *i.e.*, that it would not "diminish the integrity" of the historical sites or "change the character" of features of the Library that contribute to its

---

[5]   Plaintiffs' argument that they should have been deemed consulting parties because they were interested in the project and that interest was well-known is also without merit. The regulations expressly require parties to make a written request to become consulting parties, and gives the agency and SHPO (here the MHC) the discretion to decide whether to grant the request. 36 C.F.R. § 800.3(c)(5).

historical significance. The plaintiffs have failed to show that this finding, on which the FTA relied, was arbitrary or capricious.

Plaintiffs also urge that, even if the FTA was not arbitrary and capricious in concluding that the proposed location of the inbound elevator would not "diminish the integrity" of the library, section 800.5(a)(2), which lists specific examples of adverse effects, compels an adverse effect finding. This section provides that:

> [a]dverse effects on historic properties include, but are not limited to:
>
> (i)   Physical destruction of or damage to all or part of the property;
>
> (ii) Alteration of a property, including restoration, rehabilitation, repair, maintenance, stabilization, hazardous material remediation, and provision of handicapped access, that is not consistent with the Secretary's standards for the treatment of historic properties (36 C.F.R. Part 68) and applicable guidelines
>
> . . . .

Plaintiffs argue that locating the inbound elevator on the Library steps has an adverse effect on the Library because disturbing the Library steps constitutes "[p]hysical destruction of or damage to all or part of the property" under subpart (i).

This interpretation is inconsistent with the structure of the regulations. Under subpart (ii) adverse effects include "[a]lteration of a property, including . . . *provision of handicapped access* . . . that is not consistent with the Secretary [of the Interior's] standards for the treatment of historic properties (36 C.F.R. Part 68) and applicable guidelines." *Id.* § 800.5(a)(2)(ii) (emphasis added). Thus, subpart (ii) effectively recognizes that alterations consistent with the Secretary's regulations will not create an adverse effect if they are designed to secure handicapped access. In this respect the regulations are evidently designed to avoid potential conflicts with the requirements of the ADA. If subpart (ii) is to be given its full effect, subpart (i) cannot compel an adverse effect finding when a property is physically altered to secure handicapped access in a manner that could be said to "damage" the property. Rather, subpart (i) must be read to refer only to "damage" that does not come within the purposes enumerated in subpart (ii). In other words, alterations for the provision of handicapped access are governed exclusively by subpart (ii).

We similarly reject the plaintiffs' contentions that the placement of the inbound elevator could violate subsection (iv) ("[c]hange of the character of the property's use or of physical features within the property's setting that contribute to its historic significance") and subsection (v) ("[i]ntroduction of visual, atmospheric or audible elements that diminish the integrity of the property's significant historic features"). Again, if the project complied with subsection (ii), it cannot be argued that it failed to comply with subsections (iv) and (v).

We find no merit in plaintiffs' confusing contention that there was an adverse effect within the meaning of subpart (ii) itself. Plaintiffs have not shown that the alterations to the Library steps are inconsistent with the Secretary of the Interior's standards for the treatment of historic properties set out in 36 C.F.R. Part 68.

We finally reject plaintiffs' argument that the placement of the *outbound* elevator would have an adverse effect on Old South Church; and that placement of both elevators would have an adverse effect on the design of the Back Bay region of the city, which itself appears in the National Register of Historic Places; and that the rehabilitation of the existing wrought iron entrance would constitute an adverse effect under subpart (ii). The FTA's finding of no adverse effect encompassed the project as a whole, including both the inbound and the outbound elevator. The plaintiffs have failed to show that this finding was arbitrary or capricious.

We conclude that the agency's finding of "no adverse effect" must be sustained.

NOTES & QUESTIONS

1.   The court does not hold here that construction of an elevator on the steps of the Boston Public Library, or directly in front of the Old South Church, has no effect on the structure, but rather it holds that the elevators cannot legally be considered to have created an adverse effect under the Advisory Council on Historic Preservation regulations if they were constructed to comply with the Americans with Disabilities Act and if in conformity with the Secretary of the Interior's Standards for the Treatment of Historic Properties in 36 C.F.R. Part 68. The Secretary's Standards are general, but highly influential, statements of best practices regarding preservation, rehabilitation, restoration, and reconstruction.

How might the plaintiffs have shown that the elevators did not meet the Secretary's Standards? One standard provides that new additions shall not destroy "spatial relationships that characterize the property." 36 C.F.R. § 68.3(b)(9). Can you identify evidence recounted by the court that the elevator on the steps of the Library does or does not mar the spatial relationships of the building? Should the court have found that there would be an adverse effect on the Library or on the Church? Consider Figures 11-8 and 11-9 showing the two elevators as built: one along on the Library's side steps next to the existing wrought-iron subway entrance, the other in front of the Church.

2.   The Federal Transit Administration could still place the elevators in front of the Library and the Old South Church despite adverse effects if it considered alternatives and mitigation. Did it do so? Consider the position of a court reviewing an agency decision it considers responsible on the whole but containing technical errors.

Figures 11-8 & 11-9:
The Copley Station Elevators in Front of the Boston
Public Library and the Old South Church,
Boston, MA

3. Although the MBTA was made a defendant in the case and clearly had a large financial stake in the outcome for the litigation, only the Federal Transit Administration as a federal agency has legal duties under the terms of Section 106. As is common, the FTA relied on the MBTA and on consultants to conduct the analysis and consultation required by Section 106. The regulations leave ambiguous whether a state agency carrying out FTA's duties must or may be a defendant in a suit challenging FTA's compliance with Section 106. They provide that the federal "agency official may be a State, local, or tribal government official who has been delegated legal

responsibility for compliance with section 106 in accordance with Federal law." 36 C.F.R. § 800.2(a). They also make clear that an agency official relying on applicants or contractors "remains legally responsible for all required findings and determinations." Id. § 800.2(a)(3). Thus, the regulations impose legal duties on a state official exercising delegated federal authority, which is in some tension with the language of Section 106. Cf. National Mining Ass'n v. Fowler, 324 F.3d 752 (D.C. Cir. 2003) (setting aside as inconsistent with Section 106 Advisory Council on Historic Preservation regulations imposing duties on states exercising delegated federal permitting authority). The Back Bay court did not explicitly consider this ambiguity, instead assuming without further inquiry that MBTA was a properly added defendant.

4.   Recall in Chapter 5 the discussion on the Department of Transportation Act, and the relevant state laws. The court also considered, and rejected, the plaintiffs' claims that the transit authorities violated Section 4(f) of the Department of Transportation Act, codified at 49 U.S.C. § 303. That federal statute is an important substantive protection for historic properties, although it is limited in scope to certain federal transportation projects.

5.   Also not included in this excerpt are the plaintiff's arguments that, even if the defendants complied with Section 106, they failed to comply with Section 110, which imposes stricter procedural requirements for National Historic Landmarks than requirements for properties merely listed on the National Register of Historic Places. Which affected resources were National Historic Landmarks? Federal regulations require agencies to invite the Secretary of the Interior to consult when there "may be" an adverse effect and requires the Advisory Council on Historic Preservation to report on the outcome of the consultation process. See 36 C.F.R. §§ 800.10(c), (d). Although the court acknowledged that the defendants did not conduct this required consultation or obtain the required report, it found the language of Section 110 "ambiguous" and that since no "adverse effect" was found under Section 106, there was no need to pursue the heightened process under Section 110. Do you think this approach is adequate protection for the nation's most prized landmarks?

6.   A student commentator has used Neighborhood Ass'n of the Back Bay, Inc. as a springboard for a law review note on the tension between physical accessibility and historic preservation in two countries: the United States and England. See Christopher Parkin, A Comparative Analysis of the Tension Created by Disability Access and Historic Preservation Laws in the United States and England, 22 CONN. J. INT'L L. 379 (2007). In comparing the preservation regimes of the two countries, Parkin observes that the English regime yields some authority to local planning bodies but centralizes "considerable substantive oversight and uniformity," unlike the American regime, where "the real substantive control over preservation lies with state and local bodies." Id. at 382. What might the difference in the basic preservation regime imply about whether the ADA is uniformly enforced in this country?

5. THE FAIR HOUSING ACT

The Americans with Disabilities Act and historic preservation laws are increasingly being harmonized through regulations, official guidelines, and judicial decisions. We conclude this Part with a brief note about the disability-related provisions of the Fair Housing Act, enacted as Title VIII of the Civil Rights Act of 1968. It prohibits discrimination on the basis of race, color, religion, sex, familial status, or national origin in certain housing transactions. 42 U.S.C. §§ 3601–3631. These transactions include rental, sale, marketing, appraisal, and financing. *Id.* § 3604–06. The 1988 Amendments to the federal Fair Housing Act broadly prohibit discrimination in providing housing to persons with a "handicap," the now-disfavored term chosen by the statute's drafters over two decades ago. The Fair Housing Act now declares it unlawful for anyone:

(f)(1) To discriminate in the sale or rental, or to otherwise make unavailable or deny, a dwelling to any buyer or renter because of a handicap of—

(A) that buyer or renter,

(B) a person residing in or intending to reside in that dwelling after it is so sold, rented, or made available; or

(C) any person associated with that buyer or renter.

(2) To discriminate against any person in the terms, conditions, or privileges of sale or rental of a dwelling, or in the provision of services or facilities in connection with such dwelling, because of a handicap of—

(A) that person; or

(B) a person residing in or intending to reside in that dwelling after it is so sold, rented, or made available; or

(C) any person associated with that person.

(3) For purposes of this subsection, discrimination includes—

(A) a refusal to permit, at the expense of the handicapped person, reasonable modifications of existing premises occupied or to be occupied by such person if such modifications may be necessary to afford such person full enjoyment of the premises except that, in the case of a rental, the landlord may where it is reasonable to do so condition permission for a modification on the renter agreeing to restore the interior of the premises to the condition that existed before the modification, reasonable wear and tear excepted.

(B) a refusal to make reasonable accommodations in rules, policies, practices, or services, when such accommodations may be necessary to afford such person equal opportunity to use and enjoy a dwelling; or

(C) in connection with the design and construction of covered multifamily dwellings for first occupancy after the date that is 30 months after September 13, 1988, a failure to design and construct those dwellings in such a manner that—

(i) the public use and common use portions of such dwellings are readily accessible to and usable by handicapped persons;

(ii) all the doors designed to allow passage into and within all premises within such dwellings are sufficiently wide to allow passage by handicapped persons in wheelchairs; and

(iii) all premises within such dwellings contain the following features of adaptive design:

(I) an accessible route into and through the dwelling;

(II) light switches, electrical outlets, thermostats, and other environmental controls in accessible locations;

(III) reinforcements in bathroom walls to allow later installation of grab bars; and

(IV) usable kitchens and bathrooms such that an individual in a wheelchair can maneuver about the space.

Id. § 3604.

NOTES & QUESTIONS

1. According to the statutory excerpt above, what kinds of activities might be considered discriminatory? Is it fair to assign the burden of paying for "reasonable accommodations" on the person with the disability, as section 3604(3)(A) does? What special requirements does the Federal Housing Act impose on multifamily dwellings built since September 13, 1988?

2. The Fair Housing Act rules apply to local government ordinances regulating land use. In *City of Edmonds v. Oxford House,* 514 U.S. 725 (1995), the Supreme Court applied section 3604 to a zoning ordinance that excluded group homes of unrelated adults stipulated to being handicapped from a single-family district. The Court focused on section 3604(f)(3)(B), regarding reasonable accommodations in "rules, policies, practices, or services" to find that the city's zoning ordinance was not exempt. It could have perhaps come to the same conclusion by applying the prohibition in section 3604(f)(1) of "otherwise mak[ing] unavailable or deny[ing]" a dwelling unit to a person with a disability.

3. Consider whether, under the logic of the *City of Edmonds* case, the Fair Housing Act rules should apply to local historic district decisions. What

about a commission's decision whether to permit a resident confined to a wheelchair to alter the entrance to her protected home to facilitate access? What factors would go into such an inquiry? What kinds of exceptions to generally applicable protections for historic properties would be reasonable? Would the *ADA Accessibility Guidelines for Buildings and Facilities* provide guidance? Surprisingly, there are no reported decisions addressing the duties of a local preservation commission under section 3604 of the Fair Housing Act. Does this lack of cases reflect the ability to reach reasonable resolutions in local proceedings? Or does it suggest that legal protections for either persons with disabilities or historic properties are too weak?

4. One federal court determined a builder must prove an accommodation is "necessary" for "equal opportunity" before a zoning board (relying on a historical preservation committee's analysis) is required to prove that the accommodation was "not reasonable." *See Yates Real Estate, Inc. v. Plainfield Zoning Bd. of Adjustment*, 404 F.Supp.3d 896, 927 (D.N.J., 2019). It was noted that the City's determination of "what is essential to its zoning districts must be considered." *Id. at* 928. Does this decision imply an imbalance between federal discrimination policies and local preservation?

5. The Fair Housing Act does not apply to single-family homes sold or rented by their owners (as long as the owner owns no more than three single-family homes at any one time) or to owner-occupied apartment complexes with fewer than four independent units. *Id.* § 3603. Can you understand why these exemptions were carved out? Many historic homes were intended for multiple users; some have primary dwellings accompanied by accessory units above the garage or in the basement, while others appear to be single homes but have multiple floor-through units.

C. INTELLECTUAL PROPERTY

Intellectual property law is becoming increasingly important for creators of architecturally significant works and may soon pose puzzling issues for owners of historic properties. Generally speaking, intellectual property law protects intangible ideas and certain products of human creativity from (depending on the intellectual property being protected and the regime under which it is protected) unauthorized copying, dilution, reproduction, or appropriation. There are two classic justifications for intellectual property law. The first is the utilitarian perspective espoused by the Founding Fathers, among others: that the public goods of innovation and creation cannot arise without granting legal exclusivity to certain ideas for a period of time. Another is the natural rights perspective, descended from John Locke's *Two Treatises on Government*, that humans are entitled to benefit from their labor. Under this view, if someone puts creative energy into making a beautiful piece of art or a unique and useful product, she should have exclusive rights to benefit from her creation.

Traditional intellectual property protection comes through four distinct federal legal regimes: copyright, trademark, trade secrets, and patent. Trade secrets and patent law, which relate primarily to product design and processes, do not have significant overlap with historic preservation law and are not further discussed here. Copyright and trademark law, however, do have relevance. Two areas that overlap with historic preservation matters will be covered in this Chapter: protection for architectural design through copyright law, and protection for iconic architectural images through trademark law. For reasons that will become clear below, we consider in this section primarily individual buildings and structures, and not objects, districts, or sites. *See* 54 U.S.C. § 302101 (listing these five categories of items with potential for historic designation at the federal level).

At the moment, historic preservation law and intellectual property law do not clearly conflict. Intellectual property protections continue to expand, however, and such expansion eventually may complicate historic preservation or deter the creation of buildings worthy of being designated historic. Conversely, preservation laws may eventually limit the reach of intellectual property rights. This section aims to raise interesting questions about areas of current and potential overlap in the two areas of law.

1. PROTECTION FOR ARCHITECTURAL DESIGN THROUGH COPYRIGHT LAW

Consider the difference between architectural design—an original idea about how something should be built—and the built work itself, which is the physical manifestation of that idea. Copyright law protects the intellectual property in certain original architectural designs by prohibiting unauthorized copying of them. With copyright protection, architects may feel that their original designs will not be reused without permission and that they will be able to take advantage of any value arising from them. As a result, they may be more willing to avoid "cookie-cutter" designs, take aesthetic risks, and develop a unique style.

The extent to which architects retain intellectual property rights in their architectural designs has an impact on historic preservation. Copyright law gives architects an incentive to express themselves in original ways that may lead to the eventual historic designation of the built work. Structures built with distinctive architectural features may be eligible for historic designation by local, state, or federal authorities. At the federal level, the National Register—a list of historically significant properties maintained by the National Park Service—accepts properties "that embody the distinctive characteristics of a type, period, or method of construction, or that represent the work of a master, or that possess high artistic values, or that represent a significant and distinguishable entity whose components may lack individual distinction." 36 C.F.R. § 60.4(c). Once listed on a register, a property (the built work—not the ideas behind it) may be protected, both from demolition and other adverse affects, by the laws discussed elsewhere in this book.

Figures 11-10 & 11-11:
"Exceptionally Important" Properties:
Elvis Presley's Graceland, Memphis, TN
& Frank Lloyd Wright's Taliesin West, Scottsdale, AZ

Note that historic designation may occur relatively soon after construction for exceptional buildings whose significance is clear early on: At the federal level, for example, the Keeper of the National Register may list "[a] property achieving significance within the past 50 years if it is of exceptional importance." 36 C.F.R. § 60.4(g). Examples of such designations include the Gateway Arch in St. Louis; Graceland, entertainer Elvis Presley's Memphis home; Taliesin West, architect Frank Lloyd Wright's Scottsdale studio; and the Monroe School, the Topeka site which gave rise to *Brown v. Board of Education.* Marcella Sherfy & W. Ray Luce, *Guidelines for Evaluating and Nominating Properties that Have Achieved Significance Within the Past Fifty Years* (Nat'l Park Serv., Nat'l Register Bull. No. 22, 1990).

While historic preservation law protects built work, architectural design is protected by copyright. We now analyze that area of law more closely.

a.   ARCHITECTURAL DESIGN BEFORE 1990

Copyright law in the United States derives from the U.S. Constitution's grant of power to Congress "[t]o promote the Progress of . . . useful Arts, by securing for limited Times to Authors . . . the exclusive Right to their . . . Writings." U.S. CONST. art. I, § 8. This broad grant of power has been further articulated by Congress, initially in the Copyright Act of 1790, one of the first statutes passed by Congress. The most recent large-scale overhaul of copyright rules occurred with the passage of the Copyright Act of 1976.

The central function of copyright law is to grant copyright holders certain exclusive rights, including the rights:

(1) to reproduce the copyrighted work in copies or phonorecords;

(2) to prepare derivative works based upon the copyrighted work;

(3) to distribute copies or phonorecords of the copyrighted work to the public by sale or other transfer of ownership, or by rental, lease, or lending; * * *

(5) in the case of * * * pictorial, graphic, or sculptural works * * * to display the copyrighted work publicly.

17 U.S.C. § 106. An author of a work created after January 1, 1978 may hold the copyright for her lifetime; after her death, her estate may hold the copyright for up to seventy years. 17 U.S.C. § 302(a). Once a work is copyrighted, the holder can file suit against anyone who copies the work without permission. Although the U.S. Copyright Office processes registrations of copyrights by authors, copyrights need not be registered unless holders intend to file a suit for infringement.

For many years, the extent to which copyright law protected architectural designs remained unclear because they present special problems resulting from their dual status as both creative art and as blueprints for construction. The Copyright Act of 1976 limited protected works only to "*original* works of authorship *fixed in any tangible medium of expression.*" *Id.* § 102 (emphases added). Original architectural designs, "fixed" in blueprints or computer files, appear to meet this two-prong threshold. Beyond that threshold, the Copyright Act of 1976 lists categories for which special rules apply, including categories for dramatic works, sound recordings, and literary works. *Id.* In 1976, the most appropriate category for architectural design was the category of "pictorial, graphic, and sculptural works," which includes "two-dimensional and three-dimensional works of fine, graphic, and applied art, photographs, prints and art reproductions, maps, globes, charts, diagrams, models, and technical drawings, including architectural plans." *Id.* §§ 101 & 102(5).

At first glance, this category seems like it would be a promising avenue for copyright protection for architectural design. There is an important limitation, however, on copyright protection for pictorial, graphic, and sculptural works, which is known as the "useful article" doctrine. The Copyright Act says that works involving useful articles are only protectable if they "incorporate[ ] pictorial, graphic, or sculptural features that can be identified separately from, and are capable of existing independently of, the utilitarian aspects of the article." *Id.* § 101. The statute further defines a "useful article" as "an article having an intrinsic utilitarian function that is not merely to portray the appearance of the article or to convey information." *Id.*

The question of whether architectural blueprints could be "identified separately from" the "useful article" (that is, the building) that they depict presented challenges in interpretation. One New York district court expressed the prevailing view that "although an owner of copyrighted architectural plans is granted the right to prevent the unauthorized copying of those plans, that individual, without benefit of a design patent, does not obtain a protectable interest in the useful article depicted by those plans." *Demetriades v. Kaufmann*, 680 F.Supp. 658, 663 (S.D.N.Y. 1988). Thus, while a copyright holder could collect damages for unauthorized copying of plans, she could not collect damages if an entire building was built without her permission from those plans. This result, though perhaps required by the statute at the time, hardly seems reasonable given the nature of the intellectual property ostensibly being protected.

b. ARCHITECTURAL DESIGN AFTER 1990

Protection for architectural design became both stronger and clearer after the passage of the Architectural Works Copyright Protection Act of 1990 (AWCPA), which amended the Copyright Act. The AWCPA was passed in part to satisfy the requirements of the Berne Convention for the Protection of Literary and Artistic Works, to which the United States became a signatory in 1989.

The AWCPA added "architectural works" as a specific category of protected works, and defined the term "architectural work" as:

> the design of a building as embodied in any tangible medium of expression, including a building, architectural plans, or drawings. The work includes the overall form as well as the arrangement and composition of spaces and elements in the design, but does not include individual standard features.

17 U.S.C. § 101. By using this language, the AWCPA confirmed that in the unique case of built work, the intellectual property being protected (that is, the design) could be fixed in the medium of the "useful article" itself (that is, the building). Functional aspects of the design remain unprotected by copyright law, although they may be protectable under patent law.

The AWCPA preserved the exclusive rights for copyright holders described above and continued to allow for suits for infringement. To succeed in such a suit, a plaintiff must first show that her work was actually copied, which may be demonstrated by showing that the defendant had access to the protected work and by showing a substantial similarity between the protected and allegedly infringing works. Second, the plaintiff must show that "the copying amounts to an *improper* appropriation by demonstrating that substantial similarity to protected material exists between the two works." *Laureyssens v. Idea Group, Inc.*, 964 F.2d 131, 140 (2d Cir. 1992) (emphasis added).

It is important to note that the AWCPA imposed the following two limitations on copyright holders' rights:

> (a) Pictorial representations permitted.

> The copyright in an architectural work that has been constructed does not include the right to prevent the making, distributing, or public display of pictures, paintings, photographs, or other pictorial representations of the work, if the building in which the work is embodied is located in or ordinarily visible from a public place.

> (b) Alterations to and destruction of buildings.

> * * * [T]he owners of a building embodying an architectural work may, without the consent of the author or copyright owner of the architectural work, make or authorize the making of alterations to such building, and destroy or authorize the destruction of such building.

17 U.S.C. § 120. Keep the first limitation, in subpart (a), in mind as we consider trademark law in the next section. The second limitation, in

subpart (b), suggests that copyright holders cannot control the actions of the owners of the built work that arise from their copyrighted material.

As you think about the interplay between copyright and historic preservation law, consider the different goals and methods for protecting architectural design ideas against copying and for protecting the properties themselves against destruction. Is one more socially important than the other?

NOTES & QUESTIONS

1. The Copyright Act expressly states that it does not "annul[ ] or limit[ ] any rights or remedies under the common law or statutes of any State with respect to * * * (4) State and local landmarks, historic preservation, zoning, or building codes, relating to architectural works." 17 U.S.C. § 301(b). What possible conflicts with, or interpretations of, AWCPA were the drafters of this provision trying to address? Review section 120(b), regarding the powers of owners of buildings whose design was copyrighted under AWCPA, to see one possible area of confusion.

2. One student commentator has offered the following analysis of the laws listed in section 301(b):

> These laws will help make up for the AWCPA's failure to prevent alteration or modification of the buildings thought by the local community to be of the most aesthetic or historic worth. * * * As a practical matter, this means that state law will continue to play an important role in regulating the construction, modification, and destruction of architectural works.

> Respect for local landmark laws is founded on principles of federalism. Questions of how and when to construct or destroy buildings are questions of local concern. Similarly, questions of which buildings are considered aesthetically or historically worthy of preservation are questions that a local governing board is far better qualified to answer than federal officials or federal judges. * * * Permitting the use of federal statutes to prevent destruction or modification of buildings would distort the purposes of copyright law, and infringe on valid local concerns.

Raphael Winick, Note, *Copyright Protection for Architecture After the Architectural Works Copyright Protection Act of 1990*, 41 DUKE L.J. 1598, 1624 (1992). Does this overstate the importance of federalism? Are concerns with federal copyright different from concerns with federal protection of historic sites of national importance?

3. Consider a high-profile infringement suit brought by a student of the Yale School of Architecture, who charged that a well-known architect (David Childs) and his architecture firm (Skidmore Owings & Merrill, LLC, or SOM) had improperly copied his designs for two skyscrapers. *Shine v. Childs*, 382 F.Supp.2d 602 (S.D.N.Y. 2005). Childs had praised the student's work while serving as part of an "expert jury" critiquing student work. *Id.* at 605–06. Childs later allegedly incorporated the student's designs into SOM's

proposal for the most famous building project under construction in the United States, the Freedom Tower at the former World Trade Center site. *Id.* at 604–05. Although the student's design was eventually abandoned for another, the case continued through the court system because the copying had already been done and SOM had displayed the design publicly. The student sought an injunction to prevent further infringement and to collect damages in part stemming from SOM's profits. *Id.* at 607. After weighing the evidence, the court granted the defendants' motion for summary judgment in part because the allegedly infringing design was not probatively similar to one of the student's skyscraper designs, but denied it in part because there remained genuine issues of material fact as to whether the defendants had infringed on the student's second skyscraper design. *Id.* at 612–166.

It seems likely that the Freedom Tower—no matter what it looks like—will be designated historic under local, state, or federal law, because of its location and its place in our shared national story. What influence might copyright infringements suits such as *Shine v. Childs* have on the designation process? For example, would the very existence of such suits magnify the historical importance of the buildings in question?

On another note, how could or should prevailing parties in such suits be able to intervene in applications to public registers of historic places? For example, if a court found that the Yale student's work was improperly copied, would he—along with, or perhaps instead of, Childs and SOM—be listed as the lead designer on any register of historic places? Could this or should this issue be addressed in the AWCPA?

4.   Should architects holding copyrights to architectural plans be credited with a percentage of any proceeds (such as tax credits) later received as a result of their buildings being designated historic as a result of their unique architectural style? Copyrights can last up to seventy years after the death of the original author.

5.   What are moral rights? Unlike copyright, which protects the economic relationship an author has with her creation, moral rights protect the personal relationship between an author and her creation. Moral rights include the rights to attribution, withdrawal, integrity, and disclosure. After joining the Berne Convention, Congress enacted the Visual Artists Rights Act (VARA) in 1990 in order to protect the moral rights of the artist in visual arts only, including: paintings, drawings, sculptures, prints, and still photographs produced for exhibition. 17 U.S.C. § 106A. Because architecture is functional, buildings normally fall under "applied arts" and do not receive protection under VARA. *See* Brandon J. Pakkebier, *Form Over Function: Remedying VARA's Exclusion of Visual Art with Functional Qualities*, 103 Iowa L. Rev. 1329 (2018). Why would Congress be hesitant to apply the VARA to architectural structures? What moral rights would possibly be available to the author, and how would those rights compete with the owner of the finished project or conflict with the AWCPA?

6.   The AWCPA does not extend to buildings built before 1990, and thus it excludes from protection the designs of (among others) virtually all designated historic properties. Should its protection have been made

retroactive, and thus granted intellectual property windfalls to architects (or their estates)? Why or why not? Note that the Supreme Court upheld over a constitutional challenge a federal statute granting retroactive copyright protection to certain foreign works that were not protected in the United States when the statute passed. *See Golan v. Holder*, 565 U.S. 302 (2012). In a related case, *Eldred v. Ashcroft*, 537 U.S. 186 (2003), the Supreme Court upheld Congressional action extending existing copyrights. Based on these cases, it seems possible that the protections of the AWCPA could be extended in at least two ways. Whether such extensions are advisable as a matter of public policy is another matter.

7.   Many believe that copyright law restricts too much material and wrongly allows for powerful interests to strengthen their monopolies over aspects of our culture. Professor Lawrence Lessig and a nonprofit organization he co-founded, the Creative Commons, are at the forefront of the "copyleft" movement. When applied to architectural works, the anti-copyright arguments have some traction. Before the concept of the copyright entered modern legal regimes, architecture existed for millennia, and architects rather freely borrowed from past styles and techniques. Could the AWCPA, intended to reward creativity, backfire by having a chilling effect on architects' incorporation of and improvement upon innovative ideas?

8.   The National Historic Preservation Act and its related regulations do not delineate the extent to which nominating documents may be copyrighted by those who prepare them. But a California federal court upheld the online posting by a homeowners' association of a successful National Historic Landmark nomination against a copyright infringement challenge by the preparer of the nomination, even where the preparer had gone through the effort of registering the nomination with the U.S. Copyright Office. *Wong v. Vill. Green Owners Ass'n*, No. CV 14–03803–AB (CWx), 2015 WL 12672092 (C.D. Cal. Mar. 20, 2015). The homeowners' association had asserted a "fair use" defense, which must be reviewed pursuant to four statutory factors: the purpose and character of the use, the nature of the copyrighted work, the amount and substantiality of the portion used in relation to the copyrighted work as a whole, and the effect of the use on the potential market or value of the work. 17 U.S.C. § 107. The California court was persuaded by the fact that the association's use of the nomination was non-commercial, that the nomination contained "purely factual information" (and was not a creative work), and that the preparer could not show harm from the posting (and in fact had made it freely available on her own website). The posting of such nominations to the National Park Service website suggests that once a nomination is submitted for the public process, copyright infringement claims can no longer be brought by preparers.

2.   PROTECTABILITY OF ICONIC ARCHITECTURAL IMAGES THROUGH TRADEMARK LAW

Many historic structures are listed on public registers of historic places as part of districts whose individual components share architectural characteristics. These structures are not individually distinctive but rather represent historical architectural styles and contribute to a visually coherent ensemble. Other structures are designated individually, some for their architectural distinctiveness. Of these individually listed buildings, a handful are so iconic that their very image may merit the protection of trademark law. Indeed, about a hundred buildings have sought and attained federal trademark protection. No doubt many of these buildings, at least those over fifty years old, are registered in local, state, or national registers of historic places.

To understand how architectural images may be trademarked, a brief background of trademark law is in order. The first federal trademark statute was enacted by Congress in 1870 and most recently overhauled by the Lanham Act of 1946. *See* 15 U.S.C. §§ 1051–1141. That statute offers exclusive rights to developers of certain "marks" that are used in commerce before anyone else has used the mark. It defines "trademark" as follows:

> The term "trademark" includes any word, name, symbol, or device, or any combination thereof—
>
> (1) used by a person, or
>
> (2) which a person has a bona fide intention to use in commerce and applies to register on the principal register established by this chapter,
>
> to identify and distinguish his or her goods, including a unique product, from those manufactured or sold by others and to indicate the source of the goods, even if that source is unknown.

15 U.S.C. § 1127. Trademarks are typically used either as advertising or to identify the maker (or purveyor) of goods. They need not be registered, although marks registered with the U.S. Patent and Trademark Office received heightened protection in that they are enforceable nationwide, can be rendered incontestable after five years, and allow the holder to bring a federal cause of action without regard to diversity or minimum amounts in controversy. Registration can also establish priority, since the first to register a mark is automatically granted the trademark. Unlike copyrights, trademarks last forever, unless they are cancelled or abandoned, which usually occurs when they cease to be used in commerce.

A valid trademark allows its owner to protect the mark from certain third party activities. A trademark infringement occurs when a party either reproduces or uses a similar mark in commerce that is likely to cause confusion, to cause mistake, or to deceive. *Id.* § 1114(1). If a consumer thinks an infringer's product is the same as the trademarked product because of the marks' similarities, then a court is likely to find an infringement. In addition, a trademark owner may bring a suit for unfair competition if someone uses a mark that "is likely to cause confusion, or to cause mistake, or to deceive as to the affiliation, connection, or association of such person with another person, or as to the origin, sponsorship, or approval of his or her goods, services, or commercial activities by another person." *Id.* § 1125(a)(A). Finally, under the Federal Trademark Dilution Act, a trademark owner may obtain an injunction if another person's commercial use in commerce of a famous and distinctive mark dilutes the mark—regardless of whether confusion is likely or competition is occurring between the parties. *Id.* § 1125(c). Dilution of a famous mark may occur either by blurring or by tarnishment. Dilution by blurring occurs when "association arising from the similarity between a mark or trade name and a famous mark * * * impairs the distinctiveness of the famous mark." *Id.* § 1125(c)(2)(B). Dilution by tarnishment occurs when "association arising from the similarity between a mark or trade name and a famous mark * * * harms the reputation of the famous mark." *Id.* § 1125(c)(2)(C). Dilution does not occur during advertising that permits consumers to compare goods, parodies or critiques of the famous mark, news commentary, and noncommercial uses of the mark. *Id.* § 1125(c)(3).

A building owner may want to trademark the building's image for exclusive use in commerce for many reasons. A building may be a tourist destination, such as a house museum, and the image of the building may be used to advertise the destination itself. A building may also be a commercial property seeking to attract tenants, and a trademark of the building could be used in leasing materials. A building may be associated with an architect who designed related products, such as furniture, and the building image may be utilized to bolster sales of the related products. Although trademark law is not limited to historic buildings, it is easy to see why the owners of some historic buildings (or those with the potential to be designated historic) may seek protection in trademark law. Moreover, buildings likely will serve as trademarks only if they have significance to the public through their designs or associations with people or events, a criterion similar to that for designation as a landmark.

Two high-profile disputes involving trademarked buildings shed light on the stakes. The first involved Manhattan's famous Chrysler Building, an Art Deco skyscraper built in 1930 and listed on the National Register of Historic Places. The owners of the building registered a trademark for the spire of the structure in 1979. *See* Trademark Reg. No. 1126888 (Nov. 20, 1979). They sent a cease and desist letter to Fishs Eddy, a retailer that had developed tableware that used the New York skyline as a border. They claimed that Fishs Eddy was infringing on the Chrysler Building trademark by reproducing the building's image on the tableware without permission. Another high-profile dispute involved the New York Stock Exchange (NYSE) Building, whose façade is trademarked. The NYSE sued a Las Vegas casino, New York New York, for an exhibit featuring a replica of the NYSE (called the "New York $lot Exchange" in the exhibit). The NYSE claimed that the casino both infringed on the trademark and diluted it. For background on these disputes, see Lucia Sitar, Comment, *The Sky's The Limit? The Emergence of Building Trademarks*, 103 DICK. L. REV. 821 (1999); David W. Dunlap, *What Next? A Fee for Looking?*, N.Y. TIMES, Aug. 27, 1998. In such cases, building owners are seeking to protect the value that the public associates with the historic building.

Beyond tableware purveyors and casino owners, a much more mundane trademark infringer may lurk: photographers. Consider the following case, which involves a building that is not yet landmarked, but which clearly has the potential to be landmarked.

Rock & Roll Hall of Fame & Museum, Inc. v. Gentile Productions

134 F.3d 749 (6th Cir. 1998)

■ RYAN, CIRCUIT JUDGE.

The Rock and Roll Hall of Fame and Museum, Inc., and The Rock and Roll Hall of Fame Foundation, Inc., filed suit against Charles Gentile and Gentile Productions, alleging various trademark and unfair-competition claims under state and federal law. The plaintiffs moved for and were granted a preliminary injunction, on the authority of FED.R.CIV.P. 65. The defendants appeal, claiming, essentially, that the district court mistakenly concluded that the plaintiffs have shown a strong likelihood of succeeding on the merits. We agree and therefore vacate the entry of the preliminary injunction.

I.

In 1988, The Rock and Roll Hall of Fame Foundation registered the words, "THE ROCK AND ROLL HALL OF FAME," as its service mark, on the principal register at the United States Patent and Trademark Office. In 1991, the Foundation commissioned I.M. Pei, a world famous architect, to design a facility for The Rock and Roll Hall of Fame and Museum in Cleveland, Ohio. Pei's design was brought to life on the edge of Lake Erie, in the form of The Rock and Roll Hall of Fame and Museum which opened in September 1995. * * *

The Museum states that its building design is "a unique and inherently distinctive symbol of the freedom, youthful energy, rebellion and movement of rock and roll music." Whatever its symbolism, there can be no doubt that the Museum's design is unique and distinctive. The front of the Museum is dominated by a large, reclining, triangular facade of steel and glass, while the rear of the building, which extends out over Lake Erie, is a striking combination of interconnected and unusually shaped, white buildings. On May 3, 1996, the State of Ohio approved the registration of the Museum's building design for trademark and service-mark purposes. The Museum has similar applications pending with the United States Patent and Trademark Office.

Charles Gentile is a professional photographer whose work is marketed and distributed through Gentile Productions. In the spring of 1996, Gentile began to sell, for $40 to $50, a poster featuring a photograph of the Museum against a colorful sunset. The photograph is framed by a black border. In gold lettering in the border underneath the photograph, the words, "ROCK N' ROLL HALL OF FAME," appear above the smaller, but elongated word, "CLEVELAND." Gentile's signature appears in small blue print beneath the picture of the building. Along the right-hand side of the photograph, in very fine print, is the following explanation: "©1996 Gentile Productions . . . Photographed by: Charles M. Gentile[;] Design: Division Street Design [;] Paper: Mead Signature Gloss Cover 80#[;] Printing: Custom Graphics Inc. [;] Finishing: Northern Ohio Finishing, Inc."

In reaction to Gentile's poster, the Museum filed a five-count complaint against Gentile in the district court. The Museum's complaint contends that the Museum has used both its registered service mark, "THE ROCK AND ROLL HALL OF FAME," and its building design as trademarks, and that Gentile's poster infringes upon, dilutes, and unfairly competes with these marks. The Museum's somewhat unusual claims regarding its building design, then, are quite unlike a claim to a service-mark right in a building design that might be asserted to prevent the construction of a confusingly similar building.

Specifically, count one of the Museum's complaint alleges trademark infringement, in violation of 15 U.S.C. § 1114(1). Count two alleges unfair competition, false or misleading representations, and false designation of origin, in violation of 15 U.S.C. § 1125(a). Count three alleges dilution of trademarks, in violation of 15 U.S.C. § 1125(c) and Ohio common law. Counts four and five allege unfair competition and trademark infringement under Ohio law.

The Museum sought a preliminary injunction and the district court held a hearing on the motion. It is clear from a review of the Museum's motion and the hearing transcript that, whatever the scope of the Museum's complaint, the Museum's request for a preliminary injunction was based on the theory: (1) that the Museum has used both its building design and its service mark, "THE ROCK AND ROLL HALL OF FAME," *as trademarks*; and (2) that both the photograph of the Museum and the words identifying the Museum in Gentile's poster are uses of the Museum's trademarks that should be enjoined because they are likely to lead consumers to believe that Gentile's poster is produced or sponsored by the Museum.

Thus, in its motion, the Museum argued that, because Gentile is "using the Museum's trademarks on posters in a manner which reflects a deliberate attempt to confuse, mislead and deceive the public into believing that the posters are affiliated with the Museum, . . . [t]he Museum has an extremely strong probability of success on the merits of its claims for trademark infringement and unfair competition." Similarly, at the hearing, the Museum stated only that its motion was "about trademark infringement, [section] 43(a), violations of the Lanham Act in passing off," although its complaint was broader. Accordingly, the district court explained to Gentile that he needed to respond only to the Museum's arguments in support of its motion, not its entire complaint.

The Museum submitted several exhibits in support of its motion. Of particular concern in the present dispute is a poster the Museum sells for $20. Although the Museum's poster, like Gentile's, features a photograph of the Museum at sunset, the photographs of the building in the two posters are very different. Gentile's photograph is a ground-level, close-up view of the Museum taken at a time when the building appears to be closed. It is an artistically appealing photograph of the Museum and virtually nothing else. In contrast, the Museum's poster features a photograph of the Museum, taken from an elevated and considerably more distant vantage point, on the Museum's opening night, when red carpet stretched from the Museum's front doors, and interior lights highlighted its dramatic glass facade. There is a great deal of detail in the foreground of the Museum's photograph including the full esplanade in front of the building, and even a portion of the highway adjacent to the property. It, too, is an artistically pleasing photograph of the Museum and its surrounding environment, but it is a very different picture than Gentile's.

The Museum's poster is framed by a white border, in which the words, "The Rock and Roll Hall of Fame and Museum—Cleveland," appear beneath the photograph. To the left of these words is a small circular designation, which appears to be a trademark (the "composite mark"). In the center of this composite mark is a triangle formed by six lines fanning out from a single point. The triangle is intersected by three horizontal lines, contains two dots running vertically, and may be intended to be evocative of the Museum's building design. In a circle around this triangular design are the words, "ROCK AND ROLL HALL OF FAME & MUSEUM."

In addition to the parties' posters, the record on appeal contains color copies of photographs of several items produced by the Museum; specifically, an advertisement for the Museum's opening, a paper weight, several postcards, and two T-shirts. * * *

The Museum also submitted affidavits in support of its motion. In particular, Robert Bosak, the controller of the Museum, averred that "the Museum has used versions of the building shape trademark on T-shirts and a wide variety of products, including posters, since as early as June, 1993." According to his review of sales reports from the Museum's store, merchandise "featur[ing] the building shape have been among [the Museum's store's] top selling items." * * *

On May 30, 1996, the district court concluded that the Museum had "shown a likelihood of success in proving its federal and state claims," and it granted the Museum's motion for a preliminary injunction. *Rock and Roll Hall of Fame & Museum, Inc. v. Gentile Prods.*, 934 F.Supp. 868, 872–73 (N.D. Ohio 1996). The district court explained, *inter alia*, that

> [a]s a result of the extensive advertising and promotional activities involving the [Museum's] "ROCK AND ROLL HALL OF FAME" and building design trademarks, the public has come to recognize these trademarks as being connected with or sold by the Museum, its official licensees and/or official sponsors.

Id. at 871. The district court found that the Museum's building design was a fanciful mark, and that Gentile's use of the Museum's building design and the words, "ROCK N' ROLL HALL OF FAME," was likely to cause confusion. *Id.* at 871–72. It then determined that the balance of equities favored granting the injunction, and it ordered Gentile to refrain from further infringements of the Museum's trademarks and to "deliver . . . for destruction all copies of defendants' poster in their possession." *Id.* at 872–73.

II.

We review a district court's decision to grant a preliminary injunction for abuse of discretion. * * *

Gentile argues that the district court abused its discretion when it concluded that the Museum had shown a likelihood of success on the merits for purposes of the preliminary injunction. Specifically, Gentile argues that his photograph of the Museum is not a trademark use of the Museum's building design. Gentile also argues that his use of the words, "ROCK N' ROLL HALL OF FAME," is a non-trademark use which simply and accurately describes his non-infringing photograph of the Museum. Because we agree that the record before us does not establish a strong likelihood that Gentile has made an infringing trademark use of the Museum's name or building design, we will vacate the preliminary injunction.

A trademark is a *designation*, "any word, name, symbol, or device, or any combination thereof," which serves "to identify and distinguish [the] goods [of the mark's owner] . . . from those manufactured or sold by others and to indicate the source of the goods, even if that source is unknown." 15 U.S.C. § 1127. Although some marks are classified as inherently distinctive and therefore capable of protection, see generally *Two Pesos, Inc. v. Taco Cabana, Inc.*, 505 U.S. 763, 768–69 (1992), it is not the case that all inherently distinctive symbols or words on a product function as trademarks. Rather, in order to be protected as a valid trademark, a designation must create "a separate and distinct commercial impression, which . . . performs the trademark function of identifying the source of the merchandise to the customers." *In re Chemical Dynamics, Inc.*, 839 F.2d 1569, 1571 (Fed. Cir. 1988). * * *

At the hearing on the Museum's motion, Gentile showed the district court a poster of an illustration of the Cleveland skyline, produced by another artist, that included the Museum as one building among many. Gentile also referred to a quilt or blanket which apparently depicts "all kinds of landmarks of Cleveland," again including the Museum among several others. In response to these exhibits, the Museum stated that "they illustrate something [that the Museum does not] think . . . [is] a problem because they show a whole collage of downtown buildings and scenes around Cleveland. That's not what [the Museum is] trying to stop." However, the Museum argued that Gentile's poster features nothing but the Museum and a sunset. According to the Museum, Gentile's production of his poster was like "going into a store, getting a bottle of [C]oke, taking a picture, [of it and] putting . . . [C]oke underneath."

Although we are mindful that we are called upon to settle only the present dispute, we have found the foregoing exchange from the hearing on the Museum's motion a helpful guidepost for our discussion.

On the one hand, although Gentile's exhibits, which depict the Museum as one landmark among others or as one of several buildings in the Cleveland lakefront skyline, present easier cases, their significance is consonant with our initial impression of Gentile's poster. That is to say that, when we view the photograph in Gentile's poster, we do not readily recognize the design of the Museum's building as an indicator of source or sponsorship. What we see, rather, is a photograph of an accessible, well-known, public landmark. Stated somewhat differently, in Gentile's poster, the Museum's building strikes us not as a separate and distinct mark on the good, but, rather, as the good itself.

On the other hand, the import of the Museum's Coke bottle example is not lost upon us. Indeed, the Museum's example is not entirely concocted, see *Coca-Cola Co. v. Gemini Rising, Inc.*, 346 F.Supp. 1183 (E.D.N.Y.1972), and we accept that a photograph which prominently depicts another person's trademark might very well, wittingly or unwittingly, use its object as a trademark. However, after reviewing the record before us with this possibility in mind, we are not persuaded that the Museum uses its building design as a trademark. Thus, we are not dissuaded from our initial impression that the photograph in Gentile's poster does not function as a trademark.

The district court found that the Museum's building design is fanciful, that the Museum has used its building design as a trademark, and that "the public has come to recognize [the Museum's building design] trademark[ ] as being connected with or sold by the Museum." *Rock and Roll Hall of Fame*, 934 F.Supp. at 871. There are several problems with these critical findings. First, we find absolutely no evidence in the record which documents or demonstrates public recognition of the Museum's building design as a trademark. Such evidence might be pivotal in this case, but it is lacking. Indeed, we are at a loss to understand the district court's basis for this significant finding of fact.

Second, although no one could doubt that the Museum's building design is fanciful, it is less clear that a picture or a drawing of the Museum is fanciful in a trademark sense. Fanciful marks are usually understood as "totally new and unique combination[s] of letters or symbols" that are "invented or selected for the sole purpose of functioning as a trademark." 1 J. MCCARTHY, MCCARTHY ON TRADEMARKS AND UNFAIR COMPETITION § 11:5 (4th ed. 1997). Although the plaintiffs "invented" the Museum, the Museum's existence as a landmark in downtown Cleveland undermines its "fancifulness" as a trademark. A picture or a drawing of the Museum is not fanciful in the same way that a word like Exxon is when it is coined as a service mark. Such a word is distinctive as a mark because it readily appears to a consumer to have no other purpose. In contrast, a picture of the Museum on a product might be more readily perceived as ornamentation than as an identifier of source.

We recognize, of course, that a designation may serve both ornamental and source-identifying purposes, see, e.g., *WSM, Inc. v. Tennessee Sales Co.*, 709 F.2d 1084, 1087 (6th Cir. 1983), and this brings us to our principal difficulty with the Museum's argument and the district court's judgment. As we described *supra*, although the Museum has used drawings or pictures of its building design on various goods, it has not done so with any consistency. As Bosak stated in his affidavit, "the Museum has used *versions* of the building shape trademark on . . . a wide variety of products." (Emphasis added.) Several items marketed by the Museum display only the rear of the Museum's building, which looks dramatically different from the front. Drawings of the front of the Museum on the two T-shirts in the record are similar, but they are quite different from the photograph featured in the Museum's poster. And, although the photograph from the poster is also used on a postcard, another postcard displays various close-up photographs of the Museum which, individually and perhaps even collectively, are not even immediately recognizable as photographs of the Museum.

In this regard, this case is similar to those in which a party has claimed trademark rights in a famous person's likeness. *See, e.g., Pirone v. MacMillan, Inc.*, 894 F.2d 579, 583 (2d Cir. 1990); *Estate of Presley v. Russen*, 513 F.Supp. 1339, 1363–64 (D.N.J. 1981). In *Estate of Presley*, the court concluded that, although one particular image of Presley had been used consistently as a mark, "the available evidence [did] not support [the estate's] broad position" that all images of Presley served such a function. *Estate of Presley*, 513 F.Supp. at 1364. Similarly, in *Pirone*, the court stated that "[e]ven if [the plaintiff] could show that it has established a trademark in a particular pictorial representation of [Babe] Ruth, such a trademark would not cover all photos taken of Ruth during his career, no matter how dissimilar." *Pirone*, 894 F.2d at 583. The court explained that, given that "Ruth was one of the most photographed men of his generation, . . . [i]t cannot be said that every photograph of Ruth serves [the] origin-indicating function" of a trademark. *Id.*

In reviewing the Museum's disparate uses of several different perspectives of its building design, we cannot conclude that they create a consistent and distinct commercial impression as an indicator of a single source of origin or sponsorship. To be more specific, we cannot conclude on this record that it is likely that the Museum has established a valid trademark in every photograph which, like Gentile's, prominently displays the front of the Museum's building, "no matter how dissimilar." Even if we accept that consumers recognize the various drawings and pictures of the Museum's building design as being drawings and pictures of the Museum, the Museum's argument would still fall short. Such recognition is not the equivalent of the recognition that these various drawings or photographs indicate a single source of the goods on which they appear. Consistent and repetitive use of a designation as an indicator of source is the hallmark of a trademark. Although the record before us supports the conclusion that the Museum has used its composite mark in this manner, it will not support the conclusion that the Museum has made such use of its building design.

In the end, then, we believe that the district court abused its discretion by treating the "Museum's building design" as a single entity, and by concomitantly failing to consider whether and to what extent the Museum's use of its building design served the source-identifying function that is the essence of a trademark. As we have noted, we find no support for the factual finding that the public recognizes the Museum's building design, in any form, let alone in all forms, as a trademark. In light of the Museum's irregular use of its building design, then, we believe that it is quite unlikely, on the record before us, that the Museum will prevail on its claims that Gentile's photograph of the Museum is an infringing trademark use of the Museum's building design.

Our discussion of the district court's treatment of the Museum's building design would, of course, be much ado about nothing were we persuaded that Gentile's use of the words, "ROCK N' ROLL HALL OF FAME—CLEVELAND," was sufficient to sustain the injunction. We are not, however, persuaded. In the first place, the district court did not give separate treatment to Gentile's use of the Museum's building design— the photograph of the building itself—and to Gentile's use of words approximating the Museum's registered service mark. Thus, we cannot be certain how the district court would have viewed the use of the words in the event that the photograph was found to be non-infringing. For purposes of our review, then, we are not free to sustain the preliminary injunction on the theory that it would have been no abuse of discretion had the district court concluded that Gentile's use of the words, "ROCK N' ROLL HALL OF FAME," was alone likely to constitute a trademark violation. The district court made no such finding.

Moreover, we think Gentile's use of these words may very well constitute a fair use of the Museum's registered service mark, pursuant to 15 U.S.C. § 1115(b)(4). Section 1115(b)(4) permits a party to defend an infringement charge on the ground

> [t]hat the use of the ... term, or device charged to be an infringement is a use, otherwise than as a mark ... of a term or device which is descriptive of and used fairly and in good faith only to describe the goods or services of such party.

Although there can be no doubt that Gentile's use of the Museum's service mark presents an unusual case, his use of the words, "ROCK N' ROLL HALL OF FAME," would be nothing more than a description of his own "good," in the event that the Museum fails to prove that Gentile's photograph makes an infringing use of the Museum's building design. *See, e.g., WCVB-TV v. Boston Athletic Ass'n*, 926 F.2d 42, 46 (1st Cir. 1991); *Pirone*, 894 F.2d at 584. The critical question, then, will be whether Gentile's use of the Museum's service mark was made fairly and in good faith, and whether his use was "otherwise than as a [trade]mark." With regard to this latter inquiry, the answer will essentially turn on whether consumers view the words, "ROCK N' ROLL HALL OF FAME," as a label for Gentile's photograph, or as an indicator that Gentile's photograph originated with or was sponsored by the Museum. As always, the touchstone will be the likelihood of consumer confusion.

To summarize, then, we find that the district court did not properly consider the validity of the Museum's claim to trademark rights in its building design. In light of this error, we cannot be certain that the district court properly assessed Gentile's fair use defense in relation to his use of the Museum's service mark. Thus, we are compelled to conclude that the district court abused its discretion when it concluded that the Museum had shown a strong likelihood of proving its trademark infringement claims. Indeed, on the record before us, we are left with grave doubts as to the likelihood of the Museum's success on these claims.

III.

For all of the foregoing reasons, we VACATE the judgment of the district court, and REMAND for further consideration.

NOTES & QUESTIONS

1. What was the reasoning of the *Rock & Roll Hall of Fame & Museum* panel in determining that the district court did not properly determine that the Museum had shown a strong likelihood of prevailing on its trademark infringement claims? How did the majority incorporate the museum's status as a landmark (albeit one that is not yet designated historic) into its decision? Was this the right result on public policy grounds?

2. Let us return to a limitation on copyright law, noted above. That provision states:

The copyright in an architectural work that has been constructed does not include the right to prevent the making, distributing, or public display of pictures, paintings, photographs, or other pictorial representations of the work, if the building in which the work is embodied is located in or ordinarily visible from a public place.

17 U.S.C. § 120(a). Should similar protection against trademark infringement be extended to the images of publicly visible buildings?

3.   For historic buildings, should designation on a public register of historic places signify a kind of public right in the exterior of a building that could defeat private claims of photography-related trademark infringements? On the one hand, a "public register" defense in trademark suits could extend the utility of a historic designation to the general public. On the other, the public need to capture and/or exploit images of historic places may not be very strong.

4.   Under current law, trademarks of buildings are not limited to designated historic buildings, and the process by which the Trademarks Office evaluates the content of marks can be unclear. The Trademarks Office lists a range of trademarks that cannot be listed on the federal register, including those that are "immoral" and "scandalous," or marks that are "deceptive." 15 U.S.C. § 1052(a). Though the contents of some marks are evaluated, the Trademarks Office does not evaluate whether proposed building-related marks involve historic buildings or not. Do you see why this would be the case? Should there be a separate regime for trademarks of buildings? Why or why not?

5.   Although intellectual property issues in historic preservation primarily involve buildings and structures, consider the contentious issue of photographic rights to a famous historic object: the R.M.S. Titanic shipwreck. The shipwreck was discovered in 1985, seventy-three years after it sank in 1912 in an ill-fated transatlantic voyage. Typically, salvage law allows for those who discover shipwrecks to have exclusive rights to possess anything they find during recovery, as long as they operate continuous salvage operations. Many individuals and companies sought access to photograph the shipwreck, but the successor of the original salvor sought exclusive photographic access, no doubt to help recoup costs of the ongoing salvage operation. The Fourth Circuit rejected the salvor's request, but only after a Virginia district court sided with the salvor. See R.M.S. Titanic, Inc. v. Haver, 171 F.3d 943 (4th Cir. 1999); R.M.S. Titanic, Inc. v. Wrecked & Abandoned Vessel, 1996 WL 650135 (E.D. Va. 1996).

A student commentator has argued in favor of courts adopting the district court view, saying that "the inclusion of exclusive imagery rights within the traditional grant of possessory rights to salvors is a proper and necessary expansion of salvage principles under maritime law for historic vessels found in international waters." Justin S. Stern, Note, Smart Salvage: Extending Traditional Maritime Law to Include Intellectual Property Rights in Historic Shipwrecks, 68 FORDHAM L. REV. 2489, 2491 (2000). Which court has the better argument? How might each argument be applied beyond shipwrecks—say, to archaeological discoveries? Would granting photographic rights to archaeologists first finding artifacts create incentives for discovery, or are shipwrecks a special case?

6. What of images in virtual worlds? Programs like Second Life, which allows users to create avatars with which they can experience life in a virtual universe, may be the next frontier. In 2010, the Frank Lloyd Wright Foundation entered into a license agreement with Second Life to ensure that the Foundation controls, and receives license fees from, any uses of the image of the iconic house in Bear Run, Pennsylvania, known as Fallingwater. Fallingwater—arguably the most famous house in the United States—is on the National Register of Historic Places, and the classic image of its front façade, which includes the waterfall over which Wright so successfully nestled the house, is the subject of a registered federal trademark. The Foundation has a fairly strict photography policy for visitors to the real house: Only exterior (not interior) photography is allowed, and all photographs must be used for personal, non-commercial purposes. *See* Jennifer Dalenta, *FallingApart: The Problematic Nature of Using Private Fundraising to Preserve a Publicly Funded, But Privately Owned National Historic Landmark* (May 2011) (unpublished paper, on file with the authors).

D. GENTRIFICATION

Historic preservation is intimately related to the widespread restorations of older buildings that have been an essential part of urban revival in our time. Newcomers to deteriorated urban neighborhoods have renovated older houses, archetypically Victorian row houses or abandoned industrial lofts, and invigorated local life with farmers' markets, galleries, cafes, and civic organizations. Local historic preservation ordinances can be seen as the legal expression of this movement, both legally protecting the context within which the restoration project occurs against market, government, or indigenous incursions, and articulating a spatial identity and narrative for the renovating district.

There can be little doubt that the revival of urban neighborhoods through the practices of historic preservation has been the most significant positive influence on urban life in the past half-century or more. Moreover, what today is referred to as smart growth is largely the generalization of ideas forged in historic neighborhood restoration. At the same time, this recreation of urban life has been derided by critics as gentrification, displacing poor residents and replacing authentic urban practices with ersatz heritage. The realities are complex and only partially understood. This section seeks to provide context for discussion about the nature of preservation redevelopment and perspectives for evaluating it. For broader context of the relationship between historic preservation and affordable housing, please refer to the last section in Chapter 1.

1. HISTORICAL CONTEXT

One must begin with the problematic condition of U.S. cities in the post-World War II period. Most real estate professionals and government experts believed that the urban spaces created in the nineteenth century and frozen economically by the Depression were obsolete in the modern technological economy. Developments in transportation and communication encouraged the movement of both manufacturing and residential development to outwardly expanding suburbs. Modern highways, massively subsidized by the federal government, permitted the freeing of factories from fixed rail and port facilities and relocating larger plants to open spaces, while people could purchase new detached houses in green yards legally sheltered by zoning and subsidized by tax and other financing benefits. Cities with apparently outdated infrastructure experienced deindustrialization and depopulation. The concurrent migration of African Americans to northern cities accelerated "white flight," and racial prejudices contributed to the creation of isolated ghettos suffering extreme disinvestment and consequent social pathologies. To take an extreme case, the population of Washington, D.C., decreased from more than 800,000 in 1950 to 572,000 in 2000; even more dramatically, the District went from 72 percent white to 72 percent black from 1940 to 1970. U.S. Census Bureau, District of Columbia— Race and Hispanic Origin 1800 to 1990 (2002); U.S. Census Bureau, District of Columbia Quick Facts 2010.

Reformers seeking to modernize cities, to make them competitive with suburbs, constructed highways through them and replaced large swaths of older buildings with high-rise modernist buildings surrounded by open space, often employing eminent domain. This was urban renewal. It represented a consensus of developers, banks, and government officials in the 1950s and represented a plausible outgrowth of New Deal rationalist, big government approaches to serious problems. Large amounts of federal money financed it. In many cities, it had a racial dimension, as demolition so often targeted poor minority areas that it came to be referred to as "Negro removal," exacerbating a legacy of distrust. *See* Wendell E. Pritchett, *The "Public Menace" of Blight: Urban Renewal and the Private Uses of Eminent Domain*, 21 YALE L. & POL'Y REV. 1 (2003).

Inner city neighborhood revival, by contrast, has consisted of innumerable, grass-roots, decentralized private ventures. Individual "pioneers" or "gentrifiers" purchased older, sometimes dilapidated houses with their own funds and credit, improved the house and garden along historical lines, and also developed new community associations to represent their interests. These newcomers strongly opposed urban renewal and highway construction, seeking to preserve those features of scale and design that made their neighborhoods "urban villages." The iconic episode perhaps was the successful 1960s-era opposition, led by urban theorist Jane Jacobs, to the determination of New York's master "power broker," Robert Moses, to construct a ten-lane Lower Manhattan Expressway through the neighborhoods of Little Italy and what became SoHo. *See* ANTHONY FLINT, WRESTLING WITH MOSES (2009). In her influential 1961 book *Death and Life of Great American Cities*, Jacobs provided a stirring defense of traditional pedestrian-oriented neighborhoods composed of mixed use and mixed age buildings against modern planning orthodoxy. Over succeeding decades, revitalization of historic neighborhoods has provided a countertrend of increasing affluence and physical improvement to urban industrial decay.

What caused this striking return to city living? To some extent it reflects changes in the global economy. Manufacturing in U.S. cities has nearly disappeared and been replaced by expanding service industries and knowledge institutions congregating in urban centers and reliant on a highly educated workforce. Older neighborhoods offered these newcomers attractive older affordable housing, vacated by prior generations moving to the suburbs. But it also offered something more. The older buildings, ethnic merchants, and neighborhood stories provided a new highly educated middle class with a sense of rooted authenticity and belonging. Historian Suleiman Osman has described in penetrating detail the aspirations for a sense of place of "brownstoners," who renovated the neighborhoods of Brooklyn. They celebrated their "unslumming" neighborhoods as " 'historically diverse'—a new romantic urban aesthetic that recast older inner-city districts as sources of anti-bureaucratic authenticity." SULEIMAN OSMAN, THE INVENTION OF BROWNSTONE BROOKLYN: GENTRIFICATION AND THE SEARCH FOR AUTHENTICITY IN POSTWAR NEW YORK 94 (2011). He explains:

> In a kinetic modern city, brownstones were anchors, their heavy facades giving new white-collar workers a sense of rootedness and permanence in a transient urban environment. . . . Echoing a powerful Romantic theme, residents were reinhabiting an organic landscape, fleeing university campuses and high-rise apartments to return to a brownstone landscape middle-class forebears once called home. . . . Their stoops, street-level windows, and human-scale development also evoked for new residents the gestalt of an "urban village." . . . Brooklyn Heights represented . . . a "real neighborhood," an authentic local place where genuine human contact and ethnic folk tradition remained uncrushed by alienating modernity and capitalism.

Id., at 100–04. In their political campaigns, renovators fought against the incursion of modernist high-rise development both to protect the picturesque settings for their homes and to thwart the hegemony of dehumanizing bureaucratic and corporate structures over private lives. The enactment of New York City's Landmarks Preservation Ordinance in 1965 signaled their emerging political power, although it required alliance with traditional historic preservation advocates. Brooklyn Heights, the paradigm of the restored neighborhood, became New York

City's first historic district designated under the ordinance in the same year. Similar stories can be told of many other cities, particularly those whose economies rely primarily on an educated service and research workforce.

In light of this historical context, we turn back to legal issues. The creation of historic districts legally protected an urban form or aesthetic that encouraged individuals to invest in improvements compatible with that form and invigorated that form with a narrative that gave it meaning. Consider several ways that local historic preservation ordinances may reflect the values of neighborhood renovators. First, historic review boards typically are stand-alone agencies, largely independent of the pre-existing zoning and planning bureaucracy. Their structure reflects preservationists' distrust of the traditional authorities complicit in the "growth machine," long dominant in city politics. Second, the powers of review boards are passive. Other than providing information, they do not initiate anything, but they respond to requests for permits. This is the opposite of the active government planning and financing roles in urban renewal. It also cedes to private persons the initiative for development proposals. Third, local ordinances cover far more buildings in districts than individual landmarks. Thus, local law primarily protects neighborhoods. It protects vernacular buildings, such as row houses, which provide the settings within which private renovation occurs, and covers new construction on vacant land within the district. Such a focus helps give an identity to a neighborhood (perhaps more than it had before) and encourages neighborhood scale citizens' organizations. Practically, the effort to secure historic district designation requires documentation and articulation of neighborhood identity. Finally, and perhaps most fundamentally, local preservation ordinances protect what already exists and require new development to be compatible with existing building, thus safeguarding authentic fabric and rejecting the sharp breaks with tradition.

NOTES & QUESTIONS

1.   Recall the argument of Carol Rose, excerpted in Chapter 1, that the chief aim of modern historic preservation is community building, giving voice to community members about how their neighborhoods should be developed. Whose voices do local preservation laws favor? Do they give too much weight to owners of historic houses and not enough to lower income persons seeking affordable housing? Do they give too much weight to parochial interests and not enough to the long-term interest of the city as a whole?

2.   Does designation of a redeveloping area as a historic district raise property values? It may be difficult to separate designation from the many factors that might lead residents to seek designation, such as attractive housing stock or increasing overall population, which themselves would increase property values. PlaceEconomics, a private sector firm specializing

in the analysis of the economic impacts of historic preservation, offers the following assessment:

> There is no area of preservation economic analysis that has been done more often than measuring the impact of local historic districts on property values. Regardless of the researcher, the methodology, or the location of the study, the results of these analyses have been remarkable [EDS.: sic] consistent: In nearly every instance properties in local historic districts have greater rates of appreciation than properties elsewhere in the same city. Thirty years ago, opponents to the creation of a local historic district usually claimed, "Historic districts mean one more layer of regulation. More regulation means, prima facie, lower property values." Of course, study after study has demonstrated the opposite has been true; the values of properties have significantly benefited from local district designation.

PlaceEconomics, *Twenty-Four Reasons Historic Preservation is Good for Your Community* 6 (2020). Why should this be so? Remember the three main factors that determine the value of any piece of real estate: location, location, location. Value in urban real estate largely grows from context. Historic district protections secure an aesthetic context within which individual investment decisions may be made with confidence that neighbors can only make exterior changes that are compatible with the historic character of the district. Each individual improvement, too, should raise the appeal of the district as a whole and thus value of each constituent property. None of this guarantees an increase in property values, but it should enhance and undergird existing development impetus. *See* DONOVAN D. RYPKEMA, THE ECONOMICS OF HISTORIC PRESERVATION 63–72 (2008).

3. Does historic district restoration enshrine a sanitized version of a neighborhood's history primarily to gratify newcomers? Brooklyn renovators invented quaint pastoral names for their neighborhoods they had never borne in the past, such as Cobble Hill and Boerum Hill. OSMAN, *supra* at 23–25. One author, writing in 1971, made a more serious complaint against the interpretation of Georgetown implicit in the historic preservation of that Washington, D.C., neighborhood:

> Georgetown is a very old place, and blacks had been living there since before the Civil War. By 1930 over forty per cent of the residents of Georgetown were black. . . . There is . . . another more philosophical objection to the Georgetown . . . syndrome. It is not clear that it properly qualifies as "historic preservation" at all. The true history of Georgetown—until the preservationists' interest in it—was an integrated history. The black elements in that history have now been destroyed, resulting in a perversion and distortion of history.

Michael deHaven Newsom, *Blacks and Historic Preservation*, 36 LAW & CONTEMP. PROBS. 423, 424 (1971). Note that Georgetown was established as a historic district by the U.S. Congress in 1950, when *de jure* segregation still prevailed in Washington, D.C. How should the designation process ensure the honesty of accounts of area history, especially of poor and minorities?

4.   Newcomers to older ethnic or racial communities often are drawn to what they perceive as the authentic cultural character of the community and work self-consciously to preserve it, even as their presence changes the community. *See* JAPONICA BROWN-SARACINO, A NEIGHBORHOOD THAT NEVER CHANGES: GENTRIFICATION, SOCIAL PRESERVATION, AND THE SEARCH FOR AUTHENTICITY (2010). Recent episodes of neighborhood gentrification of areas historically important to African Americans, such as Harlem in New York and U Street in D.C., have celebrated their contributions to culture and society, even as they have diluted the black presence. One recent development is the growing visibility of African Americans returning to the city and renovating houses. *See, e.g.,* Shani O. Hilton, *Confessions of a Black Gentrifier*, WASH. CITY PAPER, Mar. 18, 2011. Urban scholar Lance Freeman, himself an African American resident of Harlem, has described a "neo-soul" aesthetic, which values

> authenticity and diversity and abhor[s] the mass-produced cookie-cutter suburbs . . . and might prefer older neighborhoods with charm like Harlem, Fort Greene, U Street, and Bronzeville. These neighborhoods have old but elegant architecture, street life, cafes where folks can meet and greet other bohos, and perhaps most important, a cultural legacy.

LANCE FREEMAN, THERE GOES THE 'HOOD: VIEWS OF GENTRIFICATION FROM THE GROUND UP 56 (2006). These aspirations are strikingly similar to those of the white gentrifiers of an earlier generation described by Suleiman Osman in his book, *The Invention of Brownstone Brooklyn*, referenced above.

An interesting variation on the interplay of race and historic preservation is provided by the controversial designation of the Kingman Park Historic District in Washington, D.C., in 2018. The modest row house neighborhood was developed during the 1920s and 1930s as segregated housing for African Americans. The impetus for designation was led by older African Americans, some of whom already had moved away, and resisted by largely white new residents seeking legal freedom to remodel their homes. The D.C. Historic Preservation Review Board has issued design guidelines for the Kingman Park Historic District that seek to conserve the ability of the district to convey the history of its long-time residents but also permit greater leeway for adaptation of buildings than typically mandated for historic districts.

2.   TERMINOLOGY AND DISPLACEMENT

Many new residents are attracted to return to city neighborhoods by their racial, ethnic, and economic diversity, which they may contrast with the bland uniformity of the suburbs (produced in no small part by traditional zoning). But some of those neighborhood denizens may resent some of the changes wrought by the newcomers and denigrate them as "gentrification." The term, gentrification, was coined by an English author, in 1964, describing middle-class people refurbishing houses in working-class neighborhoods in London "until most of the original working-class occupiers are displaced and the whole social character of the district is changed." RUTH GLASS, LONDON, ASPECTS OF CHANGE xviii–xix (1964).

It is striking that the word gentrification would be introduced in connection with concerns about displacement, because displacement, understood as the forced exodus of poorer residents from their homes and neighborhoods because of rising rents and the loss of indigenous businesses and community identity, has been the most serious and persistent critique of neighborhood renovation and associated historic preservation. Some critics of gentrification have focused on historic districting as a device for gentrification. They reason that if creation of a historic district encourages redevelopment, it will inevitably displace and exclude the poor who live there, while providing a legal defense against construction of new low income housing. *See, e.g.,* Jon C. Dubin, *From Junkyards to Gentrification; Explicating a Right to Protective Zoning in Low-Income Communities of Color,* 77 MINN. L. REV. 739, 772–73 (1993) (describing HUD investigation of historic district designation alleged to have intended to displace low income blacks); David B. Fein, Note, *Historic Districts: Preserving City Neighborhoods for the Privileged,* 60 N.Y.U. L. REV. 64, 87–88 (1985).

Displacement, however, turns out to be an ambiguous reality. While one must be troubled by landlords precipitately raising rents or even evicting tenants to cater to wealthier newcomers, it is unclear how widespread such practices are. More widespread is indirect displacement, where rents rise and renovation occurs in units voluntarily vacated for exogenous reasons. Several empirical studies have shown that residential turnover does not occur more frequently in a gentrifying neighborhood than generally, and that lower income people in a gentrifying neighborhood are actually less likely to move than people in another neighborhood. Lance Freeman & Frank Braconi, *Gentrification and Displacement in New York City,* 70 J. AM. PLANNING ASS'N 39 (2004); Jacob L. Vigdor, *Does Gentrification Harm the Poor?,* Brookings-Wharton Papers on Urban Affairs 133 (2002). A more recent study reached the same conclusion. Lei Ding, Jackelyn Hwang, & Eileen Divringi, *Gentrification and Residential Mobility in Philadelphia,* Federal Reserve Bank of Philadelphia Working Paper No. 15–36/R (2016).

These studies do not deny that demographic change occurs, but suggest that it occurs gradually and without mass evictions. At the same time, low income residents who remain will pay a larger percentage of their income in rent, which poses other burdens on them. Another empirical study using Census data concludes:

> [R]ather than dislocating non-white households, gentrification of predominantly black neighborhoods creates neighborhoods that are attractive to middle-class black households, particularly those with children or with elderly householders.

> One reasonable interpretation * * * is that because these neighborhoods are experiencing income gains, but also more diverse with regards to race/ethnicity and income than established middle-class neighborhoods, they are desirable locations for black middle-class households.

Terra McKinnish et al., *Who Gentrifies Low-Income Neighborhoods?* 67 J. URB. ECON. 180, 191–92 (2010).

Gentrification offers real benefits to cities that long have suffered from depopulation and disinvestment, and to their poor residents who have their greatest political voice in cities and who may depend on public expenditures. *See* J. Peter Byrne, *Two Cheers for Gentrification,* 46 HOW. L. J. 405 (2003). Moreover, it improves the living environment for those lower income residents who manage to remain in the gentrifying neighborhood, increasing retail choices, public safety, and educational and employment opportunities, especially in neighborhoods that have suffered the greatest previous disinvestment. LANCE FREEMAN, THERE GOES THE 'HOOD: VIEWS OF GENTRIFICATION FROM THE GROUND UP 158–60 (2006); Byrne, *supra*, at 418–24. Low income black residents, nonetheless, have mixed feelings about gentrification; although they appreciate the advantages it brings, many are cynical about the process and fear eventual displacement. Freeman, *supra*, at 92–94. The core problem is that rising rents diminish the already inadequate store of affordable housing within the neighborhood and the city generally. One can argue that the better legal response to indirect displacement is not to prevent neighborhood redevelopment but to support the provision of dispersed, mixed-income, subsidized housing throughout the city, including gentrifying areas, whose scale and appearance reflect the urban form of their neighborhoods. Byrne, *supra*, at 427–31.

CHAPTER TWELVE

INTERNATIONAL CULTURAL HERITAGE LAW

In this Chapter, we turn from domestic historic preservation law to international cultural heritage law. Studying international cultural heritage law is worthwhile because it helps situate American historic preservation law within a much broader context. One important thing to understand before proceeding is that historically significant properties like the ones covered in American law are really a subset of what international law considers to be cultural heritage. Over the last fifty years, cultural heritage has also evolved to include intangible cultureways, including music, dance, expression, and other things that cannot be reduced to ownership under American notions of property.

The desire to save historically significant properties is not peculiar to the United States, but seems a nearly universal human affection. At the same time, threats to these properties are sadly common everywhere. Transnational interest in historic places has fueled international tourism, which in some places has been a double-edged sword, enhancing awareness but also threatening the integrity of the properties. International trade in historic and cultural objects such as paintings, statuary, textiles, and pottery has resulted in commodification that puts movable objects at risk. Other threats to historic places—neglect, intentional destruction, climate change, and cultural misunderstandings—cross national boundaries.

To protect resources from these threats, nations have enacted their own protective laws suited to their legal systems and cultural priorities. Our focus in this Chapter is not the law of individual countries, but international laws that emerged in the mid-twentieth century to deal with cross border issues and to protect the "universal human value" of outstanding cultural accomplishments.

The Chapter looks first at the Hague Convention, which protects cultural resources during armed conflict. It then turns to the treaty that intersects most fully with domestic preservation laws, the World Heritage Convention. Both treaties are administered under the United Nations Educational, Scientific, and Cultural Organization (UNESCO). The Chapter then covers the universal problem of the threat of climate change to historic places, a topic we previewed in Chapter 1. It concludes with a look at the extraterritorial reach of American preservation law.

A. THE HAGUE CONVENTION

The first efforts in international law to conserve cultural resources were measures to prevent the destruction of historic buildings and objects of art during wartime. The tremendous destruction of the Second World War led to the landmark Hague Convention of 1954, a treaty imposing duties on State Parties to enact domestic laws to protect "cultural property" against destruction during armed conflict. The term "State Party" refers to any nation that has signed the treaty. The term "cultural property" is defined very broadly to include:

> movable or immovable property of great importance to the cultural heritage of every people, such as monuments of architecture, art or history, whether religious or secular; archaeological sites; groups of buildings, which, as a whole, are of historical or artistic interest; works of art; manuscripts, books and other objects of artistic, historical or archaeological interest; as well as scientific collections and important collections of books or archives or of reproductions of the property defined above.

1954 Hague Convention for the Protection of Cultural Property in the Event of Armed Conflict, May 14, 1954, 249 U.N.T.S. 240, art. 1. Note that the treaty's cultural property definition includes many more types of resources than are protected under American historic preservation law.

The 1954 Hague Convention imposes duties on State Parties both during peacetime and during armed conflict. During times of peace, State Parties must prepare for the safeguarding of cultural property "against the foreseeable effects of armed conflict." Hague Convention, art. 3. Suggested steps include designating and marking (using a distinctive Blue Shield) cultural property sites, incorporating systems and personnel within armed forces trained to protect cultural property, and providing criminal and civil penalties for people violating the Convention. During armed conflict, State Parties must avoid destroying cultural property except as may be justified by "military necessity," and prevent theft, pillage, and vandalism. Hague Convention, art. 4. They may not destroy cultural property as an act of reprisal. State Parties also must actively protect cultural property in occupied territory.

The Hague Convention is supplemented by two Protocols, which add to the duties of states that ratify them. The First Protocol, adopted at the same time as the Convention itself, addresses the export, import, and return of moveable cultural property during war, occupation, and their aftermath. The Second Protocol, adopted in 1999, addresses internal conflicts as well as international ones and strengthens protection by reducing the scope of military necessity and mandating enhanced protection for cultural property of the greatest significance. It also provides for individual responsibility for serious violations and creates the permanent Committee for the Protection of Cultural Property in the Event of Armed Conflict, consisting of twelve State Parties.

NOTES & QUESTIONS

1. As of 2021, 133 states were party to the Hague Convention of 1954, and 110 and 84 states respectively have acceded to the Protocols of 1954 and 1999. The United States participated in the negotiation of the 1954 Hague Convention but did not ratify it until 2009, after the experience of the Iraq War, when museums and archeological sites were looted. The United States has not ratified either Protocol of the Hague Convention. Why do you think the United States would not join these agreements to protect cultural property? One view is that governments like the United States do not wish to take on a commitment to protect cultural property because it is difficult and costly to succeed and may compete with other goals. *See* Eric A. Posner, *International Protection of Cultural Property: Some Skeptical Observations*, 8 CHI. J. INT'L L. 213, 220–21 (2007).

2. Documentary evidence and subsequent practice demonstrate that the Hague Convention standard for protected cultural property requires only national or local importance, not global or universal importance. *See* Roger O'Keefe, *The Meaning of "Cultural Property" Under the 1954 Hague Convention*, 46 NETHERLANDS L. REV. 26 (1999). How does the scope of significance for cultural property protected by the Hague Convention differ from preservation criteria with which you are familiar in U.S. or municipal law? Consider the following cultural resources:

- The original manuscript of the Declaration of Independence
- A 25,000-year-old cave painting
- Touro Synagogue, Newport, RI
- A replica of an infamous ship that transported enslaved persons
- Edward Hopper's painting, The Nighthawks
- Trump Tower, New York City

Are they protected under the 1954 Hague Convention? Under local historic preservation law? To the extent they have different protections, suggest why.

3. Invaders sometimes intentionally destroy cultural sites to obliterate the national identity of their enemy, as the German army notoriously sought to "eradicate [Polish] culture by destroying the most profoundly meaningful aspects of Warsaw's cityscape." ANTHONY M. TUNG, PRESERVING THE WORLD'S GREAT CITIES: THE DESTRUCTION AND RENEWAL OF THE HISTORIC METROPOLIS 79 (2001). During the breakup of the former Yugoslavia, several cultural and religious sites were intentionally attacked or destroyed, including the historic city of Dubrovnik, the Mostar Bridge, and the Jasenovac Memorial commemorating the site of a Nazi concentration camp. In response to these and other war crimes, the UN Security Council set up the International Criminal Tribunal for Yugoslavia, which led to a clearer articulation that a state's intentional destruction of properties significant to particular cultural groups was a crime against humanity. *See*

Prosecutor v. Kordić & Čerkez, IT–95–14/2–T, Judgment (Feb. 21, 2001); Prosecutor v. Jokić, IT–01–42/1–S, Sentencing Judgment (Mar. 18, 2004). What do developments suggest about the balance in international law between state sovereignty on the one hand, and a given community's enjoyment of cultural property rights on the other?

4.   In 2001, the Taliban's widespread campaign of cultural heritage elimination in Afghanistan reached a head with their destruction of two giant Buddhas that had been etched into the cliffs of Bamiyan. The Taliban claimed that the destruction was compelled by sharia (Islamic) law to prevent idol worship and that the matter was strictly an internal matter. The destruction of the Bamiyan Buddhas spurred overwhelming international interest and led to a UN General Assembly Resolution and numerous declarations by states and international bodies that the destruction violated international law. *See, e.g.*, The Destruction of Relics and Monuments in Afghanistan, G.A. Res. 55/243, U.N. Doc. A/RES/55/243 (Mar. 9, 2001). States invoked the Hague Convention to assert that the destruction was an attack on the common heritage of mankind. At the time, the Taliban had de facto control over Afghanistan. Although most states and the UN did not recognize it as the official government, this would not customarily affect its ability to claim sovereignty over a domestic property matter.

Does the Hague Convention apply to internal conflicts like that in Afghanistan? What is the "armed conflict" here? Would the international response differ if a democratically elected government destroyed cultural monuments instead of a terrorist organization? Should it? How does this differ from local governments in the United States removing memorials to the Confederacy?

5.   Recently, the international community has demonstrated a willingness to punish intentional cultural heritage destruction by apportioning individual criminal liability under international law. In a landmark case, the International Criminal Court (ICC) indicted Ahmad Al Faqi Al Mahdi for the war crime of intentional destruction of cultural heritage. Al Mahdi led a group of Tuareg rebels in northern Mali that overtook the historic city of Timbuktu in 2012. He directed his fighters to destroy ten religious sites, at least one of which was a UNESCO World Heritage property. Al Mahdi became the first defendant in the history of the ICC to make a guilty plea, and he was subsequently given nine years in prison and ordered to pay €2.7 million in "collective and symbolic reparations for the community of Timbuktu." *Prosecutor v. Al Mahdi*, ICC–01/12–01/15, Reparations Order at 60 (Aug. 17, 2017). The Court ordered these reparations for three categories of harm: damage to the properties themselves, consequential economic losses, and moral harm.

Importantly, the Al Mahdi case acknowledged the interests both of Mali and the international community as a whole (as represented by UNESCO) in Timbuktu's cultural heritage. What is the significance of the ICC recognizing a harm to the interests of the international community as a whole? Is such an interest consistent with the Court's characterization of Al Mahdi's wrongdoing as a "war crime"? What is the difference between characterizing a harm against the international community as a war crime as compared to a crime against the common heritage of mankind (the harm asserted in the case of the Bamiyan Buddhas)?

Figure 12-1:
The Historic Mostar Bridge Under Reconstruction in 2000,
Mostar, Bosnia

B. THE WORLD HERITAGE CONVENTION

The Convention Concerning the Protection of the World Cultural and Natural Heritage of 1972 (commonly referred to as the World Heritage Convention) forms the centerpiece of international cultural heritage law. The treaty has nearly universal support, with 193 signatories, known as "States Parties," and it has become the rare international legal document whose impact is recognized and understood by the public at large. The UNESCO World Heritage List created by the Convention has proven to be a powerful tool not only for preserving important heritage sites, but also for building awareness and appreciation for heritage preservation practices generally and stimulating economic development and tourism. In addition to the World Heritage List, the Convention created a World Heritage Fund, supported by States Parties' contributions, to fund protection of cultural and natural heritage around the world.

States Parties to the Convention meet every two years in a General Assembly to elect representatives from 21 countries to the World

Heritage Committee, which is responsible for the implementation of the Convention and allocations of the World Heritage Fund. Day-to-day executive functions for the Convention are coordinated by the professional staff of the World Heritage Centre, an administrative secretariat housed within UNESCO. The World Heritage Centre periodically publishes Operational Guidelines that compile the Committee's decisions in implementing the Convention and detail relevant procedures and policies. The Guidelines lack the legal force of provisions in the Convention itself but provide important clarifications and administrative guidance.

Over the years, the United States has had a complicated relationship to UNESCO. Although it fostered its founding after World War Two, the United States withdrew from UNESCO, first in 1983 under President Ronald Reagan (rejoined in 2002 under President George W. Bush) and again in 2018 under President Donald Trump. The primary impact of the American withdrawal from UNESCO has been its withholding of payments to the agency, although the United States had already frozen all payments to the World Heritage Fund in 2011, under President Barack Obama. The country's rights and obligations under the World Heritage Convention are unchanged by this action. The United States still has 24 properties inscribed on the World Heritage List, including eight Frank Lloyd Wright structures jointly inscribed in 2019.

1. ELIGIBILITY CRITERIA FOR THE WORLD HERITAGE LIST

The scope of heritage preservation under the World Heritage Convention is broader than that addressed by any U.S. law. It encompasses both cultural heritage and natural heritage sites. Article 1 of the Convention recognizes three general categories of cultural heritage—monuments, groups of buildings, and sites. Article 2 recognizes three general categories of natural heritage—natural features, geological and physiographical formations, and natural sites. Notably, the Article 1 definition of "monument" extends quite broadly to include: "architectural works, works of monumental sculpture and painting, elements or structures of an archaeological nature, inscriptions, cave dwellings and combinations of features." Additionally, the Operational Guidelines clarify that properties may be listed as mixed cultural and natural heritage, if they satisfy the definition of heritage under both Articles 1 and 2, or as "cultural landscapes." These are Article 1 sites that represent the "combined works of nature and of man" illustrating patterns of human interaction with the natural environment over time. Cultural landscapes may be intentionally created or designed by humans, evolve organically, or derive cultural significance merely from associations tied to a natural site.

For nomination to the World Heritage List, a property must demonstrate four characteristics: (1) outstanding universal value, (2) authenticity, (3) integrity, and (4) protection and management safeguards.

The Operational Guidelines define outstanding universal value (OUV) as "cultural and/or natural significance which is so exceptional as to transcend national boundaries and to be of common importance for present and future generations of all humanity." Intergovernmental Committee for the Protection of the World Cultural and Natural Heritage, UNESCO, Operational Guidelines for the Implementation of the World Heritage Convention ¶ 49 (2019) ("Operational Guidelines"). According to ten criteria set out in the Operational Guidelines, to meet the threshold of outstanding universal value, a property must:

(i)   represent a masterpiece of human creative genius;

(ii)   exhibit an important interchange of human values, over a span of time or within a cultural area of the world, on developments in architecture or technology, monumental arts, town-planning or landscape design;

(iii)   bear a unique or at least exceptional testimony to a cultural tradition or to a civilization which is living or which has disappeared;

(iv)   be an outstanding example of a type of building, architectural or technological ensemble or landscape which illustrates (a) significant stage(s) in human history;

(v)   be an outstanding example of a traditional human settlement, land-use, or sea-use which is representative of a culture (or cultures), or human interaction with the environment especially when it has become vulnerable under the impact of irreversible change;

(vi)   be directly or tangibly associated with events or living traditions, with ideas, or with beliefs, with artistic and literary works of outstanding universal significance. (The Committee considers that this criterion should preferably be used in conjunction with other criteria);

(vii)   contain superlative natural phenomena or areas of exceptional natural beauty and aesthetic importance;

(viii) be outstanding examples representing major stages of earth's history, including the record of life, significant on-going geological processes in the development of landforms, or significant geomorphic or physiographic features;

(ix)   be outstanding examples representing significant on-going ecological and biological processes in the evolution and development of terrestrial, fresh water, coastal and marine ecosystems and communities of plants and animals;

>   (x)   contain the most important and significant natural
>   habitats for in-situ conservation of biological diversity,
>   including those containing threatened species of
>   Outstanding Universal Value from the point of view of
>   science or conservation.

Id. at ¶ 77.

Note that the World Heritage Convention protects both cultural and natural sites. This is not an approach generally found in United States law, with the notable exception of the National Environmental Policy Act, covered in Chapter 4.

A property need satisfy only one criterion to be listed. However, listed properties often demonstrate OUV under multiple criteria. For example, Machu Picchu in Peru was inscribed on the World Heritage List under criteria (i) and (iii) because it is a unique artistic and architectural masterpiece, and because it bears unique and exceptional testimony to the Inca civilization. It was also designated under criteria (vii) and (ix) on account of its scenic landscape and biodiversity. UNESCO Doc. SC/83/CONF.009/8, at 9 (Dec. 9, 1983). As another example, the Blue and John Crow Mountains property was nominated and subsequently inscribed as Jamaica's first World Heritage site in 2015 under criteria (iii), (vi), and (x) because of its historical and present cultural significance as a site of refuge for people fleeing enslavement, as well as for its natural heritage by virtue of incredible biodiversity and high degree of plant endemism in the Caribbean. UNESCO Doc. WHC–15/39.COM/19, at 162–166 (July 8, 2015).

Properties demonstrating outstanding universal value are further assessed for their authenticity and integrity. The authenticity condition applies only to properties nominated under criteria (i)–(vi) and ensures that a property credibly expresses its cultural value. Operational Guidelines at ¶ 79. This condition is assessed based on sources of cultural information as well as the characteristics and accumulated meaning of the cultural heritage property. *Id.* at ¶ 80. Importantly, authenticity is judged *within* the cultural context of the heritage property and can be met by attributes that are tangible, such as design or setting, or intangible, such as spirit and feeling. *Id.* at ¶ 81.

The integrity condition applies to all properties regardless of their qualifying OUV criterion and ensures that the property is sufficiently whole or intact. *Id.* at ¶ 88. To satisfy the integrity condition, a property must include all elements necessary to express its OUV, be of adequate size to ensure a complete representation of the property's significance, and not suffer excessive adverse effects from development or neglect. *Id.* For properties nominated under criteria (vii), (viii), (ix) or (x), the elements of integrity are further defined to address specific requirements for various types of natural heritage properties. *Id.* at ¶ 90.

Figure 12-2:
Machu Picchu,
Urubamba Province, Peru

Finally, in order to be nominated for the World Heritage List, a property must be protected and managed so that its OUV, authenticity, and integrity can be safeguarded over time. *Id.* at ¶ 96. Properties must be supported by domestic legislative, regulatory, and contractual protections; delineated boundaries or buffer zones to ensure effective physical protection; and an effective management plan tailored to the property's characteristics and preservation challenges. *Id.* at ¶¶ 98–118. The Guidelines explicitly require that the protection and management condition not interfere with the continued "ecologically and culturally sustainable" use of the property. *Id.* at ¶ 119.

Properties that States Parties believe demonstrate the four elements of outstanding universal value, authenticity, integrity, and protection and management may be nominated to the tentative World Heritage List for review and assessment. The Convention provides that three external bodies will assist the World Heritage Committee: the International Council on Monuments and Sites (ICOMOS), the International Union for Conservation of Nature (IUCN), and the International Centre for the Study of the Preservation and Restoration of Cultural Property (the Rome Centre). ICOMOS assists with the preparation and evaluation of cultural properties, while IUCN assists with the preparation and evaluation of natural heritage properties. In the case of mixed cultural and natural heritage properties, both bodies play a role. The Rome Centre's primary function in relation to the Convention centers on cultural heritage training. All three advisory bodies also support the World Heritage Committee through financial review, monitoring, advisory, and capacity building competencies.

Evaluation by ICOMOS or IUCN subjects a nominated property to a rigorous expert review that follows an objective, standardized procedure. On the basis of this evaluation, the advisory bodies present the World Heritage Committee with a recommendation that the property be inscribed on the World Heritage List, not inscribed, deferred, or referred back to the State Party for resubmission. Finally, when the Committee decides to inscribe a property on the list, it concomitantly submits a Statement of Outstanding Universal Value that furnishes the legal basis for the property's future protection and management.

NOTES & QUESTIONS

1.   Scholars have lauded the Convention as groundbreaking for acknowledging a linkage between cultural and natural heritage, establishing a common preservation regime, and introducing the concept of "world heritage." *See* FRANCESCO FRANCIONI, THE 1972 WORLD HERITAGE CONVENTION: A COMMENTARY 5 (2008). This framework of heritage represented a conceptual shift that recognized heritage as conveying an "intergenerational equity" of human experience and knowledge from one generation to another. *See* JANET BLAKE, INTERNATIONAL CULTURAL HERITAGE LAW 9 (2015). Intergenerational equity in heritage creates a duty to preserve in the current generation so as to pass on to future generations.

The World Heritage Convention also helped solidify a conceptual shift toward protection of "cultural heritage," rather than "cultural property" as in the Hague Convention. Many had viewed property as providing a too narrow and culturally-bound framework for heritage conservation. *See, e.g.,* Lyndel V. Prott and Patrick J. O'Keefe, *Cultural Heritage or Cultural Property*, 1 INT'L J. CULTURAL PROP. 307 (1992). Anne-Marie Carstens notes: "The movement toward 'cultural heritage' stems from a desire to preserve not only tangible cultural artifacts and sites, but also intangible cultural expressions, customs, and modes of life not reflected in a property-oriented regime." Anne-Marie Carstens, Art, Artifacts, and Cultural Property Course 3 (2015) (unpublished teaching materials on file with authors).

Additionally, under the Convention, heritage is conceived as a global concern, embodying the patrimony of all humankind. The Pyramids of Giza, for example, are seen not just as sites of Egyptian heritage, but as that of the entire world. Is there an inherent tension between the Convention's definition of "world heritage" and the fact that, from a practical standpoint, the sites are largely administered by States Parties?

2.   Despite the Convention's novel focus on world heritage, from its early days it has been accused of imposing a preservation regime imbued with cultural bias. For example, the Convention's marquee achievement, the World Heritage List, features a vastly disproportionate number of properties

in wealthy countries able to devote resources to the lengthy nomination process. As of 2020, 529 of the List's 1,121 properties (47%) were located in Europe and North America, while only 268 (24%) were located in the Asia Pacific region and a mere 96 (9%) in Africa. UNESCO World Heritage Centre, World Heritage List Statistics (2020). These disparities disguise even starker gaps for cultural or mixed heritage properties, leading to questions about whether the Convention is living up to its mandate to preserve a world cultural heritage. How should a preservation regime address and redress underrepresentation of certain regions and cultures? What are the challenges in pursuing a more representative list? In theory, should the Convention, with its focus on "world heritage" of "outstanding universal value," concern itself with the notion of representativeness?

3.   For its part, the World Heritage Committee decided at its session in Cairns, Australia in 2000, that the Convention should focus on reducing the List's geographical and cultural imbalances. The Committee adopted the Cairns Decision, which introduced a system of quotas limiting the number of nominations each year from States Parties to one or two, among other measures designed to increase the institutional power of States Parties with no listed properties. These reforms were intended to address administrative inequities in pursuing the property nomination and inscription process between States Parties with advanced preservation and documentation regimes and those lacking such structural advantages. The Cairns Decision, which has been somewhat modified over the subsequent years, arguably frustrates the object and purpose of the Convention by introducing a constraint that limits rather than expands heritage protection in the name of representativeness, a condition outside the scope of the Convention itself. At the same time, the Cairns Decision indicates that the Committee views a regional imbalance of properties on the World Heritage List as a procedural failing, rather than a reflection of cultural bias inherent to the Convention and its institutions. Was the Committee right to adopt the quota system in the Cairns Decision? Should the imbalance of properties be addressed as a procedural or systemic failure?

4.   In general, the World Heritage Convention protects only tangible, immovable heritage; while properties may contain movable elements, they must be more immovable than movable. In fact, the Operational Guidelines specify that even the potential for future movability of immovable heritage will act as a bar to consideration for inscription on the World Heritage List. Operational Guidelines at 20. Because of the Convention's focus on immovable heritage, it lacks a specific restitution mechanism for illicitly looted or trafficked movable elements, at the same time as it increases the visibility, accessibility, and prestige of such elements for the illicit market.

Protection of movables depends on a web of other international agreements that have developed to address the intractable problem of trafficking in cultural heritage items. These include the UNESCO Convention for the Protection of Cultural Property in the Event of Armed Conflict of 1954 (the Hague Convention) and its subsequent First Protocol (1954) and Second Protocol (1999), as well as the UNESCO Convention on the Means of Prohibiting and Preventing the Illicit Import, Export and

Transfer of Ownership of Cultural Property of 1970 (the 1970 Convention) and the 1995 UNIDROIT Convention on Stolen or Illegally Exported Cultural Objects. While these agreements do not have as many States Parties as the 1972 World Heritage Convention and generally protect a narrower category of "cultural property," they buttress the scope of preservation of movable elements constituent to a property inscribed on the World Heritage List by providing various restitution mechanisms and safeguards against illicit trafficking.

5.   Although not primarily concerned with intangible heritage, the World Heritage Convention does recognize that a property's outstanding universal value may derive from its intangible associations under criterion (vi). As a subclass of Article 1 cultural landscape sites, the Committee has recognized *associative cultural landscapes* as justified for inscription "by virtue of the powerful religious, artistic or cultural associations of the natural element rather than material cultural evidence, which may be insignificant or even absent." Operational Guidelines at 83. One such property is the Uluru-Kata Tjuta National Park in Australia, which was originally inscribed on the World Heritage List under criteria for natural heritage in 1987. With an understanding that the initial listing under these criteria represented a Western perspective that prized the property for its natural and aesthetic qualities, the property was inscribed again in 1994 as a cultural landscape on the basis of the intangible but deep spiritual and cultural importance of the rock formations to the indigenous Anangu people. Graeme Calma & Lynette Liddle, *Uluru-Kata Tjuta National Park: Sustainable Management and Development*, 7 World Heritage Papers 104 (2002).

The push to safeguard intangible cultural heritage led also to the creation of the UNESCO Convention for the Safeguarding of the Intangible Cultural Heritage in 2003. This Convention counts 178 States Parties, including China and France, but not including Russia, the United States, or the United Kingdom. The 2003 Convention defines intangible heritage as "practices, representations, expressions, knowledge, skills—as well as the instruments, objects, artifacts and cultural spaces associated therewith—that communities, groups and, in some cases, individuals recognize as part of their cultural heritage." Convention for the Safeguarding of the Intangible Cultural Heritage art. 2(1), 2368 U.N.T.S. 1, 36. It goes on to recognize an intergenerational equity element as well by acknowledging that "[t]his intangible cultural heritage, transmitted from generation to generation, is constantly recreated by communities and groups in response to their environment, their interaction with nature and their history, and provides them with a sense of identity and continuity, thus promoting respect for cultural diversity and human creativity." *Id.*

6.   Think back to Chapter 2, which covered the legal process for designating historic properties to registers of places. In what sense are the criteria for the World Heritage List similar to the criteria for the National Register of Historic Places? Outstanding universal value has parallels to significance in U.S. law, but as noted above, it encompasses more than U.S. law. Authenticity and integrity as defined in the World Heritage Convention

sound a lot like different aspects of the integrity criterion in U.S. law. And while the World Heritage List requires protection and management safeguards, the National Register of Historic Places requires no such thing. Which regime has more inclusive criteria?

2.   PROTECTION PROVIDED

The World Heritage Convention's most important protective mechanisms appear in two chapters of the convention: Chapter II (Articles 4–7) and Chapter III (Articles 8–11). Chapter II of the Convention reflects the central object and purpose of the Convention and includes the key provisions setting out the scope of legal protections that States Parties are bound to implement for heritage properties under their jurisdiction. This chapter is notable for a number of reasons: first, for the obligations it places upon States Parties; second, for the roles it sets out for the international community; and third, for the recognition of a universal interest in the protection of heritage properties. Chapter III, on the other hand, reflects the procedural and administrative structure of the Convention; its most important provision is Article 11. This chapter is notable for its establishment of the World Heritage Committee and the World Heritage List, as well as the safeguards of World Heritage in Danger listing and removal from the World Heritage List. Critically, both chapters leave practical judgment about the implementation of heritage protections for properties to States Parties. Notice how this approach is embedded in Articles 4–7 and the key provisions of Article 11, reprinted below.

Excerpts from the World Heritage Convention

Chapter II.   National Protection and International Protection
of the Cultural and Natural Heritage

Article 4

Each State Party to this Convention recognizes that the duty of ensuring the identification, protection, conservation, presentation and transmission to future generations of the cultural and natural heritage referred to in Articles 1 and 2 and situated on its territory, belongs primarily to that State. It will do all it can to this end, to the utmost of its own resources and, where appropriate, with any international assistance and co-operation, in particular, financial, artistic, scientific and technical, which it may be able to obtain.

Article 5

To ensure that effective and active measures are taken for the protection, conservation, and presentation of the cultural and natural heritage situated on its territory, each State Party to this Convention shall endeavor, in so far as possible, and as appropriate for each country:

1. to adopt a general policy which aims to give the cultural and natural heritage a function in the life of the community and to integrate the protection of that heritage into comprehensive planning programmes;

2. to set up within its territories, where such services do not exist, one or more services for the protection, conservation and presentation of the cultural and natural heritage with an appropriate staff and possessing the means to discharge their functions;

3. to develop scientific and technical studies and research and to work out such operating methods as will make the State capable of counteracting the dangers that threaten its cultural or natural heritage;

4. to take the appropriate legal, scientific, technical, administrative and financial measures necessary for the identification, protection, conservation, presentation and rehabilitation of this heritage; and

5. to foster the establishment or development of national or regional centres for training in the protection, conservation and presentation of the cultural and natural heritage and to encourage scientific research in this field.

Article 6

1. Whilst fully respecting the sovereignty of the States on whose territory the cultural and natural heritage mentioned in Articles 1 and 2 is situated, and without prejudice to property right provided by national legislation, the States Parties to this Convention recognize that such heritage constitutes a world heritage for whose protection it is the duty of the international community as a whole to co-operate.

2. The States Parties undertake, in accordance with the provisions of this Convention, to give their help in the identification, protection, conservation and presentation of the cultural and natural heritage referred to in paragraphs 2 and 4 of Article 11 if the States on whose territory it is situated so request.

3. Each State Party to this Convention undertakes not to take any deliberate measures which might damage directly or indirectly the cultural and natural heritage referred to in Articles 1 and 2 situated on the territory of other States Parties to this Convention.

Article 7

For the purpose of this Convention, international protection of the world cultural and natural heritage shall be understood to mean the establishment of a system of international co-operation and assistance designed to support States Parties to the Convention in their efforts to conserve and identify that heritage.

Chapter III. Intergovernmental Committee for the Protection of the World Cultural and Natural Heritage

Article 11

1. Every State Party to this Convention shall, in so far as possible, submit to the World Heritage Committee an inventory of property forming part of the cultural and natural heritage situated in its territory and suitable for inclusion in the list provided for in paragraph 2 of this Article. This inventory, which shall not be considered exhaustive, shall include documentation about the location of the property in question and its significance.

2. On the basis of the inventories submitted by States in accordance with paragraph 1, the Committee shall establish, keep up to date and publish, under the title of "World Heritage List," a list of properties forming part of the cultural heritage and natural heritage, as defined in Articles 1 and 2 of this Convention, which it considers as having outstanding universal value in terms of such criteria as it shall have established. An updated list shall be distributed at least every two years.

3. The inclusion of a property in the World Heritage List requires the consent of the State concerned. The inclusion of a property situated in a territory, sovereignty or jurisdiction over which is claimed by more than one State shall in no way prejudice the rights of the parties to the dispute.

4. The Committee shall establish, keep up to date and publish, whenever circumstances shall so require, under the title of "List of World Heritage in Danger," a list of the property appearing in the World Heritage List for the conservation of which major operations are necessary and for which assistance has been requested under this Convention. This list shall contain an estimate of the cost of such operations. This list may include only such property forming part of the cultural and natural heritage as is threatened by serious and specific dangers, such as the threat of disappearance caused by changes in the use or ownership of the land; major alterations due to unknown causes; abandonment for any reason whatsoever; the outbreak or the threat of an armed conflict; calamities and cataclysms; serious fires, earthquakes, landslides; volcanic eruptions; changes in water level, floods and tidal waves. The Committee may at any time, in case of urgent need, make a new entry in the List of World Heritage in Danger and publicize such entry immediately. * * *

NOTES & QUESTIONS

1.   Perhaps surprisingly, neither UNESCO nor the World Heritage Committee directly "protects" properties inscribed on the World Heritage List. Article 4 of the Convention explicitly recognizes that the duty to protect a heritage property rests with the state in which it is located. This assignment of duties to the territorial state exemplifies the respect for state sovereignty seen throughout the Convention, but does it place limitations on the Convention's scope of protections? What are the consequences of Article 4's conditioning the duty to protect cultural heritage properties upon the extent of a state's resources? Does this come into tension with the Convention's universal scope of heritage protection? How should the Convention address resource shortfalls for properties located in poorer states? One way has been through international assistance from the World Heritage Fund established by Article 15.

Consider as well the implications of the Convention's recognition of a universal interest in the protection of heritage properties; how can this universal interest exist in the absence of a duty on the international community to protect sites of universal value? Can you make an argument that such a duty should exist?

2.   The strong position of states under this Convention have led to outcomes that strain the object and scope of the treaty as a whole. Consider, for example, the case of Jerusalem, the Old City of which was inscribed in 1981 under criteria (ii), (iii), and (vi). In 2000, Israel proposed an extension of the property that would include Mt. Zion under criteria (i), (ii), (iii), (iv), (v), and (vi) owing to the mountain's significance in Christianity, Judaism, and Islam, as well as a stated need to create a conservation buffer zone against encroaching urban development. UNESCO World Heritage Centre, *Jerusalem*, World Heritage Tentative List Ref. 1483 (2000). Despite resolutions from UNESCO and assurances from the Israeli delegation of the operative effect of Article 11(3) that a heritage listing would affect no disputed territorial claim, a group of Arab states led by Jordan successfully campaigned to stymie the inclusion of Mt. Zion in the Old City Jerusalem listing. Given the acknowledged significance of the mountain to all parties, could including Mt. Zion in the Old City Jerusalem property at Israel's nomination truly represent a neutral extension of heritage protection? Should states be able to prevent or impede the furtherance of heritage preservation under the Convention because of political, ideological, or cultural opposition? Can this be reconciled with the obligations of Article 6(3)?

The complex geopolitics of the region have created further challenges for heritage properties in the region. In 2017, the World Heritage Committee voted to inscribe Hebron/Al-Khalil Old Town in Palestine on both the World Heritage List and World Heritage List in Danger, simultaneously. The Committee inscribed the property under an emergency procedure after Israel blocked access to the property by experts from ICOMOS. This move angered Israel and the United States, prompting both to announce their intention to withdraw from UNESCO. As illustrated in this instance, the Convention's widespread adoption and visibility may create incentives for states to address other geopolitical concerns by proxy that have little to do with the protection of heritage properties. What does this say about the value states place on the Convention? About the role of heritage in national identity?

Some scholars have argued that the Convention's "soft" character, which affords States Parties substantial benefits from a property's inscription on the World Heritage List, while incurring only a general duty to protect, represents a source of strength. This softness encourages broader participation and generates greater visibility for the Convention's popular heritage protection regime without imposing significant negative incentives. *See* Francesco Francioni & Federico Lenzerini, *The Future of the World Heritage Convention*, in THE 1972 WORLD HERITAGE CONVENTION: A COMMENTARY 402–403 (Francesco Francioni ed., 2008).

3.   One of the foremost benefits from inscription on the World Heritage List is heightened visibility and touristic interest in a heritage property. Not only does this lend international prestige, but it frequently results in substantial economic benefits as well. Tourists bring direct economic gains to the communities and business in the vicinity of World Heritage properties, and they may provide critical funding to support heritage preservation and the continued vitality of certain cultural practices. But these benefits have cultural costs, in addition to the environmental costs discussed later in this chapter. What might some of these cultural costs of inscription on the World Heritage List entail? Does preservation of a property's outstanding *universal* value adequately protect the contextual heritage value of a property in its community? What is the role of tourism in highlighting this tension?

4.   Article 5 outlines a number of basic measures that States Parties agree to undertake for the protection, conservation, and presentation of heritage properties. While stated in broad terms with considerable latitude for a state's economic or political circumstances, the Article 5 measures establish a common minimum standard for heritage protection. In the United States, the requisite measures were incorporated into domestic law as amendments to the National Historic Preservation Act (NHPA) and the Secretary of the Interior given the responsibility for creating regulations pertaining to the nomination and protection of World Heritage properties. *See* 54 U.S.C. § 307101.

Case Study: The Dresden Elbe Valley

In the history of the World Heritage Convention, only two properties have been removed from the World Heritage List ("delisted")—the Arabian Oryx Sanctuary in Oman, delisted in 2007, and the Dresden Elbe Valley in Germany, delisted in 2009. One other property, Bagrati Cathedral in Georgia, was partially delisted in 2017. The Arabian Oryx Sanctuary was originally inscribed under criterion (x) as a breeding ground for its namesake species, among other rare fauna. After Oman unilaterally reduced the size of the protected sanctuary by 90% to drill for oil, the World Heritage Committee found that the outstanding universal value of the property had been destroyed due to habitat degradation and delisted the property. Oman consented to the property's subsequent removal from the List.

The Dresden Elbe Valley property, on the other hand, presented a messier scenario for the Committee leading up to a delisting decision. Inscribed as a cultural landscape property under criteria (ii), (iii), (iv), and (v), the Dresden Elbe Valley consists of an 18km stretch of the Elbe River through the city of Dresden in the German state of Saxony. The scenic riverfront is lined with rolling meadows, vineyards, landscaped gardens, and elegant villas from the 19th and 20th centuries. The property features a number of historic structures hearkening back to the industrial revolution, including a funicular, suspension railway, river steamship, and an 1880s steel bridge known fondly as the "Blue Wonder." *See* Sabine von Schorlemer, *Compliance with the UNESCO World Heritage Convention: Reflections on the Elbe Valley and the Dresden Waldschlösschen Bridge*, 51 GERMAN YEARBOOK OF INTERNATIONAL LAW 321–90 (2008).

At the time Germany submitted its nomination of Dresden Elbe Valley to the Committee for World Heritage listing in 2003, the Dresden City Council and Saxon state government were in the early stages of planning for the construction of a road bridge that would cross the river and provide economic development opportunities in the region. The nomination file submitted to the Committee mentioned plans for the so-called Waldschlösschen Bridge, causing minimal consternation by virtue of the "living" character of cultural landscape properties. The property was added to the World Heritage List in 2004.

Challenges arose following the property's listing, however, as a result of substantial cartographic errors and mounting local resistance to the perceived constraints imposed by the World Heritage designation. While preparing the official evaluation report required to be submitted to the Committee in advance of the listing decision regarding Dresden Elbe Valley, ICOMOS erroneously indicated the proposed site for the Waldschlösschen Bridge was 7.5km down the river from its planned location. The legal responsibility for failing to correct the cartographic error before Dresden Elbe Valley's official listing fell to Germany as the nominating state, but it contributed to an overarching lack of trust and cooperation among stakeholders.

Once inscribed, Saxony's ability to proceed with its planned construction of the bridge was met with challenges under the Convention. When the state proceeded with construction anyway, the Committee moved to place the property on the World Heritage in Danger List. These steps implicated the German federal government's international legal obligations as a State Party to the Convention, but the federal government claimed it was prevented from interfering with the matter under the German Basic Law on federalism grounds. Owing to this (disputed) legal reasoning, the German federal government adopted a mediational role between the state and local governments seeking to proceed with bridge construction on one side, and the World Heritage Committee and its advisory bodies demanding the project be converted to a tunnel on the other side. Unwilling to alter the bridge project, and buoyed by overwhelming local support, Saxon leaders went ahead with construction. The Dresden Elbe Valley was ultimately delisted in 2009 and the Waldschlösschen Bridge opened to vehicle traffic in 2013.

Although ostensibly a matter of cost and construction efficiency, in reality the Waldschlösschen Bridge debacle turned on two key issues, one legal and one ideological. The legal issue, incorporated into the Convention in Article 34, was the fundamental international law concept that a state is not freed of its international obligations because of domestic legal constraints. Here, the German federal government found itself bound by contradictory legal obligations whereby it was answerable at the international level for acts it could not intervene to address. This has a lesson for other federally-constituted states about how (not) to incorporate Article 5 heritage protections into domestic law.

The most impassioned issue in the Dresden Elbe Valley matter, however, was doubtless an ideological one based on the tension between the desire for local control over matters of local concern and preservation of a world heritage for the benefit of all humankind living and yet to come. It shows that while the purpose of the Convention and its ubiquitous World Heritage List broadly appeal to publics around the world, this heritage protection may come with high localized costs. Whether in the form of use restrictions, over-tourism, or increased illicit trafficking, communities in the vicinity of listed properties may see the World Heritage designation as more of a threat than a source of protection.

C. CULTURAL HERITAGE AND CLIMATE CHANGE

Climate change poses significant threats to cultural heritage properties. One key threat comes in the form of greater frequency of flooding or sea level rise. Wildfires, erosion, precipitation, and extreme temperature shifts have also increased in recent years. Another threat comes from cultural heritage itself, in that it drives tourism that contributes significantly to greenhouse gas emissions and hastens the effects of climate change.

Environmental and heritage preservation laws are slowly converging to respond. Protections for heritage and the environment share concerns of overseeing common resources, preserving inherent value, and transferring equity across generations. Sometimes, their protective mechanisms overlap as well. Consider the UNESCO Convention Concerning the Protection of the World Cultural and Natural Heritage of 1972 (commonly referred to as the World Heritage

Convention), which has created a World Heritage List with the support of 193 signatories (also called States Parties). Article 2 in that Convention broke new ground in extending its reach to include natural heritage properties as well as cultural heritage properties. As we discussed in Chapter 4, U.S. environmental protection laws similarly protect both natural and cultural (historic) properties. As global surface temperatures rise, the intersection between the two areas of law will likely see new attention and further development.

1. ENVIRONMENTAL THREATS TO HERITAGE SITES

International law on cultural heritage and climate change is still in its infancy, but certain key principles are starting to emerge. In the case that follows, the Supreme Court of India applies these principles to extend significant environmental protections to a trapezoidal-shaped region around the Taj Mahal. As you read, consider how the narrow scope of the environmental challenge in this case (air pollution) might affect disposition of a matter that concerns more generalized threats to a cultural heritage property due to climate change and how the specific nature of climate change might strain extant environmental protections.

Figure 12-3:
The Taj Mahal,
Agra, India

M.C. Mehta v. Union of India
(Taj Trapezium Matter)

(1997) 2 SCC 353 (India)

■ Kuldip Singh, J.

Taj Mahal—The Taj—is the "King Emperor" amongst the World-Wonders. The Taj is the final achievement and acme of the Moghul Art. It represents the most refined aesthetic values. It is a fantasy-like grandeur. It is the perfect culmination and artistic interplay of the architects' skill and the jewellers' inspiration. The marble-in-lay walls of The Taj are amongst the most outstanding examples of decorative workmanship. The elegant symmetry of its exterior and the aerial grace of its domes and minarets impress the beholder in a manner never to be forgotten. It stands out as one of the most priceless national monuments, of surpassing beauty and worth, a glorious tribute to man's achievement in Architecture and Engineering.

Lord Roberts in his work "Forty one years in India" describes The Taj as under:

> Neither words nor pencil could give to the most imaginative reader the slightest idea of all the satisfying beauty and purity of this glorious conception. To those who have not seen it, I would say, Go to India; the Taj alone is well worth the journey.

A poet describes The Taj as under: "It is too pure, too holy to be the work of human hands. Angels must have brought it from heaven and a glass case should be thrown over it to preserve it from each breath of air."

Sammuel Smith in his Book about The Taj explains the impact as under:

> We stood spell-bound for a few minutes at this lovely apparition; it hardly seems of the earth. It is more like a dream of Celestial beauty, no words can describe it. We felt that all previous sights were damned in comparison, No such effect is produced by the first view of St. Peter's or Milan or Cologne Cathedrals. They are all majestic, but this is enchantment itself. So perfect is its form that all other structures seem clumsy.

The Taj is threatened with deterioration and damage not only by the traditional causes of decay, but also by changing social and economic conditions which aggravate the situation with even more formidable phenomena of damage or destruction. A private sector preservation organisation called "World Monuments Fund" (American Express Company) has published a list of the 100 most endangered sites (1996) in the World. The Taj has been included in the list by stating as under:

The Taj Mahal—Agra—India

The Taj Mahal, Marble Tomb for Mumtaz Mahal, wife of emperor Shah Jahan, is considered the epitome of Mughal monumental domed tombs set in a garden. The environment of Agra is today beset with problems relating to the inadequacy of its urban infrastructure for transportation, water and electricity. The densest pollution near the Taj Mahal is caused by residential fuel combustion, diesel trains and buses, and back-up generators. Construction of the proposed Agra Ring Road and Bypass that would divert the estimated daily 6,50,000 tons of trans-India truck traffic awaits financing. Strict controls on industrial pollution established in 1982 are being intensively enforced following a 1993 Supreme Court Order. The Asian Development Bank's proposed $300 million loan to the Indian government to finance infrastructure improvement would provide the opportunity to solve the chronic problems.

Agra contains three World Heritage Sites, including the Taj Mahal.

According to the petitioner, the foundries, chemical/hazardous industries and the refinery at Mathura are the major sources of damage to The Taj. The sulphur dioxide emitted by the Mathura Refinery and the industries when combined with oxygen—with the aid of moisture—in the atmosphere forms sulphuric acid called "acid rain" which has a corroding effect on the gleaming white marble. Industrial/Refinery emissions, brick-kilns, vehicular traffic and generator-sets are primarily responsible for polluting the ambient air around Taj Trapezium (TTZ). The petition states that the white marble has yellowed and blackened in places. It is inside the Taj that the decay is more apparent. Yellow pallor pervades the entire monument. In places the yellow hue is magnified by ugly brown and black spots. Fungal deterioration is worst in the inner chamber where the original graves of Shah-Jahan and Mumtaz Mahal lie. According to the petitioner, The Taj—a monument of international repute—is on its way to degradation due to atmospheric pollution and it is imperative that preventive steps are taken and soon. The petitioner has finally sought appropriate directions to the authorities concerned to take immediate steps to stop air pollution in the TTZ and save The Taj.

The Report of the Expert Committee called "Report on Environmental Impact of Mathura Refinery" (Varadharajan Committee) published by the Government of India in 1978 has been annexed along with the writ petition. Para 4.1 of the conclusions therein is as under:

> There is substantial level of pollution of sulphur dioxide and particulate matter in the Agra region. The possible sources are all coal users consisting of two Power Plants, a number of small industries mainly foundries (approximately 250) and a Railway Shunting Yard. As far as suspended particulate matters are concerned, because of use of coal, contribution will be substantial. Even though the total amount of emission of sulphur dioxide from these sources may be small, on account of

their proximity to the monuments, their contribution to the air quality of the zone will be considerably high.

The Taj, apart from being cultural heritage, is an industry by itself. More than two million tourists visit The Taj every year. It is a source of revenue for the country. This Court has monitored this petition for over three years with the sole object of preserving and protecting The Taj from deterioration and damage due to atmospheric and environmental pollution. It cannot be disputed that the use of coke/coal by the industries emit pollution in the ambient air. The objective behind this litigation is to stop the pollution while encouraging development of industry. The old concept that development and ecology cannot go together is no longer acceptable. Sustainable development is the answer. The development of industry is essential for the economy of the country, but at the same time the environment and the eco-systems have to be protected. The pollution created as a consequence of development must commensurate with the carrying capacity of our eco-systems. * * *

This Court in *Vellore Citizens Welfare Forum v. Union of India*, (1996) 7 SCC 375, has defined "the precautionary principle" and the "polluter pays principle" as under:

We are, however, of the view that "the precautionary principle" and "The Polluter Pays" principle are essential features of "Sustainable Development." The "Precautionary Principle"—in the context of the municipal law—means:

> (i) Environmental measures—by the State Government and the statutory authorities—must anticipate, prevent and attack the causes of environmental degradation.

> (ii) Where there are threats of serious and irreversible damage, lack of scientific certainty should not be used as a reason for postponing measures to prevent environmental degradation.

> (iii) The "onus of proof" is on the actor or the developer/industrialist to show that his action is environmentally benign.

"The Polluter Pays" principle has been held to be a sound principle by this court in *Indian Council for Enviro-Legal Action vs. Union of India* J.T. 1996 (2) 196. The Court observed "We are of the opinion that any principle evolved in this behalf should be simple, practical and suited to the conditions obtaining in this country". The Court ruled that "Once the activity carried on is hazardous or inherently dangerous, the person carrying on such activity is liable to make good the loss caused to any other person by his activity irrespective of the fact whether he took reasonable care while carrying on his activity. The rule is premised upon the very nature of the activity carried on."

Consequently the polluting industries are "absolutely liable to compensate for the harm caused by them to villagers in the affected area, to the soil and to the underground water and hence, they are bound to take all necessary measures to remove sludge and other pollutants lying in the affected areas". The "Polluter Pays" principle as interpreted by this court means that the absolute liability for harm to the environment extends not only to compensate the victims of pollution but also the cost of restoring the environmental degradation. Remediation of the damaged environment is part of the process of "Sustainable Development" and as such polluter is liable to pay the cost to the individual sufferers as well as the cost of reversing the damaged ecology.

The precautionary principle and the polluter pays principle have been accepted as part of the law of the land. Article 21 of the Constitution of India guarantees protection of life and personal liberty. Articles 47, 48 A and 51A(g) of the Constitution are as under:

47. Duty of the State to raise the level of nutrition and the standard of living and to improve public health. The State shall regard the raising of the level of nutrition and the standard of living of its people and the improvement of public health among its primary duties and in particular, the State shall endeavour to bring about prohibition of the consumption except for medicinal purposes of intoxicating drinks and of drugs which are injurious to health.

48A. Protection and improvement of environment and safeguarding of forest and wild life. The State shall endeavour to protect and improve the environment and to safeguard the forests and wild life of the country.

51A(g). To protect and improve the natural environment including forests, lakes, rivers and wild life, and to have compassion for living creatures. . . .

In view of the above mentioned constitutional and statutory provisions we have no hesitation in holding that the precautionary principle and the polluter pays principle are part of the environmental law of the country.

Based on the reports of various technical authorities mentioned in this judgment, we have already reached the finding that the emissions generated by the coke/coal consuming industries are air-pollutants and have damaging effect on The Taj and the people living in the TTZ. The atmospheric pollution in TTZ has to be eliminated at any cost. Not even one per cent chance can be taken when—human life apart—the preservation of a prestigious monument like The Taj is involved. In any case, in view of the precautionary principle as defined by this Court, the environmental measures must anticipate, prevent and attack the causes of environmental degradation. The 'onus of proof' is on an industry to show that its operation with the aid of coke/coal is environmentally benign. It is, rather, proved beyond doubt that the emissions generated by the use of coke/coal by the industries in TTZ are the main polluters of the ambient air.

We, therefore, hold that the above-mentioned 292 industries shall as per the schedule indicated hereunder change-over to the natural gas as an industrial-fuel. The industries which are not in a position to obtain gas connections—for any reason—shall stop functioning with the aid of coke/coal in the TTZ and may relocate themselves as per the directions given by us hereunder.

NOTES & QUESTIONS

1. The *Mehta* court applies three important principles of environmental law to protect one of the world's most famous heritage properties, the Taj Mahal: the sustainable development principle, the precautionary principle, and the "polluter pays" principle. The first two point toward interesting possibilities and challenges for responding to climate change under a cultural heritage framework.

The sustainable development principle seeks to advance economic growth while minimizing or obviating negative impact to the climate or environment. This principle often drives policy responses to climate change, but can also be a focus of balancing in legal responses to climate change as well. In the realm of cultural heritage, the sustainable development principle often shows up as an issue of "buffer zones," as here, or with regard to tourism. Traditional approaches to tourism development may place great stress on cultural heritage sites, both as a direct impact and as an indirect impact due to adverse impacts on the climate and global emissions.

The precautionary principle appears in the Rio Declaration on the Environment and Development produced as part of the 1992 United Nations Conference on Environment and Development ("the Earth Summit"), as well as other subsequent major pieces of international environmental law. As laid out in the Rio Declaration, the precautionary principle requires that "[w]here there are threats of serious or irreversible damage, lack of full scientific certainty shall not be used as a reason for postponing cost-effective measures to prevent environmental degradation." This principle thus requires the State to both anticipate and address environmental degradation, while also setting a high bar to possible development or sources of environmental threat by requiring a prospective developer to prove the absence (or unlikelihood) of significant harmful effects. Additionally, the precautionary principle conditions all of this to apply notwithstanding a lack of scientific consensus or certainty regarding the environmental effects of a proposed activity. Scholars and practitioners debate whether the principle requires "strong" or "weak" precaution; that is, should the preventative action be subjected to cost-benefit analysis.

In the *Mehta* decision, the Supreme Court of India is applying these principles to a matter concerning the impacts of pollution on a cultural heritage site, not the impacts of climate change generally. Given the court's treatment of the Taj, is this distinction relevant in understanding how the precautionary principle might apply to future climate change impacts on the Taj? What support does this opinion lend for a "strong" application of the precautionary principle to activities with potential to cause environmental harm to cultural heritage properties? And support for a "weak" application of the principle?

2.   In addition to being a cultural heritage property of national importance in India, the Taj Mahal is also listed on the World Heritage List under criteria set forth in the World Heritage Convention. Specifically, the Taj satisfies criterion (i) of the cultural heritage criteria because it is a masterpiece of creative genius.

3.   With the *Mehta* decision, the Court extended substantial environmental protections to the area around the Taj. Consider what you know about the World Heritage Convention. How does this decision align with the protection regime laid out in Articles 5 and 6, excerpted above? If the Taj is a property of outstanding universal value, should a single sovereign state determine the extent of legal protections afforded it? How does the Convention balance the universal interests of world heritage preservation on the one hand and the sovereign interest of states in defining their own preservation regimes on the other?

2.   PHYSICAL THREATS FROM CLIMATE CHANGE

Climate change presents substantial challenges to culturally significant and historic properties of all kinds. According to a 2014 report of the Intergovernmental Panel on Climate Change that assessed multiple emissions scenarios, the twenty-first century will see a continued rise in the world's surface temperature under every one of them. This warming will lead to a number of direct threats to heritage properties, including: polar melting, flooding, sea level rise, desertification, and ecosystem stress.

While "ordinary" historic sites are at risk, globally significant sites are not immune from these threats. We focus here on properties listed on UNESCO's World Heritage List, which come from all over the globe, and are said to have outstanding universal value. Climate change can threaten the very basis of a property's inclusion on the World Heritage List by undermining its integrity and thus its outstanding universal value. This may be obvious for properties listed under Article 2 (natural heritage), such as the Great Barrier Reef. But climate change also threatens Article 1 (cultural heritage) properties, such as Venice and the Neolithic remains in the Orkney Islands of Scotland, both threatened by sea-level rise.

Consider the following case study of Ouadi Qadisha, a World Heritage property in Lebanon (criteria (iii) and (iv)), that was published as part of a UNESCO report on world heritage, climate change, and tourism:

UNESCO, World Heritage and Tourism in a Changing Climate

Ouadi Qadisha (the Holy Valley) and the Forest of the Cedars of God
(Horsh Arz el-Rab), Lebanon (2016)

Ouadi Qadisha, or the Holy Valley, in northern Lebanon exemplifies the spiritual character of landscapes as places where communities have woven the sacred into the fabric of their natural and built environment. Those who visited or resided in the many monasteries and hermitages of Ouadi Qadisha—some of which date back to the early years of Christianity—sought God within a remote and rugged landscape of soaring cliffs, majestic cedar forests and networks of sheltering natural caves.

Climate change and tourism development are increasing stress on the traditional livelihoods and ecological systems of Ouadi Qadisha. The valley's sacred cedars, confined to a small remnant stand of approximately 2 hectares known as the Forest of the Cedars of God (Horsh Arz el-Rab), include the oldest and largest cedars known. The Arz el-Rab forest lies near one of Lebanon's main ski resort towns, Becharre, at the foot of a mountain slope heavily overgrazed and eroded by goats. The walled grove includes individual trees of great antiquity—of the 375 or so remaining trees, two are claimed to be over 3,000 years old, and ten to be more than 1,000 years old, of which perhaps four are older than 1,500 years.

Tourism is an important component of the Lebanese economy and, although political instability has caused major drops in visits since a peak in 2009, it still contributed 25 percent of the country's gross domestic product (GDP) in 2012. In 2000, more than 200,000 tourists visited the grove—20 percent of the visitors to Lebanon that year.

The cedar of Lebanon (*Cedrus libani*) has carried a spiritual value through the millennia and is mentioned some 103 times in the Old and New Testaments, including in Psalm 104:16, which reads "God planted them, and it is He who waters them." For Christians, the trees represent the moral imperative of tending to the gifts of God from generation to generation.

Cedar wood has been prized for its strength and durability for around 5,000 years throughout the Mediterranean, and the spiritual importance of the cedar trees of Ouadi Qadisha extends well beyond the local communities—as exemplified by its use in the building of temples and sanctuaries throughout the Levant, including the First (Solomon's) and Second Temples in Jerusalem, built in the 10th and 6th centuries BC, respectively. The wood is also synonymous with the great seafaring ambitions of the ancient Phoenicians. * * *

Climate change is projected to reduce the *Cedrus libani* populations to only three refugial zones by 2100, due to higher temperatures and water stress from decreased moisture availability in the Mediterranean region. While plant communities can adapt to climate change by migrating to higher altitudes through seed dispersal and gradual replacement, most of the cedar forests of Lebanon are already isolated on or near mountain summits, with nowhere further upslope to go. The Arz el-Rab stand in the Qadisha valley is an exception, being one of the three cedar forests where there is higher-altitude habitat available for potential migration, which makes their protection all the more urgent. The cedars of Ouadi Qadisha exemplify the vulnerabilities and loss of resilience that plant communities face with habitat degradation and fragmentation.

There are currently a dozen or more *Cedrus libani* forests in Lebanon—situated at elevations of 1,100–1,925 metres on the western slopes of the Mount Lebanon range, with more than half occupying an area of less than 100 hectares—and they are zones of high biodiversity sheltering other endemic and threatened species The Lebanon cedar is itself listed as vulnerable on the International Union for the Conservation of Nature's (IUCN) Red List. The bioclimatic zone of the Arz el-Rab forest is expected to change too, affecting the spatial distribution, species composition and community structure of the cedar forest. Insect and moth attacks, fuelled by increasing aridity, are already affecting the cedar forests in Tannourine and Shouf, and threatening to spread to the Arz el-Rab sacred cedars.

The cedar of Lebanon is an emblematic species, emblazoned on the flag, currency, and stamps of Lebanon. It is an important element of the Lebanese tourist economy as well as a cultural keystone species, essential to ways of life and religious traditions.

The case of Ouadi Qadisha demonstrates the severity and diversity of threats to cultural heritage properties by the effects of climate change. Here, climate change is not just threatening the range of a single species of tree, it is threatening the deep culture, identity, religion, and lifeways that are connected to the trees in sites where they have stood for thousands of years. In a legal sense, climate change is undermining the outstanding universal value that brings the Ouadi Qadisha property its World Heritage designation and requisite protections by the territorial state.

Under the World Heritage Convention system, a property facing such threats would normally be placed on the World Heritage in Danger List and face extensive scrutiny by the Committee and subject matter experts. In extreme cases, a property could be delisted if the heritage threats were left unaddressed or unmitigated. These tools seek to focus attention, resources, and political will on addressing localized threats to heritage properties. But those same tools prove ill-suited to threats from climate change given the sheer number of properties affected and the global nature of climate threats.

States Parties to the World Heritage Convention took an initial step toward addressing these impacts in 2008, with the adoption of a Policy Document on the Impacts of Climate Change on World Heritage. That document suggested revisions to the UNESCO Operational Guidelines for the Implementation of the World Heritage Convention and legal guidance on the obligations of States Parties under the Convention regarding climate threats. Specifically, the Policy Document requires the World Heritage Committee to consider imposing tighter mechanisms for reactive monitoring and periodic reporting, as well as considering the incorporation of a precautionary approach to World Heritage decision making related to climate change. These two directives represent two of the prevailing policy approaches to climate change: a risk management approach and a precautionary approach. In practice, the Committee's responses to climate change have been more frequently colored by the former approach, even if territorial states—like India in the *Mehta* decision—adopt a precautionary principle in the face of discreet environmental challenges. Critics have complained that acquiescence to a risk management approach in the face of widespread heritage threats due to climate change is inconsistent with the Convention's object and purpose.

One analytic tool that has emerged since the 2008 document is a climate vulnerability index (CVI) developed by a group of researchers from Australia's James Cook University in conjunction with ICOMOS and other partners. First piloted in a 2019 study of Scotland's Heart of Neolithic Orkney World Heritage site, the CVI seeks to assess the vulnerability of nine World Heritage sites. First, the CVI assesses the vulnerability of a site's outstanding universal value to adverse climate impacts on the basis of its exposure and sensitivity to such impacts. Second, the CVI looks to the property's adaptive capacity to address its outstanding universal value vulnerability. Third, the CVI assesses the vulnerability of the property's associated community to the impacts of climate change on the basis of its economic, social, and cultural dependency on the property. Fourth, the CVI measures a community's adaptive capacity to address economic, social, and cultural vulnerabilities. The CVI thus provides a comprehensive measurement of a property's climate vulnerability that allows decision makers to prioritize scarce resources where they are most needed or effective. It remains to be seen whether the CVI's detailed analysis is scalable to a large number of World Heritage properties.

NOTES & QUESTIONS

1. One of the acknowledged strengths of the World Heritage Convention is its clear territorial link. Because only immovable properties

may be listed on the World Heritage List, the List encompasses resources that are all geographically-bound and place-specific, regardless of what kinds of intangible or movable elements may contribute to the property's OUV. Climate change, on the other hand, presents uniquely boundless challenges whose impacts are felt disproportionately around the globe. Can the World Heritage Convention support domestic legal arguments addressing climate change impacts? What should be the role of heritage preservation tools like the World Heritage Convention in combatting the effects of climate change? Is the original purpose of the Convention in any way in tension with a climate-related purpose?

2.   Both the Climate Vulnerability Index and the 2008 Policy Document suggest that the World Heritage Convention operates upon a risk management approach to climate change impacts. Yet the Policy Document also presses the World Heritage Committee to consider incorporating a precautionary approach into the Operational Guidelines. Some environmental law scholars see these approaches as mutually exclusive—do you think this is the case? What would a risk management approach to the current situation in Ouadi Qadisha or the pollution at the Taj Mahal look like? How about a precautionary approach?

3.   The story of Ouadi Qadisha illustrates the significant direct threats facing a World Heritage property as a result of climate change, but what about second and third order threats? Climate mitigation, adaptation, and migration pose their own challenges to heritage preservation. Consider, for example, the "Venice and its Lagoon" World Heritage property. As a result of sea level rise and the slow subsidence of the city's low-lying islands into the Venetian Lagoon, the famed Renaissance palazzos and churches lining the city's canals are experiencing flooding of increasing severity and frequency. In response, the Italian government has spent €5.5 billion on the MOSE (or "Experimental Electromechanical Module"), a system of mobile barriers designed to block the highest tides from overwhelming the lagoon. MOSE has faced a string of challenges and its potential efficacy has been called into question; the system will face its first test when it becomes fully operational in 2021. But the project may nevertheless fail World Heritage scrutiny on account of its significant impact on the integrity and authenticity of the Lagoon, itself part of the city's inscription on the World Heritage List. Does this account from Venice suggest that certain heritage components (like Renaissance architecture) should be prioritized over others (like the lagoon)? How should such determinations be made? Is such an interpretation consistent with the Convention?

4.   In addressing heritage preservation and climate change, the countervailing challenges are not merely one directional. Indeed, the current regime of international heritage preservation embodied in the World Heritage Convention may itself contribute meaningfully to hastening the effects of climate change. Much of the protections offered by territorial states for World Heritage properties are funded (either directly or indirectly) through tourism, a carbon intensive industry responsible for a full five percent of global carbon emissions and predicted to more than double in the next 25 years. *See* UNESCO, WORLD HERITAGE AND TOURISM IN A CHANGING

CLIMATE 9 (2016). While eco-tourism and sustainable development practices may present a way forward that diminishes the adverse climate impact of tourism, it is unclear whether such a shift could generate a comparable level of revenue sufficient to maintain heritage protections.

3. THE ROLE OF HERITAGE IN ADDRESSING CLIMATE CHANGE

Perhaps the most hopeful aspect of the interconnected challenges of heritage preservation and climate change is that cultural heritage can offer potential climate solutions and strategies for adaptation.

As a substantive matter, traditional cultural knowledge has equipped humans to adapt to the vast diversity of environments around the globe over millennia of ecological, societal, and industrial change. As international law begins to address climate change more systematically, the role of cultural knowledge has been a point of focus. Indeed, one influential treaty, the 1994 United Nations Convention to Combat Desertification (UNCCD), explicitly provides for the role of traditional knowledge in the research, development, adaptation, and technology (Art. 17 & 18) to combat desertification, as well as its role in advancing public awareness and capacity building (Art. 19). The "traditional knowledge" addressed in the UNCCD does not resemble the cultural heritage afforded protection by the World Heritage Convention, as it is intangible, but it would almost certainly fall within the definition of cultural heritage provided in the 2003 Convention on the Safeguarding of the Intangible Cultural Heritage. An outline of a comprehensive approach to incorporating heritage practice and knowledge into climate policy-making is presented in ICOMOS, The Future of our Pasts: Engaging Cultural Heritage in Climate Action (2019). It argues that a strong distinction between nature and culture is an impediment to addressing climate change successfully. Because greenhouse gas emissions are a result of human activity, human culture must be mobilized to address it.

Additionally, heritage properties may help focus public attention and awareness on the effects of climate change that otherwise appear too vast or incomprehensible. The very OUV of a heritage property gives greater visibility and emotional or cultural gravity to the impacts of climate change. In essence, heritage provides universal reference points to identify, track, and respond to the global climate crisis.

D. EXTRATERRITORIAL APPLICATION OF THE NATIONAL HISTORIC PRESERVATION ACT

To become a State Party to the World Heritage Convention, the United States was required to pass domestic legislation consistent with the Convention. Congress passed legislation in 1980 to implement the United States' obligations. This was accomplished by amending the

National Historic Preservation Act to include sections 401 and 402 addressing the World Heritage Convention. Pub. L. No. 95–515, 94 Stat. 2987 (now codified as amended at 54 U.S.C. § 30701). Section 402 provides:

> Prior to the approval of any undertaking outside the United States that may directly and adversely affect a property that is on the World Heritage List or on the applicable country's equivalent of the National Register, the head of a Federal agency having direct or indirect jurisdiction over the undertaking shall take into account the effect of the undertaking on the property for purposes of avoiding or mitigating any adverse effect.

54 U.S.C. § 307101(e). The language of this section resembles that of Section 106 of the National Historic Preservation Act with a few key differences. The importance of these differences remained untested until a group of concerned citizens and environmental groups brought suit on behalf of the dugong, an endangered marine mammal found in the waters around the Japanese island of Okinawa.

Figure 12-4:
A Dugong

Okinawa Dugong v. Gates

543 F.Supp. 2d 1082 (N.D. Cal. 2008)

[EDS.: All references to the National Historic Preservation Act have been recodified and often amended at title 54, Pub. L. No. 113–287, 128 Stat. 3094. We have tried to note below where specific provisions have moved.]

■ HALL PATEL, DISTRICT JUDGE.

Plaintiffs, consisting of the Okinawa dugong, three individual Japanese citizens, and six American and Japanese environmental associations, brought this action against defendants Robert Gates, Secretary of Defense, and the United States Department of Defense ("DOD") for violations of section 402 of the National Historic Preservation Act ("NHPA"), [EDS.: moved to 54 U.S.C. § 307101(e)], and the Administrative Procedure Act ("APA"), 5 U.S.C. §§ 701–706. Plaintiffs allege that defendants have approved the plans for construction of the Futenma Replacement Facility ("FRF")—a military air station off the coast of Okinawa Island—without taking into account the effect of the military facility on the Okinawa dugong, a marine mammal of cultural and historical significance to the Japanese people. Now before the court are the parties' cross-motions for summary judgment. Having considered the arguments and submissions of the parties and for the reasons set forth below, the court enters the following memorandum and order. * * *

BACKGROUND

I.   The Okinawa Dugong

The dugong (*Dugong dugon*) is a species of marine mammal related to the manatee. The waters surrounding Okinawa Island are habitat for the dugong whose range extends the costal and territorial waters of many countries in the Far East. The greatest population concentrations occur in Australia, the Philippines, and Thailand, and Japan is at the northern edge of the dugong's range. The dugong is classified as vulnerable by the World Conservation Union (IUCN) due to habitat destruction and degradation, as well as human exploitation. The Japan Ministry of the Environment recently listed the dugong as critically endangered in Japan. * * *

II.   National Historic Preservation Act * * *

Under section 106 of the NHPA, federal agencies are required, when undertaking any federally assisted action within the United States, to "take into account the effect of the undertaking on any district, site, building, structure, or object that is included or eligible for inclusion in the National Register." *Id.* § 470f [EDS.: moved to 54 U.S.C. § 306108]. The NHPA delegates to the Secretary of the Interior authority to expand and maintain a National Register of Historic Places. *Id.* § 470a(a)(1) (A). The NHPA also establishes the Advisory Council on Historic Preservation ("ACHP"), *id.* § 470i [EDS.: moved to 54 U.S.C. § 304101], and delegates to the ACHP authority to promulgate regulations necessary to implement the section 106 take into account process, *id.* § 470s [EDS.: moved to 54 U.S.C. § 304108]. The section 106 regulations promulgated by the ACHP set forth a multi-step process by which an agency takes into account the effects of an undertaking. * * *

In 1980, Congress amended the NHPA to implement the United States' participation in the Convention Concerning the Protection of the World Cultural and National Heritage ("World Heritage Convention"). Pub.L. 96–515. The amendment added to the NHPA section 402 governing undertakings outside the United States. Section 402, therefore, is the international counterpart to section 106 governing domestic undertakings. The full text of section 402 is as follows:

> Prior to the approval of any Federal undertaking outside the United States which may directly and adversely affect a property which is on the World Heritage List or on the applicable country's equivalent of the National Register, the head of a Federal agency having direct or indirect jurisdiction over such undertaking shall take into account the effect of the undertaking on such property for purposes of avoiding or mitigating any adverse effects.

16 U.S.C. § 470a–2 [EDS.: moved to 54 U.S.C. § 307101(e)]. The Secretary of the Interior is charged with directing and coordinating United States participation in the World Heritage Convention, and Congress has delegated authority to the Secretary to nominate properties to the World Heritage List. *Id.* § 470a–1. * * *

Plaintiffs argue that the court has a proper basis to review the matter and that they are entitled to summary judgment on the substantive issue of whether defendants have complied with the NHPA. They argue as a threshold matter that section 402 of the NHPA applies to the circumstances of this case because DOD's involvement in the FRF constitutes a "federal undertaking" which "may directly and adversely affect" the Okinawa dugong, a "property" protected under Japan's equivalent of the National Register. Compliance with section 402, plaintiffs argue, requires defendants to "take into account" the effects of the FRF on the Okinawa dugong by, among other things, consulting with the public and interested organizations and taking measures to mitigate or avoid adverse effects. Defendants assert that in the absence of any standards or regulations directly applicable to foreign undertakings, the DOD may determine, in the reasonable exercise of its discretion, what requirements are necessary to comply with section 402. * * *

The court will now proceed to address the substantive issues of whether the NHPA applies to the circumstances of this case, and if so, whether DOD has met its obligation to take into account. * * *

II. Applicability of NHPA Section 402

As a threshold matter, a federal agency's obligation to take into account under section 402 is triggered only when there is (1) a federal undertaking outside the United States (2) which may directly and adversely affect (3) a property which is on the applicable country's equivalent of the National Register. The court, in its March 2005 order, previously addressed the issue of whether the NHPA applies to the circumstances of this case. In that order, the court held that the Okinawa dugong is protected by Japan's Law for the Protection of Cultural Properties, the equivalent of the United States National Register, and is "property" within the meaning of section 402. *Dugong v. Rumsfeld*, 2005 WL 522106, at *6–12 (N.D. Cal. Mar. 2, 2005). The facts upon which that ruling was made remain the same, and accordingly, the court reaffirms that the Okinawa dugong is protected property under the NHPA. Because the record was undeveloped at the time of the court's March 2005 order, the court withheld judgment and ordered discovery on the two remaining issues of whether DOD's involvement in the military facility could constitute a (1) "federal undertaking" that (2) "may directly and adversely affect" the dugong. Given the more fully developed record now available, the court will proceed to address these two issues below, resolving both in favor of plaintiffs.

A. "Undertaking"

Defendants concede that their involvement in the FRF including the provision of operational requirements for the FRF and the approval of the 2006 Roadmap, constitutes a federal undertaking within the meaning of section 402. In its 2005 order, the court discussed at length the statutory definition and meaning of an "undertaking." *Dugong*, 2005 WL 522106 at *12–17. It is therefore unnecessary to repeat that discussion here, but one point deserves mention. In its 2005 order, the court surmised that "Congress may have intended a less restrictive definition of undertakings to apply to federal projects abroad." In light of the legislative history, however, it is clear that Congress intended the meaning of "undertaking" in section 402 to have the same meaning as the same term used in section 106. ("The Committee also notes that the term 'undertaking,' as it is used in other sections of the Act, is meant to be used in the same context as described in Section 106. The [ACHP] has adopted an acceptable definition within its regulations, published as 36 CFR 800.").

In light of defendants' concession, the court will only briefly summarize plaintiffs' extensive arguments and evidence in support of demonstrating a federal undertaking. The project to design, construct, relocate and operate the FRF is funded at least in part under the jurisdiction of the DOD, is carried out by and on behalf of the DOD, and requires federal approval. 16 U.S.C. § 470w(7) [EDS.: moved to 54 U.S.C. § 300320]. DOD has expended funds in the planning and design of the FRF and will bear the costs of relocating to and operating the facility once it is constructed. The FRF project is carried out by and on behalf of DOD because although the Government of Japan bears the full cost of the FRF's actual construction, the facility is being constructed for DOD's exclusive use, according to operational requirements determined by the DOD. Each phase of the FRF requires, and has in fact received, federal approval. The initial decision to relocate the Futenma air station required and received DOD approval through the U.S. Secretary of Defense's role on the bilateral Security Consultative Committee ("SCC"). At the intermediate phase, the establishment of operational requirements received independent DOD approval. Finally, the ultimate decision to design and build the FRF as a partially sea-based facility adjacent to Camp Schwab, with two runways aligned in a V-shaped pattern, also received DOD approval when the bilateral SCC approved the 2006 Roadmap. As planning and construction moves forward, additional DOD approvals, such as entry permits for engineers to enter Camp Schwab to carry out technical surveys and to begin actual construction, will be required. The court concludes that there is no issue of material fact as to whether DOD activities related to the Futenma Replacement Facility constitute a "federal undertaking" under NHPA section 402.

B.   "May Directly and Adversely Affect"

The . . . final issue related to the applicability of the NHPA to this case is whether defendants' undertaking "may directly and adversely affect" the dugong. The statute requires a threshold showing that the undertaking *may* have direct and adverse effects on the dugong, not that the undertaking necessarily *will* have effects. The term "adverse effect" is not defined in the statute, but regulations implementing section 106 domestic undertakings set forth a meaning of adverse effect that is instructive in this case. Under the domestic regulations, "an adverse effect is found when an undertaking may alter, directly or indirectly, any of the characteristics of a historic property. Adverse effects may include reasonably foreseeable effects caused by the undertaking that may occur later in time, be farther removed in distance or be cumulative." 36 C.F.R. § 800.5(a)(1). An example of an adverse effect includes "physical destruction of or damage to all or part of the property." 36 C.F.R. § 800.5(a)(2)(I).

It is undisputed that Henoko Bay is dugong habitat and that seagrass beds found in the Bay are dugong feeding grounds. It is also undisputed that dugong have been observed to feed in and traverse Henoko Bay. The record contains considerable disagreement among plaintiffs' and defendants' experts regarding the extent and degree to which the dugong would be adversely affected. But this does not disturb the undisputed fact that Henoko Bay is dugong habitat and therefore, construction and operation of a military facility in and near the Bay could have *potential* adverse effects. These potential adverse effects include physical destruction of the Okinawa dugong resulting from contamination of seagrass feeding grounds and collisions with boats and vessels, as well as long-term immune and reproductive damage resulting from exposure to toxins and acoustic pollution. That the *actual* consequences may be currently unknown is precisely the reason the NHPA requires defendants to gather, examine and assess information. Doing so allows the agency to determine, early in the process of an undertaking, whether potential consequences may crystallize into actual effects and whether the actual effects will exceed a de minimis threshold. Because it is undisputed that Henoko Bay is a dugong habitat, the court finds that there is no material issue of fact as to whether the FRF may directly and adversely affect the dugong.

III. "Take Into Account"

Having concluded that the court's review is proper and that the NHPA is applicable to the facts of this case, the court now turns to the merits of plaintiffs' claim that DOD has violated the NHPA by failing to "take into account" the effect of their undertaking on the Okinawa dugong. In its March 2005 order, the court reserved judgment on this issue until the record was more fully developed, as it is now. First, the parties dispute the meaning of "take into account" as a matter of law. Second, the parties dispute whether defendants' activities are sufficient to comply with the appropriate meaning of "take into account." The court will address each of these issues in turn.

A.   Meaning of "Take Into Account"

The meaning of "take into account" under section 402 governing foreign undertakings is an issue of first impression for the courts. The statute does not define the phrase "take into account," there are no regulations that directly define or elaborate the phrase, and neither the parties nor the court are aware of any case law construing the phrase. Defendants argue that in the absence of specific standards, criteria, or procedures, Congress delegated to the head of each federal agency the decision regarding how to comply with the "take into account" language of section 402. They argue that because the statute is silent or ambiguous with respect to the meaning of "take into account," the issue for the court is whether DOD's own interpretation of the statute—embodied in a series of internal directives and standards—is a permissible construction. Plaintiffs argue that the statute is not silent or ambiguous and that alternatively, DOD's interpretation of the statute is not a permissible construction. * * *

"When a court reviews an agency's construction of the statute which it administers, it is confronted with two questions. First, always, is the question whether Congress has directly spoken to the precise question at issue." *Chevron v. Natural Resources Defense Council*, 467 U.S. 837, 842 (1984). "If a court, employing traditional tools of statutory construction, ascertains that Congress had an intention on the precise question at issue, that intention is the law and must be given effect" by both the court and the agency. *Id.* at 842–843. If, however, the statute is silent or ambiguous, "the court does not simply impose its own construction of the statute." *Id.* at 843. Rather, "the question for the court is whether the agency's answer is based on a permissible construction of the statute." *Id.* * * * "Under *Chevron's* classic formulation, if . . . there is an express delegation of authority [by Congress] to the agency to elucidate a specific provision of the statute by regulation, [then] [s]uch legislative regulations are given controlling weight unless they are arbitrary, capricious, or manifestly contrary to the statute." *Id.* "If *Chevron* deference is inapplicable because Congress has not delegated interpretative authority to the agency, the agency's views still 'constitute a body of experience and informed judgment to which courts and litigants may properly resort for guidance.' " *Id.* "The 'fair measure of deference' may then range from 'great respect' to 'near indifference,' depending on 'the degree of the agency's care, its consistency, formality and relative expertness, and . . . the persuasiveness of the agency's position.' " *Id.*

Under *Chevron* step one, this court must determine, based on the statute's language, legislative history, structure and purpose, whether there is clear Congressional intent regarding the meaning of the phrase "take into account." On its face, the phrase "take into account" means consider, contemplate, study, and weigh. Webster's Int'l Dictionary of the English Language (3d ed. 1976) (defining the phrase "take into account" to be synonymous with "take into consideration," and in turn, defining "consider" to be synonymous with "contemplate," "study," and "weigh"). This plain meaning of "take into account" is consistent with the purposes of the NHPA to "generat[e] information about the impact of federal actions on the environment," and to "require[ ] the relevant federal agency [to] *carefully consider* the information produced," *San Carlos Apache Tribe v. United States*, 417 F.3d 1091, 1097 (9th Cir. 2005) (emphasis added), and to *"weigh* effects in deciding whether to authorize" a federal undertaking, *Save Our Heritage v. Fed. Aviation Admin.*, 269 F.3d 49, 58 (1st Cir. 2001) (emphasis added). The statutory text also contains requirements relating to *who, when,* and *what* shall be taken into account, as well as *why* an accounting is necessary. The statute states that (1) "the head of a Federal agency having direct or indirect jurisdiction over such undertaking" shall be the person charged with the task of taking into account, (2) the accounting shall occur "prior to approval" of the undertaking, and (3) the accounting shall consider the "effects of the undertaking" on the protected property. 16 U.S.C. § [EDS.: moved to 54 U.S.C. § 307101(e)]. Finally, the statute is clear regarding why the taking-into-account is required. It is conducted "for purposes of avoiding or mitigating any adverse effects." *Id.*

Although not evident from the plain language of section 402, related sections of the NHPA indicate clear Congressional intent that the take into account process involves not a federal agency acting alone, but instead, an agency acting in cooperation with relevant nations, parties, and organizations. When it enacted section 402 in 1980, Congress declared that "[i]t shall be the policy of the Federal Government, *in cooperation with other nations* and *in partnership with* the States, local governments, and Indian tribes, and *private organizations and individuals*" to "provide leadership in the preservation of the resources of the United States and the international community of nations." *Id.* § 470–1(2) [EDS.: moved to 54 U.S.C. § 300101(2)] (emphasis added); Pub. L. No. 95–515 § 101(a), Sec. 2. Similar Congressional intent is expressed in the legislative history of the 1980 amendments. The House Report states that the purpose of the World Heritage Convention—which section 402 implements for the United States—"is to establish an effective system of *collective* protection of the cultural and natural heritage." Section 402, therefore, should be read in conjunction with Congress' declaration of policy requiring cooperation, partnership, and collective participation.

The plain language of section 402, combined with express legislative purpose, reveals clear Congressional intent regarding the basic components of a take into account process under section 402. The process, at a minimum, must include (1) identification of protected property, (2) generation, collection, consideration, and weighing of information pertaining to how the undertaking will affect the historic property, (3) a determination as to whether there will be adverse effects or no adverse effects, and (4) if necessary, development and evaluation of alternatives or modifications to the undertaking that could avoid or mitigate the adverse effects. The person charged with responsibility for this basic process is the person with jurisdiction over the undertaking, and compliance with the process must occur before the undertaking is approved. In addition, a federal agency does not complete the take into account process on its own, in isolation, but engages the host nation and other relevant private organizations and individuals in a cooperative partnership.

That Congress clearly intended a take into account process to include these basic components is further supported by the context in which section 402 was enacted. In 1980 when Congress amended the NHPA to add section 402 governing foreign undertakings, the same "take into account" phrase had been used fourteen years earlier when Congress enacted section 106 governing domestic undertakings. Moreover, by the time Congress added section 402, the ACHP had already promulgated regulations elaborating what it means to take into account for purposes of section 106 domestic undertakings. 36 C.F.R. Part 800. Although the ACHP has from time to time amended the section 106 regulations, the essential elements—identification of protected properties, gathering and weighing of information, determination of adverse effect or no adverse effect, evaluation of mitigation measures if necessary, and consultation with interested parties and organizations—were in place by 1980. When identical words are used in different parts of the same act, the natural presumption is that Congress intended them to have the same meaning.

Environmental Defense v. Duke Energy Corp., 549 U.S. 561, 574 (2007). Moreover, "Congress' repetition of a well-established term carries the implication that Congress intended the term to be construed in accordance with pre-existing regulatory interpretations." *Bragdon v. Abbott,* 524 U.S. 624, 631 (1998). Here, the basic framework for a take into account process was well-understood at the time Congress used the identical phrase in section 402. This raises an inference that Congress intended the take into account process under section 402 to follow the basic structure the ACHP had already outlined for undertakings governed by section 106.

The court does not suggest, and plaintiffs do not argue, that the ACHP's regulations in 36 C.F.R. Part 800 apply verbatim to section 402 undertakings. It is clear that the section 106 process does not map directly onto the section 402 process. Congress did not include a statutory provision expressly incorporating into section 402 the ACHP's existing regulations. *Cf. Bragdon,* 524 U.S. at 631. Moreover, the statutory text of section 106, unlike that of section 402, expressly requires a federal agency to consult with the ACHP (a federal agency "shall afford the [ACHP] a reasonable opportunity to comment"), and while the ACHP is given express authority to promulgate regulations implementing section 106, it does not have comparable authority for section 402, *see* 16 U.S.C. § 470s [EDS.: moved to 54 U.S.C. § 304108]. The differing role of the ACHP in the domestic and foreign contexts, however, does not rebut the natural presumption that Congress intended the "take into account" phrase in section 402 to follow the basic outline of section 106 set forth by the ACHP. Granted, "[a] term in the same statute may take on distinct characters from association with distinct statutory objects calling for different implementation strategies." *Environmental Defense,* 549 U.S. at 574. But while Congress may have been silent on the regulatory specifics and implementation details, allowing the precise letter of the statute to be filled in by a particular agency depending on the agency's mission and undertaking, Congress was clear on the basic spirit and framework of the take into account process. There is no reason to believe that Congress intended the basic framework to differ depending on the geographic location of the undertaking and the protected property.

Congress' intent that the basic framework of the take into account process remain cohesive across a multitude of agencies and undertakings is reflected in the fact that Congress provided for a mechanism to achieve that cohesiveness. NHPA section 110 directs each federal agency to develop a preservation program. 16 U.S.C. § 470h–2(a)(2) [EDS. moved to 54 U.S.C. § 306102]. An agency's preservation program "shall ensure" that properties are considered and taken into account during both foreign and domestic undertakings pursuant to section 402 and section 106, respectively. *Id.* § [306102(b)(3)] (requiring an agency's preservation program to consider the preservation of properties in general, whether or not they are under the jurisdiction or control of the agency, and whether

or not they are affected by foreign or domestic agency actions); *id.*
§ [306102(b)(5)] (requiring an agency's preservation program to include
procedures for compliance with section 106 domestic undertakings).
Significantly, NHPA section 110 directs that "[e]ach Federal agency shall
establish, *in consultation with the Secretary [of the Interior]*, a
preservation program." *Id.* § [306102(a)] (emphasis added). In addition,
an agency's procedures for complying with section 106 domestic
undertakings must be consistent with the regulations issued by the
ACHP. *Id.* § [306102(b)(5)(A)]. In the domestic context, therefore,
Congress provided for coherency in agency preservation programs by
requiring consultation with the Secretary of the Interior, and by
specifically mandating consistency with the ACHP's section 106
regulations. In the foreign context, Congress also provided for coherency
in agency preservation programs by requiring consultation with the
Secretary of the Interior. Although there is no express mandate that an
agency's take into account procedures for foreign undertakings be
consistent with the ACHP's domestic regulations, there is no indication
that Congress intended the basic framework of foreign and domestic take
into account procedures to differ.

In developing a preservation program as required under section 110,
a federal agency consults with the Secretary of the Interior, and
accordingly, Congress has delegated to the Secretary authority to
promulgate guidance to assist agencies in fulfilling their responsibilities.
Id. § [306101(b)]. Under this authority, the Secretary of the Interior,
acting through the National Park Service, has indeed issued such
guidance, which "have no regulatory effect," but nevertheless are "the
Secretary's formal guidance." 63 Fed. Reg. 20496–20508, 20496 (April 24,
1998). With respect to foreign undertakings under section 402, the
guidelines recommend that "[e]fforts to identify and consider effects on
historic properties in other countries should be carried out in
consultation with the host country's historic preservation authorities,
with affected communities and groups, and with relevant professional
organizations." 63 Fed. Reg. at 20504 (Standard 4, Guideline (*o*)). The
guidelines advise that such consultation should involve a "process of
seeking, discussing and considering the views of others, and where
feasible, seeking agreement with them on how historic properties should
be identified, considered, and managed." *Id.* (Standard 5, Guideline (a)).
"While specific consultation requirements and procedures will vary
among agencies depending on their missions and programs, the nature
of historic properties that might be affected, and other factors,
consultation should always include all affected parties." *Id.* (Standard 5,
Guideline (d)). The guidelines also advise that consultation should occur
"early in the planning stage of any Federal action that might affect
historic properties." *Id.* (Standard 5, Guideline (c)).

As the Secretary of the Interior recognizes, "specific consultation
requirements and procedures will vary among agencies depending on

their missions and programs," and therefore, an agency has some discretion in deciding exactly who will be consulted, to what extent, and at precisely what time. Likewise, an agency has some discretion to decide exactly what information regarding effects of the undertaking it will generate, gather, and consider, and if adverse effects are found, exactly what mitigation efforts it will evaluate and pursue. Under *Chevron* step two, an agency's specific formulation of the take into account process is entitled to deference from a court. Nevertheless, under *Chevron* step one, Congress' intent that the section 402 take into account process contain basic elements—identification of protected properties, gathering and weighing of information, determination of adverse effect or no adverse effect, evaluation of mitigation measures if necessary, and consultation with interested parties and organizations—is evident. Congress explicitly declared that preservation of historic properties would be carried out in cooperation and in partnership with other nations, private organizations, and individuals. 16 U.S.C. § 470–1 [EDS.: moved to 54 U.S.C. § 300101]. Congress enacted section 402 using the same take into account phrase used previously when Congress enacted section 106, and at the time, the ACHP had already promulgated regulations setting forth a basic framework for the section 106 take into account process. 36 C.F.R. Part 800. Congress provided a mechanism, through the formal guidance of the Secretary of the Interior, to achieve coherency and consistency across the various preservation programs of different agencies. *Id.* § 470a(g) [EDS.: moved to 54 U.S.C. § 306101(b)]. It is implausible, therefore, that Congress intended the essential elements of a take into account process—whether conducted in the context of a foreign or domestic undertaking—to differ widely. Finally, the fact that the Secretary of the Interior's guidance for section 402 undertakings is consistent with the basic framework for section 106 undertakings supports the notion that the basic framework is evident from express Congressional policy and the NHPA's text, purpose, structure, and history.

B.   Compliance With "Take Into Account"

Defendants assert that information about the Okinawa dugong was taken into account during bilateral discussions to select the site for the FRF, and will continue to be taken into account as Japan moves forward with its own environmental review process. Defendants provide the declaration of Takemasa Moriya, the Japanese Administrative Vice Minister for Defense, who states that potential impacts on the dugong and its feeding grounds were of utmost importance to him and the Japanese government in selecting the site and configuration of the FRF. Because of concern for the dugong, the Japanese initially proposed a facility built completely on land, but this option was not possible due to U.S. operational requirements. Rather than shift the facility further into the shallow waters as the U.S. initially preferred, the Government of Japan developed a plan in such a way that the construction of the new facility would avoid shallow water areas to the extent possible, thereby limiting the potential impact on dugong feeding grounds.

Defendants also assert that the Government of Japan will continue to "give careful consideration to impacts on the Okinawa dugong as [Japan] proceeds with its environmental review" process required under Japanese law. Moriya explains that the Japanese environmental assessment will include specific methods for surveying, predicting and assessing the impacts of the FRF on the dugong. He explains further that the initial scoping document as well as the final results of the review will be subject to public comments, and such comments will be considered by Japanese officials as they prepare an environmental impact statement. Based on the results of the review process, Moriya explains that the Government of Japan, in consultation with the United States, will take appropriate mitigation measures, "taking comprehensively into account various factors including the opinions of the local communities, the need to meet the operational requirements of the U.S. forces, and the need to give due consideration to the natural environment."

Plaintiffs do not dispute and the court does not take issue with what Japan has or has not done with respect to the environmental assessment required under Japanese law. Indeed, as the court has already explained in connection with the act of state doctrine, the court's review is not directed at whether Japan has complied with Japanese law, but whether DOD has complied with its obligations under the NHPA. Section 402 of the NHPA is clear on its face—it assigns the obligation to take into account to "the head of a Federal agency having direct or indirect jurisdiction over such undertaking." 16 U.S.C. § 470a–2 [EDS.: moved to 54 U.S.C. § 307101(e)]. It is undisputed that, in this case, the Secretary of the Department of Defense has direct jurisdiction over the FRF project. The obligation to take into account, therefore, lies with the DOD and the DOD alone. While defendants insist that impacts on the dugong were taken into account, the court must ask not only *whether* the effects were taken into account, but *by whom*—the Department of Defense? The fact that Japan will conduct an environmental assessment pursuant to Japanese law does not relieve DOD of its independent obligation to take into account under the NHPA.

The current record contains no evidence that a single official from the DOD with responsibility for the FRF has considered or assessed the available information on the dugong or the effects of the FRF. For example, defendants provide the declaration of Richard Lawless who is the DOD official responsible for bilateral negotiations concerning the FRF and who reports to the Secretary of Defense. His declaration, while noting that the Government of Japan placed particular emphasis on preserving seagrass beds and avoiding adverse impacts to the dugong, is silent as to whether DOD also took similar concerns into account. Indeed, Lawless' declaration indicates that DOD's overarching, and perhaps only concern, was that the FRF comply with U.S. operational and safety requirements. Additional evidence in the record supports this view. An October 2005 [Futenma Replacement Site Survey] summarizing the U.S.-Japan negotiations states, "[t]he U.S. side continued to maintain that while environmental impacts were important, any FRF proposal must meet operational and safety requirements." The document continues, *"the environmental issues are primarily a question of political will since any option will affect the environment and opponents will use environment-based arguments to advance their cause."* (Emphasis added). Insofar as these statements suggest that DOD need not concern itself with environmental impacts because they are unavoidable and are simply an expedient used by opponents to obstruct the FRF, these statements evince at best, plain ignorance of, and at worst, complete defiance of DOD's obligation to consider the impacts of the FRF on the dugong. The court is unconvinced that DOD has expressed concern for, let alone taken steps to consider the effects of the FRF on the dugong. As plaintiffs argue, "[i]t is disingenuous for DOD to now claim Japan's environmental concerns as their own."

To be sure, the fact that DOD, not the Government of Japan, has the obligation to take into account under section 402 does not preclude DOD from considering information generated by Japan and coordinating with Japan to gather and compile relevant information. Indeed, as the court has already discussed, Congress' intent that a basic review process involve coordination and consultation with the host nation, interested parties, and other organizations is evident from the language, purpose and structure of the statute. Moreover, as the court alluded to when discussing the act of state doctrine, DOD need not take action that is inconsistent with or contrary to the actions of Japan. This is especially true given that, as defendants observe, the Okinawa dugong is Japan's cultural and historical property and therefore, Japan's judgment regarding how best to protect that property should be of great concern to the DOD. Duplicative, inconsistent efforts are not required. To the contrary, coordination and consultation are required in order to avoid such wasted efforts. Ultimately, however, the NHPA imposes on the DOD a responsibility to consider and weigh. DOD must determine whether the available information is sufficient, and if not, what additional information must be gathered or produced. DOD must examine that information, whether it is generated by the Government of Japan, by the DOD itself, or by outside experts and organizations. Based on that information, DOD must determine whether there will be adverse effects or no adverse effects. If there are adverse effects, DOD must consider and evaluate options to mitigate or avoid those effects. Each of these steps can be accomplished with input and cooperation from the Government of Japan and other parties, but ultimately, the responsibility rests with the DOD. * * *

In sum, the current record reflects a failure by the DOD to comply with NHPA section 402. This failure constitutes agency action that is unreasonably delayed and unlawfully withheld as provided by the APA. Defendants have failed to produce, gather and consider information necessary for taking into account the effects of the FRF on the Okinawa dugong and for determining whether mitigation or avoidance measures are necessary and possible. The current record contains an abundance of basic scientific knowledge regarding dugong behavior, migratory movements, feeding patterns, and seagrass habitats. But this information alone is insufficient because the statute is clear—the information considered must bear on the "effects of the undertaking" on the protected property, and the information must be considered for the purpose of "mitigating or avoiding any adverse effects." 16 U.S.C. § 470a–2 [EDS.: moved to 54 U.S.C. § 307101(e)]. Defendants' own declarants admit that there is insufficient evidence to evaluate the effects of the undertaking, a necessary predicate for determining whether mitigation is necessary and possible. If further information is needed in order to evaluate whether adverse impacts to the dugong will be minimal because Henoko Bay is a marginal habitat relative to other habitats around Okinawa Island, then DOD has a responsibility to ensure that such studies are conducted. If more information is needed in order to evaluate whether noise disturbance from air and water vessels during construction and subsequent operation of the FRF will adversely impact the dugong, then DOD has a responsibility to ensure that those studies are also conducted. DOD, not the Government of Japan, has the obligation to evaluate mitigation measures if it is determined that there are adverse effects, but such evaluation can occur parallel to and in conjunction with Japan's own efforts.

The court is troubled that the 2006 Roadmap embodying final plans for the construction of the FRF has received the highest levels of approvals from the U.S. Secretaries of Defense and State. Yet, the impacts of the FRF on the dugong are currently not well-understood, and other than [a] suggestion that seagrass beds might be transplanted to other locations, few mitigation measures have been studied and evaluated by the DOD. Defendants argue that insofar as the currently available information is insufficient or incomplete, any deficiencies will be addressed by Japan as it conducts a three-year environmental impact assessment pursuant to Japanese law. There is no doubt that, in satisfying its own obligations under the NHPA, defendants may consider the information generated by Japan's assessment. The critical question, however, is one of timing. It is true that, as the court stated in its 2005 order, construction of the facility has not yet begun, and the take into account process required by the NHPA can still occur. Yet, it is also true that, as the court has consistently held, the statutory text requires defendants to take into account *"prior to approval* of an undertaking." [54 U.S.C. § 307101(e)]. Congress' express inclusion of a time frame indicates that Congress intended the take into account process to occur early in the planning stages of a federal undertaking when there is still a meaningful opportunity to consider adverse impacts and mitigation measures.

Satisfaction of defendants' obligations under section 402, therefore, cannot be postponed until the eve of construction when defendants have made irreversible commitments making additional review futile or consideration of alternatives impossible.

Japan's environmental assessment has already begun and now is the time for DOD to actively participate and coordinate with Japan. Will Japan's assessment be sufficient for meeting DOD's obligations under section 402? If not, then how should Japan's assessment be supplemented? If supplemental information is necessary, then from what sources will the information be derived? These questions remain unanswered. If defendants wait to address these issues until the end of the three-year period when the Japanese environmental assessment is complete and when Japan is ready to move forward under the terms of the Roadmap, it will be too late.

Conclusion

Plaintiffs' motion for summary judgment is GRANTED.

NOTES & QUESTIONS

1.   In many ways, the language of Section 402 is similar to Section 106 in that it directs federal agencies to take into account the effects of an undertaking. However, Section 402 lacks a requirement to consult with the Advisory Council on Historic Preservation. Here, the court determines as a matter of statutory interpretation that the essential elements of the take into account process do not differ between domestic and foreign contexts while also recognizing that Section 402 does not provide for an advisory function for the ACHP in foreign matters. Given what you know about the role played by the ACHP in domestic NHPA matters, are these two findings consistent? Why or why not? What effect does this have on agency undertakings overseas going forward? Are there other possible reasons why the ACHP regulations do not address Section 402? Based on the text of Section 402 discussed in the opinion, does the Secretary of the Interior's guidance substitute for the ACHP regulations?

2.   This case was part of a decades-long effort to halt construction of the Futenma Replacement Facility in Henoko Bay. The effort included extensive litigation in both Japan and the United States, massive citizen protests, and a non-binding referendum in which 70 percent of Okinawans opposed construction. The American military presence in Okinawa has been a longstanding source of controversy among locals with roots far deeper than a disagreement over the protection of the dugong, so it is perhaps not surprising that an effort to make long-term investments in the American military presence on the island would attract significant challenges.

One reason among many for the vociferous opposition, and the subject of this case, was the protection of the Okinawa dugong. The dugong is listed on the Japanese Register of Historic Places, Places of Scenic Beauty and/or National Monuments, a register created by authority of Japan's Law for the Protection of Cultural Properties. This law defines an "object of cultural property" to include "animals (including their habitats, breeding areas and trails)." Law for the Protection of Cultural Properties, Law No. 214 of 1950, art. 2, para. 4 (Japan). The dugong is thus categorized on the Register as a "national monument" under Japanese law. The *Dugong* opinion cites a 2005 court order holding that the NHPA was applicable to the dugong by virtue of its protection under the Law for the Protection of Cultural Properties in Japan. In that earlier opinion, the court found that the Law for the Protection of Cultural Properties was equivalent to the National Register for Historic Places, triggering section 402 of the NHPA. *See Dugong v. Rumsfeld,* 2005 WL 522106 (N.D. Cal. Mar. 2, 2005).

3. In the domestic context (under section 106), the dugong would not be eligible for listing, Why not? What does this say about the notion of cultural property under the two legal systems? What are the implications of protecting a domestically ineligible property under NHPA? Does this undermine the interpretation that the Japanese law is "equivalent" to the National Register? Consider one response:

> Limiting the scope of protection to the types of properties that the National Register recognizes undermines the internationalism of § 402, which is to allow foreign nations to determine what properties—and what types of properties—are significant to their history and cultural heritage. However, the reach of § 402 should be limited to only those that are properties actually designated for their cultural or historic significance, or their necessity to the preservation of such a designated property. In that way, U.S. agencies operating overseas will know from examining the equivalent foreign register that a property must be considered. Therefore, the interpretation of "equivalent of the National Register" that hews closest to § 402's language, statutory context, and legislative purpose, is that equivalency requires, at a minimum, that a country maintain a register of culturally significant property.

Emily Monteith, Note, *Lost in Translation: Discerning the International Equivalent of the National Register of Historic Places,* 59 DEPAUL L. REV. 1017, 1051 (2010). Section 106 does not require a resource to be listed on the National Register to merit protection, it need only be eligible for listing. Should Section 402 require listing on the National Register, as this student suggests? Would doing so "hew[ ] closest to § 402's language, statutory context, and legislative purpose"? Why or why not?

4. Note how the *Dugong* court considers actions taken by the Government of Japan and the actions the DOD must take to treat these as part of the take into account process. How does the court balance the foreign affairs interest of close relations with a long-term strategic defense partner with the DOD's agency obligations under Section 402? What dangers are there in requiring American federal agencies, presumably using American legal and cultural frames, to take into account adverse effects upon a Japanese cultural property whose significance does not map clearly onto the paradigm of cultural heritage protection in the United States? In general,

what are the benefits and risks of using American law to protect heritage items of other cultures?

5.   One reason this litigation centers on the NHPA is Section 402's explicit language about extraterritorial application. This language helps cases overcome the presumption against extraterritoriality, a canon of statutory construction revived by the Supreme Court in *EEOC v. Arabian American Oil Co. (ARAMCO)*, 499 U.S. 244 (1991), that assumes Congressional intent to legislate with domestic effect in the absence of indications to the contrary. Under *ARAMCO* and its progeny, the presumption against extraterritoriality produced mixed outcomes for cases brought under other heritage preservation statutes, like NEPA. *Compare Envtl. Defense Fund, Inc. v. Massey*, 986 F.2d 528 (D.C. Cir. 1993) (presumption does not apply, allowing NEPA claim where regulated conduct occurs in the United States and effect felt in Antarctica) *with NEPA Coalition of Japan v. Aspin*, 837 F. Supp. 466 (D.D.C. 1993) (presumption did apply barring NEPA claim for military construction in Japan). In general, rebutting the presumption against extraterritoriality with NEPA presents a significant challenge without a focus on regulated agency conduct occurring domestically.

Because of this, in *Dugong* the NHPA likely presented a clearer path to surviving a motion to dismiss than NEPA or other statutes subject to the presumption against extraterritoriality. One scholar has written forcefully about the Futenma relocation controversy to argue for the extraterritorial application of NEPA and the Endangered Species Act, decrying the presumption as a form of "judicial militarism" that frustrates the pursuit of environmental justice in Okinawa. *See* Alan Ramo, *U.S. Military Accountability for Extraterritorial Environmental Impacts: An Examination of Okinawa, Environmental Justice, and Judicial Militarism*, 28 TUL. ENVTL. L. J. 53 (2014). Do you agree with this characterization? What arguments might complicate the presumption that Congress intended to address environmental problems solely as a domestic issue?

6.   As a result of the 2008 *Dugong* decision, the Department of Defense completed a report intended to satisfy its obligations under NHPA in 2014. The plaintiffs subsequently brought new litigation in 2015 to challenge the DOD's compliance with the NHPA under the Administrative Procedures Act. In a 2017 decision, the Ninth Circuit allowed litigation to proceed, reversing the district court's dismissal on standing and political question grounds. On remand, in 2018 the district court granted summary judgment for the DOD, finding that it complied with the "take into account" requirement when it consulted academic experts instead of directly consulting Japanese citizens, environmental organizations, or cultural practitioners. On appeal, in 2020 the Ninth Circuit upheld the DOD's compliance with Section 402 and finding of no adverse effect, affirming the district court's grant of summary judgment. *See Center for Biological Diversity v. Esper*, 958 F.3d 895 (9th Cir. 2020). As matters of first impression, the Ninth Circuit held that: (1) regulations implementing Section 106 do not apply to Section 402; (2) Section 402 requires only "reasonable consultation," granting flexibility to federal

agencies to determine whom to consult and in what manner; and (3) Section 402 does not require public participation. *Id.*

In a concurring opinion to *Center for Biological Diversity v. Esper*, however, Judge Bea would have thrown out the 2005 district court holding that Section 402 applied to the dugong in the first place. While finding that the Japanese law was the equivalent of the National Register, Bea would have held the dugong was not "property" within the meaning of the term in Section 402 or the World Heritage Convention, because those instruments "limit protection to specific locations and to tangible, inanimate objects." *Id.* at 918 (Bea, J., concurring). The Convention provides mixed support for the central assertion in Bea's concurrence. Article 2 expressly defines natural heritage as encompassing "precisely delineated areas which constitute the habitat of threatened species of animals," a definition that would seem to cover the dugong's habitat while not the dugong itself.

Additionally, the Operational Guidelines exclude nominations of "movable heritage" under the Convention. *See* Intergovernmental Committee for the Protection of the World Cultural and Natural Heritage, UNESCO, Operational Guidelines for the Implementation of the World Heritage Convention ¶ 48 (2019). However, the World Heritage Committee's past actions may support an alternative interpretation. Indeed, one of the cited reasons for delisting Oman's Arabian Oryx sanctuary in 2007 was the precipitous decline in herd numbers, threatening the future viability of the species. Do you agree with Judge Bea that the dugong was not property within the definition of the World Heritage Convention? Should the Convention's definition control interpretation of section 402?

7. In 2020, President Trump threatened to destroy Iranian cultural heritage sites if Iran retaliated for the killing by the United States of its top generals. Would carrying out this threat violate American law, specifically, Section 402? Would a missile attack on a heritage site without a Congressional declaration of war be an "undertaking?" Is the United States Air Force a federal agency? *See* 5 U.S.C. § 551(1)(g) (agency defined as "means each authority of the Government of the United States . . . but does not include . . . (G) military authority exercised in the field in time of war or in occupied territory"). What would compliance with Section 402 look like in a military attack on a putative enemy's cultural resources?

INDEX

References are to Pages